THE OXFORD DICTIONARY OF IDIOMS

Jennifer Speake is a freelance writer and editor of reference books, including *The Oxford Dictionary of Foreign Words and Phrases* (1997) and *The Concise Oxford Dictionary of Proverbs* (with John Simpson, 3rd edn. 1998).

Oxford Paperback Reference

The most authoritative and up-to-date reference books for both students and the general reader.

The Oxford Dictionary of

Idioms

Edited by
Jennifer Speake

OXFORD
UNIVERSITY PRESS

OXFORD
UNIVERSITY PRESS

Great Clarendon Street, Oxford OX2 6DP

Oxford University Press is a department of the University of Oxford.
It furthers the University's objective of excellence in research, scholarship,
and education by publishing worldwide in

Oxford New York

Athens Auckland Bangkok Bogotá Buenos Aires Calcutta
Cape Town Chennai Dar es Salaam Delhi Florence Hong Kong Istanbul
Karachi Kuala Lumpur Madrid Melbourne Mexico City Mumbai
Nairobi Paris São Paulo Singapore Taipei Tokyo Toronto Warsaw

with associated companies in Berlin Ibadan

Published in the United States
by Oxford University Press Inc., New York

British Library Cataloguing in Publication Data

Data available

Library of Congress Cataloging in Publication Data

Data available

ISBN 0-19-280111-2

10 9 8 7 6 5 4 3 2

Typeset in Swift and Arial
by Selwood Systems
Printed in Great Britain by
Cox & Wyman, Reading,
Berkshire

Preface

The word *idiom* entered English in the sixteenth century as part of the great surge of linguistic self-awareness that transformed the vernacular languages of Europe during the Renaissance. Both *idiom*, and the Latin equivalent *idioma*, derive from the Greek word ἴδιος meaning 'private, peculiar to oneself', and applied at first to one's native tongue: 'frame all sentences in their mother phrase, and proper *Idioma*,' exhorted the critic George Gascoigne in his 'Certayne notes of Instruction concerning the making of verse or ryme in English' (1575). The more restricted modern sense of 'a particular usage or form of speech' appears in the early seventeenth century, in John Donne's *Sermons*. The wealth of idioms in English is a reflection of the many sources, cultural and linguistic, that have fed into the mainstream of the language. Military (*spike someone's guns*), naval (*know the ropes*), sporting (*close but no cigar, saved by the bell*), musical (*run the gamut*), and other technical vocabularies have all contributed vivid forms of words to the rich mix.

An idiom, then, is a form of expression or a phrase peculiar to a language and approved by the usage of that language, and it often has a signification other than its grammatical or logical one. In practical terms this includes a wide range of expressions that have become in a sense fossilized within the language and are used in a fixed or semi-fixed way without reference to the literal meaning of their component words. Idioms are the elements in any language that are often the most recalcitrant to translation—and cause most difficulty to foreign learners.

Although some idioms degenerate into clichés and others are short-lived denizens of the twilight zones of slang or nonce usage, many others are lively contributors to a language's unique character over the long term and have revealing or perplexing histories of their own. For instance, when and why did the graphic *bees in the head* give way to the modern *bees in the bonnet*, which has the charm of alliteration but neither sense nor current dress codes to recommend it? In the case of English, the cross-fertilization between American and British usage, especially via popular twentieth-century writers such as P. G. Wodehouse and Raymond Chandler, has further enriched the flavour.

The idiomatic expressions selected for this dictionary come from various origins and in a variety of guises. In many cases, evidence for current or at least mid- to late-twentieth-century use has been a deciding factor for inclusion; thus, Victorian slang that may well have survived into the twentieth century, such as *up to the knocker* (evidenced in 1896), is generally not included. Straightforward rhyming slang is excluded (e.g. *dog and bone* 'telephone'), but expressions that rely less obviously on rhyming slang are in (e.g. *do bird*, meaning 'serve a prison sentence', alluding to *do time*, rhyming with *birdlime*).

Phrasal verbs and other usages transparent to a native speaker are not included, nor are self-explanatory similes or metaphors. However, similes in which there is a fossilized, arcane, or other non-obvious element are: for instance, the pun on *thick* in *as thick as two planks* or the mid-eighteenth-century colloquial sense (now dated) of *thick* as 'close in association, intimate' in the mid-nineteenth-century phrase *as thick as thieves*. There are also a number of quotations so familiar that they are used with no conscious reference to the original context, such as *caviar to the general*. Proverbial sayings that are used in truncated or otherwise allusive mode are also covered (*give a dog a bad name* is often heard without its savage former conclusion *and hang him*), as are numerous metaphorical phrases.

Entries are arranged in alphabetical order of keyword (shown in capital letters). The keyword is, as far as possible, the first conceptually significant unvarying word in the expression, usually a noun. Articles (*the, a*) and words such as *someone/thing* are disregarded in the alphabetization. Parts of speech are similarly ignored in the alphabetization, with no separate sequences observed for nouns and verbs.

Cross-references are provided only in cases where different readers might perceive a word other than the first noun as the most significant element or where the expression has established variants. Thus, there is no cross-reference at *tongs* to *hammer and tongs* since alphabetical placing of the idiom is obvious under the 'first noun' rule, the order of the nouns is immutable, and it is in any case unlikely that anyone would look first for the expression under the second element. *Wormwood and gall* however merits a cross-reference, as it can sometimes appear as *gall and wormwood*. Phrases on the pattern of *tower of strength*, which might equally well be looked up under *tower* or *strength*, have cross-references. Where the noun is variable but the sense identical, as in *throw in the towel* or *throw in the sponge*, the entry is at the less variable element, the verb. In some cases of adjective plus noun the entry is at the adjective, as being the more significant element as regards sense. In the few cases (e.g. *eat humble pie*), where verb, adjective, or noun might equally well be identified as the key element, comprehensive cross-references are provided.

The invariable components of the entry structure are the idiom itself with capitalized keyword and any common variants given in brackets, followed by the definition. In addition there may be a label or labels (in italics) indicating register and/or geographical area, a sentence or short paragraph covering etymological, historical and usage points of interest, and an illustrative quotation. The marking of a quotation with an asterisk indicates it is the earliest example of the use of this idiom yet traced. Dates in the history notes are given in the form E, M, or L plus the ordinal number of the century; thus, for example, E16 is the period 1500–1529, M16 is 1530–1569, L16 is 1570–1599.

Jennifer Speake

A

A 1 at Lloyds excellent, first-rate. ● In Lloyd's Register of Shipping, used of ships in first-class condition as to the hull (A) and stores (1). Now often abbreviated to simply *A 1*. The US equivalent is *A No. 1*; both have been in figurative use since M19.

from A to B from one's starting-point to one's destination; from one place to another.

> **1987** K. RUSHFORTH *Tree Planting & Management* (1990) iii. 60 The purpose of street tree planting is to … make the roads and thoroughfares pleasant in their own right, not just as places used to travel from A to B.

from A to Z over the entire range; in every particular. ● Cf. Italian *dall'A alla Zeta*.

> | *1819 J. KEATS *Otho* V. v We must obey The prince from A to Z.

take someone ABACK shock, surprise, or disconcert someone. ● The frequently used passive form of the phrase (*be taken aback*) was adopted (M19) from earlier (M18) nautical terminology, describing the situation of a ship with its sails pressed back against the mast by a headwind, preventing forward movement.

(as) easy (*or* simple) as ABC extremely easy or straightforward. ● A child's primer or first spelling and reading book was formerly (15–17) commonly called an *ABC*, hence its metaphorical use to mean the basic elements or rudiments of something.

give someone the screaming ABDABS induce an attack of extreme anxiety or irritation in someone. ● *Abdabs* (or *habdabs*) is M20 slang of unknown origin; sometimes used to mean an attack of *delirium tremens*.

ABET ▶ *see* **AID and abet**.

know what one is ABOUT be aware of the implications of one's actions or of a situation, and of how best to deal with them. *informal*

ABOVE oneself conceited; arrogant.

> **1990** V. S. NAIPAUL *India* (1991) iii. 171 I wondered whether there wasn't … even now the old religious-political feeling that it was wrong, wasteful, and provoking to the gods (and the ruler) to get above oneself.

not be ABOVE — be capable of stooping to (an unworthy act).

in ABRAHAM's bosom in heaven, the place of rest for the souls of the blessed. *dated* ● After Luke 16:22 'And it came to pass, that the beggar died, and was carried by the angels into Abraham's bosom'. In the Bible, *Abraham* was the Hebrew patriarch from whom all Jews traced their descent.

ABSENCE of mind failure to concentrate on or remember what one is doing.

ACCEPTABLE ▶ *see* **the acceptable FACE of**.

an ACCIDENT waiting to happen a potentially disastrous situation, usually caused by negligent or faulty procedures; a person certain to cause trouble.

| **1997** *Times* 23 Sept. 46/1 Accidents are often said to be 'waiting to happen'. It does not take much imagination to see that the chaotic start to the Whitbread round-the-world race … could easily have ended in tragedy.

ACCIDENTS will happen however careful you try to be, it is inevitable that some unfortunate or unforeseen events will occur. ● A shortened form of the proverbial saying 'accidents will happen in the best regulated families' (E19).

ACCIDENTS ▶ *see* **a CHAPTER of accidents**.

give a good (*or* bad) ACCOUNT of oneself make a favourable (*or* unfavourable) impression through one's performance.

there's no ACCOUNTING for tastes (*or* taste) it's impossible to explain why different people like different things, especially those things which the speaker considers unappealing. *proverbial* ● Now (since L18) the usual English form of the Latin tag *de gustibus non est disputandum* 'there is no disputing about tastes'.

settle (*or* square) ACCOUNTS with have revenge on. ● Literally, 'pay money owed to (someone)'.

have an ACE up one's sleeve have an effective resource or piece of information kept hidden until it is necessary to use it; a secret advantage. ● The *ace*, the card marked with a single pip, is the highest card in many card games, so a cheating player might well secrete one to use against an unwary opponent. A N. Amer. variant is *an ace in the hole*.

play one's ACE use one's best resource. ● See preceding entry.

within an ACE of very close to. ● *Ace* here is used figuratively with reference to the single pip on a playing card, thus a 'jot' or 'particle'. Phrase first recorded from E18.

hold (*or* have) all the ACES have all the advantages. ● Cf. ▶ **have an ACE up one's sleeve**.

an ACHILLES' heel a person's only vulnerable spot; a serious or fatal weakness. ● In Greek mythology, the nymph Thetis dipped her infant son Achilles in the water of the River Styx to make him immortal, but the heel by which she held him was not touched by the water; he was ultimately killed in battle by an arrow wound in this one vulnerable spot.

| **1998** *Times* 2 Mar. 21/1 The inclination to outlaw that of which it disapproves … is, if not the cloven hoof beneath the hem of Tony Blair's Government, certainly its Achilles' heel.

come the ACID be unpleasant or offensive, speak in a caustic or sarcastic manner.

put the ACID on seek to extract a loan or favour from (someone). *Austral. & NZ, informal*

the ACID test (of something) a situation or event which finally proves whether something is good or bad, true or false, etc. ● With allusion to the method of testing for gold with nitric acid.

| **1995** *Field* Mar. 74/3 The acid test for a new fence is in the jumping of it.

have a nodding ACQUAINTANCE with someone/thing know someone slightly; know a little about something.

| **1989** D. RADCLIFFE *Simply Barbara Bush* iii. 58 Their families had lived less than ten miles apart as they were growing up, and their fathers almost certainly had a nodding acquaintance on the golf course.

ACQUAINTANCE ▶ *see* **SCRAPE acquaintance with**.

ACRE ▶ *see* **GOD's acre**.

ACROSS the board applying to all.   ● In US horse racing (M20), denoting a bet in which equal amounts are staked on the same horse to win, place, or show in a race.

be (*or* get) ACROSS something be or become fully cognizant of the details or complexity of an issue or situation. *Austral.*

ACT of God an instance of uncontrollable natural forces in operation. ● Often used in insurance contracts to mean incidents such as lightning strikes.

clean up one's ACT behave in a more acceptable manner. *informal*

get one's ACT together organize oneself in the manner required in order to achieve something. *informal*

| **1991** J. TROLLOPE *Rector's Wife* xiv. 185 I like adolescents ... I don't at all mind that they haven't got their acts together.

get (*or* be) in on the ACT become or be involved in a particular activity, in order to gain profit or advantage. *informal*

a hard (*or* tough) ACT to follow an achievement or performance which sets a standard regarded as being difficult for others to measure up to.

| **1996** *Independent* 13 Mar. 3/2 Her determination and championing of tourism will be a tough act to follow.

ACT (noun) ▶ *see* **a CLASS act**; ▶ *see* **do a DISAPPEARING act**; ▶ *see* **READ the riot act**.

ACT (verb) ▶ *see* **act one's AGE**; ▶ *see* **play the GOAT**.

ACTION stations an order or warning to prepare for action. *dated*   ● Originally an order to naval personnel to go to their allocated positions ready to engage the enemy.

where the ACTION is where important or interesting things are happening. *informal*

| **1971** *Gourmet* Feb. 48/2 You can dine outside, weather permitting, or in the bar where the action is.

ACTION ▶ *see* **a PIECE of the action**.

your ACTUAL — the real, genuine, or important thing specified. *informal*
> **1995** L. GARRETT *Coming Plague* xi. 301 'This is your actual nightmare!' Moss said. 'The sky is falling, we know it.'

not know someone from ADAM not know or be completely unable to recognize the person in question. *informal*

the old ADAM unregenerate human nature. ● In Christian typology, fallen man as contrasted with the *second Adam*, Jesus Christ.
> **1993** *Outdoor Canada* Sept. 44/2 It is the Old Adam in us. We are descendants of a long line of dirt farmers, sheepherders … and so forth.

ADD ▶ *see* **add FUEL to the fire**; ▶ *see* **add INSULT to injury**.

ADDER ▶ *see* **DEAF as an adder**.

an ADMIRABLE Crichton a person who excels in all kinds of studies and pursuits, or who is noted for supreme competence. ● Originally with reference to James Crichton of Clunie (1560–85?), a Scottish nobleman renowned for his intellectual and physical prowess. In J. M. Barrie's play *The Admirable Crichton* (1902), the eponymous hero is a butler who takes charge when his master's family is shipwrecked on a desert island.

cast (or cut or turn) someone ADRIFT abandon or isolate someone. ● Literally, leave someone in a boat or other craft which has nothing to secure or guide it.
> **1998** *Oldie* Aug. 38/3 The various dissenting movements … should be cut adrift and left to their own devices.

any ADVANCE (on —)? any higher bid than —? ● Said by an auctioneer to elicit a higher offer; hence figuratively as a query about general progress in a matter.

ADVOCATE ▶ *see* **play DEVIL's advocate**.

AFRAID ▶ *see* **afraid of one's own SHADOW**.

for AFRICA in abundance; in large numbers. *S. Afr.*, *informal*
> **1985** *Fair Lady* 3 Apr. 137 Flowers for Africa … go to Namaqualand to see flowers in their millions.

be AFTER doing something be on the point of doing something or have just done it. *Irish*

act (or be) one's AGE behave in a manner appropriate to one's age and not to someone much younger. ● Often imperative: *act your age!*

come of AGE 1 (of a person) reach adult status. **2** (of a movement or activity) become fully established. ● In UK law a person is accounted an adult at the age of 18 (formerly 21).

feel one's AGE realize from one's physical state, prejudices, etc. that one is getting old.

AGE ▶ *see* **the AWKWARD age**; ▶ *see* **a GOLDEN age**; ▶ *see* **UNDER age**.

a hidden AGENDA a person's real but concealed aims and intentions.

AGONY ▶ *see* **PILE on the agony**; ▶ *see* **PROLONG the agony**.

AGREE ▶ *see* **agree to DIFFER**.

AGREEMENT ▶ *see* **a GENTLEMAN's agreement**.

AHEAD ▶ *see* **ahead of the GAME**; ▶ *see* **STREETS ahead**.

AID and abet help and encourage (someone to do something). ●*Abet* is also used in formal legal contexts. The word is related to an Old French term meaning 'to encourage (a hound) to bite'.

> **1986** F. PERETTI *This Present Darkness* xxxii. 292 She strained to think of ... any friend who would still aid and abet a fugitive from the law, without questions.

in AID of in support of; for the purpose of raising money for. *chiefly Brit.*

what's (all) this in AID of? what is the purpose of this? *Brit., informal*

on (*or* off) the AIR being (*or* not being) broadcast on radio or television. ●First used this sense in 1927.

take the AIR go out of doors. *dated*

(up) in the AIR (of a plan or issue) still to be settled; unresolved. ●The US slang phrase *go* (or *get*) *up in the air* (E20) means 'become angry or excited'.

walk (*or* tread) on AIR feel elated.

> **1977** B. MACLAVERTY *Secrets* (1990) 70 'I'm sure you're walking on air,' my mother said to Paul at his wedding.

AIR ▶ *see* **CLEAR the air**; ▶ *see* **HOT air**.

AIRS and graces an affectation of superior elegance of manner designed to attract or impress. ●*Air* in the sense of 'an affected manner' has been current since M17; from E18 it has been more usual in the plural in this derogatory sense.

give oneself AIRS act pretentiously or snobbishly. ●Cf. ▶ **AIRS and graces**.

> **1878** F. MARRYAT *Poor Jack* xxviii. 22/2 They haven't no rank as officers, nor so much pay as a petty officer, and yet they give themselves more airs than a lieutenant.

have people rolling in the AISLES **1** make an audience laugh uncontrollably. **2** be very amusing. *informal* ●Noel Coward in 1954 described 'had them in the aisles' as 'a theatrical phrase'. Cf. ▶ **KNOCK them in the aisles**.

> **1** *1940 P. G. WODEHOUSE *Quick Service* xii. 136 I made the speech of a lifetime. I had them tearing up the seats and rolling in the aisles.

drop one's AITCHES fail to pronounce the letter *h* at the beginning of words. ●A feature of dialect speech often formerly (L19) perceived as indicative of lack of education or inferior social class.

> **1903** G. B. SHAW *Man & Superman* II. 50 This man takes more trouble to drop his aitches than ever his father did to pick them up.

an ALADDIN's cave a place full of valuable objects. ●From the *Arabian Nights* tale of Aladdin, who found a magic lamp in a cave (see next entry).

an ALADDIN's lamp a talisman that enables its owner to fulfil every desire. ● From the oriental tale of Aladdin, who was able, by rubbing a magic lamp, to make the genie in the lamp carry out his wishes.

ALARMS and excursions confused activity and uproar. *humorous* ● The earlier spelling *alarum* represents a pronunciation of *alarm* with a rolling of the 'r'; originally a call summoning soldiers to arms (cf. Italian *allarme*). The whole phrase is used in stage directions in Shakespeare (e.g., beginning of 3 *Henry VI* V. ii) to indicate a battle scene.

ALIENATE someone's affections induce someone to transfer their affection from a person (such as a spouse) with legal rights or claims on them. *US Law*

set the world (*or* the place) ALIGHT achieve something sensational. *informal* ● Cf. ▶ **set the world on FIRE**.

ALIVE and kicking prevalent and very active. *informal*
> **1991** M. TULLY *No Full Stops in India* (1992) iv. 127 You deliberately choose unknown actors, although India is a country where the star system is very much alive and kicking.

ALIVE and well still existing or active. ● Often used to deny rumours or beliefs that something has disappeared or declined.

ALL comers anyone who chooses to take part in an activity, typically a competition.
> **1992** A. GORE *Earth in Balance* xiv. 292 He has traveled to conferences and symposia in every part of the world, argued his case, and patiently taken on all comers.

ALL in 1 with everything included. **2** *informal, dated* exhausted.

ALL of as much as. ● Often used ironically of an amount considered very small by the speaker or writer.
> **1995** B. BRYSON *Notes from Small Island* (1996) vii. 104 In 1992, a development company ... tore down five listed buildings, in a conservation area, was taken to court and fined all of £675.

ALL over the place in a state of confusion or disorganization. *informal* ● Also literally, 'everywhere'. ▶ **All over the MAP** is a N. Amer. variant of this idiom, as is ▶ **all over the LOT**. ▶ **All over the SHOP (*or* SHOW)** is mainly Brit.
> **1997** *Spectator* 13 Sept. 21/2 The government ... proposed equalising standards and making them comparable ... there could be no clearer admission that standards are all over the place.

ALL round 1 in all respects. **2** for or by each person. ● In US usage also *all around*.

ALL-singing all-dancing with every possible attribute, able to perform any necessary function. ● Applied particularly in the area of computer technology, but ultimately deriving from descriptions of show business acts.
> **1998** *Country Life* 21 May 90/1 Agromenes had hoped to celebrate the passing of the fashion for the all-singing, all-dancing mega-hospital on centralised out-of-town campus locations.

ALL there in full possession of one's mental faculties. *informal* ● Often with negative: *not all there*.

— and ALL as well. *informal* ● Used to emphasize something additional that is being referred to, as in ▶ **UNCLE Tom Cobley and all**.

for ALL — in spite of —.

ALL ▶ *see* **my EYE**; ▶ *see* **on all FOURS (with)**; ▶ *see* **be all GO**; ▶ *see* **all the RAGE**; ▶ *see* **(all) of a SUDDEN**; ▶ *see* **all SYSTEMS go**; ▶ *see* **all THINGS to all men**; ▶ *see* **be all UP with**; ▶ *see* **all the WORLD and his wife**.

give someone (*or* get) the ALL-CLEAR indicate to someone (*or* get a sign) that a dangerous situation is now safe. ● From the signal sounded in wartime to indicate that a bombing raid is over.

ALLEY ▶ *see* **a BLIND alley**; ▶ *see* **up one's STREET**.

ALLY ▶ *see* **PASS in one's ally**.

ALONG about round about (a specified time or date). *N. Amer., informal or dialect*

ALPHA and omega 1 the beginning and the end. **2** the essence or most important features. ● *Alpha* and *omega* are respectively the first and last letters of the Greek alphabet. Following Revelation 1:8 ('I am Alpha and Omega, the beginning and the ending, saith the Lord') Christians use the phrase as a title of Jesus Christ.

sacrifice someone/thing on/at the ALTAR of someone/thing cause someone or something to suffer in the interests of (someone or something else).

in the ALTOGETHER without any clothes on; naked. *informal*
| *1894 G. DU MAURIER *Trilby* I. 185 I have sat for the 'altogether' to several other people.

run AMOK behave uncontrollably and disruptively. ● Also formerly spelt *amuck*. The word comes from Malay *amuk*, meaning 'in a homicidal frenzy', in which sense it was first introduced (E16) into English.

in the final (*or* last *or* ultimate) ANALYSIS when everything has been considered. ● Used to suggest that the following statement expresses the basic truth about a complex situation.

the ANCIENT of Days God. ● In the Bible (Daniel 7:9), used as a title for God the Father.

ANCIENT ▶ *see* **ancient as the HILLS**.

the ANGEL in the house a woman who is completely devoted to her husband and family. ● The title of a collection of poems on married love by Coventry Patmore (1823–96), it is now mainly used ironically.

on the side of the ANGELS on the side of what is right. ● In a speech in Oxford in November 1864 the British statesman Benjamin Disraeli alluded to the controversy over the origins of humankind then raging in the wake of the publication of Charles Darwin's *Origin of Species* (1859): 'Is man an ape or an angel? Now I am on the side of the angels' (*Times* 26 Nov. 1864).

ANGRY young man a young man who feels and expresses anger at the conventional values of the society around him. ● Originally, a member of a group of socially conscious writers in Britain in the 1950s, including particularly the playwright John Osborne. The phrase, the title of a book (1951) by Leslie Paul, was used of Osborne in the publicity material for his play *Look Back in Anger* (1956), in which the characteristic views were articulated by the anti-hero Jimmy Porter.

ANSWER ▶ *see* **the answer's a LEMON**; ▶ *see* **a DUSTY answer**.

have ANTS in one's pants be fidgety or restless. *informal*

up (*or* raise) the ANTE increase what is at stake or under discussion, especially in a conflict or dispute. *chiefly N. Amer.* ● From Latin *ante* 'before'. As an English noun it was originally (E19) a term in poker and similar gambling games, meaning 'a stake put up by a player before drawing cards'.

> **1998** *New Scientist* 14 Mar. 12/3 This report ups the ante on the pace at which these cases need to be identified and treated.

be not having ANY (of it) be absolutely unwilling to cooperate. *informal* ● The shorter form without *of it* is mainly N. Amer.

be ANYONE's (of a person) be open to sexual advances from anyone. *informal*

ANYONE's game an evenly balanced contest.

ANYTHING ▶ *see* **anything GOES**.

APART ▶ *see* **be POLES apart**; ▶ *see* **come apart at the SEAMS**.

go APE go wild; become violently excited. *informal* ● Originally M20 North American slang, possibly with reference to the 1933 movie *King Kong*, starring a giant ape-like monster.

an APOLOGY for a very poor example of.

> **1902** W. CATHER *Treasure of Far Island* (1987) 149 He was amused to see his father appear in an apology for a frock coat and a black tie.

with APOLOGIES to used before the name of an author or artist to indicate that something is a parody or adaptation of their work.

APPEAL to Caesar appeal to the highest possible authority. ● With allusion to the claim made by the apostle Paul to have his case heard in Rome, which was his right as a Roman citizen: 'I appeal unto Caesar' (Acts 25:11).

APPEAL from Philip drunk to Philip sober ask someone to reconsider, with the suggestion that an earlier opinion or decision represented a passing mood only. ● Alluding to an anecdote told by Valerius Maximus (vi. 2) concerning an unjust judgement given by King Philip of Macedon; the condemned woman declared that she would appeal to Philip, but when he was sober.

the APPLE of one's eye a person or thing of whom one is extremely fond and proud. ● Originally (OE) denoting the pupil of the eye, considered to be a globular solid body; hence extended as a symbol of something cherished and watched over, as in Psalm 17:8.

a rotten (*or* bad) APPLE a bad person in a group, typically one whose behaviour is likely to have a corrupting influence on the rest. *informal* ● With reference to the fact that a rotten apple causes other fruit with which it is in contact to rot.

upset the APPLE CART wreck an advantageous project or disturb the status quo. ●*Apple cart* as a metaphor for a satisfactory but possibly precarious state of affairs is recorded in various expressions from L18 onwards.

> **1996** *Business Age* June 83/2 The real test will be instability in China ... Another Tiananmen Square could really upset the applecart.

(as) American as APPLE PIE typically American in character. *N. Amer.*

> **1995** *New York Times Magazine* 26 Feb. 22/2 To reward people for something beyond merit is as American as apple pie.

she's APPLES used to indicate that everything is in good order and there is nothing to worry about. *Austral., informal* ● From *apples and spice* or *apples and rice*, rhyming slang for *nice*.

APPLES and oranges (of two people or things) irreconcilably or fundamentally different. *N. Amer.*

seal (*or* stamp) of APPROVAL an indication or statement that something is accepted or regarded favourably. ● From the practice of putting a stamp (or formerly a seal) on official documents.

(tied to) someone's APRON strings (too much under) the influence and control of someone. ●Especially used to suggest that a man is too much influenced by his mother.

AREA ▶ *see* **a GREY area**; ▶ *see* **a NO-GO area**.

ARGUE the toss dispute a decision or choice already made. *chiefly Brit., informal* ●*Toss* is the tossing of a coin to decide an issue in a simple and unambiguous way according to the side of the coin visible when it lands.

out of the ARK extremely old-fashioned. ●The allusion is Noah's ark (Genesis 6–7).

cost an ARM and a leg be extremely expensive. *informal*

give an ARM and a leg for pay a high price for.

would give one's right ARM for something be willing to pay a high price for. *informal* ●Used to emphasize how much one would like to have or do something.

the long ARM of coincidence the far-reaching power of coincidence.

the long (*or* strong) ARM of the law the police seen as a far-reaching or intimidating power.

put the ARM on attempt to force or coerce (someone) to do something. *N. Amer., informal*

an ARMCHAIR critic a person who knows about a subject only by reading or hearing about it and criticizes without active experience or first-hand knowledge. ●*Armchair critic* is first recorded in 1896, but the concept was around at least a decade earlier when Joseph Chamberlain sneered at opponents as 'arm-chair politicians' (1886). Another common variant is *armchair traveller*, meaning 'someone who travels in imagination only'.

ARMED at all points prepared in every particular. ● From a First Folio variant reading of Shakespeare's *Hamlet* I. ii. 200.

ARMED to the teeth **1** carrying a lot of weapons. **2** heavily equipped.

up to one's ARMPITS deeply involved in a particular unpleasant situation or enterprise. *chiefly US*

a call to ARMS a call to make ready for confrontation.

up in ARMS protesting angrily (about something). ●Usually with preposition *about* or *over*.

> **1994** *Asian Times* 5 Nov. 13/1 A lack of checks and balances ... or legal redress for workers have trade unions up in arms.

you and whose ARMY? used as an expression of disbelief in someone's ability to carry out a threat. *informal*

have been AROUND have a lot of varied experience of the world, especially a lot of sexual experience. *informal*

a straight ARROW an honest or genuine person. *N. Amer.*

go (*or* fall) ARSE over tit fall over in a sudden or dramatic way. *vulgar slang*

not know one's ARSE from one's elbow be totally ignorant or incompetent. *vulgar slang*

ARSE ▶ *see* **LICK someone's boots**; ▶ *see* **a PAIN in the arse**.

ART for art's sake the idea that a work of art has no purpose beyond itself. ●The slogan of aestheticians who hold that the chief or only aim of a work of art is the self-expression of the individual artist who creates it. Cf. Benjamin Constant in *Journal intime* (1804), writing of a theory of aesthetics that derives ultimately from Kant: *L'art pour l'art et sans but* 'art for art's sake and without a purpose'.

be ART and part of be an accessory or participant in; be deeply involved in. ●Originally a Scottish legal expression, but now in general use: *art* referred to the contriving of an action and *part* to participation in it.

ART ▶ *see* **have something down to a FINE art**; ▶ *see* **STATE of the art**.

an ARTICLE of faith a firmly held belief. ●*Article* is in the sense of 'a statement or item in a summary of religious belief'.

> **1692** J. LOCKE *Third Letter for Toleration* i Articles of Faith (as they are called) ... cannot be imposed on any Church by the Law of the Land.

the genuine ARTICLE a person or thing considered to be an authentic and excellent example of their kind.

in the ASCENDANT rising in power or influence. ●From L16 used figuratively with reference to the technical astrological sense of *ascendant* as the point of the ecliptic (or sign of the zodiac) that at a particular moment is just rising above the eastern horizon.

rise (*or* emerge) from the ASHES be renewed after destruction. ●In classical myth, the phoenix was a fabulous bird which, when it became old, immolated itself upon a funeral pyre and was born again from the ashes with renewed youth. Hence the simile *like a phoenix from the ashes* used of someone/thing that has made a fresh start after apparently experiencing total destruction.

turn to ASHES (in one's mouth) become something that is bitterly disappointing or worthless. ● The allusion is to Dead Sea fruit (also called apple of Sodom or Dead Sea apple), which is mentioned by Josephus as having an appetizing appearance but dissolving into smoke and ashes when one attempts to eat it.

*1817 T. MOORE *Lalla Rookh* 222 Like Dead Sea fruits, that tempt the eye, But turn to ashes on the lips!

ASHES ▶ see **DUST and ashes**; ▶ see **RAKE over coals**.

ASK me another! I do not know the answer. *informal* ● Used to say emphatically that one does not know the answer to a question.

a big ASK a difficult demand to fulfil. *Austral. & NZ, informal*

don't ASK me! used to indicate that one does not know the answer to a question and that one is surprised or irritated to be questioned. *informal*

I ASK you! an exclamation of shock or disapproval intended to elicit agreement from one's listener. *informal*

ASK ▶ see **cry for the MOON**; ▶ see **ask no ODDS**.

be ASKING for trouble (*or* it) behave in a way that is likely to result in difficulty for oneself. *informal*

ASLEEP at the switch not attentive or alert; inactive. *N. Amer., informal*

1997 *High Country News* 17 Feb. 7/3 HUD officials were basically 'asleep at the switch' while corrupt tribal leaders … built luxury homes for themselves.

bust one's ASS try very hard to do something. *N. Amer., slang*

chew (someone's) ASS reprimand severely. *N. Amer., slang*

drag (*or* tear *or* haul) ASS hurry or move fast. *N. Amer., informal*

get your ASS in (*or* into) gear hurry. *N. Amer., informal* ● Usually in imperative.

kick (some) ASS (*or* kick someone's ass) act aggressively or assertively. *N. Amer., informal*

| 1995 M. AMIS *Information* (1996) 290 You got to come on strong. Talk big and kick ass.

not give a rat's ASS not care at all about something. *N. Amer., slang*

put (*or* have) someone's ASS in a sling get someone in trouble. *N. Amer., slang*

whip (*or* bust) someone's ASS use physical force to beat someone in a fight. *N. Amer., slang*

ASS ▶ see **KISS ass**; ▶ see **no SKIN off one's nose**; ▶ see **a PAIN in the arse**; ▶ see **a PIECE of ass**.

AT that in addition; furthermore. ● Originally (M19) a US colloquialism (cf.
▶ **into the BARGAIN**). Used for emphasis at the end of an utterance.
| **1884** F. M. CRAWFORD *Roman Singer* I. 226 A shoemaker, and a poor one at that.

where it's AT the fashionable place, possession, or activity. *informal*
| **1990** E. ELDMAN *Looking for Love* xi. 136 New York is where it's at, stylewise.

an ATMOSPHERE that one could cut with a knife a general feeling of
great tension or malevolence.

ATTENDANCE ▶ *see* **dance ATTENDANCE on**.

ATTITUDE ▶ *see* **STRIKE an attitude**.

AUCTION ▶ *see* **on the BLOCK**.

for AULD lang syne for old times' sake. ● Literally, 'for old long since', the
title and refrain of a song by Robert Burns.

under the AUSPICES of with the help, support, or protection of. ● *Auspice*
(since L18 almost always used in the plural), derives from Latin *auspicium*, the
act of divination carried out by an *auspex* in ancient Rome. The *auspex* foretold
the outcome of a course of action by observing the flight or behaviour of
birds, and if the omens were favourable he was seen as the protector of the
enterprise.

have something on good AUTHORITY have ascertained something from a
reliable source.

AWAKE ▶ *see* **be a WAKE-UP**.

AWAY with — let us be rid of —. ● Used as an exhortation to overcome or be rid
of something.

(get) AWAY with you! used to express scepticism. *Scottish*

AWAY ▶ *see* **FAR and away**; ▶ *see* **OUT and away**.

the AWKWARD age adolescence.

the AWKWARD squad a squad composed of recruits and soldiers who need
further training. ● Shortly before his death Robert Burns is reported to have
said, 'Don't let the awkward squad fire over me.' Now often used with *awkward*
in the sense of 'tiresome or difficult to deal with'.

have an AXE to grind have a (private, sometimes malign) motive for doing or
being involved in something. ● The expression originated in a story told by
Benjamin Franklin and was used first in the US, especially with reference to
politics, but now generally. Often in negative.
| **1997** *Times* 27 Nov. 21/3 I am a non-smoker, and have no personal axe to grind.

the AYES have it the affirmative votes are in the majority. ● *Aye* is an archaic
or dialectal word meaning 'yes', now used in standard speech only when
voting by voice. Used in giving the result of a formal vote. Cf. ▶ **the NOES
have it**.
| **1865** C. DICKENS *Our Mutual Friend* II. xvii. 304 As many as are of that opinion, say Aye,—
| contrary, No—the Ayes have it.

B

plan B an alternative strategy.

> **1997** *Spectator* 22 Nov. 28/3 Labour's most ruthless act during the campaign ... was planned all along by Labour leaders. I gather they called it 'Plan B'.

BABES in the wood inexperienced people in a situation calling for experience. ● With reference to an old ballad *The Children in the Wood*.

be someone's BABY be someone's creation or special concern. *informal* ● Used particularly of a project that has been instigated and developed by one particular person.

throw the BABY out (or away) with the bathwater discard something valuable along with other things that are inessential or undesirable. *proverbial* ● This is based on a German saying recorded from E16 but not introduced into English until M19 by Thomas Carlyle (*Nigger Question* ed. 2 (1853) 29) who identifies it as German and gives it in the form, 'You must empty out the bathing-tub, but not the baby along with it.'

> **1998** *New Scientist* 24 Jan. 45/1 It is easy to throw out the baby with the bathwater when it comes to UFO books—there are some seriously bad titles out there.

BABY ▶ *see* **be left HOLDING the baby**.

a BACK number **1** an issue of a periodical before the current one. **2** a person whose ideas or methods are out of date and who is no longer relevant or useful. ● First used in its literal sense E19; the transferred sense originated (L19) as a US colloquialism.

the BACK of beyond a very remote or inaccessible place.

> **1996** S. DEANE *Reading in Dark* (1997) vi. 221 I could tell you anywhere. Egypt? Brazil? The Atlantic Ocean? The back of beyond?

BACK to the drawing board start again to devise a new plan from the beginning because the present plan or course of action has been unsuccessful. ● An architectural or engineering project is at its earliest phase when it exists only as a plan on a *drawing board*.

> **1965** *New Yorker* 6 Nov. 122A fiery mushroom cloud, translatable by the most cretinous moviegoer as ... 'Back to the drawing board, you plucky amoebas!'

BACK to square one back to the starting-point, with no progress made. ● *Square one* may be a reference to a board-game such as Snakes and Ladders, or derive from the notional division of a football pitch into eight numbered sections for the purpose of early radio commentaries.

by (or through) the BACK door using indirect or dishonest means to achieve an objective. ● Cf. the proverb *a postern [back] door makes a thief*, recorded in English since M15.

at the BACK of one's mind not consciously or specifically thought of or remembered but still part of one's general awareness.

BACK the wrong horse make a wrong or inappropriate choice. ●A horse-racing and betting metaphor.

be on (or get off) someone's BACK nag (or stop nagging) at someone. *informal*

get (or put) someone's BACK up make someone annoyed or angry. ●In allusion to a cat's arching its back in anger.

know something like the BACK of one's hand be entirely familiar with something.

on one's BACK in bed recovering from an injury or illness.

put one's BACK into approach (a task) with vigour.

see the BACK of be rid of (an unwanted person or thing). *Brit., informal*

take a BACK seat take or be given a less important position or role. ●Cf. ▶ **in the DRIVER's seat**.

someone's BACK is turned someone's attention is elsewhere.
  | **1989** O. S. CARD *Prentice Alvin* v. 87 That prentice of yours look strong enough to dig it hisself, if he doesn't lazy off and sleep when your back is turned.

with one's BACK to (or up against) the wall in a desperate situation.

BACK (adj.) ▶ *see* **NOT in my back yard**.

BACK (adv.) ▶ *see* **GET one's own back**.

put BACKBONE into someone encourage someone to behave resolutely. ●As a metaphor for 'firmness of character' *backbone* dates from M19.
  | **1998** *Spectator* 7 Feb. 6/2 There is a widespread belief that if only Mrs Thatcher had still been in No. 10, she would have put backbone into Bush and got rid of Saddam.

a BACK-SEAT driver a passenger in a vehicle who constantly gives the driver unwanted advice on how to drive. ●Very often used figuratively for someone who lectures and criticizes the person actually in control of something.

bend (or fall or lean) over BACKWARDS to do something make every effort, especially to be fair or helpful. *informal*

know something BACKWARDS be entirely familiar with something.
  | **1991** W. TREVOR *Reading Turgenev* (1992) ii. 6 People who lived in the town knew it backwards.

bring home the BACON achieve success. *informal*
  | **1997** *Spectator* 15 Nov. 35 Mr Montgomery was able to sack Mr Hargreaves, who had evidently not brought home the bacon ...

BACON ▶ *see* **SAVE one's skin**.

a BAD quarter of an hour a short but very unpleasant period of time; an unnerving experience. ●A translation of French *mauvais quart d'heure*, which has also been current in English since M19.

BAD ▶ *see* **bad BLOOD**; ▶ *see* **be bad NEWS**; ▶ *see* **come to a sticky END**; ▶ *see* **turn up like a bad PENNY**; ▶ *see* **a bad WORKMAN blames his tools**.

BAG and baggage with all one's belongings.

a BAG of bones an emaciated person or animal. ● Cf. ▶ **be SKIN and bone.**

a BAG (*or* bundle) of nerves a person who is extremely timid or tense. *informal*

a BAG (*or* the whole bag) of tricks a set of ingenious plans, techniques, or resources. *informal*

in the BAG 1 (of something desirable) as good as secured. **2** *US, informal* drunk.

BAG ▶ *see* **be left HOLDING the baby; PACK one's bag.**

fish or cut BAIT stop vacillating and act on or disengage from something. *N. Amer., informal*

BAIT ▶ *see* **RISE to the bait.**

BAKER ▶ *see* **a baker's DOZEN.**

weigh (something) in the BALANCE carefully ponder or assess the merits and demerits (of something). ● The image is of a pair of old-fashioned scales with two pans in which the positive and negative aspects of something can be set against each other. Also *weighed in the balance and found wanting* meaning 'having failed to meet the test of a particular situation'; with allusion to the biblical book of Daniel, part of the judgement made on King Belshazzar (cf. ▶ **the WRITING is on the wall**).

BALANCE ▶ *see* **tip the SCALES.**

(as) BALD as a coot completely bald. ● The bald coot (*Fulica atra*) has a broad white shield extending upwards from the base of its bill. The history of the word *bald* is somewhat obscure, but analogies with other northern European languages suggest a connection with the idea of 'having a white patch or streak'. The simile is recorded in Lydgate (M15).

the BALL is in someone's court it is that particular person's turn to act next. ● A metaphor from tennis or a similar ball game where different players use particular areas of a marked court.

a BALL and chain a severe hindrance. ● Alluding to the heavy metal ball secured by a chain to the leg of a prisoner or convict to prevent escape.

behind the eight BALL at a disadvantage, baffled. *N. Amer.* ● The black ball is numbered eight in a variety of the game of pool.

a BALL of fire a person who is full of energy and enthusiasm. ● Also literally 'a fire-ball'; the figurative use is apparently a M20 colloquialism. An earlier (E19) slang use of the phrase was 'a glass of brandy'.

have a lot on the BALL have a lot of ability. *US*

keep the BALL rolling maintain the momentum of an activity.

keep one's eye on (*or* take one's eye off) the BALL keep (*or* fail to keep) one's attention focused on the matter in hand.

on the BALL alert to new ideas, methods, and trends. *informal* ●Originally a US colloquialism (see quot.), but in L20 also widespread in British usage.
| **1961** *Listener* 28 Dec. The B.B.C. are 'on the ball' as the Americans would say.

play BALL (with) work willingly with others; cooperate. *informal* ●The literal sense is 'play a team ball game such as baseball or cricket'.

start (*or* **get** *or* **set**) **the BALL rolling** set an activity in motion; make a start.

the whole BALL of wax everything. *N. Amer.*, *informal*

have the BALL at one's feet have one's best opportunity of succeeding. ●'He has the ball at his foot' is recorded as a Scottish saying from M17.

have a BALL enjoy oneself greatly; have fun. *informal* ●Originally US slang (M20).

a whole new BALL game a completely new set of circumstances. *orig. N. Amer.*, *informal* ●*Ball game* in North America refers to a game of baseball.
| **1998** *New Scientist* 11 July 38/3 This makes molecular anthropology 'a whole new ball game', says Zegura.

go BALLISTIC fly into a rage. *chiefly N. Amer.*, *informal*
| **1998** *New Scientist* 4 Apr. 50/2 The French nuclear industry, local authorities around La Hague and some government agencies went ballistic. Viel was fiercely condemned for his findings.

when (*or* **before**) **the BALLOON goes up** when (*or* before) the action or trouble starts. *informal* ●Probably with allusion to the release of a balloon to mark the start of an event.
| **1959** *Punch* 21 Oct. 322/1 The international rules of war are apt to be waived when the balloon goes up.

BALLOON ▶ *see* **go down like a LEAD balloon**.

in the BALLPARK in a particular area or range. *orig. US*, *informal* ●In the US a *ballpark* is a baseball ground.

the BAMBOO curtain an impenetrable political, economic, and cultural barrier between China and non-Communist countries. ●Formed after ▶ **IRON curtain**, it is primarily (M20) in political and economic use.

BANANA republic a small tropical state, esp. one in central America, whose economy is perceived as wholly dependent on its fruit-exporting trade. *derogatory*

second BANANA the second most important person in an organization or activity. *chiefly N. Amer.*, *informal* ●Originally (M20) US theatrical slang meaning the supporting comedian in a show.

top BANANA the most important person in an organization or activity. *chiefly N. Amer.*, *informal* ●Originally (M20) US theatrical slang meaning the comedian who tops the bill in a show.

BANANA SKIN ▶ *see* **SLIP on a banana skin**.

go BANANAS 1 become extremely angry or excited. **2** go mad. *informal*

> **1 1992** J. LEHRER *Bus of My Own* (1993) vi. 122 The worst was on the night I predicted John Erlichman would probably go bananas when he testified the next day.

when the BAND begins to play when matters become serious.

jump (*or* climb) on the BANDWAGON join others in doing or supporting something fashionable or likely to be successful. ●*Bandwagon* was originally the US term for a large wagon able to carry a band in a procession.

BANG for one's (*or* the) buck value for money; performance for cost. *chiefly US*

> **1995** *Desktop Publishing Journal* July 45/3 These additions to RunShare … will surely give you the most productive network, the most 'bang for your buck'.

BANG goes — used to express the sudden or complete destruction of something, especially a plan or ambition.

> **1895** G. B. SHAW *Letter* 28 Nov. Somebody will give a surreptitious performance of it: and then bang goes my copyright.

BANG (*or* knock *or* crack) (people's) heads together reprimand people severely, especially in the attempt to make them stop arguing.

get a BANG out of derive excitement or pleasure from. *chiefly N. Amer.*

> **1931** D. RUNYON *Guys and Dolls* (1932) vi. 129He seems to be getting a great bang out of the doings.

go (*or* go off) with a BANG happen with obvious success.

break the BANK 1 (in gambling) win more money than is held by the bank. **2** *informal* cost more than one can afford.

under the BANNER of 1 claiming to support a particular cause or set of ideas. **2** as part of a particular group or organization.

forbid the BANNS raise an objection to an intended marriage, especially in church following the reading of the banns. *archaic*

a BAPTISM of fire an unpleasant new experience at the start of a new undertaking. ●From the original sense of a soldier's initiation into battle.

> **1998** *Times* 9 June 33/5 Opposition spokesmen do not normally face a baptism of fire, but the Bank of England's unexpected decision … provided the Shadow Chancellor with an opportunity to make an early mark.

BAR none with no exceptions. ●Used postpositively.

> **1866** M. E. BRADDON *Lady's Mile* (edn 4) II. vii. 192 Your 'Aspasia' is the greatest picture that ever was painted—'bar none'.

the BARE bones the basic facts about something, without any detail.

would not touch someone/thing with a BARGEPOLE (*or* US ten-foot pole) would not have anything to do with someone or something. *informal* ●A *bargepole* is used on a vessel for fending. Used to express emphatic refusal or rejection.

someone's BARK is worse than their bite someone is not as ferocious as

they appear or sound. ● Earliest (E19) as a Scottish saying: 'Monkbarns's bark
... is muckle waur than his bite' (in W. Scott *Antiquary* vii (1816)). A similar
association between barking and biting however occurs in the proverb *A
barking dog never bites* which can be traced back through thirteenth-century
French (*chascuns chiens qui abaie ne mort pas* dogs that bark don't bite) to Latin:
*Adjicit deinde, quod apud Bactrianos vulgo usurpantur: canem timidum vehementius
latrare quam mordere* he then added what is commonly said among the Bactrians: that a timid dog barks more furiously than it bites (Quintus Curtius
De Rebus Gestis Alexandri Magni VII. iv. 13).

BARK up the wrong tree pursue a mistaken or misguided line of thought or
course of action. *informal* ● Originally (M19) US, the metaphor is of a dog
that has mistaken the tree in which its quarry has taken refuge and is barking
at the foot of the wrong one.
> **1898** C. G. ROBERTSON *Voces Academicae* 117 ... I calc'late we've barked up the wrong tree
> ... That comes of hazing round without a guide.

BARK (verb) ▶ *see* **bark at the MOON**.

BARN ▶ *see* **round ROBIN Hood's barn**.

BARRED ▶ *see* **no HOLDS barred**.

a BARREL of laughs a source of fun or amusement. *informal* ● Generally used
with negative.

(get someone) over a BARREL (get someone) in a helpless position; (have
someone) at one's mercy. *informal* ● Perhaps referring to the condition of a
person who has been rescued from drowning and is placed over a barrel to
clear the lungs of water; this idiom appears to have originated in the US
(M20).

BARREL ▶ *see* **SCRAPE the barrel**.

BARRELHEAD ▶ *see* **on the NAIL**.

with both BARRELS with unrestrained force or emotion. *chiefly US, informal*
● With reference to the two barrels of a firearm.

get to first BASE achieve the first step towards one's objective. *chiefly N. Amer.,
informal* ● *Base* in this and the following two idioms refers to each of the four
points in the angles of the 'diamond' in baseball, which a player has to reach
in order to score a run. Usually used with negative.
> **1962** P. G. WODEHOUSE *Service with Smile* x. 157 She gives you the feeling that you'll never
> get to first base with her.

off BASE mistaken. *N. Amer., informal*
> **1947** *Time* 20 Oct. 11/1 Your Latin American department was off base in its comparison of the
> Portillo Hotel in Chile with our famous Sun Valley.

touch BASE (with) briefly make or renew contact (with someone or something).
N. Amer., informal
> **1984** A. MAUPIN *Babycakes* (1989) xviii. 118 In search of a routine, he touched base with his
> launderette, his post office, his nearest market.

back to BASICS abandoning complication and sophistication to concentrate on the most essential aspects of something. ●Often used to suggest the moral superiority of the plain and simple, as in a speech (1993) by British Conservative leader John Major, who spearheaded the Government's campaign for the regeneration of elementary family and educational values in the 1990s.

off one's own BAT at one's own instigation; spontaneously. *Brit.* ●The *bat* is a cricket bat.

> **1995** C. BATEMAN *Cycle of Violence* xiii. 230 She doesn't have me doing anything, Marty. It's all off my own bat.

right off the BAT at the very beginning; straight away. *N. Amer.*

like a BAT (or bats) out of hell very fast and wildly. *informal* ●With reference to the rapid flight of bats when they are disturbed.

> **1998** *New Scientist* 18 Apr. 13/2 Still smaller therapods would have been able to race along … Farlow believes. 'I suspect that some of those guys could have run like bats out of hell,' he says.

not BAT (or without batting) an eyelid (or eye) show (or showing) no emotional or other reaction. *informal* ●Also *not blink an eye. Bat* in this sense is perhaps a dialect and US variant of *bate* 'lower, let down' (see quot.).

> **1879** MISS JACKSON *Shropshire Word-book* Bat, to wink, or rather to move the eyelids up and down quickly.

BAT (noun) ▶ *see* **BLIND as a bat**.

with BATED breath in great suspense; very anxiously or excitedly. ●*Baited*, which is sometimes seen, is a misspelling, since *bated* in this sense is a shortened form of *abated*, the idea being that one's breathing is lessened under the influence of extreme suspense.

an early BATH the sending off of a sports player during a game. *Brit., informal* ●The allusion is to the bath or shower taken by players at the end of a match.

take a BATH suffer a heavy financial loss. *informal*

> **1997** *Bookseller* 21 Nov. 28/3 When the yen drops in value, as it is doing right now, we take a bath. There is no way to change the prices fast enough.

pass (or hand) (on) the BATON hand over a particular duty or responsibility. ●A metaphor from athletics: the *baton* is the short stick or rod passed from one runner to the next in a relay race. Thus to *take up* (or *pick up*) *the baton* is to accept a duty or responsibility. Cf. ▶ **hand on the TORCH**.

under the BATON of (of an orchestra or choir) conducted by. ●The *baton* here is the rod used by the conductor.

have BATS in the (or one's) belfry be eccentric or crazy. *informal* ●With reference to the wild flying of bats when disturbed in an enclosed space.

> c **1901** G. W. PECK *Peck's Red-Headed Boy* 82 They all thought a crazy man with bats in his belfry had got loose.

BATTEN down the hatches prepare for a difficulty or crisis. ●Originally a nautical term meaning 'make secure a ship's hatches with gratings and tarpaulins' in expectation of stormy weather.

| **1998** *Oldie* May 22/1 They endured the hard pounding of the Seventies, when Labour battened down the hatches, and soldiered through the follies of the early Eighties.

BATTERIES ▶ *see* **RECHARGE one's batteries**.

BATTLE of the giants a contest between two pre-eminent parties. ●Perhaps with reference to the battle between the giants and gods in Greek mythology.

BATTLE royal a fiercely contested fight or dispute. ●The plural is *battles royal*.

| **1997** F. CHAPPELL *Farewell I'm Bound to Leave You* 47 The boys told no one about the fight … it was a battle royal and went on from two o'clock in the afternoon until sundown.

BATTLE stations the positions taken by military personnel in preparation for battle. *chiefly US* ●Used as a command or signal to prepare for battle.

half the BATTLE an important step towards achieving something. ●Cf. the proverbial saying *the first blow is half the battle*.

BATTLE ▶ *see* **a LOSING battle**; ▶ *see* **a PITCHED battle**; ▶ *see* **a RUNNING battle**.

bring someone/thing to BAY trap or corner a person or animal being hunted or chased. ●A medieval hunting term (OF *tenir a bay*), referring to the position of the quarry when it is cornered by the baying hounds. An animal thus cornered is said to *stand at bay*.

hold (*or* keep) someone/thing at BAY prevent someone or something from approaching or having an effect.

the BE-all and end-all a feature of an activity or a way of life that is of greater importance than any other. *informal*

BE there for someone be available to support or comfort someone who is experiencing difficulties or adversities.

-to-BE of the future. ●Used postpositively.

| **1996** D. W. BROWN *Teach Yourself Aromatherapy* v. 40 As it helps to prevent stretch marks, it is a must for the mother-to-be!

draw (*or* get) a BEAD on take aim at with a gun. *chiefly N. Amer.*

| **1831** J. AUDUBON *Ornithological Biography* I. 294 He raised his piece until the *bead* (that being the name given by the Kentuckians to the *sight*) of the barrel was brought to a line with the spot he intended to hit.

a BEAM in one's eye a fault that is greater in oneself than in the person one is finding fault with. ●With allusion to Matthew 7:3; cf. ▶ **a MOTE in someone's eye**.

off (*or* way off) BEAM on the wrong track; mistaken. *informal* ●Originally (M20) referring to the radio beam or signal used to guide aircraft. The opposite is *on the beam*.

| **1991** *Blitz* Sept. 85/1 Those who reckon that … convicted sported steroid poppers simply sit around metamorphosing into superhumans are way off beam.

on one's BEAM-ends near the end of one's resources; desperate. ●*Beam* in this sense was one of the main horizontal transverse timbers of a wooden ship; cf. ▶ **BROAD in the beam**. The phrase was originally (L18) a nautical term *on her beam-ends*, used of a ship that had heeled over on its side and was almost capsizing.

BEAM ▶ *see* **BROAD in the beam**.

not (have) a BEAN (be) penniless. ●Formerly (E19) a slang term for a golden guinea or sovereign, *bean* in the sense of 'a coin' now survives only in this phrase.

full of BEANS lively; in high spirits. *informal* ●Originally (M19) stable slang, referring to the good condition of a bean-fed horse.

a hill (*or* row) of BEANS something of little importance or value. *orig. US* ●Used with negative.
| 1863 'E. KIRKE' *My Southern Friends* v. 80l ... karn't take Preston's note—'taint wuth a hill o' beans.

know how many BEANS make five be intelligent; have one's wits about one. *Brit., informal*

BEANS ▶ *see* **SPILL the beans**.

like a BEAR with a sore head (of a person) very irritable. *Brit., informal*

loaded for BEAR fully prepared for any eventuality, typically a confrontation or challenge. *N. Amer., informal*

BEAR (verb) ▶ *see* **bear the BRUNT of**; ▶ *see* **GRIN and bear it**; ▶ *see* **have one's CROSS to bear**.

BEARD the lion in his den (*or* lair) confront or challenge someone on their own ground. ●Partly from the idea of taking a lion by the beard, partly from the use of *beard* to mean 'face'.

BEAT about the bush discuss a matter without coming to the point; be ineffectual and waste time. ●A metaphor originating in the shooting or netting of birds; cf. ▶ **BEAT the bushes**.
| 1572 G. GASCOIGNE *Works* (1587) 71 He bet about the bush, whyles other caught the birds.

BEAT someone at their own game use someone's own methods to outdo them in their chosen activity.

BEAT the bushes search thoroughly. *N. Amer., informal* ●The expression originates in the practice of hunters who walk through undergrowth with long sticks to force birds or animals hiding in the bushes out into the open where they can be shot or netted.

BEAT the clock perform a task quickly or within a fixed time limit.

BEAT one's (*or* the) meat (of a man) masturbate. *vulgar slang*

BEAT the pants off prove to be vastly superior to. *informal*
| 1990 P. AUSTER *Music of Chance* ii. 56 'Not bad, kid,' Nashe said. 'You beat the pants off me.'

BEAT a path to someone's door (of a large number of people) hasten to make contact with someone regarded as interesting or inspiring. ● From the idea of a large number of people trampling down vegetation to make a path; cf. ▶ **off the BEATEN track**.

BEAT a (hasty) retreat withdraw, typically in order to avoid something unpleasant. ● Formerly in a military context a drumbeat could be used to keep soldiers in step while retreating.

BEAT the system succeed in finding a means of getting round rules, regulations, or other means of control.

BEAT someone to it succeed in doing something or getting somewhere before someone else, to their annoyance.

if you can't BEAT them, join them if you are unable to outdo rivals in some endeavour, you might as well cooperate with them and gain whatever advantage possible by doing so. *humorous*. The US version with *lick* instead of *beat* was described (M20) as 'an old political adage'.

to BEAT all —s which is infinitely better than all the things mentioned.

to BEAT the band in such a way as to surpass all competition. *chiefly N. Amer., informal*

| **1995** P. McCABE *Dead School* (1996) 10 He was polishing away to beat the band.

BEAT (noun) ▶ *see* **MISS a beat**.

BEAT (verb) ▶ *see* **beat one's BREAST**; ▶ *see* **beat the DAYLIGHTS out of**; ▶ *see* **beat the DRUM for**.

BEATEN (*or informal* pipped) at the post defeated at the last moment. ● *Post* here is the marker at the end of a race.

off the BEATEN track (*or* path) **1** in or into an isolated place. **2** unusual.

the body BEAUTIFUL an ideal of physical beauty.

| **1992** *Mother Jones* Jan.–Feb. 26/1 About 75,000 women a year elect to have cosmetic surgery, spurred on by ubiquitous images of the body beautiful.

work like a BEAVER work steadily and industriously. *informal* ● The beaver is proverbial for the industriousness with which it constructs the dams necessary for its aquatic dwellings (cf. ▶ **an EAGER beaver**). The simile dates from M18, originating in the US. Hence *beaver (away)* as a verb (M20).

at someone's BECK and call always having to be ready to obey someone's orders immediately. ● *Beck* in the sense of 'significant gesture of command' (ME) comes from the verb *beck*, which is a shortened form of *beckon* (OE), and is now found mainly in this phrase.

BED of nails a problematic or uncomfortable situation. ● Originally a board with nails pointing out of it, as lain on by Eastern fakirs and ascetics.

a BED of roses a situation or activity that is comfortable or easy. ● Often with negative.

get out of BED on the wrong side be bad-tempered all day long.

in BED with **1** having sexual intercourse with. **2** in undesirably close association with. *informal*

one has made one's BED and must lie on (*or* in) it one must accept the consequences of one's own actions.

between you and me and the BEDPOST (*or* the gatepost *or* the wall) in strict confidence. *informal* ● The *bedpost*, *gatepost*, or *wall* is seen as marking the boundary beyond which the confidence must not go; moreover, a post itself is proverbially deaf and dumb.

BEDSIDE manner a doctor's approach or attitude to a patient.
> **1993** B. MOYERS *Healing & Mind* i. 49 Are you just talking about the old-fashioned bedside manner of a doctor who comes around and visits you when you need him?

have a BEE in one's bonnet have an obsessive preoccupation (with something). *informal* ● The expression *bees in the head* was used earlier (E16) of someone who was crazy or eccentric. The alliterative version with *bonnet* was probably known to the poet Herrick in M17, as he alludes to a bee in a 'bonnet brave' in his poem 'Mad Maud's Song' (*Hesperides*, 1648).

the BEE's knees something or someone outstandingly good. *informal* ● First used to denote something small and insignificant, then transferred to the opposite sense in US slang.

make a BEELINE for go rapidly and directly towards. ● The bee was supposed to fly in such a way when returning to its hive.
> **1997** *Bookseller* 21 Nov. 66/4 And when he heard that people might like him to sign copies of his new novel ... , he cut the small talk and made a beeline for the stall.

BEEN ▶ *see* **been THERE, done that**.

BEER and skittles amusement. *Brit.* ● From the proverbial saying (attested from M19) *life isn't all beer and skittles*. The game of *skittles* is taken as the type of light-hearted entertainment.

BEG the question assume the truth of an argument or of a proposition to be proved, without arguing it. ● In its original use in logic *begging the question* is the logical fallacy also known under its Latin name of *petitio principii*. It has recently also been widely misunderstood to mean 'raise a point that has not been dealt with' or 'invite an obvious question'.

BEGGAR belief (*or* description) be too extraordinary to be believed (*or* described).

BEGGAR on horseback a formerly poor person made arrogant or corrupt through achieving wealth and luxury. ● Cf. the proverbial saying *set a beggar on horseback and he'll ride to the devil* (M17); the phrase *beggar on horseback* was known earlier (L16).

go BEGGING **1** (of an article) be available. **2** (of an opportunity) not be taken.

BEGINNER's luck good luck supposed to attend a beginner at a particular game or activity.

the BEGINNING of the end the event or development to which the conclusion or failure can be traced.

> **1992** H. N. SCHWARTZKOPF *It Doesn't Take a Hero* ii. 24 I heard about D-Day on the radio. The announcer quoted Ohio governor John Bricker's now-famous line that this was 'the beginning of the end of the forces of evil'.

beat the BEJESUS out of someone hit someone very hard or for a long time. ● Alteration of the exclamation *by Jesus!* Often in its Anglo-Irish form *bejasus* or *bejabers*; see also next entry.

scare the BEJESUS (*or* bejabers) out of someone frighten someone very much; see previous entry.

> **1994** *Richmond Times-Dispatch* 29 Oct. E1/1 Scaring the bejabers out of people is an art.

BELL the cat take the danger of a shared enterprise upon oneself. ● In allusion to the fable in which mice or rats have the idea of hanging a bell around the cat's neck so as to have warning of its approach, the only difficulty being to find one of their number willing to undertake the task.

(as) clear (*or* sound) as a BELL perfectly clear (*or* sound).

> **1993** *Independent* 13 Feb. 40/5 We spent a few thousand on redecoration, but basically the place was sound as a bell.

ring a BELL revive a distant recollection; sound familiar. *informal* ● With preposition *with*.

BELL ▶ *see* **be SAVED by the bell**.

BELLE of the ball the most admired and successful woman on some occasion. ● Originally a girl or woman regarded as the most beautiful and popular at a dance.

BELLS and whistles attractive additional features or trimmings. *informal* ● In allusion to the various bells and whistles of old fairground organs. *Bells and whistles* in modern usage originated in computing jargon to mean 'speciously attractive but superfluous facilities'.

with BELLS on enthusiastically. *N. Amer.*, *informal*

> **1989** M. GORDON *Other Side* V. x. 384 So, everybody's waiting for you with bells on.

go BELLY up go bankrupt. *informal* ● The implied comparison is with a dead fish or other animal floating upside down in the water.

> **1998** *Times: Weekend* 19 Sept. 2/5 The single currency could well go belly-up within two or three years.

have a (*or* one's) BELLYFUL (of) become impatient after prolonged experience (of someone/thing). *informal*

BELOW stairs in the basement of a house, in particular as the part occupied by servants. *Brit.*, *dated*

below the BELT unfair or unfairly; not regarding the rules. ● From the notion of a low, and therefore illegal, blow in boxing.

BELT and braces (of a policy or action) of twofold security. *Brit.* ● From the literal *belt* and *braces* for holding up a pair of loose-fitting trousers.

tighten one's BELT cut one's expenditure; live more frugally.

under one's BELT **1** (of food or drink) consumed. **2** safely or satisfactorily achieved, experienced, or acquired.

BEND someone's ear talk to someone, especially with great eagerness or in order to ask a favour. *informal*

BEND one's elbow drink alcohol. *N. Amer.*

round (*or* US **around**) **the BEND** (*or* **twist**) crazy; mad. *informal* ● Characterized in F. C. Bowen *Sea Slang* (1929) as 'an old naval term for anybody who is mad'. The version with *twist* is an M20 British colloquial variant.

| **1998** *Spectator* 2 May 22/2 She combines a fondness for holidays in Switzerland with an amiable husband ... who saves her from going completely round the bend.

BEND (verb) ▶ *see* **bend over BACKWARDS**.

on BENDED knee (*or* **knees**) kneeling, especially when pleading or showing great respect. ● *Bended* was the original past participle of *bend*, but in ME it was superseded in general use by *bent*. It is now archaic and survives only in this phrase.

give someone/thing the BENEFIT of the doubt concede that someone/thing must be regarded as correct or justified, if the contrary has not been proved.

give someone the BENEFIT of — explain or recount to someone at length. ● Often used ironically when someone pompously or impertinently assumes that their knowledge or experience is superior to that of the person to whom they are talking.

a BENJAMIN's portion (*or* **mess**) the largest share, portion, etc. ● In the Bible, Benjamin was the youngest son of the Jewish patriarch Jacob. When Jacob's sons encountered their long-lost brother Joseph in Egypt, where he had become a high official, they failed to recognize him, but Joseph generously entertained them: 'And he took and sent messes [servings of food] unto them from before him: but Benjamin's mess was five times so much as any of their's' (Genesis 43:34)

| *1829 'AN OFFICER' *Twelve Years' Military Adventure* I. 21 [T]he majority ... were *ultra-Tweeders*, a people who, with souls too big for their native land, claim the privilege of ... securing a Benjamin's portion of the loaves and fishes, in whatever region they are to be found.

BENT out of shape angry or agitated. *N. Amer.*, *informal*

| **1994** D. SPENCER *Passing Fancy* xvi. 220 Max Corigliano was there ... and bent out of shape about having been made to wait so long.

give someone/thing a wide BERTH stay away from someone or something. ● *Berth* is a nautical term originally meaning the distance that ships should keep away from each other or from the shore, rocks, etc., in order to avoid a collision. Thus the literal meaning of the expression is 'to steer a ship well clear of something while passing it'. Earlier examples of the expression include *a clear berth* and *a good berth*, but from E19 the usual form has been *a wide berth*.

BESETTING sin a fault to which a person or institution is especially prone; a characteristic weakness. ●The somewhat archaic verb *beset* means literally 'surround with hostile intent', so the image is of a sin besieging or pressing in upon a person.

| **1974** D. SCHANNELL *Mother Knew Best* vi. 59 Mother said vanity was a besetting sin which Amy resented, to say the least of it.

BESIDE ▶ *see* **beside the POINT**.

one's BEST bet the most favourable option available in particular circumstances.

the BEST of (British) luck to someone used to wish someone well in an enterprise when one is almost sure it will be unsuccessful. *informal* ●Generally used ironically. Also abbreviated to *the best of British*.

give someone/thing BEST admit the superiority of; give way to. *Brit.*

make the BEST of it **1** derive what limited advantage one can from (something unsatisfactory or unwelcome). **2** use (resources) as well as possible. ●In British usage, sense 1 is often found in expanded form: *make the best of a bad job*, meaning 'do something as well as one can under difficult circumstances'.

six of the BEST a caning as a punishment, traditionally with six strokes of the cane. ●Formerly a common punishment in boys' schools, *six of the best* is now chiefly historical in its literal sense, but is also used figuratively and humorously.

BEST (noun) ▶ *see* **the best of both WORLDS**; ▶ *see* **the best of the BUNCH**.

BEST (adj.) ▶ *see* **best BIB and tucker**; ▶ *see* **the best thing since sliced BREAD**; ▶ *see* **put one's best FOOT forward**; ▶ *see* **with the best WILL in the world**.

don't (*or* I wouldn't) BET on it used to express doubt about an assertion or situation. *informal*

| **1973** J. MILLS *October Men* iv. 62 I suspect he wore sock suspenders, but wouldn't bet on it.

a safe BET a certainty. ●Used of a horse that is confidently expected to win a race.

| **1998** *New Scientist* 9 May 104/1 [It] is a safe bet that there was no similar abuse on the football lines out of Britain.

one can BET one's boots (*or* bottom dollar *or* life) one may be absolutely certain. *informal*

all BETS are off the outcome of a particular situation is unpredictable. *informal*

the — the BETTER used to emphasize the importance or desirability of the quality or thing specified.

BETTER the devil you know it's wiser to deal with an undesirable but familiar person or situation than to risk a change that might lead to a situation with worse difficulties or a person whose faults you have yet to discover. ● A shortened form of the (M19) proverbial saying *better the devil you know than the devil you don't (know)*.

one's BETTER half one's husband or wife. *jocular*

BETTER late than never it's preferable for something to happen or be done belatedly than not at all. ● An expression used in Latin (Livy IV. ii *potius sero quam nunquam*) and known in its current form in English from M15.

BETTER (be) safe than sorry it's wiser to be cautious and careful than to be hasty or rash and so do something that you may later regret. *proverbial* ● Apparently quite recent in this form (M20); *better be sure than sorry* is recorded from M19.

> **1998** *New Scientist* 5 Sept. 3/3 The meeting is to be commended for taking a 'better safe than sorry' attitude, and drawing up a baseline list of measures to be put in place when disease breaks out.

the BETTER to — so as to — better.

> **1986** P. MATHIESSEN *Men's Lives* (1988) III. xxii. 295 Francis ran both motors with their housings off, the better to tinker with them.

get (*or* have) the BETTER of (often of something immaterial) win an advantage over (someone); defeat or outwit.

go one BETTER **1** narrowly surpass a previous effort or achievement. **2** narrowly outdo (another person).

no BETTER than one should (*or* ought to) be perceived as sexually promiscuous or of doubtful moral character. ● First recorded in E17, the phrase was used euphemistically of a woman, but is now somewhat dated (see quot.).

> **1998** *Spectator* 7 Feb. 8/2 'She's no better than she ought to be'. (British mothers of my generation … often used that enigmatic phrase. They would use it about female neighbours of whom they disapproved, or women in low-cut dresses on television … .)

BETTER ▶ *see* **against one's better JUDGEMENT**; ▶ *see* **seen better DAYS**; ▶ *see* **so MUCH the better**.

the BETTING is (that) it is likely (that). *informal*

BETWEEN ▶ *see* **between the DEVIL and the deep blue sea**; ▶ *see* **between a ROCK and a hard place**.

BETWIXT and between neither one thing nor the other. *informal* ● *Betwixt* is now poetic or archaic and is seldom found outside this phrase.

(it's) BEYOND me (it's) too astonishing, puzzling, etc. for me to understand or explain. *informal* ● Used for emphasis.

BEYOND ▶ *see* **the BACK of beyond**.

best BIB and tucker best clothes. *informal* ● Originally used of items of women's dress: a *bib* is a garment worn over the upper front part of the body (e.g., the bib of an apron), and a *tucker* was a piece of lace formerly used to adorn a woman's bodice.

stick (*or* poke) one's BIB in interfere. *Austral. & NZ, informal*

big BICKIES a large sum of money.*Austral., informal* ● *Bickies* is a jocular use of a child's abbreviation of *biscuits*; cf. ▶ **TAKE the biscuit**.

> **1981** *Canberra Times* 30 Oct. 2/7 Appearance money is another claim which we think will succeed ... Just showing up is worth big bickies.

BIDE one's time wait quietly for a good opportunity. ● *Bide* in the sense of *await* is now obsolete except in this expression, and is superseded by *abide* in most of its other senses.

> **1991** G. SLOVO *Betrayal* xxx. 281 And so he bided his time, waiting, plotting, planning, looking for the signs that would be good for him.

a BIG cheese (*or* fish *or* gun *or* noise *or* shot *or* wheel) an important and influential person. *informal* ● The various versions of this expression are mainly self-explanatory, with the exception of *cheese*, which is of doubtful origin but may be from Persian and Urdu *chīz* 'thing'. As a phrase, *big cheese* seems to have originated in E20 US slang, as did *big noise*. *Big wheel* in this metaphorical sense (as opposed to the fairgound ride known as a Ferris wheel) and *big shot* are similarly US in origin (M20). *Big fish* may have connotations either of something it is desirable for one to catch or of the metaphorical expression *a big fish in a small pond*.

BIG deal an important event. *informal* ● Either used as an ironic exclamation or with the negative (*no big deal*) to indicate that one does not think something is as important or impressive as another person has suggested.

the BIG Three, Four, etc. the dominant group of three, four, etc. *informal*

> **1998** *Sunday Telegraph* 25 Jan. 33/5 The notion that someone outside the so-called 'Big Four'—the ministerial group which meets before Cabinet—might be given such status is uplifting.

give someone the BIG E reject someone, typically in an insensitive or dismissive way. *Brit., informal* ● *E* from *elbow*.

too BIG for one's boots (*or* *dated* breeches) conceited. *informal*

BIG ▶ *see* **Big BROTHER**; ▶ *see* **the big C**; ▶ *see* **big white CHIEF**.

get off one's BIKE become annoyed. *Austral. & NZ, informal*

> **1939** X. HERBERT *Capricornia* xxxiv. 521 'I tell you I saw no-one.'—'Don't get off your bike, son.—I know you're tellin' lies.'

on your BIKE! (*or* get on your bike) **1** go away! **2** take action! *Brit., informal* ● Sense 1 is used as an expression of annoyance. Sense 2 became a catch-phrase in 1980s Britain, used as an exhortation to the unemployed to show initiative, following a speech (Oct. 1981) by Conservative politician Norman Tebbit in which he said of his unemployed father: 'He did not riot, he got on his bike and looked for work.'

BILL and coo exchange caresses or affectionate words; behave or talk in a very loving or sentimental way. *informal*, *dated* ● The image is of two doves, a long-established symbol of mutual love. Most commonly in the phrase *billing and cooing*.

> **1842** R. H. BARHAM *Ingoldsby Legends* (2nd series) ii. 40 'Thrice happy's the wooing that's not long adoing!' So much time is saved in the billing and cooing.

fill (*or* fit) the BILL be suitable for a particular purpose. ● Originally US; *bill* in this context is a printed list of items on a theatrical programme or advertisement.

foot (*or* pick up) the BILL be responsible for paying (for something). ●Generally used of a large sum of money. Cf. ▶ **pick up the TAB**.

sell someone a BILL of goods deceive or swindle someone, usually by persuading them to accept something untrue or undesirable. ●A *bill of goods* (E20, chiefly N. Amer.) is a consignment of merchandise.

| **1968** *Globe & Mail* (*Toronto*) 17 Feb. 8/3There was no production bonus … We were sold a bill of goods.

a clean BILL of health a declaration or confirmation that someone is healthy or something is in good condition. ●A *bill of health* (M18) was an official certificate given to the master of a ship on leaving port; if *clean*, it certified that there was no infection either in the port or on board the vessel.

top (*or* head) the BILL be (advertised as) the main performer or act in a show, play, etc.

like BILLY-O very much, hard, or strongly. *Brit.*, *informal* ●*Billy-o* (L19, of unknown origin) is current only in this intensive phrase.

| **1995** J. BANVILLE *Athena* 224 This skin tone is the effect of cigarettes, I suspect, for she is a great smoker, … going at the fags like billy-o.

the BIRD has flown the person one is looking for has escaped or gone away-. ●With allusion to a bird escaping from a cage.

a BIRD in hand something that one has securely or is sure of. ●With allusion to the proverb *a bird in hand is worth two in the bush*. The proverb has been current in English since M15, but a Latin version antedated the English by two centuries.

a BIRD of passage someone who is always moving on. ●Literally, a migrant bird.

a BIRD's-eye view a view (esp. of a landscape) from above. ●Used from L18 of pictures made from this perspective, the phrase can also be used figuratively to mean a résumé of a subject.

do (one's) BIRD serve a prison sentence. *Brit.* ●*Bird* comes from rhyming slang *birdlime* 'time'.

flip someone the BIRD (*or* flip the bird) stick one's middle finger up at someone as a sign of contempt or anger. *US*

| **1994** *Washington Post Mag.* 3 July 10/1 We could simultaneously honour America, break the law and flip the bird to all the do-gooders.

give someone (*or* get) the BIRD boo or jeer at someone (*or* be booed or jeered at). *Brit.*, *informal* ●Earlier (E19) in theatrical slang as *the big bird*, meaning *goose*, because the hissing of geese could be compared to the audience's hissing at an act or actor of which it disapproved. Cf. next entry.

have a BIRD be very shocked or agitated. *N. Amer.*, *informal*

| **1992** *Globe & Mail* (Toronto) 22 Dec. A19/5 The Washington press corps would have a bird if the president-to-be appointed his wife to a real job.

a little BIRD told me I have been given some information but will not identify the source. ●Used as a teasing way of saying that one does not intend to divulge how one came to know something.

BIRD ▶ *see* **EARLY bird**.

the BIRDS and the bees basic facts about sex and reproduction as told to a child. *informal* ●A standard euphemism for human sexual functions.

BIRDS of a feather people with similar tastes, interests, etc. ●From the proverb *birds of a feather flock together*, current in this form since L16 and perhaps ultimately deriving from the Apocrypha (Ecclesiasticus 27:9).

(strictly) for the BIRDS not worth consideration; unimportant. *informal* ●Originally US army slang; explained (*American Speech* (1957) XXXII. 240) as an allusion to the way in which birds eat the droppings of horses and cattle.

BIRDS ▶ *see* **KILL two birds with one stone**.

in one's BIRTHDAY suit naked. *humorous*
> *1753 T. SMOLLETT *Ferdinand Count Fathom* II. xli. 43 He made an apology for receiving the count in his birth-day suit.

BISCUIT ▶ *see* **TAKE the biscuit**.

a BIT of all right a pleasing person or thing, especially a woman regarded sexually. *Brit., informal*

BIT of fluff (*or* skirt *or* stuff) a woman regarded in sexual terms. *informal* ●Now generally considered offensive.
> 1937 W. SOMERSET MAUGHAM *Theatre* xiv. 120 It was strangely flattering for a woman to be treated as a little bit of fluff that you just tumbled on to a bed.

BIT on the side **1** a person with whom one is unfaithful to one's partner. **2** a relationship involving being unfaithful to one's partner. **3** money earned outside one's normal job. *informal*

do one's BIT make a useful contribution to an effort or cause. *informal* ●The exhortation to *do your bit* was much used during World War I, but the expression was current in L19.

get (*or* take *or* have) the BIT between (*or* N. Amer. in) one's teeth begin to tackle a problem or task in a determined or independent way. ●The metal bit in a horse's mouth should lie on the fleshy part of its gums; if a headstrong horse grasps the bit between its teeth it can evade the control of the reins and its rider.

BIT ▶ *see* **bit of ROUGH**.

the BITCH goddess material or worldly success as an object of attainment.
> *1906 W. JAMES *Letter to H. G. Wells* 11 Sept. The moral flabbiness born of the exclusive worship of the bitch-goddess *success*.

BITE the big one die. *N. Amer., informal*

> 1989 D. KOONTZ *Midnight* I. lvii. 234 If you go, we all go with you, just like people down there at Jonestown years ago, drinking their poisoned Kool-Aid and biting the big one right along with Reverend Jim.

BITE (on) the bullet face up to doing something difficult or unpleasant; stoically avoid showing fear or distress. ● From the days before anaesthetics, when wounded soldiers were given a bullet or similar solid object to clench between their teeth when undergoing surgery.

> 1998 *New Scientist* 21 Feb. 3/2 Politicians will just have to bite on the bullet—dope will be decriminalised.

BITE the dust **1** be killed. **2** fail; come to an end. ● Earliest (L17) in English as *bite the ground*.

BITE the hand that feeds one deliberately hurt or offend a benefactor; act ungratefully.

> 1770 E. BURKE *Present Discontents* 3 This ... proposition ... that we set ourselves to bite the hand that feeds us; that with ... insanity we oppose those measures ... whose sole object is our own peace and prosperity.

BITE one's lip dig one's front teeth into one's lip in embarrassment, annoyance, or to prevent oneself from saying something.

BITE one's nails chew at one's fingernails as a nervous habit, especially when in suspense. ● Hence *nail-biting* used of a suspenseful event or situation.

BITE off more than one can chew take on a commitment one cannot fulfil. ● Originally (L19) a US colloquialism.

BITE one's tongue make a desperate effort to avoid saying something.

put the BITE on blackmail; extort money from. *N. Amer. & Austral., informal*

> 1955 R. LAWLER *Summer of Seventeenth Doll* (1965) 98 Your money's runnin' out you know you can't put the bite on me any more.

take a BITE out of reduce by a significant amount. *informal*

BITE ▶ *see* **a bite at the CHERRY**.

the BITER bit (*or* bitten) a person who has done harm has been harmed in a similar way. ● A *biter* was a L17 cant term for a fraudster or trickster, now obsolete in this sense except in this phrase.

> *1693 D'URFEY *Richmond Heiress* Epilogue Is't not fit Once in an age the Biter should be bit.

BITS and pieces (*or* bobs) an assortment of small or unspecified items. ● The precise sense of *bobs* here is unclear; the word may be primarily alliterative. A Yorkshire variant (L19) was *bits and bats*.

to BITS very much. *informal* ● Used for emphasis after a verb such as 'love'.

> 1998 *Times* 20 July 47/6 A succession of elderly ladies explained how, as young women, they had fancied him to bits.

BITTEN ▶ *see* **have the BUG**; ▶ *see* **ONCE bitten, twice shy**.

to the BITTER end persevering to the end, whatever the outcome. ● Perhaps associated with a nautical word *bitter* meaning the last part of a cable inboard of the bitts (strong bollards on a ship for securing mooring lines), and maybe influenced by the biblical sentence 'her end is bitter as wormwood' (Proverbs 5:4). Used to emphasize that one will continue doing something until it is finished, no matter what happens.

BITTER ▶ *see* **a bitter PILL**.

be in someone's BLACK books be in disfavour with a person. ●Although generally an official book in which misdemeanours and their perpetrators were noted down, the phrase perhaps originated in the black-bound book in which evidence of monastic scandals and abuses was recorded by the commissioners of Henry VIII in the 1530s before the suppression of the English monasteries.

beat someone BLACK and blue hit someone so severely that they are covered in bruises. ●*Black and blue* refers to the colour of fresh bruises. The ME form of the second word *bla* or *blo* shows it to derive from Old Norse *blá* meaning 'a dark colour between blue and black, livid', as in the colour of a *blaeberry*. Around M16 the word became obsolete apart from northern dialect (Burns has 'black and blae' in *Twa Herds*, 1785); in southern English it was replaced by the form *blew* from Old French *bleu*, giving rise to the modern *blue*.

BLACK box an automatic apparatus, the internal operations of which are mysterious to non-experts. ●*Black* does not refer to the colour of the device but to the arcane nature of its functions. Originally Royal Air Force slang for a navigational instrument in an aircraft, the phrase is now used in aviation specifically to refer to the flight-recorder; it is also used figuratively (see quot.). | **1997** *New Scientist* 15 Nov. 16/3The Higgs mechanism usually invoked is still something of a black box.

a BLACK mark (against someone) something that someone has done that is disliked or disapproved of by other people. ●Literally, a black cross or spot marked against the name of a person who has done something wrong.

the BLACK sheep (of the family) a person considered to have brought discredit upon a family or other group; a bad character. ●This metaphorical use since L18; however, black sheep had a dubious reputation since M16, and in 1598 Thomas Bastard observed: 'Till now I thought the prouerbe did but iest, Which said a blacke sheepe was a biting beast' (*Chrestoleros* xx. 90).

a BLACK spot a place that is notorious for something. ●Used especially of a place where there is a high crime or accident rate. | **1992** *Radio Times* (BBC) 16–22 May 18/1 Jonathon Porritt meets the 'green warriors' who are spearheading campaigns to clean up some of the world's worst pollution black spots.

in BLACK and white **1** in writing or in print, and regarded as more reliable, credible, or formal than by word of mouth. **2** in terms of clearly defined opposing principles or issues.

in the BLACK (of a person or organization) not owing any money; solvent. ●The opposite of ▶ **in the RED**.

not as BLACK as one is painted not as bad as one is said to be. *informal* ●Cf.

the proverb *the devil is not as black as he is painted*, first recorded in English M16 and used as a warning not to base one's fears of something on exaggerated reports.

BLACK ▶ *see* **beyond the black STUMP**.

draw a BLANK elicit no response; be unsuccessful. ● A *blank* was originally a lottery ticket that did not win a prize; the figurative use of the phrase can be traced back to E19.

write (or give someone) a BLANK cheque allow someone unlimited scope, especially to spend money. ● A *blank cheque* is literally one in which the amount of money to be paid has not been filled in by the payer.

born on the wrong side of the BLANKET illegitimate. ● An old (L18) euphemism, now somewhat dated.

BLANKET ▶ *see* **a WET blanket**.

firing BLANKS (of a man) infertile. *informal*

have kissed the BLARNEY stone be eloquent and persuasive. ● A stone, at Blarney Castle near Cork in Ireland is said to give the gift of persuasive speech to anyone who kisses it; hence the verb *to blarney* 'talk flatteringly'.

a BLAST from the past something powerfully nostalgic, especially an old pop song. *informal*
| 1997 *Time Out N.Y.* 31 July–7 Aug. 35/1 Tonight's act is a tribute to Curtis Mayfield, featuring three blasts from the past: The Impressions … The Stylistics and the Dramatics.

BLAZE a (or the) trail (or way) be the first to do something and thus set an example for others to follow. ● *Blaze* in this sense ultimately derives from an Old Norse noun meaning 'a white mark on a horse's face'. In its literal sense, *blazing a trail* refers to the practice of making white marks on trees by chipping off bits of their bark, thus indicating one's route to those who follow.

like BLAZES very fast or forcefully. *informal* ● *Blazes* in this context refers to the flames of hell; *go to blazes!* is a dated equivalent of *go to hell!*.

BLAZING ▶ *see* **with GUNS blazing**.

BLEED someone dry (or white) drain someone of all their money or re-sources. ● Since L17 *bleeding* has been a metaphor for extorting money from someone. *White* refers to the physiological effect of loss of blood.
| 1982 'W. HAGGARD' *Mischief-Makers* i. 16 Her husband had been a wealthy man, the lady's solicitors sharp and ruthless, and her husband had been bled white to get rid of her.

one's heart BLEEDS for someone one sympathizes very deeply with some-one. ● Used by Chaucer and Shakespeare to express sincere anguish, but now most commonly ironic, indicating the speaker's belief that the person referred to does not deserve the sympathy they are seeking.

BLESS ▶ *see* **not have a PENNY to bless oneself with**.

a **BLESSING in disguise** an apparent misfortune that eventually has good results.

> *1746 J. HERVEY *Reflections on Flower-Garden* 76 Ev'n Crosses from his sov'reign Hand Are Blessings in Disguise.

BLESSING ▶ *see* **a MIXED blessing**.

BLESSINGS ▶ *see* **COUNT one's blessings**.

a **BLIND alley** a course of action that does not deliver any positive results.

> 1997 *New Scientist* 15 Nov. 18/2 [T]he next person looking for the same information has to go through the process all over again—even if 1000 people have already been up the same blind alleys.

(as) BLIND as a bat having very bad eyesight. *informal* ● Probably arising from the bat's nocturnal habits and its disorientated flutterings if it is disturbed by day; an M17 collection of idioms has this expression in the form 'blind as a bat at noon'. The poor eyesight of bats (and less frequently, moles) has been proverbial since L16.

a **BLIND bit of —** the smallest bit of —; no — at all. *informal* ● Used for emphasis and usually with negative, as in *not take a blind bit of notice*.

> | 1966 'L. LANE' *ABZ of Scouse* 9Nobody could get a blind bit er sense outer 'im.

a **BLIND date** a social meeting, usually with the object of starting a romance, between two people who have not met each other before; each of the parties to such a meeting. ● E20, originally US.

turn a BLIND eye pretend not to notice. ● Said to be in allusion to Admiral Horatio Nelson (1758–1805), who lifted a telescope to his blind eye at the naval Battle of Copenhagen (1801), thus making certain that he failed to see his superior's signal to 'discontinue the action'. A less usual version, referring directly to this story, is *turn a Nelson eye*.

the BLIND leading the blind a situation in which the ignorant or inexperienced are instructed or guided by someone equally ignorant or inexperienced. ● With allusion to the proverb *when the blind lead the blind, both shall fall into the ditch*, quoting Matthew 15:14.

go it BLIND act recklessly or without proper consideration. ● Originally US (M19). Blindness and recklessness are linked in the proverbial saying *nothing so bold as a blind mare*.

a **BLIND spot** **1** an area into which one cannot see. **2** an aspect of something that someone knows or cares little about. ● These general senses appear to have developed from a cricketing term (M19) for the spot of ground in front of a batsman where a ball pitched by the bowler leaves the batsman undecided whether to play forward to it or back, but there was also a specialized sense in optics.

BLIND someone with science use special or technical knowledge and vocabulary to confuse someone.

BLIND ▶ *see* **ROB someone blind**.

BLINDER ▶ *see* **PLAY a blinder**.

BLINDING ▶ *see* **EFFING and blinding**.

in the BLINK of an eye (*or* in a blink) very quickly. *informal*
| **1995** *Daily Mail* 19 Oct. 50/1 It also has an unnerving way of flipping over from comedy to tragedy, or from tragedy to comedy, in the blink of an eye.

on the BLINK (of a machine) not working properly; out of order. *informal*
● Originally (E20) US slang. Cf. ▶ **on the FRITZ**.

BLINK ▶ *see under* **not BAT an eyelid**.

on the BLOCK for sale at auction. *chiefly N. Amer.* ● The *block* was the platform on which a slave stood to be auctioned.

put (*or* lay) one's head (*or* neck) on the BLOCK put one's position or reputation at risk by proceeding with a particular course of action. *informal*
● With allusion to the *block* of wood on which a condemned person was formerly beheaded.

a new kid on the BLOCK a newcomer to a particular place or sphere of activity. *informal* ● Originally US. The *block* is a block of buildings between streets, hence a locality.
| **1998** *Times* 20 July 29/1 Andrew Flintoff has displaced Ben Hollioake as the new kid on the block.

BLOCK ▶ *see* **a CHIP off the old block**.

put the BLOCKS on prevent from proceeding. ●A *block* of wood or other material placed in front of a wheel prevents forward movement.

BLOOD and guts violence and bloodshed, especially in fiction. *informal* ● Often attributive: *a blood-and-guts thriller*.

BLOOD and iron military force as distinguished from diplomacy. ● Translation of German *Blut und Eisen*, from a speech (Jan. 1886) by the German statesman Bismarck (1815–98) in the Prussian House of Deputies.

BLOOD and thunder unrestrained and violent action or behaviour, especially in sport or fiction. *informal* ● Originally M19 US, this is often used attributively, especially in the context of sensational literature (*a blood-and-thunder novel*). In L19 this gave rise to *penny bloods* as a term for cheap sensational novels.

BLOOD is thicker than water family loyalties are stronger than other relationships. ● The underlying idea is very old, but this form of the saying is not recorded before E19.
| **1998** *Spectator* 18 July 33/3 *Restitution* is a novel about ... whether blood is really thicker than water.

someone's BLOOD is up someone is in a fighting mood.
| *1829 G. GRIFFIN *Collegians* II. xviii. 55 To use a vulgar but forcible expression, the blood of Hardress was now completely up.

BLOOD on the carpet a serious disagreement or its aftermath. ● Used hyperbolically to suggest that there has been bloodshed.

BLOOD, sweat, and tears extremely hard work; unstinting effort. ●Cf.

Winston Churchill in a speech in the House of Commons in May 1940: 'I have nothing to offer but blood, toil, tears, and sweat.'

first BLOOD the first point or advantage gained in a contest. ● Also literally 'the first shedding of blood', especially in a boxing match or formerly in duelling with swords.

have BLOOD on one's hands be responsible for the death of someone. ● Cf. ▶ **WASH one's hands of**.

like getting BLOOD out of (*or* **from**) **a stone** (*or* N. Amer. **turnip**) extremely difficult and frustrating. ● Used with reference to obtaining something from someone. The *turnip* variant was formerly also British (see quot.).

| **1836** F. MARRYAT *Japhet* iv There's no getting blood out of a turnip.

make one's BLOOD boil infuriate one. ● In pre-modern physiology, a supposed dangerous over-reaction to strong emotion; cf. next two entries.

make one's BLOOD curdle fill one with horror. ● Cf. ▶ **make one's BLOOD run cold**. An expression with its origin in the medieval physiological scheme of the four humours in the human frame (melancholy, phlegm, blood, choler). Under this scheme blood was the hot, moist element, so the effect of horror or fear in making the blood run cold or curdling (solidifying) it was to make it unable to fulfil its proper function of supplying the body with vital heat or energy.

make one's BLOOD run cold horrify one. ● A supposed physiological reaction similar to ▶ **make one's blood CURDLE**; cf. ▶ **in COLD blood**.

new (*or* **fresh**) (*or* **young**) **BLOOD** new (*or* younger) members of a group, especially those admitted as an invigorating force.

taste BLOOD achieve an early success that stimulates further efforts.

there is bad BLOOD between — there is long-standing hostility between the parties mentioned.

BLOOD ▶ *see* **in COLD blood**; ▶ *see* **SWEAT blood**.

BLOODY (*or* **bloodied**) **but unbowed** proud of what one has achieved despite having suffered great difficulties or losses.

| **1888** W. E. HENLEY '*Invictus. In Memoriam R. T. H. B.*' Under the bludgeonings of chance My head is bloody, but unbowed.

the BLOOM is off the rose something is no longer new, fresh, or exciting. *N. Amer.* ● *Bloom* refers to the first freshness and beauty of something. Cf. the expression *take the* **BLOOM** *off* meaning 'to make stale'.

BLOT one's copybook tarnish one's good reputation. *Brit.* ● A *copybook* was an exercise book with examples of scripts, used by children to practise their handwriting.

a BLOT on the escutcheon something that tarnishes one's reputation. ● The *escutcheon* was a family's heraldic shield, hence a record and symbol of its honour.

a BLOT on the landscape something ugly that spoils the appearance of a place; an eyesore. ●E20; also applied jocularly to people.

> **1962** *Listener* 11 Jan. 90/2Charabancs and monstrous hordes of hikers are blots upon the landscape.

big (or great) girl's BLOUSE a weak, cowardly, emotionally over-sensitive man, especially one who is lacking in common sense. *Brit., informal*

BLOW someone away **1** *slang* kill, destroy, or defeat. **2** *informal* have a very strong effect on someone. ●In sense 2 cf. ▶ **BLOW someone's mind**.

> **2 1998** *Times* 18 Mar. 42/3 It blows me away the way she [a 13-year-old] is already moving through her life.

BLOW the doors off be considerably better or more successful than. *N. Amer., informal*

BLOW a fuse (or gasket) lose one's temper. ●The metaphor is of the failure of an electrical circuit or engine through overheating.

BLOW high, blow low whatever may happen. *US* ●Cf. ▶ **RAIN or shine**.

> *1774 P. V. FITHIAN *Journal* (1900) 236 Ben is in a wonderful Fluster lest he shall have no company tomorrow at the Dance—But blow high, blow low, we need not be afraid; Virginians … will dance or die!

BLOW hot and cold vacillate; be sometimes enthusiastic, sometimes unenthusiastic. ●With reference to a fable involving a traveller who was offered hospitality by a satyr and offended his host by blowing on his cold fingers to warm them and on his hot soup to cool it. From L16, often in the fuller form *blow hot and cold out of the same mouth* (or *with the same breath*). Cf. *blow cold on* 'regard (something) unfavourably'.

BLOW someone's mind affect someone very strongly. *informal* ●Originally (M20) a slang expression for the effect of hallucinatory drugs such as LSD.

BLOW something sky-high destroy something completely in an explosion. *informal* ●Also often figurative.

BLOW one's top (or chiefly N. Amer. lid or stack) lose one's temper.

BLOW up in one's face go drastically wrong with damaging effects to oneself. ●Used of an action, plan, or a situation, implying comparison with a bomb.

BLOW with the wind act according to prevailing circumstances rather than a consistent plan.

soften (or cushion) the BLOW make it easier to cope with a difficult change or upsetting news.

BLOW ▶ *see* **blow away the COBWEBS** ▶ *see* **blow great GUNS**; ▶ *see* **blow one's own HORN**; ▶ *see* **blow the GAFF**; ▶ *see* **blow the LID off**; ▶ *see* **let off STEAM**; ▶ *see* **blow a RASPBERRY**; ▶ *see* **knock someone's SOCKS off**; ▶ *see* **blow one's own TRUMPET**; ▶ *see* **blow the WHISTLE on**.

a BLOW-BY-BLOW account a detailed narrative of events as they happened.

be BLOWN away be extremely impressed. *informal*

be BLOWN off course (of a project) have one's plans disrupted by some circumstance.   ●A nautical metaphor: contrary winds deflect a sailing ship from its intended course.

be BLOWN out of the water (of a person, idea, or project) be shown to lack credibility or viability.

> **1997** *Daily Mail* 15 Jan. 52/5 Things finally seem to be looking up for Kelly—which is more than can be said for Biff, whose romantic plans are blown out of the water by Linda.

see (or know) which way the wind BLOWS work out how a situation is likely to develop.

do something until (or till) one is BLUE in the face persist in trying one's hardest at an activity but without success. *informal*   ●M19, used hyperbolically to describe the physiological effects of extreme effort.

> *1864 A. TROLLOPE *Small House at Allington* II. xvii. 175 You may talk to her until you're both blue in the face, if you please.

once in a BLUE moon very rarely, practically never. *informal*   ●*Blue* is used arbitrarily as a colour. To say that the moon is blue is recorded in the sixteenth century as proverbial for an assertion of something that could not be true.

out of the BLUE without warning; unexpectedly. *informal*   ●With reference to a blue (i.e. clear) sky, from which nothing unusual is expected. Cf. ▶ **a BOLT from the blue**; ▶ **out of a CLEAR sky**.

talk a BLUE streak speak continuously and at great length. *N. Amer., informal*   ●A *blue streak* refers to something like a flash of lightning in its speed and vividness.

true BLUE genuine.   ●J. Ray in his *English Proverbs* (1670) glosses the saying *true blue will never stain* with an observation to the effect that a good, permanent blue dye was difficult to obtain but that Coventry was particularly associated with the production of such a dye: 'true blue became a Proverb to signifie one that was always the same and like himselfe.' In the seventeenth century the colour blue was adopted by the Scottish Presbyterian party (in opposition to the royal red), but more recently it has been the colour favoured by the Tory party—hence the expression *a true blue Tory* to mean a staunch Conservative supporter.

the wide (or wild) BLUE yonder the sky or sea; the far or unknown distance.   ●From R. Crawford *Army Air Corps* (song, 1939) 'Off we go into the wild blue yonder, Climbing high into the sun'.

BLUE (noun) ▶ *see* **a BOLT from the blue**.

BLUE (adj.) ▶ *see* **between the DEVIL and the deep blue sea**; ▶ *see* **scream blue MURDER**.

a BLUE-EYED boy the favourite of someone in authority.   ●The significance of *blue eyes* may be their association with the innocence and charm of a very young child.

| **1998** *Spectator* 21 Mar. 12/2 Of the three, the arrest of Osborne, one of the blue-eyed boys of British racing, was the most striking.

BLUE-SKY research research that is not directed towards any immediate or definite commercial goal.

| **1997** *New Scientist* 2 Aug. 25/1 Bell Labs and IBM are well known for blue-sky research. They have people who are paid just to sit around and think—not about products.

call someone's BLUFF challenge someone to carry out a stated intention, in the expectation of being able to expose it as a false pretence. ● In the game of poker (which was formerly also known by the name of *bluff*), *calling someone's bluff* meant making an opponent show their hand in order to reveal that its value is weaker than their heavy betting suggests.

at first BLUSH at the first glimpse or impression. ● M17; *blush* in the sense of 'glance, glimpse' is obsolete except in this phrase.

spare (*or* save) someone's BLUSHES refrain from causing someone embarrassment.

above BOARD honest; not secret. ● Originally (E17) a gambling term, indicating fair play by players who kept their hands above the *board* (i.e. the table).

go by the BOARD (of something planned or previously upheld) be abandoned, rejected, or ignored. ● Earlier in nautical use meaning 'fall overboard', used of a mast falling past the *board* (i.e. the side of the ship).

on BOARD as a member of a team or group. *informal* ● Literally, on or in a ship, aircraft, or other vehicle, or (of a jockey) riding.

take something on BOARD fully consider or assimilate a new idea or situation. *informal* ● Cf. preceding entry.

BOARD ▶ *see* **ACROSS the board**.

be in the same BOAT be in the same unfortunate or difficult circumstances. *informal*

off the BOAT recently arrived from a foreign country. *informal* ● The implication, often offensive, is that the person concerned is naive or an outsider.

push the BOAT out be lavish in one's spending or celebrations. *Brit., informal* ● Apparently originating as M20 naval slang meaning to 'pay for a round of drinks'.

rock the BOAT say or do something to disturb an existing situation and upset other people. *informal* ● M20 in this figurative sense.

| **1998** *Oldie* Aug. 38/3 We are rejected with aggrieved dignity, bad temper or a soothing burble. 'Don't rock the boat,' says the crew, as it breaks up.

BOATS ▶ *see* **BURN one's boats**.

BOB and weave make rapid bodily movements up and down and from side to side. ● Probably with reference to evasive tactics used by a boxer.

(and) BOB's (or Bob's) your uncle everything is fine; problem solved. *Brit., informal* ● *Bob* is a pet form of the name *Robert*. The origin of the phrase is often said to be in the controversial appointment in 1887 of the young Arthur Balfour to the important post of secretary for Ireland by his uncle Lord Salisbury, whose first name was Robert. The expression is recorded in cockney speech from the 1890s. Used to express the ease with which a task can be or has been achieved.

> **1996** C. BATEMAN *Of Wee Sweetie Mice and Men* xiii. 103 I couldn't believe how easy it was to get. Just walked into a shop, signed a piece of paper, and Bob's your uncle.

know where the BODIES are buried have the security deriving from personal knowledge of an organization's confidential affairs and secrets. *informal*

ride BODKIN travel squeezed between two others.

BODY and soul involving every aspect of a person; completely.

keep BODY and soul together stay alive, especially in difficult circumstances.

over my dead BODY in the face of my total opposition. *informal* ● Often as an exclamation to emphasize that one completely opposes something and would do anything to prevent it from happening.

go off the BOIL pass the stage at which interest, excitement, activity, etc. is at its greatest. ● Cf. *on the boil* as a metaphor for being in a lively or active state; see also ▶ **keep the pot BOILING**.

BOIL (verb) ▶ *see* **make one's BLOOD boil**.

keep the pot BOILING maintain the momentum or interest value of something.

it (all) BOILS down to something signifies basically. ● Literally, *boiling down* a liquid means reducing its volume and concentrating it by evaporation.

> **1998** *Times* 25 May 46/3 And why are deals getting more complex? Unsurprisingly it all boils down to profit.

(as) BOLD as brass confident to the point of impudence. ● *Brass* is taken as a type of insensibility and lack of shame, hence *brass face* as a metaphor for 'effrontery'.

a BOLT from (or out of) the blue a sudden and unexpected event or piece of news. ● With reference to the unlikelihood of a thunderbolt coming from a clear blue sky.

have shot one's BOLT have done all that is in one's power. *informal* ● A *bolt* was a thick, heavy arrow for a crossbow.

> **1998** *Spectator* 4 July 88/1 The Britpop boom has ended, the Spice Girls have shot their bolt.

make a BOLT for try to escape by moving suddenly towards (something). ● A *bolt* is a sudden spring or start into rapid motion, typically that made by a horse breaking into an uncontrollable gallop.

BOLTED ▶ *see* **shut the STABLE door after the horse has bolted**.

go down a BOMB be very well received. *Brit., informal* ● Especially used of entertainment; cf. next entry, sense 1. The opposite of ▶ **go down like a LEAD balloon**.

go like a BOMB **1** be very successful. **2** (of a vehicle or person) move very fast. *Brit., informal*

give someone BONDI attack someone savagely. *Austral.* ● A *bondi* (also *boondie*, *bundi*, or *bundy*) is a heavy Aboriginal club.

> **1890** *Truth* (Sydney) 3 May 1/6 Buffer ... amused himself by knocking Emily Dallas down and then dancing on her and yanking her round by the hair and otherwise 'givin' her Bondi'.

a BONE of contention a subject or issue over which there is continuing disagreement. ● The idea is of a bone thrown into the midst of a number of dogs causing a fight between them. The phrase is E18, but the idea is much older (M16).

close to (*or* near) the BONE **1** (of a remark) penetrating and accurate to the point of causing hurt or discomfort. **2** (of a joke or story) likely to cause offence because near the limit of decency. ● Cf. ▶ **near the KNUCKLE**.

cut (*or* pare) something to the BONE reduce something to the bare minimum.

have a BONE to pick with someone have reason to disagree or be annoyed with someone. *informal* ● A *bone to pick* (or *gnaw*) has been a metaphor for a problem or difficulty to be thought over since M16.

not a — BONE in one's body not the slightest trace of the specified quality.

point the BONE at betray (someone); cause someone's downfall. ● Originally Australian, from an Australian aboriginal ritual, in which a bone is pointed at a victim so as to cast a curse on them to cause their sickness or death.

to the BONE affecting a person in a completely penetrating way. ● In its literal sense, used of a wound so deep as to expose the victim's bone, but often used figuratively, as in *chilled to the bone* of someone who has got very cold.

work one's fingers to the BONE work very hard. ● Often used in situations in which due recognition or reward does not ensue.

> ***1853** C. DICKENS *Bleak House* xiii Richard said that he would work his fingers to the bone for Ada.

make no BONES about something have no hesitation in stating or dealing with something, however unpleasant, awkward, or distasteful it is. ● The obsolete expression *find bones in* suggests how the meaning of this could have evolved: finding bones in meat or soup presents a difficulty in consuming it, but *making no bones* means that impediments are either ignored or overcome.

make old BONES live to a great age. *informal* ● L19; usually in a negative context.

to one's BONES (*or* to the bone) in a very fundamental way. ● Used to emphasize that a person has a specified quality as an essential or innate aspect of their personality.

BONES ▶ *see* **a BAG of bones**; ▶ *see* **the BARE bones**.

wouldn't say BOO to a goose (*or US* **not say boo**) (of a person) very shy or reticent.

> **1948** P. G. WODEHOUSE *Uncle Dynamite* xiii. 226 She looks on you as a ... poor, spineless sheep who can't say boo to a goose.

up the BOOAY completely wrong or astray. *Austral. & NZ* ● The meaning of *booay* is uncertain, though the place-name *Puhoi* in NZ has been suggested as the origin. Also spelt *boo-eye* and other variants.

bring someone to BOOK bring someone to justice; punish. ● Cf. ▶ **throw the BOOK at**.

by the BOOK strictly according to the rules.

make (*or* **open**) **a BOOK** (*US* **make book**) take bets and pay out winnings on the outcome of a race or other contest or event.

suit someone's BOOK be convenient or acceptable to someone. *Brit.* ● Originally a bookmaker's phrase.

throw the BOOK at charge or punish someone as severely as possible or permitted. *informal* ● The *book* here is one of regulations or laws.

BOOK ▶ *see* **a CLOSED book**; ▶ *see* **READ someone like a book**; ▶ *see* **take a LEAF out of someone's book**.

close the BOOKS make no further entries at the end of an accounting period; cease trading.

in someone's bad (*or* **good**) **BOOKS** in disfavour (*or* favour) with a person.

on the BOOKS contained in a list of members, employees, or clients.

BOOKS ▶ *see* **be in someone's BLACK books**; ▶ *see* **COOK the books**.

the BOOT (*or N. Amer.* **shoe**) **is on the other foot** the situation has reversed. ● Also as *the boot is on the other leg* (both M19).

get the BOOT be dismissed from one's job or position. *informal* ● From the idea of being literally kicked out. Also *give someone the boot*. A facetious expansion of this idiom is *get/give the Order of the Boot* (E20).

> **1898** C. G. ROBERTSON *Voces Academicae* 30 [A]nother blob to spoil his average. I should think he would get the boot after this—and high time too.

put the BOOT in (*or* **into someone**) treat someone brutally, especially when they are vulnerable. *Brit., informal* ● The literal sense is 'kick someone hard when they are already on the ground'.

to BOOT as well; in addition. *informal* ● *Boot* here has nothing to do with footwear but comes from an Old English word meaning 'good, profit, advantage'. It is obsolete in nearly all its senses except in this phrase and in *bootless* meaning 'unavailing, profitless'. Placed at the end of the relevant clause or phrase for emphasis.

> **1998** *New Scientist* 28 Mar. 52/2 It's an ideal first-year programming book, covering both Java and programming concepts clearly, with humour to boot.

BOOTS and all completely. *orig. Austral. & NZ, informal*

> **1947** D. M. DAVIN *Rest of our Lives* xix. 96 The next thing he'll do is counter-attack, boots and all.

one's heart sinks (*or* falls) into one's BOOTS suffer a sudden onset of depression or dismay. ● This idiom has given rise (L20) to the adjective *heart-sink*, used in the medical profession to describe a patient who has this effect upon their medical practitioner. Also *with one's heart in one's boots* referring to a state of dismay.

seven-league BOOTS the ability to travel very fast on foot. ● From the fairy story of Hop o' my Thumb, the magic boots enabling the wearer to go seven leagues at each stride.

BOOTS ▶ *see* **you can BET your boots**; ▶ *see* **DIE with one's boots on**; ▶ *see* **HANG up one's boots**; ▶ *see* **TOUGH as old boots**.

pull (*or* drag) oneself up by one's (own) BOOTSTRAPS improve one's position by one's own efforts. ● A *bootstrap* was sewn into boots to help with pulling them on. E20; *bootlaces* is sometimes substituted for *bootstraps*. This idiom has given rise to the term *bootstrapping*, meaning to 'make use of existing resources to improve one's position', hence the computer term *booting*.

shake one's BOOTY dance energetically. *slang*

> **1990** S. MORGAN *Homeboy* xxii. 135 Shakin booty at the Blue Note.

poke BORAK at make fun of (someone). *Austral. & NZ* ● *Borak*, used in Australian slang since M19, means 'nonsense'.

> **1960** E. NORTH *Nobody Stops Me* 149 I … subscribed to his ravings about women, while everybody else about the place poked borak at him.

BORN and bred by birth and upbringing. ● Often used postpositively, especially when someone is considered a typical product of a place, e.g., *a Londoner born and bred*.

not know one is BORN be unaware how easy one's life is. *informal* ● Used to say that someone is having an easy time without realizing how easy it is.

there's one (*or* a sucker) BORN every minute there are many stupid or gullible people about. *informal*. Used as a comment on a particular situation in which someone has been or is about to be deceived.

BORN ▶ *see* **born in the PURPLE**; ▶ *see* **born on the wrong side of the BLANKET**; ▶ *see* **be born with a SILVER spoon in one's mouth**; ▶ *see* **to the MANNER born**.

BORROW trouble take needless action that may have bad effects. *N. Amer.*

BORROWED plumes a pretentious display not rightly one's own. ● With reference to the fable of the jay which decked itself in the peacock's feathers.

be (living) on BORROWED time continuing to survive against expectations. ● Used with the implication that this will not be for much longer.

have it BOTH ways benefit from two incompatible ways of thinking or behaving. ● Cf. ▶ **have one's CAKE and eat it**.

| **1998** *New Scientist* 25 July 35/3 It is only now dawning on the legislators that they cannot have it both ways—that cleanliness and ecological friendliness are incompatible.

BOTH ▶ *see* **CUT both ways**.

hot and BOTHERED in a state of anxiety or physical discomfort, especially because of being pressured.

have (*or* show) (a lot of) BOTTLE have (*or* show) boldness or initiative. *Brit., informal* ● The M19 slang phrase *no bottle*, meaning 'no good, useless', is the probable origin of the M20 sense of *bottle* as 'courage, nerve'. (Hence the L20 slang expression *bottle out* meaning 'fail to do something because of loss of nerve'.)

hit (*or* be on) the BOTTLE start to drink alcohol heavily, especially as a form of spurious comfort. *informal*

be bumping along the BOTTOM (of an economy or industry) be at the lowest point in its performance without improving or deteriorating further.

the BOTTOM falls (*or* drops) out of something something fails or collapses totally. ● Similarly *knock the bottom out of something* means 'cause something to collapse'.

BOTTOM (noun) ▶ *see* **from the bottom of one's HEART**; ▶ *see* **SCRAPE the barrel**; ▶ *see* **TOUCH bottom**.

BOTTOM (adj.) ▶ *see* **you can BET your boots**; ▶ *see* **bottom DRAWER**; ▶ *see* **the bottom LINE**.

BOUNCE an idea off someone share an idea with another person in order to get feedback on it and refine it. *informal*

BOUNCE off the walls be full of nervous excitement or agitation. *N. Amer., informal*

BOUNCE ▶ *see* **a DEAD cat bounce**.

BOUND ▶ *see* **DUTY bound**; ▶ *see* **HONOUR bound**.

a (*or* one's) BOUNDEN duty a responsibility regarded by oneself or others as obligatory. ● *Bounden* as the past participle of *bind* is now archaic in all contexts and seldom found except in this phase.

BOW and scrape behave in an obsequious way to someone in authority.

make one's BOW make one's first formal appearance in a particular role.

take a BOW (of an actor or entertainer) acknowledge applause after a performance. ● Sometimes used informally in the imperative to indicate to someone that they should feel themselves worthy of applause.

BOW down in the house of Rimmon pay lip-service to a principle; sacrifice one's principles for the sake of conformity. ● *Rimmon* was a deity worshipped in ancient Damascus; the source is Naaman's request in 2 Kings 5:18 'when I bow down myself in the house of Rimmon, the Lord pardon thy servant in this thing'.

BOW (noun) ▶ *see* **have a second STRING to one's bow**.

BOWL ▶ *see* **a bowl of CHERRIES**.

get one's BOWLER hat be demobilized, retire to civilian life. *dated* ● A *bowler hat*, implicitly contrasted with a military cap, is here a metaphor for civilian life, since it was the headgear formerly worn to work by managers, clerks, and other professionals. E20 military slang.

a (warning) shot across the BOWS a statement or gesture intended to frighten someone into changing their course of action. ● Literally, a shot fired in front of the bows of a ship, not intending to hit it but to make it stop or alter course.

BOX of birds fine; happy. *Austral. & NZ*

BOX clever act so as to outwit someone. *Brit.*, *informal*

> **1950** A. BARON *There's no Home* 210 If you box clever and keep your mouth shut, ... you ought to be able to count on a suspended sentence.

a BOX of tricks an ingenious gadget. *informal*

out of the BOX unusually good. *Austral. & NZ*

out of one's BOX intoxicated with alcohol or drugs. *Brit.*, *informal*

in the wrong BOX unsuitably or awkwardly placed; in a difficulty, at a disadvantage. ● Perhaps originally with reference to an apothecary's boxes, from which a mistaken choice might have provided poison instead of medicine.

BOX ▶ *see* **BLACK box**; ▶ *see* **PANDORA's box**.

in the BOX SEAT in an advantageous position. *Austral. & NZ*

BOYS will be boys irresponsible, mischievous, or childish behaviour is typical of boys or young men. *proverbial* ● Used to indicate that such behaviour should not cause surprise when it occurs. The equivalent female proverb *girls will be girls* is far less common.

one of the BOYS accepted by a group of men.

BOY ▶ *see* **the old boy NETWORK**.

BOYS ▶ *see* **JOBS for the boys**; ▶ *see* **sort out the MEN from the boys**.

have (got) something on the BRAIN be obsessed with something. *informal*

BRAINS ▶ *see* **PICK someone's brains**; ▶ *see* **RACK one's brains**.

BRASS monkey weather (*or* brass monkeys) extremely cold. ● After the vulgar slang expression 'cold enough to freeze the balls off a brass monkey' (M20), the origin of which has been debated. One etymology relates it to brass trays known as *monkeys* on which cannon balls were stowed aboard warships in previous centuries.

come (*or* get) down to BRASS tacks start to consider the essential facts or practical details; reach the real mattter in hand. *informal* ● A L19 Amer. slang expression, E20 in Britain. Less commonly with *brass nails*.

> **1932** T. S. ELIOT *Sweeney Agonistes* 25That's all the facts when you come to brass tacks: Birth, and copulation, and death.

not a BRASS farthing no money or assets at all. *informal*

the BRASS ring success, especially as regarded as a reward for ambition or hard work. *N. Amer., informal* ● With reference to the reward of a free ride given on a merry-go-round to the person hooking a brass ring suspended over the horses.

BRASS ▶ *see* **part brass RAGS with**.

BRAVE new world a new and hopeful period in history resulting from major changes in society. ● Ultimately from Shakespeare's *Tempest* i, but more often with allusion to Aldous Huxley's ironical use of the phrase as the title of his modern dystopia *Brave New World* (1932).

BRAVE ▶ *see* **put a brave FACE on something**.

step into the BREACH take the place of someone who is suddenly unable to do a job or task. ● In military terms a *breach* is a gap in fortifications made by enemy guns or explosives; thus to *stand in the breach* is to bear the brunt of an attack when other defences or expedients have failed.

someone's BREAD and butter someone's livelihood; routine work to provide an income.

> **1998** *Times* 25 May 46/2 It is not that the smaller deal has disappeared—they remain the bread and butter of this industry.

BREAD and circuses material benefits and entertainment employed by rulers or political parties to keep the masses happy and docile. ● Translating Latin *panem et circenses* (Juvenal *Satires* x. 80), which alludes to the Roman emperors' organization of grain handouts and gladiatorial games for the populace.

break BREAD with share a meal with someone. *dated*

cast one's BREAD upon the waters do good without expecting gratitude or immediate reward. ● With allusion to Ecclesiastes 11:1 'Cast thy bread upon the waters: for thou shalt find it after many days.'

eat the BREAD of idleness consume sustenance for which one has not worked. *literary* ● Cf. the description of the virtuous woman in Proverbs 31:27 'She ... eateth not the bread of idleness.'

know (on) which side one's BREAD is buttered know where one's advantage lies. ● Recorded in Heywood's *Proverbs & Epigrams* (1562).

man cannot live by BREAD alone people have spiritual as well as physical needs. ● With allusion to Matthew 4:4 (quoting Deuteronomy 8:3); the passage continues 'but by every word that proceedeth out of the mouth of God.'

take the BREAD out of (*or* from) people's mouths deprive people of their livings especially by competition or unfair working practices.

the best (*or* greatest) thing since sliced BREAD A notable new idea, person, or thing. *informal* ● With allusion to the M20 advertising promotions for packed, pre-sliced loaves. Used to express real or ironic appreciation.

want one's BREAD buttered on both sides want more than is practicable or than is reasonable to expect.

a BREAD-AND-BUTTER letter a guest's written thanks for hospitality. ● E20, originally US; also elliptically, *a bread-and-butter*.

BREAK a butterfly on a wheel use unnecessary force in destroying something fragile or insignificant. ● After Pope's *Epistle to Dr Arbuthnot* 308. *Breaking upon the wheel* was a form of punishment or torture formerly inflicted upon criminals who were fastened to a wheel to have their bones broken or dislocated.

> **1998** *Times* 8 Sept. 22/2 But why break a butterfly upon a wheel? What harm does the Liberal Democrat leader do? Unfortunately he may be about to do a great deal.

BREAK new (*or* fresh) ground do pioneering work.

BREAK ship fail to rejoin one's ship after absence on leave.

give someone a BREAK stop putting pressure on someone about something. *informal* ● The exclamation *give me a break!* is used to express contemptuous disagreement or disbelief about what has been said.

make a BREAK for make a sudden dash in the direction of, usually in a bid to escape.

make a clean BREAK remove oneself completely and finally from a situation or relationship.

BREAK ▶ *see* **break the BANK**; ▶ *see* **break CAMP**; ▶ *see* **break COVER**; ▶ *see* **break someone's HEART**; ▶ *see* **break the ICE**; ▶ *see* **break the MOULD**; ▶ *see* **break RANK**; ▶ *see* **break STEP**.

have (*or* eat) someone for BREAKFAST deal with or defeat someone with contemptuous ease. *informal*

BREAKFAST ▶ *see* **a DOG's dinner**.

beat one's BREAST make a great show of sorrow or regret. ● Used literally in the Bible and elsewhere.

BREAST (noun) ▶ *see* **make a CLEAN breast of something**.

BREAST (verb) ▶ *see* **breast the TAPE**.

a BREATH of fresh air 1 a small amount of or a brief time in the fresh air. **2** a refreshing change, especially a new person on the scene.

the BREATH of life a thing that someone needs or depends on. ● A biblical phrase: 'And the Lord God formed man of the dust of the ground, and breathed into his nostrils the breath of life' (Genesis 2:7).

don't hold your BREATH don't expect something to happen immediately. ● Used hyperbolically to indicate that something is likely to take a long time.

save one's BREATH not bother to say something because it is pointless. ●Often in imperative and sometimes elaborated as *save your breath to cool your porridge!* (in various wordings from M17).

take one's BREATH away astonish; inspire with awed respect or delight.

*1864 R. BROWNING 'Likeness' in *Dramatis Personae* He never saw ... What was able to take his breath away, A face to lose youth for.

waste one's BREATH talk or give advice without effect.

BREATHE down someone's neck 1 constantly check up on someone. **2** follow closely behind someone.

BREATHE one's last die.

a BREED apart a kind of person or thing that is very different from the norm.

a BRICK short of a load (of a person) stupid. *informal* ●One of a number of humorous variations on the theme of someone's lacking the full complement of wits; cf. ▶ **a SANDWICH short of a picnic**.

come up against (*or* hit) a BRICK wall encounter an insuperable problem or obstacle while trying to do something.

make BRICKS without straw try to accomplish something without proper or adequate material, equipment, or information. ●With allusion to Exodus 5:6–19; 'without straw' meant 'without having straw provided' (i.e. the Israelites were required to gather the straw for themselves in order to make the bricks required by their Egyptian taskmasters). A misinterpretation has led to the current sense.

come down (on someone) like a ton of BRICKS exert crushing weight, force, or authority against someone. *informal*

cross that BRIDGE when one comes to it deal with a problem when and if it arises.

1998 *Spectator* 6 June 26/3 As to what would happen to the case for non-proliferation when the Cold War was won, the allies would cross that bridge when they came to it, which seemed at the time well beyond any foreseeable future.

BRIDGES ▶ *see* **BURN one's boats**.

hold no BRIEF for not support or argue in favour of. ●With reference to the *brief* or summary of the facts in a case used by a lawyer.

BRIGHT and early very early in the morning. ●Originally US (M19).

(as) BRIGHT as a button intelligently alert and lively. *informal* ●There is a play on *bright* in its Old English sense of 'shiny' (like a polished metal button) and *bright* in its transferred sense of 'quick-witted' (M18).

the BRIGHT lights the glamour and excitement of a big city.

BRIGHT spark clever person. ●Almost always used ironically to or of a person who has done something one considers stupid.

BRIGHT young thing a fashionable member of the younger generation (esp. in the 1920s and 1930s) noted for exuberant and outrageous behaviour.

BRIGHT-EYED and bushy-tailed alert and lively; eager. *informal* ● The image is of an animal in good health and spirits.

BRING the house down make an audience respond with great enthusiasm, especially as shown by their laughter or applause.

BRING something into play cause something to begin to have an effect; activate.

BRING ▶ *see* **bring home the BACON**; ▶ *see* **bring something HOME to someone**; ▶ *see* **bring someone to BOOK**; ▶ *see* **bring something to LIGHT**.

BROAD in the beam fat around the hips. *informal* ● Originally *beam* referred to the horizontal transverse timbers of a wooden ship, hence the greatest width of a ship, from which is derived the figurative use.

in BROAD daylight during the day, when it is light. ● Used generally in the context of surprise or outrage at someone's daring to carry out a particular act, especially a crime, when anyone could see it.

it's as BROAD as it's long there's no significant difference between two possible alternatives. *informal*

go for BROKE risk everything in an all-out effort. *informal* ● *Broke* as the past participle of *break* has been superseded by *broken* in nearly all general senses (it is also used in the US to describe a horse trained for riding); this expression represents a colloquial sense of 'without money' (E18).

BROKEN ▶ *see* **a broken REED**.

on the BROO claiming unemployment benefit. *orig. & chiefly Scottish, informal* ● A colloquial alteration of *bureau*, also spelt *buroo* (M20), meaning a labour exchange or social security office.

a new BROOM a newly appointed person who is likely to make far-reaching changes. ● With allusion to the proverb *a new broom sweeps clean*, current since M16.

a BROTH of a boy a lively boy. *informal* ● Chiefly Anglo-Irish, used as a term of approval.

BROTH ▶ *see* **too many COOKS spoil the broth**.

Big BROTHER the state perceived as a sinister force supervising citizens' lives. ● From the slogan *Big Brother is watching you* in George Orwell's novel *1984*.

(as) BROWN as a berry (of a person) very suntanned. ● The simile depends on the idea of a sun-ripened berry darkening in colour. The earliest sense of *brown* in English was simply 'dark', rather than the specific reddish or orange and black shade now generally meant.

| *c* **1386** G. CHAUCER *Cook's Tale* 4 Broun as a berye, a propre short felawe.

BROWN ▶ *see* **in a brown STUDY**.

BROWNIE point an imaginary award given to someone who does good deeds or tries to please. *informal* ● The *Brownies* are the junior wing of the Guides; the organization awards points and badges for proficiency in various activities. Generally used humorously in the context of winning favour with one's associates by public-spirited acts of a trivial nature.

bear the BRUNT of be the person to suffer the most (as the result of an attack, misfortune, etc.). ● The origin of *brunt* (first recorded E14) is unknown, and may be onomatopoeic; the sense has evolved from the specific ('a sharp or heavy blow') to the more general ('shock or violence of an attack').

on the BUBBLE (of a sports player or team) occupying the last qualifying position on a team or for a tournament, and liable to be replaced by another. *N. Amer., informal* ● From *sit on the bubble*, with the implication that the bubble may burst.

BUBBLE ▶ *see* **BURST someone's bubble**.

BUCK up one's ideas make more effort; become more energetic and hard-working. *informal* ● *Buck* here refers to a horse's action of jumping with all feet together and back arched. From this implication of liveliness, *buck up* (M19) in its modern senses of 'cheer up' and 'hurry up' evolved through school slang; Farmer and Henley's *Slang* (1890) also specifically notes the sense of 'exert yourself' at Westminster School.

make a fast BUCK earn money easily and quickly. *orig. US, informal* ● The etymology of *buck* (M19) as a slang term for 'dollar' is obscure.

the BUCK stops here (*or* with someone) the responsibility for something cannot or should not be passed to someone else. *orig. US, informal* ● Cf. ▶ **pass the BUCK**. Famously, the wording of a sign on the desk of US President Harry S. Truman.

pass the BUCK shift the responsibility for something to someone else. *orig. US, informal* ● A *buck* is an object placed as a reminder in front of the person whose turn it is to deal in the game of poker. *Pass the buck* (M19) has given rise to *buck-passing* and *buck-passer* (both M20).

> **1998** *Independent* 25 Feb. 18/1 Its management structure is a mish-mash of political and executive responsibilities … the chief executive … passes the buck.

BUCKET ▶ *see* **a DROP in the ocean**; ▶ *see* **KICK the bucket**.

(not) have BUCKLEY's (*or* Buckley's chance) someone has little or no hope of achieving a specified thing. *Austral. & NZ, informal* ● Origin obscure: who or what *Buckley* was is unknown.

> **1898 Bulletin* (Sydney) 17 Dec. 31/2 'Devil shoot me!' muttered Tim … 'if I see Buckley's chance of a shindy tonight.'

men in BUCKRAM non-existent people. *archaic* ● With allusion to Falstaff's imaginary assailants in Shakespeare's 1 *Henry IV* iv. 210–50.

in the BUFF naked. *informal* ● *Buff* is an abbreviation of *buffalo* or (obsolete) *buffle*. The dull shade of yellow commonly called *buff* is comparable to human skin colour and was associated with a particular form of dressed ox-leather formerly known as *buff leather*, used in military uniforms.

have (*or* be bitten by) the BUG develop a sudden strong enthusiasm (for something).

BUGGINS ▶ *see* **Buggins' TURN**.

BUILT on sand without secure foundations; liable to collapse. ●From the biblical parable contrasting the wise man who built his house on rock with the fool who built on sand (Matthew 7:24–7).

have (*or* get) the BULGE on have or get an advantage over. *Brit., informal*

BULGING ▶ *see* **bursting at the SEAMS**.

like a BULL at a gate hastily and without thought. ●Also used attributively: *bull-at-a-gate tactics.*

like a BULL in a china shop behaving recklessly and clumsily in a place or situation where one is likely to cause damage or injury. ●Used by Swift (E18).

take the BULL by the horns deal bravely and decisively with a difficult, dangerous, or unpleasant situation.

| **1975** S. SELVON *Moses Ascending* (1984) 59 I decided to take the bull by the horns. 'I'm going to stay in your room until the elusive Farouk turns up.'

BULL ▶ *see* **a RED rag to a bull**.

BULLET ▶ *see* **BITE the bullet; SWEAT bullets**.

BULLY for —! well done! good for (you, them, etc.)! ●This expression takes its origin from the US colloquial sense of *bully* as 'first-rate' (M19).

give someone (*or* get) the BUM's rush **1** forcibly eject someone (*or* be forcibly ejected) from a place or gathering. **2** abruptly dismiss someone (*or* be abruptly dismissed) for a poor idea or performance. *chiefly N. Amer.*

| **1** **1998** *Spectator* 4 April 24/3 When ... James Cameron wrote an uproariously funny piece about the hotel's iniquities ... he was promptly given the bum's rush.

BUMP ▶ *see* **THINGS that go bump in the night**.

BUMPER-to-bumper **1** very close together, as cars in a traffic jam. **2** (chiefly of an insurance policy) comprehensive; all-inclusive.

BUMS on seats the audience at a theatre, cinema, or other entertainment, viewed as a source of income. *informal*

BUN ▶ *see* **TAKE the biscuit**.

BUNCH of fives **1** a fist. **2** a punch. *Brit., dated, informal*

a BUNDLE of fun (*or* laughs) something extremely amusing or pleasant. *informal* ●Often with negative.

drop one's BUNDLE give up trying to succeed at or achieve something; go to pieces. *Austral. & NZ, informal* ●From obsolete *bundle* 'swag'.

go a BUNDLE on be very keen on or fond of. *Brit., informal* ●*Bundle* here is in the L19 US slang sense of a bundle of money, i.e. a large sum. Originally E20 US slang for betting a large sum of money on a horse. Now used figuratively, often with negative.

| **1968** A. DIMENT *Bang Bang Birds* I. v. 60 I don't go a bundle on being told I'm a pro.

BUNDLE ▶ *see* **a BAG of nerves**.

go BUNG **1** die. **2** fail or go bankrupt. *Austral. & NZ, slang* ●*Bung* in this sense is an Australian Aboriginal word.

> **2 1951** J. DEVANNY *Travel in North Queensland* 186 'The stations would go bung without the Abos', one of the missionaries told me.

the white man's BURDEN the supposed responsibility of whites to civilize other races. *dated* ●From Kipling's poem of that title (1899), originally in specific allusion to the United States' role in the Philippines.

give it a BURL attempt to do something. *Austral. & NZ, informal* ●*Burl* is a northern dialect variant of the onomatopoeic Scottish *birl* meaning a whirring motion and sound; cf. ▶ **give it a WHIRL**.

> **1953** T. A. G. HUNGERFORD *Riverslake* 124 Well you want to give it a burl—you want to come?

BURN one's boats (*or* bridges) commit oneself irrevocably. ●In a military campaign burning one's boats or bridges would make escape or retreat impossible.

BURN the candle at both ends **1** lavish energy or resources in more than one direction at the same time. **2** go to bed late and get up early. ●French *brusler la chandelle par les deux bouts* is earlier (E17) than the saying's appearance in English (M18).

BURN the midnight oil read or work late into the night.

go for the BURN push one's body to the extremes when practising a form of physical exercise. *informal* ●With allusion to the burning sensation caused in muscles by exertion.

slow BURN a state of slowly mounting anger or annoyance. *informal*

BURN ▶ *see* **burn DAYLIGHT**; ▶ *see* **burn one's FINGERS**; ▶ *see* **money burns a HOLE in one's pocket**; ▶ *see* **burn RUBBER**; ▶ *see* **one's EARS burn**; ▶ *see* **have MONEY to burn**.

on the back (*or* front) BURNER having low (*or* high) priority. *informal* ●A metaphor from cooking on a stove with several burners of varying heat: food cooking at a lower temperature on a back burner receives or requires less frequent attention than that cooking at high temperature on a front burner. Cf. the mainly North American expression *cook on the front burner* meaning 'be on the way to rapid success.'

BURNS ▶ *see* **MONEY burns a hole in one's pocket**.

BURNT to a cinder (*or* crisp) completely burnt through, leaving only the charred remnant.

a BURR under (*or* in) one's saddle a persistent source of irritation. *N. Amer., informal*

BURST someone's bubble shatter someone's illusions about something or destroy their sense of well-being.

BURSTING ▶ *see* **bursting at the SEAMS**.

go for a BURTON meet with disaster; be ruined, destroyed, or killed. *Brit.,* *informal* ● Origin uncertain; the expression originated in M20 airman's slang meaning 'be killed in a crash'. Suggested references to Burton's, the British men's outfitters, or Burton, a kind of ale, are folk etymologies, with no definite evidence to support them.

BURY the hatchet (*or* tomahawk) end a quarrel or conflict and become friendly. ● The source in North American Indian practice is explained in an account of peace negotiations dated 1680: 'they came to an agreement and buried two Axes in the Ground; ... which ceremony to them is more significant and binding than all Articles of Peace the Hatchet being a principal weapon with them' (*New England Historical and Genealogical Register* (1870) XXIV. 121) [abbreviations expanded].

BURY one's head in the sand ignore unpleasant realities; refuse to face facts. ● In allusion to the belief that ostriches bury their heads in the sand when pursued, thinking that as they cannot see their pursuers the pursuers cannot see them.

go BUSH leave one's usual surroundings; run wild. *mainly Austral.* ● *Bush* in the sense of 'wild, wooded, or uncleared country' became current among English speakers during the E–L19 British colonial expansion. In South Africa it may have been adopted directly from Dutch *bosch.*

BUSH ▶ *see* **BEAT about the bush**; ▶ *see* **bush TELEGRAPH**.

BUSHEL ▶ *see* **HIDE one's light under a bushel**.

BUSHES ▶ *see* **BEAT the bushes**.

the BUSINESS end the part of a tool, weapon, etc. that carries out the object's particular function. ● Often jocular.

| 1936 'R. CROMPTON' *Sweet William* ix. 227 The business end of a geometrical compass was jabbed into Douglas's arm.

do the BUSINESS **1** do what is required or expected; achieve the desired result. **2** *vulgar slang* have sexual intercourse. *Brit., informal*

in BUSINESS able to begin operations. *informal* ● The literal application of the phrase is to conducting commercial affairs, but the figurative sense is very frequent.

like nobody's BUSINESS in no ordinary way; to an extraordinarily intense degree. *informal* ● Used for emphasis.

| 1991 E. BARKER *O Caledonia* (1992) vi. 64 They spread like nobody's business. They're a really pernicious weed.

a BUSMAN's holiday a holiday or form of recreation that involves doing the same thing that one does at work. ● From the L19 a popular form of working-class recreation was to take an excursion by bus.

a BUSTED flush someone or something that has not fulfilled expectations; a failure. *orig. US, informal* ● In the game of poker, a sequence of cards of one suit that one fails to complete.

the BUTCHER, the baker, the candlestick-maker people of all kinds. ● From a traditional nursery rhyme.

have (*or* take) a BUTCHER's have a look. *Brit., informal* ● *Butcher's* from *butcher's hook*, rhyming slang for a 'look'.

look as if BUTTER wouldn't melt in one's mouth appear deceptively gentle or innocent. *informal*

have (*or* be a) BUTTERFINGERS be unable to catch deftly or hold securely. ● From the idea that hands covered with butter will be slippery, making holding onto anything difficult. There was also a dialect sense of 'unable to handle anything hot', as if one's fingers were made of melting butter. *Butter-fingers!* is often jeeringly shouted at someone who has failed to catch a ball in a game, and is used in this context in Dickens's *Pickwick Papers* (1837).

have BUTTERFLIES in one's stomach have a queasy feeling because one is nervous. *informal*

the BUTTERFLY effect the effect of a very small change in the initial con-ditions of a system which makes a significant difference to the outcome. ● From Edward N. Lorenz's question: 'Does the flap of a butterfly's wings in Brazil set off a tornado in Texas?' (from the title of a paper delivered to the American Association for the Advancement of Science, 29 Dec. 1979).

BUTTON one's lip remain silent. *informal*

on the BUTTON 1 punctually. **2** exactly right. *chiefly US, informal*

press the BUTTON initiate an action or train of events. *informal* ● During the cold war period often used with reference to the possible action of the US or Soviet presidents in starting a nuclear war.

push (*or* press) someone's BUTTONS be successful in arousing or pro-voking a reaction in someone. *informal*

BUY the farm die. *N. Amer., informal*

BUY time adopt tactics which delay an event temporarily so as to have longer to improve one's own position.

BUY ▶ *see* **sell someone a PUP**.

BY and large on the whole; everything considered.   ● Originally in nautical use, describing the handling of a ship both to the wind and off it.

let BYGONES be bygones forgive and forget past offences or causes of conflict. In this form since M17, and now often used as an invitation to reconciliation.

C

the big C cancer. *informal, euphemistic*

the whole CABOODLE (*or* the whole kit and caboodle) the whole lot (of people or things). *informal* ● Originally US, *caboodle* is perhaps from Dutch *boedel* 'possessions'.

cut the CACKLE stop talking aimlessly and come to the point. *informal* ● Usually in imperative.

have a CADENZA be extremely agitated. *S. Afr., slang* ● *Cadenza*, an Italian term for a virtuoso solo passage near the end of a piece of music; this slang sense is probably derived from Danny Kaye's humorous 1940s recording 'The Little Fiddle'.

> 1991 D. CAPEL in *Personality* 2 Sept. 18 The Conservative party is having a cadenza about 'subliminal messages' on the SABC's news logo.

CAESAR's wife a person who is required to be above suspicion. ● With reference to Plutarch's account of Julius Caesar's reason for divorcing his wife Pompeia for her indirect association with the trial of the libertine Publius Clodius for sacrilege: 'I thought my wife ought not even to be under suspicion' (*Caesar* 6). The saying *Caesar's wife must be above suspicion* has become proverbial.

CAESAR ▶ *see* **APPEAL to Caesar**.

in CAHOOTS working or conspiring together, often dishonestly; in collusion. *informal* ● Recorded (E19) from the south and west of the US in the sense of 'partnership', *cahoot* is of uncertain origin, possibly deriving either from French *cahute* 'a hut' or from *cohort*. It is often used with preposition *with*.

> 1998 *Spectator* 4 July 16/3 Labour knows that. So do the Tories and that's why the two of them are in cahoots.

raise CAIN create trouble or a commotion. *informal* ● The sense of *raise* is that of summoning a(n evil) spirit; similar sayings of varying forcefulness are *raise the devil*, *raise hell*, or (US) *raise hob*. Cain, according to the Bible, was the first murderer (Genesis 4:1–15). An M19 expression originating in the US, this form is possibly a euphemism to avoid using the words *Devil* or *hell*.

CAIN ▶ *see* **MARK of Cain**.

have one's CAKE and eat it enjoy the advantages of two mutually incompatible situations. ● Generally in the negative as a proverbial saying.

> 1611 J. DAVIES *Scourge of Folly* no. 271 A man cannot eat his cake and haue it stil.

a piece of CAKE something easily achieved. *informal* ● A M20 expression; *cake* is used in this and several other idioms as a metaphor for something pleasant or desirable.

CAKE ▶ *see* **the ICING on the cake**; ▶ *see* **a SLICE of the cake**; ▶ *see* **TAKE the biscuit**.

CAKES and ale merrymaking.

> *1601 W. SHAKESPEARE *Twelfth Night* II. iii. 124 Dost thou think because thou art virtuous there shall be no more cakes and ale?

sell (*or* go) like hot CAKES be sold quickly and in large quantities.

at (*or* on) the Greek CALENDS never. ● Translating Latin *ad Kalendas Graecas*. In the ancient Roman calendar, *kalendae* was the name given to the first day of the month, but the Greeks did not use *kalendae* in their reckoning of time. Used humorously since M17, but now dated and mainly in literary contexts.

CALF ▶ *see* **a GOLDEN calf**; ▶ *see* **kill the FATTED calf**.

CALL the shots (*or* tune) take the initiative in deciding how something should be done; be in control. *informal* ● *Call the shots* is originally US (M20). *Call the tune* alludes to the saying *he who pays the piper calls the tune* (L19).

> | 1998 *Times* 19 Aug. 23/5 That the IMF is no longer calling the shots was destabilising.

CALL (noun) ▶ *see* **call of NATURE**.

CALL (verb) ▶ *see* **call someone's BLUFF**; ▶ *see* **call it a DAY**; ▶ *see* **call someone NAMES**; ▶ *see* **call a SPADE a spade**; ▶ *see* **too CLOSE to call**.

CALM ▶ *see* **the calm before the STORM**.

open (up) a CAN of worms discover or bring to light a complicated matter likely to prove awkward or embarrassing. *informal* ● M20, especially US.

> | 1998 *New Scientist* UN officials readily accept that they have opened a can of worms, and their guidelines will only have an effect, they say, if governments act on them.

in the CAN completed and available for use. ● A metaphor from recording or film-making, meaning that something has been captured on tape or film.

CAN ▶ *see* **CARRY the can**.

cannot hold a CANDLE to be nowhere near as good as. *informal* ● The positive form of this expression (recorded M16) makes plain the literal sense of an assistant holding a candle to provide illumination for a superior to work by. The current negative version asserts that the subordinate is so far inferior as to be unfit to perform even this humble task.

not worth the CANDLE not justifiable because of the trouble or cost involved. ● The idea is that expenditure on a candle to provide light for an activity would not be recouped by the profits from that activity. The expression is of French origin (recorded E17): *Le jeu ne vaut pas la chandelle* the game is not worth the candle.

> | 1998 *New Scientist* 2 May 48/3 But what if, instead of one, … five, fifteen or fifty people … have to endure such an existence? At what point does the game cease to be worth the candle?

CANDLE ▶ *see* **BURN the candle at both ends**.

a loose CANNON a person or thing likely to cause unintentional or misdirected damage. ● Literally in former times, a piece of ordnance that had broken loose from its fastening or mounting, an accident especially dangerous on wooden ships of war.

CANOE ▶ *see* **PADDLE one's own canoe**.

in (or at) a CANTER without much effort; easily. *Brit.* ●A horse-racing metaphor: a horse has to make so little effort that it can win at the easy pace of a canter rather than having to gallop.

by a CANVAS by a small margin. ●The tapered front end of a racing boat was formerly covered with canvas to prevent water being taken on board; hence the length between the tip of the bow and the first oarsman.

CAP (or *N. Amer.* **also hat) in hand** humbly asking for a favour. ●To have one's head uncovered is a mark of respect and also subordination. The idea of the cap as a begging bowl into which coins can be dropped may also be present.

if the CAP (or *N. Amer.* **shoe) fits (wear it)** an injunction to a hearer to take as applying to himself or herself a generalized remark or criticism that the speaker feels is apposite. ●Early citations of this saying show that the *cap* in question was originally a fool's cap. The N. Amer. variant with *shoe* is slightly later (L18) than its Brit. equivalent (M18). *The cap fits* or *if the cap fits* is often used allusively.

set one's CAP at (or *US* **for)** try to attract as a suitor. *dated*. The idea is L18. The expression is attacked as 'odius' in Jane Austen's *Sense and Sensibility* (1811) by Marianne who declares 'I abhor every common-place phrase by which wit is intended. . . . Their tendency is gross and illiberal.'

cut a CAPER (or capers) make a playful skipping movement.

with a CAPITAL — emphatically —. ●Used postpositively for emphasis.
| **1991** N. WYN ELLIS *John Major* iii. 84 He is not a personality with a capital P, not flamboyant, not it seems an angry man.

have a CARD up one's sleeve have a reserve plan; a secret asset or advantage. *Brit.* ●Cf. ▶ **have an ACE up one's sleeve**.

play the — CARD exploit the specified issue or idea mentioned, especially for political advantage. ●From the view expressed by Lord Randolph Churchill that concerning Irish Home Rule 'the Orange card would be the one to play' (letter, 16 Feb. 1886).
| **1998** *Times* 11 Mar. 15/7 When in doubt, play the race card.

CARD ▶ *see* **MARK someone's card**.

get one's CARDS be dismissed from one's employment. *Brit., informal* ●*Cards* here are the national insurance card and other documents relating to an employee that are retained by the employer as long as the employment is continued. *Give someone their cards* means 'make someone redundant'.

hold all the CARDS be in the strongest or most advantageous position. ●The idea is of a winning hand in a card game.

keep (or play) one's CARDS close to one's chest (or vest) be extremely secretive and cautious about something. *informal* ●Card-players who hold their cards close to their bodies ensure that no opponent can look at them.

on (or *N. Amer.* **in) the CARDS** possible or likely. ●The allusion is probably to the practice of using playing cards or tarot cards to foretell the future.

play one's CARDS right make the best use of one's assets and opportunities.

put (*or* lay) one's CARDS on the table be completely open and honest in declaring one's resources, intentions, or attitude.

not CARE two straws care little or not at all. ● This is just one of the many traditional expressions of this sentiment. *Give* often replaces *care*; cf. ▶ **not GIVE a damn; not give a TINKER's curse**.

a magic CARPET a means of sudden and effortless travel. ● With reference to a fairytale carpet able to transport a person on it to any desired place.

on the CARPET **1** (of a topic, problem, etc.) under discussion. **2** (of a person) being severely reprimanded by someone in authority. ● *Carpet* in both senses has the meaning 'table covering', referring to 'the carpet of the council table', around which a problem is debated (sense 1) or before which one would be summoned for reprimand (sense 2). Sense 1 (E18) is an exact translation of French *sur le tapis* (also occasionally used in English). Sense 2 was originally US; cf. the M19 colloquial sense of *carpet* as a verb meaning 'reprove'.

sweep something under the CARPET conceal or ignore a problem or difficulty in the hope that it will be forgotten.

> **1996** I. PEARS *Death & Restoration* (1997) vi. 76 Many others would merely have swept all our problems under the carpet, and left them until they became too difficult to solve.

CARROT and stick the promise of reward combined with the threat of force. ● From the idea of offering a carrot to a donkey to encourage it to move and using a stick to beat it if it won't. *Carrot* has been used in this figurative sense since L19, and the combination with *stick* since M20. It is often used attributively of a course of action adopted with respect to someone (see quot.).

> **1998** *New Scientist* 30 May 53/3 And if your powers of persuasion prove insufficient, here's a carrot and stick policy.

CARRY the can take responsibility for a mistake or misdeed. *Brit., Canadian, Austral. & NZ, informal* ● The origin of this usage and the nature of the *can* involved are both uncertain, though the idiom appears to have started life as E20 naval or military slang.

> **1998** *Times* 13 May 18/2 Was this the same Mr Cook who danced on the Tories' graves for not carrying the can for errors of their officials?

CARRY ▶ *see* **carry the DAY**.

in the CART in trouble or difficulty. *Brit., informal* ● A cart was used formerly to take convicted criminals to the public gallows and to expose prostitutes and other offenders to public humiliation in the streets.

put the CART before the horse reverse the proper order or procedure of something. ● A medieval version of this expression had setting *oxen* before the *yoke*. The version with *horse* and *cart* dates from E16.

> **1998** *Spectator* 2 May 18/3 That must be a gamble ... Moreover, it's putting the cart before the horse. All history shows that if you want to create a political union, you do that first and the single currency follows.

CARVED ▶ *see* **be carved in tablets of STONE**.

be on (*or* get off) someone's CASE start (*or* stop) criticizing or hounding someone. *informal*

CASH in one's chips die. *informal* ● The counters used in various gambling games are called *chips*; they are converted into cash at the conclusion of the game.

CASH in hand payment for goods and services by money in the form of notes and coins. ● Used as distinct from a cheque, especially with reference to being paid in this way to avoid having to declare the amount earned to the tax authorities.

be CAST in a — mould be of the type specified. ● Cf. ▶ **break the MOULD**.

CAST something in someone's teeth reject defiantly or refer reproachfully to a person's previous action or statement. ● Cf. Matthew 27:44 'The thieves also, which were crucified with him, cast the same in his teeth.'

CAST ▶ *see* **cast someone ADRIFT**; ▶ *see* **cast one's BREAD upon the waters**; ▶ *see* **draw LOTS**; ▶ *see* **cast the first STONE**.

lose CASTE descend to a lower social status. ● Originally with reference to the caste system in Hindu society; a Hindu may lose the rank in society into which he or she is born by, for example, having contact with a person of low caste, by eating certain foods regarded as unclean, or by taking employment regarded as of lower status.

build CASTLES in the air (*or* in Spain) have a visionary and unattainable scheme; daydream. ● The concept was known to St Augustine (354–430): *subtracto fundamento in aere aedificare* to build on air without foundation (*Sermo II*. vi. 8). *Castles in the air* has been the version predominant in English since L16, but *castles in Spain*, reflecting Old French *château en Espagne*, was used in the late medieval period and occasionally since then. The form of the saying in Old French, known from the thirteenth century, may refer to the fact that much of Spain in the Middle Ages was under Moorish control, so any scheme to build castles there was clearly impracticable.

the CAT has got someone's tongue someone is remaining silent. ● The question *has the cat got your tongue?* is addressed particularly to a child who remains silent when required to speak.

a CAT may look at a king even a person of low status or importance has rights. ● Used proverbially since M16.
> 1998 *Times* 8 Sept. 22/6 A cat may look at a king. The cat may be wrong in its conclusions, but others, following its gaze, can draw their own.

fight like CAT and dog (of two people) be continually arguing with one another. ● The enmity between cat and dog has been proverbial since at least L16.
> 1995 E. TOMAN *Dancing in Limbo* i. 18 Her desertion of him hadn't come as a total surprise … for the pair of them had been fighting like cat and dog for the best part of a year.

let the CAT out of the bag reveal a secret, especially carelessly or by mistake. ● M18. For a similar metaphorical use of *bag* cf. French *vider le sac* literally 'empty the bag' meaning to 'tell the whole story'.
> 1996 B. CONNOLLY *Rotten Heart of Europe* (ed. 2) xiv. 380 Tim Renton, … at odds with his leader on Europe, let the cat out of the bag when he told a television audience, 'We need a strong Europe to maintain our independence from the United States and the Pacific Rim.'

like a CAT on a hot tin roof (*or Brit.* **on hot bricks**) very agitated, restless, or anxious.

like the CAT that's got (*or* **who's stolen**) **the cream** self-satisfied, having achieved one's objective. *chiefly Brit., informal*

like something the CAT brought in (of a person) very dirty, bedraggled, or exhausted. *informal*

| *1928 R. KNOX Footsteps at Lock viii. 79 Bredon felt, in an expressive modern phrase, like something the cat had brought in.

not a CAT in hell's chance no chance at all. *informal* ● Now often shortened to *not a cat's chance*.

| *1796 F. GROSE Dictionary of Vulgar Tongue (ed. 3) No more chance than a cat in hell without claws; said of one who enters into a dispute or quarrel with one greatly above his match.

play CAT and mouse with manoeuvre in a way designed alternately to provoke and to thwart an opponent. ● Alluding to the way that a cat toys with a mouse, pretending to release it and then pouncing on it again. The phrase *cat and mouse* is often used attributively, as in *cat-and-mouse game*. Most notoriously it was the name given in Britain to the Prisoners (Temporary Discharge for Ill-health) Act (1913) under which suffragettes on hunger strike in gaol were released if their health were endangered by starvation or forcible feeding, only to be rearrested as soon as their strength improved.

put (*or* **set**) **the CAT among the pigeons** say or do something that is likely to cause trouble or controversy. *Brit.* ● First recorded in J. Stevens's *New Spanish and English Dictionary* (1706), the expression is explained there as a man getting in among a group of women. The idiom ▶ **FLUTTER the dovecot(e)s** is based on the same notion of pigeons as a tranquil or harmless community.

| 1998 New Scientist 11 July 3/2 The ... study has firmly put the cat among the pigeons by claiming that most of the therapeutic effects of expensive antidepressant pills ... can be mimicked by dummy pills.

see which way the CAT jumps see what direction events are taking before committing oneself.

| 1990 D. KAVANAGH Thatcherism (ed. 2) ix. 249 I don't spend a lifetime watching which way the cat jumps I know really which way I want the cat to go.

that CAT won't jump that suggestion is implausible or impracticable. *informal* ● Originally (M19) US.

| 1965 S. TROY No More a-Roving ii. 57 If you're telling me she fell in, just like that—oh no! That cat won't jump.

turn CAT in pan change sides, be a traitor. ● The origin of the phrase is unknown. It was used (M–L16) in the form *turn the cat in the pan* with the sense of 'reverse the proper order or nature of things', but this sense seems to have become obsolete in E17, being replaced about that time with the modern sense.

CAT ▶ *see* **BELL the cat**; ▶ *see* **a DEAD cat bounce**; ▶ *see* **enough to make a cat LAUGH**; ▶ *see* **like a SCALDED cat**; ▶ *see* **no ROOM to swing a cat**.

in the CATBIRD seat in a superior or advantageous position. *N. Amer., informal*

●Said to be an allusion to a baseball player in the fortunate position of having no strikes and therefore three balls still to play (a reference made in James Thurber's short story *The Catbird Seat*).

CATCH the sun **1** be in a sunny position. **2** *Brit.* become tanned or sunburnt.

CATCH a Tartar encounter or get hold of a person who can neither be controlled nor got rid of; meet with a person who is unexpectedly more than one's match. ●The Tartars (*or* Tatars), a Mongoloid people of Central Asia, established a vast empire during the Middle Ages under the leadership of the warlord Genghis Khan, and were a byword for ferocity.

CATCH ▶ *see* **clutch at STRAWS**; ▶ *see* **catch a COLD**; ▶ *see* **catch one's DEATH**.

a CATCH-22 situation a dilemma from which the victim cannot escape. ●The classic statement of this situation is in Joseph Heller's novel *Catch-22* (1961): 'Orr would be crazy to fly more missions and sane if he didn't, but if he was sane he had to fly them. If he flew them he was crazy and didn't have to; but if he didn't want to he was sane and had to.'

> **1997** *New Scientist* 8 Nov 62/1 It's a catch-22 situation: you cannot get the job without having the relevant experience and you cannot get the experience without having first done the job.

play CATCH-UP try to equal a competitor in a sporting event.

the CAT'S WHISKERS (*or* pyjamas *or* *chiefly US* **meow)** an excellent person or thing. *informal* ●All these expressions were originally US slang (the first two E20).

make common CAUSE unite in order to achieve a shared aim. ●Followed by preposition *with*.

> **1997** A. SIVANANDRAN *When Memory Dies* I. i. 5 I was sorry that the crows, proud kings of the dung-heap, should make common cause with house-sparrows under the eaves of roofs.

a rebel without a CAUSE a person who is deeply dissatisfied with society in general but does not have a specific aim to fight for. ●From the title of a US film starring James Dean, released in 1955.

keep CAVE act as lookout. *school slang* ●*Cave* is the imperative of Latin *cavere* beware. Pronounced as one or two syllables, *cave* was the traditional warning uttered by a schoolchild to let others know that a teacher was approaching.

CAVIAR to the general a good thing that is not appreciated by the ignorant. ●From Hamlet's commendation of a play: 'the play, I remember, pleased not the million; 'twas caviar to the general' (Shakespeare *Hamlet* II. ii).

CERBERUS ▶ *see* **a SOP to Cerberus**.

stand on CEREMONY insist on the observance of formalities; behave formally. ●Usually with negative.

bad CESS to a curse on. *Anglo-Irish* ●The origin of *cess* in this expression is probably linked to the historical requirement for Irish households to provide the soldiers of their English overlords with provisions at the low prices 'assessed' by the government.

CHAFE ▶ *see* **CHAMP at the bit**.

be caught with CHAFF be easily deceived. ●*Chaff* is the husks of corn separated from the grain by threshing; cf. the proverb *you cannot catch old birds with chaff.* Used since L15 as a metaphor for being easily fooled or trapped.

CHAFF ▶ *see* **separate the WHEAT from the chaff**.

pull (*or* **yank) someone's CHAIN** tease someone, especially by leading them to believe something that isn't true. *US, informal*

CHALICE ▶ *see* **a POISONED chalice**.

as different as (*or* **as like as) CHALK and cheese** fundamentally different. *Brit.* ●The proverbial opposition of *chalk* and *cheese* hinges on their being totally different in all qualities other than their rather similar appearance.

by a long CHALK by far. *Brit.* ●The expression is based on the old custom of marking up points scored in a game with chalk on a blackboard. Cf. ▶ **not by a long CHALK**.

CHALK and talk teaching by traditional methods focusing on the blackboard and presentation by the teacher as opposed to more informal or interactive methods. *Brit.*

not by a long CHALK by no means; not at all. *Brit.* ●Cf. ▶ **by a long CHALK**.

CHALK ▶ *see* **WALK the chalk**.

CHAMP (*or* **chafe) at the bit** be restlessly impatient, especially to start doing something. ●Used literally of a spirited horse that tugs at the bit in its mouth in its eagerness to move.

CHANCE one's arm (*or* **luck)** undertake or venture on something although it may be dangerous or unsuccessful; take a risk. *Brit., informal*

CHANCE would be a fine thing desirable but unlikely. *informal* ●Used mainly in spoken English to express a belief that something desirable that has just been mentioned is unlikely to happen.

on the (off) CHANCE just in case.

> 1992 N. STEPHENSON *Snow Crash* xiii. 115 They upload staggering quantities of useless information to the database, on the off chance that some of it will eventually be useful.

CHANCE ▶ *see* **in the LAST chance saloon**; ▶ *see* **not a CAT in hell's chance**; ▶ *see* **not a CHINAMAN's chance**; ▶ *see* **not a hope in HELL**; ▶ *see* **a SPORTING chance**.

CHANGE one's tune express a very different opinion or behave in a very different way, usually in response to a change in circumstances.

get no CHANGE out of fail to get information or a desired reaction from. *Brit., informal*

CHANGE ▶ *see* **change HORSES in midstream**.

ring the CHANGES vary the ways of expressing, arranging, or doing something. ●With allusion to bell-ringing and the different sequences (*changes*) in which a peal of bells may be rung.

CHAPTER and verse an exact reference or authority. ●Originally with allusion to the numbering of passages in the Bible, now also more generally to
any (usually written) authority for something.

a CHAPTER of accidents a series of misfortunes. ●A phrase apparently
coined by Lord Chesterfield in a letter to Solomon Dayrolles (16 Feb. 1753):
'The chapter of knowledge is a very short, but the chapter of accidents is a
very long one.'

return to the CHARGE make a further attempt at something, especially in
arguing a point. *dated* ●*Charge* here means 'an impetuous attack'.

CHARITY ▶ *see* **COLD as charity**.

work like a CHARM be completely successful or effective. ●*Charm* here means
a magic spell or lucky talisman.

CHASE the dragon take heroin (sometimes mixed with another smokable
drug) by heating it in tinfoil and inhaling the fumes through a tube or roll
of paper. ●Reputedly translated from the Chinese; the expression apparently
refers to the undulating movements of the fumes up and down the tinfoil,
resembling the tail of the dragon in Chinese myths.

the CHATTERING classes articulate and educated people considered as a
social group given to the expression of (usually liberal) opinions about society
and culture. *derogatory*

CHEAP at the price well worth however much it cost. ●A frequently heard
variant of this, *cheap at half the price*, while used to mean exactly the same, is,
logically speaking, nonsense, since *cheap at twice the price* is the actual meaning
intended.

CHECK someone/thing skeef give someone or something a dirty look; look
askance at someone or something. *S. Afr.*

CHEEK by jowl close together; side by side. ●From a use of *jowl* in the sense
'cheek'; the phrase was originally *cheek by cheek*.

turn the other CHEEK refrain from retaliating when one has been attacked
or insulted. ●With allusion to Matthew 5:39 'But I say unto you, That ye
resist not evil: but whosoever shall smite thee on thy right cheek, turn to him
the other also.'

of good CHEER cheerful, optimistic. *archaic* ●The exhortation to *be of good
cheer* occurs in several passages of the New Testament in the Authorized
Version of the Bible (Matthew 9:2, John 16:33, Acts 27:22, etc.). The Late Latin
word *cara*, meaning 'face', passed into Provençal, Spanish, and Portuguese,
becoming *ch(i)ere* in Old French, from which it then passed into Middle
English. *Cheer* meaning 'face' is now obsolete, but the derived senses of
'countenance' and 'demeanour as reflected in the countenance' survive in a
number of phrases, including *in good* (or *bad*) *cheer* and the archaic *what cheer?*
(how are you?).

three CHEERS for — three successive hurrahs expressing appreciation or
congratulation of (someone or something). ●Used both literally and figura-

tively. Qualified approval or mild enthusiasm is sometimes expressed by *two cheers for —*, as in the title of E. M. Forster's book *Two Cheers for Democracy*.

CHEESE ▶ *see* **a BIG cheese**.

take the CHEQUERED FLAG finish first in a race. ● From the flag used in motor racing to signify that the winner has passed the finishing post.

a bowl of CHERRIES a very pleasant or enjoyable situation or experience. ● Cf. the 1931 song-title 'Life is just a bowl of cherries' by Lew Brown (1893–1958). Usually with negative.

a bite at the CHERRY an attempt or opportunity to do something. ● Often with negative, expressing the idea that one will not get a second chance (*a second bite at the cherry*). If one takes two attempts to do something, especially some quite small task, this is taking *two bites at the (same) cherry* or *another bite at the cherry*.

the CHERRY on the cake a desirable feature perceived as a pleasing but inessential addition to something that is already worth having.

pop someone's CHERRY have sexual intercourse with a girl or woman who is a virgin. *informal*

grin like a CHESHIRE cat have a broad fixed smile on one's face. ● Best known for its appearance (and disappearance) in Lewis Carroll's *Alice's Adventures in Wonderland* (1865), the Cheshire cat with its grin is recorded from the first half of the nineteenth century; however, the origins of the expression are uncertain.

get something off one's CHEST say something that one has wanted to say for a long time, resulting in a feeling of relief. *informal*

CHEST ▶ *see* **bottom DRAWER**.

an old CHESTNUT a joke, story, or subject that has become tedious and uninteresting because of its age and constant repetition. ● The most likely explanation of the source of this sense of *chestnut* as something that has been too often repeated is in the following exchange between two characters, Zavior and Pablo, in W. Dimond's play *Broken Sword* (1816): ZAVIOR ... When suddenly from the thick boughs of a cork tree— PABLO. (Jumping up) A chestnut, Captain, a chestnut ... Captain, this is the twenty-seventh time I have heard you relate this story, and you invariably said, a chestnut, until now (i. 13).

pull someone's CHESTNUTS out of the fire succeed in a hazardous undertaking on behalf of or through the agency of another. ● With reference to the fable of a monkey using a cat's paw (or in some versions a dog's paw) to rake out roasting chestnuts from a fire. Hence also *cat's-paw* to mean someone who is used by someone else as a tool or stooge.

CHEW the fat (*or* rag) chat in a leisurely way, usually at length; reiterate old grievances. *informal* ● Recorded from L19, this apparently originated as military slang.

> **1931** R. CAMPBELL *Georgiad* i. 17 The scavengers of letters Convene to chew the fat about their betters.

CHEW ▶ *see* **chew the CUD**.

neither CHICK nor child no children at all. *N. Amer.* or *dialect*

a CHICKEN-and-egg problem an unresolved question as to which of two things caused the other. ● From the traditional riddle, 'Which came first, the chicken or the egg?'

running (or rushing) about like a headless CHICKEN acting in a panic-stricken and undirected manner. ● A decapitated chicken may continue to flap about for a few moments.

CHICKENS come home to roost one's past mistakes or wrongdoings will eventually be the cause of present troubles. ● With allusion to the proverb *curses, like chickens, come home to roost*.

| **1998** *Spectator* 21 Mar. 55/1 Now the chickens have come home to roost, as they say in Schoenburg-Hartenstein.

CHICKENS ▶ *see* **COUNT one's chickens**.

big white CHIEF a person in authority. *humorous* ● Supposedly representing Native American speech, the expression also occurs as *great white chief* (both M20).

| **1971** R. BUSBY *Deadlock* xiii. 200 You'd think he was the bloody big white chief instead of an OB technician.

too many CHIEFS (and not enough Indians) too many people giving orders (and not enough people to carry them out).

keep one's CHIN up remain cheerful in difficult circumstances. *informal* ● Cf. ▶ **keep one's PECKER up**.

take it on the CHIN endure or accept misfortune courageously. ● A metaphor from boxing.

| **1998** *Times* 27 July 29/5 [T]he occasional 'bad 'un' [i.e. decision] is inevitable, and when it comes ... the players must take it on the chin.

not a CHINAMAN's chance not even a very slight chance. ● An E20 US colloquialism.

| **1952** F. YERBY *Woman called Fancy* x. 193 You haven't a Chinaman's chance of raising that money in Boston.

a CHINK in someone's armour a weak point in someone's character, arguments, or ideas which makes them vulnerable to attack or criticism.

a CHIP off the old block someone who resembles their parent, especially in character. *informal* ● A *chip* here perceived as something forming a portion of, or derived from, a larger or more important thing, of which it retains the characteristic qualities. Cf. Edmund Burke's comment on the younger Pitt's maiden speech (Feb. 1781): 'Not merely a chip of the old "block", but the old block itself.' E17 in the form *chip of the same block*; later *chip of the old block* (see Burke quot. above), but since E20 the variant with *off* has dominated.

a CHIP on one's shoulder a strong and usually long-standing inclination to feel resentful or aggrieved, often about a particular thing; a sense of inferiority characterized by a quickness to take offence. *informal* ● Originating in a practice described in 1830 in the *Long Island Telegraph* (Hempstead, N.Y.) 20

May 3/5: 'When two churlish boys were *determined* to fight, a *chip* would be placed on the shoulder of one, and the other demanded to knock it off at his peril.'

have had one's CHIPS be dead, dying, or out of contention. *Brit., informal* ●*Chips* here and in next entry are gambling chips; cf. ▶ **CASH in one's chips**.

when the CHIPS are down when one is in a very serious and difficult situation. *informal* ●Cf. previous entry.

CHIPS ▶ *see* **SPIT blood**.

Hobson's CHOICE no choice at all. ●This refers to the practice of Hobson, a carrier at Cambridge in E17, who would not allow his clients their own choice of horse from his stables as he insisted on hiring them out in strict rotation. Milton wrote two epitaphs on Hobson when he died in January 1631. *Hobson's choice* is also M20 British rhyming slang for 'voice'.

CHOP logic argue in a tiresomely pedantic way; quibble. ●From an obsolete use of *chop* (M16) meaning 'bandy words', later wrongly understood as 'cut into small pieces' or 'mince'.

CHOP and change change one's opinions or behaviour repeatedly and abruptly, often for no good reason. *Brit., informal* ●An alliterative phrase in which both components originally carried the idea of 'barter', 'exchange', or 'buy and sell', but as this sense of *chop* became dated (cf. ▶ **CHOP logic**) the meaning of the whole expression shifted to its present one.

not much CHOP no good; not up to much. *chiefly Austral. & NZ, informal* ●The sense of *chop* here originated in the Hindi word *chāp* (in English since E17) meaning 'official stamp'. As used by Europeans in the Far East, the word was extended to cover documents such as passports to which an official stamp or impression was attached and in China to mean 'branded goods'. From this the sense developed in L19 to mean something that has 'class' or been validated as genuine or good. Cf. ▶ **not much COP**.

| **1947** D. M. DAVIN *Gorse blooms Pale* 207I know it's not been much chop so far but we're only getting started.

bust one's CHOPS exert oneself. *N. Amer., informal*

bust someone's CHOPS nag or criticize someone. *N. Amer., informal*

strike (*or* touch) a CHORD say or do something which affects or stirs the emotions of others. ●Also *strike* (or *touch*) *the right chord with*, meaning to appeal to or arouse a particular emotion in.

CHUCK it down rain heavily. *informal*

off one's CHUMP crazy. *Brit., informal* ●The literal sense of *chump* as 'a broad, thick block of wood' gave rise (M19) to its jocose application to mean 'head', with the implication of 'blockhead'. This phrase was a L19 development along the lines of ▶ **off one's HEAD**.

close but no CIGAR (of an attempt) almost but not quite successful. *N. Amer., informal* ●A catch-phrase possibly originating as a consolatory comment to or about a man who put up a good, but not winning, performance in a sporting competition or contest of strength in which the prize was a cigar.

| **1995** N. HORNBY *High Fidelity* (1996) 33 But, you know ... you did not represent my last and best chance of a relationship. So, you know. Nice try. Close, but no cigar.

CINDER ▶ *see* **BURNT to a cinder**.

CIRCLE the wagons (of a group) unite in defence of a common interest. *N. Amer., informal* ●In South Africa the Afrikaans word *laager*, meaning 'a defensive circle of ox-wagons', is used in similar metaphorical contexts.

come (*or* **turn**) **full CIRCLE** return to a past position or situation, often in a way considered to be inevitable. ●Cf. ▶ **the wheel has come full CIRCLE**.

the wheel has turned (*or* **come**) **full CIRCLE** the situation has returned to what it was in the past, as if completing a cycle. ●With reference to Shakespeare's *King Lear* (1605–6) V. iii 'The wheel is come full circle', the allusion being to the wheel fabled to be turned by Fortune and representing mutability.

go (*or* **run**) **round in CIRCLES** be busy about something for a long time without achieving any significant progress. *informal*

a three-ring CIRCUS an uproar; an ostentatious event. *informal* ●This figurative use of *circus* originated in the US (M19).

| **1998** *Spectator* 16 May 26/1 Along the way, these meetings have lost all that might have made them worthwhile ... and have turned into a travelling three-ring circus.

CIVILIZATION ▶ *see* **the END of civilization as we know it**.

CLAIM to fame a reason for being regarded as unusual or noteworthy. ●Often used when the reason cited is comical, bizarre, or trivial.

CLAM ▶ *see* **HAPPY as a sandboy**.

CLANGER ▶ *see* **DROP a clanger**.

CLAP hold of grab someone or something roughly or abruptly. *informal* ●The meaning of *clap* in this sense is somewhat removed from the original one, widely found in N. European languages, of 'make a sudden explosive sound'; this verb came in the course of time to be used in some post-medieval English contexts to mean just 'make a sudden action', not necessarily implying any sound (see also next entry).

CLAP someone in jail (*or* **irons**) put someone in prison (*or* in chains). ●*Clap* here has the sense of doing something suddenly (cf. preceding entry).

CLAP ▶ *see* **clap EYES on**.

like the CLAPPERS very fast or very hard. *Brit., informal* ●*Clappers* here may refer to a contrivance in a mill for striking or shaking the hopper in order to make the grain move down to the millstones or to the tongues of bells. M20 RAF slang, sometimes in the form *like the clappers of hell*.

| **1959** J. BRAINE *Vodi* ix. 128 I've got to work like the clappers this morning.

a CLASS act a person or thing displaying impressive and stylish excellence. ●*Class* used attributively with the informal meaning 'of high quality' was a L19 development, apparently originally (and often still) in sporting contexts.

get one's CLAWS into enter into a manipulative and self-serving relationship with someone. *informal* ● Used especially of a woman who dominates or manipulates a man.

CLAY ▶ *see* **have FEET of clay**.

CLEAN someone's clock **1** give someone a beating. **2** defeat or surpass someone decisively. *N. Amer., informal* ● *Clock* has the slang sense of 'face'.

CLEAN house eliminate corruption or inefficiency. *N. Amer.* ● Also in the literal sense of 'do housework'.

come CLEAN be completely honest and frank. *informal* ● An E20 US expression. Cf. ▶ **make a CLEAN breast of something**.

have CLEAN hands be uninvolved and blameless with regard to an immoral act. ● Also *keep one's hands clean*. Cf. ▶ **WASH one's hands of**.

make a CLEAN breast of something (*or* **of it**) confess fully one's mistakes or wrongdoings. ● The breast was popularly supposed in former times to be the dwelling of a person's conscience.

make a CLEAN sweep **1** remove all unwanted people or things ready to start afresh. **2** win all of a group of similar or related sporting competitions, events, or matches.

Mr CLEAN an honourable or incorruptible politician.

CLEAN (verb) ▶ *see* **clean up one's ACT**.

CLEAN (adj.) ▶ *see* **clean as a WHISTLE**; ▶ *see* **a clean BILL of health**; ▶ *see* **keep one's NOSE clean**; ▶ *see* **wipe the SLATE clean**.

take someone to the CLEANERS **1** take all someone's money or possessions in a dishonest or unfair way. **2** inflict a crushing defeat on someone. ● Originally M20 US slang.

CLEAR the air defuse or clarify an angry, tense, or confused situation by frank discussion. ● From the idea that a thunderstorm makes the air less humid.

(as) CLEAR as day very easy to see or understand. ● Also *(as) clear as daylight*.

CLEAR the decks prepare for a particular event or goal by dealing with anything beforehand that might hinder progress. ● In the literal sense, obstacles or superfluous items were removed from the decks of a ship before a battle at sea.

in CLEAR not in code. ● A phrase first recorded E20, but French *en clair* had been current in English with this meaning since L19.

in the CLEAR **1** no longer in danger or suspected of something. **2** with nothing to hinder someone in achieving something.

out of a CLEAR (blue) sky as a complete surprise. ● Cf. ▶ **out of the BLUE**.

> 1992 *New Yorker* 20 July 69/1 The latest revelations ... about the marriage of the Prince and Princess of Wales may have induced disbelief, but they did not come out of a clear blue sky.

CLEAR ▶ *see* **clear as a BELL**; ▶ *see* **clear as MUD**.

be (*or* be caught) in a CLEFT stick be in a difficult situation, when any action one takes will have adverse consequences. *chiefly Brit.* ●*Cleft* is one of the forms of the past participle of *cleave*, in its basic meaning of 'to divide with a cutting blow' or 'split'. The other form still current in standard English is *cloven*, and the two words tend to be used in different contexts: thus *a cleft stick* and *a cleft palate* but ▶ **a CLOVEN hoof**.

too CLEVER by half (of a person) annoyingly proud of one's intelligence or skill. *informal* ●Used generally with the implication that such people very often overreach themselves.

CLICK into place become suddenly clear and understandable. ●Used literally of an object, especially part of a mechanism, to mean 'fall smoothly into its allotted position'.

CLICK ▶ *see* **snap one's FINGERS at**.

have a mountain to CLIMB be facing a very difficult task.

be CLIMBING the walls feel frustrated, helpless, and trapped. *informal*

at a CLIP at a time; all at once. *US, informal*

CLIP the wings of prevent (someone) from acting freely; check the aspirations of. ●From the practice of trimming the feathers of a bird so as to disable it from flight.

round (*or* around) the CLOCK all day and all night; ceaselessly.

> **1992** S. SONTAG *Volcano Lover* I. iii. 42 The mountain was ... guarded round the clock by a ring of armed soldiers mounted on nervous horses.

turn (*or* put) back the CLOCK return to the past or to a previous way of doing things, especially as a negative step.

watch the CLOCK wait eagerly for the end of working hours. ●Hence *clock-watcher* as a person who does this.

run someone CLOSE almost match the same standards or level of achievement as someone else.

too CLOSE to call (of a contest, race, etc.) so evenly balanced that it is impossible to predict the outcome with confidence. *informal*

too CLOSE for comfort dangerously or uncomfortably near.

CLOSE (verb) ▶ *see* **close the DOOR on**; ▶ *see* **close one's EYES to**; ▶ *see* **bridge the GAP**; ▶ *see* **close one's MIND to**; ▶ *see* **close RANKS**.

CLOSE (adj.) ▶ *see* **close to the BONE**; ▶ *see* **close but no CIGAR**; ▶ *see* **close to one's HEART**; ▶ *see* **close to HOME**.

a CLOSED book a thing of which one has no knowledge or understanding. ●E20 in this figurative sense; the opposite of *an open book* (M19).

> **1944** F. CLUNE *Red Heart 35* The desert is an open book to the man of the Vast Open Spaces, but to the schoolmaster it was a closed book.

behind CLOSED doors (of an action) done in a secretive or furtive way; hidden from public view.

out of the CLOSET out into the open. *informal* ● The normal North American term for 'cupboard', *closet* in the Bible typifies privacy and seclusion (cf. Luke 12:3). *Come out of the closet* means 'cease hiding a secret about oneself' or 'make public one's intentions'; it is particularly (but not invariably—see quot.) used in L20 in connection with making public one's homosexuality (cf. *closet queen* as derogatory slang for a secret homosexual).

  | **1998** *Spectator* 27 June 13/3 The Prime Minister's entourage could not conceal its glee at the results of their boss coming out of the closet.

on CLOUD nine (*or* dated **seven**) extremely happy.   ● A M20 US phrase, with reference to a ten-part classification of clouds in which *nine* was next to the highest.

under a CLOUD under suspicion; discredited.

CLOUD ▶ *see* **a SILVER lining**.

with one's head in the CLOUDS (of a person) out of touch with reality; daydreaming.

a CLOVEN HOOF an indication of evil. ● Traditional pictures of the Devil show him with head and torso of a man but the legs and cloven feet of a goat; thus a *cloven hoof* is a giveaway sign of the Devil.

  | **1959** F. MAURIAC *Women of Pharisees* xii. 162 She had been a trial to him from the beginning, and now the cloven hoof was beginning to show.

in CLOVER in ease and luxury. ● This sense of the phrase (E18) alludes to clover's being particularly attractive to livestock; cf. the simile *happy as a pig in clover*.

in the CLUB (*or* **the pudding club**) pregnant. *Brit., informal*

  | **1993** C. MACDOUGALL *Lights Below* 140 Must be serious if you're drinking with the old man. Did you stick her in the club?

join (*or* **welcome to**) **the CLUB** other people are in the same situation. *informal* ● Used as a humorous exclamation to express solidarity with someone else who is experiencing problems or difficulties that the speaker has already experienced.

CLUTCH ▶ *see* **clutch at STRAWS**.

and CO. (*or* **co.** *or* **company**) and the rest of them. *Brit., informal* ● Used after a person's name to denote those people usually associated with them. Cf. Kipling's collection of tales of schoolboy life *Stalky & Co.*

drive a COACH and horses through make something entirely useless or ineffective. *Brit.* ● Cf. the Irish lawyer Stephen Rice (1637–1715): 'I will drive a coach and six horses through the Act of Settlement.' Early versions of this idiom also refer to a space big enough *to turn a coach and six* (*or* *four*) (i.e. horses) *in*, but the context, following Rice's declaration, is very often that of rendering a law or regulation ineffective.

  | **1997** *Spectator* 29 Nov. 13/1 A coach and horses was driven through one of the guiding principles of American statecraft … .

COALS to Newcastle something brought or sent to a place where it is already plentiful. ●Coal from Newcastle upon Tyne in northern England was famously abundant in previous centuries, and *to carry coals to Newcastle* has been an expression for a superfluous activity since M17.

haul someone over the COALS reprimand someone severely. ●An expression originating in the form of torture that involved dragging the victim over the coals of a slow fire.

heap COALS of fire (up)on someone's head go out of one's way to cause someone to feel remorse. *Brit.* ●Biblical in origin: 'if thine enemy hunger, feed him; if he thirst, give him drink: for in so doing thou shalt heap coals of fire on his head' (Romans 12:20).

the COAST is clear there is no danger of being observed or caught. ●With reference to the idea that enemies guarding a sea-coast would prevent an attempt to land or embark.

ride (*or* climb *or* hang) on someone's COAT-TAILS undeservedly benefit from another's success by associating oneself closely with them. ●M19 US in origin.

| **1964** *Economist* 31 Oct. 482/2 Mr. Robert Kennedy cannot be sure of riding the coat-tails of Mr Johnson in New York.

have (*or* get) a COB on be annoyed or in a bad mood. *Brit., informal* ●*Cob* is of uncertain origin in this phrase, which was first recorded (M20 by Partridge) as ships' stewards' slang and may be northern dialect.

blow (*or* clear *or* sweep) away the COBWEBS banish a state of lethargy or ignorance; enliven or refresh. ●The figurative sense of *cobweb* as a 'musty accretion' has been current since L16, and *sweep away the cobwebs* since L17.

a COCK-and-bull story a long rambling incredible story; nonsense. ●Perhaps with reference to some unidentified fable. The French equivalent *coq à l'âne* (cock and donkey) was also known in England in M–L17. The slang use of *cock* or *bull* individually to mean 'nonsense' is later: *cock* was a shortened form of *cock-and-bull story* in M19, leading thence to its modern slang use (M20); *bull* was defined as 'hot air' in E20. In E17 *to talk of a cock and bull* was to talk nonsense, but the phrase is now more usual in attributive use (L18).

COCK one's ear listen attentively to or for something. With reference to the action of a dog in raising its ears to an erect position.

COCK of the walk someone who dominates others within a group. ●The place in which a cock bred for fighting was kept was known as a *walk*, and it would allow no other cocks within this space.

COCK (noun) ▶ *see at* **FULL cock**; ▶ *see at* **HALF cock**.

COCK (verb) ▶ *see* **cock a SNOOK at**.

knock something into a COCKED HAT **1** put a definitive end to. **2** be very much better than. ●A *cocked hat* is a hat with the brim permanently turned up, esp. the style of three-cornered hat worn L18–E19. The phrase is US in origin.

warm the COCKLES of someone's heart give someone a comforting feeling of pleasure or contentment. ●L17, of unknown origin, but perhaps deriving from the resemblance in shape between a heart and a cockle-shell.

bring something up to CODE renovate an old building or update its features in line with the latest building regulations. *N. Amer.*

COIGN of vantage a favourable position for observation or action. *literary* ●Literally, 'projecting corner' (Fr. *coin* 'corner'). Quoting Shakespeare *Macbeth* I. vi. (Duncan's description of the nesting places of the swifts at Macbeth's castle). The archaic spelling of *quoin* as *coign* barely survives outside this phrase, which seems to have been brought into general currency by the writings of Sir Walter Scott in E19.

shuffle off this mortal COIL die. *literary* ●With allusion to Shakespeare *Hamlet* III. i; used mainly humorously or euphemistically. *This mortal coil* sometimes occurs independently for 'the fact or state of being alive', with the suggestion that this is a troublesome state, since *coil* retains here its archaic sense of 'turmoil'.

| **1998** *Spectator* 25 Apr. 17/3 Whether the huge financial institutions … will be content to see another Murdoch at the top when Rupert throws off his mortal coil is another matter.

the other side of the COIN (*or* shield) the opposite or contrasting aspect of a matter. ●Cf. ▶ **the reverse of the MEDAL**.

pay someone back in their own COIN retaliate by similar behaviour.

to COIN a phrase to use a cliché. ●Generally used ironically when introducing a banal remark, but also less commonly when about to use a new expression or a variation on a familiar one.

COINCIDENCE ▶ *see* **the long ARM of coincidence**.

catch a COLD (*also* catch cold) **1** become infected with a cold. **2** *informal* encounter trouble or difficulties, especially financial ones.

(as) COLD as charity very cold. ●With reference to the perfunctory or uncaring way in which charity is often given. Cf. Wyclif's translation (1382) of Matthew 24:12 'The charite of manye schal wexe coold.'

COLD comfort poor or inadequate consolation. ●Often *be cold comfort for/to someone/thing*. *Cold* (as the reverse of 'encouraging') and *comfort* have been associated since E14, but perhaps the phrase is most memorably linked for modern readers with the title of Stella Gibbons's 1932 parody of sentimental novels of rural life, *Cold Comfort Farm*.

have (*or* get) COLD feet suffer loss of nerve or confidence. ●Originally L19 US.

the COLD shoulder a show of intentional unfriendliness; rejection. ●Hence, to *cold-shoulder someone* means to 'reject or be deliberately unfriendly to someone'.

go COLD turkey suddenly and completely stop taking drugs. ●With allusion to one of the possible unpleasant side effects of this, involving bouts of shivering and sweating that cause the bumpy condition of the skin known as *goose flesh* or *goose pimples*. An E20 US expression that has become widespread and can be used of terminating other addictive behaviours.

have someone COLD have someone at one's mercy. *US, informal*

> **1988** R. HALL *Kisses of Enemy* (1990) II. xii. 217 He waited in his office for news of violence, knowing that then he would have the troublemakers cold.

in COLD blood without feeling or mercy; ruthlessly. ● According to medieval physiology, blood was naturally hot, so this phrase refers to an unnatural state in which someone can do a (hot-blooded) deed of passion or violence without the normal heating of the blood (cf. ▶ **make one's BLOOD boil**. Since E17 in the sense of 'coolly' (cf. French *sang-froid*), and E18 in its modern sense.

leave someone COLD fail to interest or excite someone. ● This expression (in English from M19) of the idea that uninterest is cold occurs in other European languages; cf. French *cela me laisse froid* and German *das lässt mich kalt*.

out COLD completely unconscious.

(left) out in the COLD ignored; neglected. ● Cf. ▶ **COME in from the cold**.

pour (*or* throw) COLD water on be discouraging or negative about.

> **1998** *New Scientist* 24 Jan. 48/2 When I put it to … the health minister, that perhaps all clinical trial results should be published, she threw cold water on the idea.

feel someone's COLLAR arrest or legally apprehend someone. ● From using a person's collar as a means of getting a secure grip on them. Often in passive: *have one's collar felt*.

on (a) COLLISION course adopting an approach that is certain to lead to conflict with another person or group. ● An M20 phrase also used literally to mean 'going in a direction that will lead to a violent crash with another moving object or person'.

lend (*or* give) COLOUR to make something seem true or probable. ● The sense of *colour* here is 'a show of reason' or 'pretext'. Cf. ▶ **under COLOUR of**.

see the COLOUR of someone's money receive some evidence of forthcoming payment from a person.

nail (*or* pin) one's COLOURS to the mast declare openly and firmly what one believes or favours. ● Cf. ▶ **sail under false COLOURS**.

sail under false COLOURS disguise one's true nature or intentions. ● The distinguishing ensign or flag of a ship or regiment was known as its *colours* (now also *colour*); cf. ▶ **with FLYING colours**. A ship on illegal business or in time of war may fly a bogus flag in order to deceive.

show one's (true) COLOURS reveal one's real character or intentions, especially when these are disreputable or dishonourable. ● Cf. ▶ **sail under false COLOURS**.

COLOURS ▶ *see* **with FLYING colours**.

dodge the COLUMN shirk one's duty; avoid work. *Brit., informal* ● A military expression, alluding to a body of troops formed into a column to undertake a specific task.

COLUMN ▶ *see* **FIFTH column**.

as — as they COME – in a very marked degree. ● Used to describe someone or something that is a supreme example of the quality specified.

COME in from the cold gain acceptance. *informal*

> **1998** *New Scientist* 4 Apr. 41/3 Considering that the intracavity technique got off to such a slow start, it may, at last, have come in from the cold.

COME off it said when vigorously expressing disbelief. *informal* ● Usually imperative: *come off it!*

COME the — play the part of; behave like. *informal* ● Often in the imperative with negative, as in the Australian slang expression *don't come the raw prawn with me!*, i.e. 'don't attempt to deceive me!' Cf. ▶ **come the RAW prawn**

COME to that (or** if it comes to that)** in fact. *informal* ● Said to introduce an additional significant point.

COME to think of it upon reflection. ● Said when an idea or point occurs to one while one is speaking.

to COME coming, future. ● Used postpositively, as in *the life to come.*

COME ▶ *see* **come of AGE**; ▶ *see* **come APART at the seams**; ▶ *see* **come CLEAN**; ▶ *see* **come the ACID**; ▶ *see* **come to GRIEF**; ▶ *see* **come up SMELLING of roses**.

too — for COMFORT causing physical or mental unease by an excess of the specified quality.

where someone is COMING from someone's meaning, motivation, or personality. *informal*

have it COMING (to one) be due for retribution on account of something bad that one has done. *informal*

not know if one is COMING or going be confused, especially as a result of being very busy. *informal*

COMMON or garden of the usual or ordinary type. *Brit., informal* ● In this figurative sense L19, but used earlier literally to describe a plant in its most familiar domesticated form, e.g. 'the Common or Garden Nightshade' in W. Coles *Adam in Eden*, 1657.

> **1964** L. WOOLF *Letter* 3 June I certainly do not agree that the unconscious mind reveals deeper truths about someone else than plain common or garden common sense does.

the COMMON touch the ability to get on with or appeal to ordinary people. ● An obsolete sense of *common* deriving from Latin *communis* 'affable' may have influenced this phrase, also a Shakespearean phrase about the great exponent of the common touch, King Henry V, on the eve of the battle of Agincourt: 'a little touch of Harry in the night' (*Henry V* IV. Prologue). Now best known from Kipling's poem *If* (see quot.).

> **1910** R. KIPLING *If* If you can talk with crowds and keep your virtue, Or walk with Kings—nor lose the common touch ...

be (or** err) in good COMPANY** be in the same situation as someone important or respected.

COMPANY ▶ *see* **and CO**.

COMPARE notes exchange ideas, opinions, or information about a particular subject.

return the COMPLIMENT retaliate or respond in kind. ● Also in the literal sense of 'give a compliment in return for another'.

jump (*or* leap) to CONCLUSIONS (*or* the conclusion that) make a hasty judgement or decision before learning or considering all the facts.

try CONCLUSIONS with engage in a trial of skill or argument with. *formal*

be set in CONCRETE (of a policy or idea) be fixed and unalterable.

CONDUCT unbecoming unsuitable or inappropriate behaviour. ● From *Articles of War* (1872) 'Any officer who shall behave in a scandalous manner, unbecoming the character of an officer and a gentleman shall ... be cashiered'; the Naval Discipline Act, 10 Aug. 1860 uses the words 'conduct unbecoming the character of an Officer'.

a name to CONJURE with a person who is important within a particular sphere of activity. ● With reference to the magical practice of summoning a spirit to do one's bidding by invoking a powerful name or using a spell. It is to this practice that Cassius alludes in Shakespeare's *Julius Caesar* when, inciting Brutus against Caesar, he compares the names of Caesar and Brutus: 'Conjure with 'em [i.e. the names]: 'Brutus' will start a spirit as soon as 'Caesar' (I. ii.). Often used humorously.

> **1954** I. MURDOCH *Under the Net* xi. 154 His name, little known to the public, is one to conjure with in Hollywood.

CONSPICUOUS by one's absence obviously not present in a place where one should be. ● The phrase was coined by Lord John Russell in a speech in 1859. He acknowledged as his source for the idea a passage in Tacitus (*Annales* III. 76) describing an assemblage of images at a funeral, those of Cassius and Brutus being by far the most noteworthy by reason of their absence: *praefulgebant Cassius atque Brutus eo ipso quod effigies eorum non visebantur* but Cassius and Brutus outshone all of them by the very fact that their images were not to be seen.

a CONSPIRACY of silence an agreement to say nothing about an issue that should be generally known. ● Appears to have originated with the French philosopher Auguste Comte (1798–1857) (see quot.).

> ***1865** J. S. MILL *Auguste Comte and Positivism* 199 M. Comte used to reproach his early English admirers with maintaining the 'conspiracy of silence', concerning his later performances.

hold someone/thing in CONTEMPT consider someone or something to be unworthy of respect or attention. ● In formal legal contexts to *hold someone in contempt* means that they are judged to have committed the offence of contempt of court, that is they are guilty of disrespect or disobedience to the authority of a court in the administration of justice.

to one's heart's CONTENT to the full extent of one's desires. ● *Heart's content* was used by Shakespeare in *2 Henry VI* (1593) and *Merchant of Venice* (1596) in the sense of 'complete inward satisfaction', but *to one's heart's content* is not attested until L17.

CONTENTION ▶ *see* **BONE of contention**.

no CONTEST **1** a decision by the referee to declare a boxing match invalid on the grounds that one or both of the boxers are not making serious efforts. **2** a competition, comparison, or choice of which the outcome is a foregone conclusion. ● Mainly US, perhaps influenced by the plea of *nolo contendere* (I do not wish to contend) in US law, meaning that the defendant in a criminal prosecution accepts conviction but does not admit guilt.

CONTRADICTION in terms a statement or group of words associating objects or ideas which are incompatible. ● Now in general use beyond the logical or philosophical contexts in which it originated.

  *1795 T. MEEK *Sophistry Detected* He grants the possibility of a revelation, but he is not aware that his ideas of language make it absolutely impossible, which is a contradiction in terms.

CONVERT something to one's own use wrongfully make use of another's property. ● A technical legal term, now used more generally and often facetiously.

CONVICTIONS ▶ *see* **have the COURAGE of one's convictions**.

within COOEE (of) within reach (of); near (to). ● An Aboriginal word used as a shout to attract attention, *cooee* was first adopted by European settlers in Australia; thus *within cooee of* (L19) literally means 'within hailing distance of'. Both word and phrase are now used beyond Australia.

COOK the books alter records, especially accounts, with fraudulent intent or in order to mislead. *informal* ● *Cook* has been used since M17 in this figurative sense of 'manipulate' or 'tamper with'. Cf. *cook up* which has similar fraudulent connotations.

COOK someone's goose spoil someone's plans; cause someone's downfall. *informal* ● The variant '*do their goose for them* is mentioned in a letter of 1849 as 'a vulgar phrase', and *cook (some)one's goose* became current at about the same time. The underlying idea seems to be that a goose was cherished and fattened up for a special occasion.

COOK ▶ *see* **chief cook and BOTTLE-WASHER**.

the way the COOKIE crumbles how things turn out. *chiefly N. Amer., informal* ● When used in the past tense, generally suggesting that the position is undesirable but unalterable.

with one's hand in the COOKIE jar engaged in surreptitious theft from one's employer, especially a company or other organization. *chiefly N. Amer., informal* ● Cf. ▶ **have one's fingers in the TILL**.

too many COOKS spoil the broth if too many people are involved in a task or activity, it will not be done well. ● The phrase *too many cooks* is also used, alluding to this proverb.

  1997 *Times* 8 Aug. 25 Too many cooks spoil the broth and at Apple there is now the equivalent of Marco Pierre White, Anton Mosimann and Nico Ladenis.

(as) COOL as a cucumber perfectly cool or self-possessed.

  1992 R. KENAN *Let Dead Bury their Dead* vii. 181 How many men do you know, black or white, could bluff, cool as a cucumber, caught butt-naked in bed with a damn whore?

COOL ▶ *see* **cool one's HEELS**.

for (*or* in) a COON's age a very long time. *N. Amer., informal* ● *Coon* here is a colloquial abbreviation of *racoon*.

| **1951** W. STYRON *Lie Down in Darkness* (1992) iii. 90 I haven't seen him in a coon's age.

a gone COON a person or thing in desperate straits; as good as dead. *US, informal* ● Racoons were hunted for their fur, and *a gone coon* was one that had been treed or cornered so that it could not escape.

COOP ▶ *see* **FLY the coop**.

COOT ▶ *see* **BALD as a coot**.

COP hold of take hold of. *Brit.* ● A slang word for 'catch' here, *cop* is probably of northern dialect origin. Cf. also ▶ **it's a fair COP**. *Cop hold of* is mainly used as an imperative.

COP a plea engage in plea bargaining. *N. Amer.*

not much COP not very good. *Brit., informal* ● *Cop* here in the sense of 'acquisition'; for *cop* as a verb see ▶ **COP hold of**. Cf. ▶ **not much CHOP**.

| **1998** *Spectator* 4 Apr. 46/1 [S]uddenly everyone has noticed that the rest of her album ... isn't actually much cop after all.

it's a fair COP an admission that the speaker has been caught doing wrong and deserves punishment. ● For *cop* in the sense of 'capture', see under ▶ **COP hold of**. L19 underworld slang.

COPYBOOK ▶ *see* **BLOT one's copybook**.

cut the CORD cease to rely on someone or something influential or supportive and begin to act independently. ● With allusion to the cutting of the umbilical cord of a baby at birth.

CORN in Egypt a plentiful supply. ● From the aged Jacob's instructions to his sons in Genesis 42:2 'Behold, I have heard that there is corn in Egypt: get you down thither, and buy for us from thence.'

(just) around (*or* round) the CORNER likely to happen soon. ● Also literally, 'in the next street' or 'very near'.

around (*or* round) every CORNER occurring frequently and randomly. ● Used to refer to things that can happen anytime and anywhere.

fight one's CORNER defend one's position or interests. ● A boxing metaphor: opponents take diagonally opposite corners of the ring. Cf. ▶ **in someone's CORNER**.

in someone's CORNER on someone's side; giving someone support. ● A boxing metaphor: in the pauses between bouts the boxers retire to their individual corners of the ring where their trainers or assistants offer support and encouragement.

CORNER ▶ *see* **CUT the corner**; ▶ *see* **PAINT oneself into a corner**; ▶ *see* **TURN the corner**.

the four (*or* far) CORNERS of the world (*or* earth) places that are far away from each other.

CORNERS ▶ *see* **CUT corners**.

the CORRIDORS of power the senior levels of government or administration, where covert influence is regarded as being exerted and significant decisions are made. ● From the title of C. P. Snow's novel *The Corridors of Power* (1964). Although most usual with *power*, the phrase can be more specifically applied to the most influential levels of the hierarchy within a particular place or organization, esp. when they are regarded as operating covertly. The French word *coulisse* ('the wings in a theatre', but also a 'corridor') has a similar figurative sense of the corridor as a place of negotiation and behind-the-scenes scheming.

COST (noun) ▶ *see* **COUNT the cost**.

COST (verb) ▶ *see* **cost an ARM and a leg**.

wrap someone in COTTON WOOL be overprotective towards someone.

COUCH potato someone who spends leisure time passively (esp. sitting watching television or videos), eats junk food, and takes little or no physical exercise. ● A humorous coinage compounding a person with the physical shape of a *potato* slouching on a *couch*; the original American coinage relied on a pun with the second element of the slang term *boob tuber* (i.e. someone devoted to watching the *boob tube* or television).

a COUNSEL of despair an action to be taken when all else fails.

a COUNSEL of perfection advice that is ideal but not feasible.

COUNT one's chickens treat something that has not yet happened as a certainty. *informal* ● With reference to the proverbial admonition *don't count your chickens before they're hatched* (L16).

COUNT something on the fingers of one hand easily reckon up the number of occurrences because it is very small. ● Used informally to emphasize the rarity of an event or phenomenon.

out (or N. Amer. also down) for the COUNT 1 unconscious or soundly asleep. 2 defeated. ● In boxing, the *count* is the ten-second period, counted out loud by the referee, which is allowed to a boxer who has been knocked to the ground to regain his feet before he has to concede victory to his opponent. A boxer who manages to rise within the count of ten is said to 'beat the count'.

take the COUNT (of a boxer) be knocked out. ● Cf. ▶ **out for the COUNT**.

COUNT ▶ *see* **count the PENNIES**; ▶ *see* **count SHEEP**; ▶ *see* **count TEN**.

out of COUNTENANCE unpleasantly surprised. ● *Countenance* here has the sense of 'confidence of demeanour, calmness of expression'; cf. *lose countenance, keep someone in countenance*.

over the COUNTER by ordinary retail purchase, with no need for a prescription or licence. ● Often attributively as in an *over-the-counter medicine*.

under the COUNTER (*or* table) (especially of the sale of scarce goods) surreptitiously and usually illegally.

> **1994** *Coarse Fishing Today* June/July 5/2 The obvious danger is that river fish will be pinched and flogged 'under the counter.'

go (*or Brit.* hunt *or* run) COUNTER run or ride against the direction taken by a quarry.

go (*or* appeal) to the COUNTRY test public opinion by dissolving Parliament and holding a general election. *Brit.*

line of COUNTRY a subject about which a person is skilled or knowledgeable. *Brit.*

unknown COUNTRY an unfamiliar place or topic. ● The Latin equivalent, *terra incognita*, is also frequently used figuratively.

have the COURAGE of one's convictions act on one's beliefs despite danger or disapproval.

> **1998** *Times* 18 May 27/3 [The] knives were out for us and we had to have the courage of our convictions.

take one's COURAGE in both hands nerve oneself to do something that frightens one.

COURAGE ▶ *see* **DUTCH courage**.

COURSE ▶ *see* **STAY the course**.

COURT ▶ *see* **HOLD court**.

send someone to COVENTRY refuse to associate with or speak to someone. *chiefly Brit.* ● An idiom dating from M18. It is sometimes said to stem from the extreme unpopularity of soldiers stationed in *Coventry*, who were cut off from the social life of the city, or because Royalist prisoners were sent there during the English Civil War, the city being staunchly Parliamentarian.

blow someone's COVER discover or expose someone's real identity.

break COVER emerge into the open; suddenly leave a place of shelter ● Originally with reference to a hunted animal's emerging from the undergrowth in which it had been hiding.

COVER one's back (*or N. Amer.* ass) foresee and avoid the possibility of attack or criticism. *informal*

COVER one's tracks conceal evidence of what one has done.

have a COW become angry, excited, or agitated. *N. Amer., informal*

> **1990** S. NIELSEN *Wheels* xxviii. 176 'Don't have a cow,' she said huffily. 'It's no big deal.'

a sacred COW a person, idea, or institution, unreasonably held to be above questioning or criticism. ● Originally with reference to the Hindu veneration of the cow as a sacred animal.

till the COWS come home for an indefinitely long time. *informal* ● Known in this figurative sense since E17.

catch a CRAB (in rowing) effect a faulty stroke in which the oar is jammed under water or misses the water altogether.

CRACK a book open a book and read it; study. *N. Amer., informal*

CRACK a bottle open a bottle, especially of wine, and drink it.

CRACK a crib break into a house. *Brit., slang* ●*Crack* in the sense of 'housebreaking' has been thieves' slang since E19.

CRACK of doom a thunder-peal announcing the Day of Judgement. ●The idea of thunder announcing the Last Judgement comes from several passages in the book of Revelation (e.g., 6:1, 8:5). Used as a metaphor for any very loud and sudden noise.

a fair CRACK of the whip fair treatment; a chance to participate or compete on equal terms. *Brit., informal*
| **1990** *Sun* 20 Oct. 30/7 All I'm after is a fair crack of the whip.

CRACK (noun) ▶ *see* **crack of DAWN**.

CRACK (verb) ▶ *see* **BANG heads together**.

CRACKED up to be asserted to be. *informal* ●From the use of *crack* as an adjective to mean 'pre-eminent'. The earliest (L18) recorded use of *crack* in this sense relates it to Suffolk and notes that it was 'a provincial term for excellent'. Used generally in negative contexts to indicate that someone or something has been described too favourably.

go CRACKERS 1 become insane; go mad. 2 become extremely annoyed or angry. ●Sense 1 is recorded from E20.

get CRACKING (start to) act quickly and energetically. *informal* ●*Cracking* in the sense of 'vigorous' was L19 slang.

a bit of CRACKLING an attractive woman. *Brit., offensive* ●An M20 slang expression for a woman as a sexual object.
| **1968** P. DICKINSON *Skin Deep* iii. 32 'You know her?' 'I do, sir. Nice bit of crackling, she is.'

CRACKS ▶ *see* **PAPER over the cracks**.

CRAMP someone's style prevent a person from acting freely or naturally. *informal*

CRASH and burn fail spectacularly. *N. Amer., informal*
| **1994** *Hispanic* July–Aug. 22/3 But if you use Spanish, be careful not to crash and burn … the language is booby-trapped for the unwary PR professional.

stick in one's CRAW make one angry or irritated. ●For the literal sense *see* ▶ **stick in one's THROAT**. *Craw* is properly the crop of birds or insects (although cognate words in other northern European languages mean 'throat' of any animal). The transferred sense of *craw* to refer to a person's gullet, originally humorous, is now almost entirely confined to this expression. Cf. ▶ **stick in one's GIZZARD**.

CRAZY like a fox very cunning or shrewd. *orig. US* ●The fox is a proverbial type of cunning. From E20 onwards, *crazy* has been used as a term of approbation in various contexts in US colloquial speech.

CREATURE of habit a person who follows an unvarying routine.

CREDIT where credit is due praise should be given when it is deserved. ● Earlier in the form *honour where honour is due*, following the Reims and Authorized versions of the Bible, Romans 13:8 'Render therefore to all their dues: ... honour to whom honour.' Very often used in the context of conceding that praise is appropriate, even if one is reluctant to give it.

be up the CREEK (without a paddle) be in severe difficulty, usually with no means of extricating oneself from it. *informal* ● Recorded M20 as military slang for 'lost' (e.g., on a patrol).

make one's flesh CREEP feel disgust or revulsion. ● Indicating that the revulsion felt is as powerful as the literal sensation of something crawling over the skin; see next entry.

give someone the CREEPS induce a feeling of often fearful revulsion in someone. ● From the verb *creep*, with the idea that the sensation felt is similar to that which might be induced by something creeping over one's skin or by cold causing goose-pimples; cf. preceding entry.

*1849 C. DICKENS David Copperfield She was constantly complaining of the cold, and of its occasioning a visitation in her back which she called 'the creeps'.

on the CREST of a wave being very successful.

not CRICKET something contrary to traditional standards of fairness or rectitude. *Brit., informal* ● Almost always *that's not cricket!* as a protest against some infringement of principles of honest or correct behaviour. The game of cricket, with its traditional regard for courtesy and fair play, has been a metaphor for these qualities since at least M19.

put a CRIMP in have an adverse effect on; thwart. *informal* ● L19, mainly US slang.

1990 W. STEWART Right Church Wrong Pew (1991) xvi. 125 Well, that maybe puts a crimp in my theory.

CRISP ▶ *see* **BURNT to a cinder**.

shed (or weep) CROCODILE tears put on a display of insincere grief. ● With allusion to the ancient belief that crocodiles wept while luring or devouring their prey.

be CROOK on be annoyed by. *Austral. & NZ, informal* ● *Crook* in L19 Australian slang meant 'bad' or 'unpleasant'.

go CROOK 1 lose one's temper; become angry. 2 become ill. *Austral. & NZ, informal* ● Cf. preceding entry.

1950 Coast to Coast 1949–50 165 What'd you do if you were expelled? Y'r old man'd go crook, I bet.

come a CROPPER 1 fall heavily. 2 suffer a defeat or disaster. *informal* ● Sense 1 appears to have originated in M19 hunting jargon, and possibly derived from the E19 phrase *neck and crop* meaning 'bodily' or 'completely'. A British variant on this is *come a mucker*, now somewhat dated.

1980 S. HAZZARD *Transit of Venus* (1981) 219 He had seen how people came a cropper by giving way to impulse.

(as) CROSS as two sticks very annoyed or grumpy. *Brit.*, *informal* ● A play on the two senses of *cross* as (1) 'bad-tempered' and (2) 'intersecting' (M19).

at CROSS purposes with a misunderstanding of each other's meaning or intention. ● Cf. *play at cross-purposes*, that is, take part in a parlour-game in which unrelated questions and answers were linked.

CROSS one's fingers (*or* keep one's fingers crossed) hope that one's plans will be successful; trust in good luck. ● From the action of putting one's index and middle fingers across each other as a sign of hoping for good luck (cf. ▶ **HOLD one's thumbs**). The gesture, now used in entirely secular circumstances, is a scaled-down version of the Christian one of making the sign of the Cross with one's whole hand and arm as a request for divine protection. It is also superstitiously employed when telling a deliberate lie, with the idea of warding off the evil that might be expected to befall a liar.

1998 *Spectator* 15 Aug. 16/3 Since resources were limited ... the only hope the *clients* had was to hang in there, fingers crossed.

CROSS the floor join the opposing side in Parliament. *Brit.* ● The floor of the House of Commons is the open space separating members of the Government and Opposition parties, who sit on benches facing each other across it.

CROSS my heart (and hope to die) used to emphasize the truthfulness and sincerity of what one is saying or promising. *informal* ● Sometimes reinforced by making a sign of the Cross over one's chest.

CROSS someone's palm with silver pay someone for a favour or service. *often humorous* ● Originally in connection with having one's fortune told, when the client would literally trace out the sign of a cross on the hand of the fortune-teller with a silver coin. Goldsmith refers to the practice in *The Vicar of Wakefield* (1766) x.

CROSS swords have an argument or dispute. ● Originally in the literal sense of 'fight a duel', but the figurative sense has been current since L19. Often *cross swords with someone*.

have one's CROSS to bear suffer the troubles that life brings. ● In allusion to Jesus (or Simon of Cyrene) carrying the Cross before the Crucifixion; also used metaphorically in the New Testament (e.g., Matthew 10:38 'And he that taketh not his cross, and followeth after me is not worthy of me').

CROSS (verb) ▶ *see* **cross the RUBICON**.

get one's wires (*or* lines) CROSSED have a misunderstanding. ● Originally with reference to a wrong telephone connection ('a crossed line'), which resulted in another call or calls being heard.

be caught in the CROSSFIRE suffer damage or harm inadvertently as the result of the adversity of two other parties. ● Also very often in the literal sense of 'be trapped (and maybe killed) by being between two opposing sides who are shooting at each other'.

| **1998** *New Scientist* 7 Mar. 23/3 This suggested that the corneal cells are innocent victims caught in the crossfire as T cells fight the viral infection.

at a (*or* the) CROSSROADS at a critical point, when important decisions must be made.

CROSSROADS ▶ *see* **DIRTY work at the crossroads**.

as the CROW flies in a straight line. ●Generally with reference to a (shorter) distance straight across country rather than the distance as measured along a (more circuitous) road.

eat CROW be humiliated by one's defeats or mistakes. *N. Amer., informal* ●In the US 'boiled crow' has been a metaphor for something extremely disagreeable since L19.

CROWD ▶ *see* **PASS in a crowd**.

CROWNING glory 1 the best and most notable aspect of something: a triumphant culmination. **2** *chiefly jocular, dated* a person's hair. ●Cf. the Latin expression *finis coronat opus* (the end crowns the work).

be CRUEL to be kind act towards someone in a way which seems harsh but will ultimately be of benefit. ●'I must be cruel only to be kind' was Hamlet's explanation of his bullying treatment of his mother about her second marriage (Shakespeare *Hamlet* III. iv. 178).

CRUISING for a bruising heading or looking for trouble. *chiefly N. Amer., informal*

| **1998** *Times* 4 Aug. 23/2 The problem … is the unrealistic value of the Hong Kong dollar … it has been cruising for a bruising for most of last year.

CRUMBS from someone's (*or* a rich man's) table an unfair and inadequate or unsatisfactory share of something. ●Cf. the biblical description of the beggar Lazarus as 'desiring to be fed with the crumbs which fell from the rich man's table' (Luke 16:21); also Matthew 15:27.

when (*or* if) it comes to the CRUNCH when (*or* if) a point is reached or an event occurs such that immediate and decisive action is required. *informal* ●Probably influenced by *crush* and *munch*, the verb *crunch* appeared as an E19 variant of earlier and now obsolete *craunch* or *cranch*, meaning to 'grind or crush noisily with one's teeth'. The figurative sense of the noun in this idiom is apparently an M20 development.

CRUSE ▶ *see* **a WIDOW's cruse**.

CRY foul protest strongly about a real or imagined wrong or injustice. ●*Foul* in this context equates with *foul play*, a violation of the rules of a game to which attention is drawn by shouting 'foul'.

| **1998** *Times* 20 Feb. 40/7 She can't cry foul when subjected to fair and standard competition.

CRY from the heart a passionate and honest appeal or protest. ●Cf. French *cri de coeur*, also current in English since E20.

CRY stinking fish disparage one's own efforts or products. ● From the practice of street vendors crying their wares (i.e. shouting and praising their goods) to attract customers (see quot.).

*1660 J. TAYLOR *Ductor Dubitantium* (1671) 805 Does ever any man cry stinking fish to be sold?

in full CRY expressing an opinion loudly and forcefully. ● *Full cry* originated as a hunting expression referring to a pack of hounds all baying in pursuit of their quarry. *In full cry* is still used literally of hounds, but the transferred sense had developed by M17.

CRY ▶ *see* **cry for the MOON**; ▶ *see* **cry over spilt MILK**; ▶ *see* **cry WOLF**.

for CRYING out loud used to express one's irritation or surprise. *informal* ● Originally E20 US, used mainly as an impatient exclamation.

| 1941 'R. WEST' *Black Lamb* (1942) For crying out loud, why did you do it?

CUCKOO in the nest an unwelcome intruder in a place or situation. ● From the practice of the hen cuckoo's laying its eggs in other birds' nests.

CUCUMBER ▶ *see* **COOL as a cucumber**.

chew the CUD think or talk reflectively. ● A ruminant animal *chews the cud* when it brings back into its mouth and chews food that has already been partly digested. Used literally in connection with ruminant animals since early Middle English, *chew the cud* in the figurative sense dates from L14.

CUDGEL one's brain (or brains) think hard about a problem.

| *1602 W. SHAKESPEARE *Hamlet* V. i. Cudgel thy brains no more about it [a riddle].

take up the CUDGELS start to support someone or something strongly. ● Often with *in defence of* or *on behalf of*.

on CUE at the correct moment. ● *Cue* here is in the theatrical sense of 'the word or words that signal when another actor should speak or perform a particular action'.

take one's CUE from follow the example or advice of. ● See preceding entry for this sense of *cue*.

off the CUFF without preparation. *informal* ● Originating in the US (M20), the expression refers to impromptu notes made on a speaker's shirt-cuffs. Very often as a modifier, as in *an off-the-cuff remark*.

CULTURE vulture a person who spends leisure time voraciously absorbing art and culture. ● *Vulture* here is the type of a greedy and often undiscriminating feeder.

not one's CUP of tea not what one likes or is interested in. *informal* ● Recorded first (E20) as a metaphor for a person of a particular character, *cup of tea* is now generally used with the negative to indicate one's unfavourable opinion of either people or things.

in one's CUPS while drunk. *informal* ● Now used mainly as a euphemism for 'drunk', the phrase formerly could also mean 'during a drinking-bout'. Either could be intended in the passage in the Apocrypha on the strength of wine:

'And when they are in their cups, they forget their love both to friends and brethren, and a little after draw out swords' (1 Esdras 3:22).

| **1712** J. ARBUTHNOT *John Bull* II. iv She used to come home in her cups, and break the china.

a CURATE's egg something of very mixed character, partly good and partly bad. ●From a *Punch* cartoon (1895) showing a curate breakfasting with his bishop. BISHOP: I'm afraid you've got a bad egg, Mr Jones. CURATE: Oh no, my Lord, I assure you! Parts of it are excellent!

CURDLE ▶ *see* **make one's BLOOD curdle**.

make someone's hair CURL shock or horrify someone. *informal* ●A M20 colloquialism, perhaps as a dramatic or humorous variation of ▶ **make someone's HAIR stand on end**.

out of CURL lacking energy. *Brit.* ●An E20 expression based on the idea of curly hair as possessing vitality (cf. the cliché 'bouncy curls'); hence hair gone limp or *out of curl* may be thought to signify the opposite.

pass CURRENT be generally accepted as true or genuine. *Brit.* ●Originally with reference to the currency of a genuine coin, as opposed to a counterfeit one. Formerly also *pass for current* and *go current*.

CURRY favour ingratiate oneself with someone through obsequious behaviour. ●*Curry* here means 'rub down' (a horse or other animal) with a coarse brush or comb, and the phrase is an E16 alteration of the Middle English *curry favel* (which continued in use alongside the modern form until E17). *Favel* (or *Fauvel*) was the name of a chestnut horse in an E14 French romance who epitomized cunning and duplicity; hence 'to rub down Favel' meant to use on him the cunning which he personified. It is unclear whether the bad reputation of chestnut horses antedated the French romance, but the idea also existed in fifteenth-century German in the phrase *den fahlen hengst reiten* (ride the chestnut horse) meaning 'behave deceitfully'.

bring down the CURTAIN on bring to an end. ●Alluding to the screen that is lowered at the front of the stage in the theatre at the end of a performance. Hence also the colloquial expression *it's curtains for —*. An alternative sometimes used is ▶ **RING down the curtain**.

CUSTOMS ▶ *see* **old SPANISH customs**.

be CUT out for (*or* **to be)** have exactly the right qualities for a particular role, task, or job. *informal* ●The sense of *cut out* here is 'formed or fashioned by cutting' as the pieces of a garment are cut out from the fabric. Generally as past participle and usually with negative (but cf. quot.).

| **1645 J. BOND *Occasus Occidentalis* 61 It was a Country by scituation ... cut out for safety.

a CUT above superior to. *informal* ●The precise sense of *cut* in this phrase is unclear. Charles Lamb in a letter (1797) seems to allude to the expression in the sentence 'There is much abstruse science in it above my cut', and Scott has a character say in *The Heart of Midlothian* (1818) that another character is 'a cut abune me', but in both cases the context suggests that the sense is simply 'beyond me' rather than 'obviously or socially superior to me', which

is the usual modern implication. The present sense is found however by M19.
1998 *Spectator* 11 July 26/1 Samuel was a scholar ... and his contributions are a cut above the rest.

CUT and dried (of a situation, issue, or ideas) completely settled or decided. ●The distinction was originally made between the *cut and dried* herbs of herbalists' shops and growing herbs, but the phrase occurs figuratively from E18.

CUT and run make a speedy or sudden departure from an awkward or hazardous situation rather than confront it or deal with it. *informal* ●Originally a nautical phrase (E18), meaning 'sever the anchor cable because of some emergency and make sail immediately'.

CUT and thrust 1 a spirited and rapid interchange of views. **2** a situation or sphere of activity regarded as carried out under adversarial conditions. ●In fencing a *cut* is a slashing stroke and a *thrust* one given with the point of the weapon. In both senses the expression can used attributively, e.g., *a cut-and-thrust battle of wits*.

CUT both ways 1 (of a point or statement) serve both sides of an argument. **2** (of an action or process) have both good and bad effects. ●The image behind this expression is that of the double-edged weapon (see quot.).
| *1705 E. HICKERINGILL *Priest-craft* Pref. Fame, like a two-edg'd Sword, does cut both ways.

CUT corners undertake something in what appears to be the easiest, quickest, or cheapest way, often by omitting to do something important or ignoring rules. ●From the literal *cutting* (*off*) *the corner*, meaning 'taking the shortest course by going across and not round a corner'.

CUT a dash be stylish or impressive in one's dress or behaviour. ●Cf. ▶ **CUT a — figure**. L18, but earlier (E18) in the Scottish variant *cast a dash*. As a noun *dash* in the sense of 'showy appearance' is current only in this expression, but this sense survives in the adjective *dashing*.

CUT someone dead completely ignore someone. ●Although this sense of *cut* is recorded from M17, Hazlitt in 1822 (*Table-talk* II. viii) suggested that it had 'hardly yet escaped out of the limits of slang phraseology'. *Dead* is a nineteenth-century addition for emphasis.

CUT a deal come to an arrangement, especially in business; make a deal. *chiefly N. Amer., informal* ●*Cut* here relates to the E20 US slang sense of *cut* (noun) as 'share (of profits), rake-off'; the verb in this sense appears in the writings of Edgar Wallace (M20).

CUT someone down to size deflate someone's exaggerated sense of self-worth. *informal* ●Originally used literally of reducing the extent or size of something to what is appropriate.

CUT a — figure present oneself or appear in a particular way. ●The sense of *cut* here is to 'perform, execute'; cf. ▶ **CUT a dash**. The form of the expression with *cut* (M18) has superseded the older (L17) form with *make*. Always used with an adjective, as in *cut a sorry figure*.

CUT it meet the required standard. *informal* ● Cf. ▶ **CUT the mustard**. Very often in negative contexts.

  | **1998** *Spectator* 28 Mar. 29/1 Heaven knows how such people get jobs in universities; they would not cut it on *Fifteen-to-One*.

CUT it out stop it. *informal* ● Usually in imperative to ask someone to stop doing or saying something that is annoying or offensive.

CUT loose **1** distance oneself from a person, group, or system by which one is unduly influenced or on which one is over-dependent. **2** begin to act without restraint. *informal* ● Sense 2 was an E20 US slang development from sense 1.

CUT one's losses abandon an enterprise or course of action that is clearly going to be unprofitable or unsuccessful before one suffers too much loss or harm. ● The sense of *cut* here is probably *sever oneself from* rather than *reduce in size* (see quot.). Earlier (E20) also *loss*, but now always with plural.

  | *1912 Quarterly Review* Jan. 287 It is now made the basis of the argument that England should 'cut her loss', and Ireland should be sent adrift.

CUT the mustard come up to expectations; meet the required standard. *informal* ● *Mustard* appears in E20 US slang with the general meaning of 'the best of anything'. The whole phrase also dates from E20. It is often used with the negative implied or stated (see quot.).

  | **1998** *New Scientist* 14 Mar. 39/2 But if you want to go beyond this into hypersonic flight … they just don't cut the mustard.

CUT no ice have no influence or effect. *informal* ● L19 US slang in origin. Almost always in negative contexts; the positive *cut (some) ice* is less frequent.

  | **1973** J. PORTER *It's Murder with Dover* vii. 63 MacGregor remembered … that logical argument didn't cut much ice with Dover and he abandoned it.

the CUT of someone's jib the appearance or look of a person. ● Originally a nautical expression suggested by the prominence and characteristic form of the jib (a triangular sail set forward of the foremast) as the identifying characteristic of a ship. Used in this metaphorical sense since E19, but now somewhat dated.

CUT someone off (or down) in their prime bring someone's life or career to an abrupt end while they are at the peak of their abilities.

CUT a (or the) rug dance, typically in an energetic or accomplished way. *chiefly N. Amer., informal.* M20, especially referring to dancing to jazz music.

  | **1996** *Sky Magazine* Oct. 192/2 The wide-open spaces around the bar … mean, as it fills up, the place soon resembles a club and the punters are itching to cut a rug.

CUT one's teeth (on) acquire initial practice or experience of a particular sphere of activity or with a particular organization. ● The image is that of the emergence of a baby's teeth from its gums. A variant is *cut one's eye-teeth*.

CUT to the chase come to the point. *N. Amer., informal* ● *Cut* here is in the sense 'move to another part of the film', expressing the notion of ignoring any preliminaries and coming immediately to the most important part.

CUT up rough behave in an aggressive, quarrelsome, or awkward way. *Brit.*, *informal* ●*Cut up* here is in the sense of 'behave'. Found in this form in Dickens (M19); the variant *cut up savage* is found in Thackeray, but *rough* is the only word now used.

| **1998** *Spectator* 7 Feb. 12/1 The jury, knowing full well that Clodius' supporters could cut up rough, asked for and received state protection.

make (*or* miss) the CUT come up to (*or* fail to come up to) a required standard. ●In golf, a player has to equal or better a particular score in order to avoid elimination from the last two rounds of a four-round tournament.

CUT the (Gordian) knot solve a problem in an irregular but forceful and efficient way. ●With allusion to the knot with which Gordius, king of ancient Phrygia (in Asia Minor), fastened the yoke of his wagon to the pole. Its complexity was such that it gave rise to the legend that whoever could undo it would win dominion over Asia. When Alexander the Great passed that way en route to conquer the East he is said to have severed the knot with his sword.

CUT ▶ *see* an **ATMOSPHERE that one could cut with a knife**; ▶ *see* **cut it FINE**; ▶ *see* **cut someone some SLACK**; ▶ *see* **have one's WORK cut out**.

CYLINDERS ▶ *see* **FIRING on all cylinders**.

D

be a DAB (hand) at be expert at. ● The origin of *dab* as a noun in this colloquial sense (L17) is unknown.

| **1998** *Bookseller* 28 Aug. 21/2 Stephanie Cabot ... is apparently a dab hand at milking cows, according to one of those mystifying diary items in *Skateboarders' Weekly.*

rattle one's DAGS hurry up. *Austral. & NZ, informal* ● *Dags* are the excreta-clotted lumps of wool at the rear end of a sheep, which, in heavily fouled animals, rattle as they run.

at DAGGERS drawn in bitter enmity. ● With reference to the drawing of daggers as the final stage in a confrontation before actual fighting breaks out. Although found in 1668, the expression only became common from E19 onwards.

look DAGGERS at glare angrily or venomously at. ● Also *speak daggers*, after Shakespeare *Hamlet* III. ii (Hamlet's reproaches to his mother).

pushing up the DAISIES dead and buried. *informal* ● A humorous E20 euphemism, now the most frequent of several daisy-related expressions for being in one's grave; cf. *under the daisies, turn one's toes up to the daisies* (both M19).

(as) fresh as a DAISY very bright and cheerful. *informal* ● With allusion to the flower's reopening of its petals in the early morning or to its welcome appearance in springtime. The freshness of daisies has been a literary commonplace since at least L14, occurring in the writings of Chaucer.

what's the DAMAGE? how much is it? *informal* ● Used since E19 as a humorous way of asking the cost of something.

as near as DAMMIT (*or* damn it) as close to being accurate as makes no difference. *informal* ● The spelling *dammit* is used especially in comparative phrases. The word has no very precise sense here, being used rather for emphasis.

DAMN all nothing at all. *Brit., informal* ● *Damn* here is a clipped version of *damned*. Sometimes used as a less offensive alternative to *bugger all*, it is usually two words, but Joyce (*Ulysses*, 1922) has *damnall*.

DAMN with faint praise praise (someone or something) so unenthusiastically as to imply condemnation. ● From Pope's 'Epistle to Dr Arbuthnot' (1735): 'Damn with faint praise, assent with civil leer, And without sneering, teach the rest to sneer.'

| **1998** *Bookseller* 3 Apr. 21/3 Some quotes seem to damn with faint praise.

not be worth a DAMN have no value or validity at all. *informal* ● *Damn* is used vaguely, for emphasis rather than with any precise sense.

DAMN ▶ *see* **not GIVE a damn**.

DAMNED if one does and damned if one doesn't in some situations whatever one does is likely to attract criticism.

> **1998** *Spectator* 28 Mar. 9/3 Some of the media were critical of the photo ... That did not stop them all running it on the front page. You're damned if you do and damned if you don't.

do (*or* try) one's DAMNEDEST do or try one's utmost to do something. ● The superlative of the adjective *damned* is used here as a noun and can mean either 'one's worst' or (more usually now) 'one's best', depending on context. In either case the expression indicates extreme effort.

DAMON and Pythias two faithful friends. ● Phintias (the more correct form of the name) was condemned to death for plotting against Dionysius I of Syracuse (see ▶ **SWORD of Damocles**). To enable Phintias to go to arrange his affairs, Damon offered to take his friend's place in Dionysius' prison and to be executed in his stead if he failed to return. Phintias returned just in time to redeem Damon, and Dionysius was so impressed by their friendship that he pardoned and released Phintias as well.

a DAMP squib an unsuccessful attempt to impress; an anticlimax. ● From the idea that a *squib* or small firecracker will not have the desired explosive effect if damp.

put a (*or* the) DAMPER (*or* dampener) on have a depressing, subduing, or inhibiting effect on someone or something. ● *Damper* in this figurative sense is M18, while *dampener* is E20.

DAMSEL in distress any young woman in trouble. *humorous* ● With facetious reference to the ladies in chivalric romances whose *raison d'être* was to be rescued from peril by a ▶ **KNIGHT in shining armour**.

DANCE attendance on do one's utmost to please someone by attending to all their needs or requests. ● The expression originally referred to someone's waiting 'kicking their heels' until an important person summoned them or would see them (see quot.).

> ***1522** J. SKELTON *Why not to Court* 626 And Syr ye must daunce attendance, ... For my Lords Grace, Hath now no time or space, To speke with you as yet.

DANCE to someone's tune comply completely with someone's demands and wishes. ● This form of the expression (E18) has generally superseded the older *dance after someone's pipe* (M16).

lead someone a (merry) DANCE cause someone a great deal of trouble or worry. *Brit.* ● Used in this figurative sense since M16.

> **1874** T. B. ALDRICH *Prudence Palfrey* i. It was notorious that the late Maria Jane had led Mr. Wiggins something of a dance in this life.

get one's DANDER up lose one's temper; become angry. ● Originally US (M19). The sense of *dander* in this expression is uncertain, as neither *dandruff* nor *dunder* ('the ferment of molasses') seems entirely plausible, though the latter is perhaps more likely. Also *have one's dander up* and *get someone's dander up*.

keep someone DANGLING keep someone in an uncertain position. ● Used especially of a would-be suitor.

a DARK horse a person, especially a competitor, about whom little is known. ●Originally horse-racing slang (M19), used thus by Disraeli (*Young Duke*, 1831), but also soon used figuratively of a person. Cf. the title of South African poet Roy Campbell's autobiography *Light on a Dark Horse* (1951).

keep something DARK keep something secret from other people.

*1681 J. CROWNE *Henry VI* ii. 14 By your passions I read all your natures, Though you at other times can keep 'em dark.

a shot (*or* stab) in the DARK an act whose outcome cannot be foreseen; a mere guess. ●The metaphorical use of *in the dark* as 'in a state of ignorance' dates from L17. Cowper used *shooting in the dark* (*Mutual Forbearance*, 1782) metaphorically, but *a shot in the dark* is not recorded before L19.

DARKEN someone's door appear on someone's threshold as a visitor. ●Almost always used in negative and very often in the imperative (*never darken my door again!*) for humorous effect.

DATE ▶ *see* **a BLIND date**; ▶ *see* **PASS one's sell-by date**.

nothing DAUNTED without having been made fearful or apprehensive. ●The adverbial use of *nothing* to mean 'not at all' originated in Old English but is now archaic and seldom found outside this phrase or ▶ *see* **NOTHING loath**.

go to DAVY Jones's locker be drowned at sea. ●Davy Jones is identified in Smollett's *Peregrine Pickle* (1751) as 'the fiend that presides over all the evil spirits of the deep', but the origin of the name is uncertain.

the crack of DAWN very early in the morning. ●*Crack* here means the instant of time occupied by the crack of a whip, rifle, etc. Originally a dialect and US expression, *crack of dawn* appeared first (L19) as *crack of day*.

DAWN ▶ *see* **a FALSE dawn**.

all in a (*or* the) DAY's work accepted as part of someone's normal routine or as a matter of course. ●Often used to signify ironic or resigned acceptance of something unusual, burdensome, or problematic.

call it a DAY decide or agree to stop doing something, either temporarily or permanently. ●From the idea of having done a day's work. Earlier (M19) *call it half a day*.

carry (*or* win) the DAY be victorious or successful. ●The sense of *day* as 'the day's work on the field of battle' (M16) is meant here.

DAY in, day out continuously or repeatedly over a long period of time.

DAY of reckoning the time when past mistakes or misdeeds must be punished or paid for; a testing time when the degree of one's success or failure will be revealed. ●With allusion to the Day of Judgement, on which, according to traditional Christian eschatology, human beings will have to answer to God for their transgressions.

don't give up the DAY job don't recklessly abandon steady work with the idea of making a fortune by pursuing a hobby or alternative interest. *informal* ●Used as a humorous way of recommending someone not to pursue an alternative career at which they are unlikely to be successful.

from DAY one from the very beginning.

> **1996** C. BROOKMYRE *Quite Ugly One Morning* xiii. 83 The system churns out junior doctors who have paid bugger-all attention to the meat and two veg medicine they will find themselves up to their necks in from day one.

have had one's (*or* its) DAY be no longer popular, successful, or influential.

if he (*or* she, etc.) is a DAY at least. ● Especially in spoken English, appended to a statement about the age of a person or thing; recorded in Swift's *Polite Conversation* (1731–8).

> **1957** G. BELLAIRS *Death in High Provence* xiii. 149Madeleine's sister is a great age, too. Eighty, if a day.

not someone's DAY a day of successive misfortunes for someone. *informal* ● Used especially with the implication that things have been better in the past and will be so again in the future. In the context of a sporting event, cf. *the day was —'s*.

that will be the DAY something is very unlikely to happen. *informal* ● Apparently first recorded in Baker's *New Zealand Slang* (1941), where it is described as 'a cant phrase expressing mild doubt following some boast or claim by a person'. Used especially in spoken English as an expression of scepticism about a possible future event.

DAY ▶ *see* **at the END of the day**; ▶ *see* **a BLACK day**; ▶ *see* **just another day at the OFFICE**; ▶ *see* **MAKE a day of it**; ▶ *see* **MAKE someone's day**; ▶ *see* **a RED letter day**.

burn DAYLIGHT use artificial light in daytime; waste daylight.

see DAYLIGHT begin to understand what was previously puzzling or unclear.

beat the (living) DAYLIGHTS out of give (someone) a very severe beating. *informal* ● Also with other verbs of physical violence (*kick, knock,* etc.) and singular *daylight*. Used from M18 as a metaphor for 'eyes', *daylight(s)* here has the extended sense of any vital organ (see also next entry).

frighten (*or* scare) the (living) DAYLIGHTS out of give (someone) a very severe fright. ● A M20 development of the preceding, on the premiss that the effect of extreme fear is as drastic as physical violence. Mark Twain in *Huckleberry Finn* (1884) has an alternative *scare the (liver and) lights out of* (*lights* = the lungs).

> **1955** F. YERBY *Treasure of Pleasant Valley* Didn't mean to hit him … Meant to throw close to him and scare the living daylights out of him.

(just) one of those DAYS a day when several things go wrong. ● Mainly as an expression of humorous resignation, similar to ▶ **not someone's DAY.**

seen (*or* known) better DAYS be in a worse state than in the past. ● Often used as an euphemism to indicate that something has become old, worn-out, or shabby.

DEAD and buried over; finished. ● Used to emphasize that something is finally and irrevocably in the past.

a DEAD cat bounce a misleading sign of vitality in something that is really moribund. *informal* ●A dead cat will not bounce, though if it is dropped from a sufficient height it might appear to do so. The expression was coined (L20) by Wall Street traders for the situation when a stock or company on a long-term, irrevocable downward trend suddenly shows a small temporary improvement.

DEAD from the neck (*or* chin) up stupid. *informal*
> 1990 *Film Comment* Mar.–Apr. 36/2 Steward subscribes to the notion that all women are 'nitwits and lunkheads, dead from the neck up'.

DEAD in the water unable to function effectively. ●Originally used of a ship, meaning 'unable to move'.
> 1997 *Times* 28 Nov. 39/1 And Oasis? Well, they are hardly dead in the water, having sold three million copies of *Be Here Now.*

DEAD meat in serious trouble. *informal*
> 1989 T. KIDDER *Among Schoolchildren* III. ii. 100 'You're dead meat, I'm gonna get you after school'.

the DEAD of night the quietest, darkest part of the night. ●The sense of *dead* here and in the next entry developed in the sixteenth century from *dead time of* —, meaning the period most characterized by lack of signs of life or activity.

the DEAD of winter the coldest part of winter. ●Cf. preceding entry.

DEAD on one's feet extremely tired. *informal* ●A development (M20) from the hyperbolical phrase *dead tired. Dead* is also used figuratively on its own to mean 'exhausted'.

DEAD to the world fast asleep; unconscious. *informal*
> *1899 G. ADE *Doc' Horne* ii. 19 'Our host is dead to the world,' observed the actor … 'Let him rest,' said Doc'.

from the DEAD from a period of obscurity or inactivity. ●Also literally, 'from a state of death'.

wouldn't be seen (*or* caught) DEAD in (*or* with *or* at etc.) — would object strongly to being associated in any way whatsoever with the thing specified. *informal* ●Used especially in spoken English to express strong dislike or disinclination for a particular thing or situation.

DEAD ▶ *see* **dead as a DODO**; ▶ *see* **dead as a DOORNAIL**; ▶ *see* **a dead LETTER**; ▶ *see* **dead as MUTTON**; ▶ *see* **dead men's SHOES**; ▶ *see* **make a dead SET at**; ▶ *see* **over my dead BODY**.

(as) DEAF as an adder (*or* a post) completely or extremely deaf. ●The traditional deafness of an adder is based on Psalm 58:4 'the deaf adder that stoppeth her ear'.

fall on DEAF ears (of a statement or request) be ignored by others.
> 1990 E. KUZWAYO *Sit Down and Listen* 106 All efforts by her husband to dissuade her from wishing to leave fell on deaf ears.

a big DEAL a thing considered important. *informal* ●Usually with negative. *Big deal!*, used as an exclamation, expresses one's contempt for something regarded as impressive or important by another person.

a raw (or rough) DEAL a situation in which someone receives unfair or harsh treatment. *informal* ● Originally North American slang, defined in J. Sandilands' *Western Canadian Dictionary* (1912) as 'a bare-faced swindle'. The opposite is ▶ **a square DEAL** or *a fair deal*.

a square DEAL a fair bargain or treatment. ● *Square* here has the sense of 'honest', which as an adjective was associated originally with honourable play at cards; cf. the phrases *square play* (L16), *square dealing* (M17), and ▶ **on the SQUARE**. *A square deal* is L19 US in origin.

at DEATH's door so ill that one may die. ● Especially in hyperbolic use.

be the DEATH of cause someone's death. ● Generally used hyperbolically or humorously of the effects of laughter, boredom, embarrassment, or similar emotions.

| **1816** J. AUSTEN *Emma* II. iii. 56 Oh! dear, I thought it would have been the death of me!

be in at the DEATH be present when something fails or comes to an end. ● A hunting metaphor meaning 'be present when a hunted animal is caught and killed'. The literal sense (L18) is still used; cf. ▶ **be in at the KILL**.

catch one's DEATH (of cold) catch a severe cold or chill. *informal*

die a (or the) DEATH come to an end; cease or fail to be popular or successful.

do something to DEATH perform or repeat something so frequently that it becomes tediously familiar. ● L19 slang.

be frightened to DEATH be made very alarmed and fearful. *informal* ● Used hyperbolically; cf. ▶ **frighten the LIFE out of**.

like DEATH warmed up (or N. Amer. over) extremely tired or ill. *informal* ● Originally military slang, recorded from M20.

DEATH ▶ *see* **a ghost at the FEAST**; ▶ *see* **a FATE worse than death**; ▶ *see* **a matter of LIFE and death**.

not playing with a full DECK mentally deficient. *N. Amer., informal* ● A *deck* is a pack of playing cards. One of many fanciful phrases used to indicate that a person is lacking the full complement of mental abilities; e.g. ▶ **a brick SHORT of a load**.

on DECK ready for action or work. *N. Amer.* ● With allusion to a ship's main deck as the place where the crew musters to receive orders for action.

dig DEEP use one's physical, mental, or financial resources. *informal* ● This intransitive sense derives from the idea of digging deep in one's pockets to find money for something.

go off (or go in off) the DEEP end give way immediately to anger or emotion. *informal* ● An expression referred to in 1921 as 'the slang of the moment' (*Times Literary Supplement*) and explained in 1927 as a 'very common phrase since the war ... evidently taken from the deep end of a swimming-bath where the diving board is' (W. E. Collinson *Contemporary England*). In the US the phrase has also developed to mean 'go mad', but in either sense the underlying idea is of a sudden explosive loss of self-control.

in DEEP water (or waters) in trouble or difficulty. *informal* ●A biblical metaphor; cf. Psalm 69:14 'let me be delivered from them that hate me, and out of the deep waters.'

jump (or be thrown) in at the DEEP end face a difficult problem or undertaking with little experience of it. *informal* ●In the deep end of a swimming pool one will either ▶ **SINK or swim**.

DELIVER the goods provide something promised or expected. *informal*

DELUSIONS of grandeur a false impression of one's own import-ance. ●Current in English since E20, the equivalent of the French phrase *folie de grandeur*, which came into English in L19 and remains current.

DEMON ▶ *see* **like the DEVIL**.

out of one's DEPTH in the position of lacking the ability or knowledge to cope. ●Literally, 'in water too deep to stand in'. Also with *beyond* instead of *out of*, the form used by Shakespeare in *Henry VIII* (1613).

have a DERRY on someone be prejudiced against someone. *Austral. & NZ* ●Re-ferring to the traditional song refrain *derry down*, this was a L19 adaptation of the expression ▶ **have a DOWN on**.

have DESIGNS on have a plan to appropriate something, usually in an under-hand way. ●Often used to express a sexual interest in someone who does not reciprocate one's interest.

a (or the) DEUCE of a — something very bad or difficult of its kind. ●Introduced probably from Low German in M17, *deuce* was used at first in various exclamatory expressions in which it was equated with 'bad luck' or 'mischief', since in playing at dice two (= *deuce*) is the lowest and most unlucky throw. From this there soon (by E18) developed the sense of *deuce* as 'the devil' (i.e. bad luck or mischief personified). *Deuce* as a euphemistic synonym for the devil occurs in a number of expressions, including this one and the two following entries.

like the DEUCE very fast. ●For the use of *deuce* for *devil* see preceding entry.

the DEUCE to pay trouble to be expected. ●Euphemistic for ▶ **the DEVIL to pay**.

leave someone to their own DEVICES leave someone to do as they wish without supervision. ●*Device* in the sense of 'inclination' or 'fancy' is now obsolete in the singular. The plural survives only in this expression or in the phrase *devices and desires* quoted from the General Confession in the Book of Common Prayer.

between the DEVIL and the deep blue sea caught in a dilemma; trapped between two equally dangerous alternatives. ●An obsolete variant is *between the devil and the dead sea*; *between the devil and the deep sea* is occasionally found.

DEVIL-may-care cheerfully or defiantly reckless. ●Originally an exclamation *devil may care!*, used attributively since M19, as in *a devil-may-care attitude*.

a (*or* the) DEVIL of a — something very large or bad of its kind. *informal*

> **1919** K. MANSFIELD *Letter* 27 Oct. We had the devil of a great storm last night, lasting for hours, thunder, lightning, rain & I had appalling nightmares!

the DEVIL to pay serious trouble to be expected. ● With allusion to the bargain formerly alleged to be made between magicians and the devil, that they would receive extraordinary powers or wealth in return for their souls.

the DEVIL's own — a very difficult or great —. *informal* ● Especially in *the devil's own job*.

like the DEVIL (*or* a demon) with great speed or energy.

play DEVIL'S advocate take a side in an argument that is the opposite of what one really wants or thinks. ● Translating modern Latin *advocatus diaboli*, *devil's advocate* is the popular name for the official in the Roman Catholic Church who puts the case against a candidate for canonization or beatification; he is more properly known as *promotor fidei* 'promoter of the faith'.

> **1885** J. BONAR *Malthus* I. i. 7 The father made it a point of honour to defend the 'Enquirer'; the son played devil's advocate.

play the DEVIL (*or* Old Harry) with damage or affect greatly. ● *Old Harry* is mentioned first in Brandt's *Popular Antiquities* (1777) as being a nickname for the devil in northern England.

raise the DEVIL make a noisy disturbance. *informal* ● Cf. ▶ **raise CAIN,** ▶ **raise HOB**.

speak (*or* talk) of the DEVIL said when a person appears just after being mentioned. *proverbial* ● From the superstition that the devil will appear if his name is spoken. Noted by Torriano in *Piazza Universale* (1666) as an English saying in the form *talk of the Devil, and he's presently at your elbow*.

sup (*or* dine) with the DEVIL have dealings with a malevolent or wily person. ● Cf. the proverb *he who sups with the devil should have a long spoon*, used especially to urge caution upon someone undertaking such contacts. The saying was known to Chaucer (*Squire's Tale* 602).

DEVIL ▶ *see* **SELL one's soul**.

DIALOGUE of (*or* between *or* among) the deaf a discussion in which each party is unresponsive to what the others say. ● Cf. French *dialogue des sourds*, which is also sometimes used in English.

DIAMOND cut diamond a situation in which a sharp-witted or cunning person meets their match. *Brit.*

> **1863** C. READE *Hard Cash* xxv He felt … sure his employer would outwit him if he could; and resolved it should be diamond cut diamond.

DIAMOND ▶ *see* **ROUGH diamond**.

DICE with death take serious risks. ● *Dice with* used here in the general sense of 'play a game of chance with'. In M20 *dice with death* was a journalistic cliché used to convey the risks taken by racing drivers; the expression seems for some time to have been especially connected with motoring, although it is now used of other risky activities. It gave rise to the use of *dicing* as a slang word among drivers for 'driving in a race'. Cf. also the air-force slang word *dicey* (M20) meaning 'dangerous'.

no DICE used to refuse a request or indicate no chance of success. *chiefly N. Amer., informal*

| **1990** P. AUSTER *Music of Chance* vii. 166 Sorry kid. No dice. You can talk yourself blue in the face, but I'm not going.

DICE ▶ *see* **LOAD the dice against**.

not a DICKY BIRD no news from someone; someone is not revealing any information. *informal* ●*Dicky bird* is rhyming slang for 'word'.

cut DIDOES perform mischievous tricks or deeds. ●The phrase occurs in dialect and US slang, but the origin of *dido* is uncertain. See quot. at ▶ **a DUTCH uncle**.

DIE hard disappear or change very slowly. ●Quoted in the *Gentleman's Magazine* in 1784 as a 'Tyburn phrase', the expression seems to have been used first of criminals who died resisting to the last on the Tyburn gallows in London. At the battle of Albuera in 1811, during the Peninsular War, William Inglis, commander of the British 57th Regiment of Foot, exhorted his men to 'die hard'; they did so with such heroism that the regiment earned the nickname *Die-hards*. The appellation was attached later in the century to various groupings in British politics determinedly opposed to change; it is still used both attributively *die-hard* and as a noun (*diehard*) of someone who is stubbornly conservative or reactionary.

DIE in (one's) bed suffer a peaceful death from natural causes. ●Contrasted with both ▶ **DIE with one's boots on** and ▶ **DIE in harness**.

DIE in harness die before retirement. ●The implicit comparison is between a person at work and a horse in harness drawing a plough or cart.

| **1992** *Harper's Magazine* 70/2 Don't overly concern yourself with the union pension fund. Musicians mostly die in harness.

DIE in the last ditch die desperately defending something, die fighting to the last extremity. ●From a remark attributed to King William III of Great Britain and Ireland (1650–1702); asked whether he did not see that his country was lost, he is said to have responded, 'There is one way never to see it lost, and that is to die in the last ditch'. Hence *last-ditch* is used attributively to mean 'desperately resisting to the end'.

the DIE is cast an event has happened or a decision has been taken that cannot be changed. ●With allusion to Julius Caesar's remark reported by Suetonius (*jacta alea esto* let the die be cast) as he was about to ▶ **cross the RUBICON**.

DIE on the vine be unsuccessful at an early stage. ●Cf. ▶ **WITHER on the vine**.

DIE with one's boots on die while actively occupied. ●Apparently first used (L19) of the deaths of cowboys and others in the American West killed in gun battles or being hanged.

(as) straight as a DIE 1 absolutely straight. 2 entirely open and honest.

| **1** **1920** *Blackwood's Magazine* Jan. 107/2 The ... Ganges Canal ... runs straight as a die between its wooded banks.

to DIE for extremely good or desirable. *informal* ● Used postpositively.

DIE ▶ *see* **die a DEATH**; ▶ *see* **die like FLIES**.

agree to DIFFER cease to argue about something because neither party will compromise or be persuaded.

DIFFERENT ▶ *see* **different STROKES for different folks**.

DIG the dirt (*or* dig up dirt) discover damaging information about a public figure or enemy. *informal* ● *Dirt* is commonly used as a metaphor for unsavoury gossip or scandal; cf. ▶ **DISH the dirt**.

DIG oneself into a hole (*or* dig a hole for oneself) get oneself into an awkward or restrictive situation. ● Cf. ▶ **in a HOLE**.

DIG in one's heels (*or* toes *or* feet) resist stubbornly; refuse to give in. ● With reference to the action of a horse or other animal when obstinately refusing to be led or ridden forwards.

DIG ▶ *see* **dig someone in the RIBS**; ▶ *see* **dig a PIT for**; ▶ *see* **dig one's own GRAVE**.

(be) beneath one's DIGNITY be of too little importance or value for one to do it. ● Often ironical. *Infra dig.* (a jocular abbreviation of the Latin equivalent, *infra dignitatem*) is sometimes used in informal contexts.

stand on one's DIGNITY insist on being treated with due respect.

DIM ▶ *see* **take a dim VIEW of**.

a DIME a dozen very common and of no particular value. *US, informal* ● A small coin worth ten cents, *dime* occurs in various US expressions as a metaphor for cheapness and/or smallness.

| **1998** *New Scientist* 29 Aug. 47/1 Of course, medical breakthroughs are not a dime a dozen.

get off the DIME be decisive and show initiative. *US, informal*

| **1992** DARYL F. GATES *Chief: My Life in the LAPD* viii. 133 That was fine with me; all I wanted to do was get them off the dime, make a decision.

on a DIME **1** (of a manoeuvre that can be performed by a moving vehicle or person) within a small area or short distance. **2** quickly or instantly. *US, informal* ● The British equivalent to sense 1 is ▶ **on a SIXPENCE**.

DIME ▶ *see* **DROP the dime on**.

the law of DIMINISHING returns the principle by which, after a certain point, the level of profits or benefits to be gained is reduced to less than the amount of money or energy invested. ● Originating in E19 with reference to the profits from agriculture, this expression is predominantly used in economics, but it is also used figuratively in more general contexts.

fair DINKUM **1** genuine or true. **2** (of behaviour) acceptable. *chiefly Austral & NZ* ● As a noun *dinkum*, recorded from L19, was an English dialect word meaning 'hard work, honest toil'; it now mainly features as an adjective in various Australian and New Zealand expressions.

done like (a) DINNER utterly defeated or outwitted. *Austral. & Canadian, informal*

| 1978 C. GREEN *The Sun is up* 11 I had old Splinters Maloney the fishing inspector knocking on me door wanting to see me licence. Of course I was done like a dinner.

hand (*or* turn *or* pass) in one's DINNER PAIL die. *informal* ● With reference to the bucket in which a workman formerly carried his dinner; cf. ▶ **kick the BUCKET**. E20 US slang.

more — than someone has had hot DINNERS one's experience of a specified activity or phenomenon is vastly greater than someone else's. *Brit., informal*

by DINT of by means of. ● *Dint* in the sense of 'blow' or 'stroke' is now obsolete, and in the sense of 'application of force' survives only in this phrase.

DIP one's pen in gall write unpleasantly or spitefully. ● *Gall* is an obsolete term for *bile*, the bitter secretion of the liver; it was used in the Bible *passim* as a metaphor for bitterness or affliction: cf. ▶ **WORMWOOD and gall**.

DIP one's toe(s) into (*or* in) something begin to do or test something cautiously. ● From the action of putting one's toe(s) briefly into water to check the temperature.

do someone DIRT harm someone maliciously. *informal*

| 1951 J. C. FENNESSY *Sonnet in Bottle* i. 245 It was doing dirt to one of their own people.

eat DIRT suffer insults or humiliation. *informal* ● In the US (L19) also with the sense of 'make a humiliating retraction' or 'eat one's words' (cf. ▶ **eat CROW**).

treat someone like DIRT treat someone contemptuously or unfairly. ● Used to express anger at such treatment.

| 1983 A. WALKER *Everything is Human Being* in *Living Word* (1988) 147 The Earth is treated 'like dirt'—its dignity demeaned by wanton dumpings of lethal materials.

DIRT ▶ *see* **DRAG someone through the dirt**.

DIRTY work at the crossroads illicit or underhand dealing. *humorous* ● Possible explanations of this expression may relate to a crossroads as either symbolizing a point at which a decision as to one's future path has to be made or as the haunt of highwaymen or as the place where suicides were traditionally buried.

| *1914 P. G. WODEHOUSE *Man Upstairs* 269 A conviction began to steal over him that ... some game was afoot which he did not understand, that—in a word—there was dirty work at the crossroads.

the DIRTY end of the stick the difficult or unpleasant part of a task or situation. *chiefly Brit., informal*

| 1936 P. G. WODEHOUSE *Laughing Gas* v. 62 I mean what's downtrodden and oppressed and gets the dirty end of the stick all the time. That's me.

do the DIRTY on someone cheat or betray someone. *Brit., informal*

get one's hands DIRTY (*or* dirty one's hands) 1 do manual, menial, or other hard work.   **2** *informal* become directly involved in dishonest or dishonorable activity.

| **2 1998** *Spectator* 9 May 20/1 Unlike its sister churches in the West, the Catholic Church in the Philippines is not afraid to get its hands dirty.

play DIRTY act in a dishonest or unfair way. *informal*

talk DIRTY speak about sex in a way considered to be coarse or obscene. *informal*

DIRTY ▶ *see* **wash one's dirty LINEN in public**.

do a DISAPPEARING act go away without being seen to go, especially when someone is looking for one. ● The suggestion is that the person has vanished as completely and inexplicably as things vanish in a magician's act.

be a recipe for DISASTER be almost certain to have unfortunate consequences.

DISH the dirt reveal or spread scurrilous information or gossip. *informal*

| **1997** *New Scientist* 8 Nov. 54/2 We love revisionist biographies that dish the dirt on our icons.

DISHWATER ▶ *see* **DULL as dishwater**.

go the DISTANCE complete a difficult task or endure an ordeal. ● A metaphor from boxing meaning, when used of a boxer, 'complete a fight without being knocked out' or, when used of a boxing match, 'last the scheduled length'. In the US there is an additional baseball-related sense: 'pitch for the entire length of an inning'.

| **1998** *Times* 13 Apr. 27/5 'Everyone wants to see an amateur who can go the distance,' another spectator said. Kuchar has certainly gone the distance.

within spitting DISTANCE (of) within a very short distance (of).

| **1991** *Time* 11 Feb. 80/2 His reputation as a hard-boiled novelist is within spitting distance of Hammett's and Chandler's.

within striking DISTANCE (of) near enough to hit or achieve.

DITCHWATER ▶ *see* **DULL as dishwater**.

all of a DITHER in a state of extreme agitation or vacillation. *informal* ● *Dither* (verb) was originally a northern dialect word. As a noun it was recorded in 1819 in this expression in Lancashire speech ('I'm aw on o' dither'). Similar to ▶ **all of a DOODAH**.

say DITTO to agree with; endorse. *informal*

take a DIVE   **1** (of a boxer or footballer) pretend to fall so as to deceive an opponent or referee.   **2** *informal* (of prices, hopes, fortunes, etc.) fall suddenly and significantly.

| **2 1998** *New Scientist* 30 May 23/3 When the DOJ announced its action, Microsoft's stock price took a dive, knocking $10 billion off the firm's market value.

DIVIDE and rule (*or* conquer) the policy of maintaining supremacy over one's opponents by encouraging dissent between them, thereby preventing them from uniting against one. ● This is a maxim associated with a number of rulers: Latin *divide et impera*, German *entzwei und gebiete*. Since E17 English writers have often wrongly attributed it to the Italian political philosopher Niccolò Machiavelli (1469–1527).

(a house) DIVIDED against itself (a group which should be coherent) split by factional interests. ●With reference to Jesus's observation, 'every city or house divided against itself shall not stand' (Matthew 12:25).

whistle DIXIE engage in unrealistic fantasies; waste one's time. *US* ●The origin of the nickname *Dixie* applied to the southern United States is obscure; it featured in a popular song (1859) by D. D. Emmett.

> **1992** *Discover* Feb. 46/2 You're never going to understand what happened to the Neanderthals … until you see how these people coped with their world. Until you nail that down, you're just whistling Dixie.

DO a — behave in a manner characteristic of (a specified person or thing). *informal*

DO one's head (or nut) in (or do one's head) be extremely angry, worried, or agitated. *Brit., informal*

DO or die persist in the face of great danger, even if death is the result. ●Also used as a modifier to describe a crisis where one's actions may result in victory or defeat: *a do-or-die situation.*

DO ▶ *see* **do the HONOURS**; ▶ *see* **do someone PROUD**; ▶ *see* **do something to DEATH**; ▶ *see* **do the TRICK**.

in DOCK out of action for repairs. *Brit., informal* ●Originally in its literal sense applied to a ship in a (dry) dock and therefore out of action, but now also used of a person in hospital and of a vehicle in a garage for repairs.

in the DOCK (of a person or thing) under investigation or scrutiny for suspected wrongdoing or harm caused. *Brit.* ●In a court of law the dock is the enclosure where the defendant is placed during a trial.

be (just) what the DOCTOR ordered be very beneficial or desirable under the circumstances. *informal*

> **1948** G. VIDAL *City and Pillar* I. i. 16 The waiter brought her a drink. 'Just what the doctor ordered,' she said, smiling at him.

go for the DOCTOR make an all-out effort. *Austral., informal*

DODGE ▶ *see* **dodge the COLUMN**.

(as) dead as a (or the) DODO 1 no longer alive. 2 no longer effective, valid, or interesting. *informal* ●The name *dodo*, applied to the large flightless bird of Mauritius that was wiped out by visiting European sailors, comes from Portuguese *duodo* 'stupid'. The dodo's fate has made it proverbial for something that is long dead. *Dodo* has been used metaphorically since L19 for an old-fashioned, stupid, or unenlightened person.

DOG-and-pony show an elaborate display or performance designed to attract people's attention. *mainly N. Amer.*

> **1998** *Spectator* 24 Jan. 24/1 Happy as I always am to help the Bank of England, I have … supplied the script for its euro dog and pony show.

the DOG's bollocks (of a person or thing) the best of its kind. *Brit., vulgar slang*

a DOG's dinner (*or* breakfast) a poor piece of work; a mess. *Brit.*, *informal* ●Referring to a dog's meal being jumbled-up scraps. Also used of someone's appearance with the implication that the mess is the result of an attempt at ostentation (see quot.). Cf. ► **dressed like a DOG's dinner**.

*1934 'C. L. ANTHONY' *Touch Wood* ii. ii. 66 Why have you got those roses in your hair? You look like a dog's dinner.

DOG eat dog a situation of fierce competition in which people are willing to harm each other in order to succeed. ●With allusion to the proverb *dog does not eat dog*, which dates back to M16 in English but before that to Latin *canis caninam non est* a dog does not eat dog's flesh (Varro *De Lingua Latina* vii. 32).

1998 *Spectator* 24 Jan. 20/1 It was now Holy Week and, on the dog-does-not-eat-dog principle, all Santeria ceremonies were suspended.

DOG in the manger a person inclined to prevent others from having or using things that they do not want or need themselves. ●With allusion to 'cruell Dogges liying in a Maunger, neither eatyng the Haye theim selues ne sufferyng the Horse to feed thereof hymself' (W. Bullein *Dialogue against the Fever Pestilence*, 1564). Also used as modifier: e.g., *a dog-in-the-manger policy*.

a DOG's life an unhappy existence full of problems or unfair treatment. ●One can *lead a dog's life* oneself and also *lead someone (else) a dog's life*.

1987 F. FLAGG *Fried Green Tomatoes at Whistle Stop Cafe* 344 The judge's daughter had just died a couple of weeks ago, old before her time and living a dog's life on the outskirts of town.

DOG tired extremely tired; utterly worn out. *informal* ●Also *dog weary*, that is, exhausted as a dog is after a long chase or hunt. *Dog* — and (*as*) — *as a dog* are used for emphasis of a number of physical conditions; cf. ► **SICK as a dog**.

dressed (up) like a DOG's dinner wearing ridiculously smart or ostentatious clothes. *Brit.*, *informal*

give a DOG a bad name it is very difficult to lose a bad reputation, even if it is unjustified. ●With allusion to the proverb *give a dog a bad name and hang him*, known from E18.

in a DOG's age a very long time. *N. Amer.*, *informal* ●Cf. ► **for a COON's age**.

keep a DOG and bark oneself pay someone to work for one and then do the work oneself.

*1583 B. MELBANCKE *Philotimus* 119 It is smal reason you should kepe a dog, and barke your selfe.

let the DOG see the rabbit let someone get on with work they are ready and waiting to do. *informal* ●A catch-phrase derived from dog racing.

like a DOG with two tails showing great pleasure; delighted. ●From the wagging of a dog's tail as a manifestation of happiness. A M20 simile used informally to emphasize how pleased someone is.

not a DOG's chance no chance at all. ●*Dog* is used for emphasis or as an intensifier in a number of expressions; cf. ► **DOG tired**.

put on the DOG behave in a pretentious or ostentatious way. *N. Amer., informal* ● *Dog* was L19 US slang for 'style' or a 'flashy display'.

| 1962 'A. GILBERT' *No Dust in Attic* xiv. 190 Matron put on a lot of dog about the hospital's responsibility.

DOG ▶ *see* **the HAIR of the dog**; ▶ *see* **SICK as a dog**.

DOGBOX ▶ *see* **in the DOGHOUSE**.

it's DOGGED as does it persistence succeeds. ● With allusion to the tenacity of a dog when following a trail. *Dogged* is here pronounced as two syllables.

lie DOGGO remain motionless or quiet. *Brit.* ● A L19 slang expression of uncertain origin, but probably from a dog's habit of lying motionless or apparently asleep but nonetheless alert. Also sometimes with *stay* or *play* instead of *lie*.

(be) in the DOGHOUSE (*or* dogbox) (be) in disgrace or disfavour. *informal* ● Originally M20 US slang.

| 1963 P. H. JOHNSON *Night & Silence* ix. 55 He'd been getting bad grades, he was in the doghouse as it was.

DOGS of war 1 the havoc accompanying military conflict. *literary* 2 mercenary soldiers. ● Quoting Shakespeare *Julius Caesar* III. i. 273: 'let slip the dogs of war.' The image is of hunting dogs being loosed from their leashes to pursue their prey.

| 2 1998 *Times* 13 May 18/2 The good guys … may have broken the rules by employing dogs of war.

go to the DOGS deteriorate shockingly, especially in behaviour or morals. *informal* ● A greyhound-race meeting was formerly considered a scene of moral peril and financial loss. The 1846 edition of *The Swell's Night Guide* equates *gone to the dogs* with 'become poor in circumstances' and 'gone to pot'. However, in 1927 the *Daily Mail* (28 July) observed that literally ' "Going to the dogs" has … lost … its old suggestion of a descent to dissipation and ruin', though the old derogatory associations remain fossilized in this idiom.

| 1998 *Spectator* 4 July 82/3 [T]he artistic, classical expressiveness of Blasis's 'ideal beauty' had already gone to the dogs long before our gloomy days.

throw someone to the DOGS discard someone as worthless.

DOGS ▶ *see* **RAIN cats and dogs**; ▶ *see* **let SLEEPING dogs lie**.

DOLLAR ▶ *see* **one can BET one's boots**.

be DOLLARS to doughnuts that be a certainty that. *N. Amer., informal* ● Earlier (from L19) with other nouns in place of *doughnuts*.

| 1936 J. CURTIS *Gilt Kid* xiii. 131 If he were seen it was dollars to doughnuts that he would be arrested.

a DONE deal a plan or project that has been finalized or accomplished. *US*

| 1991 *New Yorker* 2 Sept. 92/1 The French are still overreacting to German unification, even though it is a done deal.

DONE for in a situation so bad that it is impossible to get out of it. *informal*

DONE in (*or* up) extremely tired. *informal*

for DONKEY's years for a very long time. *informal* ● A pun alluding to the length of a donkey's ears and playing on the pronunciation (formerly considered uneducated) of *years* as *ears* (see quot.).

> *1916 E. V. LUCAS *Vermilion Box* lxxvii. 86 Now for my first bath for what the men call 'Donkey's ears', meaning years and years.

all of a DOODAH very agitated; excited. ● The nonsense word *doo-da(h)* is the refrain of the plantation song 'Camptown Races'. E20 slang; cf. ▶ **all of a DITHER**.

DOOM and gloom a general feeling of pessimism or despondency. ● Also as *gloom and doom*, the phrase was particularly pertinent to fears about a nuclear holocaust during the cold war period of the 1950s and 1960s. It became a catch-phrase in the 1968 film *Finian's Rainbow*.

till DOOMSDAY for ever. ● *Doomsday* means literally 'judgement day' (Old English *dōm* = judgement), thus the Last Judgement in Christian eschatology.

close (*or* shut) the DOOR on (*or* to) exclude the opportunity for; refuse to consider.

DOOR to door **1** (of a journey) from start to finish. **2** visiting all the houses in an area to sell or publicize something. ● Also as modifier *door-to-door*.

lay something at someone's DOOR regard or name someone as responsible for something. ● Perhaps with reference to the practice of leaving an illegitimate baby on the doorstep of the man to be identified as its father.

leave the DOOR open for ensure that there is still an opportunity for something.

open the DOOR to create an opportunity for.

> 1995 *Kindred Spirit* Sept.–Nov. 60/3 By recreating the space in which you live or work, Feng Shui can open the door to abundance, wellbeing and a Renewed Sense of Purpose!

DOOR ▶ *see at* DEATH's door; ▶ *see* a TOE in the door.

(as) dead as a DOORNAIL completely dead. ● A *doornail* was one of the large iron studs formerly much used on doors for strength or ornamentation; it was proverbially considered an archetypical insensate object, and the word occurred in various alliterative phrases (e.g., *deaf as a doornail* and *dour as a doornail*) of which *dead as a doornail* is now the only one in common use.

on one's (*or* the) DOORSTEP very near; close at hand.

> 1998 *New Scientist* 11 July 38/2 The solution to Underhill's problem was on his doorstep.

DOS and don'ts rules of behaviour. ● The plural of the noun *do* in this sense (an injunction to do something specified) is normally only found when coupled with *don'ts* in this phrase.

> *1902 'STANCLIFFE' (*title*) Golf do's and don'ts.

like a DOSE of salts very fast and efficiently. *Brit., informal* ● The *salts* here are laxatives, so the verb most associated with this simile is *go through* (see quot.).

> *1837 *Crockett's Almanac* 3 I'll go through the Mexicans like a dose of salts.

DOSE ▶ *see* a dose of one's own MEDICINE.

in small DOSES experienced or engaged in a little at a time.

> 1994 *American Spectator* June 69/2 In small doses, ironical detachment is as necessary for getting along in life as ... any of the other human qualities.

DOT and carry one the action of a person with one lame leg and one sound one; the person who moves thus. *informal* ●Earlier (L18) as *dot and go one*. *Dot and carry one* was used first (L18) as a schoolboy description of a form of elementary arithmetic and was humorously transferred to its current sense in M19, eventually superseding *dot and go one*.

DOT the i's and cross the t's ensure that all details are correct. *informal* ●Recorded in this form from L19.

on the DOT exactly on time. *informal* ●With reference to a dot on a clock-face marking the hour.

> 1998 *Oldie* Aug. 8/2 The Conditions of Sale state that the buyer has to pay the auctioneer on the dot.

the year DOT a very long time ago. *Brit.*, *informal* ●Used of a date too long ago to be particularized.

> 1998 *Spectator* 10 Jan. 15/2 From the year dot there has been an uneasy relationship between press and police.

at (*or* on) the DOUBLE at running speed; very fast. ●The modern generalized sense has developed from the M19 military use of *double pace* to mean twice the number of steps per minute of *slow pace*.

DOUBLE or nothing (*or Brit.* quits) a gamble to decide whether a loss or debt should be doubled or cancelled.

a DOUBLE-EDGED sword (*or* weapon) a course of action or situation having both positive and negative effects.

a DOUBTING Thomas a person who refuses to believe something without incontrovertible proof; a sceptic. ●From the biblical story of the apostle Thomas, who said that he would not believe that Christ had risen from the dead until he had seen and touched his wounds (John 20:24–9).

DOVECOTES ▶ *see* **FLUTTER the dovecotes**.

DOWN and dirty **1** unprincipled; unpleasant. **2** energetically earthy, direct, or sexually explicit. *N. Amer.*, *informal*

DOWN and out beaten in the struggle of life, completely without resources or means of livelihood. ●With allusion to a boxer who is felled by a blow and knocked out. Since E20 the noun *down-and-out* has been used to designate a person in such a hopeless situation.

DOWN in the mouth unhappy; dejected. *informal* ●Used of a person or a facial expression, with mouth turned down in the opposite of a smile.

DOWN on one's luck experiencing a period of bad luck. *informal*

DOWN tools stop work, typically as a form of industrial action. *Brit.*, *informal*

have a (*or* be) DOWN on disapprove of; feel hostile or antagonistic towards. *informal* ●Apparently originating in M19 Australia.

have (or put) someone/thing DOWN as judge someone/thing to be (a particular type or class of person or thing).

> **1914** M. A. VON ARNIM *Pastor's Wife* (1987) ii. 13 The other excursionists were all in pairs; they thought Ingeborg was too, and put her down at first as the German gentleman's wife because he did not speak to her.

on the DOWNGRADE in decline. *N. Amer.* ● *Downgrade* was originally (M19) used literally of a downward slope, but was in figurative use by L19 (see quot.).

> **1876** J. MILLER *Life amongst Modocs* vi. 76 He [*sc.* the stage-driver] … said:—'Boys, I am on the down grade and can't reach the brake!' and sank down and died. And so it is that 'the down grade', an expression born of the death of the old stage-driver, has a meaning with us now.

go DOWNHILL become worse; deteriorate.

DOWNWARDLY ▶ *see* **downwardly MOBILE**.

a baker's DOZEN thirteen. ● The thirteenth loaf traditionally represented the retailer's profit.

talk nineteen to the DOZEN talk incessantly. *Brit.* ● No convincing reason has been put forward as to why *nineteen* should have been preferred in this idiom rather than *twenty* or any other number larger than twelve.

> *****1785** E. SHERIDAN *Journal* 7 Aug. The Mother good humour'd and Civil but talks nineteen to the dozen.

DRAG one's feet or heels (of a person or organization) be deliberately slow or reluctant to act. ● From the literal sense of walking slowly and wearily or with difficulty.

> **1994** *Nature Conservancy* Jan.–Feb. 18/1 We can't afford to drag our feet until a species is at the brink of extinction.

DRAG (the name of) someone (or something) through the dirt (or mud) slander or denigrate someone publicly; give someone or something a bad reputation through despicable behaviour.

> **1998** *Economist* 14 Mar. 35/1 The deputy prime minister … is having his name dragged through the mud.

sow (or plant) DRAGON's teeth take action that is intended to prevent trouble, but which actually brings it about. ● In Greek legend Cadmus killed a dragon and sowed its teeth, which sprang up as armed men; these all then killed one another, leaving just five survivors who became the ancestors of the Thebans.

DRAGON ▶ *see* **CHASE the dragon**.

down the DRAIN totally wasted or spoilt. *informal* ● Used also literally, but in the figurative sense especially of wasted money.

> | **1930** W. S. MAUGHAM *Breadwinner* i. 52 All his savings are gone down the drain.

make a DRAMA out of exaggerate the importance of a minor problem or incident. *informal*

feel the DRAUGHT experience an adverse change in one's (esp. financial) circumstances. *informal*

DRAW someone's fire attract hostility or criticism away from a more important target.

DRAW the (*or* a) line at set a limit of what one is willing to do or accept, beyond which one will not go.

> **1995** K. ATKINSON *Behind Scenes at Museum* She even manages to persuade Gillian not to cheat, ... although Gillian draws the line at not screaming when she loses.

DRAW stumps cease doing something. ● In the game of cricket, the stumps are taken out of the ground at the close of play.

quick on the DRAW very fast in acting or reacting. ● The *draw* is the action of taking one's pistol or other weapon from its holster.

DRAW (noun) ▶ *see* **the LUCK of the draw**.

DRAW (verb) ▶ *see* **draw a BEAD on**; ▶ *see* **draw a BLANK**; ▶ *see* **draw LOTS**; ▶ *see* **draw the short STRAW**.

bottom DRAWER the collection of linen, clothes, and household items assembled by a woman in preparation for her marriage. ● Called after the traditional place of storage of such goods (L19). The US equivalent is *hope chest* (E20).

on the DRAWING board (of an idea, scheme, or proposal) under consideration; not yet put into practice. ● To *get something off the drawing board* is to put something into action or to realize the first stages of a project.

DRAWING ▶ *see* **BACK to the drawing board**.

beyond one's wildest DREAMS bigger, better, or to a greater extent than would be reasonable to expect or hope for.

in someone's DREAMS not likely ever to happen. ● Used as a rejoinder in spoken English to assert that some desirable thing that has been mentioned is unlikely.

> **1997** J. OWEN *Camden Girls* 1 Look, you know me I'd go to the openin of an envelope if I thought I was on the guest list ... yeah yeah right up your alley ... in your dreams sunshine.

in one's wildest DREAMS in one's most fanciful imaginings. ● Used with negative to emphasize that something is beyond the scope of one's imagination.

> **1996** *Daily Star* 26 Feb. 19/1 Never in his wildest dreams did he think the cheers were to welcome the opening goal of a match.

like a DREAM very well or successfully. *informal*

DRESSED ▶ *see* **dressed to KILL**; ▶ *see* **dressed to the NINES**.

DRINK someone under the table consume more alcohol than one's drinking companion without becoming as drunk. *informal*. Cf. ▶ **under the TABLE**.

DRINK ▶ *see* **drink the three OUTS**.

let DRIVE attack with blows, missiles, or criticism.

> **1926** *Travel* Nov. 58/2 I let drive for the point of his chin, and he went down and out for a full count.

DRIVE ▶ *see* **drive a COACH and horses through**: ▶ *see* **drive something HOME**.

in the DRIVER's (or driving) seat in charge of a situation.
| **1998** *Times* 11 Aug. 23/1 [T]he deal would propel the no-nonsense Lancastrian into the driving seat at the UK's biggest generator.

what someone is DRIVING at the point that someone is attempting to make.
| **1986** R. SPROAT *Stunning the Punters* 13 Martin is always saying things where I can't see what he's driving at.

at the DROP of a hat without delay or good reason. *informal* ● Originally an M19 US colloquialism.
| **1991** *Independent* 5 Jan. 25/1 These days Soviet visas are issued at the drop of a hat.

DROP one's aitches omit the 'h' sound, especially from the beginning of words. ● In Britain traditionally regarded as a sign that the speaker belongs to an inferior social class.

DROP the ball make a mistake; mishandle things. *N. Amer., informal* ● With allusion to mishandling in baseball.

DROP a brick make an indiscreet or embarrassing remark. *Brit., informal* ● Cf. next entry.

DROP a clanger make an embarrassing or foolish mistake. *Brit., informal* ● Dropping something that makes a loud clang attracts attention; this M20 expression is therefore used especially for a social blunder that elicits adverse comment.
| **1998** *Spectator* 21 Mar. 26/2 Yet he never escaped from his own nagging suspicion that he had somehow overachieved … and that he was likely to drop a huge clanger at any moment.

DROP dead die suddenly and unexpectedly. ● In informal speech used in the imperative as an expression of intense scorn or dislike, but also as an emphatic modifier as in *drop-dead gorgeous*.

DROP the (or a) dime on inform on (someone) to the police. *US, informal*
| **1990** S. TUROW *Burden of Proof* III. xlvi Dixon says he's thought it over, the best course for him is just to drop the dime on John.

DROP a hint (or drop hints) let fall a hint (or hints), as if casually or unconsciously.

a DROP in the ocean (or in a bucket) a very small amount compared with what is needed or expected. ● *Bucket* is older than *ocean* in this idiom, occurring in Wyclif's translation (1382) of Isaiah 40:15 'as a drope of a boket' (retained in the Authorized Version of 1611). *Of* seems to have been replaced by *in* during the nineteenth century (but cf. quot., which is an early example with *ocean*).
| **1829** 'AN OFFICER' *Twelve Years' Military Adventure* I. x. 158 … [O]ur handful of men … was but as a drop to the ocean.

DROP someone a line send someone a note or letter in a casual manner.

DROP one's trousers deliberately let one's trousers fall down, especially in a public place.

have the DROP on have the advantage over. *informal* ● An M19 US expression originally used literally to signify having the opportunity to shoot before one's opponent can use their weapon.

| **1893** J. H. MCCARTHY *Red Diamonds* II. 27 It was my own fault for letting them get the chance to have the drop on me.

DROP ▶ *see* **lower one's GUARD**; ▶ *see* **drop someone/thing like a HOT potato**; ▶ *see* **drop NAMES**; ▶ *see* **drop the PILOT**.

DROWN one's sorrows forget one's problems by getting drunk.

like a DROWNED rat extremely wet and bedraggled.

a DRUG on the market an unsaleable or valueless commodity. ● *Drug* in the sense of 'a commodity for which there is no demand' is recorded from M17, but its history does not make it unequivocally clear that it is the same word as the medicinal substance. The phrase is M19. Earlier also as *a drug in the market*.

| **1998** *Spectator* 24 Jan. 24/2 Merchant banks are a drug on the market these days.

beat (*or* bang) the DRUM for (*or* of) be ostentatiously in support of.

DRUM ▶ *see* **MARCH to a different tune**.

(as) DRUNK as a lord (*or* fiddler *or* skunk) extremely drunk. ● These are the more usual variants of this simile, but many others exist or have existed, particularly referring to animals, e.g., a mouse, rat, sow, etc.

come up DRY be unsuccessful. *N. Amer.*

| **1988** J. TREFIL *Dark Side of Universe* iii. 48 Attempts to see this decay with extremely sensitive experiments have so far come up dry.

(as) DRY as dust **1** extremely dry. **2** extremely dull. ● Sense 2 is exemplified in the fictitious character of the antiquarian Dr Jonas Dryasdust, to whom Scott addressed the prefatory epistle of *Ivanhoe* and some other novels.

there wasn't a DRY eye (in the house) everyone in the audience (of a film, play, speech, etc.) was moved to tears.

DUCK and dive use one's ingenuity to deal with or evade a situation.

| **1998** *New Scientist* 20 June 36/3 You don't last for over 100 million years without some capacity to duck and dive.

(like) a dying DUCK in a thunderstorm having a dejected or hopeless expression. *informal* ● The miserable demeanour of ducks during thunder has been proverbial since L18.

| **1933** A. CHRISTIE *Lord Edgware Dies* xxii. 183 You did look for all the world like a dying duck in a thunderstorm.

lame DUCK a person or thing that is powerless or in need of help. *informal* ● Earliest (M18) in a stock-market context, with reference to a person or company who cannot fulfil financial obligations, but also specifically (M19) with reference to US politicians who are not eligible for re-election.

| **1998** *Spectator* 29 Aug. 11/1 [A]t some point in his second and final term, every president becomes a lame duck: as the man himself matters less, so does the office.

take to something like a DUCK to water take to something very readily.

> **1960** C. DAY LEWIS *Buried Day* vi. 107 I had taken to vice like a duck to water, but it ran off me like water from a duck's back.

(like) water off a DUCK's back a remark or incident which has no apparent effect on a person. ● As a simile traditional since E19. Cf. preceding entry.

DUCKLING ▶ *see* **an UGLY duckling**.

get (*or* have) one's DUCKS in a row get (*or* have) one's facts straight; get (*or* have) everything organized. *N. Amer.*

> **1996** *Brew Your Own* July 54/1 You really want to have all your ducks in a row before the meeting.

play DUCKS and drakes with trifle with; treat frivolously. ● From the game of *duck and drake* (now usually plural), played by throwing a flat stone across the surface of water in such a way as to make it skim and skip before it finally sinks. The game was known by this name by L16, and it was already a metaphor for an idle or frivolous activity in E17.

DUCKS ▶ *see* **fine WEATHER for ducks**.

in high DUDGEON in a state of deep resentment. ● *Dudgeon* is recorded in various forms since L16 (see quot.), and although in its modern form it is identical to an obsolete word for a type of wood formerly used to make dagger- or knife-handles, no connection of sense has ever been proved between the two. The origin of *dudgeon* in the sense of 'ill humour' is therefore unknown. Use of *dudgeon* as a freestanding noun is now not common; it is almost always used in this phrase and qualified by an adjective, though *deep*, *great*, etc. may be substituted for *high*.

> ***1573** G. HARVEY *Letter-book* 28 Who seem'd to take it in marvelus great duggin.

up the DUFF pregnant. *Brit., informal*

> **1994** *Daily Telegraph* 26 Sept. 115/3 At 19, he was married ('only because she was up the duff' he explains gallantly).

DUKE it out fight it out. *N. Amer., informal* ● The L19 slang usage of *dukes* or *dooks* for 'fists' gave rise to this M20 expression.

(as) DULL as dishwater (*or* ditchwater) extremely dull. ● The point of the simile is perhaps the unattractive colour of the two liquids. *Ditchwater* is by far the older expression, occurring also in the obsolete ME expression *digne as ditchwater* 'haughty as ditchwater' (i.e. stinking with pride, like a foul ditch), and in *dull as ditchwater* since M19.

DULL the edge of make less sensitive, interesting, or effective. ● With reference to the idea of making blunt a knife-edge.

sell someone a (*or* the) DUMMY deceive an opponent. ● Used since E20 with reference to the tricking of an opponent in the game of rugby by a feigned pass or kick (*dummy*).

into the DUMPER into a bad or worse state or condition. *N. Amer., informal*

> **1991** *Tucson Weekly* 25–31 Dec. 3/1 J. Fife III peaked well before his run for governor ... and has been sliding into the dumper ever since.

(down) in the DUMPS (of a person) depressed or unhappy. *informal* ● The only context in which the E16 noun *dump* meaning 'a fit of depression' survives.

turn to DUST and ashes (in one's mouth) (of pleasure or success) become a source of great disappointment or disillusionment. ● *Dust and ashes* is used in the Bible as a metaphor for worthlessness; e.g., Genesis 18:27, Job 30:19. The attractive appearance of the Sodom apple or Dead Sea fruit tempted people to eat it, but the taste of its flesh was of dust and ashes. Cf. Milton *Paradise Lost* (1667): 'The Frutage fair to sight ... not the touch, but taste Deceav'd; they ... instead of Fruit Chew'd bitter Ashes' (x. 561–6).

in DUST and ashes abject(ly). ● Cf. Job 42:6 'I abhor myself, and repent in dust and ashes.'

the DUST settles things quieten down.

| **1998** *New Scientist* 9 May 104/1 The dust is settling on the chaos which ensued when the French sold 110 000 tickets to the World Cup football matches by phone.

eat someone's DUST fall far behind someone in a competitive situation. *N. Amer., informal*

| **1927** Z. GREY *Valley of Wild Horses* (1964) xiv. 175 Aw, I'm sick eatin' his dust.

gather (*or* collect) DUST remain unused.

not see someone for DUST find that a person has made a hasty departure.

| **1978** P. GRACE *Mutuwhenua* (1988) xii. 87 You didn't see this Maori for dust ... . Out the door, on the bike, and away.

raise (*or* kick up) a DUST create a disturbance. *Brit.*

DUST ▶ *see* DRY as dust.

be done and DUSTED (of a project) be completely finished or ready.

a DUSTY answer a curt and unhelpful reply. *Brit.* ● Probably quoting George Meredith's *Modern Love* (1862): 'Ah, what a dusty answer gets the soul When hot for certainties in this our life!'

that beats the DUTCH that is extraordinary or startling. *US* ● L18; in 1939 *American Speech* (XIV. 267) recorded 'beats the Jews' as an alternative.

DUTCH courage bravery induced by drinking alcohol. ● With allusion to the long-standing British belief that the Dutch are extraordinarily heavy drinkers.

go DUTCH share the cost of something equally. ● Hence an excursion or entertainment paid for in this way is *a Dutch treat* and sharing the cost of a meal in a restaurant is *eating Dutch*.

| **1993** *Vanity Fair* Jan 133/1 He insists on buying his own tickets, 'going Dutch', as he puts it.

in DUTCH in trouble. *US, dated*

| **1939** R. CHANDLER *Big Sleep* (1976) xviii. 106 And for that amount of money you're willing to get yourself in Dutch with half the law enforcement of this country?

a DUTCH uncle a kindly but authoritative figure. ● *Dutch* here probably means no more than that the person described is not a genuine blood relation. In M19 *I will talk to him like a Dutch uncle* (meaning 'I will give him a lecture') was noted as being an American expression. Most often used in the context of giving friendly advice or guidance to a younger person (see quot.).

| *1838 J. C. NEAL *Charcoal Sketches* 201 If you keep a cutting didoes, I must talk to you both like a Dutch uncle.

(or) I'm a DUTCHMAN (or) I am something that I am obviously not. *Brit.* ● Used mainly in spoken English to express one's strong (dis)belief in a preceding assertion.

| 1856 C. READE *Never Too Late* lii. If there is as much gold … as will make me a wedding-ring, I am a Dutchman.

(in) DUTY bound obliged by one's sense of duty.

in a DWAAL in a dreamy, dazed, or absent-minded state. *S. Afr.*

| 1985 P. SLABOLEPSKY *Saturday Night at Palace* 15 Yassas—Carstens!! Wake up, man. You in a real dwaal tonight.

DYED in the wool (of a person) completely and permanently fixed in a particular belief or opinion; inveterate. ● With allusion to the fact that yarn was dyed in the raw state, producing a more even and permanent colour.

to one's DYING day for the rest of one's life.

| 1967 G. MACKAY BROWN *Calendar of Love* (1978) 106 This one always was and ever will be to his dying day a garrulous long-winded old man.

put one's finger in the DYKE attempt to stem the advance of something undesirable which threatens to overwhelm one. *informal* ● From a story of a small Dutch boy who saved his community from flooding by placing his finger in a hole in a dyke.

E

the three Es economy, efficiency, and effectiveness.

an EAGER beaver a person who is (too) enthusiastic about work. *informal* ● Often used disparagingly; cf. ▶ **work like a BEAVER**.

have someone's EAR have access to and influence with someone.

> **1993** *Olympian* (Olympia, Washington) 18 July c1/2 About 50 of the freshman congressman's constituents had his ear for more than two hours.

have (or keep) an EAR to the ground be well-informed about events and trends. ● From the idea that putting one's ear against the ground would enable one to hear approaching footsteps.

in (at) one EAR and out (at) the other heard but disregarded or quickly forgotten. ● L16 in this form, but the idea goes back to E15.

listen with half an EAR not give one's full attention.

out on one's EAR dismissed or ejected ignominiously. *informal*

> **1997** *Accountancy* Apr. 59/2 At the age of 47, he found himself out on his ear, victim of Lord Hanson's policy of taking over companies … and replacing senior management.

EAR ▶ *see* **LEND an ear**; ▶ *see* **make a PIG's ear of**; ▶ *see* **make a SILK purse out of a sow's ear**; ▶ *see* **turn a DEAF ear**.

EARLY bird a person who rises, arrives, or acts before the usual or expected time. ● Alluding to the saying *the early bird catches the worm*.

it's (or these are) EARLY days it is too soon to be sure how a situation will develop. *chiefly Brit., informal*

EARN one's corn put in a lot of effort for one's wages. *Brit., informal*

EARN one's keep be worth the time, money, or effort spent on one.

a nice little EARNER a profitable activity or business. *Brit., informal*

> **1997** *Independent* 30 Nov. 8/6 [T]he Tories … initiated the proliferation of the quango state … keeping their friends in 'nice little earners'.

be all EARS be listening eagerly and attentively. *informal* ● Cf. ▶ **be all EYES**.

bring something about one's EARS bring something, especially misfortune, down on oneself.

one's EARS burn be conscious of being talked about, especially in one's absence. ● The superstition that one's ears (earlier, *left ear* only) tingled when one was being talked about is recorded from M16.

have something coming out of one's EARS have a substantial or excessive amount of something. *informal*

> **1997** *Daily Express* 19 Feb. 17/3 (Advt.) In terms of advice, … Jill's had suggestions coming out of her ears.

up to the (*or* **one's**) **EARS** (*or* **eyes**) **in** very busy with or deeply involved in. *informal*

EARS ▶ *see* **fall on DEAF ears**.

bring someone back (*or* **or come back**) **(down) to EARTH (with a bump)** make someone return (*or* return) (suddenly) to reality after a period of daydreaming or euphoria.

cost (*or* **charge** *or* **pay**) **the EARTH** cost (*or* charge *or* pay) a large amount of money. *chiefly Brit.*, *informal*

the EARTH moved for an orgasm was experienced by. *informal* ● In spoken English usually as a question: *did the earth move for you?*

go to EARTH go into hiding. ● Used literally of a hunted animal hiding in a burrow or earth. Cf. ▶ **go to GROUND**; ▶ **RUN someone/thing to earth**.

like nothing on EARTH very strange. *informal*

> **1942** P. LARKIN *Letter* 13 Dec. (1992) 49 I've had a day or so in bed feeling like nothing on earth, pissing golden syrup, no appetite etc.

EARTH ▶ *see* **promise the MOON**; ▶ *see* **RUN someone/thing to earth**.

not stand (*or* **have**) **an EARTHLY** have no chance at all. *Brit.*, *informal*, *dated* ● *Chance* is understood as *an earthly chance*.

come EASY to present little difficulty to.

> **1989** T. PARKER *Place called Bird* iv. 44 College was a lot harder than High School, book work didn't come easy to me there.

EASY come, easy go what is acquired without effort or difficulty may be lost or spent casually and without regret. *proverbial* ● Although recorded in this exact form only from M19, *easy come, easy go* had parallels in medieval French and in the English sayings *light come, light go* (M16) and *quickly come, quickly go* (M19). Frequent in spoken English, it is now far more common than either of the latter two.

EASY does it go carefully and slowly. *informal* ● Mainly as an exclamation (recorded from M19) counselling steadiness and a relaxed approach to a task. Also *gently does it*.

EASY on the eye (*or* **ear**) pleasant to look at (*or* listen to). *informal* ● *Easy on the eye* originated (L19) as a US expression used of a pretty woman, a context in which it still often features.

go (*or* **be**) **EASY on someone** be less harsh on or critical of someone. *informal*

go EASY on (*or* **with**) **something** be sparing or cautious in one's use or consumption of something. *informal*

have it EASY be free from difficulties, especially those normally associated with a situation or activity. *informal*

of EASY virtue (of a woman) promiscuous. ● *Easy* in the sense of 'sexually compliant' occurs in Shakespeare's *Cymbeline* II. iv: 'Not a whit, Your lady being so easy.' *A woman of easy virtue* as a euphemism for 'an unchaste woman' is now somewhat dated.

take the EASY way out extricate oneself from a difficult situation by choosing a course of action offering the least effort, worry, or inconvenience, even though a more honourable alternative exists.

take it EASY **1** approach a task or activity gradually or carefully. **2** relax.

EASY ▶ *see* **easy as ABC**; ▶ *see* **(as) easy as FALLING off a log**; ▶ *see* **easy as PIE**; ▶ *see* **a soft TOUCH**.

EAT someone alive **1** (of insects) bite someone many times. **2** exploit someone's weakness and completely dominate them. *informal*

EAT one's heart out suffer from excessive longing, especially for someone or something unattainable. ● In informal use in spoken English *eat your heart out, —!* is used to indicate that one thinks a particular person, either present or absent, would be very envious of something.

EAT someone out of house and home eat a lot of someone else's food. *informal*

EAT ▶ *see* **eat CROW**; ▶ *see* **eat DIRT**; ▶ *see* **eat someone's DUST**; ▶ *see* **eat HUMBLE pie**; ▶ *see* **you can't have your CAKE and eat it**; ▶ *see* **eat SALT with**; ▶ *see* **eat one's WORDS**.

have someone EATING out of one's hand have someone completely under one's control.

> **1987** B. MACLAVERTY *The Great Profundo* (1989) 101 One of my main difficulties is that I'm not good with an audience. There's guys can come out and have a crowd eating out of their hand right away with a few jokes.

at a low EBB in an especially poor state.

EBB and flow a recurrent or rhythmical pattern of coming and going or decline and regrowth. ● With reference to the regular movement of the tides.

applaud (*or* cheer) someone to the ECHO applaud (*or* cheer) someone enthusiastically.

in ECLIPSE losing or having lost significance, power, or prominence; in decline. ● Also used literally of a heavenly body that is obscured by another or the shadow of another.

ECONOMICAL with the truth dissimulating; not entirely frank or truthful. ● The phrase *economy of truth* was used earlier by the orator Edmund Burke (1729–97), and Mark Twain observed 'Truth is the most valuable thing we have. Let us economize it' (*Following the Equator*, 1897). The present phrase, now often used as a euphemism for 'lying', became current after being used in the 'Spycatcher' trial in the New South Wales Supreme Court: Robert Armstrong, head of the British Civil Service, was reported (*Daily Telegraph* 19 Nov. 1986) as saying of a letter 'It contains a misleading impression, not a lie. It was being economical with the truth.' The phrase is also found in the jocular version *economical with the actualité*.

> **1998** *Oldie* July 45/1 Keith Waterhouse wrote a brilliant novel called *Billy Liar*, about a youthful undertaker's assistant who was economical with the truth.

on the EDGE of one's seat (*or* chair) very excited and giving one's full attention to something. *informal*

set someone's teeth on EDGE cause someone to feel intense discomfort or irritation. ●An expression used in the Bible of the unpleasant sensation caused by eating something bitter or sour: 'every man that eateth the sour grape, his teeth shall be set on edge' (Jeremiah 31:30). Now used also of the effect of an unpleasant sound or just figuratively.

take the EDGE off something reduce the intensity or effect of something, especially something unpleasant or severe.

get a word in EDGEWAYS contribute to a conversation with difficulty because the other speaker talks almost without pause. ●Very often with negative.

EFFING and blinding using vulgar expletives; swearing. ●*Effing* and *blinding* here stand for the initial letters of taboo or vulgar slang words.

go suck an EGG go away. *N. Amer., informal* ●Used as an expression of dismissal, anger, or contempt, mainly as imperative.

> **1993** *Virginian Pilot & Ledger-Star* (Norfolk, Va.) 6 July D1/1 A place [in the country] where you can drop a line in the water from your back yard and tell the rest of the world to go suck an egg.

lay an EGG be completely unsuccessful; fail badly. *N. Amer., informal*

with EGG on one's face appearing foolish or ridiculous. *informal*

EGG ► *see* a CURATE's egg; ► *see* kill the GOOSE that lays the golden egg.

putting (*or* having) all one's EGGS in one basket risking everything on the success of one venture. ●The warning against *putting all one's eggs in one basket* was first noted as a proverbial expression in English in M17.

> **1998** *New Scientist* 30 May 46/2 Type 1a supernovae are one of the most promising means of measuring the Hubble constant … But would I put all of my eggs in that basket? Absolutely not.

EGGS ► *see* SURE as eggs is eggs.

one over the EIGHT slightly drunk. *Brit., informal* ●From the presumption that a drinker can reasonably be expected to consume eight glasses of beer without becoming drunk. Armed forces' slang (E20), now used euphemistically.

EIGHT ► *see* behind the eight BALL.

give someone the ELBOW reject or dismiss someone. *informal* ●From the action of nudging someone aside in a rough or contemptuous manner.

lift one's ELBOW consume alcohol to excess.

out at (*or* at the) ELBOWS 1 (of a coat) worn out. 2 (of a person) ragged, poor.

up to one's ELBOWS in deeply involved in. *informal* ●Literally, 'with one's hands plunged into something'.

in (*or* out of) one's ELEMENT in (*or* out of) one's accustomed or preferred environment, where one feels confident and at ease, often in performing a particular activity.

see the ELEPHANT see the world, get experience of life. *US* ● An *elephant* is the type of something remarkable.

> **1994** *Fighting Firearms* Autumn 72/1 These men have all seen the elephant and represent a typical cross-section of the Gunsite staff in general.

ELEPHANT ▶ *see* **a WHITE elephant**.

at the ELEVENTH hour at the latest possible moment. ● Originally with allusion to Jesus's parable of the labourers hired right at the end of the day to work the vineyard (Matthew 20:1–16).

the ELYSIAN Fields heaven. *literary* ● Homer describes the *Elysian Fields* (called *Elysium* by Latin writers) as the happy land which is the abode of blessed spirits in the afterlife.

EMPTY nester a person whose children have grown up and left home. *informal* ● Cf. ▶ **FLY the nest**.

be running on EMPTY have exhausted all one's resources or sustenance.

> **1998** *New Scientist* 19 Sept. 5/1 Bateson concluded that a hunted deer may be running on empty for 90 minutes, but Harris argues that this period will be just a few minutes.

EMPTY ▶ *see* **on an empty STOMACH**.

big ENCHILADA a person or thing of great importance. *N. Amer., informal* ● *Enchilada* is American Spanish for a tortilla served with chilli sauce.

the whole ENCHILADA the whole situation; everything. *N. Amer., informal*

> **1992** *New York Times* 15 Nov. IX. 3/4 [H]igh-tech gadgetry is best viewed as the spice, but not the whole enchilada.

at the END of the day when everything is taken into consideration. *informal, chiefly Brit.*

END in tears have an unhappy or painful outcome. ● Frequently as a warning: *it will all end in tears*.

END it all commit suicide. *euphemistic*

> **1993** R. SHELL *iCED* 173 Quentin thought … he'd jump off the Brooklyn Bridge and make the papers. At least he'd end it all in a blaze of media glory.

the END justifies the means wrong or unfair methods may be used if the overall goal is good. ● Cf. Ovid *Heroides* ii. 85 *exitus acta probat* 'the outcome justifies the actions'. Very commonly used in the negative.

the END of civilization as we know it the complete collapse of ordered society. ● Supposedly a cinematic cliché, and actually used in the film *Citizen Kane* (1941): 'a project which would mean the end of civilization as we know it'. Often used ironically in contexts indicating that someone is being alarmist or is overreacting to a trivial inconvenience or blunder as if it were enormously significant and catastrophic.

the END of the road (*or* line) the point beyond which progress or survival cannot continue.

at the END of one's tether (*or* N. Amer. **rope**) having no patience, resources, or energy left to cope with something. ● The image is that of a grazing animal tethered on a rope that allows it a certain range in which to move but which at full stretch prohibits further movement.

the END of the world a complete disaster. *informal* ● From the idea of the termination of life on earth as the ultimate catastrophe. Very often used with the negative as reassurance that a misfortune or a mistake is not important: *it's not the end of the world*.

get (or** have) one's END away** have sex. *Brit.*, *vulgar slang*

keep (or** hold) one's END up** perform well in a difficult or competitive situation. *informal*

never (or** not) hear the END of something** be continually reminded of an unpleasant topic or cause of annoyance.

> **1994** *Homiletic & Pastoral Review* Feb. 32/1 We'll never hear the end of their harping on our inconsistency.

no END to a great extent; very much. *informal*

no END of something a vast number or amount of something. *informal*

the sharp END **1** *informal* the most important or influential part of an activity or process. **2** *informal* the side of a system or activity which is the most unpleasant or suffers the chief impact. **3** *Brit.*, *humorous* the bow of a ship.

a — to END all —s something so impressive of its kind that nothing that follows will have the same impact. *informal* ● Often in *the war to end all wars*, with reference to a widely held mistaken belief about World War I.

> **1971** B. HEAD *Maru* (1987) ii. 121 It was a wedding to end all weddings.

END ▶ *see* **at a LOOSE end**; ▶ *see* **at one's WIT's end**; ▶ *see* **be on the RECEIVING end**; ▶ *see* **be thrown in at the DEEP end**; ▶ *see* **the BEGINNING of the end**; ▶ *see* **the DIRTY end of the stick**; ▶ *see* **get the WRONG end of the stick**; ▶ *see* **end of STORY**; ▶ *see* **go off the DEEP end**; ▶ *see* **make someone's HAIR stand on end**; ▶ *see* **a MEANS to an end**; ▶ *see* **the thin end of the WEDGE**; ▶ *see* **to the BITTER end**.

all ENDS up completely. *informal* ● E20, originally chiefly in sporting contexts.

> **1921 A. W. MYERS *Twenty Years Lawn Tennis* 19 Barrett beat him 'all ends up' in an early round.

make (both) ENDS meet earn or have enough money to live without getting into debt.

> **1996** A. GHOSH *Calcutta Chromosome* (1997) x. 64 Actually I think she's having trouble making ends meet, now that she's retired.

ENDS ▶ *see* **BURN the candle at both ends**.

public ENEMY number one a notorious wanted criminal. *orig.* US

> **1995** *Independent* (*section 2*) 24 Nov. 8/3 So foods that pile on the pounds are seen as Public Enemy Number One.

be one's own worst ENEMY act contrary to one's own interests; be self-destructive.

> **1993** R. LOWE & W. SHAW *Travellers* 161 We convinced ourselves that everything was against us but the truth was we were probably our own worst enemies.

ENGRAVED ▶ *see* **be engraved in STONE**.

ENOUGH is enough no more will be tolerated.

> **1997** *Earthmatters* Winter 2/1 13/1 Unless we say 'enough is enough' and start to take habitat protection seriously, the future of the world's wildlife is in jeopardy.

ENOUGH said there is no need to say more; all is understood. ● Used in spoken English to put an end to discussion, especially on an embarrassing or troublesome subject.

ENOUGH ▶ *see* **enough to make a cat LAUGH**.

ENTER one's head (*or* mind) (of a thought or idea) occur to one.

the back of an ENVELOPE the place where rough calculations or sketchy plans may be jotted down.

push the ENVELOPE (*or* the edge of the envelope) approach or extend the limits of what is possible. *informal* ● Originally aviation slang, relating to graphs of aerodynamic performance etc.

ÉPATER les bourgeois shock the conventionally minded. ● The French phrase is generally used in English, there being no exact English equivalent. 'Je les ai épatés, les bourgeois' is attributed to Alexandre Private d'Anglemont (d. 1859).

> **1995** *Times* 7 Sept. 16/2 Because it takes more than a urinal to *épater les bourgeois* now, the real things that are being hauled into galleries grow ever more provocative: turds, frozen foetuses and used sanitary towels ...

other (*or* all) things being EQUAL if other related factors remain the same. ● Used to indicate that a situation can be accurately predicted or stated provided that circumstances do not alter.

(the) first among EQUALS having the highest status in a group. ● Latin *primus inter pares*, of which this is the usual English rendering, is also used in English.

ERR on the right side act so that the most likely mistake to be made is the least harmful one.

ERR on the side of act with a specified bias towards something. ● Often *err on the side of caution*.

make good one's ESCAPE succeed in breaking free from confinement.

ESCUTCHEON ▶ *see* **a BLOT on the escutcheon**.

of the ESSENCE critically important. Especially with reference to time.

ETERNAL triangle a relationship between three people, usually two of one sex and one of the other, involving sexual rivalry (E20).

an EVEN break a fair chance. *informal* ● W. C. Fields's catch-phrase 'Never give a sucker an even break', said to have originated in the 1923 musical *Poppy*, was also the title of one of Fields's films (1941).

EVEN Stephens an even chance. ● A rhyming jingle, used as an intensifier for *even* in various senses. Also *Steven(s)* and without initial capital.

get (*or* be) EVEN with inflict similar trouble or harm on someone as they have inflicted on oneself. *informal* ● Cf. ▶ **don't GET mad, get even**.

on an EVEN keel (of a person or situation) functioning normally after a period of difficulty. ● Used literally of a ship (or more recently, aircraft) to mean 'not tilting to one side'.

it was EVER thus (*or* so) nothing has changed. *informal* ● Used as a wry or humorous observation that despite claims of things having been better in the past nothing much alters.

| **1998** *Bookseller* 10 Apr. 66/1 [C]urious and surprising (to say the least) and depressing things happen. But it was ever so.

EVERY last (*or* every single) used to emphasize every member of a group.

| **1991** C. DEXTER *Jewel That was Ours* ii. 229 One clue unfinished in a *Listener* puzzle, and he would strain the capacity of every last brain-cell to bursting point until he had solved it.

EVERY man for himself everyone must take care of themselves and their own interests, safety, etc. ● Originally a proverbial saying in its own right (see quotation), but from M16 often expanded as *every man for himself and the devil take the hindmost* or, less commonly, *every man for himself and God for us all*.

| *c* **1386** G. CHAUCER *Knight's Tale* 1182 At the kynges court, my brother, Ech man for hymself, ther is noon oother.

EVERY which way in all directions; in a disorderly fashion. *N. Amer., informal* ● Also *every whichaway*.

EVERY ▶ *see* **every INCH a —**.

in EVIDENCE noticeable; conspicuous.

put off the EVIL day (*or* hour) postpone (something unpleasant) for as long as possible.

the EXCEPTION that proves the rule a particular case that is so unusual that it is evidence of the validity of the rule that generally applies. ● From the Latin legal maxim *exceptio probat regulum in casibus non exceptis* 'Exception proves the rule in the cases not excepted', in which the sense of *exception* originally intended ('the action of excepting') is popularly taken to mean 'a person or thing who does not conform to the general rule affecting other individuals of that class'. In the modern form since M17, but the Latin maxim was known E17.

| **1998** *Spectator* 28 Mar. 7/2 The success of *The Full Monty* in the United States is an exception which proves the rule. On such lucky breaks, industries and economies are not built.

EXEUNT omnes everyone leaves or goes away. ● Latin for 'all go out', used originally as a stage direction in a printed play to indicate that all the actors leave the stage; now humorously of a collective or mass departure.

EXHIBIT A the most important piece of evidence relating to a matter in question. ●From legal usage, denoting the first exhibit submitted as evidence in a trial.

be EXPECTING be pregnant. *informal* ●More fully, *be expecting a baby*. Both expressions are somewhat euphemistic and dated.

what can (or do) you EXPECT? there was nothing unexpected about a person or event. ●Used to express disappointment heavily tinged with cynicism, as the person or thing concerned has acted entirely in character. A more elaborate statement of the same sentiment is the proverbial *what can you expect from a pig but a grunt?*

an EYE for an eye (and a tooth for a tooth) retaliation in kind. ●With allusion to the *lex talionis* or law of retribution in the Old Testament (Exodus 21:24). Often used to express the view that the appropriate way to deal with an offence or crime is to exact retribution in kind.

the EYE of the storm the most intense part of a tumultous situation. ●From the meteorological phenomenon of the calm region at the centre of a storm or hurricane.

| **1998** *Times* 25 Aug. 16/7 He [Mr Yeltsin] was now our heroic figure in the eye of the storm, preaching defiance ... from the top of a tank outside the White House.

the EYE of a needle a very small opening or space. ●With allusion to Matthew 19:24 'It is easier for a camel to go through the eye of a needle, than for a rich man to enter the kingdom of God.' Used metaphorically to emphasize the impossibility of a projected endeavour.

—'s-EYE view a view from the position or standpoint of the person or thing specified. ●Most usually in ▶ **BIRD's-eye view** or ▶ **WORM's-eye view**.

get (or keep) one's EYE in become (or remain) able to make good judgements about a task or occupation in which one is engaged. *Brit.*

give someone the (glad) EYE look at someone in a way that clearly indicates one's sexual interest in them. *informal* ●An E20 British colloquialism.

| **1923** W. L. GEORGE *Hail, Columbia!* iv. 119 I have never seen an American girl give to a man in the street what the English call the 'glad eye'.

half an EYE a slight degree of perception or attention.

| **1962** C. EKWENSI *Burning Grass* (1990) iv. 20 His sandals were new because it was market day; or perhaps he had half an eye to some maiden.

have an EYE for be able to recognize, appreciate, and make good judgements about a particular thing.

have (or with) an EYE for (or on or to) the main chance look or be looking for an opportunity to take advantage of a situation for personal gain, especially when this is financial. ●The *main chance* literally, in the game of hazard, is a number (5, 6, 7, or 8) called by a player before throwing the dice.

hit someone in the EYE (or between the eyes) be very obvious or impressive. *informal*

keep an EYE out (*or* open) for look out for something with particular attention.

| 1996 *Guardian: Weekend* 21 Sept. 61/3 Keep an open eye for kingklip, a delectable fish, and the superb local hake.

my EYE (*or* all my eye and Betty Martin) nonsense. *informal*, *dated* ● Who or what *Betty Martin* was has never been satisfactorily explained. Another version of the saying also current in L18 was *all my eye and my elbow*. Used especially in spoken English to indicate scepticism about something.

| *1781 S. CRISPE *Letter* 16 Oct. Physic, to old, crazy Frames, like ours, *is all my eye and Betty Martin*—(a sea phrase that Admiral Jemm frequently makes use of).

one in the EYE for a disappointment or setback for someone or something. ● Used especially when the setback is perceived as being well deserved.

see EYE to eye have similar views or attitudes to something; be in full agreement.

| 1997 A. SIVANANDRAN *When Memory Dies* III. xi. 338 We don't see eye to eye about anything—work, having children, what's going on in the country.

with one EYE on giving some but not all one's attention to.

EYE ▶ *see* **a GLEAM in someone's eye**; ▶ *see* **keep one's eye on the BALL**; ▶ *see* **more to someone/thing than MEETS the eye**; ▶ *see* **turn a BLIND eye**.

EYEBALL to eyeball face to face with someone, especially in an aggressive way. ● Often as modifier: e.g., *an eyeball-to-eyeball confrontation*.

up to the (*or* one's) EYEBALLS very deeply involved. *informal* ● Generally used to emphasize the extreme degree of an undesirable situation or condition.

raise one's EYEBROWS (*or* an eyebrow) show surprise, disbelief, or mild disapproval.

by an EYELASH by a very small margin.

be all EYES be watching eagerly and attentively. ● Cf. ▶ **be all EARS**.

| 1955 N. NABOKOV *Annotated Lolita* (1970) II. ii. 165 The lesser nymphet ... would be all eyes, as the pavonine sun was all eyes on the gravel under the flowering trees.

clap (*or* lay *or* set) EYES on see. *informal* ● The sense of *clap* here suggests a sudden impression (cf. ▶ **CLAP hold of**).

close (*or* shut) one's EYES to refuse to notice or acknowledge something unwelcome or unpleasant.

EYES (out) on stalks full of eager curiosity or amazement. *informal*

have EYES bigger than one's stomach have asked for or taken more food than one can actually eat.

have EYES in the back of one's head observe everything that is happening, even when this is apparently impossible.

keep one's EYES open (*or* peeled *or* Brit. **skinned)** be on the alert; watch carefully or vigilantly for something.

make EYES at someone look at someone in a way that makes it clear one finds them sexually attractive.

open someone's EYES enlighten someone about certain realities; cause someone to realize or discover something.

shut one's EYES to be wilfully ignorant of.

| **1996** E. LOVELACE *Salt* iii. 40 Leave your father ... Just shut your eyes to everything around you and go.

EYES ▶ *see* **have SQUARE eyes**; ▶ *see* **pull the WOOL over someone's eyes**; ▶ *see* **up to the EARS**.

give one's EYE-TEETH for go to any lengths in order to obtain something. ●*Eye-teeth* are the two canine teeth in the upper jaw, under the eyes.

*1930 W. S. MAUGHAM *Cakes & Ale* i. 13 He'd give his eye-teeth to have written a book half as good.

EYE-TEETH ▶ *see* **CUT one's teeth**.

F

the acceptable FACE of the tolerable or attractive manifestation or aspect of. ●Very often negative; cf. British Prime Minister Edward Heath talking about the activities of the Lonrho company: 'the unpleasant and unacceptable face of capitalism' (*Hansard*, 1973).

someone's FACE fits someone has the necessary qualities for something.
| **1992** *Looks* July 41/2 My face fits and I've got the job!

FACE the music be confronted with the unpleasant consequences of one's actions. ●Recorded from M19 US, but still regarded in UK as a 'vulgar colloquialism' in 1897.

get out of someone's FACE stop harassing or annoying someone. *US*, *informal* ●Usually as imperative.

have the (brass) FACE to have the effrontery to (do something). *dated* ●Cf. ▶ BOLD as brass.

in your FACE aggressively obvious; assertive. ●Often as modifier: *in-your-face incivility*.
| **1996** *Sunday Telegraph* 4 Feb. 3/1 The … campaign reflects a growing trend of aggressive and 'in your face' advertisement that is alarming many within the industry.

lose FACE suffer a loss of respect; be humiliated. ●Originally associated with China and translating the Chinese expression *tiu lien*. Hence also *loss of face*.

make (or pull) a FACE (or faces) produce an expression on one's face that shows dislike, disgust, or some other negative emotion, or that is intended to be amusing.

off one's FACE very drunk or under the influence of illegal drugs. *informal*
| **1998** *Times Magazine* 15 Aug. 21/2 I've been accused of being off my face many times but you just go, by osmosis, with the people that you're with.

put a brave (or bold or good, etc.) FACE on something act as if something unpleasant or upsetting is not as bad as it really is.

save FACE retain respect; avoid humiliation. ●Cf. ▶ **lose FACE**. Also *save someone's face* 'enable someone to avoid humiliation'.
| **1994** T. BOSWELL *Cracking Show* II. iv. 28 And Rose got to save face, at least in his own eyes, with one last brassy news conference.

set one's FACE against oppose or resist with determination.

throw something back in someone's FACE reject something in a brusque or ungracious manner.

FACE ▶ *see* **not just a PRETTY face**.

the FACTS of life information about sexual functions and practices, especially as given to children or teenagers.

do (*or* take) a FADE run away. *informal*

without FAIL absolutely predictably; with no exception or cause for doubt. ● *Fail* as a noun in the sense of 'failure, deficiency' (from Old French *fail(l)e*) is obsolete apart from this phrase.

not have the FAINTEST have no idea. *informal* ● *Faintest* here is short for 'faintest idea'. Cf. ▶ **not have the FOGGIEST**.

a FAINT heart timidity or lack of willpower preventing one from achieving one's objective. ● *Faint heart never won fair lady* is a proverbial expression dating in this wording from E17; the idea, however, was current at least two centuries earlier.

FAIR and square 1 with absolute accuracy. **2** honestly and straight-forwardly. ● Also with the more usual adverbial forms *fairly and squarely*.

a FAIR deal equitable treatment.

FAIR dos just treatment. *Brit., informal* ● *Dos* (plural of *do*, noun) is pronounced du:z. Used mainly as a request to be treated fairly.

FAIR's fair used to request just treatment or assert that an arrangement is just. *informal*

a FAIR field and no favour equal conditions in a contest.

for FAIR completely and finally. *US, informal*
> **1967** J. BARTH *Sot-Weed Factor* (1987) II. v. 142 And when the matter of hostages arose, the mother had said 'Pray God they will take Harry, for then we'd be quit of him for fair, and not a penny poorer'.

no FAIR unfair. *N. Amer., informal* ● Often used in or as a petulant protestation.

FAIR ▶ *see* **a fair CRACK of the whip**; ▶ *see* **fair DINKUM**; ▶ *see* **it's a fair COP**.

(away) with the FAIRIES giving the impression of being mad, distracted, or in a dreamworld.

FAITH ▶ *see* **PUNIC faith**.

FALL in (*or* into) line conform with others or with accepted behaviour. ● With reference to military formation.

FALL off (the back of) a lorry (of goods) be acquired in illegal or unspecified circumstances. ● From the traditional bogus excuse given to the police by someone caught in possession of stolen goods.
> **1991** *Time Out* 13 Mar. 16/3 People buy so much stolen stuff that ... you can ... buy a video in Dixons and take it round the corner to a pub, say it fell off the back of a lorry and get 50 quid more than it cost you.

FALL (*or* land) on one's feet achieve a fortunate outcome to a difficult situation. ● From the supposed ability of cats always to land on their feet.
> **1980** S. HAZZARD *Transit of Venus* (1981) 123 In the postwar scramble, the Major had been lucky; had, as he explained, fallen on his feet.

FALL short (of) be deficient or inadequate; fail to reach a required goal. ● Used literally of a missile that fails to reach its target.

take the FALL receive blame or punishment, typically in the place of another person. *N. Amer., informal* ● Very similar to ▶ **take the RAP**. In L19 criminals' slang *fall* could mean an 'arrest', and this was later extended to mean 'term of imprisonment'. Cf. the US term *fall guy* (E20) for a scapegoat.

FALL ▶ *see* **come APART at the seams**; ▶ *see* **fall between two STOOLS**; ▶ *see* **fall from GRACE**; ▶ *see* **fall on DEAF ears**; ▶ *see* **fall on STONY ground**; ▶ *see* **bend over BACKWARDS**; ▶ *see* **fall PREY to**; ▶ *see* **fall VICTIM to**.

a FALSE dawn a misleadingly hopeful sign. ● A transient light in the sky which precedes the true dawn by about an hour, especially in eastern countries.

| **1998** *Times* 6 Mar. 34/8 Unfortunately, BTR's investors have seen other false dawns.

the (*or* one's) FAMILY jewels a man's genitals. *informal*

in the FAMILY way pregnant. *informal*

sell (*or* sell off) the FAMILY silver part with a valuable resource for immediate advantage. ● With reference to a speech by the former British prime minister Harold Macmillan to the Tory Reform Group in 1985 on privatization (the selling off of nationalized industries to private companies), likening it to the sales of heirlooms undertaken by impoverished aristocratic families: 'First of all the Georgian silver goes ...'

FAMOUS for fifteen minutes (especially of an ordinary person) enjoying a brief period of fame before fading back into obscurity. ● From a remark by pop artist Andy Warhol (1927–87): 'In the future everybody will be world famous for fifteen minutes' (quoted in *Andy Warhol*, 1968). Short-lived celebrity or notoriety is often referred to as *fifteen minutes of fame* (see quot.).

| **1998** *Spectator* 21 Mar. 23/1 I have had my 15 minutes of fame.

FAMOUS last words an overconfident assertion that may well soon be proved wrong by events. ● Apparently originated as a catch-phrase in M20 forces' slang. It is used as an ironic comment or reply when someone has made such an assertion.

FANCY one's (*or* someone's) chances believe that one (*or* someone else) is likely to be successful.

FANTASTIC ▶ *see* **TRIP the light fantastic**.

be a FAR cry from be very different from.

| **1987** *National Geographic* Sept. 302/2 'I walk out and hire a helicopter ... an expensive way to mine.' And a far cry from the ancient Maori canoe expeditions ... to hunt for jade.

FAR and away by a very large amount. ● An more emphatic way of saying *by far*.

FAR be it from (*or* for) me to I am very reluctant to—. ● Used to express hesitation, especially about doing something which one thinks may be resented.

so FAR so good progress has been satisfactory up to now.

> **1998** *New Scientist* 26 Sept. 31/3 The project has just now reached a rigorous testing phase, and the researchers say so far, so good.

to a FARE-THEE-WELL to perfection; thoroughly. ● Also *to a fare-you-well*. L18 US in origin.

> **1911** R. D. SAUNDERS *Col. Todhunter* i. 3 The fight's begun, and we've got to rally around old Bill Strickland to a fare-you-well.

FARM ▶ *see* **BUY the farm**.

pull a FAST one try to gain an unfair advantage by rapid action of some sort. *informal* ● Originally E20 US slang; also *put over a fast one*.

> **1943** H. BOLITHO *Combat Report* 107l said … that they must not try to pull a fast one on me.

the FAT is in the fire something has been said or done that is about to cause trouble, anger, etc. ● In this current sense with reference to the sizzling and spitting caused by a spillage of cooking fat into an open flame. The expression is recorded from M16 in the sense that something has gone irretrievably wrong.

live off (*or* on) the FAT of the land have the best of everything. ● Cf. Genesis 45:18, Pharaoh's invitation to Joseph's brothers: 'ye shall eat the fat of the land.' *Fat* meaning 'the best part' or 'choicest produce' is obsolete except in this expression.

a FATE worse than death a terrible experience, especially that of seduction or rape. ● Formerly euphemistic, now often humorous.

seal someone's FATE make it inevitable that something unpleasant will happen to someone.

FATE ▶ *see* **TEMPT fate**.

founding FATHER someone who establishes an institution. ● Used in particular (often with initial capitals) of an American statesman at the time of the Revolution, especially a member of the Federal Constitutional Convention of 1787.

how's your FATHER sexual intercourse. *Brit., slang* ● A pre-World War I music-hall catch-phrase, it was earlier used to mean 'nonsense' before acquiring its present sexual sense. It is now used also of a penis.

> **1992** A. LAMBERT *Rather English Marriage* (1993) v 94 And my name is Agnes Odejayi and you may call me Aggie like everyone else … But you may *not* call me Mrs Owsyerfather.

like FATHER, like son a son's character or behaviour can be expected to resemble that of his father. ● Cf. the Latin tag *qualis pater, talis filius*. The female equivalent, *like mother, like daughter*, is based on Ezekiel 16:44.

kill the FATTED calf produce a lavish celebratory feast. ● The participial adjective *fatted* is an archaism, and it has been superseded by *fattened* in other contexts. The allusion is to the New Testament story of the prodigal son (Luke 15:11–32), in which the forgiving father orders his best calf to be killed in order to make a feast to celebrate the return of his wayward son.

to a FAULT to an extent verging on excess. ● Used of someone who strongly displays a commendable quality such as generosity.

do someone a FAVOUR do something for someone as an act of kindness. *Brit.*, *informal* ● In imperative (*do me a favour!*) used as a way of expressing brusque dismissal or rejection of a remark or suggestion.

FAVOURITE son a famous man who is particularly popular and praised for his achievements in his native area. ● In the US the term is used specifically of a person supported as a presidential candidate by delegates from the candidate's home state.

put the FEAR of God in (*or* into) someone cause someone to be very frightened.

without FEAR or favour not influenced by any consideration of the people involved in a situation; impartially.
> **1906** R. KIPLING 'Children's Song' in *Puck of Pook's Hill* 19 That we, with Thee, may walk uncowed By fear or favour of the crowd.

a ghost (*or* spectre *or* skeleton *or* death's head) at the FEAST someone or something that brings gloom or sadness to an otherwise pleasant or celebratory occasion. ● The *ghost* or *spectre* of Banquo at Macbeth's feast (Shakespeare *Macbeth* III. iv) is the most famous literary instance of this phenomenon. The version of the expression with *skeleton* (M19) probably refers to the ancient Egyptian practice of having the coffin of a dead person, adorned with a painted portrait of the deceased, present at a funeral banquet. A *death's head* or skull was formerly used a *memento mori*.

FEAST one's eyes on gaze at with pleasure.

FEAST or famine either too much of something or too little.

FEAST of reason intellectual talk. ● From Alexander Pope's description of congenial conversation in *Imitations of Horace* II. I: 'The feast of reason and the flow of soul'.

a movable FEAST an event which takes place at no regular time. ● With reference to a religious feast day (especially Easter Day and the other Christian holy days whose dates are related to it) which does not occur on the same calendar date each year.

a FEATHER in one's cap an achievement to be proud of. ● This phrase was earlier used derogatorily; cf. B. E. *A New Dictionary of the ... Canting Crew* (pre-1700), s.v. Feather where 'He has a Feather in his Cap' is defined as 'a Periphrasis for a Fool'. However, by M18 it was acquiring its modern laudatory sense.
> **1998** *Times* 11 Aug. 40/3 [T]o take six wickets in the last innings of the game was a feather in his cap.

FEATHER one's (own) nest make money, usually illicitly and at someone else's expense. ● With reference to the habit of some birds of using feathers (their own or another bird's) to line the interior of their nest. First recorded use in this metaphorical sense by P. Stubbes in his *Anatomie of Abuses* (1583).

> **1998** *Spectator* 4 July 16/3 It won't solve a damned thing except feather the nests of a lot of dodgy pen-pushers and party hacks.

in fine (or high) FEATHER in good spirits. ● With allusion to a bird in its breeding plumage as being in peak condition, neither moulting nor moping.

FEATHER ▶ *see* **show the WHITE feather**.

FED UP to the teeth (or back teeth) extremely annoyed.

off one's FEED having no appetite. *informal* ● An expression used of a horse or other domestic animal and only humorously of a person.

FEEL ▶ *see* **feel one's AGE**; ▶ *see* **feel someone's COLLAR**; ▶ *see* **feel the DRAUGHT**; ▶ *see* **feel one's OATS**; ▶ *see* **feel the PINCH**; ▶ *see* **feel the PULSE of**.

have FEET of clay have a fatal flaw in a character that is otherwise powerful or admirable. ● With reference to the statue seen in a dream by Nebuchadnezzar, king of Babylon, which although it was almost entirely constructed from fine metals had feet of clay; when these were smashed, the whole image was brought down and destroyed (Daniel 2:31–5).

have (or keep) one's FEET on the ground be (or remain) practical and sensible.

think on one's FEET be quick-witted. *informal*

FEET ▶ *see* **be RUN off one's feet**; ▶ *see* **DIG in one's heels**; ▶ *see* **DRAG one's feet**; ▶ *see* **FALL on one's feet**; ▶ *see* **KEEP one's feet**; ▶ *see* **SIX feet under**; ▶ *see* **VOTE with one's feet**.

in (or at) one FELL swoop all in one go. ● Quoting Shakespeare *Macbeth* (1605): 'Oh hell-kite! ... All my pretty chickens, and their dam At one fell swoop?' (IV. iii)

over the FENCE unreasonable or unacceptable. *Austral. & NZ, informal*

> **1964** *Sydney Morning Herald* 18 Sept. 11/1 Some publications which unduly emphasize sex were 'entirely over the fence'.

sit on the FENCE avoid making a decision or choice. ● The two sides of a fence are seen in this and related idioms as representing the two opposing or conflicting positions or interests involved in a particular debate or situation.

> **1998** *Spectator* 13 June 7/1 If Stephen Dorrell ... was tempted to outflank Labour from the Left ... his successors seem to be seeking a handy fence to sit on.

FENCES ▶ *see* **MEND fences**.

FETCH and carry go backwards and forwards bringing things to someone in a servile fashion. ● Used originally of the activity of a retrieving dog. Also as a noun *fetch-and-carry*.

> ***1591** W. SHAKESPEARE *Two Gentlemen of Verona* III. i. She hath more qualities then a Water-Spaniell ... Imprimis: Shee can fetch and carry.

in fine (or good or high) FETTLE in very good condition. ● *Fettle* was recorded in an M18 glossary of Lancashire dialect as meaning 'dress, case, condition'. Now seldom found outside this phrase and its variants.

FEW and far between scarce; infrequent.

have a FEW drink enough alcohol to be slightly drunk. *informal* ● *Drinks* is understood after *few*.

FIDDLE while Rome burns be concerned with relatively trivial matters while ignoring the serious or disastrous events going on around one. ● With allusion to Suetonius' description (*Nero* xxxviii) of the behaviour of the Roman emperor Nero during the great fire that destroyed much of Rome in AD 64.

(as) fit as a FIDDLE in very good health. ● Earlier also *fine as a fiddle*; both versions of the simile used in E17.

on the FIDDLE engaged in cheating or swindling. *informal* ● *Fiddle* was L19 US slang for a 'swindle'.

play second FIDDLE to take a subordinate role to someone or something. ● The expression derives from the respective roles of the fiddles or violins in an orchestra. Both *to play first fiddle* and *to play third fiddle* are much less common. The implication of *playing second fiddle* is often that it is somewhat demeaning.

> *1809 B. H. MALKIN tr. *Gil Blas* x. xi. I am quite at your service to play second fiddle in all your laudable enterprises.

a face as long as a FIDDLE a dismal face.

hold the FIELD avoid being superseded.

play the FIELD avoid an exclusive commitment, especially indulge in a series of sexual relationships without committing oneself to anyone. *informal*

> *1936 L. LEFKO *Public Relations* ii. 18 He hasn't any steady. He plays the field—blonde, brunette, or what have you.

FIELD ▶ *see* **a FAIR field and no favour**.

something FIERCE to a great and almost overwhelming extent; intensely or furiously. *chiefly N. Amer., informal*

FIFTEEN ▶ *see* **FAMOUS for fifteen minutes**.

FIFTH column an organized body sympathizing with and working for the enemy within a country at war or otherwise under attack. ● Translating Spanish *quinta columna*; during the Spanish Civil War, an extra body of supporters was claimed by General Mola as being within Madrid when he besieged the city with four columns of Nationalist forces in 1936.

take the FIFTH (amendment) (in the US) exercise the right of refusing to answer questions in order to avoid incriminating oneself. ● The allusion is to Article V of the ten original amendments (1791) to the Constitution of the United States, which states that 'no person ... shall be compelled in any criminal case to be a witness against himself.'

not give (*or* care) a FIG not have the slightest concern about. ● *Fig* was formerly used in a variety of expressions to signify something valueless or contemptible, esp. in the scornful exclamation *A fig for —!*

in full FIG wearing the smart clothes appropriate for an event or occasion. ● In the sense of 'dress, equipment', *fig* is used solely in this phrase (M19).

FIGHT fire with fire use the weapons or tactics of one's enemy or opponent, even if one finds them distasteful.

> **1998** *New Scientist* 19 Sept. 3/3 [M]any opponents of biotechnology might say that they are simply fighting fire with fire. After all, the biotechnology industry is not averse to misquoting people when it suits them.

FIGHT a losing battle be fated to fail in one's efforts.

FIGHT shy of be unwilling to undertake or become involved with.

FIGHT or flight the instinctive physiological response to a threatening situation, which readies one either to resist violently or to run away.

FIGHT ▶ *see* **fight like CAT and dog**; ▶ *see* **fight TOOTH and nail**.

FIGURE of fun a person who is considered ridiculous.

> **1990** R. CRITCHFIELD *Among British* vii. 390 [Reagan] was the first American leader in my lifetime who was widely regarded over here as a figure of fun.

FILL someone's shoes (or boots) take over someone's function or duties and fulfil them satisfactorily. *informal*

FILL ▶ *see* **fill the BILL**.

FINAL ▶ *see* **the last STRAW**.

FIND one's feet **1** stand up and become able to walk. **2** establish oneself in a particular situation or enterprise.

FIND God experience a religious conversion or awakening.

FIND it in one's heart to do something allow or force oneself to do something. ● Often with negative.

FINDERS keepers (losers weepers) whoever finds something by chance is entitled to keep it (and the person who lost it will just have to lament its loss). *informal* ● Mainly used humorously, this expression has been current since E19, although the idea goes back much further and is found in the Roman dramatist Plautus. A variant sometimes heard is *findings keepings*.

cut (or run) it (or things) FINE allow a very small margin of something, usually time.

FINE feathers beautiful clothes. ● Alluding to the proverb *fine feathers make fine birds*, meaning that an eye-catching appearance makes a person seem beautiful or impressive. Known in England since L19, it is recorded in E16 in French: *les belles plumes font les beaux oiseaux*.

have (or get) something down to a FINE ART achieve a high level of skill, facility, or accomplishment in some activity through experience.

not to put too FINE a point on it to speak bluntly.

one FINE day at some unspecified or unknown time.

the FINER points of the more complex or detailed aspects of.

—'s FINEST the police of a specified city. *informal* ● Used humorously or ironically; originally and especially North American.

> **1998** *Oldie* July 7/2 We are quite sure that Wakefield's finest are familiar with the expression *O spurie! Noli me tangere!*—but more usually in its English translation: 'Don't touch me, you bastard!'

one's FINEST hour the time of one's greatest success.

> **1940** W. S. CHURCHILL *Speech to House of Commons* 18 June Let us therefore brace ourselves to that duty, and so bear ourselves that, if the British Commonwealth and its Empire lasts for a thousand years, men will still say, 'This was their finest hour'.

get (or pull) one's FINGER out cease prevaricating and start to act. *Brit., informal*

give someone the FINGER make a gesture with the middle finger raised as an obscene sign of contempt. *N. Amer., informal* ● Since 1976 sometimes called the Rockefeller Gesture after Nelson Rockefeller was seen making it on a news film. Cf. ▶ **flip someone the BIRD**.

have a FINGER in every pie (or many pies) be involved in a large and varied number of activities or enterprises. ● Also *have a finger in the pie* (M17), which often has the implication of being involved in an annoying or interfering way.

have (or keep) one's FINGER on the pulse be aware of all the latest news or developments.

lay a FINGER on someone touch someone, usually with the intention of harming them. ● Usually in the context of warning someone against employing physical force.

POINT the finger openly accuse someone or apportion blame.

> **1998** *Spectator* 2 May 12/3 Reason suggests that one should point the finger at those who whipped up the emotion in the first place.

put the FINGER on inform against someone to the authorities. *informal*

put one's FINGER on something identify something exactly.

twist (or wind or wrap) someone around one's little FINGER have the ability to make someone do whatever one wants.

be all FINGERS and thumbs (or all thumbs) be clumsy or awkward in one's actions. *Brit., informal* ● Earlier (M16) in the obsolete form *each finger is a thumb*; hence *all thumbs*, an M–L19 colloquialism indicating complete lack of dexterity.

burn one's FINGERS (or get one's FINGERS burned/burnt) suffer unpleasant consequences as a result of one's actions. ● Used especially in financial contexts (see quot.).

> **1998** *Times* 4 Aug. 23/5 [An] American buyer remains a possibility, although it is not entirely clear why any would want to risk getting their fingers burnt twice.

click one's FINGERS make a sharp clicking sound between a finger and the thumb, typically in order to attract attention in a peremptory way or to accompany the beat of music.

snap one's FINGERS at make a clicking sound with one's fingers as a gesture of contempt towards somone or something.

FINGERS ▶ *see* **CROSS one's fingers**; ▶ *see* **have one's fingers in the TILL**; ▶ *see* **work one's fingers to the BONE**.

at one's FINGERTIPS readily available. ● Used especially of information.

by one's FINGERTIPS only with difficulty; barely.
| **1990** *Current History* Jan. 20/2 In early 1988, United States Assistant Secretary of State Elliott Abrams said that General Noriega was clinging to power 'by his fingertips'.

to one's FINGERTIPS totally; completely.

a fight to the FINISH a fight, contest, or match which only ends with the complete defeat of one of the parties involved.

breathe FIRE be fiercely angry. ● The implied comparison is with a fire-breathing dragon.

catch FIRE become interesting or exciting. ● From literally going up in flames.

FIRE and brimstone the supposed torments of hell. ● In the Bible the means of divine punishment of the wicked (e.g., Genesis 19:24, Revelation 21:8). *Brimstone* (from OE *brynstán* = burning stone) is an obsolete word for 'sulphur' and now seldom occurs outside this phrase, except as the name of a species of sulphur-yellow butterfly.

FIRE in the (*or* one's) belly a powerful sense of ambition or determination.
| **1951** N. ANNAN *L. Stephen* ix. 275 There is no fire in the belly, no sense of urgency.

go through FIRE (and water) face any peril. ● Originally with reference to the medieval practice of trial by ordeal, which could take the form of making an accused person hold or walk on red-hot iron or of throwing them into water.

light a FIRE under someone stimulate someone to work or act more quickly or enthusiastically. *N. Amer.*

set the world (*or Brit.* Thames) on FIRE do something remarkable or sensational. ● Very often with an implied or expressed negative. Cf. ▶ **set the HEATHER on fire**.
| **1976** D. FRANCIS *In Frame* (1983) iv. 66 He was the same sort of man my father had been, middle-aged, middle-of-the-road, expert at his chosen job but unlikely to set the world on fire.

under FIRE being rigorously criticized. ● Literally, being shot at.
| **1993** *Albuquerque* (New Mexico) *Journal* 22 Jan. A1/3 Zoe Baird, under fire for hiring illegal aliens to work in her home, has withdrawn her name as President Clinton's nominee for US Attorney General.

where's the FIRE? what's the hurry? *informal* ● Used jocularly to someone in a hurry or state of agitation.

> **1963** J. F. STRAKER *Final Witness* xvi. 174 'Where's the fire, dear boy?' he drawled. 'Do we really have to run for it?'

FIRE ▶ *see* **PLAY with fire**.

FIRING on all (four) cylinders working or functioning at a peak level. ● A metaphor from an internal-combustion engine: a cylinder is said to be firing when the fuel inside it is ignited. Also with other verbs (see quot.).

> **1932** P. G. WODEHOUSE *Hot Water* xv. 245 His smiling face, taken in conjunction with the bottle of wine which he carried, conveyed to Gordon Carlisle the definite picture of a libertine operating on all six cylinders.

FIREMAN ▶ *see* **VISITING fireman**.

be on FIRM ground be sure of one's facts or secure in one's position, especially in a discussion.

a FIRM hand (on the reins) strict discipline or control. ● From controlling a horse through one's handling of the reins.

FIRST come, first served used to indicate that people will be dealt with strictly in the order in which they arrive or apply.

FIRST off as a first point; first of all. *chiefly N. Amer., informal*

> **1880* 'MARK TWAIN' *Tramp Abroad* xx. 193 First-off, I thought it would certainly give me the botts.

FIRST past the post   **1** (of a contestant, especially a horse, in a race) winning a race by being the first to reach the finishing line.   **2** *Brit.* denoting an electoral system whereby a candidate or party is selected by achievement of a simple majority. ● In sense 2 often attributive, as in *the first-past-the-post system* (in contrast to *proportional representation* or a *transferable vote*).

FIRST thing early in the morning; before anything else.

FIRST things first important matters should be attended to before anything else. ● The title of a book by G. Jackson, subtitled 'Addresses to young men' (1894).

FIRST up   **1** first of all.   **2** at the first attempt. *Austral.*

of the FIRST order (*or* magnitude) used to denote something that is excellent or considerable of its kind. ● Stars *of the first magnitude* are the most brilliant. Cf. French *du premier ordre*.

FIRST ▶ *see* **first among EQUALS**; ▶ *see* **first BLOOD**; ▶ *see* **get to first BASE**; ▶ *see* **not KNOW the first thing about something**; ▶ *see* **of the first WATER**.

a big FISH in a small (*or* little) pond a person seen as important and influential only within the limited scope of a small organization or group.

drink like a FISH drink excessive amounts. ● Now used to indicate that a person is habitually consuming too much alcohol.

> **1744* T. GRAY *Letter* 26 Apr.Mr. Trollope and I are in a course of Tar-water; ... I drink like a fish.

FISH in troubled waters make a profit out of trouble or upheaval.

a FISH out of water a person in a completely unsuitable environment or situation.

> *1613 S. PURCHAS *Pilgrimage* VI. xii. The Arabians out of the desarts are as Fishes out of the Water.

have other (*or* bigger) FISH to fry have other or more important matters to attend to.

> 1985 G. BENFORD *Artifact* IV. iv. 243 Kontos can throw a fit back there, chew the rug, anything— it won't matter. His government has bigger fish to fry.

like shooting FISH in a barrel done very easily.

> 1992 L. COLWIN *Home Cooking* (1993) xxvii. 133 I fear that's the urgency of greed. Picking cultivated berries is like shooting fish in a barrel.

neither FISH, flesh, nor good red herring of indefinite character and difficult to identify or classify. ● With allusion to distinctions made in dietary laws formerly laid down by the Church. For *red herring* see ▶ **a RED herring**. Proverbial since M16. Very similar is *neither fish, flesh, nor fowl*.

there are plenty more FISH in the sea there are many other people in the world. ● With allusion to the proverb *there are as good fish in the sea as ever came out of it*. Used especially as a consolatory remark to someone whose romantic relationship has ended.

> 1987 J. HIGGINS *Little Death Music* xvii.'Cheer up,' she said. 'There are plenty more fish in the sea.'

FISH ▶ *see* **a BIG cheese**; ▶ *see* **a pretty KETTLE of fish**.

a FISHING expedition a search or investigation undertaken with the hope, though not the stated purpose, of discovering information.

> 1961 E. S. GARDNER *Case of Bigamous Spouse* xv. I am not going to permit counsel to go on a fishing expedition.

make a good (*or* poor etc.) FIST of (or at) do something well (*or* badly *or* as specified). *informal*

FIST ▶ *see* **an IRON hand in a velvet glove**.

FIT for the gods excellent; extremely pleasing.

FIT to be tied very angry. *informal*

FIT to bust with great energy.

> 1992 D. GLAZER *Last Oasis* 149 I'd be rushing back at night, pedalling on my bike fit to bust.

give someone a FIT greatly shock, frighten, or anger someone. *informal* ● *Have* (or *throw*) *a fit* is used with similar hyperbolical sense.

FIT (verb) ▶ *see* **fill the BILL**; ▶ *see* **fit like a GLOVE**.

FIT (adj.) ▶ *see* **fit as a FIDDLE**; ▶ *see* **fit as a FLEA**.

in FITS in a state of hysterical amusement. *informal*

in (*or* by) FITS and starts with irregular bursts of activity.

take FIVE take a short break, relax. ●*Five* here is 'a five-minute break'.

FIX someone's WAGON bring about someone's downfall, spoil someone's chances of success. *US*

> **1951** T. CAPOTE *Grass Harp* i. 13She said her brother would fix my wagon, which he did; ... I've still got a scar where he hit me.

get a FIX on assess or determine the nature or facts of: obtain a clear understanding of. *informal* ●From the action of determining the position of an aircraft, ship, etc., by visual or radio bearings or astronomical observation.

fly the FLAG 1 (of a ship) be registered to a particular country and sail under its flag. **2** represent or demonstrate support for one's country, political party, or organization, especially when one is abroad. ●In sense 2 also *show* or *carry* or *wave the flag* (see quot.).

> **1963** *Times* 7 Feb. 18/6 This was a genuine effort ... to show the flag at a time when they thought it should be shown. A series of six British products would be advertised.

keep the FLAG flying 1 represent one's country or organization, especially when abroad. **2** show continued commitment to something, especially in the face of adversity. ●From the practice in naval warfare of lowering the flag on a defeated ship to signify a wish to surrender. Sense 1 is very similar to sense 2 of ▶ **fly the FLAG**. Sense 2 is represented in the 1914 song-title *Keep the Old Flag Flying*.

put the FLAGS (*or* flag) out celebrate publicly. ●Cf. the title of a novel by Evelyn Waugh, *Put Out More Flags* (1942), with an epigraph from the Chinese, part of which reads 'a drunk military man should order gallons and put out more flags in order to increase his military splendour.'

show the FLAG make a gesture of support for or solidarity with one's country, political party, or organization, especially when one is abroad or among outsiders. ●Used literally of a naval vessel making an official visit to a foreign port, especially as a show of strength. See also ▶ **fly the FLAG** sense 2.

wrap oneself in the FLAG make an excessive show of one's patriotism, especially for political ends. *chiefly N. Amer.*

run something up the FLAGPOLE test the popularity of a new idea or proposal. ●The idea is of hoisting a particular flag to see who salutes.

an old FLAME a former lover. *informal*

FLAMES ▶ *see* **SHOOT someone/thing down in flames**.

someone's ears are FLAPPING someone is listening intently in order to overhear something not intended for them. *informal*

FLASH in the pan a thing or person whose sudden but brief success is not repeated or repeatable. ●With allusion to priming of a firearm, the flash being from an explosion of gunpowder within the lock.

> **1998** *New Scientist* 28 Mar. 53/2 But Java ... may turn out to be flash in the pan: books on human–computer interaction struggle to stay abreast of rapid developments in computing.

(as) quick as a FLASH very quickly. ●Used especially of a person's response or reaction.

fall FLAT fail completely to produce the intended or expected effect.

fall FLAT on one's face **1** fall over forwards. **2** fail in an embarrassingly obvious way.

FLAT out **1** as fast or as hard as possible. *informal* **2** *chiefly N. Amer.* without hesitation or reservation; unequivocally.

on the FLAT **1** on level ground as opposed to uphill. **2** (of a horse-race) on an open course as opposed to one with jumps. ● In sense 2 also *on the Flat*.

FLAT ▶ *see* **flat as a PANCAKE**.

catch someone FLAT-FOOTED take someone by surprise or at a disadvantage. *informal* ● The opposite of *flat-footed* in this metaphorical use is ▶ **on one's TOES**.

| **1998** *Field* Apr. 36/1 Farming and forestry were both caught flat-footed when fashion changed.

FLATTER to deceive encourage on insufficient grounds and cause disappointment.

| **1913** *Field* 15 Nov. 1046/2 Two furlongs from home Maiden Erlegh looked most dangerous, but he flattered only to deceive.

go FLATTING leave the family home to live in a flat. *Austral. & NZ*

FLAVOUR of the month someone or something that enjoys a short period of great popularity; the current fashion. ● The phrase originated in a marketing campaign in US ice-cream parlours in the 1940s, when a particular flavour of ice cream would be singled out for the month for special promotion.

(as) fit as a FLEA in very good health. ● With reference to a flea's agility.

a FLEA in one's ear a sharp reproof. ● Formerly *a flea in one's ear* also meant something that agitates or alarms one; cf. French *avoir la puce à l'oreille*. Now often *give someone a flea in the ear* or *send someone away with a flea in their ear*.

go the way of all FLESH die or come to an end. ● *All flesh* in the Authorized Version of the Bible is used of all human and animal life. Cf. the dying words of King David in 1 Kings 2:2 'I go the way of all the earth' (in the Douay Bible (1609), 'I enter into the way of all flesh').

in the FLESH in person rather than via a telephone, film, article, etc.

make someone's FLESH creep (or crawl) cause someone to feel fear, horror, or disgust. ● Cf. ▶ **give someone the CREEPS**.

one's (own) FLESH AND BLOOD near relatives; close family.

put FLESH on (the bones of) something add more details to something which only exists in a draft or outline form. ● Also *flesh something out*.

FLESH ▶ *see* **one's POUND of flesh**.

FLEX ▶ *see* **flex one's MUSCLES**.

FLEXIBLE ▶ *see* **flexible FRIEND**.

give someone the FLICK (or get the flick) reject (or be rejected) in a casual or offhand way. *chiefly Austral., informal*

die (*or* drop) like FLIES die or collapse in large numbers.

drink with the FLIES drink alone. *Austral. & NZ, informal*

> **1963** D. WHITTINGTON *Mile Pegs* 177 'Have a drink?' the larrikin invited. 'Or do you prefer drinking with the flies?'

there are no FLIES on — the person mentioned is very quick and astute.
● Early instances of this expression suggest that this originated with reference to cattle who were so active that no flies settled on them. Noted in M19 as being very common in Australia as a general expression of approbation. In the US it could also have the sense that the person concerned is of superior breeding or behaves honestly.

in full FLIGHT running (away) as rapidly as possible.

> **1938** *Life* 6 June 22/3 A week later General Cedillo was reported in full flight through the bush, with Federal troops hot on his heels.

FLIP one's lid (*or* chiefly US **wig)** suddenly go mad or lose one's self-control. *informal*

do a moonlight FLIT make a hurried, usually nocturnal, removal or change of abode, especially in order to avoid paying one's rent. *informal* ● *Make a moonlight flitting* is recorded from E19 and appears to have originated in northern England or Scotland. The expression is now often shortened to *do a moonlight*.

FLOG a dead horse waste energy on a lost cause or unalterable situation.

> **1971** *Cabinet Maker & Retail Furnisher* 1 Oct. 14/2 If this is the case, we are flogging a dead horse in still trying to promote the scheme.

be in full FLOOD have gained momentum; be at the height of activity. ● Used in the literal sense of a river that is swollen and overflowing its banks, and figuratively especially of someone talking volubly (cf. ▶ **in full FLOW** sense 1).

from the FLOOR (of a speech or question) delivered by an individual member at a meeting or assembly, not by a representative on the platform.

take the FLOOR **1** begin to dance on a dance floor. **2** speak in a debate or assembly.

FLOOR ▶ *see* **CROSS the floor**.

FLOTSAM and jetsam useless or discarded objects. ● Respectively referring to things found floating in the water and things thrown into the water. In figurative use since M19. The two nouns are almost always associated and are seldom used independently.

go with the FLOW be relaxed; accept a situation. *informal* ● From going with the current of a stream rather than trying to swim against it.

in full FLOW **1** talking fluently and easily and showing no sign of stopping. **2** performing vigorously and enthusiastically.

the FLOWER of the finest individuals out of a number of people or things.
● Middle and Early Modern English did not recognize the modern distinction

in spelling and sense between *flower* and *flour*, and the earliest instances of this expression relate to the sense that in Modern English would be spelt *flour*, the idea being that of the finest part of the wheat (see quot.).

| **1508** W. DUNBAR *Poems* vii. 81Prynce of fredom, and flour of gentilnes.

FLUFF ▶ *see* **BIT of fluff**.

in the first FLUSH in a state of freshness and vigour. ● The exact origins of *flush* as a noun are obscure; early senses share the idea of a sudden rush or abundance of something (e.g. water, growth of grass, emotion, etc.). Usually followed by *of*.

FLUSH ▶ *see* **a BUSTED flush**.

FLUTTER the dovecot(e)s alarm, startle, or upset a sedate or conventionally-minded community. ● Also *cause a flutter among the dovecotes* (or *in the dovecote*); cf. ▶ **put the CAT among the pigeons**. Possibly with allusion to Shakespeare *Coriolanus* v. v. 115: 'like an eagle in a dove-cote, I Fluttered your Volscians in Corioli.'

| **1998** *Spectator* 25 Apr. 18/3 Such a move would cause far too much fluttering in the Whitehall dovecote.

FLUTTER one's eyelashes at flirt with. ● From the action of opening and closing one's eyes rapidly in a coyly flirtatious manner.

FLY the coop make one's escape. *informal*

| **1991** J. PHILLIPS *You'll Never Eat Lunch* 415 Has David left? Nah, he would want to make sure I'm really ensconced, or I might fly the coop.

FLY high be very successful; prosper. ● Hence the noun *high-flyer* (or *high-flier*) (M17) applied to a successful and ambitious person.

a FLY in amber a curious relic of the past, preserved into the present. ● Alluding to the bodies of insects often found preserved in amber.

FLY in the face of be openly at variance with what is usual or expected.

FLY a kite **1** make a kite rise and remain suspended in the air. **2** *informal* try something out to test opinion. ● A historical sense of the phrase was 'raise money by an accommodation bill' i.e. raise money on credit, and this sense of testing public opinion of one's creditworthiness gave rise to the current (M20) figurative sense 2. The imperative *go fly a kite!* is a mainly US colloquialism meaning *go away!*

FLY the nest (of a young person) leave their parent's home to set up home elsewhere. *informal* ● The literal sense relates to a young bird's departure from its nest on becoming able to fly. Cf. ▶ **EMPTY nester**.

a FLY in the ointment a minor irritation or other factor that spoils the success or enjoyment of something. ● With allusion to Ecclesiastes 10:1 'Dead flies cause the ointment of the apothecary to send forth a stinking savour.'

| **1998** *Times* 18 May 49/5 Before you conclude that I have become a raging Europhile, let me say that there is a fly in the ointment.

FLY off the handle lose one's temper suddenly and unexpectedly. *informal* ● With reference to the flying off of a loose head of an axe.

a FLY on the wall an unnoticed observer of a particular situation. ●Very often as a modifier, as in *fly-on-the-wall documentary*, which refers to a film-making technique whereby events are merely observed and presented realistically with minimum interference rather than acted out under direction.

a FLY on the wheel a person who overestimates his or her own influence. ●With reference to Aesop's fable of a fly sitting on the axletree of a moving chariot and saying, 'See what a dust I raise.'

on the FLY **1** while in motion. **2** while busy or active. **3** (of an addition or modification in computing) carried out during the running of a program without interrupting the run.

like a blue-arsed FLY in an extremely hectic or frantic way. *Brit. vulgar slang* ●With reference to the frenetic buzzing about of a bluebottle.

someone/thing wouldn't hurt (*or* harm) a FLY someone/thing is inoffensive and harmless.

FLY ▶ *see* fly the **FLAG**.

take a FLYER take a chance. *chiefly N. Amer.*
| **1998** *Times* 17 July 22/3 Or we [i.e. journalists] can take a flyer: share a hunch and risk coming a cropper.

with FLYING colours with distinction. ●In former military parlance, *flying colours* meant having the regimental flag flying as a sign of success or victory; a conquered army usually had to *lower* (or *strike*) *its colours*.

FOAM ▶ *see* **FROTH** at the mouth.

in a FOG in a state of perplexity; unable to think clearly or understand something.

not have the FOGGIEST (idea *or* notion) have no idea at all. *chiefly Brit., informal*

FOLLOW one's nose **1** trust to one's instincts. **2** move along guided by one's sense of smell. **3** go straight ahead.

FOLLOW suit **1** (in bridge, whist, and other card games) play a card of the suit led. **2** conform to another's actions.

FOLLOW ▶ *see* follow in someone's **FOOTSTEPS**.

FOOD for thought something that warrants serious consideration or reflection.

FOOL's gold something deceptively attractive and promising in appearance. ●*Fool's gold* is the name popularly given to any yellow metal, such as pyrite or chalcopyrite, that may be mistaken for gold.

be no (*or* nobody's) FOOL be a shrewd or prudent person.

more FOOL — a specified person is unwise to behave in such a way. ●Used as an exclamation when one is told about someone's imprudent actions.

get (or start) off on the right (or wrong) FOOT make a good (or bad) start at something, especially a task or relationship.

> **1998** *Spectator* 24 Jan. 14/3 This relationship got off on the wrong foot ..., when Mr Cook's scathing attack on the government over the arms-to-Iraq affair was felt to include some officials as well.

have a FOOT in both camps have an interest or stake in two parties or sides without commitment to either.

have (or get) a FOOT in the door gain or have a first introduction to a profession or organization.

have one FOOT in the grave be near death through old age or illness. *informal* ● Generally humorous.

put one's best FOOT forward embark on an undertaking with as much speed, effort, and determination as possible.

put FOOT hurry up; get a move on. *S. Afr., informal*

put one's FOOT down 1 adopt a firm policy when faced with opposition or disobedience. 2 *Brit., informal* make a motor vehicle go faster by pressing the accelerator pedal with one's foot.

put one's FOOT in it (or put one's foot in one's mouth) say or do something tactless or embarrassing; commit a blunder or indiscretion. *informal* ● Hence *foot-in-mouth* as an adjective (see quot.).

> **1998** *Spectator* 25 Apr. 7/3 How must they despair ... of the Duke's Palmerstonian attitude towards foreigners, which has earned him the title of Britain's Foot-in-Mouth Ambassador.

put a FOOT wrong make any mistake in performing an action. ● Usually with negative.

FOOT ▶ *see* **foot the BILL**.

FOOTLOOSE and fancy-free without commitments or responsibilities; free to act or travel as one pleases. ● *Footloose* used literally in L17 to mean 'free to move the feet', was originally US (L19) in this figurative sense. The collocation with *fancy-free* (*fancy* in the sense of 'love' or 'object of one's affections') is M20.

play FOOTSIE (with someone) work with someone in a cosy and covert way. ● *Footsie* (M20; also *footy-footy, footsie-footsie* and other variants) is touching someone's feet lightly with one's own feet, usually under a table, as a playful expression of romantic interest.

follow (or tread) in someone's FOOTSTEPS do as another person did before, especially in making a journey or following an occupation.

be FOR it be in imminent danger of punishment or other trouble. *Brit., informal*

there's (or that's) — FOR you that is a particularly good example of (a quality or thing mentioned). ● Often ironic.

FORBIDDEN fruit a thing that is desired all the more because it is not allowed. ● The fruit forbidden to Adam: 'But of the tree of the knowledge of good and evil, thou shalt not eat of it' (Genesis 2:17).

FORCE someone's hand make someone do something they dislike or act prematurely.

FORCE the issue compel the making of an immediate decision.

FORCE the pace adopt a fast pace in a race in order to tire out one's opponents quickly.

in FORCE in great strength or numbers.

> **1989** A. WILENTZ *Rainy Season* (1990) vi. 160 They turned out in force, armed with machetes and cocomacaques.

FORCED march a rapid march carried out under compulsion over a long distance, especially by soldiers.

FORCES ▶ *see* **JOIN forces**.

take time by the FORELOCK seize an opportunity. *literary* ● The Latin fabulist Phaedrus described Opportunity or Occasion as being bald except for a long forelock, a personification that was illustrated in Renaissance emblem books and was applied also to Time.

> **1594** E. SPENSER *Amoretti* lxx Tell her the ioyous time wil not be staid Unlesse she doe him by the forelock take.

touch (or tug) one's FORELOCK indicate respect or deference. ● From the action of raising a hand to one's forehead in deference when meeting a person of higher social rank.

Morton's FORK a situation in which there are two choices or alternatives whose consequences are equally unpleasant. ● John Morton (*c.*1420–1500) was Archbishop of Canterbury and chief minister of Henry VII. *Morton's fork* was the argument used by Morton to extract loans: the obviously rich must have money and the frugal must have savings, so neither could evade his demands.

with (a) FORKED tongue untruthfully; deceitfully. *humorous* ● With reference to the forked tongue of a snake.

a FORLORN hope a faint remaining hope or chance; a desperate attempt. ● M16 from Dutch *verloren hoop* 'lost troop'. The phrase originally denoted a band of soldiers picked to begin an attack, many of whom would not survive; the equivalent French phrase is *enfants perdus* 'lost children'. The current sense (M17), derives from a misunderstanding of the etymology.

FORM ▶ *see* **a MATTER of form**.

FORTY winks a short sleep or nap, especially during the day. *informal* ● This expression is an E19 colloquialism, but *wink* in the sense of 'a closing of the eyes for sleep' dates from L14.

FOUL one's (own) nest do something damaging or harmful to oneself or one's own interests. ● Cf. the proverbial condemnation, current in English since E15 and before that in Latin, of a person who vilifies their own country or family: *it's an ill bird that fouls its own nest*.

FOUR ▶ *see* **to the WIND**.

on all FOURS (with) equal (with); presenting an exact analogy (with).

> 1931 *Economist* 8 Aug. 277/1 The railways maintain that conditions in Great Britain and America are not on all fours.

the FOURTH estate the Press. ● The three traditional Estates of the Realm (the Crown, the House of Lords, and the House of Commons) are now viewed as having been joined by the Press, regarded as having power in the land equivalent to that of the others; cf. Lord Macaulay in 1843: 'The gallery in which the reporters sit has become a fourth estate of the realm.'

FOX ▶ *see* **CRAZY like a fox**.

be in (*or* out of) the FRAME 1 be (*or* not be) taking part or the centre of attention. 2 under suspicion or wanted (*or* not) by the police.

FRANKENSTEIN's monster something which has developed beyond the management or control of its originator. ● *Frankenstein* was the title of a novel (1818) by Mary Shelley whose eponymous main character constructed and gave life to a human monster.

> 1991 J. KINGDOM *Local Government & Politics in Britain* ii. 26 The factories of the bourgeoisie had created another dangerous by-product, a Frankenstein's monster posing a constant sense of threat—the working class.

for FREE without cost or payment; free of charge. *informal* ● This and similar pleonastic uses are mainly US (cf. ▶ **for REAL**), recorded from L19 onwards. A more emphatic variant is *free, gratis, and for nothing* (M19).

> 1957 G. SMITH *Friends* 147 Back home we pay if we're ill … You don't expect to be ill for free.

FREE and easy informal and relaxed. ● As an adjectival phrase from L17. Hence the noun *free-and-easiness* (M19).

FREE, white, and (over) twenty-one independent; not subject to another person's authority. *dated* ● *Twenty-one* was formerly the age at which legal adult status was attained in Britain.

it's a FREE country something is not illegal or forbidden. ● Since L19, usually in justifying one's own actions or expressing tolerance of someone else's.

make FREE of treat without ceremony or proper respect; take liberties with.

FREE ▶ *see* **free REIN**; ▶ *see* **there's no such thing as a free LUNCH**.

FREEZE one's blood fill one with feelings of fear or horror. ● For the physiology behind this expression see ▶ **in COLD blood**. Hence *my blood froze*, used hyperbolically of one's feelings of extreme fear or horror.

FREEZE ▶ *see* **BRASS monkey weather**.

(if you'll) excuse (*or* pardon) my FRENCH used to apologize for swearing. *informal* ● *French* has been used since L19 as a euphemism for bad language.

> 1992 A. LAMBERT *Rather English Marriage* iii. 49 'A *loony* can change a bloody toilet-roll, pardon my French.'

take FRENCH leave make an unannounced or unauthorized departure. ● From the custom prevalent in eighteenth-century France of leaving a reception or entertainment without taking leave of one's host or hostess.

be FRESH out of something have just sold or run out of a supply of something. *informal*

FRESH ▶ *see* **new BLOOD**; ▶ *see* **break new GROUND**; ▶ *see* **a BREATH of fresh air**; ▶ *see* **fresh as a DAISY**.

a fair-weather FRIEND someone who cannot be relied on in a crisis.

> 1998 *Spectator* 5 Sept. 24/2 The Americans gave up supplying gold on demand to other countries' central banks at $35 an ounce … when their fair-weather friends from London threatened to turn up and clean them out.

flexible FRIEND a credit card. ● From the advertising slogan, 'Access—your flexible friend'.

a FRIEND at court a person in a position to use influence on one's behalf.

FRIENDS in high places people in senior positions who are able and willing to use their influence on one's behalf.

look a FRIGHT have a dishevelled or grotesque appearance. *informal*

FRIGHTEN ▶ *see* **frighten the DAYLIGHTS out of**; ▶ *see* **frighten the LIFE out of**.

FRIGHTENED ▶ *see* **afraid of one's own SHADOW**; ▶ *see* **be frightened out of one's WITS**; ▶ *see* **be frightened to DEATH**.

put the FRIGHTENERS on threaten or intimidate. *Brit.*, *informal* ● *Frightener* in M20 criminal slang is a thug who intimidates victims on behalf of a gang or racket.

go (*or* be) on the FRITZ (of a machine) stop working properly. *N. Amer.*, *informal* ● The nature of any connection with *Fritz*, the derogatory nickname for a German, is uncertain. Hence *put the fritz on* is to 'put a stop to' something. Like ▶ **on the BLINK**, E20 in origin.

have a FROG (in one's throat) lose one's voice or find it hard to speak because of hoarseness or an apparent impediment in one's throat. *informal*

FRONT of house **1** the parts of a theatre in front of the proscenium arch. **2** the business of a theatre that concerns the audience, such as ticket sales. ● As modifier usually *front-of-house*.

FRONT ▶ *see* **on the back BURNER**.

FROTH (*or* foam) at the mouth be very angry. ● From the involuntary production by a person or animal of large amounts of saliva from the mouth in a bodily seizure.

bear FRUIT have good results. ● A biblical metaphor (e.g., Matthew 13:23).

out of the FRYING pan into the fire from a bad situation to one that is worse. ● *Leap out of the frying pan into the fire* is included in J. Heywood's collection of English proverbs and epigrams (1546).

FUCK all absolutely nothing. *Brit.*, *vulgar slang* ● Cf. ▶ **SWEET Fanny Adams**.

FUDGE factor a figure included in a calculation to account for some unquantified but significant phenomenon or to ensure a desired result. ● *Fudge*, apparently originating in M18 as an exclamation of disgust or irritation, acquired a specific verbal sense in printers' jargon (L18), meaning to 'do work imperfectly or as best one can with the materials available'.

add FUEL to the fire (or flames) (of a person or circumstance) cause a situation or conflict to become more intense, especially by provocative comments.

at FULL cock (of a firearm) with the cock lifted to the position at which the trigger will act. ● Cf. ▶ **at HALF cock**.

FULL of years having lived to a considerable age. ● A biblical (AV) expression, now archaic: 'an old man, and full of years' (Genesis 25:8).

FULL steam (or speed) ahead proceed with as much speed or energy as possible. ● A metaphor from steam-powered rail engines. Often as a command or encouragement to proceed immediately.

FULL ▶ see **full PELT**; ▶ see **at full STRETCH**; ▶ see **come full CIRCLE**; ▶ see **the full MONTY**; ▶ see **full as a GOOG**; ▶ see **full of BEANS**; ▶ see **top WHACK**; ▶ see **give full WEIGHT to**; ▶ see **CRY**; ▶ see **in full FIG**; ▶ see **in full FLIGHT**; ▶ see **in full FLOW**; ▶ see **under full SAIL**; ▶ see **in full SWING**; ▶ see **in full VIEW**; ▶ see **not the full QUID**; ▶ see **not playing with a full DECK**; ▶ see **on a full STOMACH**.

to the FULL to the greatest possible extent.

the FULLNESS of one's (or the) heart overwhelming emotion. *literary*

in the FULLNESS of time after a due length of time has elapsed; eventually. ● A biblical (AV) expression (e.g. Ephesians 1:10).

FUN ▶ see **POKE fun at**.

in FUNDS having money to spend. *Brit.*

it's (or that's) someone's FUNERAL an unwise act or decision is the initiator's own responsibility. *informal* ● Used to warn someone of the possible consequences of their action or as a comment on a third party's action.

FUNNY old strange and unexpected. ● Generally in the comment *it's a funny old world* (after the W. C. Fields quip in the film *You're Telling Me* (1934): 'It's a funny old world—a man's lucky if he gets out of it alive') or *it's a funny old life*.

the FUNNY thing is the strangest aspect is. ● Used in speech to draw attention to what follows as the most curious or piquant part of a story or situation.

see the FUNNY side (of something) appreciate the humorous aspect of a situation or experience.

FUR and feather game animals and birds.

the FUR will fly there will be serious, perhaps violent, trouble. *informal* ● The image is of a furious dog-or cat-fight. Originally E19 US slang.

FURIOUSLY ▶ see **give someone furiously to THINK**.

part of the FURNITURE a person or thing that has been somewhere so long as to seem a permanent, unquestioned, or invisible feature of the scene. *informal*

nothing could be FURTHER from one's mind (or thoughts) used to deny that one has been thinking about something. ● Very often used insincerely or ironically.

like FURY with great energy or effort. *informal* ●M19, but *fury* has been used of things that operate with irresistible force since L16 (e.g. 'the fury of the sea').

1994–5 *Game Gazette* Dec.–Jan. 54/1 I was to fish it for the legendary Tiger fish ... that ... has a mouth of teeth like a canteen of cutlery and fights like fury.

FUSE ▶ *see* **LIGHT the fuse**.

FUTURE shock a state of distress or disorientation due to rapid social or technological change. ●From Alvin Toffler in *Horizon* (1965), 'The dizzying disorientation brought on by the premature arrival of the future'; definition of *future shock*.

G

---

on (or upon) the GAD on the move; going about. ● Now somewhat archaic, *gad* in this sense is current only in this expression. It derives from the ME verb *gad* meaning 'to roam about idly, especially in search of pleasure'.

blow the GAFF (on) reveal a plot or secret. ● *Gaff* here is E19 slang of uncertain origin.

GAIETY of nations general cheerfulness or amusement. *Brit.* ● Samuel Johnson in his *Lives of the English Poets* 'Edmund Smith' wrote of the death of the great actor David Garrick (1717–79) that it 'has eclipsed the gaiety of nations and impoverished the public stock of harmless pleasure.' Now often used ironically.

go one's (or one's own) GAIT pursue one's own course. ● Also in the Scottish variant *gang your gait*.

> **1940** H. READ *Annals of Innocence* II. ii. 82 These are qualities to be enjoyed by non-poetic people: the poet must go his own gait.

GALL ▶ *see* **DIP one's pen in gall**; ▶ *see* **WORMWOOD and gall**.

play to the GALLERY act in an exaggerated or histrionic manner, especially in order to appeal to popular taste. ● From M17 the uppermost seating in a theatre was called the gallery, and it was here that the cheapest seats—and the least refined members of the audience—were to be found. This figurative use dates from L19.

ahead of the GAME ahead of one's competitors or peers in the same sphere of activity.

> **1996** *Daily Telegraph* 4 Nov. 16/2 The smart money headed for Chinatown, where you can pick up all those Eastern looks the designers are promoting for next spring ahead of the game.

(as) GAME as Ned Kelly very brave. *Austral.* ● Ned Kelly (1855–80), a famous Australian bushranger, was the leader of a band of horse and cattle thieves and bank raiders operating in Victoria; he was eventually hanged at Melbourne.

the GAME is up the plan, deception, crime, etc. is revealed or foiled.

GAME over said when a situation is regarded as hopeless or irreversible. *chiefly N. Amer., informal* ● Probably from the use of the phrase at the conclusion of a computer game.

off (or on) one's GAME playing badly (or well).

on the GAME involved in prostitution. *Brit., informal* ● The phrase itself is apparently L19, but *game* in the sense of 'amorous sport' is much older; cf. Shakespeare (1606) 'daughters of the game' (*Troilus and Cressida* IV. v) and the E–M17 use of *gamester* for a lewd person.

the only GAME in town the best or most important of its kind; the only thing worth concerning oneself with. *informal*

> **1998** *Spectator* 11 July 20/3 But there is … a sense of resentment that the big set-piece political interviews are not now the only game in town.

play someone's GAME advance another's plans, whether intentionally or not.

play the GAME behave in a fair or honourable way; abide by the rules or conventions.

> **1993** A. McNAB *Bravo Two Zero* (1994) ii. 21 Shorncliffe was a nightmare, but I learned to play the game. I had to—there was nothing else for me.

what's your (or the) GAME? what's going on?; what are you up to? *informal*

GAME ▶ *see* **BEAT someone at their own game**; ▶ *see* **the NAME of the game**; ▶ *see* **TWO can play at that game**.

play GAMES (with) deal with (someone or something) in a way that lacks due seriousness or respect or deviates from the truth.

run the GAMUT experience, display, or perform the complete range of something. ● *Gamut* is a contraction of medieval Latin *gamma ut*, *gamma* being the lowest note in the medieval musical scale and *ut* the first of the six notes forming a hexachord; hence the full range of notes of which a voice or instrument is capable. Usually followed by *of* or *from*.

> **1883** *Harper's Magazine* 822/2 The stocks … were running … up and down the gamut from $1 to $700 a share.

go GANGBUSTERS proceed very vigorously or successfully. *N. Amer.* ● A *gangbuster* literally is a person who assists in the vigorous or violent breakup of criminal gangs, from which the more general sense of 'a successful person' has developed. Similarly, *like gangbusters* means 'vigorously and successfully'.

> **1994** *Wall Street Journal* 13 May c1/2 Sotheby's glamorous semi-annual black tie auction of contemporary art was going gangbusters.

GARBAGE in, garbage out incorrect or poor quality input inevitably produces faulty output. ● Often abbreviated as GIGO, this expression originated in computing (M20) and is now applied in other spheres.

> **1987** *Washington Times* 10 Sept. F4 The computer rule 'garbage in, garbage out' applies to the human mind just as much as it does to the computer.

cultivate one's GARDEN attend to one's own affairs. ● After Voltaire *Candide* (1759) xxx: 'il faut cultiver notre jardin'.

everything in the GARDEN is lovely all is well. *informal* ● An E20 catchphrase, originating in a song popularized by the English music-hall artiste Marie Lloyd (1870–1922) used as an expression of general satisfaction and contentment.

lead someone up (or N. Amer. down) the GARDEN path give someone misleading clues or signals. *informal* ● Earliest (E20) as just *garden*, which suggests the original context of someone enticing someone whom they wish to seduce or flirt with out into the garden.

all Sir GARNET highly satisfactory. *informal, dated* ● Sir Garnet Wolseley (1833–

1913), leader of several successful military expeditions, was associated with major widespread reforms to the army.

| *1894 *Sporting Times* 1 Sept.1/4The start was all 'Sir Garnet'.

all GAS and gaiters a satisfactory state of affairs. *informal* ●Also with the sense of 'pomposity' in some contexts. As the title of a British TV series, both possible meanings were implied.

| *1839 C. DICKENS *Nicholas Nickleby* xlix. 489 She is come at last—at last—and all is gas and gaiters!

run out of GAS run out of energy; lose momentum. *N. Amer., informal* ●Literally, 'run out of petrol'.

step on the GAS press on the accelerator to make a car go faster. *N. Amer., informal*

blow a GASKET lose one's temper. *informal* ●Literally, 'suffer a leak in a gasket of an engine'.

one's (or the) last GASP the point of exhaustion, death, or completion. ●Also *last-gasp* as modifier, meaning 'done or completed just in time or in the short time remaining'.

get (or be given) the GATE be dismissed from a job. *N. Amer., informal*

GATEPOST ▶ *see* **between you and me and the BEDPOST**.

throw down (or take up) the GAUNTLET issue (or accept) a challenge. ●From the medieval custom of issuing a challenge by throwing one's glove or gauntlet to the ground; whoever picked it up was deemed to have accepted the challenge.

run the GAUNTLET go through an intimidating or dangerous crowd, place, or experience in order to reach a goal. ●With reference to the former military practice of punishing a wrongdoer by forcing him to run between two lines of men armed with sticks, who beat him as he passed.

in the GAZETTE have one's bankruptcy published. ●*Gazette* is the title of an official journal in Britain containing public notices, including lists of bankruptcies.

change GEAR begin to move or act differently, usually more rapidly. ●From literally engaging a different gear of a motor vehicle in order to alter speed. Cf. *in gear* (with a gear engaged, and thus ready for action) and its opposite *out of gear*. To *move up a gear* means literally 'change to a higher gear', often used figuratively for increasing the volume, speed, etc. of one's activities.

all someone's GEESE are swans someone habitually exaggerates the merits of undistinguished people or things. ●There are several variants on this expression, all depending on the traditional antithesis between geese and swans (cf. ▶ **an UGLY duckling**).

let the GENIE out of (or put the genie back in) the bottle let loose (or bring back under control) an unpredictable force, course of events, etc. ●A *genie* or *jinnee* in Arabian stories is a spirit that can adopt various forms and take a mischievous or benign hand in human affairs; it generally inhabits a lamp (cf. ▶ **ALADDIN's lamp**) or bottle from which someone can release it by the appropriate words or actions. The Arabic word appears in English in various transliterations; *genie* is owed to the French translators of *The Arabian Nights* who used *génie* (from Latin *genius* meaning 'a tutelary spirit') as being similar in sound and sense to the Arabic word.

| **1997** *New Scientist* 6 Dec. 3/3 They should realise, though, that no amount of legislation can put the genie back in the bottle.

a **GENTLEMAN'S agreement** an agreement between two or more people that relies upon honour rather than being a legally enforceable contract.

| **1991** C. ANDERSON *Grain: Entrepreneurs* xvi. 158 There had been a 'gentleman's agreement' by the Grain Growers not to enter the markets of Saskatchewan Wheat Pool's predecessor.

the little **GENTLEMAN in the velvet coat** the mole. *humorous* ● A Jacobite toast, because the death of King William III was brought about by complications following a fall from his horse, reputedly caused by its stumbling over a molehill. In various forms: e.g., *the wee gentleman in black velvet*.

in **GERM** not yet developed. ● The figurative use of *germ* (Latin *germen* 'seed') dates back to M16; *germ* as a disease-causing micro-organism is a L19 development.

(as) — as all GET out to a great or extreme extent. *N. Amer., informal*

be out to GET someone be determined to punish or harm someone.

GET it together get oneself or a situation organized or under control. *informal.* Cf. ▶ *see* **get one's ACT together**.

don't GET mad, get even used to advise in favour of revenge rather than fruitless rage. *orig. US, informal* ● A saying popularized by US president John F. Kennedy, who called it 'that wonderful law of the Boston Irish political jungle' (in B. Bradlee *Conversations with Kennedy*, 1975).

| **1998** *New Scientist* 14 Feb. 5/1 The Wellcome Trust doesn't get mad, it gets even.

GET one's own back have one's revenge; retaliate. *Brit., informal*

GET-up-and-go (*or US* **get)** energy, enthusiasm, and initiative. *informal* ● An M19 US colloquialism was 'get up and get'.

the **GHOST in the machine** the mind viewed as distinct from the body. ● A phrase coined by the British philosopher Gilbert Ryle in *The Concept of Mind* (1949). *The ghost in the machine* is frequently used derogatorily by critics of the kind of dualism exemplified by Descartes' distinction between the material body and the immaterial soul.

the **GHOST walks** money is available and salaries will be paid. ● The expression has been explained in theatrical phrase books by the story that an actor playing the ghost of Hamlet's father refused to 'walk again' until the cast's overdue salaries had been paid.

give up the GHOST 1 (of a person) die. **2** (of a machine) stop working; break down, especially permanently. **3** stop making an effort; give up hope. ● It is only in this idiom that *ghost* is still found in its Old English sense of 'the soul or spirit as the source of life'. Cf. ▶ **the GHOST in the machine**.

look as if one has seen a GHOST look very pale and shocked.

not have (*or* stand) the GHOST of a chance have no chance at all.

the GIFT of the gab the ability to speak with eloquence and fluency. ● *Gab* (L18) was an informal word for 'conversation, prattle'; in Scotland it was associated with *gab* (E18), a dialect variant of *gob* 'mouth'.

God's (own) GIFT to — a godsend or extraordinary benefit to someone or something. ● Generally used ironically.

> **1998** *Spectator* 4 July 16/2 Their [the English] hooligans, their pressmen, hell, even their footballers behave as if they were God's own gift to sport.

in the GIFT of in the power of someone to award. ● Used especially of a church living or official appointment.

look a GIFT horse in the mouth find fault with what has been given or be ungrateful for an opportunity. ● The Latin version of the proverb *don't look a gift horse in the mouth* (*noli ... equi dentes inspicere donati*) was known to St Jerome in the early 5th century AD. The sixteenth-century English form was *do not look a given horse in the mouth*.

> **1998** *New Scientist* 9 May 19/2 The *JAMA* paper offers this advice to researchers involved in industry-funded studies: 'At times it may be prudent ... to look a gift horse in the mouth.'

GIFT ▶ *see* **the gift of TONGUES**.

GILD the lily try to improve what is already beautiful or excellent. ● Adapting Shakespeare: 'To gild refined gold, to paint the lily, ... Is wasteful and ridiculous excess' (*King John* IV. ii).

green about (*or* around *or* at) the GILLS sickly-looking. *informal* ● *Gills* in the context of a person refer to the flesh between the jaw and the ears (E17). Other colours are occasionally used to indicate a sickly hue; much less common is *rosy about the gills* indicating good health.

GILT ▶ *see* **take the gilt off the GINGERBREAD**.

GINGER group a small number of people who stimulate an organization or movement into action. *informal* ● An old horse-coper's trick (recorded from L18) to make a broken-down animal look lively was to insert ginger into its anus. Hence the metaphorical phrase *to ginger up*, meaning 'to put spirit or mettle into', which is what a *ginger group* (E20) does.

> **1970** *New Society* 5 Feb. 210/2 The appearance of ginger groups to fight specific proposals, is not a bad thing—particularly if the established bodies aren't prepared to fight.

take the gilt off the GINGERBREAD make something no longer attractive or desirable. ● Gingerbread was traditionally made in decorative forms that were then ornamented with gold leaf.

GIRD (up) one's loins prepare oneself for physical or mental effort. ● Of biblical origin, the idea being that the long loose garments worn in the ancient Orient had to be hitched up to avoid impeding one's actions. Cf. 1 Kings 18:45-6 'And Ahab rode, and went to Jezreel. And ... Elijah ... girded up his loins, and ran before Ahab to the entrance of Jezreel.' Adopted as a metaphor in the New Testament: 'Wherefore gird up the loins of your mind, be sober ...' (1 Peter 1:13).

GIRL ▶ *see* **PAGE three girl**.

GIVE and take **1** mutual concessions and compromises. **2** exchange of words and views. ● Cf. the L18 saying *give and take is fair* (*play*). The collocation of the verbs *give* and *take* is at least as early as E16 (in Horman's *Vulgaria* (1519)), hence the use of the phrase as a verb, meaning to 'make concessions and compromises'.

GIVE as good as one gets respond with equal force or vehemence when attacked.

GIVE the game (or show) away inadvertently reveal something secret or concealed.

GIVE it to scold or punish (someone). *informal*

GIVE me — (any day) I prefer or admire a specified thing.

GIVE or take — the figure given or the statement made is only an estimated one. *informal*

GIVE someone what for punish or scold someone severely. *Brit.*, *informal*

not GIVE a damn (or hoot etc.) not care at all. *informal*

GIVE ▶ *see* **give oneself AIRS**; ▶ *see* **give someone/thing BEST**; ▶ *see* **give someone furiously to THINK**; ▶ *see* **put one's MIND to**; ▶ *see* **give up the GHOST**.

stick in one's GIZZARD be a source of great and continuing annoyance. *informal* ● Cf. ▶ **stick in one's CRAW**.

GLAD ▶ *see* **give someone the EYE**; ▶ *see* **give someone the glad HAND**; ▶ *see* **in one's glad RAGS**.

the (or just the) GLASSY the most excellent person or thing. *Austral.*, *informal* ● In M20 surfing parlance *glassy* is an extremely smooth wave offering excellent surfing conditions.

a GLEAM (or twinkle) in someone's eye **1** a barely formed idea. **2** *humorous* a child who has not yet been conceived.

GLOOM ▶ *see* **DOOM and gloom**.

go to GLORY die; be destroyed. *euphemistic*

in one's GLORY in a state of extreme joy or exaltation. *informal*

GLORY ▶ *see* **CROWNING glory**.

fit like a GLOVE (of clothes) fit exactly.
| **1771** T. SMOLLETT *Humphrey Clinker* 10 June Letter i The boots … fitted me like a glove.

GLOVE ▶ *see* **throw down the GAUNTLET**.

the GLOVES are off (or with the gloves off or take the gloves off) used to express the notion that something will be done in an uncompromising or brutal way, without compunction or hesitation. ● Contrasted with the idea of the gloved hand as handling things gently or in a civilized way.

in a GLOW hot or flushed; sweating. *informal* ● Also *all of a glow*. Formerly often euphemistic for 'sweating'.

a GLUTTON for punishment a person who is always eager to undertake hard or unpleasant tasks. ● *Glutton of* — was used figuratively from E18 for someone who is inordinately fond of the thing specified, esp. translating the Latin phrase *helluo librorum* 'a glutton of books'. The possible origin of the present phrase is E19 sporting slang: Moore (*Tom Crib*, third edn., 1819) describes *glutton* as 'the classical phrase at Moulsey-Hurst, for one who ... takes a deal of punishment before he is satisfied'. In a similar vein, Kipling (1895) has 'a glutton for work', a phrase which is also still current.

GNASH one's teeth feel or express anger or fury. ● Often in association with *weeping* or *wailing*, as used in the Bible *passim* to express a mixture of remorse and rage (e.g. Matthew 8:12).

| **1998** *Times* 20 Apr. 46/1 Prepare yourself for the usual wailing and gnashing of teeth after tomorrow's retail prices index figures.

GNAT ▶ *see* **STRAIN at a gnat**.

GNOMES of Zurich Swiss financiers or bankers, regarded as having sinister influence. *derogatory* ● From a remark made by British politician Harold Wilson in a speech in 1956: 'all the little gnomes in Zurich ... about whom we keep on hearing'.

GO down with (all) guns firing fail or be beaten, but continue to offer resistance until the end.

be all GO be (a situation in which people are) very busy or active. *informal*

from the word GO from the very beginning. *informal* ● A M19 US colloquialism, now also in Brit. usage.

| *1834 D. CROCKETT *Narrative of Life* 59 I was plaguey well pleased with her from the word go.

GO-as-you-please untrammelled; free.

GO figure! said to express the speaker's belief that something is inexplicable. *N. Amer., informal*

GO halves (*or* shares) share something equally.

GO (to) it act in a vigorous, energetic, or dissipated way. *Brit., informal*
| **1606** W. SHAKESPEARE *King Lear* IV. vi. The wren goes to't, and the small gilded fly Does lecher in my sight.

have a GO at attack or criticize (someone). *chiefly Brit.*

make a GO of be successful in something. *informal* ● An Australian and New Zealand variant is *make a do of it* (E20).
| **1987** E. E. SMITH *Miss Melville Returns* (1988) viii. 65 He'd been unable to make a go of life in the city, and so he'd returned to the small New England village he came from.

on the GO very active or busy. *informal*

to GO (of food or drink from a restaurant or café) to be eaten or drunk off the premises. *N. Amer.*

GO ▶ *see* **go APE**; ▶ *see* **go BALLISTIC**; ▶ *see* **go BANANAS** ; ▶ *see* **go great GUNS**; ▶ *see* **go POSTAL**; ▶ *see* **go the way of all FLESH**; ▶ *see* **go the whole HOG**; ▶ *see* **all SYSTEMS go**.

score an own GOAL do something that has the unintended effect of harming one's own interests. *informal* ● In football, an *own goal* is one scored by mistake against the scorer's own side.

move the GOALPOSTS unfairly alter the conditions or rules of a procedure during its course.

get someone's GOAT irritate someone. *informal*
> **1919** H. JEMKINS *John Dene of Toronto* (1920) iv. 70 There are some things in this country that get my goat.

play (or act) the (giddy) GOAT act irresponsibly; fool around.

GOD's acre a churchyard. ● German *Gottesacker* 'God's seed-field' in which the bodies of the dead are 'sown' (cf. 1 Corinthians 15:36–7).

GOD willing used to express the wish that one will be able to do as one intends or that something will happen as planned. ● An expression found in many cultures: cf. Latin *deo volente* or Arabic *inshallah*.

little tin GOD a self-important person. ● *Tin* is implicitly contrasted with precious metals. The phrase seems to have originated in an Indian context with Kipling, who was thinking of idols that he considered were given undeserved veneration.
> **1888** R. KIPLING *Plain Tales from Hills* 'Germ-Destroyer' (*epigraph*) Pleasant it is for the Little Tin Gods When great Jove nods; But Little Tin Gods make their little mistakes In missing the hour when great Jove wakes.

play GOD behave as if all-powerful or supremely important.

GODDESS ▶ *see* **the BITCH GODDESS**.

GODS ▶ *see* **in the LAP of the gods**.

anything GOES there are no rules about acceptable behaviour, dress, etc. ● Earlier (L19) as *everything goes*.

as (or so) far as it GOES bearing in mind something's limitations. ● Used when qualifying praise of or enthusiasm about something.

what GOES around comes around the consequences of one's actions will have to be dealt with eventually. ● A L20 proverb of US origin, now also current in Brit. English.

who GOES there? said by a sentry as a challenge.

GOING, going, gone! this is the last chance to have something. *informal* ● From an auctioneer's traditional announcement that bidding is closing or closed.

GOING on — (also *Brit.* **going on for)** approaching a specified time, age, or amount. *humorous*

have — GOING for one have a specified factor or factors in one's favour. *informal*

while the GOING is good while conditions are favourable.

go GOLD (of a recording) achieve sales meriting a gold disc.

pot (*or* crock) of GOLD (at the end of the rainbow) a large but distant or illusory reward. ●With allusion to the folklore tradition that a crock of gold is supposedly to be found by anyone reaching the end of a rainbow.

like GOLD DUST very valuable and rare.

GOLD ▶ *see* **FOOL's gold**; ▶ *see* **worth one's WEIGHT in gold**.

a GOLDEN age a period in the past when things were at their best, happiest, etc. ●According to Greek and Roman mythology, the Golden Age was the earliest and best age of the world, when humanity lived in a state of perfect happiness. The Ages of Silver, Brass, and Iron represented successive stages of a descent into barbarism and misery.

a GOLDEN calf something, especially wealth, as an object of excessive or unworthy worship. ●From the story in Exodus 32 of the idol made and worshipped by the Israelites in disobedience to Moses.

a GOLDEN handshake a sum of money paid by an employer to a retiring or redundant employee. ●On the same principle, a L20 coinage is *a golden hello*, explained in an Appointments section of *New Scientist* (1998): 'Employers ... especially in the financial sector, are offering "golden hellos". These are advances of up to £2000, sometimes given on acceptance of a job offer or with the first month's salary.'

the GOLDEN mean the avoidance of extremes. ●Latin *aurea mediocritas*, from Horace *Odes* II. x.

the GOLDEN section the division of a line so that the whole is to the greater part as that part is to the smaller part. ●A mathematical term for a proportion known since the fourth century and mentioned in Euclid. It has been called by several names, but the M19 German one *goldene Schnitt*, translating Latin *sectio aurea*, has given rise to the current English term.

GONE ▶ *see* **gone with the WIND**.

GONG ▶ *see* **KICK the gong around**.

all to the GOOD to be welcomed without qualification.

as GOOD as very nearly. ●Used especially when a predicted outcome will inevitably follow.

(as) GOOD as gold extremely well-behaved.

(as) GOOD as new (of a person or thing) in a very good condition or state, especially close to the original state after damage, injury, or illness.

be — to the GOOD have a specified amount of profit or advantage.

GOOD and used as an intensifier before an adjective or adverb. *informal* ●Originally (L19) a US colloquialism.

| **1969** B. KNOX *Tallyman* ii. 22 [It] can wait until we're good and ready.

GOOD oil reliable information. *Austral., informal*

in GOOD time **1** with no risk of being late. **2** in due course but without haste. ●In sense 2 also *all in good time*, often used as a exclamation to rebuke someone's impatience.

make GOOD be successful. ●A non-standard variant of this is *done good*.

no GOOD to gundy no good at all. *Austral.*, *informal* ●The origin of this expression remains unexplained, although attempts have been recorded since 1906, when the Sydney *Bulletin* (19 Dec. 14/1) linked it to a Welsh verb meaning 'to steal'. In 1945 S. J. Baker (*Australian Language* iv. 90) associated it with the old US phrase 'according to Gunter' (equivalent to the E19 Brit. 'according to Cocker', meaning that something is in accordance with the rules); Edward Gunter (1581–1626) was a renowned mathematician whose measuring devices were a byword for accuracy. None of this is entirely convincing; the phrase's lasting appeal is perhaps based simply on alliteration.

| **1955** N. PULLIAM *I Traveled Lonely Land* 324 Just cards and races and booze—and fightin'. No good to Gundy!

take (something) in GOOD part not be offended by something.

up to no GOOD doing or intending to do something wrong. *informal*
| **1985** R. AWAD translating Mahfouz's *Beginning and End* (1989) xxxvii. 171 On every corner there is a thug, a man who is up to no good, or a debauched drunkard.

GOOD ▶ *see* **be good NEWS**; ▶ *see* **good SAMARITAN**; ▶ *see* **have a MIND to do something**; ▶ *see* **in someone's bad BOOKS**; ▶ *see* **be in good COMPANY**; ▶ *see* **one good TURN deserves another**.

come up with (*or* deliver) the GOODS do what is expected or required of one. *informal*

get (*or* have) the GOODS on someone obtain (*or* possess) information about a person which may be used to their detriment. *informal*

(as) full as a GOOG very drunk. *Austral.*, *slang* ●*Goog* is slang of uncertain origin for 'egg'.

(kill) the GOOSE that lays (*or* laid) the golden egg(s) (destroy) a reliable and valuable source of income. ●With allusion to one of Aesop's fables, in which the owner of the goose, dissatisfied with its production of just one egg a day, kills it in the expectation of finding a large quantity of gold inside it.
| **1998** *Times* 6 Mar. 34/6 Fairview Homes is clearly the goose that lays the golden egg.

GOOSE ▶ *see* **COOK someone's goose**; ▶ *see* **what's SAUCE for the goose is sauce for the gander**.

GORDIAN ▶ *see* **CUT the knot**.

one's GORGE rises one is sickened or disgusted. ●*Gorge* is an obsolete term from falconry, meaning 'a meal for a hawk'; from this derives the more general sense of the contents of the stomach, now found almost exclusively in this phrase and the following entry.

cast the GORGE at reject with loathing. *Brit.* ●Cf. preceding entry.

GORY details explicit details. *humorous*

> **1988** D. CARPENTER *God's Bedfellows* vi. 93 She starts telling me some of the gory details ... everybody knew he was dying.

GOSPEL truth the absolute truth. *informal* ●The truth or truths contained in the New Testament. An emphatic way of asserting the truth of what one is saying.

GOTHAM ▶ *see* **a WISE man of Gotham**.

out of one's GOURD 1 out of one's mind; crazy. **2** under the influence of alcohol or drugs. *N. Amer., informal*

> **2 1993** S. KING *Gerald's Game* xxxvii. 432 I was 'on medication' (this is the technical hospital term for 'stoned out of one's gourd').

up for GRABS available; obtainable. *informal* ●Originally M20 US slang, relating especially to a woman who is open to sexual advances.

fall from GRACE fall from favour. ●Also in the strict theological sense of 'fall into a state of sin'.

with good (*or* bad) GRACE in a willing and happy (*or* resentful and reluctant) manner.

be in someone's good (*or* bad) GRACES be regarded by someone with favour (*or* disfavour).

make the GRADE succeed; reach the desired standard. *informal*

against the GRAIN contrary to the natural inclination or feeling of someone or something. ●With allusion to the fact that wood is easier to cut along the line of the grain than across or against it.

a GRAIN of mustard seed a small thing capable of vast development. ●With allusion to the great height attained by black mustard in Palestine, as in Matthew 13:31–2 'mustard seed ... indeed is the least of all seeds: but when it is grown, it is the greatest among herbs.'

in GRAIN thorough, genuine, by nature, downright, indelible. ●*In grain* comes from *dyed in the grain*; the galls of the kermes oak (known as *grain* on account of their having formerly been mistaken for seeds) were the source of a particularly indelible crimson dye.

a (*or* the) GRAND old man of a man long and highly respected in (a particular field). ●Recorded from 1882, and popularly abbreviated as GOM, *Grand Old Man* was the sobriquet of the British statesman William Ewart Gladstone (1809–98), who went on to win his last election in 1892 at the age of eighty-three.

GRANDEUR ▶ *see* **DELUSIONS of grandeur**.

teach one's GRANDMOTHER to suck eggs presume to advise a more experienced person. *proverbial* ●Used since E18 as a caution against any attempt by the ignorant or inexperienced to instruct someone wiser or more knowledgeable.

GRAPES ▶ *see* **SOUR grapes**.

hear on the GRAPEVINE acquire information by rumour or by unofficial communication. ●Originally from an American Civil War expression, when news was said to be passed 'by grapevine telegraph'. Cf. ▶ **bush TELEGRAPH**.

GRASP the nettle tackle a difficulty boldly. *Brit.* ●With reference to a belief (recorded L16 onwards) enshrined in a rhyme quoted in S. O'Casey's *Juno and the Paycock* (1925) i. 35: If you gently touch a nettle it'll sting you for your pains; grasp it like a lad of mettle, an' as soft as silk remains.

> **1998** *New Scientist* 11 Apr. 3/3 The problem was that governments failed to grasp the nettle and scrap the system.

GRASP ▶ *see* **clutch at STRAWS**.

the GRASS is always greener other people's lives or situations always seem better than one's own. *proverbial* ●A shortened form of the saying 'the grass is always greener on the other side of the fence', usually used as a caution against dissatisfaction with one's own lot in life. There are a number of sayings along these lines about the attractions of something distant or inaccessible: e.g. *Blue are the faraway hills. The Grass is Greener* is the title of a 1959 play by H. and M. Williams.

not let the GRASS grow under one's feet not delay in acting or taking an opportunity. ●Variants of this expression have been current since M16.

put out to GRASS force (someone) to retire; make redundant. *informal* ●Used literally of putting a horse or other animal out to graze. In figurative use since L16, the earlier form of the expression was with *turn (out)* rather than *put out*.

at the GRASS roots at the level of the ordinary voter, among the rank and file of a political party. ●Originally US (E20) in this political sense.

GRASSHOPPER ▶ *see* **KNEE-HIGH to a grasshopper**.

dig one's own GRAVE do something foolish which causes one to fail or be ruined.

> **1934** F. SCOTT FITZGERALD *Letter* 8 Dec.A man digs his own grave and should, presumably, lie in it.

(as) silent (*or* quiet) as the GRAVE extremely quiet.

take the (*or* one's etc.) secret to the GRAVE die without revealing a secret.

turn (*N. Amer. also* turn over) in one's GRAVE (of a dead person) supposed to be likely to react thus with shock or anger.

> **1998** *Spectator* 11 Apr. 47/2 There was a lot of buzz at Jeff Koons's studio ... But the grinding noise one heard was Peter Fuller turning in his grave.

white man's GRAVE equatorial West Africa. *dated* ●An area traditionally regarded as being particularly unhealthy for whites.

GRAVE ▶ *see* **DANCE on someone's grave**; ▶ *see* **have one FOOT in the grave**.

GRAVEN ▶ *see* **a graven IMAGE**.

board the GRAVY train obtain access to an easy source of financial gain. *informal* ● *Gravy* is slang for 'money easily acquired'. *Gravy train* is perhaps an alteration of *gravy-boat* a boat-shaped vessel for serving gravy.

GREASE (*or* oil) someone's palm bribe someone. *informal* ● From the practice of applying grease to something to make it run smoothly; cf. ▶ *see* **GREASE the wheels**. The same expression exists in French (*graisser la patte*). The form with *palm* is now predominant but *hand(s)* appears in the earliest recorded versions of the idiom (E–L16).

| **1998** *Economist* 14 Mar. 51/2 Licences to run a shop [in Italy] ... have caused many an official's palm to be greased.

GREASE the wheels make things run smoothly, especially by paying the expenses.

GREASED ▶ *see* **like LIGHTNING**.

GREASY spoon a cheap and inferior restaurant or café. ● Originally E20 US slang.

| **1968** L. DEIGHTON *Only when I Larf* viii. 110 Bob said he was hungry and wanted to pull up at every greasy spoon we passed.

the GREAT and the good distinguished and worthy people collectively. ● Most often used ironically.

| **1998** *New Scientist* 14 Mar. 16/1 But last year, an ad hoc committee of the Internet's great and good unveiled its own plan.

GREAT and small of all sizes, classes, or types. ● Used postpositively, as in *all creatures great and small*.

a GREAT one for a habitual doer of; an enthusiast for.

| **1994** R. GUNESEKERA *Reef* (1998) 23 Early on I learned the value of making lists from watching Mister Salgado. He was a great one for lists.

GREAT ▶ *see* **the UNWASHED**.

(all) GREEK to me incomprehensible to me. *informal*

| **1601** W. SHAKESPEARE *Julius Caesar* I. ii. Ay, he spoke Greek ... .those that understood him smiled at one another, and shook their heads; but for mine own part, it was Greek to me.

GREEK ▶ *see* **at the Greek CALENDS**.

beware (*or* fear) the GREEKS bearing gifts if rivals or enemies show apparent generosity or kindness, one should be suspicious of their motives. ● A proverbial saying alluding to Virgil's '*timeo Danaos et dona ferentes*' (*Aeneid* ii. 49), the point in the narrative of the fall of Troy at which the Trojan priest Laocoon warns his countrymen against taking into their city the gigantic wooden horse that the Greeks have left behind on their apparent departure.

give (*or* get) the (*or* a) GREEN light encourage or allow (*or* be encouraged or allowed) to proceed. ● From the green light in traffic signals indicating that traffic is free to move forward. Red and green lights were much earlier (L19) in use in railway signals, but this figurative use of *green light* appears to date from M20.

| **1997** *New Scientist* 29 Nov. 58/2 Zemin even got the green light to buy nuclear power plants.

GREEN ▶ *see* **green about the GILLS**.

the GREEN-EYED monster jealousy. *literary* ● Quoting Shakespeare *Othello* III. iii. 166.

a GREY area an area of law, morality, etc. which does not fall into any predefined category and which is a matter of uncertainty. ● In the 1960s, *grey areas* in British planning parlance referred to places that were not in as desperate a state as slums but which were in decline and in need of rebuilding.

come to GRIEF have an accident; meet with disaster. ● An M19 euphemism.

> **1998** A. TROLLOPE *Sir Harry Hotspur of Humblethwaite* (1991) xxii. 227 If he went on living as he was living now, he would 'come to grief'.

give someone GRIEF be a nuisance to someone. *informal*

> **1998** *Times: Weekend* 4 Apr. 33/8 One of the passengers who'd been giving the cabin crew grief started yelling, 'We've had a near miss.'

(as) merry (or lively) as a GRIG full of fun; extravagantly lively. ● The meaning and origin of *grig* are obscure. Samuel Johnson conjectured in his *Dictionary* that it refers to 'anything below the natural size'. A sense that squares with the *lively* version of this idiom is 'a young or small eel in fresh water'. The phrases *merry grig* and *merry Greek*, meaning 'a lively, frolicsome person', were both current in M16, but it is impossible to establish the precise relationship between them or be certain which may be a corruption of the other.

like (or for) GRIM death with intense determination.

GRIN and bear it deal with one's pain or misfortune in a stoical manner. ● The usual modern sense of *grin* (= broad smile) is less sinister than earlier in the word's history, when it (and its obsolete cognate *girn*) primarily meant 'an act of showing the teeth' or 'a snarl'. From M17 to M18, a *grin* was generally used derogatorily or in unfavourable contrast to a cheerful *smile*. The sense of *grin* in *grin and bear it* retains the earlier associations with showing one's teeth in a grimace of pain or anger. *Grin and abide* is recorded as a proverb in L18; the modern version dates from L19.

GRIND to a halt (or come to a grinding halt) move, function, or occur at a slower and slower rate before finally stopping.

> **1998** *New Scientist* 29 Aug. 47/1 [You would] be better off on Mars when it [i.e.the year 2000] happens. Everything here will grind to a halt.

keep one's nose to the GRINDSTONE work hard and continuously. ● A *grindstone* was a thick revolving disc of stone on which knives were sharpened, tools ground, etc. In various forms since M16, this idiom originally referred to getting mastery over someone else by compelling them to toil unremittingly, holding them like a knife-blade against the grindstone.

come (or get) to GRIPS with begin to deal with or understand. ● Literally, engage in physical combat with someone.

get a GRIP keep or recover (one's self-)control. ● Also *get* (or *take*) *a grip on* *oneself*. Often in imperative. The opposite is *lose one's grip* become unable to control oneself or one's situation.

| **1998** *Times* 17 July 22/6 [D]ecent fellow; seems to have got a grip.

GRIST to the mill experience, material, or knowledge which can be turned to good use. ●*Grist* in the sense of 'corn that is to be ground', is current now only in this phrase (used metaphorically since L16) and in the proverb *all is grist that comes to the mill*; the word is related to Old Saxon *gristgrimmo* meaning 'gnashing of teeth'.

true GRIT strength of character; stamina. *informal* ●*Grit* in this colloquial sense was originally E19 US slang.

GRODY to the max unspeakably awful. *US, slang* ●*Grody* is probably an alteration of *grotesque* and *to the max* of *to the maximum point*. Identified in *Life* Autumn 1989 as 'San Fernando Valspeak'.

in (or into) the GROOVE 1 performing well or confidently, especially in an established pattern. 2 relaxed and spontaneously enjoying. *informal* ●*Groove* refers to the spiral cut in a gramophone record that forms the path for the needle. M20 slang, originally from the US music scene. This gave rise to the adjective *groovy* which initially meant the state of mind conducive to playing well.

by the GROSS in large numbers or amounts. ●A *gross* was formerly widely used as a unit of quantity equalling twelve dozen.

break new (or fresh) GROUND do something innovative which is considered an advance or positive benefit. ●Literally, 'do preparatory digging or other work prior to building or planting something'. In North America the idiom is *break ground*.

cut the GROUND from under someone's feet do something which leaves someone without a reason or justification for their actions or opinions. *informal*

get in on the GROUND floor become part of an enterprise in its early stages. *informal*

get off the GROUND (or get something off the ground) start or cause to start happening or functioning successfully. *informal*

go to GROUND (of a person) hide or become inaccessible, usually for a prolonged period. ●Used literally of a fox or other animal that enters its earth or burrow to hide, esp. when being hunted. Cf. ▶ **go to EARTH**.

on the GROUND in a place where real, practical work is done.

on one's own GROUND on one's own territory or concerning one's own range of knowledge or experience.

prepare the GROUND make it easier for something to occur or be developed.

thick (or thin) on the GROUND existing (or not existing) in large numbers or amounts.

work (*or* run) oneself into the GROUND exhaust oneself by working or running very hard. *informal*

GROUND ▶ *see* **have one's FEET on the ground**; ▶ *see* **RUN someone/thing to earth**.

GROVES of Academe the academic community. *literary* ● After Horace *Epistles* II.ii. 45 (*Atque inter silvas Academi quaerere verum* 'and seek for truth in the groves of Academe'). The Academia was a grove near ancient Athens where a number of philosophers, Plato among them, taught their pupils.

GROW on trees be plentiful or easily obtained. ● Used since M17 in the context of commodities that are scarce and desirable, usually with negative, as in *money doesn't grow on trees*.

lower (*or* drop *or* let down) one's GUARD **1** relax one's defensive posture, leaving oneself vulnerable to attack. **2** reduce one's level of vigilance or caution. ● An expression connected in its literal sense with boxing, as is its opposite *raise one's guard* meaning to 'adopt a defensive posture'.

get a GUERNSEY **1** be selected for a football team. **2** gain recognition or approbation. *Austral., informal* ● A *guernsey* is a type of knitted shirt or sweater, the word being applied in Australian slang specifically to a football shirt.

anybody's GUESS a totally unpredictable matter. *informal*
| **1998** *New Scientist* 22 Aug. 46/1 How this happens is anybody's guess.

by GUESS and by God without specific guidance or direction. ● Originally nautical, meaning to steer blind, without guidance of landmarks.

be my GUEST please do. *informal* ● An invitation to do or continue doing something.

GULLET ▶ *see* **stick in one's THROAT**.

up a GUM TREE in a predicament; in great difficulties. *informal* ● Now mainly in British English, the phrase is recorded in E19 from the US, where *possum up a gum tree* was the title of a song or dance.

jump the GUN act before the proper or appropriate time. *informal* ● In athletics a contender who *jumps the gun* sets off before the starting pistol has been fired. Earlier (E20) *beat the gun*.

top GUN a (*or* the) most important person.

under the GUN under great pressure. *N. Amer., informal*

GUN ▶ *see* **a BIG cheese**. ▶ *see* **SMOKING gun**.

blow great GUNS be very windy. *informal*

go great GUNS perform forcefully or vigorously or successfully. *informal*
● Apparently originally a sporting idiom, it is almost always used with the present participle (see quot.).

| **1913** *Field* 3 May 849/3 A moment later Louvois shot out, passed Sanquhar and Fairy King, and going great guns ... beat the favourite by a head.

stick to one's GUNS refuse to compromise or change, despite criticism. *informal* ● With allusion to maintaining one's position under enemy fire.

| **1998** *New Scientist* 22 Aug. 46/1 [R]esearchers have bravely stuck to their guns as they went about seeking public funds.

with (all) GUNS blazing with great determination and energy, often without thought for the consequences. *informal*

GUNS ▶ *see* **GO down with guns firing**.

— one's GUTS out perform some action as hard as possible. *informal* ● Frequently in *sweat* (or *work*) *one's guts out*.

hate someone's GUTS feel a strong hatred for someone. *informal*

have someone's GUTS for garters punish or rebuke someone severely. *informal* ● A humorous hyperbole often used as a threat, current since L16.

come a GUTSER come a cropper, fail from miscalculation. *informal* ● *Gutser* (or *gutzer*) is explained in Fraser and Gibbons *Soldier and Sailor Words* (1925) as 'pre-war slang, and an old term among Scottish boys for falling flat on the water in diving, instead of making a clean header'. In air force slang *come* (or *fetch*) *a gutser* was 'to crash'. The expression also appears in Australian and New Zealand colloquial speech.

give someone GYP cause pain or severe discomfort to someone. *Brit., informal* ● *Gyp* is apparently a dialect contraction of *gee-up*, a word of command to a horse to get it to move faster, here used as a noun. *Gyp* thus is something that deprives one of rest.

H

kick the HABIT stop engaging in a habitual practice. *informal*

> **1992** *Economist* 7 Mar. 78/3 Perhaps it is time for ex-French West Africa to choose its own forms of government … and kick the habit of turning to France whenever trouble starts.

HACKING cough a short dry frequent cough. ● One of the senses of *hack* as an intransitive verb (E19) is to cough in this way.

make someone's HACKLES rise make someone angry or indignant. ● *Hackles* are the long feathers on the neck of a fighting cock or the hairs on the top of a dog's neck, which are raised when the animal is angry or excited.

HAIL-fellow-well-met friendly in an easygoing way. ● Often with the implication that the familiarity is excessive or out of place (see quot.).

> **1581** G. PETTIE *Guazzo's Civil Conversation* iii. (1586) 171 The maister … being as you say haile fellow well met with his servant.

HAIR of the dog (that bit one) a small quantity of alcohol taken as a remedy for a hangover. *informal* ● So called because the supposed cure is a small amount of the cause of the problem; thus, hair from a rabid dog was considered to be a remedy against the effects of its bite.

> ***1546** J. HEYWOOD *Proverbs* I pray the leat me and my felow haue A heare of the dog that bote us last night.

in (or out of) someone's HAIR annoying (or ceasing to annoy) someone. *informal*

keep one's HAIR on remain calm; not get angry. *Brit.*, *informal* ● Usually in imperative: *keep your hair on!*

let one's HAIR down behave wildly or uninhibitedly. *informal*

make someone's HAIR stand on end alarm or horrify someone. ● From the physical reaction of hair rising from the skin under the stimulus of strong emotion.

not turn a HAIR remain apparently unmoved or unaffected.

put HAIR (or hairs) on one's chest (of alcoholic drink or food) revive one's strength. *informal* ● With the idea of a man's masculinity being indicated by his chest hair.

HAIR ▶ *see* **neither HIDE nor hair of**.

split HAIRS make small and overfine distinctions. ● First recorded L17. *Split straws* (M19) is a less frequent version.

a — and a HALF a particular person or thing considered as an impressive example of the kind specified. *informal*

at HALF cock when only partly ready. *informal* ● Used of a firearm with the cock lifted but not to the position at which the trigger will act. Usually in *go off at half cock* or *go off half-cocked* meaning 'go ahead without proper preparation and therefore fail'. Cf. ▶ **at FULL cock**.

HALF a chance the slightest opportunity. *informal*

| **1970** N. BAWDEN *Birds on Trees* (1991) viii. 139 [G]ive her half a chance and she'll make you think black's white.

HALF a loaf not as much as one wants but better than nothing. ●With allusion to the proverb *half a loaf is better than no bread*. The proverb has been current since M16.

the HALF of it the most important part or aspect of something. *informal* ●Usually with negative.

not HALF 1 *informal* not nearly as. **2** *informal* not at all. **3** *Brit.*, *informal* to an extreme degree; very much so. ●Senses 1 and 2 are used with either *as* or *so*. Sense 3 can also stand alone as an emphatic response to another speaker's statement.

HALF ▶ *see* **one's BETTER half**; ▶ *see* **half the BATTLE**; ▶ *see* **half an EYE**; ▶ *see* **half the TIME**; ▶ *see* **have a MIND to do something**; ▶ *see* **how the OTHER half lives**.

a HALFWAY house 1 a compromise. **2** the halfway point in a progression. **3** a place where ex-prisoners, mental patients, etc. can stay while they become reaccustomed to normal life. ●Literally in L18, an inn or other establishment halfway between two places or at the midpoint of a journey.

go HALVERS agree to have a half share each. *chiefly Scottish*, *N. Engl.*, & *N. Amer.*, *informal*

HAMLET without the prince a performance or event taking place without the principal actor. ●The allusion is to Shakespeare's *Hamlet*, a play in which the eponymous hero is all-important.

come (*or* go) under the HAMMER be sold at an auction.

HAMMER and tongs with great energy and noise. ●With reference to a blacksmith's blows on the hot iron taken with the tongs from the fire of the forge. Usually *go at something hammer and tongs*.

HAMMER ▶ *see* **drive something HOME**.

take a HAMMERING 1 be subjected to harsh treatment. **2** be heavily defeated. *informal*

bind (*or* tie) someone HAND and foot severely restrict someone's freedom to act or make decisions. ●From literally tying someone's hands and feet together.

get (*or* keep) one's HAND in become (*or* remain) practised in something.

give someone the glad HAND offer someone a cordial handshake or greeting. *orig. US, informal* ●L19; often used with the implication that the cordiality is bogus or facile.

give (*or* lend) a (helping) HAND assist in an action or enterprise.

HAND in glove in collusion or association. ●Earlier *hand and glove* (L17); the current form gained ground from L18.

HAND to mouth (*or* from hand to mouth) satisfying only one's immediate needs because of lack of money for future plans and investments. ●Dating from E16. Often as modifier *hand-to-mouth*.

a HAND's turn a stroke of work. *informal* ●An E19 dialect phrase, usually now in negative contexts.

make (*or* lose *or* spend) money HAND over fist make (*or* lose *or* spend) money very rapidly. *informal* ●Earliest (M18) in nautical contexts as *hand over hand*, with reference to the movement of a person's hands when rapidly climbing a rope or hauling it in. By M19 *hand over hand* was used figuratively to mean 'advancing continuously and rapidly', especially in the context of one ship pursuing another. *Hand over fist* too is first (E19) recorded in the nautical context, but was soon used more generally to indicate rapidity, especially in the handling of money (see quot.), until in 1901 the *Daily Chronicle* (27 Dec.) referred to *making money hand-over-fist* as 'a phrase common to the Anglo-Saxon'. *Hand over hand* has reverted to literal use in the context of climbing or hauling ropes.

| **1833** S. SMITH *Life of Major J. Downing* (1834) 116 They … clawed the money off of his table, hand over fist.

the right HAND doesn't know what the left hand's doing there is a state of confusion or a failure of communication within a group or organization.

set (*or* put) one's HAND to (the plough) start work on. ●In the full version, with allusion to Luke 9:62 'No man, having put his hand to the plough, and looking back, is fit for the kingdom of God.'

take a HAND become influential in determining something; intervene. ●Followed by preposition *in*.

| **1988** R. HALL *Kisses of Enemy* (1990) iv. 480 But as long as money people take a hand in our economy under the name of IFID, I say: Oho look out.

turn one's HAND to something undertake an activity different from one's usual occupation.

| **1994** B. ANDERSON *All Nice Girls* ii. 24 Win had always told him he was an able man, a fixer, one who could turn his hand to anything.

wait on someone HAND and foot attend to all someone's needs or requests. ●Used especially where such service is regarded as unreasonable.

| **1955** L. P. HARTLEY *Perfect Woman* He has everything he wants and servants who wait on him hand and foot.

do something with one HAND (tied) behind one's back do something easily.

HAND ▶ *see* **be a DAB hand at**; ▶ *see* **have one's fingers in the TILL**; ▶ *see* **with one's hand in the COOKIE jar**.

all HANDS the entire crew of a ship. ●Used of the entire workforce in other contexts. A US variant is *all hands and the cook*, meaning 'absolutely everyone available', since the cook would not normally be expected to do the work of other team members, whether on a cattle ranch or on a ship, except in cases of dire emergency. Hence *all hands on deck* or *all hands to the pumps*, besides their literal shipboard senses, are used to indicate that all members of a team are or should be involved.

HANDS down (especially of winning) easily and decisively. ● Originally a horse-racing expression, *to win hands down* meant that a jockey was so certain of victory in the closing stages of a race that he could lower his hands, thus relaxing his hold on the reins and ceasing to urge on his mount.

HANDS off! do not touch or interfere with something.   ● Generally used as an exclamation of warning. Also as modifier *hands-off* (E20), meaning 'not involving or requiring direct control or intervention'. Cf. ▶ **HANDS-ON**.

on (or off) someone's HANDS having (*or* not having) to be dealt with or looked after by the person specified.

put one's HANDS together applaud; clap. ● Often as instruction given by a master of ceremonies: *put your hands together for —*.

put one's HANDS up raise one's hands in surrender or to signify assent or participation. ● Also as an order or instruction: *hands up!*

a safe pair of HANDS someone who is capable, reliable, or trustworthy in the management of a situation. ● A sporting metaphor, originally (M19) and especially in a cricketing context, used to denote someone's reliability in the act of catching a ball.

HANDS ▶ *see* **get one's hands DIRTY**; ▶ *see* **put one's HANDS up**; ▶ *see* **SIT on one's hands**; ▶ *see* **WASH one's hands of**.

HANDSHAKE ▶ *see* **a GOLDEN handshake**.

HANDSOME is as handsome does character and behaviour are more important than good looks. *proverbial* ● Dating in this form from M17. *Handsome* describing behaviour is properly 'chivalrous' or 'genteel', though in the context of this proverb it is taken to refer to good looks. The original sense is made clear in the earlier *goodly is he that goodly dooth*, recorded *c.*1580 as an 'ancient adage'.

HANDS-ON 1 involving or offering active participation rather than theory. **2** (in computing) involving or requiring personal operation at a keyboard.

get the HANG of something learn how to operate or do something. *informal* ● Originally an M19 US colloquialism.

| **1990** R. DOYLE *Snapper* (1993) 194 He was pretending to time them ... because he couldn't get the hang of the stop-watch Bertie'd got him.

HANG fire delay or be delayed in taking action or progressing. ● Originally (L18) a term used for the action of a firearm that was slow in communicating the fire through the vent to the charge and so did not go off immediately.

HANG a left (or right) make a left (or right) turn. *US, informal*

HANG of a — (or a hang of) to a very high degree; very great. *S. Afr., Austral., & NZ, informal* ● *Hang* here probably stands as a euphemism for *hell*. Used as an intensifier (like *hell of a*), with the spelling sometimes reflecting pronunciation (*hangava, hanguva*).

| **1945** F. SARGESON *When Wind Blows* ii. 16 All this was because Charlie was hang of a funny to be with.

HANG someone out to dry leave someone in a difficult or vulnerable situation. *chiefly N. Amer., informal* ● From suspending wet washing from a clothesline to dry. The idea of 'flapping uselessly or ineffectually' like clothes drying in the wind is also contained in the cricketing metaphor *hanging one's bat out to dry* (L19) for having one's bat away from one's body at an ineffectual angle.

| **1998** *Spectator* 7 Mar. 10/2 We point out that another MP ... has been hung out to dry for failing to declare what was (relative to this) a minuscule interest.

HANG tough be or remain inflexible or firmly resolved. *N. Amer.*

| **1992** R. KENAN *Let Dead Bury their Dead* v. 89 Obviously, he intended to hang tough at first, but apparently Miss Jesse's psychic bullwhip lashed out and snap-crackled his brain.

HANG up one's boots cease working, retire. *informal* ● *Boots* here are considered as part of one's working clothes; cf. ▶ **die with one's BOOTS on.**

| **1997** *Farmers Weekly* 18 July 92/1 The hard fact is that all farmers, whether the pension scheme is attractive or not, are, mostly, reluctant to hang their boots up.

let it all HANG out be uninhibited or relaxed. *informal* ● Originally M20 US slang.

not care (*or* give) a HANG not care at all. *informal* ● *Hang* here is a L19 euphemism for *damn*.

HANG ▶ *see* **hang by a THREAD**; ▶ *see* **hang LOOSE**.

a HANGING offence a fault or crime so serious that the perpetrator should be executed.

| **1998** *Spectator* 20 June 9/2 It is hardly a hanging offence to overlook telegrams about a small African country, but surely the Prime Minister must read JIC reports?

(as) HAPPY as a sandboy (*or* Brit. Larry *or* N. Amer. a clam) extremely happy; perfectly contented with one's situation. ● An 1823 dictionary describes a *sandboy* as an urchin who hawked sand around the streets, but the expression *as jolly as a sandboy* was already proverbial by that date for 'a merry fellow who has tasted a drop'. *Larry* is a pet name for *Lawrence*, and the saying is sometimes connected with the renowned boxer Larry Foley (1847–1917); on the other hand, it may owe something to *larry*, a dialect word used by Hardy, meaning 'a state of excitement'. The US form with *clam* apparently originated (E19) on the east coast, where clams are plentiful, and the full version *happy as a clam at high water* explains the source of the clam's satisfaction.

HAPPY hunting ground a place where success or enjoyment is obtained. ● Originally referring to the hope of Native Americans that the afterlife will be spent in a country abounding with game for hunting.

be HARD put (to it) find it very difficult. ● Usually followed by infinitive.

| **1998** *Times* 17 July 22/6 The praetorian guard around Mr Blair begins to look rather vulnerable; a couple of them trip and ... he is hard-put [*sic*] to save them.

(as) HARD as nails **1** very hard. **2** (of people) insensitive, callous; without pity.

(as) HARD as the nether millstone callous and unyielding. ●The *nether millstone*, the lower of the two millstones by which corn is ground; with allusion to Job 41:24 in the Geneva version of the Bible (1560): 'His heart is as strong as a stone, and as hard as the nether millstone.'

HARD at it busily working or occupied. *informal*

> **1997** *Independent* 13 June 3/4 I leave home ... just after 6am each day and I'm hard at it by 7.30.

a HARD case **1** a tough or intractable person. **2** *Austral. & NZ* an amusing or eccentric person.

the HARD way through suffering or learning from the unpleasant consequences of mistakes.

play HARD to get deliberately adopt an aloof or uninterested attitude, typically in order to make oneself more attractive or interesting. *informal*

put the HARD word on ask a favour of (someone), especially a sexual or financial favour. *Austral. & NZ, informal*

HARD ▶ *see* **drive a hard BARGAIN**; ▶ *see* **a tough NUT**; ▶ *see* **a hard ROW to hoe**.

run with the HARE and hunt with the hounds try to remain on good terms with both sides in a conflict or dispute. *Brit.* ●A metaphor current since M15.

start a HARE raise a topic of conversation. *Brit., dated* ●The rapid twisting and running of a hunted hare is here a metaphor for the pursuit of a topic in an animated conversation, especially one in which the participants hold strong views.

HARE ▶ *see* **MAD as a hatter**.

out of HARM's way in a safe place.

> **1996** F. McCOURT *Angela's Ashes* (1997) iii. 101 Take down the Pope and hide him in the coal hole ... where he won't be seen and he'll be out of harm's way.

there is no HARM in — the course of action specified may not guarantee success but is at least unlikely to have unwelcome repercussions.

HARM ▶ *see* **someone/thing wouldn't hurt a FLY**.

in HARNESS **1** in the routine of daily work. **2** working closely with someone to achieve something. ●From a horse or other animal being used for driving or draught work.

HARP on the same string dwell tediously on one subject.

under the HARROW in distress. ●A *harrow* is a heavy frame set with iron teeth or tines, drawn over ploughed land to break up clods and root up weeds. The situation of a frog (L14) or toad (E19) under a harrow is the epitome of misery; cf. Kipling 'Pagett, MP' (1886): 'The toad beneath the harrow knows Exactly where each tooth-point goes.'

HARRY ▶ *see* **play the DEVIL with**.

make a HASH of make a mess of; bungle. *informal* ● *Hash* comes from French *hacher* 'to chop up small'. A *hash* is a dish of meat, usually previously cooked, cut up small and warmed up with gravy; hence the derogatory sense of a jumble of incongruous elements.

settle someone's HASH deal with and subdue a person very forcefully. *informal* ● E19, possibly boxing slang.

HASH ▶ *see* **SLING hash**.

more HASTE, less speed one makes better progress with a task if one doesn't try to do it too quickly. ● The primary meaning of 'speed' in this proverbial saying was 'success in the performance of an activity', rather than 'rapidity of movement', though it is the latter that is now generally assumed to be meant. Until E20 the usual form of the proverb was *the more haste the less (or worse) speed*.

keep something under one's HAT keep something a secret.

pass the HAT round (or N. Amer. **pass the hat)** collect contributions of money from a number of people for a specific purpose.

pick something out of a HAT select something, especially the winner of a contest, at random.

throw one's HAT in (or into) the ring indicate willingness to take up a challenge or enter a contest.

> **1998** *Times* 24 Feb. 52/4 We have been anticipating that South Africa would throw its hat into the ring for some time and have a high regard for the candidacy.

under (the) HATCHES concealed from public knowledge. ● Literally, below deck in a ship.

HATCHES, matches, and despatches the births, marriages, and deaths columns in a newspaper. *humorous, dated*

HATCHES ▶ *see* **BATTEN down the hatches**.

do a HATCHET job on criticize savagely.

HAUL ▶ *see* **haul someone over the COALS**.

HAVE had it **1** be in a very poor condition; be beyond repair or past its best. **2** be extremely tired. **3** have lost all chance of survival. **4** be unable to tolerate someone or something any longer. *informal*

HAVE it away (on one's toes) leave quickly. *Brit., informal*

HAVE it away (or off) (with) have sexual intercourse (with). *Brit., vulgar slang*

> **1998** *Oldie* July 45/2 Today, young Billy would be having it off with all three young ladies on a rota basis.

HAVE (got) it in for have a particular dislike of (someone) and behave in a hostile manner towards them. *informal*

HAVE (got) it in one (to do something) have the capacity or potential (to do something). *informal*

HAVE it out (with someone) attempt to resolve a contentious matter by confronting someone and engaging in a frank discussion or argument. *informal*

HAVE (got) nothing on someone/thing be not nearly as good as someone or something, especially in a particular respect.

HAVE ▶ *see* **have it BOTH ways**; ▶ *see* **have NONE of**; ▶ *see* **have one too MANY**.

play HAVOC with completely disrupt; cause serious damage to.

> **1989** V. SING *In Search of River Goddess* 47 I hate contractors who come from the plains, chop down trees, play havoc with our lives.

watch someone like a HAWK keep a vigilant eye on someone, especially to check that they do nothing wrong.

hit the HAY go to bed. *informal* ● E20; cf. ▶ *see* **hit the SACK**

make HAY make good use of an opportunity while it lasts. ● A shortened version of the proverb *make hay while the sun shines* (M16).

> **1969** B. HEAD *When Rain Clouds Gather* (1989) v. 69 He was often away from home, making hay with his former sweethearts.

make HAY of throw into confusion.

bang (*or* knock) one's HEAD against a brick wall doggedly attempt the impossible and have one's efforts repeatedly and painfully rebuffed.

be hanging over one's HEAD (of something unpleasant) threaten to affect one at any moment. ● Cf. ▶ **SWORD of Damocles**.

be on someone's (own) HEAD be someone's sole responsibility.

bite (*or* snap) someone's HEAD off reply sharply and brusquely to someone.

do someone's HEAD in cause someone to feel annoyed, confused, or frustrated. *Brit., informal*

get one's HEAD down **1** sleep. **2** concentrate on the task in hand. *Brit., informal*

get one's HEAD round (*or* around) something understand or come to terms with something. *informal*

give someone his (*or* her) HEAD allow someone complete freedom of action. ● From allowing a horse to go as fast as it wants rather than checking its pace with the bit and reins; cf. ▶ **allow free REIN to**.

go to one's HEAD **1** (of alcohol) make one dizzy or slightly drunk. **2** (of success) make one conceited.

HEAD and shoulders above by far superior to. *informal*

— one's HEAD off laugh, talk, shout, etc. with a complete lack of restraint or without stopping.

HEAD over heels upside down; turning over completely in forward motion, as in a somersault. ●The earlier (more logical) version of this phrase was *heels over head*; the normal modern form is L18. Often used figuratively of a disordered condition, as in *head over heels in love* 'madly in love' or *in debt* 'deeply in debt'.

hold (*or* put) a gun (*or* a pistol) to someone's HEAD force someone to do something by using threats.

keep (*or* lose) one's HEAD remain calm.

> 1910 R. KIPLING If you can keep your head when all about you Are losing theirs and blaming it on you.

keep one's HEAD above water avoid succumbing to difficulties, especially falling into debt.

keep one's HEAD down remain inconspicuous in difficult or dangerous times. *informal* ●The opposite of *show one's head above the parapet*.

make HEAD or tail of understand at all. ●Usually with negative expressed (*make neither head nor tail of*) or implied.

need one's HEAD examined be foolishly irresponsible. ●With the implication that the examination will reveal proof of insanity.

off (*or* out of) one's HEAD **1** crazy. **2** extremely drunk or severely under the influence of illegal drugs. *informal*

off the top of one's HEAD without careful thought or investigation. *informal*

> 1988 J. KINKAID *Small Places* 5 He apologises for the incredible mistake he has made in quoting you a price off the top of his head which is so vastly different (favouring him) from the one listed.

over one's HEAD **1** beyond one's ability to understand. **2** without one's knowledge or involvement, especially when one has a right to this. **3** with disregard for one's own (stronger) claim. ●Also in sense 1 *above one's head*.

put something into someone's HEAD suggest something to someone.

do something standing on one's HEAD do something very easily.

stand (*or* turn) something on its HEAD completely reverse the principles or interpretation of an idea, argument, etc.

take it into one's HEAD decide impetuously. ●Followed by infinitive. Usually used in contexts suggesting that the ensuing action is unwise or uncharacteristic.

turn someone's HEAD make someone conceited.

HEAD ▶ *see* **with one's head in the CLOUDS**; ▶ *see* **KING Charles's head**; ▶ *see* **KNOCK someone/thing on the head**; ▶ *see* **have one's head SCREWED on**;

hit (*or* make) the HEADLINES (*or* papers) be written about or given attention as news.

HEADS roll people are dismissed or forced to resign.

| **1997** R. BOWEN *Evans Above* iii. 33 The Home Secretary is livid. Heads are going to roll.

put HEADS together consult and work together.

turn HEADS attract a great deal of attention or interest.

at the top (*or* **bottom) of the HEAP** (of a person) at the highest (*or* lowest) point of a society or organization.

be struck all of a HEAP be extremely disconcerted. *informal*

HEAP ▶ *see* **heap COALS of fire on someone's head**.

be unable to HEAR oneself think be unable to think clearly as a result of an excessive amount of noise. *informal*

after one's own HEART of the type that one likes or understands best; sharing one's tastes.

from the bottom of one's HEART (*or* **from the heart)** with sincere feeling. ● Cf. Latin *ab imo pectore*.

have the HEART be insensitive or hard-hearted enough. ● Usually with negative and with infinitive (see quot.).

| **1990** N. BISSOONDATH *Eve of Uncertain Tomorrows* (1991) 17 Miguel doesn't have the heart
| to force her to do what he knows she should be doing.

have (*or* **put) one's HEART in** be (*or* become) keenly involved in or committed to (an enterprise etc.).

have one's HEART in one's mouth be greatly alarmed or apprehensive.

have one's HEART in the right place be sincere or well-intentioned.

HEART and soul with great energy and enthusiasm.

a HEART of gold a generous nature.

HEART of oak a courageous nature. ● Literally, the solid central part of the tree used for timber.

| **1759** D. GARRICK *Heart of Oak* (song-title) Heart of oak are our ships, Heart of oak are our
| men.

HEART of stone a stern or cruel nature.

one's HEART's desire someone or something that is greatly wished for.

HEART to heart candidly, intimately. ● Often attributively, as in *a heart-to-heart talk*.

in one's HEART of hearts in one's inmost feelings.

take to HEART take seriously, be much affected or upset by.

wear one's HEART on one's sleeve make one's feelings apparent. ● From Shakespeare's *Othello* I. i. 64.

| **1998** *Spectator* 4 July 75/1 He ... is not suffering from compassion fatigue, yet neither does he
| wear his heart on his sleeve.

HEART ▶ *see* one's heart BLEEDS for someone; ▶ *see* one's heart sinks into one's BOOTS; ▶ *see* to one's heart's CONTENT.

a HEARTBEAT (away) from very close to; on the verge of.

HEARTH and home home and its comforts.

HEARTS and minds emotional and intellectual support or commitment.

in the HEAT of the moment while temporarily angry, excited, or engrossed, and without stopping for thought.

turn the HEAT on someone/thing concentrate pressure or criticism on. *informal*

turn up the HEAT intensify pressure or criticism. *informal*

set the HEATHER on fire be very exciting. *Scottish* ● Cf. ▶ **set the world on FIRE**.

HEAVE in sight (*or* into view) come into view. *informal* ● *Heave* meaning to 'rise up' as on the swell of a wave occurs in several nautical expressions; here the allusion is to the way that objects appear to rise up over the horizon at sea.

in seventh HEAVEN in a state of ecstasy. ● According to pre-modern cosmography the heavens were thought to be divided into spherical shells, one outside the other and varying in number from seven to eleven. Both Talmudic and Muslim authorities considered the seventh heaven to be the highest, where a state of eternal bliss was to be enjoyed.

move HEAVEN and earth make extraordinary efforts. ● Usually with infinitive.

the HEAVENS opened it started to rain suddenly and very heavily.

stink (*or* smell) to high HEAVEN have a very strong and unpleasant odour.

HEAVY on using a lot of.
> **1984** S. TERKEL *Good War* (1985) I. v. 137 We were heavy on the Italian feeling in America. We were more Italian than Italians.

HEAVY ▶ *see* make heavy WEATHER.

a HECK of a — very bad, great, etc. *informal* ● Of dialect origin, *heck* is a L19 euphemism for *hell*. Used for emphasis in various statements or exclamations.

HEDGE one's bets try to minimize the risk of being wrong or incurring loss by pursuing two courses of action at the same time. ● *Hedging* (formerly *hedging in* or *off*) one's financial liabilities, especially bets, meant limiting potential losses by putting money on the other side in such a way as more or less to balance any potential loss on the first transaction. In betting terms this means in practice putting money on more than one runner in a race.
> **1998** *New Scientist* 9 May 35/2 And just to hedge its bets, the Wilmut team has asked another unnamed lab to look at the length of Dolly's telomeres.

at (*or* to) HEEL (of a dog) close to and slightly behind its owner. ● Thus to *bring someone to heel* is to get them under control and make them act subserviently.

down at HEEL **1** (of a shoe) with the heel worn down. **2** (of a person, place, or thing) with a poor, shabby appearance.

turn on one's HEEL(S) turn sharply round.

under the HEEL of dominated or controlled by.

HEEL ► *see* **ACHILLES'** heel.

cool (or *Brit.* **kick) one's HEELS** be kept waiting.

kick up one's HEELS have a lively, enjoyable time. *chiefly N. Amer.*

set (or rock) someone back on their HEELS astonish or discomfit someone.

take to one's HEELS (or legs) run away.

HEELS ► *see* **DIG** in one's heels; ► *see* **DRAG** one's feet.

a (or one) HELL of a — a very bad, great, etc. *informal* ● L18, used for emphasis in various statements or exclamations. Sometimes spelt *helluva*.

all HELL broke (or was let) loose suddenly there was chaos or uproar. *informal*

be HELL on be unpleasant or harmful to.

come HELL or high water no matter what difficulties may occur. ● *High water* is the tide at its fullest. Also *hell and high water* (E20); the current version is M20.

for the HELL of it just for fun. *informal*

from HELL obnoxious. *informal* ● Generally for humorous emphasis.
  | **1998** *Times* 18 Mar. 55/7 As for Ellie Sykes, who calls herself 'the skating mum from hell', she's pushier still.

get the HELL out (of) escape from (a place or situation) very quickly. *informal*

give someone (or get) HELL reprimand someone (or be reprimanded) severely. *informal*

go to (or through) HELL and back endure an extremely unpleasant or difficult experience.

go to HELL in a handbasket undergo a rapid process of deterioration. *N. Amer., informal* ● Recorded E20; variants include *in a handcart* and *in a basket*.
  | **1990** *Nature Conservancy* Sept.–Oct. 5/3 I read widely on environmental issues and often feel that 'the world is going to hell in a handbasket'.

HELL for leather as fast as possible. ● Originally (L19) with reference to riding on horseback at reckless speed.

HELL's half acre a great distance. *N. Amer.*

not a hope (or chance) in HELL no hope (or chance) at all. *informal* ● An elaboration is *not a snowball's chance in hell* (M20).

play (merry) HELL with throw into turmoil; disrupt. *informal*

raise HELL **1** make a noisy disturbance. **2** complain vociferously. ● *informal*

there will be HELL to pay serious trouble will occur, as a result of a previous action. *informal* ● *Hell to pay* meaning 'serious trouble' dates from E19.

until (or till) HELL freezes over for an extremely long time; forever. *informal* ● As a subscription to a letter E20: 'Yours till hell freezes'.

HELLO ▶ *see* **a golden HANDSHAKE**.

so HELP me (God) used to emphasize that one means what one is saying. *N. Amer* ● With allusion to the oath taken by witnesses in court when they swear to tell 'the truth, the whole truth, and nothing but the truth'.

like a HEN with one chick(en) absurdly fussy, overanxious.

rare (or scarce) as HEN's teeth extremely rare. ● As hens do not possess teeth, the implication is that something is rare to the point of non-existence. Originally (M19) a US colloquialism.

HER indoors a humorous reference to one's wife or a housewife. *Brit., informal*

HERD ▶ *see* **RIDE herd on**.

HERE today, gone tomorrow soon over or forgotten; short-lived; transient.

neither HERE nor there of no importance or relevance.
| **1998** *Spectator* 5 Sept. 18/3 The fact that it's an idiot question … is neither here nor there.

out-HEROD Herod behave with extreme cruelty or tyranny. ● In medieval miracle plays Herod, the ruler of Judaea at the time of Jesus' birth who was responsible for ordering the massacre of boy babies in his realm, was portrayed as a blustering tyrant. The phrase is Shakespeare's: 'I would have such a fellow whipp'd for o'erdoing Termagant; it out-herods Herod' (*Hamlet* II. ii).

HERRING ▶ *see* **a RED herring**.

HEWERS of wood and drawers of water menial drudges; labourers. ● With reference to Joshua 9:21, the story of how the Israelites on their invasion of the Promised Land were tricked into sparing the lives of some of the indigenous inhabitants.

HIDDEN ▶ *see* **a hidden AGENDA**.

HIDE one's light under a bushel keep quiet about one's talents or accomplishments. ● With allusion to Matthew 5:15 'neither do men light a candle, and put it under a bushel, but on a candlestick.'
| **1997** *Spectator* 22 Nov. 56/1 Actors are not naturally people who believe in hiding their light under a bushel.

neither HIDE nor hair of (someone) not the slightest trace of someone. ● Also *neither hair nor hide*.

on a HIDING to nothing unlikely to succeed, or in a position to gain no advantage if one does. *Brit.*
| **1998** *Spectator* 28 Feb. 42/2 Which only goes to show that even the most reflexive liberal panderer is on a hiding to nothing in this territory.

be for the HIGH jump be about to be severely punished. *Brit., informal* ●With reference to execution by hanging. Recorded in E20 as a military expression meaning to 'be put on trial before one's commanding officer'.

HIGH and dry **1** out of the water. **2** in a difficult position, especially without resources. ●In its literal sense 1 used especially of ships left stranded by the sea as the tide ebbs. In both senses usually with the verb *leave* (*left high and dry*).

HIGH and low in many different places.

| **1993** *Independent* 8 Feb. 12/2 As the world's press hunted for him high and low, he was holed up in a country hotel.

HIGH and mighty **1** important and influential. **2** *informal* thinking or acting as though one is more important than others; arrogant. ●In sense 1 formerly used when respectfully addressing or referring to a king or prince. Also as plural noun: *the high and mighty*.

HIGH days and holidays special occasions. *informal* ●In the Church's calendar a *high day* was the day of an important festival. A *holiday* (originally *holy day*) was similar but less specific; the sacred origins of *holiday* are now submerged in its various secular senses, so *holy day* is used if a specifically religious occasion is intended.

| ***1865** M. ARNOLD *Essays in Criticism* iii. 105 Here, the summer has, even on its highdays and holidays, something mournful.

HIGH old (of a time or state) most enjoyable or remarkable. *informal*

| **1955** J. POTTS *Death of Stray Cat* ii. 11 You probably had a high old time chasing blondes.

HIGH, wide, and handsome expansive and impressive; stylish and carefree in manner. *informal* ●Originally E20 US; *Yankee Slang* (1932) identifies 'Ride him, Cowboy, high, wide and handsome' as a shout commonly heard at rodeos.

hit the HIGH spots visit places of entertainment. *informal* ●High spot was E20 slang meaning 'the best or most exciting aspect of something'.

on a HIGH in a state of euphoria. *informal* ●Originally M20 US slang referring specifically to the euphoria induced by drugs.

HIGH ▶ *see* **high on the HOG**; ▶ *see* **in fine FEATHER**; ▶ *see* **RUN high**.

take a HIKE go away. *chiefly US, informal* ●Usually in imperative as an expression of irritation or annoyance.

over the HILL past one's best; declining. *informal*

HILL ▶ *see* **a hill of BEANS**; ▶ *see* **UP hill and down dale**.

(as) ancient (*or* old) as the HILLS of very long standing or very great age. ●*Hills* in the Bible are a metaphor for permanence. Often used hyperbolically.

(up) to the HILT completely. ●From the idea of plunging a knife-blade deeply into something leaving only the hilt visible.

HIND ▶ *see* **on one's hind LEGS**.

HINT ▶ *see* **DROP a hint**.

in someone's HIP POCKET completely under someone's control. *N. Amer.*

HIRE and fire engage and dismiss, especially as indicating a position of established authority over other employees.

the rest is HISTORY used to indicate that the events succeeding those already related are so well known that they need not be recounted again.

HIT and miss done or occurring at random; succeeding by chance rather than through planning. ● Often as modifier: *hit-and-miss*.
> **1998** *New Scientist* 25 Apr. 11/1 But not all species of mosquitoes carry malaria and identifying the culprits is difficult, making control hit and miss.

HIT-and-run **1** (of a person) causing accidental or wilful damage and escaping before being discovered or stopped. **2** (of an incident or accident) in which damage is caused in this way.

HIT (someone) below the belt behave deviously (towards someone), especially so as to gain an unfair advantage. ● In boxing, delivering a blow below an opponent's waistline is illegal.

HIT the ground running proceed at a fast pace with enthusiasm and dynamism. *chiefly N. Amer., informal* ● A L20 expression which achieved cliché status in the 1990s, this seems likely to refer to military personnel disembarking rapidly from a ship or helicopter, but it cannot be definitely traced back to either World War II or the Vietnam conflict.

HIT it off feel a liking; be friendly. *informal* ● With preposition *with*.

HIT the mark be successful in an attempt or accurate in a guess. ● *Mark* here is a target in shooting.

HIT the nail on the head state the truth exactly; find exactly the right answer.
> **1998** *Spectator* 18 Apr. 36/3 Yet his conceit and knack of hitting nails on heads meant that even his best performances made him as many enemies as friends.

HIT or miss as likely to be unsuccessful as successful. ● Also as modifier: *hit-or-miss*.

HIT the road (or US trail) set out on a journey; depart. *informal*

HIT where one lives struck at one's vital point.

HIT ▶ *see* **hit the BOTTLE**; ▶ *see* **hit someone for SIX**; ▶ *see* **hit the HAY**; ▶ *see* **hit the HEADLINES**; ▶ *see* **hit HOME**; ▶ *see* **hit the JACKPOT**; ▶ *see* **hit the right NOTE**; ▶ *see* **hit the ROOF**; ▶ *see* **hit the SACK**; ▶ *see* **hit the SILK**; ▶ *see* **hit the SPOT**.

HITCH horses together get on well together, act in harmony. *US*

HITCH one's wagon to a star make use of powers higher than one's own. ● Used by Emerson (*Society and Solitude* 'Civilization', 1870) in the context of idealistic aspiration; modern usage generally has the more cynical implication of attaching oneself to someone successful or famous in order to profit from the association (see quot.).

1998 *Spectator* 18 Apr. 36/2 [Francis Bacon] was among the first to hitch his wagon to the star of the repulsive George Villiers ... James I's next favourite.

play (*or* raise) HOB cause mischief; make a fuss. *N. Amer.* ● *Hob* (in this sense since M15) is short for *hobgoblin* and equates with *the devil* in this M19 expression. Cf. ▶ **raise CAIN**, ▶ **raise the DEVIL**.

1911 J. C. LINCOLN *Cap'n Warren's Wards* vi. 88 Theoph's been raising hob because the Odd Fellows built on to their building.

HOBSON ▶ *see* **Hobson's CHOICE**.

in HOCK 1 having been pawned. **2** in debt (to). ● *Hock* here from Dutch *hok* 'hutch' or 'prison'. Originally M19 US slang, now also Brit., *hock* in this sense occurs only in this phrase or, rarely, *out of hock*.

2 1998 *Spectator* 21 Feb. 38/2 [O]ur conservatoires are still in hock to the Germano-Austrian symphonic tradition.

go the whole HOG do something completely or thoroughly. *informal* ● The origin is uncertain, but a fable in Cowper's *The Love of the World: Hypocrisy Detected* (1779) is sometimes mentioned in this connection: certain Muslims, forbidden pork by their religion but tempted to indulge in some, maintained that Muhammad had had in mind only one particular part of the animal; they could not agree which part that was, and as 'for one piece they thought it hard From the whole hog to be debarred' they between them ate up the whole beast, each salving his conscience that his own particular portion was not the one that had been forbidden. Recorded as a political expression in the US in E19; an 1835 source maintains that it originated in Virginia 'marking the democrat from a federalist'.

(live) high on (*or* off) the HOG (live) in luxury. *N. Amer.*

1991 N. MAILER *Harlot's Ghost* II. vi. 310 Even the Joint Chiefs' flunkies live high on the military hog.

HOIST ▶ *see* **hoist with one's own PETARD**.

HOLD the clock on time (a sporting event etc.).

HOLD court be the centre of attention amidst a crowd of one's admirers. ● With reference to a royal court or household revolving around the king, prince, etc.

HOLD the fort take responsibility for a situation while another person is temporarily absent.

HOLD someone's hand give a person comfort, guidance, or moral support in a sad or difficult situation.

HOLD hard used to exhort someone to stop or wait. *Brit.* ● Originally an exclamation warning riders in the hunting field to pull hard on the reins to make their horses stop. Usually in imperative. Cf. ▶ **HOLD one's horses**.

HOLD one's horses wait a moment; restrain one's enthusiasm. *informal* ● Usually in imperative.

HOLD the line **1** not yield to the pressure of a difficult situation. **2** maintain the telephonic connection during a break in the conversation. ● Sense 1 is a military metaphor from a line of soldiers withstanding an attack without moving from their positions.

> **1 1980** S. HAZZARD *Transit of Venus* (1981) 159 But if we made one exception we would naturally be in no position to hold the line on similar cases.

HOLD one's thumbs fold one's fingers over one's thumbs to bring good luck; hope for luck or success. *S. Afr.*

> **1987** *Sunday Times* (South Africa) 12 Apr. 21 They say they are holding thumbs for her and praying that the pregnancy will be trouble-free.

HOLD one's tongue remain silent. *informal* ● Often in imperative.

HOLD water (of a statement, theory, or line of reasoning) appear to be valid, sound, or reasonable. ● Often with negative.

there is no HOLDING someone someone is particularly determined or cannot be prevented from doing something.

be left HOLDING the baby (*or* US **bag**) be left with an unwelcome responsibility, often without warning.

HOLD ▶ *see* **don't hold your BREATH**; ▶ *see* **hold someone/thing at BAY**; ▶ *see* **hold the FIELD**; ▶ *see* **hold one's GROUND**; ▶ *see* **hold one's HAND**; ▶ *see* **hold one's OWN**; ▶ *see* **hold one's PEACE**; ▶ *see* **hold the STAGE**; ▶ *see* **hold someone/thing to RANSOM**.

no HOLDS barred no rules or restrictions apply in a particular conflict or dispute. ● Originally in wrestling, having no restrictions on the kinds of holds used.

blow a HOLE in ruin the effectiveness of something.

in a HOLE in an awkward situation from which it is difficult to escape. *informal* ● This figurative use of *hole* has been current since M18 (cf. ▶ **DIG oneself into a hole**). The fun in English politician Denis Healey's 'first law of holes' remark (1988) ('if you are in one, stop digging') is the playful juxtaposition of the figurative and literal.

in the HOLE in debt. *N. Amer.* ● Cf. the slang sense of *hole* as a cell for solitary confinement.

need something like a HOLE in the head used to emphasize that someone has absolutely no need or desire for something. *informal*

HOLE ▶ *see* **MONEY burns a hole in one's pocket**; ▶ *see* **a square PEG in a round hole**.

pick HOLES (in) criticize.

a Roman HOLIDAY an event occasioning enjoyment or profit derived from the suffering or discomfort of others; a pitiable spectacle. ● From Byron's description of the dying gladiator, 'Butchered to make a Roman holiday' (*Childe Harold's Pilgrimage* iv. 141).

HOLIER than thou characterized by an attitude of self-conscious virtue and piety. ● From Isaiah 65:5 'Stand by thyself, come not near to me; for I am holier than thou.'

beat someone HOLLOW defeat or surpass someone completely or thoroughly.

in the HOLLOW of one's hand entirely in one's power.

HOLY of holies a place or thing regarded as sacrosanct. ● With reference to the Hebrew phrase for the inner chamber of the sanctuary in the Jewish Temple at Jerusalem, separated by a veil from the outer chamber.

bring something HOME to someone make someone realize the full significance of something.

close (or near) to HOME (of a remark or topic of discussion) relevant or accurate to the point that one feels uncomfortable or embarrassed.

come HOME to someone (of the significance of something) become fully realized by someone.

> **1883** R. BROUGHTON *Belinda* (1984) 173 She has long known in theory that he must have been frequently in London ... but never before has it come home to her with cruel practical certitude.

drive (or hammer or press or ram) something HOME make something clearly and fully understood by the use of repeated or forcefully direct arguments.

hit (or strike) HOME **1** (of a blow or a missile) reach an intended target. **2** (of a person's words) have the intended, often unsettling or painful, effect on their audience. **3** (of the significance or true nature of a situation) become fully realized by someone.

HOME and dry successful in achieving one's objective. *chiefly Brit.* ● M20. A fuller version is *home and dry on the pig's back.* Cf. ▶ **HOME and hosed** and ▶ **HOME free**.

HOME and hosed successful in achieving one's objective. *chiefly Austral. & NZ* ● Cf. ▶ **HOME and dry** and ▶ **HOME free**.

> **1998** *Times* 15 Apr. 42/2 The championship was over, Manchester United were home and hosed.

HOME free successful in achieving one's objective. *mainly N. Amer.* ● Cf. ▶ **HOME and dry** and ▶ **HOME and hosed**.

a HOME from (or N. Amer. away from) home a place where one is as happy, relaxed, or at ease as in one's own home.

HOME, James (and don't spare the horses)! used as a humorous way of exhorting the driver of a vehicle to drive home quickly. *dated* ● Parodying the instruction given to a coachman in the days of horse and carriage, this was the title of a popular song by F. Hillebrand in 1934.

who's — when —'s at HOME a humorously emphatic way of asking about someone's identity. *Brit.*

an HONEST broker a disinterested intermediary or mediator. ● Translating German *ehrlicher Makler*; in a speech in 1878 the German statesman Bismarck

(1815–98) recommended adopting this role in peace-making, and the phrase became one of his sobriquets.

earn (*or* turn) an HONEST penny earn money by fair means, especially by hard work.

make an HONEST woman of marry (esp. a pregnant woman). ● *Honest* here originally meant 'respectable', but was probably associated with the archaic sense 'chaste, virtuous'. Now dated and used mainly humorously.

do the HONOURS perform a social duty or small ceremony for others. ● Often used to describe the serving of food or drink to a guest.

HONOURS are even there is equality in the contest. *Brit.*

(in) HONOUR bound obliged by one's sense of honour.

on the HOOF 1 (of livestock) not yet slaughtered. **2** without great thought or preparation.

> **2 1997** *Times* Are we not witnessing an example of Tony Blair making policy on the hoof, … with a decision to match the circumstances, not the principle?

by HOOK or by crook by one means or another; by fair means or foul. ● That *hook* is a bill-hook or heavy curved pruning knife, rather than the (now obsolete) word for a shepherd's crook, is borne out by one of the earliest recorded instances of this phrase (in Gower's *Confessio Amantis*, 1390) which has the rare word *hepe* (pruning knife) in place of *hook*. Various folk etymologies of the expression have been put forward, none of them entirely convincing. William Cobbett in 1822 wrote of people who lived near woodland being allowed, under the ancient forest law of England, to gather dead branches for fuel, which they may have brought down from the trees literally *by hook or by crook*. *With hook or crook* is recorded from L14. *By hook or by crook* is always used in contexts that imply resorting to devious means to overcome obstacles in achieving one's ends.

get (*or* give someone) the HOOK be dismissed from a job (*or* dismiss someone from a job). *N. Amer., informal*

HOOK it run away. *Brit., informal*

HOOK, line, and sinker entirely; without reservation. *informal* ● A fishing metaphor: all three are items attached to a fisherman's rod and might be thought likely to be gulped down by a greedy fish. Current since M19, always with the implication that the action thus carried out is regrettable and often used with *fall (for)* in cases where someone is deceived (see quot.).

> **1936** N. COWARD *To-night at 8.30* II. 58 I fell for it hook, line and sinker.

off the HOOK 1 *informal* no longer in difficulty or trouble. **2** (of a telephone receiver) not on its rest, and so not receiving incoming calls. ● *Hook* in sense 1 is a longstanding (M15) figurative use of the word to mean in general 'something by which one is caught and trapped', as a fish-hook catches a fish. Sense 2 is a fossilized expression from the early years of telephony (L19), when the receiver literally hung on a hook.

on the HOOK for (in a financial context) responsible for. *N. Amer.*, *informal*

> **1992** *New York Times* 8 Nov. III. 6/2 I think Clinton is on the hook to deliver some help for the economy fast.

sling (*or* take) one's HOOK leave; go away. *Brit.*, *informal* ● *Sling your hook* appears in a slang dictionary of 1874 where it is defined as 'a polite invitation to move-on'.

> **1998** *Times: Weekend* 25 July 3/7 I now realise that Sylvia hasn't heard from him since she told him to sling his hook.

play HOOKEY stay away from school without permission or explanation; play truant. *N. Amer.*, *informal*

off the HOOKS dead. *Brit.*, *informal*

put someone (*or* go) through the HOOPS make someone undergo (*or* be made to undergo) a difficult and gruelling test or series of tests.

not care (*or* give) a HOOT (*or* two hoots) not care at all. *informal*

> **1990** K. LAWRENCE *Springs of Living Water* iii. 70 Never think about anybody but yourself, do you? Never give two hoots about your poor little sister following you around.

HOP the twig (*or* stick) 1 depart suddenly. **2** die. *Brit.*, *informal*

on the HOP unprepared. *Brit.*, *informal* ● Usually in *catch someone on the hop*.

HOPE against hope cling to a mere possibility.

HOPE springs eternal it is human nature to always find fresh cause for optimism. ● A shortened version of Alexander Pope's line: 'Hope springs eternal in the human breast' (*Essay on Man* i. 95).

> **1992** A. LAMBERT *Rather English Marriage* (1993) viii. 145 Hope springs eternal—she smiled wryly—even in Tunbridge Wells.

HOPE ▶ *see* **bottom DRAWER**.

on the HORIZON just imminent or becoming apparent.

blow (*or* toot) one's own HORN talk boastfully about oneself or one's achievements. *N. Amer.* ● Cf. ▶ **blow one's own TRUMPET**.

on the HORN on the telephone. *N. Amer.*, *informal*

a HORNETS' nest a situation fraught with trouble, opposition, or complications. ● This figurative use has been current since L16. Now often with *stir up*.

> **1739–40** S. RICHARDSON *Pamela* I. xxvi. 78 I have rais'd a Hornet's Nest about my Ears, that … may have stung to Death my Reputation.

draw (*or* pull) in one's HORNS become less assertive or ambitious; draw back. ● With reference to the snail's habit of drawing in its retractile tentacles when disturbed.

on the HORNS of a dilemma faced with a decision involving equally unfavourable alternatives. ● T. Wilson in *Logike* (1551) described *dilemma* as 'a horned argument' (after scholastic Latin *argumentum cornutum*), the idea being that if one avoided one 'horn' of the argument one ended up impaled on the other.

eat like a HORSE eat heartily and greedily.

(straight) from the HORSE's mouth from the person directly concerned or another authoritative source. ● With reference to the presumed ideal source for a racing tip and hence of other useful information.

> **1998** *New Scientist* 6 June 56/2 PhD students will be able to learn these subjects direct from the horse's mouth.

a HORSE of another (*or* different) colour a thing significantly different.

> **1980** S. HAZZARD *Transit of Venus* (1981) 123 Your average tourist is not a big reader. Guidebooks now—well, there you're on to a horse of a different colour.

on one's HIGH horse in a supercilious or indignant mood. *informal*

HORSE ▶ *see* **a DARK horse**; ▶ *see* **a TROJAN horse**.

change HORSES in midstream change one's mind or tactics midway through a course of action. *proverbial* ● Quoted by Abraham Lincoln in 1864 as the saying of 'an old Dutch farmer' (*Collected Works* (1953) VII. 384). Early versions (M19–M20) have *swap* instead of *change*.

HORSES for courses different people are suited to different things or situations.

> **1891 A. E. T.* WATSON *Turf* vii. A familiar phrase on the turf is 'horses for courses' ... The Brighton Course is very like Epsom, and horses that win at one meeting often win at the other.

wild HORSES won't drag someone to something (*or* something from someone) nothing will make someone go to a particular place (*or* divulge particular information). *informal* with reference to the punishment of tying someone to one or more wild horses to be dragged to death or pulled apart.

> **1998** *Times* 13 Mar. 35/7 As things stand, wild horses wouldn't drag them [children] to a symphony concert.

HORSES ▶ *see* **HITCH horses together**.

a HOSTAGE to fortune an act, commitment, or remark which is regarded as unwise because it invites trouble or could prove difficult to live up to. ● The original *hostages to fortune* were a man's family, with allusion to Francis Bacon's *Essays* (1625) 'Of Marriage': 'He that hath wife and children hath given hostages to fortune.'

go HOT and cold experience sudden feelings of fear, embarrassment, or shock.

> **1973** A. PRICE *October Men* v. 64 His wife had said ... that she had gone 'all hot and cold' after nearly being run over.

HOT air impressive promises or boasting without any substance.

> **1998** *Times* 18 Mar. 37/2 If a chief executive is convinced that a day spent hot-air ballooning is a more effective way of motivating the troops than a lot of hot air from him or her, then anything goes.

HOT on the heels of following closely.

HOT under the collar angry, resentful, or embarrassed.

| 1997 'Q' *Dead Meat* 25 I cut him short and said I was coming back later that night. He got hot under the collar.

drop someone/thing like a HOT potato quickly abandon someone/thing. *informal* ●*Drop* here is used literally, but also in the figurative sense of 'terminate a social acquaintance (with someone)' (see quot.). A *hot potato* can be used independently as a metaphor for a controversial or awkward issue or problem that no one wants to handle.

| 1930 W. S. MAUGHAM *Cakes and Ale* xiv. 169 She dropped him, but not like a hot brick or a hot potato.

in HOT water in a situation of difficulty, trouble, or disgrace.

make it (or things) HOT for someone make life difficult for someone.

too HOT to hold one (of a place) not safe to remain in because of one's past misconduct.

HOT ▶ see **BLOW hot and cold**; ▶ see **sell like hot CAKES**.

have the HOTS for be sexually attracted to. *informal* ●Originally M20 US slang, similar to E20 US slang *have hot pants*.

| 1951 W. H. AUDEN *Nones* 18Jack likes Jill who worships George Who has the hots for Jack.

keep late (or regular) HOURS do the same thing, typically getting up and going to bed, late (or at the same time) every day.

till all HOURS till very late. *informal*

HOURS ▶ see **the SMALL hours**.

get on (or along) like a HOUSE on fire have a very good and friendly relationship.

HOUSE and home a person's home. ●A duplication of sense used for emphasis.

a HOUSE divided a group or organization weakened by internal dissensions. ●Alluding to Matthew 12:25 'every city or house divided against itself shall not stand,' i.e. will be unable to withstand external pressures.

a HOUSE of cards an insecure or overambitious scheme. ●Literally, a structure of playing-cards balanced together.

on the HOUSE free. ●Used of drinks or a meal in a bar or restaurant taken at the management's expense.

put (or set or get) one's HOUSE in order make necessary reforms. ●Cf. 2 Kings 20:1 'Set thine house in order'.

HOUSE ▶ see **EAT someone out of house and home**.

not give something HOUSEROOM be unwilling to have or consider something. *Brit.* ●*Houseroom* (L16) is literally 'accommodation in a house'.

go round (or all round) the HOUSES 1 take a circuitous route to one's destination. 2 take an unnecessarily long time to get to the point.

(as) safe as HOUSES thoroughly or completely safe. *Brit.*

proclaim (or shout) from the HOUSETOPS announce publicly. ●Cf. Luke 12:3 'that which ye have spoken in the ear in closets shall be proclaimed upon the housetops.'

according to HOYLE according to plan or the rules. ● Edmond Hoyle (1672–1769) wrote a number of authoritative books about whist and other card games; his name, at first synonymous with expert opinion on card games, became a metaphor for the highest authority generally.

HUFF and puff 1 breathe heavily with exhaustion. **2** express one's annoyance in an obvious or threatening way.

HUM and haw (*or* ha) hesitate; be indecisive. *Brit.* ● M16. The word *hum* had been used as an inarticulate syllable in hesitant speech since Chaucer; *ha* appeared in a similar role from E17.

eat HUMBLE pie make a humble apology and accept humiliation. ● *Humble pie* is from a pun (M19) based on *umbles* 'offal', considered inferior food.

| **1998** *Spectator* 11 Apr. 30/3 [A] white youth behind us did shout racial abuse. But ... after the game was over his companions forced him to come up to Darcus to eat humble pie.

live on one's HUMP be self-sufficient. *informal* ● With allusion to the camel, which is famous for surviving on the fat in its hump without feeding or drinking.

over the HUMP over the worst.

HURT ▶ *see* **someone/thing wouldn't hurt a FLY**.

HUSTLE one's butt (*or* buns *or* vulgar slang **ass)** move or act quickly. *N. Amer., informal*

I

I ▶ *see* **DOT the i's and cross the t's**.

break the ICE help people begin to feel at ease in a social situation by making conversation, introducing them, etc.

on ICE **1** (especially of a plan or proposal) held in reserve for future consideration. **2** (of wine or food) kept chilled by being surrounded by ice. **3** (of an entertainment) performed by skaters.

(skating) on thin ICE in a precarious or risky situation.

the tip of an (*or* the) ICEBERG the small perceptible part of a situation or problem, of which much the larger part remains hidden. ● With allusion to the fact that only about one-fifth of the mass of an iceberg is visible above the surface of the sea.

> **1998** *New Scientist* 4 Apr. 4/3 This leaves pressure groups wondering whether there are further breaches still waiting to be discovered. Sue Mayer of Gene Watch asks: 'Is it the tip of the iceberg?'

the ICING (*N. Amer. also* frosting) on the cake an attractive but inessential addition or enhancement.

get IDEAS be ambitious or rebellious. *informal*

give someone IDEAS **1** give someone expectations or hopes that may not be realized. **2** cause someone to think about another in a sexual way.

IF anything it may be the case that. ● Used to suggest tentatively that something may be so, often the opposite of something previously stated or implied.

be under the ILLUSION believe mistakenly. ● Followed by *that* and clause.

be under no ILLUSION (*or* illusions) be fully aware of the true state of affairs. ● Often with *about*.

> **1992** *Christian Scientist Monitor* 7 Jan. 19 It is crucial to the nation's security ... that we be under no illusions about reasons for this zero-loss rate.

a graven IMAGE an object of misdirected worship; an idol. ● With allusion to the second of the Ten Commandments: 'Thou shalt not make unto thee any graven image' (Exodus 20:4).

IMPROVE the shining hour make good use of time; make the most of one's time. *literary* ● After Isaac Watts (1674–1748): 'How doth the little busy bee Improve each shining hour.'

be IN for have good reason to expect (typically something unpleasant).

have it IN for someone have hostile feelings towards someone. *informal*

be IN on be privy to (a secret).

IN with enjoying friendly relations with. *informal*

> **1990** J. MASSON *Final Analysis* (1991) vi. 124 I was in demand everywhere ... simply because I was in with the right people.

give someone an INCH once a concession has been made or a sign of weakness shown to someone this is likely to result in their making further demands. ● The full form of the saying is *give him* (or *her*, etc.) *an inch and he* (or *she*, etc.) *will take a mile*. Formerly *ell* (an obsolete measure of length equal to a little over a metre) was also used instead of *mile*.

(to) within an INCH of one's life almost to the point of death.

INCLINE one's ear listen favourably. *literary* ● In the Bible *passim*, e.g. Psalms 17:6, Proverbs 2:2. Often followed by *to*.

INDIAN summer a tranquil or productive period in someone's later years. ● Since L18, the name given to a period of calm dry warm weather in late autumn in the northern US (now also elsewhere).

> **1930** V. SACKVILLE-WEST *Edwardians* iii. 100 Meanwhile she was quite content that Sebastian should become tanned in the rays of Sylvia's Indian summer.

under the INFLUENCE affected by alcoholic drink, especially beyond the legal limits for driving a vehicle; drunk. *informal* ● Short for *under the influence of alcohol*.

honest INJUN honestly; really. ● *Injun* and *Injin* are dialect or colloquial forms of *Indian*. Perhaps originally from an expression of good faith elicited from US Indians, now somewhat dated.

do oneself an INJURY suffer physical harm or damage. *informal* ● Cf. ▶ **do someone a MISCHIEF**.

have had a good INNINGS have enjoyed a long period of fulfilling action or opportunity. *Brit., informal* ● A metaphor from cricket; an *innings* is the period that a team or batsman spends batting and *a good innings* is one during which a lot of runs are scored. Said when someone is near death (or has died) or has done a job well for a long time and is about to leave (or has left).

> **1870** MISS BRIDGMAN *Robert Lynne* I. vi. 81 She's had remarkably good innings, and persons can't expect to live for ever.

in all INNOCENCE without knowledge of something's significance or possible consequences.

the INS and outs all the details (of something). ● In M17 as *in and outs*; the current version since E19.

know something (or someone) INSIDE OUT know someone or something very thoroughly.

add INSULT to injury act in a way that makes a bad or displeasing situation worse. ● From Edward Moore's *The Foundling* (1748) 'This is adding insult to injuries.'

> **1998** *Times* 8 Sept. 22/3 To add insult to this injury Downing Street squeaks that 'this report has nothing to do with the Government'.

to all INTENTS and purposes practically; virtually.

> **1992** *London Review of Books* 26 Mar. 3/1 For if in 1976 pianists really were about to lose the skill of polyphonic piano-playing, then to all intents and purposes the skill of playing the piano was at an end.

declare an (*or* one's) INTEREST make known one's financial interests in an undertaking before it is discussed.

run INTERFERENCE intervene on someone's behalf, typically so as to protect them from distraction or annoyance. *N. Amer. informal* ● A metaphor from American football.

the IRON entered into someone's soul someone became deeply and permanently affected by imprisonment or ill-treatment. *literary* ● The version of Psalm 105:18 in the Book of Common Prayer, 'the iron entered into his soul', translates a Latin mistranslation of the Hebrew, which is accurately rendered in the AV as 'he was laid in iron', i.e. he was fettered.

an IRON curtain an impenetrable barrier, esp. (*Iron Curtain*) the physical and other barriers preventing the passage of people and information between the Soviet bloc and the West during the cold war. ● In L18 an *iron curtain* was literally a fire-curtain in a theatre, but the figurative sense was current from E19. The phrase was thus in use well before Winston Churchill made it famous in the cold war sense when he observed in a speech in March 1946 that 'an iron curtain has descended across the Continent [of Europe].'

an IRON hand (*or* fist) in a velvet glove inflexibility or ruthlessness masked by a gentle or urbane appearance or manner.

IRON out the wrinkles resolve all minor difficulties and snags. ● From smoothing fabric with a hot iron after washing, *iron out* (in figurative use since M19) also often occurs with other nouns, especially *differences*.

> **1984** *New Yorker* 14 May 43 Willa had sold her story to Universal Pictures and was in California ironing out some wrinkles in the deal.

IRON ▶ *see* **STRIKE while the iron is hot**.

have many (*or* other) IRONS in the fire have many (*or* a range of) options or courses of action available or be involved in many activities or commitments at the same time. ● Various implements made of iron were called *irons* (now usually with a defining word; e.g., *grappling-iron*). The metaphor is of a blacksmith or other labourer who heats iron objects in a fire until they reach the critical temperature at which they can be shaped or used. First recorded M16 in the metaphorical sense.

new off the IRONS newly made or prepared; brand-new. ● *Irons* here are the dies used in striking coins.

an ITCHING palm a rapacious nature.

get (*or* have) ITCHY feet be restless; have a strong urge to move or travel. *informal*

J

before one can say JACK Robinson very quickly or suddenly. *informal* ● The present expression was in use in L18, and an E19 popular song about *Jack Robinson* and some M19 attempts to identify the eponymous *Jack Robinson* fail to throw light on its origins.

every man JACK each and every person. *informal* ● *Jack* is the pet-name form of the forename John, influenced perhaps by the medieval diminutive form *Jankin* and possibly by French *Jacques*. It was used sometimes in US colloquial speech as a form of address to a man whose name one did not know, and as a generic name for any ordinary or working-class man (see also following entries). Used for emphasis.

I'm all right, JACK used to express or comment upon selfish complacency. *informal* ● An E20 catchphrase which became the title of a 1959 British film.

JACK of all trades (and master of none) a person who can do many different types of work (but who is not necessarily very competent at any of them). ● *Jack* here is in the sense of a 'general labourer' or 'odd-job man' (M19).

on one's JACK on one's own. *Brit., slang* ● This an abbreviation of the rhyming slang expression *on one's Jack Jones* (E20).

hit the JACKPOT **1** win a jackpot. **2** *informal* have great or unexpected success, especially in making a lot of money quickly. ● Originally, the *jackpot* (L19) was the pot or pool in draw-poker that has to accumulate until a player can open the betting with a pair of jacks or higher. It is now used of any large money prize that accumulates until it is won.

JAM tomorrow a pleasant thing which is often promised but rarely materializes. *Brit.* ● From Lewis Carroll's *Through the Looking-Glass* (1871) v. 'The rule is jam to-morrow and jam yesterday—but never jam today.'

plain JANE an unattractive girl or woman. ● The use of *Jane* as a generic name for a woman (esp. US) dates from about the same time as this phrase (both E20).

> **1912** C. MACKENZIE *Carnival* ii. 14 She sha'n't be a Plain Jane and No Nonsense, with her hair screwed back like a broom, but she shall be Jenny, sweet and handsome.

and all that JAZZ and such similar things. *informal, chiefly derogatory* ● *Jazz* was used colloquially for 'meaningless talk' within a decade of the word's first appearance in its musical sense. This phrase was an M20 development, with *jazz* here being synonymous with 'nonsense'.

JEKYLL and Hyde a person alternately displaying opposing good and evil personalities. ● From *The Strange Case of Dr. Jekyll and Mr. Hyde* by R. L. Stevenson (1886), in which the physician Jekyll, in order to indulge his evil instincts, uses a drug to create the persona of Hyde, which at first he can put on and off at will but which gradually gains control of him.

the JEWEL in the (*or* someone's) crown the most attractive or successful part of something. ●Originally (E20) a rhetorical phrase for the colonies of the British empire, hence used by Paul Scott (1920–78) as the title of the first novel (1966) of his Raj Quartet about British India.

JIB ▶ *see* **the CUT of someone's jib**.

in JIG time extremely quickly; in a very short time. *N. Amer.*, *informal*

the JIG is up the scheme or deception is revealed or foiled; the game is up. *N. Amer.*, *informal* ●Jig here is in the sense of 'jest' or 'sportive trick' (L16). *The jig is over* is recorded from L18 US, with this usual modern form of the idiom only slightly later.

the whole JINGBANG the whole lot (of people or things). *informal* ●The origin of *jingbang* and its variant *jimbang*, which occur only in this phrase, is uncertain, although the word was first recorded as M19 Banffshire dialect.

do a JOB on someone do something which harms or defeats an opponent. *informal*

a JOB's comforter a person who aggravates distress while purporting to offer comfort. ●Job was the much-afflicted biblical patriarch, who responded to the exhortations of his friends, 'miserable comforters are ye all' (Job 16.2).

more than one's JOB's worth not worth risking one's job for. ●Hence the name *Jobsworth* is applied to the kind of person, usually a minor official, who says 'it's more than my job's worth' to justify insisting that rules are followed exactly, without allowing any latitude in their interpretation.

JOB ▶ *see* **make the BEST of it**.

JOBS for the boys the giving of paid employment to one's friends, supporters, or relations. *Brit.*, *informal* ●M20, always used derogatorily.

JOIN the great majority die. *euphemistic* ●From Edward Young *The Revenge* (1721): 'Death joins us to the great majority.' The idea of the dead being the majority antedates Young, being found in Latin in Petronius' *Satyricon* ('Cena Trimalchionis' xlii. 5): *abiit ad plures*.

JOIN ▶ *see* **join the CLUB**.

out of JOINT **1** (of a specified joint) out of position; dislocated. **2** in a state of disorder or disorientation. ●Cf. ▶ **put someone's NOSE out of joint**.
| **2** 1601 W. SHAKESPEARE *Hamlet* I. v. 188 The time is out of joint.

the JOKE is on someone someone looks foolish, especially after trying to make someone else look so. *informal*
| **1998** *Spectator* 25 Apr. 5/1 He turned out to be as right as rain, … so the joke was on us.

the JOKER in the pack a person or factor likely to have an unpredictable effect on events. ●The *joker* is the extra, or fifty-third, card in a pack of playing cards, which is not part of the four suits (clubs, diamonds, hearts, and spades) and is usually ornamented with the figure of a jester; it is used in some card games as a trump and in poker as a wild card.

keep up with the JONESES try to maintain the same social and material standards as one's friends or neighbours. ● From a comic-strip title, 'Keeping up with the Joneses—by Pop' in the New York *Globe* 1913. *Jones*, one of the most frequent British family names, is used as a generic name for one's neighbours or presumed social equals.

JOURNEY ▶ *see* **a SABBATH day's journey**.

full of the JOYS of spring lively and cheerful.

wish someone JOY (of) congratulate someone (on something). *Brit.* ● Almost always used ironically.

JUDAS ▶ *see* **a Judas KISS**.

against one's better JUDGEMENT contrary to what one feels to be wise or sensible.

go for the JUGULAR be aggressive or unrestrained in making an attack. ● That is, go for the throat, since the jugular vein runs in the throat.

get (or have) the JUMP on get (or have) an advantage over someone as a result of one's prompt action. *chiefly N. Amer., informal*
> 1912 G. ADE *Knocking Neighbors* 123 Rufus was sinfully Rich … his Family had drilled into him the low-down Habit of getting the Jump on the Other Fellow.

go (and) JUMP in the lake go away and stop being a nuisance. *informal* ● Often in imperative.
> 1998 *New Scientist* 24 Jan. 43/2 He is in some unexplained way independent of his genes: … if they don't like what he does, his genes can go jump in the lake.

JUMP someone's bones have sexual intercourse with someone. *N. Amer., vulgar slang*

JUMP down someone's throat respond to what someone has said in a sudden and angrily critical way. *informal*

JUMP out of one's skin be extremely startled. *informal*

JUMP the queue (or US jump in line) **1** push into a queue of people in order to be served or dealt with before one's turn. **2** take unfair precedence over others.

JUMP the rails (or track) (of a train) become dislodged from the track; be derailed.

JUMP ship **1** (of a sailor) leave the ship on which one is serving without having obtained permission to do so. **2** suddenly abandon an organization, enterprise, etc.

JUMP through hoops be obliged to go through an elaborate or complicated procedure in order to achieve an objective.

JUMP (or leap) to conclusions (or the conclusion) form an opinion precipitately, before one has learned or considered all the facts.

one JUMP ahead one step or stage ahead of someone else and so having the advantage over them.

JUMP ▶ *see* **jump the GUN**; ▶ *see* **jump on the BANDWAGON**.

be JUMPING up and down be very angry, upset, or excited. *informal*

the law of the JUNGLE the principle that those who are strong and apply ruthless self-interest will be most successful. ● The supposed principle of survival in jungle life.

> **1989** B. HEAD *Tales, Tenderness & Power* (1990) 37 And at the beer tank the law of the jungle prevailed, the stronger shoving the weaker.

the JURY is (still) out a decision has not (yet) been reached.

> **1998** *New Scientist* 14 Feb. 30/2 The jury is still out, but it looks as if there are no significant changes in the cosmic dust flux during past climate cycles.

do oneself JUSTICE perform as well as one is able to.

do someone/thing JUSTICE (*or* do justice to someone/thing) treat or represent someone or something with due fairness or appreciation.

poetic JUSTICE the ideal distribution of rewards and punishments supposed to befit a poem or other literary work; well-deserved retribution. ● From Pope's *Dunciad* i. 52 'Poetic Justice, with her lifted scale'.

rough JUSTICE **1** treatment, especially punishment, that is approximately fair. **2** treatment that is not at all fair or not in accordance with the law.

K

have KANGAROOS in the (*or* one's) top paddock be mad or eccentric. *Austral.*, *informal*

| **1985** P. CAREY *Illywacker* 53 'And he was a big man too, and possibly slow-witted.' 'Leichhardt?' 'No, Bourke ... He had kangaroos in his top paddock.'

(as) KEEN as mustard extremely eager or enthusiastic. *Brit.*, *informal* ● *Keen* here is in the sense of 'operating on the senses like a sharp instrument'.

you can't KEEP a good man (*or* woman) down a competent person will always recover well from setbacks or problems. *informal*

KEEP one's feet (*or* legs) manage not to fall.

KEEP open house provide general hospitality.

KEEP ▶ *see* **keep the BALL rolling**; ▶ *see* **keep one's eye on the BALL**; ▶ *see* **keep the SHOW on the road**; ▶ *see* **on one's TOES**; ▶ *see* **keep under WRAPS**; ▶ *see* **keep up with the JONESES**.

a different KETTLE of fish a completely different matter or type of person from the one previously mentioned. *informal* ● This phrase is M20; see next entry for earlier usages.

a pretty (*or* fine) KETTLE of fish an awkward state of affairs. *informal* ● The phrase was used (M18) by Fielding to mean a 'muddle', but a *kettle of fish* was also literally a large saucepan of fish, mainly freshly caught salmon, cooked at Scottish picnics in L18, and hence also the name given to such a picnic.

KETTLE ▶ *see* **the POT calling the kettle black**.

in (*or* out of) KEY in (*or* out of) harmony.

put the KIBOSH on put an end to; thwart the plans of. *informal* ● The meaning and origin of *kibosh*, which is very seldom used outside this expression, is debated. 'Put the kye-bosk [*sic*] on her' appears as vulgar London slang (used by 'a pot-boy') in Dickens's *Sketches by Boz* (1836). In British speech the accent always falls on the first syllable, but in the US the accent tends to be on the second.

| **1914** A. ELLERTON (*song-title*) Belgium put the kibosh on the Kaiser.

KICK (some) ass (*or* butt) act in a forceful or aggressive manner. *N. Amer.*, *informal*

KICK someone's ass (*or* butt) beat, dominate, or defeat someone. *N. Amer.*, *informal*

a KICK at the can (*or* cat) an opportunity to achieve something. *Canadian*, *informal*

KICK the bucket die. *informal* ● *Bucket* here may mean a 'pail'; cf. ▶ **hand in one's DINNER pail**. However, another suggestion is that it means a 'beam' on which something can be hung up. In Norfolk dialect the beam from which a slaughtered pig was suspended by its heels could be called a *bucket*, hence *kick the bucket*. Recorded from L18.

KICK the gong around smoke opium. *slang* ●*Gong* is E20 US slang for a narcotic drug, especially opium.

a KICK in the pants (*or* up the arse *or* backside) something that prompts or forces fresh effort. *informal*

a KICK in the teeth a grave setback or disappointment, especially one seen as a betrayal. *informal*

KICK something into touch remove something from the centre of attention or activity. *Brit., informal* ● A football idiom: the touchlines mark the sides of the playing area and if the ball is kicked beyond these (*into touch*) it is no longer in play.

> **1998** *New Scientist* 20 June 53/2 The British public is more interested in these matters than many politicians think. Such issues cannot be kicked into touch.

KICK a man when he's down cause further misfortune to someone who is already in a difficult situation.

KICK up a fuss (*or* a stink) register strong disapproval; object loudly to something. *informal*

KICK someone upstairs remove someone from an influential position in a business by giving them an ostensible promotion. *informal*

KICK ▶ *see* **kick against the PRICKS**; ▶ *see* **kick down the LADDER**; ▶ *see* **cool one's HEELS**; ▶ *see* **kick over the TRACES**; ▶ *see* **kick up one's HEELS**.

more KICKS than halfpence more harsh treatment than rewards. *informal* ● Grose (*Dictionary of Vulgar Tongue*, 1785) calls this 'monkey's allowance', probably with reference to the monkey used by a travelling showman or musician to attract a paying audience.

handle (*or* treat) someone/thing with KID gloves deal with someone or something very gently or tactfully.

KID ▶ *see* **a new kid on the BLOCK**.

KIDS' stuff something that is childishly simple or naive. *informal, derogatory*

be in at the KILL be present at or benefit from the successful conclusion of an enterprise. ● A hunting metaphor; cf. ▶ **be in at the DEATH**

dressed to KILL wearing attractive and flamboyant clothes in order to make a striking impression.

go (*or* move in *or* close in) for the KILL take decisive action to turn a situation to one's advantage. ● From a predator making the final moves to kill its prey.

KILL oneself laughing be overcome with laughter.

KILL or cure (of a remedy for a problem) likely to either work well or fail catastrophically, with no possibility of partial success. *Brit.*

KILL two birds with one stone achieve two aims at once. ●Proverbial, recorded from M17 onwards.

KILL with (or by) kindness spoil with over-indulgence. ●Cf. the title of Thomas Heywood's play *A Woman Killed with Kindness* (1607).

KILL ▶ *see* **kill the FATTED calf**; ▶ *see* **the GOOSE that lays the golden egg**.

make a KILLING have a great financial success, especially on a stock exchange.

if it KILLS one whatever the problems or difficulties involved. *informal*

in KILTER balanced and in harmony. ●*Kelter* or *kilter* (E17) was a dialect word of obscure origin meaning 'frame, order'. Now found commonly in the usual US spelling *kilter*, it is used only in this phrase and its opposites *out of kilter* and *off kilter*.

KIN ▶ *see* **NEXT of kin**.

KING Charles's head an obsession, an *idée fixe*. ●With reference to 'Mr Dick', in Dickens's *David Copperfield*, who could not write or speak on any matter without the subject of King Charles's head intruding.

KING or Kaiser any powerful earthly ruler.

KING ▶ *see* **a king's RANSOM**; ▶ *see* **take the King's SHILLING**.

come into (or to) one's KINGDOM achieve recognition or supremacy.

till (or until) KINGDOM come for ever. *informal* ●*Kingdom come* is the next world, eternity; from the clause in the Lord's Prayer *thy kingdom come*.

to KINGDOM come into the next world. *informal* ●See preceding entry.

a Judas KISS an act of betrayal. ●Judas Iscariot was the disciple who betrayed Jesus to those who came to arrest him; 'And he that betrayed him gave them a sign, saying, Whomsoever I shall kiss, that same is he: hold him fast' (Matthew 26:48).

KISS and make up become reconciled.

> 1991 *Economist* 3 Aug. 46/2 [China] and Vietnam are preparing to kiss and make up in the cause of socialist solidarity.

KISS and tell recount one's sexual exploits, especially to the media concerning a famous person. *chiefly derogatory* ●Also as modifier as in *kiss-and-tell memoirs*.

KISS ass behave in an obsequious or sycophantic way. *N. Amer., vulgar slang*

KISS something goodbye accept the certain loss of something. *informal* ●Also *kiss goodbye to something*. *Kiss someone goodbye* is also used literally of making one's farewells with a kiss.

KISS of death an action or event that causes certain failure for an enterprise. ●Perhaps with reference to the kiss of betrayal given by Judas to Jesus in the Garden of Gethsemane (Matthew 26:48–9). Used particularly in cases where the action appears at first to be well-intentioned.

| **1998** *Spectator* 23 May 12/3 I commend the Commission's recent Green Paper and its efforts to introduce an enlightened, evolutionary discussion—although I hope my saying so will not be the kiss of death.

KISS the dust submit abjectly; be overthrown.

KISS the ground prostrate oneself as a token of respect. ● From the action, practised particularly in courts of the ancient oriental world, of throwing oneself on the ground in front of a monarch.

KISS the rod accept punishment submissively. ● From the practice of making a child kiss the rod with which it was beaten.

| **1592–3** W. SHAKESPEARE *Two Gentlemen of Verona* I. ii. 55 How wayward is this foolish love That, like a testy babe, will scratch the nurse And presently all humbled kiss the rod.

KISS ▶ *see* **have kissed the BLARNEY stone**.

play KISSY-FACE (*or* kissy-kissy) behave in an excessively friendly way in order to gain favour.

everything but the KITCHEN sink everything imaginable. *informal, humorous* ● Identified by Partridge (1948) as forces' slang used in the context of an intense bombardment in which the enemy fired everything they had *except the kitchen sink* (or *including the kitchen sink*).

| **1965** 'E. MCBAIN' *Doll* x. 128 Brown began searching. 'Everything in here but the kitchen sink,' he said.

(as) high as a KITE intoxicated with drugs or alcohol. ● A play on *high* meaning 'lofty' and its slang sense 'intoxicated'. M20 US slang, now general in informal speech.

KITH and kin one's relations. ● *Kith*, an Old English word meaning 'native land' or 'one's countrymen', is now obsolete except in this phrase, which itself dates back to L14. Also *kith or kin*.

have KITTENS be extremely nervous or upset. *Brit., informal* ● Originally (E20) US slang.

scoop the KITTY gain everything, be completely successful. ● In gambling, the *kitty* is the pool of money that is staked.

at one's mother's (*or* father's) KNEE at an early age.

KNEE ▶ *see* **on BENDED knee**.

KNEE-HIGH to a grasshopper very small or very young. *informal, humorous* ● In this form apparently M19, but E19 US versions include *to a toad* and *to a mosquito*.

bring someone/thing to their/its KNEES reduce someone or something to a state of weakness or submission.

weak at the KNEES overcome by a strong emotion.

ring the KNELL of announce or herald the end of. ● From the tolling of a bell to announce a death or funeral.

get one's KNICKERS in a twist become upset or angry. *Brit.*, *informal* ● Originally used specifically of women; the jocular masculine equivalent is *get one's Y-fronts in a twist*.

| **1998** *Times* 30 Sept. 19/4 I'm not as anxious as I was … Most things these days, I'm really not going to get my knickers in a twist about.

before you can say KNIFE very quickly; almost instantaneously. *informal*

get (*or* stick) one's KNIFE into (*or* in) someone do something hostile or aggressive to someone. *informal* ● Also *put in the knife*.

like a (hot) KNIFE through butter very easily; without any resistance.

twist (*or* turn) the KNIFE deliberately make someone's grief or problems worse.

KNIFE ▶ *see* **an ATMOSPHERE that one could cut with a knife**.

on a KNIFE-EDGE (*or* razor edge) in a tense situation, especially one finely balanced between success and failure.

a KNIGHT in shining armour an idealized or heroic person, especially a man who comes to the rescue of a woman in distress or in a difficult situation. ● Often used ironically of someone who presents himself in this guise but is inadequate to the role. A variant is *a knight on a white charger*; cf. also ▶ **a WHITE knight**.

KNIGHT of the road a man who frequents the roads, for example a travelling representative, lorry or taxi driver, or tramp. ● Originally (M17) used ironically of a highwayman. The commercial traveller sense is L19.

KNIGHT ▶ *see* **a WHITE knight**.

stick to the (*or* one's) KNITTING (of an organization) concentrate on a known core area of business activity rather than diversify into other areas in which it has no experience. *informal*

with KNOBS (*or* brass knobs) on and something more. *Brit.*, *informal* ● Sometimes used for returning and strengthening an insult.

| **1998** *Times* 12 Mar. 52/4 He was blunt and ungushing; himself, with knobs on.

KNOCK someone's block off hit someone very hard in anger. *informal* ● *Block* is in its slang sense of 'head'.

KNOCK someone dead greatly impress someone. *informal*

| **1991** J. PHILIPS *You'll Never Eat Lunch* 261 I'm good at public speaking. I've been knocking them dead at seminars.

KNOCK someone into the middle of next week hit someone very hard. *informal*

KNOCK it off stop doing something. *informal* ● Used to tell someone to cease doing something that one finds tiresome or foolish.

KNOCK on (*or* at) the door seek to join a particular group or sphere of action. ● Often used to suggest that the person is persistent or very close to achieving their aim.

KNOCK someone/thing on the head decisively prevent an idea, plan, or proposal from being held or developed. *Brit., informal* ● From literally stunning or killing someone or something by a blow on the head.

KNOCK someone sideways affect someone very severely; make someone severely depressed or unable to cope. *informal*

KNOCK spots off easily outdo. *informal* ● May be in reference to shooting out the pips (spots) on a playing card in a pistol-shooting competition. Originally US, it was used with the definite article (*knocks the spots off*) and the gloss 'as we say here' in *Spirit of the Times*, 1856. Now mainly Brit.

> **1997** *Spectator* 11 Oct. 62/1 [Walter Laut Palmer's] 'Morning in Venice' is a *tour-de-force* … It knocks spots off the neighbouring, deeply unattractive, Monet of a gondola.

KNOCK them in the aisles amaze and impress people. *informal* ● Cf. ▶ **have people rolling in the AISLES**.

take a KNOCK suffer a material or emotional setback.

KNOCK ▶ *see* **hit someone for SIX**; ▶ *see* **bang one's HEAD against a brick wall**; ▶ *see* **BANG heads together**; ▶ *see* **knock something into a COCKED hat**; ▶ *see* **lick someone/thing into SHAPE**; ▶ *see* **touch WOOD**; ▶ *see* **knock someone's SOCKS off**.

you could have KNOCKED me (*or* her, him, etc.) down with a feather I (*or* she, he, etc.) was greatly surprised. *informal* ● The idea occurs in Richardson's *Pamela* in 1741 ('you might have beat me down with a feather'); the modern form of the expression with *knock* is M19.

on the KNOCKER 1 going from door to door, usually canvassing, buying, or selling. **2** *Austral. & NZ, informal* (of payment) immediately; on demand.

the school of hard KNOCKS painful or difficult experiences that are seen to be useful in teaching someone about life. ● Cf. ▶ **the UNIVERSITY of life**.

tie the KNOT get married. *informal*

KNOT ▶ *see* **CUT the knot**.

at a rate of KNOTS very fast. *Brit., informal* ● A *knot* is a nautical unit of speed, being one nautical mile per hour.

tie oneself (*or* someone) (up) in KNOTS make completely confused. *informal*

— as we KNOW it as is familiar or customary in the present. ● Cf. ▶ **the END of civilization as we know it**.

be in the KNOW be aware of something known only to a few people.

KNOW better than be wise, well-informed, or well-mannered enough to avoid doing something specified. ● With infinitive.

KNOW (*or* not know) from nothing be totally ignorant, either generally or concerning something in particular. *N. Amer., informal*

KNOW someone in the biblical sense have sexual intercourse with someone. *informal, humorous* ● *Know* is a Hebraism (e.g. Genesis 4:1) which has passed into modern languages; cf. German *erkennen*, French *connaître*.

KNOW the ropes be thoroughly acquainted with the way in which something is done. *informal* ● An expression going back in its literal sense to the days of sailing ships, when skill in handling ropes was essential for any sailor. The idiom in various forms (*learn/understand* or *show/teach someone the ropes*) is attested as a slang expression from M19; the 1874 edition of J. C. Hotten's *Dictionary of Modern Slang, Cant, and Vulgar Words* records its figurative extension: ' "To know the ropes," is to be conversant with the minutiae of metropolitan dodges, as regards both the streets and the sporting world.'

KNOW what's what have enough knowledge or experience. *informal*
| **1992** *More* 28 Oct.–10 Nov. 62/2 I know what's what at work, so no-one's going to trip me up.

KNOW who's who be aware of the identity and status of each person.

not KNOW what hit one be hit, killed, or attacked by someone or something without warning.

not KNOW what to do with oneself be at a loss as to what to do, typically through boredom, embarrassment, or anxiety.

not KNOW where (*or* which way) to look feel great embarrassment and not know how to react.

KNOW ▶ *see* **not know someone from ADAM**. ▶ *see* **know something like the BACK of one's hand**; ▶ *see* **know where the BODIES are buried**.

there is no KNOWING no one can tell.

KNOWN ▶ *see* **seen better DAYS**.

before one KNOWS where one is (*or* before one knows it) with baffling speed. *informal*

for all someone KNOWS used to express the limited scope or extent of one's information.

go the KNUCKLE fight; punch. *Austral., informal*

near the KNUCKLE verging on the indecent or offensive. *Brit., informal* ● L19 in the more general sense of 'close to the permitted limit' (of behaviour).

KNUCKLES ▶ *see* **RAP on the knuckles**.

L

a LABOUR of Hercules a task requiring enormous strength or effort. ●In Greek mythology, the hero Heracles (Hercules), in perfomance of a penance imposed upon him for killing his children in a fit of madness, was set a series of twelve seemingly impossible tasks or labours by King Eurystheus of Tiryns.

a LABOUR of love a task done for the love of a person or for the work itself.

LABOUR the point explain or discuss something at excessive or unnecessary length.

kick down the LADDER reject or disown the friends or associates who have helped one to rise in the world, especially with the idea of preventing them from attaining a similar position.

it isn't over till the fat LADY sings there is still time for a situation to change. ●With allusion to the saying *the opera isn't over till the fat lady sings*, which originated (L20) in the US; it is doubtful whether any particular operatic production or prima donna was ever intended.

LADIES who lunch women with the money and free time to meet for social lunches. *informal* ●With allusion to the title of a song (1970) by Stephen Sondheim: 'A toast to that invincible bunch ... Let's hear it for the ladies who lunch.' Used of women who raise money for charity by organizing fashionable lunches, but also often derogatorily of women with the money and leisure to lunch at expensive restaurants.

give it LALDY do something with vigour or enthusiasm. ●*Laldy* or *laldie* means 'punishment', as in *give someone laldy* 'beat someone'; it appears only in this context (recorded from L19).

> **1993** I. WALSH *Trainspotting* (1994) 175 A chorus ... echoes throughout the pub. Auld, toothless Willie Shane is giein it laldy.

on the LAM in flight, especially from the police. *N. Amer., informal*

like a LAMB to the slaughter as a helpless victim. ●Cf. Isaiah 53:7 'he is brought as a lamb to the slaughter', an image later applied to Jesus.

LAME ▶ *see* **lame DUCK**.

LAMP ▶ *see* **SMELL of the lamp**.

how the LAND lies what the state of affairs is. ●Also *the lie of the land* (L17) used both literally ('the way in which an area's features or characteristics present themselves') and figuratively.

in the LAND of the living alive or awake. *humorous* ●A biblical idiom: e.g. Job 28:13, Psalms 27:13, 52:5.

LAND of Nod a state of sleep. ●A pun, with allusion to the biblical place name *Nod* (Genesis 4:16), the land to which Cain was exiled after the killing of Abel; after Swift *Polite Conversation* (1731–8) 'I'm going to the Land of Nod.'

live off the LAND (*or* the country) subsist on whatever fruit, animals, etc. one can find or kill.

> **1995** *Empire* Nov. 137/2 Harrison Ford is the frazzled father who ups his family from cosy suburbia in an effort to live off the land, get back to nature, etc.

LAND (noun) ▶ *see* **NO man's land**.

LAND (verb) ▶ *see* **FALL on one's feet**.

LANDSCAPE ▶ *see* **a BLOT on the landscape**.

speak the same LANGUAGE understand one another as a result of shared opinions, values, etc.

fall (*or* drop) into someone's LAP (of something pleasant or desirable) come someone's way without any effort having been made.

in the LAP of the gods (of the success of a plan or event) open to chance; depending on factors that one cannot control. ● From an expression used in several passages in Homer (e.g. *Odyssey* i. 267; the Greek refers to the 'knees' of the gods, possibly because suppliants laid gifts on the knees of those who were sitting in judgement upon them.

in the LAP of luxury in conditions of great comfort and wealth.

LARES and penates the home. ● In ancient Rome the *lares* and *penates* were the protective gods of a household, and thus by metonymy both could also be used to signify the home itself. The phrase *lares and penates* (Latin *lares et penates*) is generally used of the essential elements of someone's home; thus in 1775 Horace Walpole wrote in a letter 'I am returned to my own Lares and Penates—to my dogs and cats.'

LARGE ▶ *see* **large as LIFE**.

up with the LARK up very early in the morning. ● The (sky)*lark*'s song, for which it is renowned, is to be heard especially soon after dawn; there is also a play on *up*, as the lark sings from high up in the sky.

LARRY ▶ *see* **HAPPY as a sandboy**.

(drinking) in the LAST chance saloon having been allowed one final opportunity to improve, get something right, etc. *informal* ● From the fanciful idea of a saloon bar with this name.

> | **1998** *Times* 20 May 48/1 Gascoigne has finally found himself in the Last Chance Saloon.

— one's LAST do something for the last time. ● Especially in *breathe one's last* or *look one's last*.

LAST but not least last in order of mention or occurrence but not of importance.

the LAST of the Mohicans the sole survivor(s) of a particular race or kind. ● With allusion to *The Last of the Mohicans*, a novel (1826) by J. F. Cooper (1789–1851). The Mohegans (*Mohicans*) were an Algonquian people formerly inhabiting Connecticut and Massachusetts.

LAST thing late in the evening, especially as a final act before going to bed.

be the LAST word be the most fashionable or up-to-date. ● Usually with preposition *in*. Cf. French *le dernier cri*, current in English since L19, which appeared in L20 literally translated as *the last cry* in this sense.

> **1966** *Listener* 6 Jan. 12/2 The Trombay establishment is the last word in nuclear sophistication.

have the LAST word 1 make or have the right to make the final decision about something. **2** carry out a final and conclusive action in a process or course of events.

LAST ▶ *see* **DIE in the last ditch**; ▶ *see* **FAMOUS last words**. ▶ *see* **one's last GASP**; ▶ *see* **on one's last LEGS**; ▶ *see* **PAY one's respects**; ▶ *see* **the last STRAW**;

LATE in the day (*or N. Amer.* **game**) at a late stage in proceedings, especially too late to be useful.

LATE ▶ *see* **the late UNPLEASANTNESS**.

enough to make a cat LAUGH extremely ridiculous or ironic. *informal* ● M19 associated with the story of *Puss in Boots*, but the idea of something being 'enough to make a cat speak' is E18.

good for a LAUGH guaranteed to amuse or entertain.

> **1998** *Spectator* 21 Mar. 26/2 I'm now ashamed to admit it, but the fact remains that in 1979 voting Tory did seem good for a laugh.

have the last LAUGH be finally vindicated, thus confounding earlier scepticism. ● With allusion to various proverbial expressions such as *he laughs best who laughs last*.

LAUGH all the way to the bank make a great deal of money with very little effort. *informal*

> **1998** *Country Life* 21 May 90/3 In the Taw Valley they don't need to say 'cheese' to raise a smile—they just whisper 'environment' and laugh all the way to the bank.

LAUGH in someone's face show open contempt for someone by laughing rudely at them in their presence.

the LAUGH is on me (*or you or him, etc.*) the situation is reversed and now the other person is the one who appears ridiculous.

LAUGH like a drain laugh raucously; guffaw. *Brit., informal* ● M20 forces' slang.

a LAUGH a minute very funny. ● Very often used ironically.

LAUGH on the other side of one's face (*or N. Amer.* **out of the other side of one's mouth**) be discomfited after feeling satisfaction or confidence about something.

LAUGH someone/thing out of court dismiss with contempt as being obviously ridiculous.

LAUGH oneself silly (*or* **sick**) laugh uncontrollably or for a long time.

LAUGH someone/thing to scorn ridicule someone or something. ● A biblical idiom: e.g. Job 12:4, Matthew 9:24.

LAUGH up one's sleeve be secretly or inwardly amused. ●*Up* is recent; the expression dates from M16 in the form *laugh in one's sleeve*.

be LAUGHING be in a fortunate or comfortable situation. *informal* ●M20 forces' slang.

no LAUGHING matter something serious that should not be joked about.

play something for LAUGHS (of a performer) try to arouse laughter in an audience, especially in inappropriate circumstances.

look to one's LAURELS be careful not to lose one's superior position to a rival. ●In ancient Greece a wreath made of bay-tree (laurel) leaves was awarded as a mark of distinction and, in particular, to victors at the Pythian Games held at Delphi.

rest on one's LAURELS be so satisfied with what one has already done or achieved that one makes no further effort. ● See preceding entry.

LAVENDER ▶ *see* **LAY up in lavender**.

be a LAW unto oneself behave in a manner that is not conventional or predictable.

lay down the LAW issue instructions to other people in an authoritative or dogmatic way.

take the LAW into one's own hands punish someone for an offence according to one's own ideas of justice, especially in an illegal or violent way.

take someone to LAW initiate legal proceedings against someone.

there's no LAW against it an assertion that one is doing nothing wrong. *informal* ●Used in spoken English, especially in response to an actual or implied criticism.

LAW ▶ *see* **the law of the JUNGLE**; ▶ *see* **the law of the MEDES and Persians**.

LAY a charge make an accusation.
> **1989** T. PARKER *Place Called Bird* ix. 108 We have domestic assaults. The complainant lays a charge.

LAY a (*or* the) ghost get rid of a distressing, frightening, or worrying memory or thought. ●From exorcising an unquiet or evil spirit.

LAY someone low 1 (of an illness) reduce someone to inactivity. **2** bring to an end the high position or good fortune formerly enjoyed by someone.

LAY something on thick (*or* with a trowel) grossly exaggerate or over-emphasize something. *informal* ●A *trowel* here is the one used by a bricklayer or plasterer.

LAY something to rest soothe and dispel fear, anxiety, grief, and similar unpleasant emotions. ●When used of a dead person, a euphemism for burying them in their grave.

LAY up in lavender preserve carefully for future use. ●The flowers and stalks of lavender were traditionally used as a preservative for stored clothes.

LAY ▶ *see* **lay something at someone's DOOR**; ▶ *see* **lay down the LAW**; ▶ *see* **clap EYES on**; ▶ *see* **lay it on the LINE**; ▶ *see* **burn RUBBER**; ▶ *see* **lay something on the TABLE**; ▶ *see* **set STORE by**; ▶ *see* **lay WASTE to**.

LEAD someone by the nose control someone totally, especially by deceiving them. *informal* ●The image is of an animal being controlled by a restraint around or in the nose (see quot.).

> **1604** W. SHAKESPEARE *Othello* I. iii. The Moor ... will as tenderly be led by th'nose As asses are.

LEAD from the front take an active role in what one is urging and directing others to do.

LEAD with one's chin behave or speak incautiously. *informal* ●With reference to a boxer's stance that leaves his chin unprotected. M20 boxing slang.

get the LEAD out move or work more quickly; hurry up. *chiefly N. Amer.*, *informal* ●Renowned for its weight, the metal *lead* appears in a number of expressions as a metaphor for inertness or heaviness (e.g. ▶ **go down like a LEAD balloon**, ▶ **SWING the lead**). This one is M20 jazz slang, meaning to 'play allegro'. The fuller version is *get the lead out of one's pants*.

LEAD in one's pencil vigour or energy, especially sexual energy in a man. *informal* ●Recorded in 1941 as Australian slang.

> **1972** D. LEES *Zodiac* 107 The couscous is supposed to put lead in your pencil but with Daria I needed neither a talking point nor an aphrodisiac.

go down (or N. Amer. over) like a LEAD balloon fail; be a flop. *informal* ●That is, plummet as heavily as a balloon made of lead would. An M20 colloquialism, apparently of US origin, used especially of a speech, proposal, joke, etc. that is poorly received; the humorously punning opposite of *go down well* or ▶ **go down a BOMB**.

> **1962** L. DEIGHTON *Ipcress File* xxv. 158 With this boy it [the greeting] went over like a lead balloon.

LEAD (noun) ▶ *see* **SWING the lead**.

LEAD (verb) ▶ *see* **lead someone a DANCE**; ▶ *see* **lead someone up the GARDEN path**.

shake (or tremble) like a LEAF tremble greatly, especially from fear.

take a LEAF out of someone's book closely imitate or emulate someone in a particular way.

> ***1809** B. H. MALKIN *Gil Blas* VII. ii. 12 I took a leaf out of their book.

turn over a new LEAF improve one's conduct or performance. ●The *leaf* is a page of a book. Used in this metaphorical sense since L16, it now always means to alter for the better, but it could previously also mean just to alter or even alter for the worse.

have (or take) a LEAK urinate. *slang*

LEAK ▶ *see* **SPRING a leak**.

LEAN ▶ *see* **bend over BACKWARDS**.

a LEAP in the dark a daring step or enterprise whose consequences are unpredictable.

LEAP to the eye be immediately apparent. ● Used especially of words seen in writing or of a mistake.

by LEAPS and bounds with startlingly rapid progress.

a new LEASE of (or N. Amer. on) life a substantially improved prospect of life or use after rejuvenation or repair.

LEASH ▶ see **STRAIN at the leash**.

LEAST said, soonest mended a difficult situation will be resolved more quickly if there is no more discussion of it. ● Proverbial in various versions since M15; this standard modern version dates from L18.

not LEAST notably; in particular. ● Used for emphasis followed by *because* and clause.

to say the LEAST (or the least of it) putting a condemnatory statement in the mildest way. ● Used as an understatement or euphemism to imply that the reality is far worse.

> **1997** *Spectator* 22 Nov. 37/2 References in Mr Cole's letter to the 'bottle' were, to say the least, distasteful.

LEAVE someone cold fail to interest someone.

> **1993** J. MERRILL *Different Persons* ix. 110 I might have waxed sentimental over the ruins of Catullus's *garçonnière* but places that 'breathe History' have always left me cold.

LEAVE much (or a lot) to be desired be highly unsatisfactory.

LEAVE ▶ see **take FRENCH leave**; ▶ see **take leave of one's SENSES**.

like a LEECH persistently or clingingly present. ● From the strong attachment by suction of a leech to the person or animal from which it is sucking blood.

make up (the) LEEWAY struggle out of a bad position, especially by recovering lost time. *Brit.* ● *Leeway* (M17) was the nautical term for the lateral drift of a ship towards the side downwind of its course. The figurative use dates from E19.

be LEFT at the post fail to compete. *informal* ● With allusion to the situation of a race horse that fails to leave the starting post in contention with its rivals.

have two LEFT feet be clumsy or awkward.

LEFT, right, and centre (also left and right or right and left) on all sides.

LEFT (noun) ▶ see **HANG a left**.

LEFT (verb) ▶ see **be left HOLDING the baby**.

get one's LEG over (of a man) have sexual intercourse. *vulgar slang*

not have a LEG to stand on have no facts or sound reasons to support one's argument or justify one's actions.

a LEGEND in one's own lifetime a very famous or notorious person. ● Someone whose fame is comparable to that of a hero of legend or about whom similar stories are told.

go LEGIT begin to behave honestly after a period of illegal activity. ● *Legit* was originally an L19 theatrical abbreviation meaning a 'a legitimate actor', i.e. one who acts in 'legitimate theatre' (conventional or serious drama).

feel (or find) one's LEGS become able to stand or walk.

have the LEGS of someone or something be able to go faster or further than. *Brit.*

on one's hind LEGS standing up to make a speech. *Brit., informal*

on one's last LEGS near the end of life, usefulness, or strength.

> **1987** E. NEWBY *Round Ireland in Low Gear* (1988) xvii. 274 It is certainly difficult to imagine how anyone who is in any way infirm, and some of the pilgrims who make the climb are literally on their last legs, can reach the top.

LEGS ▶ *see* **KEEP one's feet**; ▶ *see* **take to one's HEELS**.

lady (or man or gentleman) of LEISURE a woman or man of independent means or whose time is free from obligations to others.

the answer's a LEMON the response or outcome is unsatisfactory. *informal* ● A *lemon* is the type of a bad, unsatisfactory, or disappointing thing (E20 US slang), apparently deriving from a gambling machine which would deliver either a prize or its opposite—a lemon. See also next entry.

hand someone a LEMON pass off a substandard article as good; swindle someone.

LEND an ear (or one's ears) listen sympathetically or attentively.

LEND one's name to something allow oneself to be publicly associated with.

LEND ▶ *see* **give a HAND**.

LENTEN fare meagre rations without meat. ● Food appropriate to *Lent*, the Christian season of fasting between Ash Wednesday and Holy Saturday in commemoration of Jesus's 40 days of fasting in the wilderness.

in LESS than no time very quickly or soon. *informal*

the LESSER evil (or the lesser of the two evils) the less harmful or unpleasant of two bad choices or possibilities. ● Cf. Cicero *De Officiis* III. xxix: *minima de malis* '[choose] the least among evils'; the advice is also found in Aristotle (*Nicomachean Ethics* II. ix. 1109a).

LET someone down gently seek to give someone bad news in a way that avoids causing them too much distress or humiliation. ● Earliest (M18) with *eas(il)y*.

LET something drop (or fall) casually reveal a piece of information.

LET oneself go **1** act in an unrestrained or uninhibited way. **2** neglect oneself or one's appearance; become careless or untidy in one's habits.

LET it drop (*or* rest) say or do no more about a matter or problem.

LET it go (*or* pass) choose not to react to an action or remark.

LET or hindrance obstruction or impediment. *formal* ● *Let* in its Middle English sense of 'something that impedes' is now archaic and rarely occurs outside this phrase, in which it duplicates the sense of *hindrance*, except in sports such as badminton and tennis.

LET ▶ *see* **let off STEAM**; ▶ *see* **let RIP**; ▶ *see* **let SLIP**.

a dead LETTER a law or practice no longer observed. ● Originally with reference to passages in the biblical epistles in which St Paul compares the life-giving spirit of the New Testament with what he sees as the dead 'letter' of the Mosaic law. Later (until L19) *Dead-letter Office* was the name given to the organization that dealt with unclaimed mail or mail that could not be delivered for any reason. The expression has been used metaphorically for an obsolete or unobserved law since M17.

> **1998** *Spectator* 23 May 24/3 They were saying on the news … that some provision of the Stormont agreement might end up a dead letter.

to the LETTER with adherence to every detail. ● Cf. French *au pied de la lettre*, used in English since L18.

a man (*or* woman) of LETTERS a male (*or* female) scholar or writer.

do one's LEVEL best do one's utmost; make all possible efforts.

a LEVEL playing field a situation in which everyone has a fair and equal chance of succeeding.

> **1998** *Times* 11 Aug. 25/1 Most damagingly, the Brussels-centred concept of 'the level playing field' had also proved a wonderfully convenient alibi for protectionist lobbies.

on the LEVEL honest; truthful. *informal*

> **1890–1901** S. CRANE *Tales, Sketches & Reports* 335 If you aint on the level, you get a swift, hard throw-down sooner or later.

take LIBERTIES (with) 1 behave in an unduly familiar manner (towards a person). 2 treat (something) freely, without strict faithfulness to the facts or to an original.

take the LIBERTY venture to do something without first asking permission.

LICENCE to print money a very lucrative commercial activity, typically one perceived as requiring little effort.

at a LICK at a fast pace. *informal* ● *Lick* in this sense was originally (M19) dialect US, or Australian.

a LICK and a promise a hasty performance of a task, especially of cleaning something. *informal*

> **1993** S. STEWART *Ramlin Rose* iv. 28 A lick-n-a-promise … before we dropped into bed last thing at night, then oop at first light and into stinkin coaly clothes.

LICK someone's boots (*or* vulgar slang **arse)** be excessively obsequious towards someone, especially to gain favour.

LICK one's lips (or chops) look forward to something with eager antici-pation. ● With allusion to an animal salivating in expectation of food.

LICK one's wounds retire to recover one's strength or confidence after a defeat or humiliating experience. ● With allusion to an animal's behaviour after being injured.

LICK ▶ *see* **if you can't BEAT them;** ▶ *see* **lick someone/thing into SHAPE**.

blow the LID off remove means of restraint and allow something to get out of control. *informal*

keep a (or the) LID on 1 keep (an emotion or process) from going out of control. 2 keep secret. *informal*

put the (or a) LID on put a stop to. *informal*
| **1996** *Observer* 29 Dec. 1/3 Nothing's final. I haven't put the lid on anything.

put the LID (or the tin lid) on be the culmination of a series of acts or events that makes things unbearable. *Brit., informal*

take (or lift) the LID off (or lift the lid on) reveal unwelcome secrets about. *informal*

LID ▶ *see* **FLIP one's lid**.

give the LIE to something serve to show that something seemingly apparent or previously stated or believed is not true.

I tell a LIE (or that's a lie) an expression used to immediately correct oneself when one realizes that one has made an incorrect remark. *informal*

let something LIE take no action regarding a controversial or problematic matter.

LIE in state (of the corpse of a person of national importance) be laid in a public place of honour before burial.

LIE like a trooper tell lies constantly and flagrantly. ● Cf. ▶ **SWEAR like a trooper**.

LIE through one's teeth (or in one's throat) tell an outright lie without remorse. *informal*

live a LIE lead a life that conceals one's true nature or circumstances.

LIE (noun) ▶ *see* **how the LAND lies**; ▶ *see* **NAIL a lie**.

LIE (verb) ▶ *see* **let SLEEPING dogs lie**.

as far as in me LIES to the best of my power.

(do) anything for a quiet LIFE (make) any concession to avoid being disturbed.

for dear (or one's) LIFE as if or in order to escape death.

for the LIFE of me however hard I try; even if my life depended on it. *informal*
● With modal and negative; similar in use to ▶ **to save one's LIFE**.

frighten the LIFE out of terrify. ● Used hyperbolically; cf. ▶ **be frightened to DEATH**.

get a LIFE start living a fuller or more interesting existence. *informal* ● Often in imperative.

> **1998** *Spectator* 11 Apr. 23/2 There are people on the wireless as well as on television who talk about 'getting a life' and 'finding themselves'.

(as) large as LIFE (of a person) conspicuously present. *informal* ● Originally used literally with reference to the size of a statue or portrait relative to the original: in M18 Horace Walpole described a painting as being 'as large as the life'. The humorous M19 elaboration of the expression, *large as life and twice as natural*, used by Lewis Carroll and others, is still sometimes found; it is attributed to the Canadian humorist T. C. Haliburton (1796–1865).

larger than LIFE **1** (of a person) attracting attention because their appearance or behaviour is more flamboyant than that of ordinary people. **2** (of a thing) seeming disproportionately important. ● Also attributive *larger-than-life* (see quot.).

> **1950** *New Yorker* 23 Dec. 42 Mr. Churchill ... the living, larger-than-life embodiment of the British people's opposition to appeasement.

life and LIMB life and all bodily faculties. ● Often in the context of *risking life and limb*.

the LIFE and soul of the party a person whose vivacity and sociability makes a party enjoyable.

LIFE in the fast lane an exciting and eventful lifestyle, especially a wealthy one. *informal* ● With allusion to the motorway lane used by the fastest traffic.

a matter of LIFE and death a matter of vital importance.

not on your LIFE absolutely not. *informal*   ● Said to emphasize one's refusal to comply with some request.

see LIFE gain a wide experience of the world, especially its more pleasurable aspects.

take one's LIFE in one's hands risk being killed.

this is the LIFE an expression of contentment with one's present circumstances.

> **1995** N. WHITTAKER *Platform Souls* (1996) xxiii. 180 This is the life, nothing to do but read and look out of the window.

to the LIFE exactly like the original.

to save one's LIFE even if one's life were to depend on it. ● With modal and negative; cf. ▶ **for the LIFE of me**.

LIFE ▶ *see* the **FACTS** of life; ▶ *see* a new **LEASE** of life; ▶ *see* the **TIME** of one's life; ▶ *see* **WALK** of life; ▶ *see* within an **INCH** of one's life.

throw a LIFELINE to (or throw someone a lifeline) provide (someone) with a means of escaping from a difficult situation.

of a LIFETIME (of a chance or experience) such as does not occur more than once in a person's life; exceptional.

LIFT (or stir) a finger (or hand) make the slightest effort to do something, especially to help someone. ● Usually with negative.

be LIGHT on be rather short of.

be LIGHT on one's feet (of a person) be quick or nimble.

go out like a LIGHT fall asleep or lose consciousness suddenly. *informal*

in the LIGHT of (or N. Amer. in light of) drawing knowledge or information from; with regard to.

LIGHT at the end of the tunnel a long-awaited indication that a period of hardship or adversity is nearing an end.

LIGHT the (or a) fuse (or touchpaper) do something that creates a tense or exciting situation. ● With reference to lighting a fuse attached to gunpowder, fireworks, etc. in order to cause an explosion. A *touchpaper*, which is used in the same way as a fuse, is a twist of paper impregnated with saltpetre to make it burn slowly.
| **1998** *Times* 1 Sept. 41/5 [T]he rejection of global capitalism may light a touchpaper in all those countries battered by the crisis.

the LIGHT of one's life a much-loved person.

make LIGHT (or little) of treat as unimportant.
| **1990** *Vanity Fair* Aug. 159/3 Ian says they still hope to marry someday, and tries to make light of their non-wedding.

make LIGHT work of accomplish (a task) quickly and easily. ● The opposite of ▶ **make heavy WEATHER of**.

stand (or be) in someone's LIGHT be situated between someone and a source of light.

LIGHT (noun) ▶ *see* **HIDE one's light under a bushel**.

LIGHT (verb) ▶ *see* **light a FIRE under someone**; ▶ *see* **light the FUSE**.

LIGHTNING never strikes twice calamity never occurs twice. ● Alluding to the folk belief that lightning never strikes the same spot twice.
| **1983** P. LIVELY *Perfect Happiness* (1985) iv. 38 It's nasty, isn't it? … Having to go to the same airport. Though in a way you can't help thinking well lightning never strikes twice.

like LIGHTNING (or like greased lightning) very quickly.

punch someone's LIGHTS out beat someone up.

LIKE —, like — as — is, so is —. ● Two familiar sayings cast in this form are *like father, like son* (Latin *qualis pater, talis filius*), recorded in this form from E17 onwards, and *like mother, like daughter*, based on Ezekiel 16:34.

LIKE it or not willy-nilly. *informal* ● Used to indicate that someone has no choice in a matter.

| **1998** *New Scientist* 19 Sept. 3/3 Like it or not, people expect more honesty from those who claim to be on the side of the environment.

a LIKELY story used to express disbelief of an account or excuse.

the LIKES of a similar type of person or thing. *informal* ● Usually derogatory.

LILY ▶ *see* **GILD the lily**.

out on a LIMB **1** isolated or stranded. **2** without support. ● *Limb* here is the projecting branch of a tree. Also *go out on a limb*, meaning 'take a risk' or 'act boldly and uncompromisingly'.

| **1 1997** *Spectator* Without an inquiry of this sort everyone is left out on a limb.

tear LIMB from limb violently dismember (someone). ● Can be used literally, but more often humorous.

be the LIMIT be intolerably troublesome or irritating. *informal*

the bottom LINE the final reality; the important conclusion. ● Literally, the final total in an account or balance sheet.

come (or bring someone/thing) into LINE conform (*or* cause someone or something to conform).

come down to the LINE (of a race) be closely fought right until the end.

end of the LINE the point at which further effort is unproductive or one can go no further. ● M20 in figurative use. Also literally of the end of a rail or other transport route; Cf. the Canadian expression (E20) *end of steel*.

get a LINE on learn something about. *informal*

| **1939** R. CHANDLER *Big Sleep* (1976) xxv. 152 I was trying to get a line on you, sure.

lay (or put) it on the LINE speak frankly.

(draw) a LINE in the sand (state that one has reached) a point beyond which one will not go.

step out of LINE act inappropriately, disreputably, or illegally. *chiefly N. Amer., informal* ● To describe someone as *out of line* (M20 US) is to indicate that they are behaving unacceptably.

LINE one's pocket (or pockets) enrich oneself, usually by dishonest means.

LINE ▶ *see* **the line of least RESISTANCE**; ▶ *see* **TOE the line**.

wash one's dirty LINEN in public discuss or argue about one's personal affairs in public. ● E19 in English; the equivalent French prohibition on publicizing *linge sale* is attributed to Napoleon.

a LION in the way a danger or obstacle, especially an imaginary one. *literary* ● After Proverbs 22:13 'The slothful man saith, There is a lion without, I shall be slain in the streets.'

the LION's share the largest part of something.

| **1998** *Times* 21 May 31/3 Rich countries generally seize the lion's share of trade.

throw someone to the LIONS cause someone to be in an extremely dangerous or unpleasant situation.   ● With reference to the imperial Roman practice of throwing Christians and other religious or political dissidents to the wild beasts.

bite one's LIP repress an emotion; stifle laughter, a retort, etc.

curl one's LIP raise a corner of one's upper lip to show contempt; sneer.

pay LIP service to something express approval of or support for something without taking any significant action.

| **1998** *New Scientist* 15 Aug. 48/1 Green organisations are having great difficulty maintaining their membership, and politicians pay lip service to environmental problems.

hang on someone's LIPS listen attentively to someone.

lick (or smack) one's LIPS look forward to something with relish; show one's satisfaction.

pass someone's LIPS be eaten, drunk, or spoken by someone.

LIPS ▶ *see* **someone's lips are SEALED**.

enter the LISTS issue or accept a challenge.   ● In medieval times the *lists* were the enclosed area in which knights fought each other in tournaments.

quite the LITTLE — used when condescendingly or ironically recognizing that someone has a particular quality or accomplishment.

LITTLE ▶ *see* **make LIGHT of**.

LIVE and breathe something be extremely interested in or enthusiastic about a particular subject or activity; spend a great deal of one's time pursuing a particular interest.

LIVE and learn one is always learning something new.   ● Used, especially in spoken English, to express surprise at some new or unexpected discovery or piece of information.

| **1984** J. MINAHAN *Great Diamond Robbery* xi. 'Y' want *steins*, gov, go to Germany; 'ere we only got *pints*.' Live and learn.

LIVE and let live you should tolerate the opinions and behaviour of others so that they will similarly tolerate your own.   ● Often imperative. It appears not to be a native English saying, as it was referred to as a Dutch proverb (*Leuen ende laeten leuen*) on its first appearance in English in 1622 and it appears a little later (1641) in this exact form as a Scottish proverb.

LIVE in the past   1 have old-fashioned or outdated ideas and attitudes.   **2** dwell on or reminisce at length about past events.

LIVE it up spend one's time in an extremely enjoyable or extravagant way. *informal*

LIVE out of a suitcase live or stay somewhere on a temporary basis and with only a limited selection of one's belongings, typically because one's occupation requires a great deal of travelling.

LIVE over the shop live on the premises where one works. ● Small shopkeepers used literally to live in rooms above their shops, but the expression is now used rather more loosely.

LIVE one's own life follow one's own plans and principles; be independent of others.

LIVE rough live and sleep outdoors as a consequence of having no proper home.

LIVE to fight another day survive a certain experience or ordeal. ● The idea, found in the Greek comic playwright Menander, is expressed in the English proverbial jingle *He who fights and runs away Lives to fight another day*.

LIVE to tell the tale survive a dangerous experience and be able to tell others about it.

LIVE ▶ *see* **live by one's WITS**; ▶ *see* **live for the MOMENT**; ▶ *see* **HAND to mouth**; ▶ *see* **live a LIE**; ▶ *see* **live off the FAT of the land**; ▶ *see* **live off the LAND**.

LIVELY ▶ *see* **merry as a GRIG**; ▶ *see* **LOOK lively**.

where one LIVES at, to, or in the right, vital, or most vulnerable spot. *N. Amer.* ● Cf. ▶ **HIT where one lives**.

be (the) LIVING proof that (or of) show by one's or something's existence and qualities that something is the case.

in (or within) LIVING memory within or during a time that is remembered by people still alive.

the LIVING image of an exact copy or likeness of.

LIVING ▶ *see* **be on BORROWED time**.

get (or have) a LOAD on become drunk. *chiefly N. Amer., informal*

LOAD the dice against (or in favour of) someone put someone at a disadvantage (or advantage).

> **1995** *Maclean's* 24 Apr. 53/2 What global warming has done is load the dice in favor of warmer-than-normal seasons and extreme climatic events.

take a (or the) LOAD off one's feet sit or lie down.

take a LOAD off someone's mind bring someone relief from anxiety.

LOADED ▶ *see* **loaded for BEAR**.

use one's LOAF use one's common sense. *Brit., informal* ● Probably from *loaf of bread*, rhyming slang for 'head'.

LOAF ▶ *see* **HALF a loaf**.

LOATH ▶ *see* **NOTHING loath**.

have a LOCK on have an unbreakable hold or total control over. *N. Amer.*, *informal* ● With allusion to a *lock* or hold in wrestling.

> **1974** P. ERDMAN *Silver Bears* xiii.He would sooner see the whole bank go down the drain ... than get beaten by us. Unless we develop an even better lock on him—and that won't be easy.

LOCK horns engage in conflict. ● From the way that two bulls fight head-to-head with their horns. Originally M19 US in both literal and figurative uses. Used with preposition *with*.

LOCK, stock, and barrel including everything; completely. ● With reference to the complete mechanism of a firearm.

under LOCK and key securely locked up. ● From L16 in this form, but the collocation of *lock* and *key* appears in various phrases from M13 onwards to emphasize the idea of security: e.g. Hoccleve *Minor Poems* (1413) 'He, of thy soules helthe, is lok and keye.'

LOCKER ▶ *see* **go to DAVY Jones's locker**; ▶ *see* **a SHOT in the locker**.

(as) easy as falling off a LOG very easy. *informal* ● M19 US, now in general use. Used by Mark Twain (*c*.1880) in the alternative form *rolling off a log*.

at LOGGERHEADS in violent dispute or disagreement. ● Possibly a use of *loggerhead* in the L17 sense of 'long-handled iron instrument for heating liquids and tar', perhaps wielded as a weapon. Often with preposition *with* (someone) or *over* (something).

LOINS ▶ *see* **GIRD one's loins**.

LOITER with intent stand or wait around with the intention of committing an offence. *Brit.* ● A legal phrase derived from an 1891 Act of Parliament, it is also used figuratively and humorously of anyone who is waiting around for some unspecified purpose.

all LOMBARD Street to a China orange great wealth against one ordinary object; virtual certainty. *informal* ● *Lombard Street* in London was originally occupied by Lombard bankers, and it still contains a number of London's principal banks. Used in the context of making a bet, either explicitly or implicitly.

a LONDON particular a dense fog formerly affecting London. ● From Dickens's *Bleak House* (1853).

by (*or Brit.* **on) one's LONESOME** all alone. *informal* ● An L19 colloquialism.

in the LONG run (*or* **term)** over a long period of time; eventually.

> **1997** *New Scientist* 6 Dec. 21/3 But as the economist Maynard Keynes pointed out, in the long run we are all dead.

the LONG and the short of it **1** all that can or need be said. **2** the eventual outcome.

LONG in the tooth rather old. ● Originally said of horses, from the recession of the gums with age.

not be LONG for this world have only a short time to live. ● First recorded in a letter by Byron (1822); often used euphemistically of someone who is close to death; almost always in this negative form.

> **1933** J. MASEFIELD *Bird of Dawning* 43 He was shocked by the roaring wash of the water coming into the after hold. 'She's not long for this world,' he muttered.

over the LONG haul over an extended period of time. *chiefly N. Amer.*

LONG ▶ *see* **by a long CHALK**; ▶ *see* **by a long SHOT**; ▶ *see* **not by a long CHALK**; ▶ *see* **not by a long SHOT**.

draw the LONGBOW make exaggerated claims or statements. *dated* ● The *longbow* was the national weapon of England from the fourteenth century until the introduction of firearms, and prowess in its use was highly prized. In this metaphorical sense since M17.

LOOK down one's nose at despise. *informal* ● Also just *look down on*.

LOOK someone in the eye (*or* face) look directly at someone without showing embarrassment, fear, or shame.

LOOK lively (*or* dated alive) be quick in doing something. *informal* ● Used in the imperative to tell someone to hurry up.

LOOK the other way deliberately ignore wrongdoing by others.

> **1998** *Economist* 14 Mar. 44/1 The Greek government looked the other way as lorries ... switched documents the minute they crossed the border.

LOOK sharp be quick.

> **1953** M. KENNEDY *Troy Chimneys* (1985) 64 I had ... begun an idle flirtation with Maria, ... then, perceiving that I should be caught if I did not look sharp, I kept out of her way.

LOOK (noun) ▶ *see* **not LIKE the look of**.

LOOK (verb) ▶ *see* **LOOK lively**; ▶ *see* **look DAGGERS**; ▶ *see* **LOOK down one's nose at**; ▶ *see* **look for TROUBLE**.

be on the LOOKOUT **1** keep searching for (someone or something that is wanted). **2** be alert to (danger or trouble). ● Naval and military in origin, *lookout* (or *look-out*) applied first (L17) to sentries or other persons employed to keep watch; the sense of 'the action of keeping watch', as here, is M18. Usually with preposition *for*. A common alternative in both senses is *keep a lookout*.

in (*or* out of) the LOOP aware (*or* unaware) of information known to only a limited number of people. *chiefly US*

> **1998** *Times* 31 Mar. 18/5 An insider suggests to a favoured, helpful journalist that the said minister is out of the loop and on the skids.

throw (*or* knock) someone for a LOOP surprise or astonish someone; catch someone off guard. *N. Amer.*

hang (*or* stay) LOOSE be relaxed; refrain from taking anything too seriously. *informal* ● Often as imperative.

at a LOOSE END (*or* N. Amer. at loose ends) having nothing to to; not knowing what to do.

LOOSE ▶ *see* **a loose CANNON**.

LORRY ▶ *see* **FALL off a lorry**.

LOSE one's mind (*or informal* **one's marbles**) become insane or irrational.

LOSE sleep worry. ●Usually with negative and preposition *over* or *about*.

LOSE one's (*or* **the**) **way** no longer have a clear idea of one's purpose or motivation in an activity or business. ●From literally becoming lost on a journey, a usage recorded from 1530 in J. Palsgrave *Lesclarcissement* ('I wander, as one dothe who hath loste his waye').

LOSE ▶ *see* **lose FACE**; ▶ *see* **lose one's GRIP**; ▶ *see* **lose one's HEAD**; ▶ *see* **give one's HEART**; ▶ *see* **lose one's RAG**; ▶ *see* **lose one's SHIRT**; ▶ *see* **lose TOUCH**; ▶ *see* **lose TRACK**.

be on (*or* **on to**) **a LOSER** be involved in a course of action that is bound to fail. ●Probably with reference to betting on a horse that loses.

a LOSING battle a struggle that is bound to end in failure.

all is not LOST used to suggest that there is still some chance of success or recovery.
| **1667** J. MILTON *Paradise Lost* I. 105 What though the field be lost? All is not lost.

be LOST for words be so surprised, confused, or upset that one cannot think what to say. ●Also *be at a loss for words*.

be LOST on someone fail to influence or be noticed or appreciated by someone.

give someone up for LOST stop expecting that a missing person will be found alive.

LOST ▶ *see* **a lost SOUL**; ▶ *see* **be lost in the SHUFFLE**.

all over the LOT in a state of confusion or disorganization. *US, informal* ●Cf. ▶ **ALL over the place**.

fall to someone's LOT become someone's task or responsibility. ●From deciding something by drawing or casting lots.

throw in one's LOT with decide to ally oneself closely with and share the fate of (a person or group).

for the LOVE of Mike used to accompany an exasperated request or to express dismay. *Brit., informal* ●*Mike*, the shortened form of the male forename Michael, perhaps here as the generic name for an Irishman; cf. *mickey* as in ▶ **take the MICKEY out of**. E20, used by James Joyce in *Ulysses*.

not for LOVE or money not in any circumstances. *informal*
| **1998** *Spectator* 15 Aug. 25/3 I am told that you cannot get a plasterer for love or money, but that the going rate is a big kiss and £1,000 a week.

there's no (*or* **little** *or* **not much**) **LOVE lost between** there is mutual dislike between (two or more people mentioned).

the LOWEST of the low those regarded as the most immoral or socially inferior of all.

> **1995** N. WHITTAKER *Platform Souls* (1996) xviii. 152 And fare dodgers, well, they're the lowest of the low, and should be strung up.

LOWER the boom on **1** treat severely. **2** put a stop to (an activity). ● M20 N. Amer. slang; *Western Folklore* (1950) explained the expression as 'knock[ing] out your adversary with one punch' in a fight.

LOWER the tone diminish the general spirit or moral character of a conversation, place, etc. ● *Tone* here is the 'distinctive class' of a group of people (M17).

LOWER ▶ *see* **raise one's SIGHTS**.

as LUCK would have it used to indicate the fortuitousness of a situation.

one's LUCK is in (or out) one is fortunate (or unfortunate) on a particular occasion.

the LUCK of the draw the outcome of chance rather than something one can control. ● Often used in an expression of resignation (*it's the luck of the draw*) when something turns out contrary to one's wish.

make one's own LUCK be successful through one's own efforts and opportunism.

ride one's LUCK let favourable events take their course without taking undue risks.

try one's LUCK (at something) do something that involves risk or luck, hoping to succeed.

you'll, he'll, etc. be LUCKY (or I, you, etc. should be so lucky) used to say that someone's wishes or expectations are unlikely to be fulfilled.

LULL ▶ *see* **the lull before the STORM**.

a LUMP in the throat a feeling of tightness or dryness in the throat caused by strong emotion, especially grief.

take (or get) one's LUMPS suffer punishment; be attacked or defeated. *chiefly N. Amer., informal*

> **1971** B. MALAMUD *Tenants* 130 Now I take my lumps, he thought. Maybe for not satisfying Mary.

do LUNCH meet for lunch. ● *chiefly N. Amer., informal*

there's no such thing as a free LUNCH one never gets something for nothing; any benefit received has eventually to be paid for. ● Originally (M20) a US axiom relating to economics and finance.

> **1996** *Washington Times* 14 Aug. A18 Europeans are now learning some hard facts of life about socialized medicine: There's no such thing as a free lunch.

LUNCH ▶ *see* **LADIES who lunch**; ▶ *see* **OUT to lunch**.

leave in the LURCH leave (an associate, friend, etc.) abruptly and without assistance or support when they are in a difficult situation. ● *Lurch* as a noun in the sense of 'a state of discomfiture' (M16) has long been obsolete except in this idiom.

> **1987** E. DUNLOP *House on Hill* (1990) vi. 36 What have Gilmores ever done but leave her in the lurch? Poor Jane, she just can't run the risk of being hurt again.

take something LYING DOWN accept an insult or injury without attempting retaliation.

wax LYRICAL about (*or* over) talk in an effusive or enthusiastic way about. ● *Wax* (Old English *weaxan*) was the usual verb meaning 'increase in size' right through until Early Modern English, but since then it has been superseded in all general contexts by *grow* (originally specific to vegetative contexts). It now survives only in certain fossilized expressions, especially with reference to the moon's monthly increase and decrease (*waxing and waning*).

> **1998** *New Scientist* 5 Sept. 53/1 Even as they wax lyrical about the perils of a changing climate, Clinton and Gore are presiding over the most massive expansion of oil exploration and drilling since ... the Trans-Alaska Pipeline twenty years ago.

M

the real McCOY the real thing; the genuine article. *informal* ● The origin is unknown, but it appears in the form 'the real Mackay' in a letter by R. L. Stevenson (1883). *McKie* is another variant. *McCoy* is found glossed as 'genuine liquor' in the *American Mercury* of 1930.

> **1992** J. TORRINGTON *Swing Hammer Swing!* xxix. 247 'How d'you know the armour's real?' 'Oh, I'm sure it's the real McCoy.'

(as) MAD as a hatter (*or* a March hare) completely crazy. *informal* ● *Hatter* refers to Lewis Carroll's character, the Mad Hatter, in *Alice's Adventures in Wonderland* (1865). Hatters were thought to suffer from the effects of mercury poisoning because of the fumes arising from the use of mercurous nitrate in the manufacture of felt hats. The *March hare* version refers to the leaping and running of hares in the breeding season.

far from the MADDING crowd secluded or removed from public notice. ● In allusion to the phrase's use in Gray's *Elegy*; also the title of one of Thomas Hardy's novels (1874). *Madding* is now only poetical.

that way MADNESS lies it is ill-advised to pursue a particular course of action as it will cause distress or anxiety. ● Quoting Lear's self-pitying exclamation when contemplating the ingratitude of his daughters (Shakespeare *King Lear* III. iv). Used especially in spoken English as a warning to others or as an explanation of the speaker's intention not to do something.

MAGIC ▶ *see* **a magic CARPET**.

MAGNITUDE ▶ *see* **of the FIRST order**.

by MAIN force through sheer strength. ● *Main* derives from Old English *mægen* or its Old Norse cognate (not from French *main* hand). As an epithet of *strength* or *force*, meaning 'exerted to the full', it is a very ancient usage: 'mægenstrengo' occurs in the Anglo-Saxon epic *Beowulf*.

MAJORITY ▶ *see* **JOIN the great majority**; ▶ *see* **the SILENT majority**.

MAKE a day (*or* night) of it devote a whole day (*or* night) to an activity, typically an enjoyable one.

MAKE someone's day make an otherwise ordinary or dull day pleasingly memorable for someone. ● Sometimes used ironically as a warning that an action will give pleasure to someone hostile, as in a notice inviting burglars to 'Break in. Make his day' displayed under a picture of a guard dog.

MAKE do manage with the limited or inadequate means available. ● With preposition *with*. Also absolute in *make do and mend*, a UK slogan from the 1940s. Hence also *make-do* as a noun (L19).

MAKE like pretend to be; imitate. *N. Amer., informal*

> **1939** J. STEINBECK *Grapes of Wrath* xxiii. 396 This rich fella ... makes like he's poor.

MAKE or break (*or* chiefly Brit. **mar)** be the factor which decides whether (something) will succeed or fail. ● The collocation of *make* and *mar* is recorded from E15, but since M19 *break* has become the more common. Also as modifier *make-or-break*.

| **1998** *Spectator* 24 Jan. 22/1 1998 would be the make-or-break year in Paris's increasingly desperate attempt to beat off foreign competition.

on the MAKE 1 *informal* intent on gain, typically in a rather unscrupulous way. 2 *informal* looking for a sexual partner.

put the MAKE on make sexual advances to. *N. Amer., informal*

| **1993** A. RIVER SIDDONS *Hill Town* (1994) vii. 145 Put the make on you, did she, Joe? I should have warned you. Past a certain blood alcohol level Yolie gets snuggly.

MAKE ▶ *see* **make a BEELINE for**; ▶ *see* **make the CUT**.

meet one's MAKER die. *humorous* or *euphemistic* ● With allusion to the Christian belief that the soul goes after death to be judged by God who made it.

be the MAKING of someone ensure their success or favourable development.

(with) MALICE aforethought (having) wrongful intent beforehand, especially as an element in murder.

the MAMMON of unrighteousness wealth ill-used or ill-gained. ● From Luke 16:9; *Mammon* is ultimately from Hebrew *māmōn* money, wealth. In early use, it was (the proper name of) the devil of covetousness; later it was used as the personification of wealth regarded as an idol or an evil influence.

as — as the next MAN as — as the average person.

MAN about town a fashionable male socialite. ● This is the predominant form of this idiom since M19 (used e.g. by Dickens), but it was used earlier with nouns other than *man* (e.g. in a letter *c*.1645 James Howell described himself as having been 'a youth about the Town').

MAN and boy throughout life from youth. ● The Scottish poet Dunbar used the phrase *baith man and lad* (E16), but the modern usage follows Shakespeare (see quot.).

| **1602** W. SHAKESPEARE *Hamlet* V. i. 155 I have been sexton here, man and boy, thirty years.

a MAN for all seasons a man who is ready to cope with any contingency and whose behaviour is always appropriate to every occasion. ● Said of the English statesman and scholar Sir Thomas More (1478–1535) by Robert Whittington in *Vulgaria*, part 2 (1521), and used by Robert Bolt as the title of his play (1960) about More.

the MAN in the moon someone regarded as out of touch with real life. ● Used, especially in comparisons, to refer to the imagined likeness of a face seen on the surface of a full moon.

the MAN in (*or* US on) the street an ordinary person, usually with regard to their opinions, or as distinct from an expert. ● A specifically Brit. variation is ▶ **the MAN on the Clapham omnibus**.

MAN of the cloth a clergyman. ● Swift used *cloth* as a colloquial term for the *clerical profession* in E18, but *cloth* was in use earlier as a metonym for other professions or occupations for which distinctive clothing was worn (e.g. by lawyers or liveried servants). *Man of the cloth* is now mainly jocular.

MAN of God **1** a clergyman. **2** a holy man or saint.

MAN of the moment a man of importance at a particular time.

MAN of straw **1** a person compared to an effigy stuffed with straw, especially someone undertaking a financial commitment without adequate means; a sham. **2** a sham argument set up to be defeated, usually as a means of avoiding having to tackle an opponent's real arguments. ● Also *straw man*, particularly in sense 2 (see quot.).

> **1991** *Past & Present* Aug. 171 By making the representativeness of the case-studies into the crucial issue, Rubinstein is erecting a straw man which he can easily demolish without addressing the basic criticisms of his sources and methodology.

the MAN on the Clapham omnibus the average man, especially with regard to his opinions. *Brit.* ● A legal fiction, attributed to English judge Lord Bowen (1835–94), who used it as a metaphor for the ordinary reasonable person— such as a juror is expected to be. Clapham is a district in south London.

MAN's best friend an affectionate or jocular way of referring to a dog.

a MAN's man a man whose personality is such that he is more popular and at ease with other men than women. ● Apparently earliest in G. Du Maurier (*Martian*, 1897), who defines the *man's man* as 'a good comrade par excellence, a frolicsome chum, a rollicking boon-companion, a jolly pal'. A *man's woman* (E20) is a woman who is more at ease with men than with other women. Both expressions are perhaps somewhat dated (see quot.).

> **1991** *Men's Health* Nov.–Dec. 88/3 Masculinity used to be simple to define. If you had hair on your chest and a deep voice, and belonged to a club that excluded women, you were masculine, or, as was the phrase of the time, 'a man's man'.

MAN to man in a direct and frank way between two men; openly and honestly. ● Also as modifier: *man-to-man*. In a team ball game, *man-to-man* designates a type of defensive strategy in which each player is responsible for marking one member of the opposing team.

MAN ▶ *see* be one's **OWN** man (*or* woman); ▶ *see* **EVERY** man for himself; ▶ *see* **every** man has his **PRICE**; ▶ *see* a man of **LETTERS**; ▶ *see* a man of the **WORLD**.

MANGLE ▶ *see* **put someone through the WRINGER**.

in a MANNER of speaking in some sense; so to speak. ● *Manner of speaking* is recorded from M16; cf. French *façon de parler*, current in English since E19.

to the MANNER born naturally at ease in a specified way of life, job, situation, etc. ● With allusion to Shakespeare's *Hamlet* I. iv. 14 'though I am native here And to the manner born'. Punning on this expression, *to the manor born* refers to someone of aristocratic origins or lifestyle.

son (*or* daughter) of the MANSE the child of a minister, especially a Presbyterian.

be too (*or* one too) MANY for outwit, baffle.

have one too MANY become slightly drunk. ● That is, have one too many drinks.

MANY's the — used to indicate that something happens often.

all over the MAP in a state of confusion or disorganization. *N. Amer., informal* ● Cf. ▶ **ALL over the place**.

off the MAP (of a place) very distant or remote. ● Cf. ▶ **off the BEATEN track**.

put something on the MAP make something prominent or important.

wipe something off the MAP obliterate something totally.

lose one's MARBLES go insane; become irrational or senile. *informal* ● *Marbles* as slang for 'mental faculties' appears to be E20 North American slang. The underlying reference is apparently to the children's game played with multicoloured glass balls (see also next entry).

| **1998** *Spectator* 11 July 24/3 At least, that is how I recall the event, but I am losing my marbles.

pick up one's MARBLES and go home withdraw petulantly from an activity after having suffered a setback. *informal, chiefly US* ● With allusion to a child who refuses sulkily to continue playing the game of marbles.

MARCH to (the beat of) a different tune (*or* drum *or* drummer) consciously adopt a different approach or attitude to the majority of people; be unconventional. *informal* ● The *drummer* version refers ultimately to Thoreau (*Walden*, 1854): 'If a man does not keep pace with his companions, perhaps it is because he hears a different drummer' ('Conclusion').

| **1997** *New Scientist* 15 Nov. 49/1 In formulating his ideas about the composition of the fundamental building blocks of matter ... Sternglass has marched to the beat of an entirely different drum.

MARCH ▶ *see* **MAD as a hatter**.

MARE ▶ *see* **a mare's NEST**.

tell that to the MARINES (*or* the horse marines) a scornful expression of incredulity. ● The saying may have originated in a remark of King Charles II, recommending that unlikely reports should be referred to sailors who, from their knowledge of distant places, might be the people best qualified to endorse or discount them. *Horse-marines* (E19) were an imaginary corps of cavalry, soldiers mounted on horseback on board ship being a humorous image of ineptitude or of people out of their natural element. In 1823 Byron noted that *That will do for the marines, but the sailors won't believe it* was an 'old saying', and the following year Scott used *Tell that to the marines — the sailors won't believe it!* in *Redgauntlet* (xiii). The *horse-marines* variant is L19.

| **1998** *Times* 18 Mar. 42/3 Truth is the issue, say the apologists, not the grope. You can tell that to the marines. The issue is the grope.

be quick (*or* slow) off the MARK be fast (*or* slow) in responding to a situation or understanding something. ● The *mark* here is the line or marker from which a competitor starts a race; cf. next entry and ▶ **on your MARKS**.

get off the MARK get started. ● Cf. preceding entry.

leave (or make) its (or one's or a) MARK have a lasting or significant effect. ●In British usage *make one's mark* means also 'become famous and successful'.

the MARK of Cain the stigma of a murderer, a sign of infamy. ●God placed a sign upon Cain after the murder of Abel, originally as a sign of divine protection in exile (Genesis 4:15).

MARK someone's card give someone information. *slang* ●A horse-racing idiom; the *card* is a *race-card*, the list of runners at a race meeting, so to *mark someone's card* is to give them tips for possible winners. From M20.

MARK time pass one's time in routine activities until a more favourable or interesting opportunity presents itself. ●Used literally of troops when they march on the spot without moving forward.

near (or close) to the MARK almost accurate. ●*Mark* in this and the two following entries is a target or goal.

off (or wide of) the MARK **1** a long way away from an intended target. **2** (of calculations etc.) inaccurate.

on the MARK correct; accurate.

up to the MARK **1** of the required standard. **2** (of a person) as healthy or in as good spirits as usual. *dated* ●In sense 2 usually with negative.

MARK (noun) ▶ *see* **a BLACK mark**.

MARK (verb) ▶ *see* **mark with a WHITE stone**.

be in the MARKET for wish to buy.

MARKET ▶ *see* **a DRUG on the market**.

on your MARKS used to instruct competitors in a race to prepare themselves in the correct starting position.

MARRIAGE of convenience a marriage concluded to achieve a practical purpose. ●Used by Addison in E18, translating French *mariage de convenance*, which has also been current in English since M19.

> **1949** G. B. SHAW *Buoyant Billions* iv. 53 The proportion of happy love marriages to happy marriages of convenience has never been counted.

to the MARROW (of one's bones) right through. ●From the idea of the marrow of one's bones representing one's innermost self.

> **1994** M. GEE *Crime Story* (1996) iii. 50 Moral corruption, the lawyer said. Men who are greedy to the marrow of their bones.

MARRY money marry a rich person. *informal*

> **1991** *Bookseller* 16 Aug. 403 Never marry money but go where money is.

MARRY with the left hand marry morganatically, i.e. without the marriage partner of lower rank becoming entitled to the higher rank of their partner.

go to the MAT vigorously engage in an argument or dispute, typically on behalf of a particular person or cause. ● Alluding to the thick mat in a gymnasium on which wrestling is practised.

> **1924** P. G. WODEHOUSE *Leave it to Psmith* i. 28 I ... heard ... you and Aunt Constance going to the mat about poor old Phyllis.

on the MAT being reprimanded by someone in authority. *informal* ● A military reference: the orderly room mat was where a soldier accused of some misdemeanour would stand before the commanding officer.

meet one's MATCH encounter one's equal in strength or ability.

MATCH ▶ *see* **the whole SHOOTING match**.

waltz (or walk) MATILDA carry a bundle of one's personal possessions as one travels the roads. *Austral.* ● The female forename *Matilda* was one of a number of names given to the swag or pack carried by itinerants. The expression was famously used by A. B. ('Banjo') Paterson (1864–1941) in his 1903 song *Waltzing Matilda*.

a MATTER of form mere routine. ● Originally a legal phrase, signifiying a point of correct procedure.

the MATTHEW principle the principle that more will be given to those who already have. ● After the gospel passage: 'Unto every one that hath shall be given, and he shall have abundance' (Matthew 25:29).

to the MAX to the highest degree possible. *N. Amer., informal*

make a MEAL of 1 consume (food) as a meal. **2** *Brit.* treat (a task or occurrence) with more attention or care than necessary.

> **2 1961** C. WILLOCK *Death in Covert* iv. 93 Dyson ... was making a meal of everything. He had carefully paced the distance.... He had stuck sticks in the ground.

MEAN to say really admit or intend to say. ● Usually either in direct questions (*Do you mean to say ... ?*), but sometimes used by speakers as a padding phrase similar to *I mean* to fill a pause or hesitation.

no MEAN — a very good —. ● A common example of litotes, the figure of speech by which something is affirmed by using the negative of the contrary. Most famously used by St Paul: 'I am ... a Jew of Tarsus ..., a citizen of no mean city' (Acts 21:39).

MEAN ▶ *see* **the GOLDEN mean**.

not know the MEANING of the word behave as if unaware of the concept referred to or implied. *informal*

a MEANS to an end a thing that is not valued or important in itself but is useful in achieving an aim. ● *End* and *means* are compared or contrasted in several proverbial sayings (e.g. ▶ **the END justifies the means** and *he who wills the end wills the means*).

for good MEASURE in addition to what has already been done, said, or given.

get (or take or have) the MEASURE of assess or have assessed the character, nature, or abilities of someone or something.

MEASURE one's length (of a person) fall flat on the ground. *dated*

be MEAT and drink to be a source of great pleasure or encouragement to.

easy MEAT a person or animal overcome, outwitted, or persuaded without difficulty. *informal*

MEAT and potatoes ordinary but fundamental things; basic ingredients.

MEAT ▶ *see* **DEAD meat**.

the reverse of the MEDAL (*or* shield) the opposite view of a matter. ● Cf. ▶ **the other side of the COIN**.

the law of the MEDES and Persians something which cannot be altered. ● With biblical allusion to Daniel 6:12.

a dose (*or* taste) of one's own MEDICINE the same bad treatment that one has given to others. ● *One's own medicine* has been in metaphorical use since M19; cf. *take one's medicine* meaning 'submit to something disagreeable such as punishment'.

> **1894** P. L. FORD *Hon. Peter Stirling* xxvii. 150 'He snubbed me ... ,' explained Miss De Voe, smiling slightly at the thought of treating Peter with a dose of his own medicine.

(as) MEEK as Moses (*or* a lamb) very meek. ● A biblical allusion: 'Now the man Moses was very meek' (Numbers 12:3).

MEET the case be adequate.

MEET one's eye (*or* ear) be visible (*or* audible).

MEET someone's eye (*or* eyes *or* gaze) look directly at someone.

MEET someone halfway make a compromise with someone.

MEET ▶ *see* **make ENDS meet**; ▶ *see* **meet one's MAKER**; ▶ *see* **meet one's MATCH**; ▶ *see* **meet one's WATERLOO**.

a MEETING of minds an understanding or agreement between people.

there's more to someone or something than MEETS the eye a person or situation is more complex or interesting than they appear.

the whole MEGILLAH a long and detailed story, esp. one that is tedious or complicated. *slang* ● The Hebrew word for 'scroll', *megillah* refers particularly to each of five books of the Jewish Scriptures (the Song of Solomon, Ruth, Lamentations, Ecclesiastes, and Esther) appointed to be read in the synagogue on certain important days.

do a MELBA **1** return from retirement. **2** make several farewell appearances. *Austral. & NZ, informal* ● The allusion is to the Australian operatic soprano Nellie Melba (stage name of Helen Mitchell, 1861–1931).

MELT in the mouth (of food) be unusually and delectably soft and smooth in texture. Also literally of food that dissolves or disintegrates in the mouth with little or no chewing.

take a trip (*or* walk) down MEMORY lane deliberately recall pleasant or sentimental memories. ● *Down Memory Lane* (1949) was the title of a compilation of Mack Sennett comedy shorts.

MEN in suits business executives; bureaucrats. *derogatory* ●Used to make a humorous equation of the executives with their working wear, and thus to imply that they are faceless functionaries in an organization rather than autonomous individuals. The phrase is sometimes abbreviated to just *suits*.

MEN in white coats doctors or hospital attendants. *humorous* ●White coats are the working dress of medical personnel. Used often in the jocular suggestion that someone is crazy and so *will be taken away by men in white coats*.

separate (*or* sort out) the MEN from the boys act as a test to distinguish those who are capable (of doing an exacting task) from those who are not.

| **1968** *House & Garden* May 36/4 The Dry Martini … is a drink that will quickly separate the men from the boys and the girls from their principles.

MEN ▶ *see* **TWELVE good men and true**.

MEND (one's) fences make peace with a person. ●Originally L19 US, with reference to a member of Congress returning to his home to keep in touch with the voters and to look after his interests there. Cf. the saying *good fences make good neighbours* (in this form in Robert Frost's 'North of Boston' (1914), but the idea has been current since M17).

on the MEND improving in health or condition; recovering.

MEND one's pace go faster; alter one's pace to another's.

MEND ▶ *see* **MAKE do and mend**.

be MENTIONED in dispatches be commended for one's actions. *Brit.* ●From the military practice in official reports from the front line by which any soldiers who have been responsible for particular acts of bravery are commended by name.

be thankful (*or* grateful) for small MERCIES be relieved that an unpleasant situation is alleviated by minor advantages.

MERRY ▶ *see* **merry as a GRIG**; ▶ *see* **lead someone a merry DANCE**; ▶ *see* **play HELL with**.

MESS with someone's head cause someone to feel frustrated, anxious, or upset. *US, informal*

MESS ▶ *see* **sell something for a mess of POTTAGE**.

get the MESSAGE infer an implication from a remark or action. *informal*

| **1993** I. OKEPWHO *Tides* 191 I think he got the message, because he flashed me a look from the corner of his eye.

send the right (*or* wrong) MESSAGE make a significant statement, either implicitly or by one's actions.

shoot (*or* kill) the MESSENGER treat the bearer of bad news as if they were to blame for it. ●Often imperative: *don't shoot the messenger*. Being the bearer of ill tidings has been a traditionally thankless task from the time of Sophocles (*Antigone* 277 'No man loves the messenger of ill'), through Shakespeare (*Antony and Cleopatra* I. ii 'The nature of bad news infects the teller').

there is METHOD in one's madness there is a sensible foundation for what appears to be foolish or strange behaviour. From Shakespeare's *Hamlet* II. ii. 211.

be on one's METTLE be ready or forced to prove one's ability to cope well with a demanding situation. ● Originally the same word as *metal*, *mettle* was no more than a variant spelling that gradually became particularly associated with figurative uses of the word ('quality of temperament', hence 'natural spirit' or 'courage'). These senses eventually developed so far from the literal senses that the words' identity was no longer apparent. The distinctive uses of *metal* and *mettle* were orthographically acknowledged by E18, though not necessarily universally applied until the following century. *Be (up)on one's mettle* and ▶ **put someone (up)on their METTLE** are both recorded with this spelling in M18.

put someone on their METTLE (of a demanding situation) test someone's ability to face difficulties in a spirited and resilient way.

MEXICAN ▶ *see* Mexican **OVERDRIVE**.

take the MICKEY (out of) tease or ridicule (someone), especially in an unkind or persistent way. *chiefly Brit., informal* ● The origin is unknown. *Mick(e)y* is a (particularly Irish) pet name for Michael; cf. ▶ **for the LOVE of Mike**. *Take* (or *extract*) *the Michael* is a humorously formal variant.

slip someone a MICKEY Finn give someone a drugged or otherwise adulterated drink. ● Apparently a personal name, but of unknown origin. Originally E20 US slang.

come under the MICROSCOPE being examined critically.

the MIDAS touch the ability to turn one's actions to financial advantage. ● In classical legend, *Midas* was a king of Phrygia (in Asia Minor) whose touch was said to turn all things to gold.

the MIDDLE of nowhere somewhere very remote and isolated. *informal* ● One of several derogatory expressions concerning rural life as viewed from an urban perspective: cf. ▶ **the BACK of beyond** and ▶ **in the STICKS**.

steer (*or* take) a MIDDLE course adopt a policy which avoids extremes.
| 1991 J. NEVILLE in *Dance Research* 4 [A courtier] had to steer a middle course between sloppiness and wooden concentration.

MIDNIGHT ▶ *see* **BURN the midnight oil**.

in MIDSTREAM (of an activity or process, especially one that is interrupted) part-way through its course; unfinished. ● Literally, in the middle of a stream or river. Cf. ▶ **change HORSES in midstream**.

with MIGHT and main with all one's force. ● *Main* derives from Old English *mægen* 'physical strength' (cf. ▶ **by MAIN force**). The collocation of the two nouns *might* and *main* dates from M15; except in this phrase, *main* in this sense is obsolete in modern English. The use of two nouns of almost identical meaning is a duplication for emphasis.

MIGHT is right those who are powerful can do what they wish unchallenged, even if their action is in fact unjustified. *proverbial* ● An observation made by both Greek and Latin writers and known in this form in English in E14.

MIKE ▶ *see* **for the LOVE of Mike**.

go the extra MILE be especially assiduous in one's attempt to achieve something. ● Ultimately in allusion to the New Testament injunction 'And whosoever shall compel thee to go a mile, go with him twain' (Matthew 5:41). Cf. also the revue song (1957) by Joyce Grenfell, 'Ready … To go the extra mile'.

a MILE a minute very quickly. *informal* ● As a noun, *mile a minute* is a popular nickname for the quick-growing climbing plant *Polygonum baldschuanica* (Russian Vine).

run a MILE show that one is frightened and horrified by something. *informal* ● Used hyperbolically to suggest a rapid distancing of oneself from a disagreeable situation or prospect.

see (or tell or spot) something a MILE off recognize something very easily. *informal*

stand (or stick) out a MILE be very obvious. *informal*

be MILES away be lost in thought and so unaware of what is happening around one. *informal*

cry over spilt (or US spilled) MILK lament or make a fuss about a misfortune that has happened and is irretrievable. ● Very often in the proverbial admonition *it's no use crying over spilt milk* (first recorded M17).

MILK and honey prosperity and abundance. ● With allusion to the prosperity of the Promised Land of Israel in the Bible (Exodus 3:8).

MILK and water feeble, insipid, mawkish. ● With reference to the thin and flavourless liquid that results from the dilution of milk with water.

the MILK in the coconut a puzzling fact or circumstance. ● Originally an M19 US colloquialism.

MILK of human kindness care and compassion for others. ● With allusion to Lady Macbeth's soliloquy about her husband in Shakespeare's *Macbeth* (I. iv).

go (or put someone) through the MILL undergo (or cause someone to undergo) an unpleasant experience.

MILL ▶ *see* **RUN of the mill**.

gone a MILLION (of a person) completely defeated or finished. *Austral.*, *informal* | 1976 *Australian* (Sydney) 1 Mar. 1/2 Gough's gone. Gone a million. He's had it.

look (or feel) (like) a MILLION dollars (of a person) look or feel extremely good. *informal*

a MILLSTONE round one's neck a very severe impediment or disadvantage. ● A *millstone* was one of the large circular stones used in the grinding of corn. The phrase alludes to a method of executing people by throwing them into deep water with a heavy stone attached to them, a fate believed to have been suffered by several early Christian martyrs.

MILLSTONE ▶ *see* **HARD as the nether millstone**.

not MINCE words (*or* matters *or* one's words) speak candidly and directly, especially when criticizing someone or something.

make MINCEMEAT of defeat decisively or easily in a fight, contest, or argument. *informal*

cast one's MIND back think back; recall an earlier time.

close (*or* shut) one's MIND to (*or* against) refuse to consider or acknowledge. ● Also *have a closed mind* 'be prejudiced'.

come (*or* spring) to MIND (of a thought or idea) occur to someone; be thought of.

have a (*or* a good *or* great *or* half a) MIND to do something be very much inclined to do something.

have a MIND of one's own **1** be capable of independent opinion or action. **2** (of an inanimate object) seem capable of thought and desire, especially by behaving contrary to the will of the person using it.

have on one's MIND be troubled by the thought of.

in one's MIND's eye in one's imagination or mental view.

MIND over matter the power of the mind asserted over the physical universe; the use of willpower to overcome physical problems.

MIND one's Ps and Qs be careful to behave well and avoid giving offence. ● Various suggestions have been made concerning the significance of P and Q. One obvious one is that a child learning to read or write might have difficulty in distinguishing between the two tailed letters *p* and *q*.

MIND the shop have charge of affairs temporarily.

MIND your back (*or* backs) used to warn inattentive bystanders that someone wants to get past. *informal*

not pay someone any MIND not pay someone any attention. *N. Amer.*

on someone's MIND preoccupying someone, especially in a disquieting way.

open one's MIND to be prepared to consider or acknowledge; be receptive to. ● Also *have an open mind* 'be unprejudiced'.

out of one's MIND **1** having lost control of one's mental faculties; insane. **2** used to express a belief in someone's foolishness or mental turmoil. **3** *informal* suffering from the specified condition to a very high degree.

put one's MIND to (something) start to concentrate on (something).

MIND ▶ *see* **give someone a PIECE of one's mind**; ▶ *see* **READ someone's mind**.

be in (*or* chiefly *N. Amer.* of) two MINDS be unable to decide between alternatives.

in a MINOR key (especially of a literary work) understated.
| **1995** *Independent* 23 Oct. 3/4 He was a moralist in a minor key.

in MINT condition (of an object) new or as if new; in pristine condition. ●With reference to the state of a newly minted coin.

one MINUTE to midnight the last moment or opportunity. *informal*
| **1998** *New Scientist* 23 May 3/2 It's one minute to midnight for the discredited WHO.

all done with MIRRORS an apparent achievement with an element of trickery. ●Alluding to explanations of conjuring tricks; cf. ▶ **SMOKE and mirrors**.

do someone (*or* oneself) a MISCHIEF injure someone or oneself. *informal* ●This archaic sense of *mischief* as an evil or injury caused by an agent is now virtually confined to this expression.

make MISCHIEF create trouble or discord. ●L19; antedated by *mischief-maker* and *mischief-making* (both E18).

put something out of its MISERY end the suffering of a creature in pain by killing it.
| *1792 J. WOODFORDE *Diary* 16 May My poor old Horse, Punch ... was shot by Ben this Morning to put him out of his Misery.

put someone out of their MISERY release someone from suspense or anxiety, especially by telling them something they are anxious to know. *informal* ●Used earlier (M19) in its literal sense: 'end the suffering of someone in pain by killing them'.

give something a MISS decide not to do or have something. *Brit.*, *informal*

MISS a beat hesitate or falter, especially in demanding circumstances or when making a transition from one activity to another. ●Usually with negative.

MISS the boat (*or* bus) be too slow to take advantage of an opportunity. *informal*
| **1987** K. LETTE *Girl's Night Out* (1989) 143 He'll never get divorced and marry her. She'll miss the boat.

not MISS much be alert to or aware of everything that is happening around one. *informal*

not MISS a trick never fail to take advantage of a situation. *informal*
| **1965** *Harper's Bazaar* Feb. 66/1 Fenwicks ... never misses a trick when it comes to picking up a new accessory idea.

MISS ▶ *see* **make the CUT**.

and no MISTAKE without any doubt. *informal* ●Used in spoken English to emphasize a preceding statement.

make no MISTAKE (about it) do not be deceived into thinking otherwise. *informal*
| **1974** *Times* 22 Mar. 11/7 Make no mistake. We had a major work of television last night.

there is no MISTAKING someone/thing it is impossible not to recognize someone or something.

MITE ▶ *see* **a WIDOW's mite**.

get one's MITTS on obtain possession of. *informal* ● *Mitt* (abbreviated from *mitten*) was L19 US slang for a hand.

a MIXED blessing something good which nevertheless has some disadvantages. ● Cf. ▶ **a CURATE's egg**.

MIX and match select and combine different but complementary items, as clothing, colours, pieces of equipment etc., to form a coordinated set. ● Also as modifier *mix-and-match*.

the MIXTURE as before the same treatment repeated. *Brit.* ● With allusion to an instruction formerly written on a medicine bottle. Now often humorous.

downwardly (*or* upwardly) MOBILE moving to a lower (*or* higher) social position; losing (*or* gaining) wealth and status. ● The idea of social mobility was explored in 1927 in a book of that title by P. A. Sorokin.

put the MOCKER(S) on 1 put an end to; thwart. 2 bring bad luck to. ● E20 Brit. slang. An Austral. variant (also E20) is *put the mock(s) on*.

> **1** 1966 L. DAVIDSON *Long Way to Shiloh* (1968) V. iv. 82 Shimshon and the judo both seemed to have put the mockers on this particular idyll. We left soon after.

> **2** 1970 J. PORTER *Dover Strikes Again* ii. 36 This investigation had got the mockers on it from the start.

make a MOCKERY of something make something seem foolish or absurd.

> 1998 *New Scientist* 29 Aug. 46/2 In some fisheries, waste makes up about half of the landed catch, which makes a mockery of most population models.

MOLEHILL ▶ *see* **make a MOUNTAIN out of a molehill**.

MOMENT of truth a crisis; a turning-point when a decision has to be made or a crisis faced. ● With allusion to the final sword-thrust in a bullfight: Spanish *el momento de la verdad*.

have one's (*or* its) MOMENTS have short periods that are better or more impressive than others.

MONDAY morning quarterback a person who is wise after the event. *N. Amer.* ● A *quarterback* in American football is the player stationed behind the centre who directs the team's attacking play, hence a person who analyses and criticizes a game retrospectively.

be in the MONEY have or win a lot of money. *informal*

for my MONEY 1 in my opinion or judgement. 2 for my preference or taste.

have MONEY to burn have so much money that one can spend as lavishly as one wants.

MONEY burns a hole in one's pocket (*or* purse) one has an irresistible urge to spend money as soon as one has it.

> 1529 T. MORE *Dyaloge of Ymagys* II. x. Hauyng a lytell wanton money whyche hym thought brennyd out the botom of hys purs.

MONEY for jam (*or* old rope) 1 money earned for little or no effort. 2 an easy task. *Brit., informal* ● The *jam* version was explained in 1919 (*Athenaeum* 8

Aug.) as arising from 'the great use of jam in the Army'. *Old rope* is another item that might be considered valueless.

on the MONEY accurate; correct. *chiefly N. Amer.*

put MONEY (*or* put one's money) on have confidence in (the truth or success of something). ● Also literally, 'place a bet on'.

put one's MONEY where one's mouth is take action to support one's statements or opinions. *informal* ● Explained (*American Speech* (1951) XXVI) as a phrase from poker and equated with ▶ **PUT up or shut up**.

throw good MONEY after bad incur further loss in a hopeless attempt to recoup a previous loss.

throw MONEY at something try to solve a problem by recklessly spending more money on it, without due consideration of what is required.

MONEY ▶ *see* **see the COLOUR of someone's money**.

have a MONKEY on one's back **1** have a burdensome problem. **2** be dependent on drugs. *informal* ● Sense 2 is M20 US slang; it can also refer to withdrawal symptoms.

like a MONKEY on a stick restless and agitated. ● With reference to a child's toy consisting of the figure of a monkey able to slide up and down a stick.

make a MONKEY of (*or* out of) someone humiliate someone by making them appear ridiculous.

not give a MONKEY's be completely indifferent or unconcerned. *informal* ● Vulgar slang variants are *a monkey's fuck* and *a monkey's toss*.

(as) artful (*or* clever *or* mischievous) as a wagonload (*or* cartload) of MONKEYS extremely clever or mischievous. *Brit., informal*

MONSTER ▶ *see* **FRANKENSTEIN's monster**; ▶ *see* **the GREEN-EYED monster**.

a MONTH of Sundays a very long, seemingly endless period of time. ● Possibly alluding to Sundays traditionally passing slowly because of religious restrictions on activity or entertainment; cf. the allusion to the absence of mail deliveries on Sundays in a letter by G. E. Jewsbury (29 Mar. 1849): 'If I don't get a better letter from you, ... you may pass "a month of Sundays" at breakfast without any letter from me.'

1998 *Country Life* 10 Sept. 129/2 All in all, the Ministry of Agriculture is gaining the no-nonsense, get-your-coats-off atmosphere that Jack Cunningham could not have managed in a month of Sundays.

the full MONTY everything which is necessary or appropriate. *informal* ● *Monty* is an alternative spelling of Spanish *monte* 'mountain', used as a cardplayers' term for the stack of cards remaining after the deal. It was the name of a card game played in E19 Mexico and mentioned in 1850 as 'the favorite game in California'. The L19 Austral. & NZ slang use of *monte* or *monty* for a certainty, esp. a horse considered sure to win a race, probably also refers to the gambling game. The *-y* spelling antedates by over sixty years the World War II general Montgomery with whom a fanciful Brit. etymology associates the expression.

bark at the MOON clamour or make an outcry to no effect. ● The barking of dogs at a full moon has been a metaphor for futile activity since M17.

cry (or ask) for the MOON ask for what is unattainable or impossible. *Brit.* ● The *moon* here stands for something distant and unattainable. Cf. ▶ **promise the MOON**. Current in various forms since M16.

over the MOON extremely happy; delighted. *informal* ● From *The Cow jumped over the Moon*, a line from a nursery rhyme (M18).

promise (someone) the MOON (or earth) promise something that is unattainable. *Brit.* ● Cf. ▶ **cry for the MOON**.

| **1998** *New Scientist* 24 Jan. 44/2 Scientists tend to promise taxpayers the moon, and then not deliver.

MOON ▶ *see* **once in a BLUE moon**.

MOONLIGHT ▶ *see* **do a moonlight FLIT**.

many MOONS ago a long time ago. *informal* ● With reference to the phases of the moon marking out the months.

MORNING, noon, and night all of the time; constantly.

| **1993** T. PARKER *May Lord in His Mercy be Kind to Belfast* vi. 67 [I]t was the sort [of relationship] where nothing else matters for you except to be with that other person morning, noon and night.

MORTAL ▶ *see* **shuffle off this mortal COIL**.

MORTON ▶ *see* **Morton's FORK**.

a MOTE in someone's eye a trivial fault in someone which is less serious than one in someone else who is being critical. ● With allusion to Matthew 7:3–5, critics of motes in other people's eyes being castigated there as hypocrites; cf. ▶ **a BEAM in one's eye**.

like a MOTH to the flame irresistibly attracted to someone or something.

in MOTHBALLS unused but kept in good condition for future use. ● With allusion to the practice of storing clothes, furnishings, etc. with pellets of naphthalene to repel fabric-eating moths.

MOTHER ▶ *see* **every mother's SON**.

go through the MOTIONS 1 do something perfunctorily, without any enthusiasm or commitment. 2 simulate an action; act out something.

wear MOTLEY play the fool. ● With allusion to the particoloured clothes worn by a court jester in former times.

break the MOULD put an end to a pattern of events or behaviour, especially one that has become rigid and restrictive, by doing things in a markedly different way. ● Originally with reference to casting artefacts in moulds (cf. the metaphorical use of *in the same mould*); destroying a mould ensured that no further identical examples could be produced. The image was used in Italian of Nature's creativity: Ariosto *Orlando Furioso* (1532) X. 84 *Natura il fece, e poi roppe la stampa* (translated by Harington (1591) as 'This is the goodly impe whom nature made ... And after brake the mould' (X. 70). The earliest occurrence in English was in William Painter's *Palace of Pleasure* (1566). The expression became a catchphrase in Britain in the early 1980s with the foundation of the Social Democratic Party, which its founders promoted as breaking the 'out-of-date mould' of British politics (Roy Jenkins in a speech 9 June 1980).

if the MOUNTAIN won't come to Muhammad, Muhammad must go to the mountain if one party will not compromise, the other party will have to make the extra effort. ● With allusion to the story that Muhammad was once challenged to demonstrate his credentials as a prophet by summoning Mount Safa to the place where he was. When the mountain did not move in response to the summons, Muhammad observed that had the mountain moved it would undoubtedly have overwhelmed him and all his followers and that therefore he would go to the mountain to give thanks to God for his mercy in not allowing this disaster to happen. The second half of the sentence is often used allusively on its own.

make a MOUNTAIN out of a molehill foolishly or pointlessly exaggerate the importance of something trivial. ● The contrast between the smallness of molehills and the largeness of mountains has been made in this and related expressions since L16.

MOVABLE ▶ *see* **a movable FEAST**.

move MOUNTAINS 1 achieve spectacular and apparently impossible results. **2** make every possible effort. ● In sense 1, with allusion to 1 Corinthians 13:2 'though I have all faith, so that I could remove mountains'.

a better MOUSETRAP an improved version of a well-known article. ● From an observation attributed (1889) to Ralph Waldo Emerson, though also claimed by Elbert Hubbard: 'If a man write a better book, preach a better sermon, or make a better mousetrap than his neighbour, tho' he build his house in the woods, the world will make a beaten path to his door.'

all MOUTH (and no trousers) (of a person) who talks or boasts a lot but cannot or will not act on their words. *informal*
| **1998** *Oldie* May 51/1 What was the point of the Sitwells? … The *image* was the point, transcending mere achievement … The Sitwells were all mouth and no trousers.

make someone's MOUTH water cause someone an intense desire to possess something. ● With reference to salivating at the prospect of appetizing food.

put words in (*or* into) someone's MOUTH 1 falsely report what someone has said. **2** prompt or encourage someone to say something.

take the words out of someone's MOUTH say what someone else was about to say.

give someone a MOUTHFUL talk to or shout at someone in an angry, abusive, or severely critical way; swear at someone. *Brit., informal*

say a MOUTHFUL make a striking or important statement; say something noteworthy. *N. Amer., informal*

get a MOVE on hurry up. *informal* ● Often in imperative.
| **1992** L. TUTTLE *Lost Futures* 294 So stop worrying, sweetheart, and let's get a move on … I don't want to be late.

make a MOVE 1 take action. **2** *Brit.* start on a journey; leave somewhere.

make a MOVE on (*or* put the moves on) make a proposition to (someone), especially of a sexual nature. *informal*

MOVE with the times keep abreast of current thinking or developments.

MOVE ▶ *see* **change GEAR**; ▶ *see* **move the GOALPOSTS**; ▶ *see* **move HEAVEN and earth**; ▶ *see* **move MOUNTAINS**; ▶ *see* **not move a MUSCLE**.

MOVES ▶ *see* **the SPIRIT moves someone**.

a MOVER and shaker someone at the centre of events who makes things happen; a powerful person.   ● From *movers and shakers*, a phrase from 'Ode', by Arthur O'Shaughnessy (1874).
| **1998** *Times* 9 June 33/6 [T]en years from now his name will again be high on the list of movers and shakers to watch in the decade.

not(hing) MUCH in it little difference between things being compared.

so MUCH the better (*or* worse) it is better (*or* worse) for that reason.
| **1995** *Guardian: Weekend* 29 July 32/3 If you can get a tropical fruit juice … so much the better.

much of a MUCHNESS very similar; nearly the same. *informal* ● *Muchness*, used in Middle English with the sense 'large size, bigness' is now very seldom used outside this expression, which dates from E18.

as common as MUCK of low social status. *Brit., informal*

make a MUCK of handle incompetently; bungle. *Brit., Austral., & NZ, informal*

MUCKER ▶ *see* **come a CROPPER**.

(as) clear as MUD not at all easy to understand. *informal, humorous*

someone's name is MUD someone is in disgrace or unpopular. *informal* ● *Mud* was an obsolete slang term for a fool (E18–L19). 'J. Bee' in *Slang* (1823) records this expression as being exclaimed 'upon the conclusion of a silly oration'.
| **1998** *Times: Magazine* 4 Apr. 91/3 Just because I smoked a few lousy cigarettes every hour for 25 years, my name is mud in the insurance business.

fling (*or* sling *or* throw) MUD make disparaging or scandalous remarks or accusations. *informal* ● With allusion to the proverb *throw dirt (or mud) enough, and some will stick*, attributed to the Florentine statesman Machiavelli.

MUD ▶ *see* **DRAG someone through the dirt**.

MUDDY the waters make an issue or a situation more confusing and harder to understand by introducing complications. ● The figurative use of *muddy* (= make turbid) occurs in Shakespeare; *muddy the waters* dates from M19.

a MUG's game an activity in which it is stupid to engage because it is likely to be unsuccessful or dangerous. *informal* ● *Mug* was M19 slang for a fool, in particular the dupe of a card-sharper or criminal. *Mug's game* appeared in E20 and has been applied to a wide variety of activities, especially horse-racing and betting on horses.
| **1930** G. B. SHAW *Apple Cart* II. 77 I am going out of politics. Politics is a mug's game.

poke MULLOCK at ridicule (someone). *Austral. & NZ, informal* ● The Middle English sense of *mullock* as 'refuse matter, rubbish' is now only dialect, but in Australia (M–L19) it was used of rock that either does not contain gold or from which the gold had been extracted. It is used figuratively to mean 'worthless information'. This phrase E20; cf. ▶ **poke BORAK at**.

cover a MULTITUDE of sins conceal or gloss over a lot of problems or defects. ● With reference to 1 Peter 4:8 'For charity shall cover the multitude of sins.'

keep MUM remain silent about something; not reveal a secret. *informal* ● In this and ▶ **MUM's the word**, *mum* (L14, now obsolete) stands for an inarticulate sound made with pursed lips indicating either unwillingness or inability to speak.

MUM's the word say nothing; don't reveal a secret. *informal* ● Used as a request, command, or warning.

get away with MURDER succeed in doing whatever one chooses without being punished or suffering any disadvantage. *informal*

MURDER will out murder cannot remain undetected. ● Similar in construction to another proverbial saying: *truth will out* (M15). In both these there is ellipsis of the intransitive verb *come*.

| *c.1386 G. CHAUCER *Prioress's Tale* 576 Mordre wol out, certeyn, it wol nat faille.

scream (or yell) blue (or N. Amer. bloody) MURDER make an extravagant and noisy protest. *informal*

| **1995** I. BANKS *Whit* (1996) xxiii. 375 I was now left with the ticklish problem of how to let my great-aunt know there was somebody there in the room with her without … causing her to scream blue murder.

MURPHY's law if anything can go wrong it will. ● *Murphy's law* is said to have been the inspiration of a Californian project manager for the firm Northrop, referring to a remark made in 1949 by a colleague, Captain E. Murphy of the Wright Field-Aircraft Laboratory. In 1955 *Aviation Mechanics Bulletin* explained Murphy's Law as 'If an aircraft part can be installed incorrectly, someone will install it that way.' However, various aphoristic expressions of the apparent perverseness and unreasonableness of things, which would now be seen as examples of Murphy's Law, were in circulation long before Murphy and his colleague: a classic is Kipling's 'The bread never falls but on its buttered side' (in *Beast and Man*, 1891).

flex one's MUSCLES give a show of strength or power.

| **1998** *Times* 6 Mar. 35/6 Mr Prescott is flexing his muscles and the City is wondering just how far he is prepared to go.

like MUSHROOMS suddenly and in great numbers. ● Alluding to the sudden overnight appearance of mushrooms in a field.

MUSIC to one's ears something that is very pleasant or gratifying to hear or discover.

MUSTARD ▶ *see* **CUT the mustard**; ▶ *see* **a GRAIN of mustard seed**.

pass MUSTER be accepted as adequate or satisfactory. ● In origin a military expression, meaning 'come through a review or inspection without censure'. Earlier (L16–L17) in the now obsolete form *pass (the) musters*; figurative since L16.

(as) dead as MUTTON quite dead.

MUTTON dressed as lamb a middle-aged or old woman dressed in a style suitable for a much younger woman. *Brit., informal* ● *Mutton* as a slang term for a prostitute is recorded from E16, and the word occurs in various derogatory contexts relating to women, e.g. *hawk one's mutton* (solicit).

*1895 R. KIPLING *Brushwood Boy* Look at young Davies makin' an ass of himself over mutton-dressed-as-lamb old enough to be his mother!

N

a NAIL in the coffin an action or event regarded as likely to have a detrimental or destructive effect on a situation, enterprise, or person.

> **1981** R. LANCASTER *Plant Hunting in Nepal* (1983) xiv. 165 A major nail in the coffin of the plant hunter, so some people believe, is the growing importance placed on plant conservation in the wild.

NAIL a lie expose as a falsehood. ● *Nail* in this context has the sense associated with such practices as *nailing to the counter* (the method adopted formerly by shopkeepers of exposing forged coins and putting them out of circulation) or *nailing to the barn door* (pinning up dead vermin as a deterrent to others).

on the NAIL (or N. Amer. **on the barrelhead)** (of payment) without delay. ● The origins of this phrase are obscure.

> **1993** J. GASH *Paid and Loving Eyes* (1994) xiii. 98 Illegal syndicates pay cash on the nail.

right on the NAIL with complete accuracy.

NAIL (noun) ▶ *see* **HIT the nail on the head**.

NAIL (verb) ▶ *see* **nail one's colours to the MAST**.

NAILS ▶ *see* **HARD as nails**; ▶ *see* **SPIT blood**.

the NAKED truth the plain truth, without concealment or embellishment. ● Perhaps originally with allusion to Horace's *nudaque veritas* (*Odes* I. *xxiv*) or to any of various fables that personify Truth as a naked woman in contrast to the elaborate dress and artifice of Falsehood.

give one's NAME to invent, discover, or found something which then becomes known by one's name.

something has one's NAME on it one is destined or particularly suited to receive or experience a specified thing. ● Cf. ▶ **have someone's NUMBER on it**.

have to one's NAME in one's possession. ● Often with negative.

in all but NAME existing in a particular state but not formally recognized as such.

in NAME only by description but not in reality.

> **1993** *Harper's Magazine* Jan. 42/2 In Western Europe the Communist parties shrank year after year, … they had become small-bourgeois capitalist parties, Communist in name only.

make a NAME for oneself become famous.

NAME and shame identify wrongdoers by name with the intention of embarrassing them into improving their behaviour. ● A stronger version of ▶ **NAME names**.

> **1998** *New Scientist* 4 Apr. 4/1 I'm all for naming and shaming, as this is worth many times more than fines.

the NAME of the game the main purpose or most important aspect of a situation. *informal*

NAME names mention specific names, especially of people involved in something wrong or illegal. ● The use of *name* with the cognate object probably derives from the Bible (e.g. Wyclif's translation (1382) of 2 Timothy 2:19). A less accusatory action than ▶ **NAME and shame**. Cf. ▶ **NAME no names**.

NAME no names refrain from mentioning the names of people involved in an incident etc. ● More formal than ▶ **no NAMES, no pack drill**. Often as phrase *naming no names*, used with the implication that the hearer or reader would be able to supply the names for themselves.

> ***1792** F. BURNEY *Journal* June She desired he would name no names, but merely mention that some of the ladies had been frightened.

put a NAME to know or manage to remember what someone or something is called.

what's in a NAME? names are arbitrary labels. ● With allusion to Shakespeare's *Romeo and Juliet* II. ii. 43.

you NAME it whatever you can think of. *informal* ● Generally used at the conclusion of a list that has been either explicitly recited or implied.

> **1991** A. CARTER *Wise Children* (1992) i. 23 The streets of tall, narrow houses were stuffed to the brim with stand-up comics; adagio dancers; soubrettes; conjurers; fiddlers; speciality acts with dogs, doves, goats, you name it.

call someone NAMES insult someone verbally.

drop NAMES refer frequently to well-known people in such a way as to imply that they are close acquaintances. ● Hence *name-dropper* and *name-dropping*.

no NAMES, no pack drill blame or punishment cannot be meted out if names and details are not mentioned. ● *Pack drill* is a form of military punishment in which an offender has to perform parade-ground exercises while carrying a heavy pack. This E20 expression is often used as an aside to indicate that reticence is desirable over a particular subject.

NAME ▶ *see* **drag someone through the MUD**; ▶ *see* **someone's name is MUD**; ▶ *see* **take someone's name in VAIN**.

catch someone NAPPING (of an action or event) find someone off guard and unprepared to respond. *informal*

go NAP **1** win all the matches or games in a series. **2** risk everything in one attempt. ● From the card game *nap* (abbreviation of Napoleon) in which a player attempts to take all five tricks.

not go NAP on not be too keen on; not care much for. *Austral., informal* ● Cf. preceding entry.

a NASTY piece (*or* bit) of work an unpleasant or untrustworthy person. *informal*

NASTY ▶ *see* **a bad TASTE in the mouth**; ▶ *see* **something nasty in the WOODSHED**.

one NATION a nation not divided by social inequality. ● Often as modifier: *one-nation*. A political slogan of the 1990s associated with the British Conservative Party (see quot.).

| **1998** *Times: Weekend* 4 Apr. 40 (*comic strip caption*) We Toreens [i.e. Tories] are now a united one-nation force.

go NATIVE (of a person living away from their own country or region) abandon one's own culture, customs, or way of life and adopt those of the country or region one is living in. ● Generally humorous and/or derogatory.

one's better NATURE the good side of one's character; one's capacity for tolerance, generosity, or sympathy.

| **1965** M. FRAYN *Tin Men* i. 9 Appeal to their better natures.

call of NATURE a need to urinate or defecate. ● An M19 euphemism.

get (*or* go) back to NATURE return to the type of life (regarded as being more in tune with nature) that existed before the development of complex industrial societies.

in the NATURE of things inevitable; inevitably.

| **1894** R. KIPLING *My First Book* 92 All my verses … came without invitation, unmanneredly, in the nature of things.

in a state of NATURE **1** in an uncivilized or uncultivated state. **2** totally naked. **3** (in Christian theology) in a morally unregenerate condition, unredeemed by divine grace.

the NATURE of the beast the inherent or essential quality or character of something, which cannot be changed and must be accepted. *informal* ● Generally used of undesirable characteristics.

NATURE ▶ *see* **RED in tooth and claw**.

contemplate one's NAVEL spend time complacently considering oneself or one's own interests; concentrate on one issue at the expense of a wider view.

one's NEAREST and dearest one's close friends and relatives. ● Often used ironically.

so NEAR and yet so far a rueful comment on a situation in which one has narrowly failed to achieve an aim.

a NECESSARY evil something that is undesirable but must be accepted.

| *1547 W. BALDWIN *Treatise of Morall Phylosophie* III. XV A woman is a necessary euyll.

break one's NECK to do something exert oneself to the utmost to achieve something. *informal* ● Used hyperbolically of intense effort, with the implication that physical damage, perhaps fatal, could be caused.

get (*or* catch) it in the NECK be severely criticized or punished. *informal*

have the (brass) NECK to do something have the impudence or nerve to do something. *informal*

NECK and neck level in a race, competition, or comparison. ● Originally with reference to racing horses.

> **1998** *Spectator* 2 May 14/2 [The Republicans] had a 30-point lead over the Democrats; today, the Democrats are neck and neck on what's supposed to be a bedrock conservative issue.

NECK or nothing risking everything on success.

the same NECK of the woods the same small geographical area or community. *orig. US* ● *Neck* in the sense of 'narrow strip of woodland' is recorded from L18. The phrase occurs in M19 US usage, and in 1871 it was glossed as 'the name applied to any settlement made in the well-wooded parts of the South-west especially.' (S. De Vere *Americanisms* 178). In current speech *neck* is sometimes used elliptically for the whole phrase.

> **1998** *Spectator* 23 May 22/1 Both [letters] come from the same neck of the woods, both are on the same subject and both are cries for help which are being ignored.

up to one's NECK in **1** heavily involved in something onerous or unpleasant. **2** very busy with. *informal*

win by a NECK succeed by a small margin. ● In horse racing, a *neck* is the length of the head and neck of a horse as a measure of its lead in a race.

NECK ▶ *see* **STICK one's neck out**.

NED KELLY ▶ *see* **GAME as Ned Kelly**.

a NEEDLE in a haystack something almost impossible to find because it is concealed by so many other similar things.

> **1998** *New Scientist* 11 July 38/1 Looking for variation on the Y chromosome with conventional techniques of DNA sequencing is like searching for a needle in a haystack.

NEEDLE ▶ *see* **SHARP as a needle**.

must NEEDS do something **1** cannot avoid or help doing something. **2** foolishly insist on doing something. ● For *needs*, cf. next entry.

NEEDS must sometimes you are forced to take a course of action you would have preferred to avoid. ● A shortened form of the proverb *needs must when the Devil drives*. As an adverb *needs* (= of necessity) is now used mainly in elliptic phrases with *must*. The full version of the saying dates from M15.

not on your NELLY certainly not. ● Originally as *not on your Nelly Duff*, British rhyming slang for 'puff' (i.e. breath of life); modelled on the phrase *not on your life*.

strain every NERVE make every possible effort. ● From the earlier sense of *nerve* as 'tendon, sinew'.

touch (*or* hit) a (raw) NERVE provoke a reaction by referring to a sensitive topic.

get on someone's NERVES irritate or annoy someone. *informal*

have NERVES of steel not be easily upset or frightened.

live on one's NERVES (*or* one's nerve ends) be extremely anxious or tense.

NERVES ▶ *see* a BAG of nerves; ▶ *see* a WAR of nerves.

NESSUS' shirt (*or* shirt of Nessus) used to refer to a destructive or expurgatory force or influence. *literary* ● In Greek mythology, the centaur Nessus, when fatally wounded by the hero Heracles (Hercules), told Deianira, Heracles' wife, that his blood would act as a love charm by which she would always be able to retain her husband's love. When Deianira later had cause to doubt Heracles' affection, she steeped a shirt in Nessus' blood and gave it to Heracles to wear, but the blood was a powerful poison that corroded his body and as he tried to tear it off ripped away chunks of his flesh.

a mare's NEST a wonderful discovery which proves or will prove to be illusory. ● The type of something fantastical, it is recorded from E17, but the obsolete *horse nest* is found in L16.

NESTER ▶ *see* EMPTY nester.

slip (*or* fall) through the NET escape from or be missed by something organized to catch or deal with one.

| 1977 M. DRABBLE *Ice Age* i. 67 Britain is, after all, a welfare state, and not many slip through its net.

NET ▶ *see* SURF the net.

NETTLE ▶ *see* GRASP the nettle.

the old boy NETWORK mutual assistance, especially preferment in employment, shown among those with a shared social and educational background.

NEVER-never land an imaginary utopian place or situation. ● Often with allusion to the imaginary country in J. M. Barrie's *Peter Pan* (1904). The term was used earlier to denote the unpopulated northern part of the Northern Territory and Queensland in Australia (from which one might never return).

NEVER ▶ *see* never say DIE.

a NEW one on (me, him, etc.) an account, idea, or joke not previously encountered by me, him, etc. *informal*

NEW ▶ *see* a new BROOM; ▶ *see* a new kid on the BLOCK; ▶ *see* new off the IRONS; ▶ *see* turn over a new LEAF; ▶ *see* a whole new BALL GAME.

be bad NEWS be a problem or handicap. *informal*

be good NEWS be an asset; be commendable or admirable. *informal*

NEXT in line immediately below the present holder of a position in order of succession. ● Used with preposition *for* or *to*.

the boy (*or* girl) NEXT DOOR a person or the type of a person perceived as familiar, approachable, and dependable, typically in the context of a romantic partnership.

NEXT ▶ *see* next to no TIME.

his NIBS a self-important man, especially one in authority. *informal* ● Origin obscure; *nabs*, with a possessive pronoun, was used earlier (L18) as a slang or jocular term for a person. Used humorously as a mock title since M19.

make NICE (*or* nice-nice) be pleasant or polite to someone, typically in a hypocritical way. *N. Amer., informal*

NICE work if you can get it used to express envy of what is perceived to be another person's more favourable situation, especially if they seem to have reached it with little effort. *informal* ● The title of an Ira Gershwin song (1937).

to a NICETY precisely.

in good NICK in good condition. *Brit., informal* ● Originally dialect slang (E20). *In bad nick* and other variants occur.

in the NICK of time only just in time; just at the critical moment. ● *Nick* here is in the sense of 'the precise moment of an occurrence or an event'. This form of this phrase dates from M17, but *in the (very) nick* is recorded from L16.

> **1985** N. HERMAN *My Kleinian Home* 18 Time and again, when all seemed lost, I somehow won through in the nick of time.

NICK someone for cheat someone of something, typically a sum of money. *N. Amer., informal*

accept a wooden NICKEL be fooled or swindled. *US* ● A *wooden nickel* is a worthless or counterfeit coin.

not worth a plugged NICKEL of no value. *US* ● A *plugged* coin has had a portion removed and the space filled with base material.

a NIGGER in the woodpile a hidden cause of trouble. *informal* ● Originally an M19 US colloquialism, also found in the version *a nigger in the fence*. Now often considered offensive.

> **1990** *New York Times* 11 Jan. B1/1 He suggested to a racially mixed audience in Brooklyn that critics of government were 'always looking for a nigger in the woodpile'.

NIGHT of the long knives a ruthless or decisive action held to resemble this. ● Originally a treacherous massacre, as (according to legend) of the Britons by Hengist in 472, or of Ernst Roehm and his associates by Hitler on 29—30 June 1934 (the phrase occurs in a Nazi marching song). In Britain the phrase is particularly associated with Prime Minister Harold Macmillan (see quot.)

> **1991** J. BARBER *Prime Ministers since 1945* vii. 70 Macmillan had had an even more damaging experience in July 1962—the 'night of the long knives'. His 'unflappable' reputation disintegrated as he dismissed a third of his Cabinet at one stroke.

NIGHT ▶ *see* **MAKE a day of it**.

dressed to (*or Brit.* up to) the NINES dressed very smartly or elaborately. ● *To the nine* (L18), later *nines*, at first meant 'to perfection, to the greatest degree' in a general sense, but by M19 was particularly associated with smart dress.

NINE to five typical office hours. ● Often as modifier: *a nine-to-five job*. Frequently used to express an idea of routine or predictability.

NINE ▶ *see* **a nine days' WONDER**; ▶ *see* **on CLOUD nine**.

no more than NINEPENCE in the shilling of low intelligence. *dated* ● With the decimalization of the British coinage, this phrase is heading for obsolescence, but there are numerous other jocular variations on the theme of someone's lacking a full complement of wits: cf. ▶ **a SANDWICH short of a picnic**.

go down (or drop or fall) like NINEPINS topple or succumb in large numbers.

| **1998** *Spectator* 15 Aug. 24/1 [M]isuse of Viagra by oldies is knocking them over like ninepins.

NINETEEN ▶ *see* **talk nineteen to the DOZEN**.

NIP something in the bud suppress or destroy something at an early stage. ●With allusion to the horticultural practice of pinching out plant buds so as to prevent the development of shoots or flowers. *Nip* in this sense was used figuratively in L16, and *nip in the bud* in E17.

pick NITS look for and criticize small or insignificant faults or errors. ●With allusion to painstakingly removing tiny parasitic *nits* (lice or lice eggs) from someone's hair. Originally (M20) chiefly N. Amer. Also in the back formation *nit-pick*.

keep NIT keep watch or act as a guard. *Austral.* ●*Nit* here possibly an alteration of *nix*, a warning signal by schoolchildren that a teacher is approaching; *keep nix* is a parallel use.

NO man's land an intermediate or ambiguous area of thought or activity. ●Used literally in L16 for a piece of land without an owner, but particularly associated with the terrain between the German trenches and those of the Allied forces in World War I. Figurative usage dates from L19.

not (or never) take NO for an answer persist in spite of refusals.

— or NO — regardless of the person, thing or quality specified.

NO ▶ *see* **no SOONER said than done**.

the NOBLE art (or science) (of self-defence) boxing. *archaic* or *humorous*

NOBODY ▶ *see* **be nobody's FOOL**; ▶ *see* **like nobody's BUSINESS**.

be on NODDING terms know someone slightly. ●With preposition *with*. Also ▶ **have a nodding ACQUAINTANCE with someone/thing**.

get (or give someone/thing) the NOD **1** be selected or approved (or select or approve someone or something). **2** get (or give someone) a signal or information.

a NOD's as good as a wink there's no need for further elaboration or explanation. ●With allusion to the proverb *a nod is as good as a wink to a blind horse* (L18), used to convey that a mere hint or suggestion can be or has been understood. Also *a nod and a wink* meaning 'a hint' or 'innuendo'.

on the NOD by general agreement and without discussion. *Brit., informal*

the NOES have it the negative votes are in the majority. ●Cf. ▶ **the AYES have it**.

a NO-GO area a zone that is not entered (by specified people) because it would be too dangerous to do so. ●As a noun *no-go* was first used (L19) in the sense

of 'an impracticable situation', but its attributive use in this phrase, with
the sense of 'no entry', is particularly associated with Northern Ireland in
the 1970s.

> **1971** *Guardian* 13 Nov. 1/6 For journalists and others, the Bogside and Creggan estates are
> 'no-go areas', with the IRA in total effective control.

make a NOISE speak or act in a way designed to attract a lot of attention or
publicity.

NOISE ▶ *see* **a BIG cheese**.

NONE ▶ *see* **be none the WISER**; ▶ *see* **none the WORSE**.

go NON-LINEAR become very excited or angry, especially about a particular
obsession. *informal* ●Perhaps originating as a humorous play on ▶ **go off
the RAILS**.

make NONSENSE (*or* **a nonsense) of** reduce the value of something to a
ridiculous degree.

every NOOK and cranny every part or aspect of something.

put one's head in a NOOSE bring about one's own downfall.

up NORTH to or in the north of a country. *informal* ●Cf. ▶ **down SOUTH**.

by a NOSE (of a victory) by a very narrow margin. ●In horse racing, the nar-
rowest margin by which a horse can win.

cannot see further than one's NOSE (of a person) be unwilling or fail to
consider different possibilities or to foresee the consequences of one's actions.

cut off one's NOSE to spite one's face disadvantage oneself in the course
of trying to disadvantage another. ●Proverbial for self-defeating malice in
both medieval Latin and medieval French, and in English since M16.

get up someone's NOSE irritate or annoy someone. *informal*

give someone a bloody NOSE inflict a resounding defeat on someone.

keep one's NOSE clean stay out of trouble. *informal*

keep one's NOSE out of refrain from interfering in (someone else's affairs).

on the NOSE 1 to a person's sense of smell. 2 *chiefly N. Amer., informal* precisely.
3 *Austral., informal* distasteful; offensive.

put someone's NOSE out of joint embarrass, disconcert, frustrate, or sup-
plant someone; make someone look foolish. *informal*

turn up one's NOSE at show distaste or contempt for something. *informal*

under someone's NOSE (of an action) committed openly and boldly,
but without someone noticing or noticing in time to prevent it. *informal*
●Literally, directly in front of someone.

with one's NOSE in the air haughtily.

> **1994** *Time* 30 May 35/1 Charles de Gaulle arrived in the U.S. with his nose in the air; he
> considered Jackie empty and much too beau monde.

NOSE ▶ *see* **keep one's nose to the GRINDSTONE**; ▶ *see* **LEAD someone by the nose**.

count NOSES count people, typically in order to determine the numbers in a vote.

NOT in my back yard expressing an objection to the siting of something regarded as undesirable in one's own neighbourhood, with the implication that it would be acceptable elsewhere. ● Originating in the US in derogatory references to the attitude of anti-nuclear campaigners, in Britain it is particularly associated with reports of the then Environment Secretary Nicholas Ridley's opposition in 1988 to housing developments near his own home. The phrase has given rise to the acronym *nimby*.

NOT ▶ *see* **not HALF**; ▶ *see* **not LEAST**.

hit (or strike) the right (or wrong) NOTE say or do something in exactly the right (or wrong) way.

strike (or sound) a — NOTE express a feeling or view of a particular kind. ● For instance, to *strike a false note* is to appear insincere or inappropriate.

be as NOTHING (compared) to be insignificant in comparison with.

> **1998** *Oldie* Aug. 38/2 Believe me, being pronounced anathema is as nothing compared to the earful you get from a liberal who considers himself insufficiently appreciated.

have NOTHING on someone/thing **1** have much less of a particular quality or ability than someone or something; be inferior to someone or something in a particular respect. **2** (especially of the police) have no incriminating information about someone. *informal*

NOTHING doing **1** there is no prospect of success or agreement. **2** nothing is happening. *informal*

NOTHING (or nothing else) for it no alternative. *Brit.*

NOTHING less than very; entirely. ● Used to emphasize how extreme something is.

NOTHING loath quite willing.

> ***1667** J. MILTON *Paradise Lost* Her hand he seis'd, and to a shadie bank ... He led her nothing loath.

NOTHING to it very simple to do. *informal*

you ain't seen NOTHING yet there is something even more extreme or impressive in store. *informal* ● Cf. the title of an Al Jolson song (1919) *You Ain't Heard Nothing Yet*, referring to an earlier remark of his before an encore.

NOTHING ▶ *see* **nothing DAUNTED**; ▶ *see* **nothing MUCH in it**; ▶ *see* **STOP at nothing**.

sweet NOTHINGS words of affection exchanged by lovers.

at short (or a moment's) NOTICE with little warning or time for preparation.

put someone on NOTICE (or serve notice) warn someone of something about or likely to occur, often formally or threateningly.

NOW or never an expression of urgency.

a road to NOWHERE a situation or course of action offering no prospects of progress or advancement.

NOWHERE ▶ *see* **in the MIDDLE of nowhere**.

to the NTH degree to any extent; to the utmost.

a NUDGE and a wink encouragement given secretly or implicitly; covert support. ● Both *nudge* and *wink* are covert signs of complicity, with *wink* also having the implication of 'shutting one's eyes' to something.

| 1998 *Times* 13 May 18/3 There was a nudge and a wink at some mercenary help that in the end proved unnecessary.

NUDGE nudge (wink wink) used to draw attention to an innuendo, especially a sexual one, in the previous statement. *informal*

NUDGE ▶ *see* **dig someone in the RIBS**.

NUFF said there is no need to say any more. ● *Nuff* is a colloquial or dialect shortening of *enough*. An M19 US colloquialism.

make a NUISANCE of oneself cause trouble and annoyance, usually deliberately or avoidably.

do a NUMBER on treat someone badly, typically by deceiving, humiliating, or criticizing them in a calculated and thorough way. *N. Amer., informal*

have someone's NUMBER understand a person's real motives or character and thereby gain some advantage. *informal* ● M19, also with *get* or *take*.

have someone's (name and) NUMBER on it (of a bomb, bullet, or other missile) be destined to hit a specified person. *informal* ● With reference to a lottery number or a number, such as that given to a soldier, by which one may be identified.

make one's NUMBER to report one's arrival, pay a courtesy call, or report for duty. ● With reference to ships' making themselves known by signal under the number by which they were registered. An M19 nautical expression that was recorded by Partridge (1942) as passing into civilian slang. Used with preposition *with*.

someone's NUMBER is up the time has come when someone is doomed to die or suffer some other disaster or setback. *informal* ● Either with reference to a lottery number or to the various biblical passages on the 'number of one's days [i.e. of one's life]' (e.g. Job 38:21).

take care of (or look after) NUMBER one be selfishly absorbed in protecting one's own person and interests. *informal*

without NUMBER too many to count.

| 1990 B. BRYSON *Mother Tongue* xv. 228 The varieties of wordplay available in English are almost without number—puns, tongue-twisters, anagrams, riddles, cryptograms ...

NUMBER ▶ *see* **a BACK number**; ▶ *see* **public ENEMY number one**.

someone's (or something's) days are NUMBERED someone or something will not survive or remain in a particular position for much longer.

by NUMBERS following simple instructions identified by numbers; mechanically. ●With allusion to *painting by numbers*, a painting kit with a canvas on which numbers have been marked to indicate which colour of paint should be applied at which place.

do one's NUT be extremely angry or agitated. *Brit.*, *informal* ●*Nut* here and in the next entry is slang for 'head'.

off one's NUT out of one's mind; crazy. *informal*

a tough (or hard) NUT (to crack) someone who is difficult to deal with or hard to beat; a formidable person. *informal*

NUT ▶ *see* **take (or use) a SLEDGEHAMMER to crack a nut**.

a wooden NUTMEG a false or fraudulent thing. *US* ●A piece of wood shaped to resemble a nutmeg and fraudulently sold as the real thing; the deception was particularly associated with the inhabitants of Connecticut, giving rise to the sobriquet 'the Nutmeg State'.

be NUTS about (or Brit. on) be very enthusiastic about or fond of. *informal*
| 1934 D. HAMMETT *Tin Man* (1989) xxii. 123 She told me she had this job with Wynant and he was nuts about her and she was sitting pretty.

for NUTS even tolerably well. *Brit.*, *informal* ●Following negative (see quot.).
| 1934 A. THIRKELL *Wild Strawberries* xi. 237 That Miss Stevenson can't play for nuts.

NUTS and bolts the basic practical details. *informal* ●Also as modifier: *nuts-and-bolts* or *nut and bolt*.
| 1998 *Spectator* 28 Mar. 24/3 [P]erhaps his ennobled successor ... is more at home in the nut and bolt belt around Birmingham than in the Ritz Hotel.

in a NUTSHELL in the fewest possible words. ●A *nutshell* is a traditional metaphor for a very small space; cf. Shakespeare *Hamlet* II. ii. 'I could be bounded in a nutshell, and count myself a king of infinite space.'

(as) NUTTY as a fruitcake completely crazy. *informal* ●*Nutty* meaning 'not right in the head, crazy' dates from L19, and this phrase, punning on the sense of 'full of nuts', is M20. From this comes the slang usage of *fruitcake* to mean 'a crazy or eccentric person'.

O

stick (*or* poke *or* put) one's OAR in give an opinion, advice, etc. without being asked. *informal*

> **1992** *Daily Telegraph* 24 July 13/7 My only minor fault is I sometimes like putting my oar in ... and my advice can be a little brutal.

rest (*US* lay) on one's OARS relax one's efforts. ●Literally, cease rowing by leaning on the handles of one's oars, thus lifting them horizontally out of the water.

feel one's OATS feel lively and buoyant. *US*, *informal* ●With reference to *oats* as a feed that makes horses lively.

get one's OATS have sexual intercourse. *informal*

> **1965** w. DICK *Bunch of Ratbags* 188 I was kissing her excitedly and passionately ... Cookie, you're gonna get your oats tonight for sure, I thought to myself.

sow one's wild OATS go through a period of wild or promiscuous behaviour while young. ●The *wild oat* (*Avena fatua*) is a cornfield weed resembling the cultivated oat, traditionally supposed to have been deliberately sown there to mar the crop (cf. the parable of the wheat and the tares in Matthew 13). The expression has been current since L16.

off one's OATS lacking an appetite. *informal*

no OBJECT not influencing or restricting choices or decisions. ●Used post-positively in phrases: e.g., *money no object*.

OCCAM's razor the principle that in explaining something no more assumptions should be made than are necessary. ●An ancient philosophical principle often attributed to the English scholastic philosopher William of Occam (*c*.1285–1349), but earlier in origin.

ODD one (*or* man) out **1** someone or something that is different to the others. **2** someone who is not able to fit easily or comfortably into a group or society.

by all ODDS certainly. *N. Amer.*

ask no ODDS ask no favours. *US*

it makes no ODDS it does not matter. *chiefly Brit.*, *informal* ●From an earlier use of *odds* in the sense 'difference in advantage or effect'.

lay (*or* give) ODDS be very sure about something. ●Literally, offer a bet with odds favourable to the other better. Cf. *take odds* offer a bet with odds unfavourable to the other better.

over the ODDS above what is generally considered acceptable, especially for a price. *Brit.*

what's the ODDS? what does it matter? ●From an earlier (M17) sense of *odds* as 'difference in advantage'; cf. *it makes no odds*. *informal*

be in good (*or* bad) ODOUR with someone be in or out of favour with someone.

ODOUR of sanctity **1** a state of holiness. **2** *derogatory* sanctimoniousness. ● Translating French *odeur de sainteté*; a sweet or balsamic odour was reputedly emitted by the bodies of saints at or after death.

OFF and on (*also* on and off) intermittently; now and then.

OFFENCE ▶ *see* **a HANGING offence**.

just another day at the OFFICE boring routine. ● Also often used ironically as a humorous way of saying that an event or job was the opposite of routine.
| **1997** *Times* 6 Aug. 17/1 Professional cricket has been reduced to just another day at the 'office'.

good OFFICES help and support, often given by exercising one's influence.

in the OFFING nearby; likely to happen or appear soon. ● A nautical term for a distance offshore, beyond a harbour or anchoring-ground. Used figuratively since L18.

no OIL painting not very attractive. *Brit.*, *informal*

OIL and water two elements, factors, or people that do not agree or blend together. ● With allusion to the mutual repulsion of water and oily substances.

OIL the wheels help something go smoothly.

OIL (noun) ▶ *see* **BURN the midnight oil; POUR oil on troubled waters**.

OIL (verb) ▶ *see* **GREASE someone's palm**.

the OLD days a period in the past, often seen as significantly different from the present. ● Usually in contexts where the past is viewed as noticeably better or worse than the present: *the good old days* or *the bad old days*.

OLD enough to be someone's father (*or* mother) of a much greater age than someone. *informal* ● Especially used to suggest that a romantic or sexual relationship between the people concerned is inappropriate.

an OLD one a familiar joke.

of the OLD school traditional; old-fashioned.
| **1818** M. EDGEWORTH *Letter* 19 Sept. Lord Bathurst is an *agreeable* diplomatist … dry faced— of the old school.

OLD ▶ *see* **the old ADAM**; ▶ *see* **make old BONES**; ▶ *see* **play the DEVIL with**; ▶ *see* **ancient as the HILLS**; ▶ *see* **the old boy NETWORK**; ▶ *see* **come the old SOLDIER**; ▶ *see* **old SPANISH customs**; ▶ *see* **an old wives' TALE**; ▶ *see* **the old school TIE**.

hold out (*or* offer) an OLIVE branch offer a token of peace or goodwill. ● A branch of an olive tree was an emblem of peace; with allusion to the token brought by a dove to Noah to indicate that God's anger was assuaged and that the flood had abated (Genesis 8:11).

be ON about talk about tediously and at length. *Brit.*, *informal*

be ON at someone nag or grumble at someone. *Brit., informal*

be ON to someone be close to discovering the truth about an illegal or undesirable activity that someone is engaging in. *informal*

be ON to something have an idea or information that is likely to lead to an important discovery. *informal*

it's not ON it's impractical or unacceptable. *informal*

ON it drinking heavily. *Austral., informal*

ON side supporting or part of the same team as someone else.
| **1997** *Spectator* 1 Nov. 25 And while clearly 'on side' with New Labour, he has never been a closely quartered insider.

you're ON said by way of accepting a challenge or bet. *informal*

ON ▶ *see* **OFF and on**.

ONCE a —, always a — a person cannot change their fundamental nature. ● A formula that has almost limitless applications, often but not necessarily used in derogatory contexts, as in 'once a whore, always a whore'.

ONCE and for all (*or* **once for all**) now and for the last time; finally.

ONCE and future denoting someone or something that is eternal, enduring, or constant. ● From T. H. White's *Once and Future King* (1958).

ONCE bitten, twice shy a bad experience makes one wary of the same thing happening again. ● L19 in this form. A variant common in the US is *once burned, twice shy*.

ONCE (*or* **every once**) **in a while** from time to time; occasionally.
| **1989** A. DILLARD *Writing Life* vii. 99 Every once in a while Rahm saw a peephole in the clouds and buzzed over for a look.

get something in ONE understand or succeed in guessing something immediately. *informal*

ONE on one (*or* **one to one**) denoting or referring to a situation in which two parties come into direct contact, opposition, or correspondence.

the ONE that got away something desirable that has eluded capture. ● From the angler's traditional way of alluding to a large fish that has managed to escape after nearly being caught: 'you should have seen the one that got away'.

ONE ▶ *see* **have had one over the EIGHT**; ▶ *see* **public ENEMY number one**; ▶ *see* **ROLLED into one**; ▶ *see* **take care of NUMBER one**.

know one's ONIONS be fully knowledgeable about something. *informal* ● Perhaps short for rhyming slang *onion rings* = 'things'. E20.

be OPEN with speak frankly to; conceal nothing from.

in (*or* **into**) **the OPEN** **1** out of doors; not under cover. **2** not subject to concealment or obfuscation; made public.

OPEN sesame a (marvellous or irresistible) means of achieving access to what would normally be inaccessible. ● In the tale of Ali Baba and the Forty Thieves in the *Arabian Nights*, the door of the robbers' cave was made to open by this magic formula.

with one's eyes OPEN (*or* with open eyes) fully aware of the risks and other implications of an action or situation.

OPEN ▶ *see* **a CLOSED book**.

OPEN-AND-SHUT (of a case or argument) admitting no doubt or dispute; straightforward and conclusive.

for OPENERS to start with; first of all. *informal*

OPPORTUNITY knocks a chance of success occurs. ● Alluding to the proverb *opportunity never knocks twice at any man's door* or *opportunity knocks but once*. The form of the saying with *opportunity* dates from L19, but *fortune* was used in E19 and a version of the saying is recorded in medieval French.

keep (*or* leave) one's OPTIONS open not commit oneself.
> **1996** C. BATEMAN *Of Wee Sweetie Mice and Men* xxiv. 189 Have it your way. We'll go to Princetown. But I'm keeping my options open. If there's any more trouble, … we're out, we're home.

ORANGE ▶ *see* **all LOMBARD Street to a China orange**.

into ORBIT into a state of heightened performance, activity, anger, or excitement. *informal*

out of ORDER **1** not in normal sequence. **2** (of a machine) not working. **3** *informal* (of behaviour) improper or unacceptable. *informal*

ORDER ▶ *see* **a TALL order**.

ORDERS are orders commands must be obeyed, however much one may disagree with them.

how the OTHER HALF lives the way of life of a different group in society, especially a wealthier one. *Brit., informal*

OUT and about (of a person, especially after an illness) engaging in normal activity.

OUT and away by far.

OUT for having one's interest or effort directed to; intent on.

OUT to lunch crazy, insane. *informal* ● Originally M20 North American slang.

OUT with — an exhortation to expel or dismiss someone or something unwanted.

OUT with it say what you are thinking. ● Often imperative in speech.
> **1993** T. PARKER *May Lord in His Mercy be Kind to Belfast* iv. 51 So he came out with it: he was an intelligence officer in the UVF.

OUT ▶ *see* **out at ELBOWS**; ▶ *see* **out-HEROD Herod**; ▶ *see* **out of BOUNDS**; ▶ *see* **out of DRAWING**; ▶ *see* **out of HAND**; ▶ *see* **out of ORDER**; ▶ *see* out of **POCKET**; ▶ *see* **out of the QUESTION**; ▶ *see* **out of SORTS**; ▶ *see* **out of this WORLD**.

the great OUTDOORS the open air; outdoor life. *informal* ● *Out-door* (M18) and *out-of-door*(s) (E19) were both initially used adjectivally, but Keats had *out-of-doors* as a noun in a letter in 1819, and *out-doors* came into use as a noun only slightly later (M19). *The great outdoors* is commonly found in contexts that make ironic allusion to enthusiasm for all things sporting.

at OUTS (*or N. Amer.* **on the outs**) at variance or enmity.
> **1997** A. SIVANANDRAN *When Memory Dies* I. i. 11 Now the land had been taken from him … He was at outs with the world.

drink the three OUTS get very drunk. ● Drink until one is out of wit, out of money, and out of alcohol.

get OUTSIDE of eat or drink. *slang*

on the OUTSIDE looking in (of a person) excluded from a group or activity.

OVER and done with completely finished.

go OVERBOARD **1** be highly enthusiastic. **2** behave immoderately; go too far. ● The idea behind this is recklessly jumping over the side of a ship into the water. Often in sense 1 with preposition *for* and in sense 2 with preposition *with*.

throw something OVERBOARD abandon or discard something. ● With the idea that something thrown over the side of a ship is irrevocably lost.

Mexican OVERDRIVE the neutral gear position used when coasting downhill. *US, informal* ● M20, especially truckers' slang.

OVER-EGG the pudding (*or* **cake**) go too far in embellishing, exaggerating, or doing something. ● Excessive quantities of egg in a pudding could either make it too rich or cause it not to set or cook correctly.
> **1998** *Spectator* 18 July 34/1 This is a noble end, but in her eagerness to reach it Duffy somewhat over-eggs the cake.

OVERPLAY one's hand spoil one's chance of success through excessive confidence in one's position. ● Literally, in a card game, play a hand on the basis of an overestimate of one's strength.

OVERSHOOT (*or* **overstep**) **the mark** go beyond what is intended or proper; go too far.

OWE ▶ *see* **bear a GRUDGE**.

OWE someone one feel indebted to someone. *informal*

OWE someone a living someone is entitled to be supported or provided for. ● Usually in negative contexts, referring to people who consider that they should be looked after by the rest of society either on account of their merits or simply because they exist.

as if one OWNS the place in an overbearing or self-important manner. *informal*

be one's OWN man (*or* woman *or* person) act independently and with confidence.

come into its (*or* one's) OWN become fully effective, used, or recognized.

get one's OWN back take action in retaliation for a wrongdoing or insult. *informal* ● Usually used in the context of a relatively trivial insult or offence.

hold one's OWN retain a position of strength in a challenging situation; not be defeated or weakened. ● Often with preposition *against*.

| **1953** M. KENNEDY *Troy Chimneys* (1985) 55 A young man so gifted may hold his own very well.

the world is one's OYSTER one is in a position to take the opportunities that life has to offer.

| **1998** *Times: Magazine* 21 Feb. 83/1 I was never brought up thinking, 'You are an Asian woman so you can't do things.' I was always given the impression that the world was my oyster.

P

P ▶ *see* **MIND one's Ps and Qs**.

change of PACE a change from what one is used to. *chiefly N. Amer.*

off the PACE behind the leader or leading group in a race or contest.

set the PACE **1** start off a race as the fastest. **2** lead the way in doing or achieving something.

stand (*or* stay) the PACE be able to keep up with another or others.

put someone (*or* something) through their (*or* its) PACES make someone (*or* something) demonstrate their (*or* its) qualities or abilities.

go to the PACK deteriorate; go to pieces. *Austral. & NZ, informal* ● Cf. *send to the pack*, defined in 1916 as 'relegate to obscurity'.

> **1980** F. MOORHOUSE *Days of Wine and Rage* 357 All the places overseas where the British have pulled out are going to the pack.

PACK one's bag (*or* bags) put one's belongings in a bag or suitcase in preparation for one's imminent departure.

PACK heat carry a gun. *N. Amer., informal*

PACK it in stop what one is doing. *informal*

PACK a punch **1** be capable of hitting with skill or force. **2** have a powerful effect.

send someone PACKING make someone leave in an abrupt or peremptory way. *informal*

PAD ▶ *see* **a SNAKE in the grass**.

PADDLE one's own canoe be independent and self-sufficient. *informal* ● Current in figurative use from E19, *Paddle Your Own Canoe* was the title of a popular song (1854) by Sarah T. Bolton.

PAGE three girl a model whose nude or semi-nude photograph appears as part of a regular series in a tabloid newspaper. ● So called after the page on which such photographs appear in the British tabloid newspaper the *Sun*.

on the same PAGE (of two or more people) in agreement. *US*

put PAID to stop abruptly; destroy. *informal*

no PAIN, no gain suffering is necessary in order to achieve something. *chiefly N. Amer.* ● There has been a proverbial association between *pain* and *gain* since at least L16 (N. Breton, *Works of Young Wit* (1577): 'They must take pain that look for any gayn'), and Herrick had *No Paines, no Gaines* as a poem title in

Hesperides (1648). The modern form (L20) apparently originated as a slogan in fitness classes.

> **1997** *American Spectator* May 47 As the cliché goes, no pain, no gain. In fact, in our confessional age, you can make quite a lot of gains for very little pain.

a PAIN in the arse (*or US* **ass** *or* **backside, etc.**) an intensely annoying person or thing. *vulgar slang*

a PAIN in the neck an annoying or tedious person or thing. *informal*

like watching PAINT dry (of an activity or experience) extremely boring.

PAINT oneself into a corner leave oneself no means of escape or room to manoeuvre.

PAINT the town red go out and enjoy oneself flamboyantly. *informal*

PAINTING the Forth Bridge undertaking a task that can never be completed. ●The steel structure of the Forth Bridge in Scotland has required continuous repainting.

PAINTING ▶ *see* **no OIL painting**.

PAIR of hands a person seen as suitable for performing a task.

PAIR ▶ *see* **another pair of SHOES**.

PALE into insignificance lose importance or value.

beyond the PALE outside the bounds of acceptable behaviour. ●*Pale* (from Latin *palus* a stake) means a long thin board pointed at the top and used for fencing ('paling') and hence any fenced enclosure. *Beyond the pale* thus meant literally the untamed area beyond the fence. The expression is sometimes specifically associated with the historical Pale in Ireland, the area (which varied in extent over time) under English law and administration. The earliest writer to refer to the Pale in Ireland as such (Andrew Boorde in his *Introduction to Knowledge*, 1547) draws the contrast between Ireland's two parts: the English Pale and the 'wyld Irysh'.

have (or hold) someone in the PALM of one's hand have someone under one's control or influence.

read someone's PALM tell someone's fortune by looking at the lines on their palm.

PALM ▶ *see* **CROSS someone's palm with silver**; ▶ *see* **GREASE someone's palm**.

go down the PAN reach a stage of abject failure or uselessness. ●*Pan* is short for *lavatory pan*. Defined M20 as a 'Cockney equivalent' of ▶ **down the DRAIN**.

(as) flat as a PANCAKE completely flat.

a PANDORA's box a thing which once activated will give rise to intractable problems. ●In Greek mythology, the box was the gift of Jupiter to Pandōra ('all-gifted'). The first mortal woman, she was made by Vulcan and was given gifts by all the gods and goddesses; in the box were enclosed all human ills, which flew out when she foolishly opened it. According to a later version, it contained all the blessings of the gods, which with the exception of hope escaped and were lost when the box was opened.

| **1997** *Spectator* 29 Nov. 63/2 Drummond's series ... has opened a Pandora's box of complaints ... about the tide of mediocrity engulfing the art.

press (or push or hit) the PANIC BUTTON respond to a situation by panicking. *informal* ● A *panic button* is a security device to raise the alarm in an emergency.

catch someone with their PANTS (or trousers) down catch someone in an unprepared state or sexually compromising situation. *informal*

scare (or bore etc.) the PANTS off someone make someone extremely scared, bored, etc. *informal*

wearing (or in) short PANTS very young. *informal* ● A little boy was traditionally dressed in shorts before attaining a certain age, when he would be allowed to wear long trousers.

PANTS ▶ *see* **BEAT the pants off**; ▶ **by the SEAT of one's pants**.

not worth the PAPER it is written on (of an agreement, promise, etc.) of no value or validity whatsoever.

on PAPER **1** in writing. **2** in theory rather than in reality.

PAPER over the cracks disguise problems or divisions rather than trying to solve them. ● The image of applying wallpaper to hide fissures on an unsound wall was used by the German statesman Bismarck (1815–98): 'Wir arbeiten eifrig an Erhaltung des Friedens und Verklebung der Risse im Bau' (*Letter* 14 Aug. 1865). The 1910 edition of *Encyclopaedia Britannica* refers to 'papered over the cracks' as being 'Bismarck's phrase'.

someone couldn't — their way out of a PAPER BAG a person is completely unable to do something, either through ineptitude or weakness. *informal*

PAPER tiger an apparently dangerous but actually ineffectual person or thing. ● Phrase used of the atom bomb and 'reactionaries' by the Chinese Communist leader Mao Zedong (1893–1976) in an interview in 1946.

| **1998** *Oldie* Mar. 8/2 We fear that the Rail Regulator and the Consultative Committee are paper tigers and a waste of time.

PAPERS ▶ *see* **hit the HEADLINES**.

above PAR **1** at a premium. **2** better than average. ● A stock exchange idiom. *Par* is Latin for 'equal' (see also following entries).

at PAR at face value.

below (or under) PAR **1** at a discount. **2** worse than usual, often in relation to a person's health. ● *Under par* in golfing terms however means better than usual (cf. ▶ **PAR for the course**).

on a PAR with equal in importance or quality to; on an equal level with.

> **1998** *Spectator* 1 Aug. 55/1 Imagine learning that the MCC had been used for 200 years as a front for procuring under-age boys ... The scandal of the Tour de France is roughly on a par with such a revelation.

PAR for the course what is normal or expected in any given circumstances. *informal* ● In golf, *par* is the number of strokes that a first-class player would normally require to get round a particular course.

up to PAR at an expected or usual level or quality.

> **1989** R. KENAN *Visitation of Spirits* (1996) 97 Why not him? Did he not look okay? Did he smell bad? Have bad breath? Were his clothes not up to par?

pass the PARCEL a situation in which movement or exchange takes place, but no one gains any advantage. ● A children's game in which a parcel is passed round to the accompaniment of music, the child holding the parcel when the music stops being allowed to open it.

> **1998** *Times* 6 Mar. 35/8 People who won the initial franchises have made the money ... Any movement from now on is just a game of pass the parcel, really.

PARE ▶ *see* **cut something to the BONE**.

in PARENTHESIS as a digression or afterthought.

PART and parcel an essential feature or element. ● Both nouns derive ultimately from Latin *pars* 'part' and in this phrase have virtually identical senses. Used in M16 legal parlance and now in general contexts to emphasize that the item mentioned is absolutely integral to the whole.

> **1998** *Spectator* 13 June 14/3 It's not enough for people just to shrug their shoulders and say, 'Well, that is part and parcel of being in public life.'

PART company **1** (of two or more people) cease to be together; go in different directions. **2** (of two or more parties) cease to associate with each other, usually as the result of a disagreement. **3** disagree with someone about a particular subject. ● In senses 2 and 3 with preposition *over*.

PART (noun) ▶ *see* **take in GOOD part**.

PART (verb) ▶ *see* **part brass RAGS with**.

PARTICULAR ▶ *see* **a LONDON particular**.

a (*or* the) PARTING of the ways a point at which two people must separate or at which a decision must be taken. ● After Ezekiel 21:21 'the king of Babylon stood at the parting of the way, at the head of the two ways.'

a man of (many) PARTS a man showing great ability in many different areas.

the PARTY's over a period of success, good fortune, etc. has come to an end. *informal*

> **1998** *Independent* 11 Aug. 3/4 Until the Government decided yesterday that the party's over, it was seemingly routine procedure for our hospital consultants to have ... the Committee on Distinction Awards, which is dominated by the consultants, look after their interests.

come to a pretty PASS reach a bad or regrettable state of affairs.

> **1998** *Spectator* 11 Apr. 17/1 [I]t's a pretty pass when something as absurdly titled as 'Cool Britannia' is believed in with a collectively straight face by ... the British.

PASS by on the other side avoid having anything to do with something that should demand one's attention or concern. ● With allusion to the parable of the good Samaritan (Luke 10: 31–2).

PASS one's eye over read (a document) cursorily.

PASS in one's ally die. *Austral.* ● An *ally* is a choice playing-marble, originally of marble or alabaster, later also of glass or other material.

PASS in a CROWD be not conspicuously below the average, especially in appearance.

PASS one's sell-by date reach a point where one is useless or worn out. *informal* ● With allusion to the date stamped on perishable goods indicating the latest date on which they may be sold.

> **1998** *Spectator* 25 Apr. 17/1 [He] would probably have to turn on them [his colleagues] when, in his view, they had passed their sell-by date.

PASS ▶ *see* **pass the BATON**; ▶ *see* **pass the BUCK**; ▶ *see* **pass the HAT round**; ▶ *see* **pass someone's LIPS**; ▶ *see* **pass MUSTER**; ▶ *see* **pass the PARCEL**; ▶ *see* **pass the TIME of day**.

head (or cut) someone/thing off at the PASS forestall someone or something, especially at a critical moment or at the last possible moment. ● For the sense of *pass* see next entry.

sell the PASS betray a cause. *Brit.* ● *Pass* here is in the sense of a narrow route through mountains viewed as a strategic point in time of war. *Selling the pass* was supplying information to the enemy that would enable them to circumvent or otherwise get through the obstacle (*turn the pass*). In M19 it was considered to be an Irish expression meaning 'betray one's fellow countrymen by selling information to the authorities'.

PASSAGE of (or at) arms a fight or dispute.

work one's PASSAGE work in return for a free place on a voyage.

not put it PAST someone believe someone to be psychologically capable of doing something, especially something one considers wrong or rash.

PAST it too old to be of any use or any good at anything. *informal*

put someone out to PASTURE force someone to retire. ● Cf. ▶ **put out to GRASS**.

PAT someone on the back express approval of or admiration for someone. ● Both this expression and *a pat on the back* have been current in their figurative senses since E19.

have something off (or down) PAT have something memorized perfectly.

stand PAT stick stubbornly to one's opinion or decision. *chiefly N. Amer.* ● In the card games poker and blackjack *standing pat* is retaining one's hand as dealt, without drawing other cards.

on one's PAT on one's own. *Austral.*, *informal* ● Rhyming slang: *Pal Malone/alone*.

not a PATCH on greatly inferior to. *Brit.*, *informal*

> **1991** M. NICHOLSON *Martha Jane & Me* (1992) xxi. 172 We thought the uniform of our soldiers was 'pathetic', not a patch on the American soldiers' uniform.

PATCH ▶ *see* **a PURPLE patch**.

PATH ▶ *see* **lead someone up the GARDEN path**; ▶ *see* **the line of least RESISTANCE**.

the PATTER of tiny feet the presence of a young child. ● With reference to the sound of young children running. Often used in a periphrasis for the expectation of the birth of a child.

give PAUSE to someone (*or* **give pause for thought**) cause someone to think carefully or hesitate before doing something.

PAVE the way for create the circumstances to enable something to happen or be done.

PAY the piper pay the cost of an enterprise. *informal* ● With reference to the proverb *he who pays the piper calls the tune* (cf. ▶ **CALL the shots**). Used with the implication that the person who has paid expects to be in control of whatever happens.

PAY one's respects make a polite visit to someone. ● Also often *pay one's last respects*, that is, show respect towards a dead person by attending their funeral.

PAY through the nose pay much more than a fair price. *informal*

> **1998** *Country Life* 9 July 91/1 [W]e pay a lot of money for a fairly ordinary garment in order to advertise a name that is only well-known because we pay through the nose for the huge advertising budget.

PAY its (*or* **one's**) **way** (of an enterprise or person) earn enough to cover its or one's costs.

it (always) PAYS to — it produces good results to do a particular thing.

> **1994** *Guns & Shooting* 13/2 A custom handgun can be a big investment so it always pays to choose the right pistolsmith.

you PAYS your money and you takes your choice used to convey there is little to choose between one alternative and another. ● Both *pays* and *takes* are non-standard, colloquial forms, retained from the original version of the saying in a *Punch* joke of 1846.

like PEAS (*or* **like as two peas**) **in a pod** so similar as to be indistinguishable.

hold one's PEACE remain silent (about something). *dated*

keep the PEACE refrain or prevent others from disturbing civil order.

PEACE ▶ *see* **no peace for the WICKED**.

a PEACH of a — a particularly excellent or desirable thing of the kind specified. *informal* ● *Peach* has been used since M18 as a slang term for an attractive young woman and more generally since M19 for anything of exceptional quality.

1998 *Spectator* 18 Apr. 47/1 Neil Pollard … rode a peach of a race … to win the two-mile marathon.

PEACHES and cream (of a person's complexion) of a cream colour with downy pink cheeks.

cast (or throw) PEARLS before swine give or offer valuable things to people who do not appreciate them. ● Quoting Matthew 7:6.

PEARLY whites a person's teeth. *Brit.*, *informal*

go PEAR-SHAPED go wrong. *informal*   ● Originally RAF slang as a humorously exaggerated allusion to the shape of an aircraft that has crashed nose-first.

1998 *Spectator* 11 Apr. 51/1 Unfortunately it all went pear-shaped because the programme to which I was going to peg my babblings … just wasn't interesting enough to sustain a whole review.

not the only PEBBLE on the beach not the only person to be considered in a particular situation; not unique or irreplaceable. ● From a song-title (1897): *You're not the Only Pebble on the Beach*. The original context was romantic: the way to advance one's courtship was to make it plain to the lady that 'she's not the only pebble on the beach', but it is also used more generally as a warning against selfish egocentricity.

keep one's PECKER up remain cheerful. *Brit.*, *informal* ● *Pecker* probably in the sense 'beak, bill', hence 'countenance'. Current in British English since M19, the expression has rather different connotations in the US, where *pecker* is a slang term for *penis* (E20). Cf. ▶ **keep one's CHIN up**.

with the PEDAL to the metal with the accelerator of a car pressed to the floor. *N. Amer.*, *informal*

PEED off annoyed; irritated. *slang* ● *Pee* represents the initial letter of *piss*. Used euphemistically as a slightly less vulgar expression than ▶ **PISSED off**.

off the PEG (or N. Amer. rack) (of clothes) ready-made as opposed to specially made for a particular person. *chiefly Brit.* ● Also often as modifier: *off-the-peg*.

a PEG to hang a matter (or idea etc.) on something used as a pretext or occasion for the discussion or treatment of a wider subject.

a square PEG in a round hole a person in a situation unsuited to their abilities or character. ● Less commonly, *a round peg in a square hole*.

take someone down a PEG or two make someone realize that they are less talented or important than they think they are.

pile (or heap) PELION on Ossa add an extra difficulty, task, etc. to an already difficult situation or undertaking. ● With reference to the Greek legend of how the giants in their war against the Olympian gods attempted to stack the Thessalian mountains of Ossa and Pelion on top of each other in order to scale the heavens and overthrow the gods.

(at) full PELT with great speed; as fast as possible. *Brit.*, *Austral.*, & *NZ*

PEN ▶ *see* **DIP one's pen in gall**.

count (*or* watch *or* US pinch) the (*or* your) PENNIES be careful about how much one spends.

not have two PENNIES to rub together lack money; be very poor.

PENNIES from heaven unexpected benefits, especially financial ones. ● From the title of a 1936 song by US songwriter Johnny Burke (1908–64).

not have a penny to BLESS oneself with be completely impoverished. *dated* ● Alluding either to the cross on the silver pennies which circulated in England before the reign of Charles II or to the practice of crossing a person's palm with silver for luck.

the PENNY drops someone finally realizes or understands something. *chiefly Brit., informal* ● With allusion to the operation of a *penny-in-the-slot* machine.

a PENNY for your thoughts what are you thinking? *informal* ● Used in spoken English to get the attention of someone who seems absorbed in silent thought.

PENNY WISE and pound foolish a small saving or economy may lead to much greater, enforced expenditure. ● Current in this form since E17.

a pretty PENNY a large sum of money. *informal*

> **1989** R. BANKS *Affliction* xix. 284 You can probably get a pretty penny for that place in a year or two.

spend a PENNY urinate. *Brit., informal* ● With reference to the old-fashioned coin-operated locks on the doors of public lavatories. A common but somewhat dated euphemism for urination.

turn up like a bad PENNY someone or something unwelcome will always reappear or return. ● A *bad penny* is a counterfeit coin which circulates rapidly as people try to pass it on to someone else.

two (*or* ten) a PENNY plentiful or easily obtained and consequently of little value. *chiefly Brit.*

PENNY ▶ *see* **earn an HONEST penny**.

play the PERCENTAGES (*or* the percentage game) choose a safe and methodical course of action when calculating the odds in favour of success. *informal* ● With reference to calculating the percentage of successes from statistics.

knock someone off their PERCH cause someone to lose a position of superiority or pre-eminence. *informal*

PERISH the thought the suggestion or idea is completely ridiculous or unwelcome. *informal* ● Used, often as an ironic exclamation or aside, mainly in spoken English.

— PERMITTING if the specified thing does not prevent one from doing something. ● Often in *weather permitting*.

PERSON ▶ *see* **be one's OWN man**.

in (*or* out of) PERSPECTIVE 1 (of a work of art) showing the right (*or* wrong) relationship between visible objects.   **2** correctly (*or* incorrectly) regarded in terms of relative importance.

hoist with (*or* by) one's own PETARD have one's plans to cause trouble for others backfire on one.   ●From Shakespeare's *Hamlet* III. iv. A *petard* was a small bomb. *Hoist* is the past participle of the verb *hoise*, obsolete except in this expression.

PHOENIX ▶ *see* **rise from the ASHES**.

go PHUT (especially of a scheme or plan) fail; break down. *informal*   ●Usually considered to be imitative of a dull, abrupt sound, like that made by a rifle or perhaps by a machine breaking down, but in its earliest use, by Kipling in L19, the Indian context makes it likely that it was an Anglo-Indian word from Hindi and Urdu *phatnā* 'to burst'.

get PHYSICAL   **1** become aggressive or violent.   **2** become sexually intimate with someone.   **3** become physically fit; exercise. *informal*

PICK and choose select only the best or most desirable or appropriate from among a number of alternatives.

PICK someone's brains (*or* brain) question someone who is better informed about a subject than oneself in order to obtain information. *informal*

PICK something clean completely remove the flesh from a bone or carcass.

PICK up the pieces restore one's life or a situation to a more normal state, typically after a shock or disaster.

PICK up the threads resume something that has been interrupted.

PICK ▶ *see* **the best of the BUNCH**.

be no PICNIC be difficult or unpleasant. *informal*   ●L19 especially in military contexts.

be (*or* look) a PICTURE (of a person, scene, or thing) be beautiful.

get the PICTURE understand a situation. *informal*

in the PICTURE fully informed about something.   ●Often in *put someone in the picture* 'brief someone fully'.

out of the PICTURE no longer involved; irrelevant.

a (*or* the) PICTURE of — the embodiment of a specified state or emotion such as health, misery, etc.

(as) pretty as a PICTURE very pretty.

PIDGIN ▶ *see* **be someone's PIGEON**.

(as) easy as PIE very easy. *informal*   ●*Pie* as a metaphor for something pleasant was originally L19 US slang. Cf. also ▶ **nice as PIE**, ▶ **PIE in the sky**.

(as) nice (*or* sweet) as PIE extremely nice (*or* agreeable).

a piece (*or* slice) of the PIE a share in an amount of money or business regarded as something to be divided up.

PIE in the sky something that is agreeable to contemplate but very unlikely to be realized. *informal* ● With reference to a song (1911) by the US labour leader Joe Hill (1879–1915) in which 'the preacher' tells 'the slave': 'Work and pray, live on hay, You'll get pie in the sky when you die.'

PIE ▶ *see* **eat HUMBLE pie**.

all of a PIECE (with something) entirely consistent (with something).

give someone a PIECE of one's mind tell someone what one thinks, especially when one is angry about their behaviour.

in one PIECE unharmed or undamaged, especially after a dangerous journey or experience.

a PIECE (*or* slice) of the action **1** a share in the excitement of something. **2** a share in the profits accruing from something. ● *informal*

a PIECE of ass (*or* tail) a woman regarded in sexual terms. *chiefly US*, *offensive slang* ● Cf. Brit. ▶ **a BIT of fluff**.

say one's PIECE give one's opinion or a prepared statement.

PIECE ▶ *see* **a piece of CAKE**.

go to PIECES become so nervous or upset that one is unable to behave or perform normally.

pick (*or* pull *or* tear) (someone/thing) to PIECES criticize (someone or something) in a severe or detailed way.

PIERCE someone's heart affect someone keenly or deeply.

bleed like a (stuck) PIG bleed copiously.

in a PIG's eye expressing scornful disbelief at a statement. *chiefly N. Amer.*, *informal*

make a PIG of oneself overeat. *informal*

> **1991** F. KING *Ant Colony* (1992) xvii. 147 I do love chocolates. Always make a pig of myself over them.

make a PIG's ear of bungle; make a mess of. *Brit.*, *informal* ● Probably with humorous reference to its traditional opposite: ▶ **make a SILK purse out of a sow's ear.**

PIG (*or* piggy) in the middle a person who is placed in an awkward situation between two others. *chiefly Brit.* ● With reference to one of several games of this name, in which two people attempt to throw a ball to each other without a third person in the middle catching it.

a PIG in a poke something that is bought or accepted without knowing its value or seeing it first. ● A *poke* was a small sack or bag.

PIGS might (*or* can) fly impossible; an impossibility. *chiefly Brit.* ● Used ironically to express disbelief. *Pigs fly in the air with their tails forward* was a proverbial saying (E–L17). Another variation on the theme of flying pigs is *pigs have wings*, which is also the title of a book (1952) by P. G. Wodehouse.

> **1973** 'J. HIGGINS' *Prayer for Dying* xii. 165 'Something could come out of that line of enquiry.' 'I know … Pigs might also fly.'

squeal (*or* yell) like a stuck PIG squeal or yell loudly and shrilly. ● A *stuck pig* is one that is being butchered by having its throat cut.

sweat like a PIG sweat profusely. *informal*

be someone's PIGEON (*or* pidgin) be someone's concern or affair. ● *Pidgin* represents Chinese pronunciation of English *business*. *Pidgin/pigeon* has been current in English meaning 'occupation' or 'affair(s)' since E19. The spelling *pidgin* in this sense has gradually been superseded since E20 by *pigeon*.

come down the PIKE appear on the scene; come to notice. *N. Amer.* ● *Pike* here is 'a turnpike road, a highway'.

> **1983** E. McCLANAHAN *Natural Man* (1984) ii. 18 He was, in a word, the most *accomplished* personage who'd yet come down the pike in all the days of Harry's ladhood.

(as) plain as a PIKESTAFF 1 very obvious. **2** ordinary or unattractive in appearance. ● Alteration of *as plain as a packstaff* (M16), the staff being that of a pedlar, on which he rested his pack of wares. The version with *pikestaff* was already in use in L16, but *packstaff* also remained current until L17.

make a (*or* one's) PILE become rich. *informal* ● *Pile* here is a 'pile of money'.

PILE it on exaggerate for effect. *informal*

PILE on the agony exaggerate or aggravate a bad situation. *informal*

PILE ▶ *see* **at the top of the HEAP**.

a bitter PILL (to swallow) an unpleasant or painful necessity (to accept).

sugar (*or* sweeten) the PILL make an unpleasant or painful necessity more acceptable. ● From literally making bitter medicine palatable with sugar.

from PILLAR to post from one place to another. ● Perhaps with reference to the rebounding of a ball around a real-tennis court. Current from M16 in this form, but earlier (E15) as *from post to pillar*. The modern version may have come about to provide a rhyme with *tossed*, *toss* being a verb with which the phrase is frequently associated. It is also used with other verbs (e.g. *drive*, *chase*, *run*), always in contexts implying repulse or harassment.

a PILLAR of society a person regarded as a particularly responsible citizen. ● *Pillar* in the sense of a person regarded as a mainstay or support for something is recorded from Middle English; *Pillars of Society* was the English title (1888) of a play by Ibsen.

drop the PILOT abandon a trustworthy adviser. ● From *Dropping the Pilot*, the caption to Tenniel's famous cartoon, and the title of poem, on Bismarck's dismissal as German Chancellor by the young Kaiser Wilhelm II (in *Punch* 29 Mar. 1890).

(as) clean (*or* neat) as a new PIN extremely clean or neat.

for two PINS I'd, she'd, etc. — used to indicate that one is very tempted to do something, often out of annoyance.

> **1997** *Spectator* 29 Nov. 31/1 Certainly it is a fierce dog ... What is more, for two pins it would bite us again.

one could hear a PIN drop there was absolute silence or stillness.

on PINS and needles in an agitated state of suspense. ●*Pins and needles* is the pricking or tingling sensation in a limb recovering from numbness.

PIN one's ears back listen carefully.

PIN ▶ *see* **nail one's colours to the MAST**.

at (*or* N. Amer. **in) a PINCH** if necessary; in an emergency.

feel the PINCH experience stress or poverty as if a physical pain.

PINCH ▶ *see* **take with a pinch of SALT**.

the rough end of the PINEAPPLE bad treatment. *Austral. & NZ, informal*

> **1981** P. BARTON *Bastards I Have Known* 114 There was no way that I was going to get 'the rough end of the pineapppple' from Wally, so I kept out of his way.

in the PINK in extremely good health and spirits. *informal* ●Thomas Tusser applied the word *pink* to species of *Dianthus* in L16, and was followed in this by other herbalists such as Gerard; since the wild pinks are a pale blush hue, the word *pink* for this colour was later derived from the flower. How Tusser arrived at this name for the flower is uncertain, though a plausible link would be to the Dutch word for them: *pinck oogen* 'little eyes' (cf. French *oeillet*). The present phrase is an ellipsis for *in the pink of condition, health, etc.* where *pink* is a synonym for *flower*. Shakespeare spells this out in *Romeo and Juliet* (possibly because the word was still quite a new one—just the kind of novelty to be seized upon by the punning Mercutio): MERCUTIO. Nay, I am the very pinck of curtesie. ROMEO. Pinke for flower. Thus *pink* is used metaphorically, like *flower*, to mean the 'most excellent condition of —' in expressions.

give someone the PIP make someone irritated or depressed. *informal, dated.* ●*Pip* is a disease of fowls; the word was also used, often humorously, of various ill-defined or minor ailments in people and hence as a slang term for 'ill humour'.

> **1976** *Scotsman: Weekend Supplement* 24 Dec. 1/5I feel it's my duty but I'm not keen. My grandchildren give me the pip.

PIP someone at (*or* **to) the post** defeat someone at the last moment. ●*Pip* is L19 slang for 'defeat'; it is uncertain from which sense of *pip* as a noun it derives. *Post* here is the winning post; cf. ▶ **BEATEN at the post**.

put that in one's PIPE and smoke it someone should accept what has been said, even if it is unwelcome. *informal* ●E19 slang, used chiefly as a retort in spoken English.

> **1947** W. S. MAUGHAM *Creatures of Circumstance* 296 I'm engaged to her, so put that in your pipe and smoke it.

in the PIPELINE being processed or completed; about to happen.

> **1992** *Sunday Times of India* 19 Apr. 3/2 In effect, this means that two bio-pics on Buddha are in the pipeline for release in 1993.

PIPING hot very hot. ● *Piping* (as in *blowing the pipe*) describes the hissing or sizzling noise made by food taken very hot from the oven. When referring to food, the phrase advertises that the dish is very freshly cooked, but it is also used of weather (*a piping hot day*) and of new commodities (Browning *Up at a Villa* ix: 'the new play, piping hot').

> ***c.1386** G. CHAUCER *Miller's Tale* 193 And wafres, pipyng hoot out of the gleede.

squeeze someone until the PIPS squeak extract the maximum amount of money from someone. *Brit.* ● With allusion to a speech (1918) by the British politician Sir Eric Geddes about Germany's payment of indemnities after World War I: 'The Germans ... are going to pay every penny; they are going to be squeezed as a lemon is squeezed—until the pips squeak.'

not have a pot to PISS in be very poor. *N. Amer., vulgar slang*

a piece of PISS a very easy thing to do. *Brit., vulgar slang*

PISS in the wind do something that is ineffective or a waste of time. *vulgar slang*

take the PISS (out of someone/thing) mock (someone or something). *Brit., vulgar slang*

> **1998** *Spectator* 11 Apr. 17/2 It must be admitted, however, that any child who tried nowadays to follow my priggish example would, probably rightly, be accused at once of taking the piss.

(as) PISSED as a newt (*or* fart) very drunk. *vulgar slang*

PISSED off annoyed; irritated. *vulgar slang* ● Also ▶ **PEED off**.

dig a PIT for try to trap. ● A common biblical metaphor: cf. Jeremiah 18:20 'they have digged a pit for my soul'; also Psalm 35:7, Proverbs 26:27, etc.

the PIT of one's (*or* the) stomach an ill-defined region of the lower abdomen seen as the seat of strong feelings, especially anxiety.

make a PITCH make a bid to obtain a contract or other benefit. ● *Pitch* in the L19 slang sense of a sales pitch. With preposition *for*.

a PITCHED battle a fierce fight. ● Literally, a battle fought on a predetermined ground (*pitch*), as opposed to either a casual skirmish or ▶ **a RUNNING battle**. Earlier (pre-1600) with *pight*, the archaic past participle of *pitch*.

PITCHFORKS ▶ *see* **RAIN cats and dogs**.

be the PITS be extremely bad or the worst of its kind. *informal* ● M20 US slang for 'armpits', *pits* has the suggestion of body odour, hence an obnoxious person.

more's the PITY unfortunately. *informal* ● Used especially in spoken English to express regret about something that has just been said.

PLACE in the sun a position of favour or advantage. ● Associated with German nationalism on account of a speech in the Reichstag by Prince Bernhard von

Bülow in 1897 ('we desire to throw no one into the shade [in East Asia], but we also demand our place in the sun'). The phrase was however earlier recorded in the writings of Pascal (English translation 1688).

| **1998** *Times* 23 July 47/3 But it seems that Pollock will not be denied his place in the sun.

go PLACES be increasingly successful. *informal* ● Also literally, 'travel'.

(as) PLAIN as day (*or* **the nose on one's face**) very obvious. *informal* ● Cf. ▶ **(as) plain as a PIKESTAFF**.

PLAN ▶ *see* **plan B**.

walk the PLANK lose one's job or position. ● From the traditional fate of the victims of pirates: to be forced to walk blindfold along a plank over the side of a ship to one's death in the sea.

PLANK ▶ *see* **THICK as two planks**.

on a PLATE with little or no effort from the person concerned. *informal* ● Generally with the verbs *hand* or *give*.

on one's PLATE occupying one's time or energy. *chiefly Brit.*

go PLATINUM (of a recording) achieve sales meriting a platinum disc.

make a PLAY for attempt to attract or attain. *informal*

make (great) PLAY of (*or* **with**) draw attention to in an ostentatious manner, typically to gain prestige or advantage.

PLAY a blinder perform very well. *informal* ● *Blinder* (M20) is sporting slang for a 'dazzlingly good piece of play', especially in rugby football or cricket.

| **1998** *Spectator* 13 June 23/1 In purely political terms … the Paymaster General would seem to have played the proverbial blinder.

PLAY both ends against the middle keep one's options open by supporting or favouring opposing sides.

PLAY something by ear **1** perform music without having to read from a score. **2** proceed instinctively according to results and circumstances rather than according to rules or a plan. *informal* ● In sense 2 often *play it by ear*.

PLAY by the rules follow what is generally held to be the correct line of behaviour.

PLAY fair observe principles of justice; avoid cheating.

PLAY someone false prove treacherous or deceitful towards someone; let someone down.

PLAY fast and loose behave irresponsibly or immorally.

| **1998** *Spectator* 4 Apr. 27/3 Fingers may point at those custodians playing fast and loose with the national treasure.

PLAY favourites show favouritism towards someone or something. *chiefly N. Amer.*

PLAY for time use specious excuses or unnecessary manoeuvres to gain time.

PLAY a (*or* one's) hunch make an instinctive choice.

PLAY oneself in become accustomed to the circumstances and conditions of a game or activity; get into a rhythm or pattern of working or performing. *Brit.*

PLAY into someone's hands act in such a way as unintentionally to give someone an advantage.

PLAY it cool make an effort to be or appear to be calm and unemotional.
   ● *informal*

PLAY the market speculate in stocks.

PLAY (*or* play it) safe (*or* for safety) take precautions; avoid risks.

PLAY with fire take foolish risks.

PLAY ▶ *see* play one's **ACE**; ▶ *see* play **BALL**; ▶ *see* keep one's **CARDS close to one's chest**; ▶ *see* play one's **CARDS right**; ▶ *see* play the **DEVIL with**; ▶ *see* play **DUCKS and drakes with**; ▶ *see* play the **FIELD**; ▶ *see* play the **FOOL**; ▶ *see* play to the **GALLERY**; ▶ *see* play the **GAME**; ▶ *see* play the **GOAT**; ▶ *see* play **GOD**; ▶ *see* play **HAVOC with**; ▶ *see* play **HELL with**; ▶ *see* play **HOOKEY**; ▶ *see* play **POSSUM**.

PLAYING ▶ *see* not playing with a full **DECK**; ▶ *see* a **LEVEL** playing field.

as — as you PLEASE used to emphasize the degree to which someone or something possesses the specified quality, especially when this is seen as surprising. *informal*

PLEASED ▶ *see* pleased as **PUNCH**.

at Her (*or* His) Majesty's PLEASURE detained in a British prison.

sign (*or* take) the PLEDGE make a solemn undertaking to abstain from alcohol.

PLIGHT one's troth pledge one's word in marriage or betrothal. ● *Plight* in this sense (ME) is now virtually obsolete apart from this context, as is *troth*.

lose the PLOT lose one's ability to understand what is happening; lose touch with reality. *informal*
   | 1997 *Spectator* 22 Nov. 60/3 The truth is that we've lost the plot of great painting and have entered a new phase in which the criteria for judging work are … demonstrably shallow and trivial.

the PLOT thickens the situation becomes more difficult and complex. ● From the burlesque drama by George Villiers, 2nd Duke of Buckingham, *The Rehearsal* (1671): 'now the plot thickens very much upon us' (iii. 2).

PLOUGH a lonely (*or* one's own) furrow follow a course of action in which one is isolated or in which one can act independently.

PLOUGH the sand labour uselessly. ● *Ploughing the sand* has been a proverbial type of fruitless activity since L16.

put (*or* set) one's hand to the PLOUGH undertake a task. ● With allusion to Luke 9:62.

PLUG ▶ *see* **PULL the plug**.

like a ripe PLUM (*or* ripe plums) obtainable with little or no effort.

have a PLUM in one's mouth have a rich-sounding voice or affected accent. *Brit.*

out of PLUMB not exactly vertical.

> **1984** T. C. BOYLE *Budding Prospects* (1985) II. i. 52 His bad eye, I noticed, had gone crazy. Normally it was just slightly out of plumb.

PLUMB the depths **1** reach the extremes of evil or unhappiness. **2** inquire into the most obscure or secret aspects of something.

PLUMES ▶ *see* **BORROWED plumes**.

take the PLUNGE commit oneself to a course of action about which one is nervous. *informal* ● With allusion to the idea of diving into water.

PLUS-minus more or less; roughly. *S. Afr.*

> **1992** *Weekend Post* 20 June 9 He expected 'plus-minus' 1000 files would eventually be forwarded for 'possible prosecution'.

POACH on someone's territory encroach on someone else's rights.

POACHER turned gamekeeper someone who now protects the interests which they previously attacked. ● Cf. the saying *an old poacher makes the best gamekeeper*, the principle behind which was known to Chaucer (*Physician's Tale* 83–5).

in POCKET **1** having enough money or money to spare; having gained in a transaction. **2** (of money) gained by someone from a transaction.

in someone's POCKET dependent on someone financially and therefore under their influence; closely involved with someone.

out of POCKET having lost money in a transaction.

pay out of POCKET pay for something with one's own money, rather than from a particular fund or account. *US*

put one's hand in one's POCKET spend or provide one's own money.

have deep POCKETS have large financial resources. *informal*

> **1998** *Spectator* 23 May 30/3 In any case, it was never in any danger of going out of business: … there were several other putative proprietors with deep pockets waiting in the wings.

POETIC ▶ *see* **poetic JUSTICE**.

POINT of no return the point in a journey or enterprise at which it becomes essential or more practical to continue to the end.

take someone's POINT concede that a person has made a valid contention. *chiefly Brit.*

ask (*or* tell, etc.) someone POINT-BLANK ask (*or* tell, etc.) someone something very directly, abruptly, or rudely. ● The origin of *point-blank* has been conjectured to be the white spot in the centre of a target, but there is no evidence for this in French or any other Romance language, and this usage appears to be peculiar to English. The likelihood is that *blank* is the white itself and *point* the action of levelling a gun or arrow horizontally at the target, and in its original use *point-blank range* was the very short distance over which it was thought that a bullet or arrow would travel horizontally to the *blank* or white. First used (L16) as noun and adjective in contexts involved with shooting, *point-blank* in its modern figurative use was given, along with 'forthright', as the translation of the Italian adverbial phrase *a dirittura* in Florio's *World of Words* (1598).

score POINTS (off) deliberately make oneself appear superior (to someone else) by making clever remarks.

win on POINTS win by accumulating a series of minor gains rather than by a single dramatic feat. ● In boxing, a fighter wins *on points* by having the referee and judges award him more points than his opponent, rather than by a knockout.

POINT (verb) ▶ *see* **point the BONE at**; ▶ *see* **point the FINGER**.

POINTS (noun) ▶ *see* **the FINER points of**.

a POISONED chalice something that is apparently desirable but likely to be damaging to the person to whom it is given.

> **1998** *New Scientist* 26 Sept. 22/1 Anyone who discovers a superconductor that works at room temperature may be handing the world a poisoned chalice … the material might be too toxic to be usable.

POKE fun at tease or make fun of. ● Cf. Australian *poke borak at*.

> **1989** B. H. KERBLAY *Gorbachev's Russia* vi. 116 They used to poke fun at his boorish ways.

POKE one's nose into take an intrusive interest in; pry into. ● *informal*

take a POKE at someone **1** hit or punch someone. **2** criticize someone.

POKE (noun) ▶ *see* **buy a PIG in a poke**.

POKE (verb) ▶ *see* **dig someone in the RIBS**; ▶ *see* **stick one's BIB in**; ▶ *see* **stick one's OAR in**.

in POLE position in an advantageous position. ● In motor racing, the position on the front row of the starting grid which will give the driver the inside of the first bend (M20); taken over from its earlier use (M19) in horse racing to mean the starting position nearest the inside rails.

be POLES apart differ greatly in nature or opinion.

play POLITICS act for political or personal gain rather than from principle. *derogatory*

POMP and circumstance ceremonial formality surrounding an event.

PONY ▶ *see* **on SHANKS's pony**.

(as) POOR as a church mouse (*or* **as church mice**) extremely poor. ● *Church mice* may be considered to be particularly poor in that they do not have the pickings from a kitchen or larder. A German *church mouse* (*kirchenmaus*) is also said to be very poor, and the saying exists too in other languages.

POOR little rich girl (*or* boy) a wealthy young person whose money brings them no contentment. ●After *Poor Little Rich Girl*, a song (1925) by Noel Coward. Often used as an expression of mock sympathy.

the POOR man's — an inferior or cheaper substitute for the thing specified.
| 1991 *Canberra Times* 31 Jan. 5/5 Just as alarming is the prospect of FAEs, Fuel-Air Explosives, ... known as the poor man's atom bomb.

POOR relation a person or thing that is considered inferior or subordinate to others of the same type or group.

POOR ▶ *see* **take a dim VIEW of**.

— a POP costing a specified amount per item. *N. Amer.*, *informal*

have (*or* take) a POP at **1** physically attack. **2** criticize. *informal*
| **2** 1998 *Spectator* 13 June 14/2 That's why it's so easy for them to have another pop at me.

in POP in pawn. *Brit.*, *informal* ●*Pop* (verb) in this slang sense dates from M18; *in pop* is M19.

POP one's clogs die. *informal*
| 1998 *Oldie* Mar. 5/1 We cannot claim any credit for foreseeing that Enoch was about to pop his clogs.

POP the question propose marriage. *Brit.*, *informal*

POPPY ▶ *see* **a TALL poppy**.

any PORT in a storm in adverse circumstances one welcomes any source of relief or escape. ●Literally true of a ship seeking shelter from rough weather, but current as a proverb from at least M18.

POSE ▶ *see* **STRIKE an attitude**.

like someone POSSESSED very violently or wildly, as if under the control of an evil spirit.

play POSSUM **1** pretend to be asleep or unconscious when threatened. **2** feign ignorance. ●*Possum* is the aphetic form of *opossum*, an American marsupial that feigns death when threatened. Originally E19 US.

POST ▶ *see* **BEATEN at the post**; ▶ *see* **DEAF as an adder**; ▶ *see* **FIRST past the post**; ▶ *see* **be LEFT at the post**; ▶ *see* **from PILLAR to post**; ▶ *see* **PIP someone at the post**.

go POSTAL become homicidal. *US*
| 1998 *Spectator* 21 Feb. 45/1 Post office employees [in the US] regularly go berserk and kill their colleagues, to the extent that the phrase 'going postal' ... has passed into the language.

keep someone POSTED keep someone informed of the latest developments or news. ●*Posted-up* was a M19 Americanism meaning 'well-informed'.

for the POT for food or cooking.

> **1992** D. LESSING *African Laughter* 39 That was when we shot for the pot, just shooting what we needed.

go to POT deteriorate through neglect. *informal* ● From the idea of chopping ingredients up into small pieces before putting them in the pot for cooking, thus to be ruined or destroyed. Since M19 without the definite article, but earlier in the form *to the pot* (M16).

the POT calling the kettle black someone making criticisms about someone else which could equally well apply to themselves. ● Generally as a noun phrase, but see quot.

> **1998** *Times* 20 Feb. 40/7 Yet as *Guardian* insiders point out, the pot can't call the kettle black. She can't cry foul when subjected to fair and standard competition.

put someone's POT on inform on a person. *Austral. & NZ, informal*

shit (or piss) or get off the POT get on with doing something. *vulgar slang* ● Used to tell someone to stop wasting time and either do something themselves or make way for another person to do it.

POT ▶ *see* **keep the pot BOILING**;   ▶ *see* **pot of GOLD**.

POTATO ▶ *see* **COUCH potato**;   ▶ *see* **drop someone/thing like a HOT potato**.

POTATOES ▶ *see* **SMALL potatoes**.

POTEMKIN ▶ *see* **a Potemkin VILLAGE**.

take POTLUCK eat whatever food has been prepared or is available. ● *Potluck* (L16) is also used generally to mean whatever is available, but since L18 is most usually found in this phrase.

sell something for a mess of POTTAGE sell something for a ridiculously small amount. ● With allusion to the story of Esau who sold his birthright to his brother Jacob in return for a dish of lentil broth (Genesis 25:29–34). *Mess* is an archaic term for a portion of pulpy food. The phrase *mess of pottage* does not actually appear in the text of the Authorized Version of the Bible (1611). However, as early as 1526 it was in use with reference to the Esau story, and it appears in the chapter heading to Genesis, chapter 25 in the Bibles of 1537 and 1539 and the Geneva Bible of 1560.

one's POUND of flesh an amount one is legally entitled to, but which it is morally offensive to demand. ● With allusion to Shylock's bond with the merchant Antonio in Shakespeare's *Merchant of Venice* and the former's insistence that he should receive it, even at the cost of Antonio's life.

POUND the pavement move about on foot at a steady, regular pace in a town or city.

> **1992** *New York Times* 21 July A 15/6 Put yourself in the shoes of someone who … is now out pounding the pavement wondering what to settle for in a low-wage job.

POUR it on progress or work quickly or with all one's energy. *N. Amer., informal*

POUR oil on troubled waters try to settle a disagreement or dispute with words intended to placate or pacify those involved. ●With allusion to the flattening effect of a film of oil on the agitated surface of water.

POUR ▶ *see* **pour COLD water on**.

POURS ▶ *see* **it never RAINS but it pours**.

keep one's POWDER dry be ready for action; remain alert for a possible emergency. ●With allusion to a remark attributed to the English statesman and general Oliver Cromwell (1599–1658) who is said to have exhorted his troops when they were about to cross a river: 'Put your trust in God; but mind to keep your powder dry.' *Powder* here is 'gunpowder'.

> **1998** *Independent* 25 Feb. 18/1 Instead of keeping its powder dry for the important things, New Labour's political fate is being inextricably bound up with events over which mere politicians can have no control.

POWDER one's nose (of a woman) go to the lavatory. ●An E20 euphemism, now somewhat dated. Hence *powder-room* (M20) for a ladies' lavatory in a hotel, restaurant, etc.

> **1972** L. P. DAVIES *What did I do Tomorrow?* 72 I'll use your bathroom. To powder my nose, as nice girls say.

take a POWDER depart quickly, especially in order to avoid a difficult situation. *N. Amer., informal* ●M20; also *take a run-out powder* (E20).

do someone/thing a POWER of good be very beneficial to someone or something. ●*informal*

more POWER to your elbow! said to encourage someone or express approval of their actions. *Brit.*

POWER behind the throne a person who exerts authority or influence without having formal status.

the POWERS that be the authorities. ●With allusion to Romans 13:1 'the powers that be are ordained of God'. Now often used facetiously.

PRACTICE makes perfect regular exercise of an activity or skill is the way to become proficient in it. ●Proverbial in this form from M18, but the idea had been around much earlier (M16). Used especially when encouraging someone to further endeavours.

PRACTICES ▶ *see* **old SPANISH customs**.

PRACTISE what one preaches do what one advises others to do. ●The complaint against those who do not practise what they preach goes back in English at least as far as Langland's *Piers Plowman* (1377), but 'We must practise what we preach' occurs first in R. L'Estrange's *Seneca's Morals* (1678).

PRAWN ▶ *see* **come the RAW prawn**.

not have a PRAYER have no chance at all of succeeding at something. *informal*

> **1998** *Oldie* Mar. 49/3 Show them you can re-programme the computer to eliminate the Millennium Problem and you are in. Confess that you don't even know how to turn it on, and you haven't a prayer.

PREACH to the converted advocate something to people who already share one's convictions about its merits or importance.

PRECIOUS little (*or* few) extremely little (*or* few). ● Used for emphasis.

a PREGNANT pause (*or* silence) a pause or silence that is laden with significance.

put (*or* place) a PREMIUM on regard as or make particularly valuable or important.
> **1998** *New Scientist* 18 Apr. 28/3 Enormous forces would have acted upon the skull and neck, putting a premium on size and strength.

PRESENCE of mind calmness and self-command in the face of sudden difficulty or danger.

all PRESENT and correct used to indicate that not a thing or person is missing. ● Often humorous.
> **1982** B. MACLAVERTY *Time to Dance* (1985) 141 She began to check it, scraping the coins towards her quickly and building them into piles. 'All present and correct,' she said.

(there is) no time like the PRESENT used to suggest that something should be done now rather than later.

PRESENT company excepted excluding those who are here now. ● Used in spoken English when the speaker thinks that someone present might take a remark personally and be offended by it.

PRESS (the) flesh (of a celebrity or politician) greet people by shaking hands. *chiefly US*, *informal* ● Generally derogatory, with the implication of a contrived or bogus friendliness.

PRESS ▶ *see* **press CHARGES**; ▶ *see* **drive something HOME**.

not just a PRETTY face intelligent as well as attractive. ● Often used ironically or as a parodic comment on traditional male expectations about pretty women.

sitting PRETTY in an advantageous position or situation. *informal*

PRETTY ▶ *see* **come to a pretty PASS**; ▶ *see* **a pretty PENNY**.

fall PREY to be vulnerable to or overcome by. ● Used literally of animals, meaning 'be hunted and killed'.

everyone has their PRICE everyone can be won over by money.
> *1734 W. WYNDHAM in Bee VIII. 97 'It is an old Maxim, that every Man has his Price,' if you can but come up to it.

a PRICE on someone's head a reward offered for someone's capture or death.

PRICE someone out of the market eliminate someone from commercial competition by charging prohibitive prices. ● Often reflexive: *price oneself out of the market*.

what PRICE —? **1** so much for —; what is the value of —? **2** how about —?

● When used rhetorically in sense 1 it suggests that something has or will become worthless.

| **1** *1893 P. H. EMERSON *Signor Lippo* xiv. 52 What price you, when you fell off the scaffold?

PRICK (up) one's ears (of a person) become suddenly attentive. ● Used literally of a horse or dog that makes its ears stand erect when on the alert.

a spare PRICK at a wedding a person who is out of place or has no role in a particular situation. ● *Brit., vulgar slang*

a PRICKING in one's thumbs a premonition, a foreboding. ● With allusion to Shakespeare *Macbeth* IV. i. 44: 'By the pricking of my thumbs, Something wicked this way comes.'

kick against the PRICKS hurt oneself by persisting in useless resistance or protest. ● With allusion to the words Saul heard on the road to Damascus: 'It is hard for thee to kick against the pricks' (Acts 9:5). The image is that of an ox or other beast of burden fruitlessly kicking out when it is pricked by a goad or spur.

one's PRIDE and joy someone or something of which one is very proud and which is a source of great pleasure.

PRIDE goes (or comes) before a fall if you're too conceited or self-important, something will happen to make you look foolish. ● Adapted from Proverbs 16:18 ('Pride goeth before destruction, and an haughty spirit before a fall'). *Goes before* here is in the sense of 'precedes'.

PRIDE of place the most prominent or important position amongst a group of things.

| 1995 A. GURNAH *Paradise* 81 He was brought up in a devout Sikh household in which the writings of the great Gurus had pride of place in the family shrine.

PRIME the pump stimulate or support the growth or success of something, especially by supplying it with money. ● Used literally of a mechanical pump into which a small quantity of water needs to be poured before it can begin to function.

| 1977 T. SHARPE *Great Pursuit* xiii. 124 Significance is all ... Prime the pump with meaningful hogwash.

PRIMROSE path the pursuit of pleasure, especially when it is seen to bring disastrous consequences. ● With allusion to Shakespeare's 'the primrose path of dalliance' (*Hamlet* I. iii. 50).

PRINCE (or princess) of the blood a man (or woman) who is a prince (or princess) by right of his (or her) royal descent.

PRISONER of conscience a person detained or imprisoned because of his or her religious or political beliefs. ● Originally used by Amnesty International.

take no PRISONERS be ruthlessly aggressive or uncompromising in the pursuit of one's objectives.

| 1998 *Times* 15 June 37/5 The transition from Formula One to front-wheel drive saloon cars was never going to be easy ... especially in a series where drivers are not known for taking prisoners.

a PROCRUSTEAN bed something designed to produce conformity by unnatural or violent means. ● In Greek myth Procrustes was a robber who tied his victims to a bed, either stretching or lopping their limbs, to make them fit it.
| **1998** *Spectator* 14 Feb. 6/3 Intellectuals often employ their intellects for foolish purposes, forcing facts onto a Procrustean bed of theory.

on the PROD looking for trouble. *N. Amer., informal*

PRODIGAL son a spendthrift who subsequently regrets such behaviour; a returned and repentant wanderer. ● From the parable in Luke 15, the story of the wastrel younger son who repented and was joyfully welcomed back by his father (see also ▶ **kill the FATTED calf**).

make a PRODUCTION of do something in an unnecessarily elaborate or complicated way.

the oldest PROFESSION the practice of working as a prostitute. *humorous* ● Politics or the law is sometimes jocularly awarded the status of 'second oldest profession', with the sarcastic implication that their practitioners are as immoral and mercenary as society traditionally considered prostitutes to be.

PROLONG the agony cause a difficult or unpleasant situation to last longer than necessary.

on a PROMISE (of a person) confidently assured of something, especially of having sexual intercourse with someone. *informal*

PROMISE ▶ *see* **promise the MOON**.

PROMISES, promises used to indicate that the speaker is sceptical about someone's stated intention to do something. *informal*

above PROOF (of alcohol) having a stronger than standard strength.

the PROOF of the pudding is in the eating the real value of something can be judged only from practical experience or results and not from appearance or theory. ● *Proof* here means 'test', rather than 'verification'. *The proof of the pudding* is also used allusively on its own.
| *1623 W. CAMDEN Remains (ed. 3) 266 All the proofe of a pudding, is in the eating.

PROP up the bar spend a considerable time drinking in a public house. *informal* ● With humorous allusion to a drinker's leaning on the bar for support.

not a PROPOSITION unlikely to succeed; not a viable option.

the PROS and cons the arguments for and against something. ● *Pro* is Latin for 'for'; *con* the abbreviation of Latin *contra* 'against'.

under PROTEST after expressing one's objection or reluctance; unwillingly.
| **1997** *Independent* 13 Jan. ii. 7/1 Jon Benet would come to the Griffin house for her lessons on deportment, disappearing into the basement—sometimes under protest—to practise Dior turns.

do someone PROUD **1** act in a way that gives someone cause to feel pleased or satisfied. **2** treat someone with lavish generosity or honour. *informal*

not PROVEN not certainly proved one way or the other. ●In Scots law, a verdict that there is insufficient evidence to establish guilt or innocence.

PROVIDENCE ▶ *see* **TEMPT fate**.

PRUNES and prisms (marked by) prim affectation of speech. ●Offered by Mrs General in Dickens's *Little Dorrit* (1857) as a phrase giving 'a pretty form to the lips'.

go PUBLIC 1 become a public company. 2 reveal details about a previously private concern. ●In sense 2 often with preposition *with*.

in the PUBLIC eye the state of being known or of interest to people in general, especially through the media.

PUBLIC ▶ *see* **public ENEMY number one**.

PUBLISH or perish used to refer to an attitude or practice existing within academic institutions, whereby researchers are under pressure to publish material in order to retain their positions or to be deemed successful. ●Also as modifier: *the publish-or-perish ethos*.

in the PUDDING club pregnant. *Brit.*, *informal*

in all one's PUFF in one's whole life. *chiefly Brit.*, *informal*

PULL someone's leg deceive someone playfully; tease someone.

PULL the other one (*or* **leg**) (**it's got bells on**) used to express a suspicion that one is being deceived or teased. *Brit.*, *informal*
> 1997 *Spectator* 11 Oct. 32/2 'Britain to join European monetary union in first wave': pull the other leg, old boy, it's got bells on.

PULL the plug (on) prevent (something) from happening or continuing; put a stop to (something). *informal* ●With allusion to an older type of lavatory flush which operated by the pulling out of a plug to empty the contents of the pan into the soil pipe.
> 1997 *New Scientist* 29 Nov. 58/2 And with the first elements of the ISS set for launch next year, it's hardly likely Congress will pull the plug on the project.

PULL (one's) punches be less forceful, severe, or violent than one could be. ●Usually with negative.

PULL strings (*or chiefly US* **wires)** make use of one's influence and contacts to gain an advantage unofficially or unfairly. ●The image in this and the next entry is of a puppeteer manipulating a marionette by means of strings.
> 1998 *New Scientist* 11 Apr. 3/3 Behind the scenes, there is invariably a democratic government or two pulling strings to keep the cigarette barons in power.

PULL the strings be in control of events or of other people's actions.

PULL together cooperate in a task or undertaking.

PULL oneself together recover control of one's emotions.

PULL one's weight do one's fair share of work.

PULL ▶ *see* **make a FACE**; ▶ *see* **pull a FAST one**; ▶ *see* **draw in one's HORNS**;

▶ *see* pull **RANK**; ▶ *see* pull one's **SOCKS up**; ▶ *see* pull out all the **STOPS**;
▶ *see* pull the **WOOL** over someone's eyes.

like PULLING teeth extremely difficult or laborious to do. *informal*

> 1976 H. MACINNES *Agent in Place* xix. 202 It was like pulling teeth. But we did learn something important.

beat (*or* smash) someone to a PULP beat someone severely.

feel (*or* take) the PULSE of ascertain the general mood or opinion of. ● From literally determining someone's heart rate by feeling and timing the pulsation of an artery.

PUMP iron exercise with weights. *informal*

beat someone to the PUNCH anticipate or forestall someone's actions.

PUNCH above one's weight engage in an activity or contest perceived as being beyond one's capacity or abilities. ● A metaphor from boxing, in which contests are arranged between opponents of nearly equal weight.

> 1998 *Spectator* 14 Feb. 8/2 Post-imperial Britain retains an imperial habit of mind, ... we entertain ... an ambition to 'punch above our weight'.

PUNCH the (time) clock **1** (of an employee) clock in or out. **2** be employed in a conventional job with regular hours. *N. Amer.*

(as) pleased (*or* proud) as PUNCH feeling great delight or pride. ● With allusion to the self-congratulatory glee displayed by the grotesque, hook-nosed Punch, anti-hero of the Punch-and-Judy puppet show.

PUNCH ▶ *see* punch someone's **LIGHTS** out; ▶ *see* punch one's **TICKET**.

PUNCHES ▶ *see* **PULL** punches; ▶ *see* **ROLL** with the punches.

PUNIC faith treachery. ● From Latin *Punica fides* 'Carthaginian trustworthiness', reflecting the Romans' opinion of their traditional enemy, Carthage (e.g. Sallust *Jugurtha* cviii).

take (*or* have) a PUNT at have a go at; attempt. *mainly Austral. & NZ*

> 1998 *Times: Magazine* 4 Apr. 91/3 However cheerfully positive I can be about the future, the man from the Pru isn't going to take a punt on me living the full term.

sell someone (*or* buy) a PUP swindle someone (*or* be swindled), especially by selling (*or* buying) something worthless. *Brit., informal* ● E20 slang; the idea is that the purchaser is given or has an inflated perception of a useless object's potential or future value.

> 1930 W. S. MAUGHAM *Cakes and Ale* xiv. 165 The public has been sold a pup too often to take unnecessary chances.

in PURDAH in seclusion. ● From the curtain (*parda*) used in traditional Hindu and Muslim households, especially in the Indian subcontinent, to conceal wives and daughters from the eyes of strangers. The transferred use of this expression to refer to medical quarantine or to seclusion generally dates from E20.

> 1998 *Times* 13 Mar. 2/1 Treasury ministers are, of course, in purdah.

(as) PURE as the driven snow completely pure. ●*Driven* as used of snow means that it has been piled into drifts or made smooth by the wind. Famously parodied by actress Tallulah Bankhead: 'I'm as pure as the driven slush' (1947).

PURE and simple and nothing else. ●L19, but the French *pur et simple* was current in English earlier (M19). Used postpositively.

PURE ▶ *see* **the real SIMON Pure**.

come (or go) a PURLER fall heavily, especially head first. ●The verb *purl* was in dialect or colloquial use in M19 with the sense of 'turn upside down', 'capsize', or 'go head over heels'. Hence the noun *purler*, also used figuratively in the sense of 'disaster'.

born in (or to) the PURPLE born into a reigning family or privileged class. ●In antiquity, garments of *purple* were the prerogative of royal and imperial families because of the rarity and costliness of the dye. The variant using *in* may have specific reference to the practice of the Byzantine emperors, whose empresses gave birth in a room in the palace at Constantinople the walls of which were decorated with purple; hence the appellation 'the Porphyrogenitos' (or 'Porphyrogenita') for a prince (or princess) born after his (or her) father became emperor.

a PURPLE patch an ornate or elaborate passage in a literary composition. ●Translating Horace *Ars Poetica* (15–16): *Purpureus ... pannus*.

accidentally on PURPOSE apparently by accident but in fact intentionally. *humorous*

hold the PURSE strings have control of expenditure. ●From the medieval and later pattern of a purse as a small bag with drawstrings that were pulled tight to hold the mouth of the bag closed. Also *tighten* (or *loosen*) *the purse strings*, meaning to restrict (or increase) the amount of money available to be spent.

PURSE ▶ *see* **make a SILK purse out of a sow's ear**.

PURSUIT ▶ *see* **in HOT pursuit**.

at a PUSH if necessary; in an emergency. *Brit.*
| **1997** *Trail* May 107/2 It's roomy for one person, but can take two at a push.

give someone (or get) the PUSH (or shove) dismiss someone (or be dismissed) from a job; reject someone (or be rejected) in a relationship. *Brit., informal*

PUSH at (or against or on) an open door have no difficulty in accomplishing a task; fail to realize how easy something is.
| **1998** *New Scientist* 21 Mar. 50/2 So promoting safer behaviour among HIV-positive people should be like pushing on a half-open door—a matter of finding the best way to encourage an existing inclination.

PUSH one's luck act rashly or presumptuously on the assumption that one will continue to be successful or in favour. *informal*

when PUSH comes to shove when action must be taken; if the worst comes to the worst. *informal* ●Originally an M20 N. Amer. colloquialism.

| **1998** *Times* 8 Apr. 16/7 For the truth is that when push came, literally, to shove, Franklin Delano Roosevelt couldn't hold a candle to Anthony Charles Lynton Blair.

PUSH ▶ *see* **push the BOAT out**; ▶ *see* **push someone's BUTTONS**.

PUSHING ▶ *see* **pushing up the DAISIES**.

not know where to PUT oneself feel deeply embarrassed. *informal*

| **1986** R. SPROAT *Stunning the Punters* 68 He was begging and pleading with me ... with tears rolling down his cheeks so I didn't know where to put myself.

PUT something behind one get over a bad experience by distancing oneself from it.

PUT it (or oneself) about be sexually promiscuous. *Brit., informal*

PUT it to make a statement or allegation to (someone) and challenge them to deny it. ●With clause.

PUT one over on deceive (someone) into accepting something false. *informal* ●Identical to the somewhat dated *put it across (someone)*.

PUT up or shut up defend or justify oneself or remain silent. *informal* ●Originally (L19) and chiefly US. Usually in imperative.

PUT ▶ *see* **put BACKBONE into someone**; ▶ *see* **put one's best FOOT forward**; ▶ *see* **put the BOOT in**; ▶ *see* **put a brave FACE on something**; ▶ *see* **put one's FINGER on something**; ▶ *see* **put the FINGER on**; ▶ *see* **put one's FOOT down**; ▶ *see* **put one's FOOT in it**; ▶ *see* **put one's HANDS together**; ▶ *see* **put one's HANDS up**; ▶ *see* **put one's MIND to**; ▶ *see* **put the SCREWS on**; ▶ *see* **put a SOCK in it**; ▶ *see* **set STORE by**; ▶ *see* **put to BED**; ▶ *see* **put TWO and two together**; ▶ *see* **put the WIND up**; ▶ *see* **put someone WISE**; ▶ *see* **put words in someone's MOUTH**.

be (like) PUTTY (or wax) in someone's hands be easily manipulated or dominated by someone.

| **1975** S. SELVON *Moses Ascending* (1984) 104 Bob was there, and I gave him a little bit of crumpet, and afterwards he was like putty in my hands.

PYRRHIC victory a victory gained at too great a cost. ●With allusion to that of Pyrrhus, king of Epirus, over the Romans at Asculum (279 BC), when he lost his finest troops.

Q

on the Q.T. secretly or secret; without anyone noticing. *informal* ●Humorous abbreviation of *quiet*, thus *on the quiet*.

QUAKE ▶ *see* **SHAKE in one's shoes**.

get (*or* fit) a QUART into a pint pot attempt to do the impossible, especially when this takes the form of trying to fit something into a space that is too small. *Brit.* ●Also used proverbially since L19.

QUARTER ▶ *see* **a BAD quarter of an hour**.

QUEEN ▶ *see* **take the King's SHILLING**.

the QUEENSBERRY Rules standard rules of polite or acceptable behaviour. ●With reference to a code of rules drawn up in 1867 under the supervision of Sir John Sholto Douglas (1844–1900), eighth Marquis of Queensberry, to govern the sport of boxing in Great Britain.

in QUEER Street in difficulty, especially by being in debt. *Brit., informal, dated.* ●*Queer Street* was an imaginary street where people in difficulties were supposed to live. Used since E19 to indicate various kinds of misfortune, but the sense of 'financial distress' has become the predominant one. The use of 'queer' to mean 'a male homosexual' is a separate development.

> **1952** A. WILSON *Hemlock and After* III. i. 208 He enjoys a little flutter … and if he finds himself in Queer Street now and again, I'm sure no one would grudge him his bit of fun.

QUEER someone's pitch spoil someone's chances of doing something, especially secretly or maliciously. *Brit.* ●M19 slang; early examples of use suggest that *pitch* here refers to the place where an itinerant showman sets up a performance (see quot.), although it could equally well refer to the site of a market trader's stall.

> **1875** T. FROST *Circus Life* xvi. 278 The spot they select for their performance is their 'pitch', and any interruption of their feats, such as an accident, or the interference of a policeman, is said to 'queer the pitch'.

be a QUESTION of time be certain to happen sooner or later.

QUESTION ▶ *see* **the SIXTY-FOUR thousand dollar question**.

cut someone to the QUICK cause someone deep distress by a hurtful remark or action. ●*Quick* is an area of flesh that is well supplied with nerves and therefore very sensitive to touch or injury.

QUICK ▶ *see* **quick on the DRAW**; ▶ *see* **quick as a FLASH**; ▶ *see* **be quick off the MARK**.

not the full QUID not very intelligent. *Austral. & NZ, informal* ●*Quid*, L17 of unknown origin, is a slang term for a pound sterling (earlier a sovereign or guinea). M20. Cf. ▶ **not the full SHILLING**.

| **1960** N. HILLIARD *Maori Girl* III. vi. 213 Not that she was simple in the sense that she was short of the full quid.

be QUIDS in be in a position where one has profited or is likely to profit from something. *Brit., informal* ● *Quids* (cf. ▶ **not the full QUID**) is not found except in this phrase, the normal plural being *quid*.

(as) QUIET as a mouse (*or* lamb) (of a person or animal) extremely quiet or docile.

| **1982** R. DAVIES *Rebel Angels* (1983) i. 9 I shall be as quiet as a mouse. I'll just tuck my box … in this corner, right out of your way.

QUIET ▶ *see* **anything for a quiet LIFE**; ▶ *see* **on the Q.T.**; ▶ *see* **silent as the GRAVE**.

call it QUITS **1** agree or acknowledge that terms are now equal, especially on the settlement of a debt. **2** decide to abandon an activity or venture, especially so as to cut one's losses. ● The origin of the *-s* in *quits* is uncertain, but is possibly connected with medieval Latin *quit(t)us* meaning 'discharged', used on receipts. L19, but earlier *cry quits* (M17).

an arrow in the QUIVER one of a number of resources or strategies that can be drawn on or followed.

on the QUI VIVE on the alert or lookout. ● French *qui vive?* (used in English since L16) means literally '(long) live who?', originating in a sentry's demand that persons approaching his post declare their allegiance.

| **1976** J. E. WEEMS *Death Song* (1991) xxiii. 249 They came in groups of four, five, or six—'all on the *qui vive*, apprehensive of treachery, and ready to meet it'.

QUOTE—unquote to begin quoting—to end quoting. *informal* ● Used parenthetically in spoken English to indicate the beginning and end (*or* just the beginning) of a statement or passage that one is repeating, especially to emphasize one's detachment from or disagreement with the original.

R

the three Rs reading, (w)riting, and (a)rithmetic, regarded as the fundamentals of elementary education.

work the RABBIT's foot on cheat, trick. *US* ● A *rabbit's foot* is carried as a good-luck charm.

breed like RABBITS reproduce prolifically. ● *informal*

be in the RACE have a chance of success. *Austral. & NZ, informal* ● Usually with negative.

> **1953** T. A. G. HUNGERFORD *Riverslade* 227 'See that bloke?' He pointed down the road after the vanished car. 'A few years ago he wouldn't have been in the race to own a car like that.'

a RACE against time a situation in which someone attempts to do or complete something before a particular time or before something else happens.

at RACK and manger amid abundance or plenty. ● A *rack* is a frame in which hay is placed, and a *manger* also holds food for horses to eat. The collocation of *rack* and *manger* dates from L14 in both literal and figurative senses.

on the RACK suffering intense distress or strain. ● See next entry.

RACK one's brains (*or* brain) make a great effort to think of or remember something. ● A *rack* was a medieval instrument of torture, and *rack* here refers to torturing someone by stretching them on the rack.

> **1998** *Spectator* 4 July 97/2 If I rack my brains for something nice to say about our weather, I suppose it does at least enable us to grow better grass than they do in California.

go to RACK and ruin gradually deteriorate in condition because of neglect: fall into disrepair. ● *Rack*, a variant of *wrack* meaning 'destruction', is the standard spelling in this expression. Current since L16.

> **1998** *Oldie* Aug. 49/3 The allotment below mine looks set to go to rack and ruin from its previous well-tended state.

RACK ▶ *see* **off the PEG**.

a (whole) RAFT of — a large collection; a lot. ● *Raft* was originally a dialect variant (also found in the US) of *raff* meaning 'a great quantity'. Early examples of the phrase *a whole raft of —* suggest that it was formerly used disparagingly.

> ***1830** W. A. FERRIS *Life in Rocky Mountains* (1940) vi. 29 We ... would have fought a whole raft of them.

lose one's RAG lose one's temper. *informal*

> **1998** *New Scientist* 28 Mar. 32/1 In boxing as in medieval theology, anger is a sin. Lose your rag and you are likely to lose the match.

RAG ▶ *see* **CHEW the fat**; ▶ *see* **a RED rag to a bull**; ▶ *see* **TAG, rag, and bobtail**.

all the RAGE very popular or fashionable. ●*Rage* here in the sense of a widespread (and often temporary) fashion.

| **1998** *New Scientist* 11 July 55/1 The weather people call this repetition 'ensemble forecasting', and it has been all the rage since an unexpected storm blew in late one evening and ripped through southern Britain in October 1987.

run someone RAGGED exhaust someone by making them undertake a lot of physical activity.

in one's glad RAGS in one's smartest clothes; in formal evening dress. *informal* ●Originally E20 US slang.

| **1922** H. B. HERMON-HODGE *Up against it in Nigeria* v. 76 We all turned out in our glad rags to join in the procession.

part brass RAGS with quarrel and break off a friendship with. ●The expression is explained in W. P. Drury's *Tadpole of Archangel* (1898): 'When [sailors] desire to prove the brotherly love ... with which each inspires the other, it is their ... custom to keep their brasswork cleaning rags in a joint ragbag. But should relations ... become strained between them, the bag owner casts forth upon the deck ... his sometime brother's rags; and with the parting of the brassrags hostilities begin.' L19 nautical slang.

(from) RAGS to riches (from) extreme poverty to wealth, especially in a rapid or otherwise remarkable manner. ●Often attributive (see quot).

| **1998** *Spectator* 1 Aug. 47/3 We all love rags-to-riches stories but once they become the rule rather than the exception they become very, very tedious.

go off the RAILS begin behaving in a strange, abnormal, or wildly uncontrolled way. *informal* ●An expression used literally of rail trains; cf. ▶ **JUMP the rails**.

| **1998** *New Scientist* If you had ... asked him what he was doing, you might have thought he'd gone off the rails.

on the RAILS **1** *informal* behaving or functioning in a normal or regulated way. **2** (of a racehorse or jockey) in a position on the racetrack nearest the inside fence.

RAILS ▶ *see* **RIDE the rails**.

(as) right as RAIN (of a person) perfectly fit and well, especially after a minor illness or accident. *informal*

| **1995** P. McCABE *Dead School* (1996) 25 You just make sure to give him this medicine and come tomorrow night he'll be right as rain.

RAIN cats and dogs (or pitchforks or Brit. stair-rods) rain very hard. ●Despite much speculation, there is no consensus as to the origin of *rain cats and dogs*. Suggestions range from the supernatural (cats being associated with witches who were credited with raising storms, dogs being attendants upon Odin, the Scandinavian storm-god) to the down-to-earth (animals in medieval times drowning in flooded streets in times of heavy rain and their bodies being assumed by the credulous to have fallen from the skies). The enmity between cat and dog was proverbial (cf. ▶ **fight like CAT and dog**). The versions with *pitchforks* (E19) and *stair-rods* (M20) are comparatively straightforward, reflecting the shaft-like appearance of heavy rain. *Rain cats and dogs* is first recorded in Swift's *Polite Conversation* (1738).

RAIN on somone's parade prevent someone from enjoying an occasion or event; spoil someone's plans. *chiefly N. Amer., informal*

(come) RAIN or shine whether it rains or not; whatever the circumstances. ● Cf. ▶ **BLOW high, blow low**.

> **1994** *BBC Top Gear Magazine* Aug. 71 (caption) But come rain or shine, there is a torrent of new convertibles about to reach the UK.

RAINBOW ▶ *see* **pot of GOLD**.

chase RAINBOWS (*or* a rainbow) pursue an illusory goal. ● Cf. ▶ **pot of GOLD**.

take a RAINCHECK (on) retain the option of accepting an invitation or doing something at a later date. *orig. US* ● A *raincheck* is a ticket given to spectators at US sporting events enabling them to claim a refund of entrance money or admission on another occasion if the event is cancelled because of rain. The raincheck system is mentioned as operating in US sports grounds in L19; the figurative use of the word is E20.

> **1976** L. DEIGHTON *Twinkle, Twinkle, Little Spy* xiv. 141 'Let me take a rain-check.' 'On a love affair?' I said.

it never RAINS but it pours misfortunes or difficult situations tend to follow each other in rapid succession or to arrive all at the same time. ● Cf. J. Arbuthnot's title *It cannot rain but it pours* (1726), perhaps referring to an already current proverb. *But* is used here somewhat archaically to introduce an inevitable accompanying circumstances.

a RAINY day a possible time of need, usually financial need, in the future. ● Usually in the context of hoarding or preserving something for use at such a time. The expression may have its origins in casual farm labourers needing formerly to save a proportion of their wages 'for a rainy day' when the weather would prevent them from working and earning.

RAISE a dust **1** cause turmoil. **2** obscure the truth. *Brit.*

RAISE one's hat to someone admire or applaud someone. ● From the gesture of briefly removing one's hat as a mark of courtesy or respect to someone.

RAISE the roof make or cause someone to make a lot of noise inside a building, for example through cheering.

> **1995** *Daily Mail* 2 Jan. 78/3 The fans were patient and understanding and when I finally scored against Swansea they raised the roof.

RAISE the wind procure money for a purpose. *Brit.* ● The *wind* is considered here as a motive power. In medieval times spirits or witches were commonly thought to be capable of causing winds to blow to help or hinder shipping; the figurative use of this phrase is much later (L18).

RAISE ▶ *see* **raise CAIN**; ▶ *see* **raise the DEVIL**; ▶ *see* **raise one's EYEBROWS**; ▶ *see* **raise HELL**; ▶ *see* **raise HOB**.

RAKE over (old) coals (or rake over the ashes) revive the memory of a past event which is best forgotten. *chiefly Brit.*

(as) thin as a RAKE (of a person or animal) very thin. ● Alluding to ribs sticking out like the tines of a rake.

RAKE's progress a progressive deterioration, especially through dissipation. ● From the title of a series of engravings (1735) by William Hogarth (1697–1764).

RAM ▶ *see* **drive something HOME**.

break RANK (or ranks) fail to maintain solidarity. ● Literally, of soldiers or police officers, 'fail to remain in line'.

pull RANK take unfair advantage of one's seniority or privileged position.

close RANKS unite in order to defend common interests. ● Literally, of soldiers or police officers, 'come closer together in a line'.
> **1998** *Country Life* 9 July 91/4 [T]he farming community stands to lose those privileges unless it closes ranks against the few who let the side down.

rise through (or from) the RANKS **1** (of a private or a non-commissioned officer) receive a commission. **2** advance from a lowly position in an organization by one's own efforts.

hold someone/thing to RANSOM **1** hold someone prisoner and demand payment for their release. **2** demand concessions from a person or organization by threatening damaging action.

a king's RANSOM a huge amount of money; a fortune. ● In feudal times prisoners of war were freed for sums consonant with their rank, so a king, as the highest-ranking individual, commanded the greatest ransom.

beat the RAP escape punishment for or be acquitted of a crime. *N. Amer., informal* ● Cf. ▶ **take the RAP**.

RAP someone on (or over) the knuckles rebuke or criticize someone. ● Formerly an accepted way of disciplining schoolchildren, a *rap over the knuckles* is a light punishment for a comparatively trivial offence.

take the RAP be punished or blamed, especially for something that is not one's fault or for which others are equally responsible. ● Cf. ▶ **take the FALL**. The L18 slang use of *rap* to mean 'criticism' or 'rebuke' was exntended in E20 US slang to various criminal senses, including 'a criminal charge' and 'a prison sentence'.

blow a RASPBERRY make a derisive sound with one's lips, imitating the emission of air from the anus. ● From rhyming slang *raspberry tart* a fart.
> **1997** *Spectator* 11 Oct. 32/3 — is now flying round and round in ever-decreasing circles. One of these days it will disappear up its own share register and blow raspberries at its pursuers.

come up (or be given) with the RATIONS (of a medal) be awarded automatically and without regard to merit. *military slang*

RATS deserting a sinking ship people hurrying to get away from an enterprise or organization that is failing. *informal* ●*A sinking ship* is also used in other contexts as a metaphor for a failing enterprise.

RATTLE someone's cage make someone feel angry or annoyed, usually deliberately. *informal* ●A humorous comparison is implied between the person thus annoyed and a dangerous caged animal.

RATTLE sabres threaten to take aggressive action. ●Often *sabre-rattling* (noun and modifier).

come the RAW prawn attempt to deceive someone. *Austral., informal* ●*Prawn* applied to people is a derogatory term meaning 'idiot'. An M20 colloquialism. With prepositions *over*, *on*, or *with*.

1959 E. LAMBERT *Glory Thrown In* v. 41 Don't ever come the raw prawn with Doc, mate. He knows all the lurks.

in the RAW 1 in its true state; not made to seem better or more palatable than it actually is. **2** *informal* (of a person) naked.

touch someone on the RAW upset someone by referring to a subject about which they are extremely sensitive.

(little) RAY of sunshine someone or something that brings happiness into the lives of others. ●Often used facetiously or ironically.

1997 *Trail* May 110 Don't worry … let our Knowledge experts bring a ray of sunshine into your lives with their radiant personalities and shining answers.

RAZOR ▶ *see* **OCCAM's razor**; ▶ *see* **on a KNIFE-EDGE**.

READ between the lines look for or discover a meaning that is hidden or implied rather than explicitly stated.

1994 *American Spectator* Sept. 72/2 Those familiar with the virulent animosity in this element of black racism can read between the lines to get a fuller picture.

READ someone like a book be able to understand someone's thoughts and motives clearly or easily. ●Cf. ▶ **a CLOSED book**.

READ my lips listen carefully. *N. Amer., informal* ●Used to emphasize the importance of the speaker's words or the earnestness of their intent. Most famously used by US president George Bush in an election campaign pledge in 1988: 'Read my lips: no new taxes' (*New York Times* 19 Aug.).

take something as READ assume something without the need for further discussion.

you wouldn't READ about it used to express incredulity, disgust, or ruefulness. *Austral. & NZ, informal*

READ the riot act give someone a strong warning that they must improve their behaviour. ●In Britain, the Riot Act, passed (1715) under George I, was used until 1967 to prevent unlawful assemblies of twelve or more people; under its provisions a person in authority was to read out a certain portion of the Act as a warning, and if the people did not then disperse within an hour they were accounted felons and the authorities could act against them.

READY for (the) off (of a person or vehicle) fully prepared to leave. *informal*

READY to roll (of a person, vehicle, or thing) fully prepared to start functioning or moving. *informal*

for REAL actually or seriously; genuine.   *N. Amer., informal* ● Cf. ▶ **for FREE**. Another N. Amer. colloquialism is *for real?* in a question to express surprise.
> **1992** M. BISHOP *Count Geiger's Blues* xi. 203 The man ... radiated only bluster and uncertainty. If challenged, he'd run. The other man facing Xavier was for real. He'd fight.

get (*or* **be**) **REAL** stop being ludicrously optimistic or idealistic. *chiefly N. Amer., informal* ● Used as an exclamation or command telling someone to face facts.
> **1998** *LM* Mar. 13 And can any journalist really be so naive as to believe that people would trust any president to be truthful, honest and open about sex? ... Be real!

REAL ▶ *see* **the real McCOY**; ▶ *see* **the real SIMON Pure**.

REAM someone's ass (*or* **butt**) criticize or rebuke someone. *N. Amer., vulgar slang*

REAP the harvest (*or* **fruits**) **of** be affected by the results or consequences of.

you REAP what you sow you eventually have to face up to the consequences of your actions.   ● A proverbial saying that exists in various forms, with allusion to Galatians 6:7.

REAR its head (of an unpleasant matter) emerge; present itself.

their's (*or* **our's**) **not to REASON why** it is not someone's place to question a situation, order, or system.   ● With allusion to Tennyson's poem *The Charge of the Light Brigade* (1854), which describes how, in a notorious incident in the Crimean War, the British cavalry unquestioningly obeyed a suicidal order to ride straight at the Russian guns.

see REASON (*or* **sense**) realize that one has been wrong and adopt a sensible attitude.

(it) stands to REASON it is obvious or logical.

for REASONS best known to himself (*or* **herself, etc.**) inexplicably. *chiefly humorous* ● Used when recounting someone's behaviour to suggest that it is puzzling or perverse.

on the REBOUND while still affected by the emotional distress caused by the ending of a romantic or sexual relationship. ● *Rebound* is used literally of a ball's bouncing back after striking a hard surface or object.

be at (*or* **on**) **the RECEIVING end of** (**something**) be subjected to something unpleasant. *informal*

RECHARGE one's batteries regain one's strength and energy by resting and relaxing for a time.

a — to be RECKONED with (*or* **to reckon with**) a thing or person of considerable importance or ability that is not to be ignored or underestimated.

for the RECORD so that the true facts are recorded or known. ● Cf. ▶ **off the RECORD**.

a matter of RECORD something that is established as a fact through being officially recorded.

off the RECORD not made as an official or attributable statement. ●Cf. ▶ **on RECORD**.

> **1990** C. ALLEN *Savage Wars of Peace* (1991) 264 I went to see him very much as somebody going in just to have a chat with him off the record after the interrogation.

on RECORD (*also* **on the record**) **1** used in reference to the making of an official or public statement. **2** officially measured and noted. **3** recorded on tape and reproduced on a plastic record. ●Cf. (in senses 1 and 2) ▶ **off the RECORD**.

put (*or* set) the RECORD straight give the true version of events that have been reported incorrectly; correct a misapprehension.

better dead than RED the prospect of nuclear war is preferable to that of a Communist society. ●A cold-war slogan that was reversed by the nuclear disarmament campaigners of the late 1950s as *better red than dead*.

in the RED in debt, overdrawn, losing money. ●*Red* ink was traditionally used to indicate debit items and balances in accounts. Cf. ▶ **in the BLACK**.

(as) RED as a beetroot (*or* N. Amer. beet) (of a person) red-faced, typically through embarrassment.

a RED herring something that diverts attention from the main business or argument. ●The colour of a *red herring* is imparted to it in the process of curing by smoking. Smoked herrings were formerly an important product of English fishing ports such as Yarmouth. Because of the strong smell of a smoked herring it was formerly recommended as an aid to teaching hounds to follow a trail; hence the idea of a red herring's being drawn across a trail as a distraction.

RED in tooth and claw involving savage or merciless conflict or competition. ●Originally quoting Tennyson: 'Nature, red in tooth and claw' (*In Memoriam* (1850) canto 56).

> **1998** *Spectator* 23 May 11/3 Life is sharper on the shop floor, too; and for small business it is red in tooth and claw.

RED letter day a pleasantly memorable, fortunate, or happy day. ●In Church calendars, a saint's day or church festival was traditionally distinguished by being written in red letters.

(like) a RED rag to a bull an object, utterance, or act which is certain to provoke someone. ●The colour red was traditionally supposed to provoke a bull, and is the colour of the cape used in bull-fighting. Cf. ▶ **see RED**.

> **1998** *Times* 3 July 31/4 Such talk is like a red rag to a bull at the Soil Association.

see RED become very angry suddenly. *informal*

RED ▶ *see* **PAINT the town red**.

RED-LIGHT district a district where commercialized sexual activities are concentrated. ●From the use of a *red light* to signify a brothel.

REDRESS the balance take action to restore equality in a situation.

REDS under the bed (exaggerated fear of) the pervasive presence and influence of Communist sympathizers in a society. ● Used mockingly during the cold war with reference to people who were obsessed with hunting out supposed Communists.

REDUCE someone to the ranks punish with loss of status. ● From demoting a non-commissioned officer to an ordinary soldier.

in REDUCED circumstances in the state of being poor after being relatively wealthy. *euphemistic*

a broken REED a weak or ineffectual person, especially one on whose support it is foolish to rely. ● With reference to Isaiah 36:6, the taunt of the Assyrian general to King Hezekiah of Jerusalem about the latter's supposed ally, the Egyptian pharaoh: 'Lo, thou trusteth in the staff of this broken reed, on Egypt.'

allow (or give) (a) free REIN to permit freedom of action or expression to. ● From the action of loosening one's grip on the reins of a horse, allowing it to choose its own course and pace.

keep a tight REIN on exercise strict control over; allow little freedom to. ● The opposite of ▶ **allow free REIN to**.

REINVENT the wheel waste a great deal of time or effort in creating something that already exists or doing something that has already been done.

RELIEVE one's feelings use strong language or vigorous behaviour when annoyed.

get RELIGION be converted to religious belief and practices. *informal* ● Usually derogatory.

it REMAINS to be seen something is not yet known or certain.

> **1996** *Scientific American* June 42/2 It remains to be seen how well Russian and U.S. spacefarers will work together … in the more demanding environment of a space station under construction.

— in RESIDENCE a person with a specified occupation (especially an artist or writer) paid to work for a time in a college or other institution.

the line (or path) of least RESISTANCE an option avoiding difficulty or unpleasantness; the easiest course of action. ● Literally, the shortest distance between a buried explosive charge and the surface of the ground.

in the last RESORT whatever else happens or is the case; ultimately. ● Suggested by French *en dernier ressort*.

be no RESPECTER of persons treat everyone the same, without being influenced by their status or wealth. ● Cf. Acts 10:34 'God is no respecter of persons.'

RESPECTS ▶ *see* **PAY one's respects**.

give it a REST stop doing or talking about a particular thing. *informal* ● Used mainly in imperative to someone who is being tediously persistent in their actions or talk.

REST one's case conclude one's presentation of evidence and arguments in a lawsuit. ●Used humorously to show that one believes that one has presented sufficient evidence for one's views.

REST (noun) ▶ *see* **no peace for the WICKED**; ▶ *see* **the rest is HISTORY**.

REST (verb) ▶ *see* **rest on one's LAURELS**; ▶ *see* **rest on one's OARS**.

RETREAT ▶ *see* **BEAT a retreat**.

REVERSE ▶ *see* **the reverse of the MEDAL**.

go to one's REWARD die. ●A euphemism based on the idea that people receive their just deserts after death.

REWRITE history select or interpret events from the past in a way that suits one's own particular purposes.

REWRITE the record books (of a sports player) break a record or several records.

RHYME or reason logical explanation or reason. ●The two have been associated since M17 and almost always used with the negative; cf. French *ni rime ni raison.*

cut a (*or* the) RIBBON perform an opening ceremony, usually by formally cutting a ribbon strung across the entrance to a building, road, etc.

cut (*or* tear) something to RIBBONS **1** cut (*or* tear) something so badly that only ragged strips remain. **2** damage something severely.

dig (*or* nudge *or* poke) someone in the RIBS prod someone in the side with one's elbow, often to draw attention to something or as a warning.

a bit RICH rather impudent; absurd. ●*Rich* in the senses of 'humorous, ironic, amusing' is an M18 development.
> **1998** *Times* 8 Sept. 22/3 It is also a bit rich for Mr Hames to reprove Buckingham Palace for its 'new, slick, emphasis on presentation', while speaking for the organisation that invented 'rebranding Britain'.

be well RID of be in a better state for having removed or disposed of a troublesome or unwanted person or thing.

good RIDDANCE it is good to have got free of a troublesome or unwanted person or thing. ●Said as an exclamation of relief. Sometimes *good riddance to bad rubbish!*

talk (*or* speak) in RIDDLES express oneself in an ambiguous or puzzling manner.

for the RIDE joining in with something for pleasure or interest, rather than because of any serious involvement.

let something RIDE take no immediate action over something.

RIDE for a fall act in a reckless or arrogant way that invites defeat or failure.

informal ● An L19 horse-riding expression, meaning to ride a horse, especially in the hunting field, in such a way as to make an accident likely.

| ***1884** E. W. HAMILTON *Diary* 16 Jan. (1972) II. 544 He believes that C. is 'riding for a fall' and has doubts as to his loyalty towards Mr G.

RIDE herd on keep watch over. ● In its literal sense of guarding or controlling a herd of cattle by riding on its perimeter, this North American expression was being used metaphorically by L19.

RIDE off into the sunset achieve a happy conclusion to something. ● From a conventional closing scene in films.

RIDE the pine (*or* bench) (of an athlete) not participate in a game or event, typically because of poor form. *N. Amer., informal*

RIDE the rails travel by rail, especially without a ticket. *N. Amer.*

RIDE shotgun   **1** travel as a guard in the seat next to the driver of a vehicle.   **2** ride in the passenger seat of a vehicle.   **3** act as a protector. *chiefly N. Amer.*

a rough (*or* easy) RIDE a difficult (*or* easy) time doing something.

take someone for a RIDE deceive or cheat someone. *informal*

RIDE ▶ *see* ride **BODKIN**; ▶ *see* **ride on someone's COAT-TAILS**; ▶ *see* **ride ROUGHSHOD over**; ▶ *see* **have a TIGER by the tail**.

— RIDES again someone or something has reappeared unexpectedly and with new vigour. ● Cf. the 1939 film title *Destry Rides Again*.

(in) full RIG (wearing) smart or ceremonial clothes. *informal*

put (*or* set) someone RIGHT   **1** restore someone to health.   **2** make someone understand the true facts of a situation.

RIGHT enough certainly; undeniably. ● *informal*

a RIGHT one a silly or foolish person. *Brit., informal*

she's (*or* she'll be) RIGHT that will be all right; don't worry. *Austral., informal*

somewhere to the RIGHT of Genghis Khan holding right-wing views of the most extreme kind. ● Genghis Khan (1162–1227), the founder of the Mongol empire, is the type of a repressive and tyrannical ruler. The name of the early fifth-century warlord Attila the Hun also occurs in this expression.

RIGHT ▶ *see* **be as right as RAIN**; ▶ *see* **right as a TRIVET**.

bang (*or* N. Amer. **dead) to RIGHTS** (of a criminal) with positive proof of guilt. *informal*

the life of RILEY (*or* Reilly) a luxurious or carefree existence. *informal* ● *Reilly* or *Riley* is a common Irish surname. A popular song (1919) by H. Pease entitled *My Name is Kelly* had the lines 'Faith and my name is Kelly Michael Kelly, But I'm living the life of Reilly just the same'; however it is uncertain whether this is the source of the expression or whether Pease was drawing on an already existing catchphrase.

> **1978** *Daily Telegraph* 8 Feb. 6/7 It is simply not true that we don't pay tax and are living the life of Riley.

RIMMON ▶ *see* **BOW down in the house of Rimmon**.

before (*or* since) the RINDERPEST a long time ago (*or* for a very long time). *S. Afr.* ●*Rinderpest* is a contagious viral disease of cattle that periodically caused heavy losses in much of Africa; the 1896 epidemic was so devastating that it was treated as a historical landmark.

hold the RING monitor a dispute or conflict without becoming involved in it.

> **1991** M. TULLY *No Full Stops in India* (1992) x. 302 The police no longer attempt to hold the ring between the farmers and landless labourers fighting for just the paltry minimum wage.

RING down (*or* up) the curtain mark or bring about the end (*or* the beginning) of an enterprise or event. ●Alluding to the ringing of a bell in a theatre as the signal to raise or lower the stage curtain at the beginning or end of a perfomance. Cf. ▶ **bring down the CURTAIN on**.

RING in one's ears (*or* head) linger in the memory.

RING off the hook (of a telephone) be constantly ringing due to a large number of incoming calls. *N. Amer.*

RING (noun) ▶ *see* **throw one's HAT in the ring**.

RING (verb) ▶ *see* **ring a BELL**; ▶ *see* **ring the CHANGES**; ▶ *see* **ring the KNELL of**.

run (*or* make) RINGS round (*or* around) someone outclass or outwit someone very easily. *informal*

RIOT ▶ *see* **READ the riot act**.

let RIP **1** do something or proceed vigorously or without restraint. **2** express oneself vehemently or angrily. *informal* ●Often followed by preposition *with*.

let something RIP **1** allow something, especially a vehicle, to go at full speed. **2** allow something to happen forcefully or without interference. **3** express something forcefully and noisily. *informal*

get (*or* take) a RISE out of provoke an angry or irritated response from (someone), especially by teasing. *informal* ●Cf. ▶ **RISE to the bait**.

RISE and shine get out of bed smartly; wake up. *informal* ●Usually in imperative. Originally (E20) an expression used in the armed forces.

RISE to the bait react to a provocation or temptation exactly as intended. ●Used literally of the action of a fish when it comes to the surface to take a bait, fly, etc. Cf. ▶ **get a RISE out of**.

> **1966** *Listener* 6 Oct. I should perhaps apologise for having risen to the bait of Mr Wilkinson's provocative letter.

RISE with the sun (*or* lark) get up early in the morning.

RISE ▶ *see* **rise from the ASHES**.

RISING ▶ *see* **someone's STAR is rising**.

RITE of passage a ceremony or event marking an important stage in someone's life, especially birth, initiation, marriage, and death. ● *Rite de passage* was a term invented by the French ethnographer Arnold van Gennep (1873–1957) who published *Les Rites de passage* in 1909.

put on the RITZ make a show of luxury or extravagance. ● The hotels in Paris, London, and New York founded by Swiss-born hotelier César Ritz (1850–1918) became synonymous with opulence. This expression dates from the heyday of these grand hotels in E20.

sell someone down the RIVER betray someone, especially so as to benefit oneself. *informal* ● Originally US, with reference to the practice in the slave-owning states of selling troublesome slaves to owners of sugar-cane plantations on the lower Mississippi, where conditions were harsher than those in the more northerly states.

> **1998** *Bookseller* 3 Apr. 12/4 Once you have lost it with the first three the last lot will sell you down the river so fast it isn't true.

up the RIVER to or in prison. *chiefly N. Amer., informal* ● With allusion to Sing Sing prison situated up the Hudson River from the city of New York.

down the ROAD in the future. *chiefly N. Amer., informal*

in (or out of) the (or one's) ROAD in (or out of) someone's way. *informal* ● *Out of the road* often in imperative.

one for the ROAD a final drink, especially an alcoholic one, before leaving for home. *informal*

take to the ROAD (or take the road) set out on a journey or series of journeys.

ROAD ▶ *see* **the END of the road**; ▶ *see* **HIT the road**; ▶ *see* **a road to NOWHERE**.

ROADS ▶ *see* **all roads lead to ROME**.

do a ROARING trade (or business) sell large amounts of something; do very good business. *informal*

ROB someone blind get a lot of money from someone by deception or extortion. *informal*

ROB Peter to pay Paul take something away from one person to pay another, leaving the former at a disadvantage; discharge one debt only to incur another. ● Probably with reference to the apostles SS Peter and Paul, who are often shown together as equals in Christian art and who therefore may be presumed equally deserving of honour, devotion, etc.; it is uncertain if a specific allusion is intended, and the phrase shows some variations such as *unclothe Peter and clothe Paul, borrow from Peter ...* , etc.

> **1997** *New Scientist* 29 Nov. 58/2 So far, NASA has been able to rob Peter to pay Paul, taking money from the shuttle and science programmes to keep the ISS on track ...

round ROBIN Hood's barn by a circuitous route. ● Robin Hood is the legendary outlaw of English popular tradition famous since medieval times. *Robin*

Hood's barn typifies an out-of-the-way place. This expression is recorded from M19, and seems to have originated in the dialect speech of the English Midlands, the area in which Robin Hood is said to have operated.

between a ROCK and a hard place in a situation where one is faced with two equally difficult or unpleasant alternatives. *chiefly N. Amer., informal*

> **1998** *Times* 26 Jan. 20/7 They are saying now, as they once said of Richard Nixon, that Bill Clinton is 'between a rock and a hard place'.

ROCK ▶ *see* **rock the BOAT**.

off one's ROCKER crazy. *informal* ● *Rocker* here is a concave piece of wood or metal placed under a chair, cradle, etc., enabling it to rock. L19 slang.

> **1932** E. WAUGH *Black Mischief* v. 195 It's going to be awkward for us if the Emperor goes off his rocker.

up (*or* rise) like a ROCKET (and down (*or* fall) like the stick) rise suddenly and dramatically (and subsequently fall in a similar manner). ● The origin of this is a gibe by Thomas Paine about Edmund Burke's oratory in a House of Commons debate (1792) on the subject of the French Revolution: 'As he rose like a rocket, he fell like the stick.'

get one's ROCKS off **1** have an orgasm. **2** obtain pleasure or satisfaction. *vulgar slang*

on the ROCKS **1** (of a relationship or enterprise) experiencing difficulties and likely to fail. **2** (of a drink) served undiluted and with ice cubes. *informal*

the ROCKY road to — a difficult progression, especially to success.

> **1957** F. O'CONNOR *Letter* 6 Apr. Whereas the writer himself is traveling the rocky road, and feels every individual bump.

make a ROD for one's own back do something likely to cause difficulties for oneself later. ● Heywood's *Proverbs* (1546) has 'a rod made for his owne tayle', but the idea goes back at least as far as Malory (L15).

a ROD in pickle a punishment in store. ● *In pickle* means 'preserved ready for use'. This form (M17) has superseded an earlier variant *rod in piss* (M16).

rule someone/thing with a ROD of iron control or govern someone or something very strictly or harshly. ● From Psalm 2:9.

ROD ▶ *see* **KISS the rod**.

a ROLAND for an Oliver an effective or appropriate retort or response; tit for tat. *archaic* ● The phrase alludes to the evenly matched single combat between Roland, the legendary nephew of Charlemagne, and Oliver, another of Charlemagne's knights (paladins), out of which there grew a strong friendship between them. According to the French medieval epic the *Chanson de Roland*, Roland was in command of the rearguard of Charlemagne's army when it was ambushed at Roncesvalles (now Roncevaux) in the Pyrenees in 778; despite the urging of Oliver that he should blow his horn to summon aid, Roland refused to do so until too late, and they were slain along with the rest of the rearguard.

a ROLL in the hay (*or* the sack) an act of sexual intercourse. *informal*

> **1998** *Bookseller* 10 Apr. 66/4 And those who fancy a roll in the hay this summer could do worse than study 'Grass Identification', run in Epping Forest.

on a ROLL experiencing a prolonged spell of success or good luck. *informal*

> **1998** *Oldie* Apr. 11/1 Western economists cottoned on to basic 'flaws' in the [Indonesian] economy which they hadn't noticed (or didn't want to notice) while it was on a roll.

ROLL of honour **1** a list of those who have died in battle. **2** a list of people whose deeds or achievements, typically in sport, are honoured.

ROLL one's own make one's own cigarettes from loose tobacco. *informal* ●Originally US: *rolls its own* was listed as a colloquialism in *American Speech* in 1930. The expression is also used figuratively in the sense of 'do something oneself without assistance' (see quot.).

> **1941** *N. Y. Times* 25 July 14/5 'Ghosting' is routine in public papers in the United States, and has been since our history began … Mr. Roosevelt proved again today that he can roll his own whenever he has the time and the inclination.

ROLL up one's sleeves prepare to fight or work.

ROLL with the punches adapt oneself to adverse circumstances. ●In boxing, a boxer *rolls* (*with*) *the punch* by moving his body away from an opponent's blow so as to lessen the impact.

> **1988** B. STERLING *Islands in Net* (1989) ii. 48 Or else these data sharks wouldn't be here now, trying to roll with the punches.

(all) ROLLED into one (of characteristics drawn from different people or things) combined in one person or thing.

> **1907** G. B. SHAW *Major Barbara* 167 My methods … would be no use if I were Voltaire, Rousseau, Bentham, Mill, Dickens, Carlyle, Ruskin, George, Butler, and Morris all rolled into one.

be ROLLING (in money) be very rich. *informal* ●*Rolling in* (i.e. 'turning over and over in') here has the sense of 'luxuriating in'. The idea of wallowing in riches, money, etc. has been current since L16.

ROLLING drunk so drunk as to be swaying or staggering.

a ROLLING stone a person who does not settle in one place, job, way of life, etc. ●Alluding to the proverb *a rolling stone gathers no moss*, meaning that a restless or feckless person will not accumulate wealth, status, friends, etc. In E16 Erasmus included Greek and Latin versions of this in his *Adages*, and it was current in English by M16.

ROLLING ▶ *see* **have people rolling in the AISLES**.

strike someone off the ROLLS (*or* roll) debar a solicitor from practising after dishonesty or other misconduct. ●*Rolls* here are the official lists or records, so called from the time when such records were literally kept on parchment or paper scrolls.

all roads lead to ROME there are many different ways but all reach the same goal or conclusion. ●An ancient saying based on Rome's having been the point of convergence of the main roads of the Roman empire and after that of the medieval pilgrimage routes through Europe; cf. medieval Latin *mille vie ducunt hominem per secula Romam* a thousand roads lead a man forever towards Rome.

ROME was not built in a day a complex or ambitious task is bound to take a long time and should not be rushed. ●A proverbial warning against rashness and impatience current in English since M16.

when in ROME (do as the Romans do) when abroad or in an unfamiliar environment you should adopt the customs or behaviour of those around you. ●Perhaps ultimately derived from St Ambrose of Milan (d. 397), who is quoted in a letter of St Augustine as saying that when he was in Rome he fasted as they did there, on a Saturday, but when he was in Milan he did not fast on a Saturday. A medieval Latin saying expresses this idea as *si fueris Romae, Romano vivito more; si fueris alibi, vivito sicut ibi*, if you are at Rome, live in the Roman manner; if elsewhere, live as they do there. The first three words are often used allusively on their own.

go through (*or* hit) the ROOF 1 (of prices or figures) reach extreme or unexpected heights; become exorbitant. 2 suddenly become very angry. *informal*

the ROOF falls in a disaster occurs, everything goes wrong.

ROOF ▶ *see* **RAISE the roof**.

shout something from the ROOFTOPS make something previously secret completely public. ●Adapted from Luke 12:3 'that which ye have spoken in the ear in closets shall be proclaimed upon the housetops.'

in a smoke-filled ROOM (of political bargaining or decision-making) conducted privately by a small group of influential people rather than openly or democratically. ●Originating in a news report (12 June 1920) about the selection of Warren Harding of Ohio as the Republican presidential candidate.

no (*or* not) ROOM to swing a cat a very confined space. *humorous* ●*Cat* here refers to a 'cat-o'-nine-tails', a form of whip with nine knotted thongs for lashes.

ROOM at the top opportunity to join an elite or the top ranks of a profession. ●The expression is attributed to the American politician Daniel Webster (1782–1852) who was cautioned against attempting to enter the overcrowded legal profession and is said to have replied: 'There is always room at the top.'

ROOT and branch of a thorough or radical nature; thoroughly or entirely. ●Suggested by a biblical metaphor for total destruction: 'it shall leave them neither root nor branch' (Malachi 4:1). The 1640 petition to the English Parliament for the total abolition of episcopal government in the Church was nicknamed 'the Root-and-branch petition', and the phrase has also been attached to some later radical movements or parties.

strike at the ROOT (*or* roots) of have a potentially destructive effect on. ●Cf. a biblical metaphor for imminent destruction: 'And now also the axe is laid unto the root of the trees' (Matthew 3:10).

take ROOT become fixed or established. ● Alluding to a plant beginning to grow and spread its roots through the soil; see also next entry.

put down ROOTS begin to lead a settled life in a particular place.

give someone enough ROPE (*or* **plenty of rope**) give a person enough freedom of action to bring about their own downfall. ● With allusion to the proverb *give a man enough rope and he will hang himself* (in various forms since M17).

a ROPE of sand something that provides only illusory security or coherence.
     ● *literary*

on the ROPES in a desperate position; in a state of near collapse or defeat.
     ● An idiom from boxing, alluding to the situation of a losing boxer who is forced back by his opponent against the ropes that mark the sides of the boxing ring. Originally used in its literal sense in E19, the phrase has been used figuratively since at least the 1920s.

ROPE ▶ *see* **MONEY for jam**.

ROPES ▶ *see* **KNOW the ropes**.

(there is) no ROSE without a thorn every apparently desirable situation has its share of trouble or difficulty. ● Proverbial since M15 in various versions. Cf. Claudian *armat spina rosas* a thorn arms roses (*In Nuptias Honorii … Fescennina* iv. 10).
     | *1430–40 J. LYDGATE *Bochas* Prol. ix There is no rose … in garden, but there be sum thorne.

under the ROSE in confidence; under pledge of secrecy. ● The origin of the rose as emblem of secrecy is uncertain, but the concept may have originated in Germany (cf. German *unter der rose*), and there was a similar expression in Early Modern Dutch. *Under the rosse* appears in a State Paper (1546) of Henry VIII, with a gloss that suggests that it was then a new or unfamiliar expression. Latin *sub rosa* has also been very commonly used in English since M17 in this metaphorical sense.

come up ROSES (of a situation) develop in a very favourable way. *informal* ● An M20 idiom, one of a number of rose-related expressions referring to favourable or pleasant circumstances: cf. ▶ **everything's ROSES,** ▶ **ROSES all the way**.

everything's (*or* **it's all**) **ROSES** everything is going well. *informal* ● Also *everything in the garden's roses*.

not all ROSES not entirely perfect or agreeable. *informal*
     | 1938 G. GREENE *Brighton Rock* VII. i. 283 'Sometimes he's bad to me … it's not all roses'.

ROSES, (roses,) all the way very successful or pleasant. ● Quoting the first line of Robert Browning's *Patriot* (1855), describing the literal throwing of roses at a popular hero as he passed through the streets.
     | 1977 *World of Cricket Monthly* June 42/2 Although Australia lost the Ashes, it was roses, roses, all the way for him.

ROSES ▶ *see* **BED of roses;** ▶ *see* **come up SMELLING of roses;** ▶ *see* **SMELL the roses**.

the ROT sets in a rapid succession of (usually unaccountable) failures begins.

bit of ROUGH a (usually male) sexual partner whose toughness or lack of sophistication is a source of attraction. *informal*

> **1998** *Spectator* 31 Jan. 20/1 The programme dwelt at length on the maestro's interest in extramarital sex, particularly with below-stairs women—what would be called these days a bit of rough.

ROUGH and ready **1** rough or crude but effective. **2** (of a person or place) unsophisticated or unrefined.

ROUGH around the edges having a few imperfections. ● Also *rough edges* meaning 'slight imperfections in someone or something that is basically satisfactory'.

a ROUGH diamond a person who has genuinely fine qualities but uncouth manners. *informal* ● Literally, a diamond before cutting and polishing. Also (N. Amer.) *diamond in the rough.*

the ROUGH edge (*or* side) of one's tongue a scolding. ● Usually *give someone the rough edge of one's tongue.*

a ROUGH passage (*or* ride) a difficult time or experience.

sleep ROUGH sleep in uncomfortable conditions, usually out of doors. *Brit.*

take the ROUGH with the smooth accept the difficult or unpleasant aspects of life as well as the good.

ROUGH ▶ *see* **rough JUSTICE**.

ride ROUGHSHOD over carry out one's own plans or wishes with arrogant disregard for others.

> **1977** *Times Literary Supplement* 11 Feb. 148/3 Sociologists are notorious for their use of generalizing terms that ride roughshod over the particularities of history.

go the ROUND (*or* rounds) (of a story or joke) be passed on from person to person.

in the ROUND **1** (of sculpture) standing free with all sides shown, rather than carved in relief against a ground. **2** treated fully and thoroughly; with all aspects shown or considered. **3** (of a theatrical performance) with the audience placed on at least three sides of the stage.

ROUND (adj.) ▶ *see* **a square PEG in a round hole**.

ROUND (prep.) ▶ *see* **round the BEND**.

a hard (*or* tough) ROW to hoe a difficult task. ● *Hoeing a row* of crop plants is here a metaphor for unremitting toil. Originally an M19 US colloquialism.

ROYAL road to way of attaining without trouble. ● With allusion to the riposte by the Alexandrian Greek mathematician Euclid (end of fourth century BC) to the Egyptian ruler Ptolemy I, who had asked whether geometry could not be made easier: 'There is no royal road to geometry.' Generally in the negative. *There is no royal road to learning* has proverbial status, but other goals or endeavours are sometimes substituted.

not have two — to RUB together have none or hardly any of the specified items, especially coins. *informal*

> **1991** W. TREVOR *Reading Turgenev* in *Two Lives* (1992) iv. 23 She was marrying him for his money, since it was a known fact that the Dallons hadn't two coins in the house to rub together.

RUB one's hands show keen satisfaction or expectation. ● From the gesture of rubbing one's hands together as a sign of pleasure.

RUB someone's nose in something emphatically or repeatedly draw someone's attention to an embarrassing or painful fact. *informal* ● From the mistaken belief that the way to house-train a puppy or kitten is to rub their noses in their faeces or urine if they have made a mess indoors. Also *rub it in*.

> **1963** P. M. HUBBARD *Flush as May* xiii. 121 I'm sorry. I've said I'm sorry ... Don't rub my nose in it.

RUB noses rub one's nose against someone else's in greeting. ● From a form of greeting traditional among Maoris and some other peoples.

RUB shoulders (*or US* **elbows**) associate or come into contact with another person.

> **1943** G. GREENE *Ministry of Fear* (1963) I. iii. 40 It wasn't exactly a criminal world, though eddying along its dim and muted corridors you might possibly rub shoulders with genteel forgers.

RUB someone (*or Brit.* **rub someone up**) **the wrong way** irritate or repel someone. ● With reference to stroking an animal against the lie of its fur.

there's (*or* **here's**) **the RUB** that is the crucial difficulty, problem, etc. *literary* ● A *rub* (L16) in the game of bowls is an impediment that prevents the bowl from running smoothly. This expression is from Shakespeare's *Hamlet* III. i. 65.

> **1998** *Times* 13 May 18/2 Even worse, and here is the rub, nobody could say who put what paper in which tier of whose red box.

burn (*or US* **lay**) **RUBBER** drive very quickly. *informal*

> **1998** *Times* 3 July 31/1 Monsanto is burning rubber on a racetrack to become world leader in life sciences.

cross the RUBICON take an irrevocable step. ● The Rubicon was a small river in north-east Italy which in the first century BC marked the boundary of Italy proper with the province of Cisalpine Gaul; by taking his army across it into Italy in 49 BC, Julius Caesar broke the law forbidding a general to lead an army out of his own province, and so committed himself to war against the Senate and Pompey. See also ▶ **the DIE is cast**.

RUFFLE someone's feathers cause someone to become annoyed or upset. ● Alluding to the apparent discomfort of birds when their feathers are blown about.

smooth someone's RUFFLED feathers make someone less angry or irritated by using soothing words.

pull the RUG (from under someone) abruptly withdraw support (from someone).

RUG ▶ *see* **CUT a rug**

RULE of thumb a broadly accurate guide or principle, based on experience or practice. ●The phrase has been current since L17, explicitly or implicitly contrasted with theory or formal methodology.

> **1998** *New Scientist* [The] best forecast of tomorrow's weather in any one place often comes not from a supercomputer, but from the rule of thumb that says: tomorrow it will be similar to today.

— RULE(s), OK? used to express one's enthusiasm for someone or something. *informal, humorous* ●Very often found in the form of graffiti.

RULE the roost be in complete control. ●The original expression was *rule the roast*, common from M16 onwards; however, none of the early examples of its use throws any light on its source, though it could be surmised as being 'master of a feast' and hence 'in sole authority'. The version with *roost* begins to be attested in M18 and became predominant over the succeeding century, so that by the time Fowler (*Modern English Usage*, 1926) researched the idiom, none of the three people he asked had ever heard of *rule the roast*, but stated that *rule the roost* came from a cock's keeping his hens in order.

run the RULE over examine cursorily for correctness or adequacy. *Brit.*

> | **1998** *Spectator* 28 Mar. 24/3 [A] committee of directors will run the rule over would-be bidders.

RUMOUR has it it is rumoured. ●Usually with *that*, indicating that the speaker is doubtful about the truth of the following statement.

be RUN off one's feet be kept extremely busy. *informal*

give someone/thing a (good) RUN for their money provide with challenging competition or opposition.

> **1997** *Rugby World* Aug. 94/1 Beaten Welsh Cup finalists Swansea gave them a good run for their money for much of the campaign before fading away.

have a (good) RUN for one's money derive reward or enjoyment in return for one's outlay or efforts. ●Originally from horse racing.

(try to) RUN before one can walk attempt something difficult before one has grasped the basic skills required. ●The opposite is the less frequently used *walk before one can run*.

RUN dry (especially of a source of money or information) be completely used up. ●From the drying up or ceasing to flow of a well, spring, or river.

(make a) RUN for it attempt to escape someone or something by running away.

RUN foul (*or chiefly* N. Amer. **afoul) of come into conflict with; go against. ●A nautical expression used when a ship collides or becomes entangled with an obstacle or another vessel; both literal and figurative uses were current by L17.

RUN someone close almost defeat a person or team in a contest.

RUN high be strong or tumultuous. ●From the rising of waves, tides, etc. above their normal height, especially in stormy conditions.

RUN into the sand come to nothing.

RUN of the mill the ordinary or undistinguished type. ●The material produced from a mill before sorting. Also often attributive *run-of-the-mill*.

RUN off at the mouth talk excessively or indiscreetly. *N. Amer., informal*

RUN someone out of town force someone to leave a place. *chiefly N. Amer.*

RUN someone/thing to earth (or ground) find someone or something, usually after a long search. ●An idiom from hunting, especially foxhunting, meaning to chase a quarry to its lair and corner it there.

RUN ▶ *see* **run a BLOCKADE**; ▶ *see* **run its COURSE**; ▶ *see* **cut it FINE**; ▶ *see* **run the GAUNTLET**; ▶ *see* **work oneself into the GROUND**; ▶ *see* **run with the HARE and hunt with the hounds**; ▶ *see* **run a MILE**; ▶ *see* **run RINGS round**; ▶ *see* **go to SEED**; ▶ *see* **run WILD**.

give someone the RUN-AROUND deceive and confuse someone; avoid answering someone's questions directly. *informal*

read the RUNES try to forecast the outcome of a situation by analysing all the significant factors involved. *Brit.* ●The *runes* were an ancient Germanic alphabet in use in northern Europe, each character of which was supposed to have a secret magical significance.

do a RUNNER leave hastily, especially to avoid paying for something or to escape from somewhere; abscond. *Brit., informal*

> **1998** *Oldie* Aug. 18/1 [H]e thought that the landlord had done a runner. A chilly reminder that running a pub is not a short cut to a fortune.

a RUNNING battle a continuous struggle. ●Literally, a fight that is constantly changing its location, the opposite of ▶ **a PITCHED battle**. The phrase *running fight* was originally (L17) in use for a naval engagement in which the fight was continued as one party retreated or fled; *running battle* appears to be of M20 date.

in (or out of) the RUNNING in (or no longer in) contention for an award, victory, or a place in a team.

make the RUNNING set the pace in a race or activity.

(go and) take a RUNNING jump go away. ●Usually as imperative, when angrily rejecting or disagreeing with someone.

> **1998** *Oldie* Aug. 3/2 Get back to the studio and tell the focus groups to take a running jump!

take up the RUNNING take over as pacemaker in a race.

RUSH one's fences act with undue haste. *Brit.* ●An equestrian metaphor: in the hunting field to *rush one's fences*, rather than tackling the obstacles steadily, is to risk a fall.

a RUSH of blood (to the head) a sudden attack of wild irrationality in one's thinking or actions.

RUSH ▶ *see* **give someone the BUM's rush**.

in a RUT following a fixed (especially tedious or dreary) pattern of behaviour that is difficult to change. ●*Rut* here is the deep groove worn by a wheel travelling perpetually along the same track.

> **1995** N. HORNBY *High Fidelity* (1996) 13 I should have spotted that we were in a rut, that I had allowed things to fester to such an extent that she was on the lookout for someone else.

S

a SABBATH day's journey a short and easy journey. ●Originally with reference to the distance that rabbinical law allowed an observant Jew to travel on the Sabbath (about a kilometre); thus in the Bible Mount Olivet is described as being 'from Jerusalem a sabbath day's journey' (Acts 1:12).

hit the SACK go to bed. *informal* ●M20; Cf. ▶ **hit the HAY**.

hold the SACK bear an unwelcome responsibility. *N. Amer.*

SACK ▶ *see* **a ROLL in the hay**.

in SACKCLOTH and ashes manifesting grief or repentance. ●With allusion to wearing sackcloth and sprinkling ashes on one's head, as a sign of penitence or mourning (e.g. Esther 4:1). Now most often as a humorous hyperbole.

SACRED ▶ *see* **a sacred COW**.

in the SADDLE **1** on horseback. **2** in office or control.

to be on the SAFE side in order to have a margin of security against risks.

SAFE ▶ *see* **a safe BET**; ▶ *see* **BETTER safe than sorry**; ▶ *see* **a safe pair of HANDS**; ▶ *see* **safe as HOUSES**.

(there's) SAFETY in numbers being in a group of people makes you feel more confident or secure. *proverbial* ●Probably adapting Proverbs 11:14 'In the multitude of counsellors there is safety', but now much wider in its application and with a somewhat different emphasis (see quot.).

| *1816 J. AUSTEN *Emma* II. i She determined to call upon them and seek safety in numbers.

SAIL close to (or near) the wind come close to breaking a rule or the law; behave or operate in a risky way. ●A nautical expression meaning 'sail as nearly against the wind as possible'.

SAILS ▶ *see* **take the WIND out of someone's sails**.

SALOON ▶ *see* **in the LAST chance saloon**.

rub SALT into the (or someone's) wound make a painful experience even more painful for someone.

SALT a mine introduce extraneous ore or other material into a mineral sample to make the source seem rich. ●*informal*

the SALT of the earth a person or group of people of great kindness, reliability, or honesty. ●With allusion to Matthew 5:13.

sit below the SALT be of lower social standing or worth. ●From the former custom of placing a large salt-cellar midway down a long dining table at which people were seated in order of rank.

take with a pinch (*or* grain) of SALT regard as exaggerated; believe only part of.

> **1998** *Bookseller* 3 Apr. 21/3 Meanwhile, ... readers should take the quotes they see with a pinch of salt.

worth one's SALT good or competent at the job or profession specified.

eat SALT with be a guest of. ● *Brit.*

put SALT on the tail of capture. ● With reference to jocular instructions given to young children for catching a bird.

SALT the books show receipts as larger than they really have been. *informal* ● *Salt* is also used of other dubious commercial practices: e.g. *salting an account* is setting an extremely high or low price for articles. Cf. ▶ **SALT a mine**.

SALTS ▶ *see* **like a DOSE of salts**.

good SAMARITAN a charitable or helpful person. ● With allusion to the parable of the Samaritan who came to the aid of the man who had fallen among thieves (Luke 10:30–6).

one and the SAME the same person or thing. ● Used for emphasis.

SAME difference (it is) all the same; essentially similar. *informal* ● Used to express the speaker's belief that two or more things are essentially the same, in spite of apparent differences.

SAME here the same applies to me. *informal*

> **1993** A. McNAB *Bravo Two Zero* (1994) x. 297 'I've still got my map and compass,' I said. 'Yeah, same here.'

SAME ▶ *see* **by the same TOKEN**.

SAND ▶ *see* **BUILT on sand**; ▶ *see* **BURY one's head in the sand**; ▶ *see* **ROPE of sand**; ▶ *see* **RUN into the sand**.

SANDBOY ▶ *see* **HAPPY as a sandboy**.

the SANDS (*of time*) are running out the allotted time is nearly at an end. ● With reference to the movement of sand in an hourglass.

the meat (*or* filling) in the SANDWICH a person who is awkwardly caught between two opposing factions.

a SANDWICH (*or* two sandwiches) short of a picnic (of a person) stupid. *informal* ● Cf. ▶ **a BRICK short of a load**.

packed like SARDINES crowded very close together. ● With reference to the way sardines are packed in tins.

what's SAUCE for the goose is sauce for the gander what is appropriate in one case is also appropriate in the other case in question. *proverbial* ● Although also applied in general contexts (see quot.), it is most often used as a statement that what is right (*or* wrong) for one sex is right (*or* wrong) for the other as well. John Ray, who was the first to record this saying (in *English Proverbs* 1670), remarked 'This is a woman's Proverb.'

| **1998** *New Scientist* 4 July 51/1 What is sauce for the US goose is sauce for the Iraqi gander!

have eyes like SAUCERS have one's eyes opened wide in amazement.

not a SAUSAGE nothing at all. *Brit., informal*

SAVE the day (*or* **situation**) find or provide a solution to a difficulty or disaster.

| **1990** R. CRITCHFIELD *Among British* i. 22 When the postwar social fabric started to tear, amid a stagnant economy and global decline, ... Edward Heath ... was supposed to save the day. He failed to deliver.

be unable to do something to SAVE one's life be very incompetent at doing something. ● Used hyperbolically in trivial contexts to indicate that the person in question would be unable or reluctant to take the action specified even under the threat of death.

| *1848 A. TROLLOPE *Kellys and O'Kellys* III. v. 106 If it was to save my life and theirs, I can't get up small talk for the rector and his curate.

SAVE one's skin (*or* **neck** *or* **bacon**) escape from imminent danger or difficulty. ● The variant with *bacon* has been in use since M17; the expression can also be used with an object: *save someone's skin.*

SAVE ▶ *see* **save one's BREATH**; ▶ *see* **save FACE**.

SAVED by the bell preserved from danger narrowly or by an unexpected intervention. ● In boxing matches a floored contestant can be saved from being counted out by the ringing of the bell to mark the end of a round. Often as an exclamation of relief at a last-minute escape.

have something (*or* **nothing**) **to SAY for oneself** contribute (*or* fail to contribute) to a conversation or discussion.

SAY the word give permission or instructions to do something.

go without SAYING be too well known or obvious to need mention. ● L19, translating French (*cela*) *va sans dire.*

there is no SAYING it is impossible to know.

throw away the SCABBARD abandon all thought of making peace. ● From the proverb *who draws his sword against his prince must throw away the scabbard.*

like a SCALDED cat at a very fast speed.

| **1997** *T3* Feb. 70/3 If you're in a desperate hurry you can bury the accelerator ... and take off like a scalded cat.

throw something on (*or* **into**) **the SCALE** cause to be a factor in a contest or debate.

the SCALES fall from someone's eyes someone is no longer deceived. ● The expression used to describe St Paul's recovery from blindness (Acts 9:18).

tip (*or* **turn**) **the SCALES at** have a weight of (a specified amount). ● With allusion to the arm of an old-fashioned pair of scales with a pan suspended at either end.

turn the SCALES (*or* balance) alter the probability of the outcome. ●With allusion to the critical moment or weight at which the arm of the scales tilts in one direction or the other. Usually with *against* or *in favour of —*.

make oneself SCARCE surreptitiously disappear; keep out of the way. *informal*

SCARE ▶ *see* **frighten the DAYLIGHTS out of**.

behind the SCENES in private; secretly. ●With reference to the area out of sight of the public at the back of the stage in a theatre. Also as modifier: *behind-the-scenes*.

change of SCENE (*or* scenery) a move to different surroundings.

not one's SCENE not something one is interested in. *informal*

set the SCENE **1** describe a place or situation in which something is about to happen. **2** create the conditions for a future event.

on the SCENT in possession of a useful clue in a search or investigation. ●Literally, referring to a dog or other animal following the scent of its quarry.

put (*or* throw) off the SCENT mislead in the course of a search or investigation.

the SCHEME of things the organization of things in general; the way the world is.

> **1859** E. FITZGERALD *Rubaiyat of Omar Khayyam* lxxiii.Ah Love! could Thou and I with Fate conspire To grasp this sorry Scheme of Things entire, Would we not shatter it to bits!

the whole SCHMEAR everything possible or available; every aspect of something. *N. Amer., informal* ●*Schmear* (also *schmeer, shmear, shmeer*), from Yiddish *schmirn* to grease, flatter, means 'bribery' or 'flattery'. *Schmear* may have originated (M20) in show business jargon.

> **1970** L. SANDERS *Anderson Tapes* v. 23I want a complete list ... Any thing and everything ... The whole shmear.

SCHOOL of thought a particular philosophy, opinion, or way of thinking, often one disputed by the speaker.

SCHOOL ▶ *see* **of the OLD school**; ▶ *see* **school of hard KNOCKS**; ▶ *see* **the old school TIE**.

SCIENCE ▶ *see* **BLIND someone with science**.

know the SCORE be aware of the essential facts about a situation. *informal*

on that (*or* this) SCORE so far as that (*or* this) is concerned.

settle (*or* pay) a (*or* the) SCORE take revenge on someone for something damaging that they have done in the past. ●With allusion to paying off a debt or other obligation. Also *settle with someone* or *pay off old scores*.

SCORE ▶ *see* **score an own GOAL**; ▶ *see* **score POINTS**.

SCOUT's honour a binding obligation to behave honourably. *informal* ●With allusion to the oath taken by a Scout. Used in spoken English to associate one's own moral standard with the ideal code of the Scouts, with the intention of reassuring someone that one will stand by a promise or tell the truth.

SCRAPE (an) acquaintance with contrive to get to know. *dated*

> **1892** J. FISKE *Letter* 28 May A very nice San Franciscan girl scraped acquaintance with me last evening and said she had been to my lectures.

SCRAPE the barrel (*or* the bottom of the barrel) be reduced to using things or people of the poorest quality because there is nothing else available. *informal*

from SCRATCH from the very beginning, especially without utilizing or relying on any previous work for assistance. ●In sporting parlance the *scratch* (M19) is the starting point for a competitor who receives no odds.

SCRATCH a — and find a — an investigation of someone or something soon reveals their true nature. ●First in English E19, translating French *grattez le Russe et vous trouverez le Tartare* (scratch the Russian and you will find the Tartar), attributed to Napoleon.

SCRATCH one's head **1** think hard in order to find a solution to something. **2** feel or express bewilderment. *informal*

SCRATCH the surface **1** deal with a matter only in the most superficial way; address only a small part of a subject or problem. **2** initiate the briefest investigation to discover something concealed.

up to SCRATCH up to the required standard; satisfactory.

you SCRATCH my back and I'll scratch yours if you do me a favour, I will return it. *proverbial* ●Mutual (back)scratching as a metaphor for reciprocity has been current since E18.

have a SCREW loose be slightly eccentric or mentally disturbed. *informal* ●Used since L19 to indicate something mildly amiss in a person's mental faculties.

a (final *or* last) turn of the SCREW an additional amount of pressure or hardship applied to a situation that is already extremely difficult to bear. *informal*

tighten (*or* turn) the SCREW (*or* screws) exert strong pressure on someone. ●*informal*

have one's head SCREWED on (the right way) have common sense. *informal*

put the SCREWS on exert strong psychological pressure on (someone) so as to intimidate them into doing something. *informal*

by the SCRUFF of the (*or* one's) neck (*or* collar) holding the back of a person or animal's neck (*or* collar) in a rough or brutal way. ●*Scruff* (L18) was a northern dialect word for the nape of the neck.

SCYLLA and Charybdis two dangers of which the attempt to avoid one increases the risk from the other. *literary* ●In classical mythology, *Scylla* was a fearful monster and *Charybdis* a whirlpool; they were associated with two dangerous rocks in the straits between Italy and Sicily.

(all) at SEA confused or unable to decide what to do.

> **1993** S. STEWART *Ramlin Rose* iii. 23 She had a lot of bodily sufferin. Mr Statham and the Girls couldn't stand it; they was all at sea.

put (*or* set) the SEAL on put the finishing touch to. ● With allusion to the former practice of stamping one's personal seal on a document or letter when it is finished.

set (*or* put) one's SEAL to (*or* on) authorize or confirm in a position. ● From the use of a personal seal as an authenticating device; cf. preceding entry.

someone's lips are SEALED a person is obliged to keep a secret.

bursting (*or* bulging) at the SEAMS (of a place or building) full to overflowing. *informal* ● In this and the following entry the *seams* are the lines along which pieces of fabric or the planks of a boat are joined and which are perceived as the points most vulnerable to failure.

come (*or* fall) apart at the SEAMS **1** (of a thing) fall to pieces. **2** *informal* (of a person) collapse; have an emotional breakdown. ● The figurative sense **2** is M20.

SEASONS ▶ *see* a MAN for all seasons.

by the SEAT of one's pants by instinct rather than logic or knowledge. *informal* ● First in M20 aviation slang, meaning 'relying on human judgement rather than navigational instruments', and still, though not exclusively, used in the context of piloting a plane or driving a vehicle.

> **1977** M. WALKER *National Front* i. 17 Mussolini had governed by the seat of his pants, guided in part by his early Socialism, in part by his … bombastic nationalism.

SECOND childhood enfeebled old age; dotage. ● Cf. Latin *senex bis puer*, which translates as the (obsolete) English proverb *an old man is twice a child*. Shakespeare has 'second childishness and mere oblivion' as the last of the seven ages of man in *As You Like It* II. vii.

SECOND to none surpassed by no other.

> **1961** J. HELLER *Catch-22* (1962) xi. 112 He would stand second to none in his devotion to country.

SECOND ▶ *see* play second FIDDLE to.

in (on) the SECRET among the small number of people who know something.

SECTION ▶ *see* the GOLDEN section.

SEE a man about a dog keep a private undisclosed appointment. *humorous* ● Said euphemistically when leaving to go to the lavatory or if one wishes not to disclose the nature of the errand one is about to undertake.

SEE one's way clear to do (*or* doing) something find that it is possible or convenient to do something. ● Often used in polite requests: *would you see your way clear to —?*

SEE someone coming recognize a person who can be fooled or deceived. *informal*

SEE something coming foresee or be prepared for an event, typically an unpleasant one.

SEE someone right make sure that a person is appropriately rewarded or looked after. *Brit., informal*

SEE ▶ *see* **the BACK of**; ▶ *see* **see EYE to eye**; ▶ *see* **see REASON**.

go (or run) to SEED **1** (of a plant) cease flowering as the seeds develop. **2** deteriorate in condition, strength, or efficiency.

SEED ▶ *see* **SOW the seed**.

be SEEING things be hallucinating.
> **1987** R. MISTRY 'One Sunday' in *Tales from Firozsha Baag* (1992) 43 How much fun they made of me. Calling me crazy, saying it is time for old ayah to go back to Goa, ... she is seeing things.

SEEING is believing you need to see something before you can accept that it really exists or occurs. *proverbial* ● Current in this form since M17.

SEEN ▶ *see* **seen better DAYS**.

SEIZE the day make the most of the present moment. ● Translating Horace *Odes* I. xi. 8: *carpe diem*.

SELL someone/thing short fail to recognize or state the true value of.
> **1998** *Times* 8 Sept. 22/2 Mr Ashdown may secure his seat in the Cabinet, but he will have bought it by selling liberal principles short.

SELL one's soul (or oneself) (to the devil) do or be willing to do anything, no matter how wrong, in order to achieve one's objective. ● With allusion to the contract with the devil that certain German people (most famously the German scholar Faust celebrated in plays by Marlowe and Goethe) were formerly believed to have made: the devil would grant them all their desires in this life and would receive in return their souls for eternity.

SELL ▶ *see* **sell someone a BILL of goods**; ▶ *see* **sell someone down the RIVER**; ▶ *see* **sell someone a DUMMY**; ▶ *see* **sell like hot CAKES**; ▶ *see* **sell the PASS**; ▶ *see* **sell someone a PUP**.

SEND someone flying cause someone to be violently flung to the ground.

SEND ▶ *see* **send someone PACKING**; ▶ *see* **send someone to COVENTRY**.

SENSE ▶ *see* **see REASON**.

bring someone to their SENSES cause someone to think and behave reasonably after a period of folly or irrationality.

come to one's SENSES become reasonable after acting foolishly.

take leave of one's SENSES go mad.

go one's SEPARATE ways **1** leave in a different direction from someone with whom one has just travelled or spent time. **2** end a romantic, professional, or other relationship.

SEPARATE ▶ *see* **separate the MEN from the boys**; ▶ *see* **separate the SHEEP from the goats**; ▶ *see* **separate the WHEAT from the chaff**.

SERVE one's time (*chiefly US also* serve out one's time) **1** hold office for the normal period. **2** spend time in office, an apprenticeship, or prison. ●In sense 2 also *serve time*, particularly with reference to a prison sentence.

SERVE two masters take orders from two superiors or follow two conflicting or opposing principles or policies at the same time. ●With allusion to the biblical warning against trying to serve both God and Mammon (Matthew 6:24).

SESAME ▶ *see* **OPEN sesame**.

make a dead SET at make a determined attempt to win the affections of. *Brit.* ●Originally a sporting idiom (E19), referring to the manner in which a dog such as a setter or pointer stands stock still with its muzzle pointing in the direction of the prey.

SET one's heart (*or* hopes) **on** have a strong desire for or to do.

SET little (*or* much *or* a great deal) **by** consider to be of little (*or* great) value.

SET out one's stall display or show off one's abilities, attributes, or experience in order to convince someone of one's suitability for something. ●From a street trader's setting up a stall to display goods for sale.

SET one's teeth 1 clench one's teeth together. **2** become resolute.

SET the wheels in motion do something to begin a process or put a plan into action.

SET ▶ *see* **be carved in STONE**; ▶ *see* **clap EYES on**; ▶ *see* **set one's FACE against**; ▶ *see* **set one's HAND to**; ▶ *see* **put PEN to paper**; ▶ *see* **set the SCENE**; ▶ *see* **set the STAGE for**; ▶ *see* **set STORE by**.

SETTLE ▶ *see* **settle someone's HASH**; ▶ *see* **settle a SCORE**.

SEVEN-LEAGUE ▶ *see* **seven-league BOOTS**.

SEVENTH ▶ *see* **in seventh HEAVEN**.

a SHADE — a little; a small amount. *informal*
| **1984** A. MAUPIN *Baby-Cakes* (1989) xlix. 316 Shall we go a shade lighter … Pink it up a bit?

SHADES of — used to suggest reminiscence of or comparison with someone or something specified. ●*Shades* here in the sense of 'shadows' or 'ghosts'.

afraid (*or* be frightened) **of one's own SHADOW** be unreasonably timid or nervous.
| **1995** E. TOMAN *Dancing in Limbo* i. 21 You're afraid of your own shadow! What harm is there in putting it to them as a business proposition.

wear oneself to a SHADOW completely exhaust oneself through overwork.

a SHAGGY-dog story a long, rambling story or joke, especially one that is amusing only because it is absurdly inconsequential or pointless. ●Invented as a literary sub-genre in the US (M20).

| **1993** *New York Times Book Review* 21 Mar. 7/3 [T]he book has the unhurried pace of the best of the shaggy dog stories; the pleasure is all in the journey rather than the destination.

get (*or* give someone) a fair SHAKE get (*or* give someone) just treatment or a fair chance. *informal*

more than one can SHAKE a stick at a very large number. *informal* ●Used with humorous imprecision to emphasize the largeness of an amount.

SHAKE the dust off one's feet leave indignantly or disdainfully. ●From the instructions of Jesus to his disciples: 'And whosoever shall not receive you ... when ye depart out of that house or city, shake off the dust of your feet' (Matthew 10:14).

SHAKE (*or* quake) in one's shoes (*or* boots) tremble with apprehension.

SHAKE a leg make a start; rouse oneself. *informal*

in two SHAKES (of a lamb's tail) very quickly.

no great SHAKES not very good or significant. ●*informal* Since E19, possibly alluding to the shaking of a dice.

| **1989** G. VANDERHAEGHE *Homesick* vi. 74 I got specs now. Catch better with them than before, but still am no great shakes at ball.

drown the SHAMROCK drink, or go drinking on St Patrick's day. ●The *shamrock* was said to have been used by St Patrick to illustrate the doctrine of the Trinity; hence adopted as the national emblem of Ireland.

on SHANKS's pony with one's own legs as a means of transport. ●*Shank* (from Old English *sceanca* leg bone) is now used jocularly in the plural for 'legs'. As a verb, *shank* or *shank it* was a dialect expression for travel on foot. *Shanks's mare* (L18) predates the more usual modern *pony*.

get into SHAPE (*or* get someone into shape) become (*or* make someone) physically fitter by exercise. ●Also *in good shape* (physically fit) and *in poor shape* (unfit).

lick (*or* knock *or* whip) someone/thing into SHAPE act forcefully to bring someone or something into a fitter, more efficient, or better organized state. ●The form of the expression with *lick* harks back to the belief propagated by medieval bestiaries that bear cubs were born as formless lumps and were literally licked into shape by their mother.

the SHAPE of things to come the way the future is likely to develop. ●The title of a novel (1933) by H. G. Wells.

SHAPE up or ship out someone must improve their performance or behaviour or face being made to leave. *informal, chiefly N. Amer.* ●Used as an ultimatum.

SHARE and share alike have or receive an equal share; share things equally.

(as) SHARP as a needle extremely quick-witted.

SHARP (adj.) ▶ *see* **the sharp END**.

SHARP (adv.) ▶ *see* **LOOK sharp**.

who's SHE—the cat's mother? **1** used as a mild reproof, especially to a child, for impolite use of the pronoun *she* when a person's name would have been more well-mannered. **2** expressing the speaker's belief that a woman or girl has a high opinion of herself or is putting on airs. *Brit., informal*

count SHEEP count imaginary sheep jumping over a fence one by one in an attempt to send oneself to sleep. ● The idea of imagining sheep jumping seems to have been known as a soporific from at least M19.

> **1977** H. PITCHER *When Miss Emmie was in Russia* x. 75 Did you know that if you count sheep, it is watching the sheep *jump* that sends you off?

make SHEEP's eyes at someone look at someone in a foolishly amorous way.

separate the SHEEP from the goats divide people or things into superior and inferior groups. ● With allusion to the parable of the Last Judgement in Matthew 25:32–3.

SHEEP ▶ *see* **the BLACK sheep**.

two (or three) SHEETS to (or in) the wind drunk. *informal* ● A nautical idiom. *Sheets* here are the ropes attached to the corners of a ship's sail and used for controlling the extent and direction of the sail; if they are hanging loose in the wind, the vessel is likely to be out of control or taking an erratic course. The earlier form of the expression was *two sheets in the wind*.

off the SHELF not designed or made to order but taken from existing stock or supplies.

on the SHELF **1** (of people or things) no longer useful or desirable. **2** (of a music recording or a film) awaiting release on the market after being recorded. ● Sense 1 is typically used of a woman who is past an age when she might expect to have the opportunity to marry.

come out of (or retreat into) one's SHELL become less (or more) shy and retiring.

two sides of a SHIELD two ways of looking at something, two sides to a question.

SHIELD ▶ *see* **the other side of the COIN**; ▶ *see* **the reverse of the MEDAL**.

make SHIFT do what one wants to do in spite of not having ideal conditions; get along somehow.

SHIFT for oneself manage as best one can without help.

SHIFT one's ground say or write something that contradicts something one has previously written or said.

not the full SHILLING not mentally alert or quick-thinking. ● Cf. ▶ **not the full QUID**.

take the King's (or Queen's) SHILLING enlist as a soldier. *Brit.* ● With reference to the former practice of paying a shilling to a man who enlisted as a soldier.

take the SHINE off spoil the brilliance or excitement of; overshadow.

take a SHINE to take a fancy to; develop a liking for. *informal* ●Originally an M19 US colloquialism.

hang out one's SHINGLE begin to practise a profession. *N. Amer.* ●The main and oldest (ME) sense of *shingle* is 'a wooden roofing tile' but in E19 it could also be used generally of 'a piece of board' and in the US it developed the particular sense of 'a small sign-board'.

when someone's SHIP comes in (*or* home) when someone's fortune is made. ●An expression dating back to the period of Britain's maritime empire, when the safe arrival of a valuable cargo meant an instant fortune for the owner and those who had taken shares in the enterprise.

SHIP ▶ *see* **run a TIGHT ship**; ▶ *see* **RATS deserting a sinking ship**.

SHIPS that pass in the night transitory acquaintances. ●From H. W. Longfellow's *Tales of a Wayside Inn* part 3 (1874).

SHIPSHAPE and Bristol fashion with everything in good order. ●Bristol was formerly a major port in the west of England; this originally nautical expression (M19) alluded to the good order of its shipping.

keep your SHIRT on don't lose your temper; stay calm. *informal*

lose one's SHIRT lose all one's possessions, especially as the result of unwise financial transactions. *informal* ●In this and the following two entries *shirt* represents what is nearest and most essential to oneself.

put one's SHIRT on bet all one has on; be sure of. *Brit., informal*

the SHIRT off one's back one's last remaining possessions as offered to another. ●A proverbial instance of generosity.

in (one's) SHIRTSLEEVES wearing a shirt with nothing over it.

not know SHIT from Shinola be very ignorant or innocent. *US vulgar slang* ●*Shinola* is the proprietary name of a US brand of boot polish.

up SHIT creek in an awkward predicament. *vulgar slang*

when the SHIT hits the fan when a situation becomes critical; when the disastrous consequences of something become public. *vulgar slang*

be scared (*or* bored) SHITLESS be extremely frightened (*or* bored). *vulgar slang*

be SHITTING bricks be extremely nervous or frightened. *vulgar slang*

short, sharp SHOCK 1 a brief but harsh custodial sentence imposed on offenders in an attempt to discourage them from committing further offences. 2 a severe measure taken in order to effect quick results. ●A phrase used by characters in W. S. Gilbert's *The Mikado* (1885) on the prospect of being beheaded: 'Awaiting the sensation of a short, sharp shock From a cheap and chippy chopper on a big black block'. As a form of corrective treatment for young offenders, in which the deterrent value was seen in the harshness of the regime rather than the length of time served, it was advocated by the

Home Secretary, William Whitelaw, to the Conservative Party Conference in 1979.

SHOCK ▶ *see* **FUTURE shock**.

where the SHOE pinches where one's difficulty or trouble is.

> **1580** G. HARVEY *Letter-book* (Camden) 85 Subtle enemyes, that knowe … where the shooe pinchith us most.

wait for the other SHOE to drop wait for the next or final thing to happen. *N. Amer.*

SHOE ▶ *see* **if the CAP fits, wear it**.

another pair of SHOES quite a different matter or state of things.

be in another person's SHOES be in another person's situation or predicament.

dead men's SHOES property or a position coveted by a prospective successor but available only on a person's death. ●The phrase has been used in this sense since M16; cf. the proverb *it is ill waiting for dead men's shoes* (E19 in this form).

SHOOT the breeze (or the bull) have a casual conversation. *N. Amer., informal*

SHOOT one's cuffs pull one's shirt-cuffs out to project beyond the cuffs of one's jacket or coat.

SHOOT someone/thing down in flames forcefully destroy an argument or proposal. ●From the literal sense of shooting at an aircraft to cause it to burst into flames and crash.

> **1992** A. LAMBERT *Rather English Marriage* (1993) iv. 66 Ought to have shot the idea down in flames straightaway.

SHOOT from the hip react suddenly or without careful consideration of one's words or actions. *informal*

SHOOT oneself in the foot inadvertently make a situation worse for oneself; demonstrate gross incompetence. *informal*

> **1997** *Spectator* The only thing the Royal Opera seems to have done successfully is shoot itself in the foot …

SHOOT it out engage in a decisive confrontation, typically a gun battle. *informal*

SHOOT a line describe something in an exaggerated, untruthful, or boastful way. *Brit., informal*

SHOOT one's mouth off talk boastfully or indiscreetly. *informal*

the whole SHOOTING match everything. *informal* ●Also used literally, but in this figurative sense since L19, superseding the other L19 slang expression *the whole shoot*.

> **1989** P. O'BRIAN *Thirteen Gun Salute* (1992) vi. 170 I have seen all the great houses brought down, Coutts, Drummonds, Hoares, the whole shooting match.

all over the SHOP (or show) **1** everywhere; in all directions. **2** in a state of disorder or confusion. **3** wildly or erratically. ●Informal in all its senses, *all over the shop* was first recorded as British 'pugilistic slang' in Hotten's *Slang Dictionary* (1874): to inflict severe punishment on an opponent was 'to knock him all over the shop'. Cf. ▶ **ALL over the place**.

talk SHOP discuss matters concerning one's work, especially in circumstances where this is inappropriate.

> 1990 G. G. LIDDY *Monkey Handlers* x. 169 Lawyers talk shop, bounce ideas off one another all the time.

SHOP ▶ *see* **LIVE over the shop**.

be caught (*or Brit.* **taken) SHORT** **1** be put at a disadvantage. **2** *Brit.*, *informal* urgently need to urinate or defecate.

bring (*or* **pull) someone up SHORT** make someone check or pause abruptly.

get (*or* **have) someone by the SHORT and curlies (***or* **short hairs)** have complete control of a person. *informal* ●L19 military slang. A periphrasis for the vulgar slang expression *get someone by the balls*.

in SHORT order immediately; rapidly. *chiefly US*

in the SHORT run (*or* **term)** over a brief period of time.

make SHORT work of accomplish, consume, or destroy quickly.

SHORT and sweet brief and pleasant. ●Chiefly used ironically of something that is short or quick but certainly not agreeable.

the SHORT END of the stick the disadvantage in a situation; a bad deal.

> 1994 *Hispanic* July–Aug. 6/2 Latinas are getting the 'short end of the stick' when it comes to equality in the business world and seeking financing for their businesses.

SHORT ▶ *see* **a BRICK short of a load**; ▶ *see* **in SHORT order**; ▶ *see* **a SANDWICH short of a picnic**; ▶ *see* **short, sharp SHOCK**.

by a long SHOT by far; outstandingly. *informal* ●Cf. ▶ **not by a long SHOT**.

get (*or* **be) SHOT of** get (or be) rid of. *Brit.*, *informal*

give it one's best SHOT try as hard as one can to do something. *informal*

like a SHOT without hesitation; willingly. *informal*

not by a long SHOT by no means.

> 1991 Z. EDGELL *In Times Like These* I. 275 Even though we had a very good crowd at the meeting tonight we weren't at full strength, not by a long shot.

a SHOT in the arm stimulus or encouragement. *informal*

a SHOT in the locker a thing in reserve but ready for use. *Brit.* ●The literal sense relates to naval gunnery. Frequently in negative: (*left*) *without a shot in one's locker*.

SHOT to pieces (*or* **to hell)** ruined. *informal*

SHOT ▶ *see* **a BIG cheese**; ▶ *see* **a shot across the BOWS**; ▶ *see* **a shot in the DARK**.

SHOTGUN ▶ *see* **RIDE shotgun**.

SHOTS ▶ *see* **CALL the shots**.

look over one's SHOULDER be anxious or insecure about a possible danger.
> **1990** *Daily Star* 23 Oct. 28/2 [The] chief executive … toasted the lifting of the takeover threat. 'Now they can get on with running the business while not looking over their shoulders,' says one city analyst.

be on someone's SHOULDER keep a close check on someone. *informal*
> **1998** *Times* 20 May 48/3 No England manager can control his players … I can't be on their shoulder week in and week out.

put one's SHOULDER to the wheel set to work vigorously. ● Literally, shove with one's shoulder against the wheel of a cart or other vehicle that has become stuck.

a SHOULDER to cry on someone who listens sympathetically to someone's problems.

SHOULDER to shoulder **1** side by side. **2** acting together towards a common aim: with united effort. ● Sense 2 developed out of the notion of soldiers or others standing side by side in unbroken ranks.

SHOULDER ▶ *see* **STRAIGHT from the shoulder**.

SHOULDERS ▶ *see* **RUB shoulders with**.

in with a SHOUT having a good chance. *informal*

SHOUT the odds talk loudly and opinionatedly.

all over bar the SHOUTING (of a contest) almost finished and therefore virtually decided. *informal*

SHOVE ▶ *see* **if PUSH comes to shove**.

give the (whole) SHOW away demonstrate the inadequacies or reveal the truth of something.

get (or keep) the SHOW on the road start (*or* keep going) an enterprise or organization. *informal*
> **1997** *Spectator* 8 Nov. 34/1 Much rarer … is the journalist who helps to keep the national show on the road.

the only SHOW in town the only or most significant thing.
> **1998** *New Scientist* 8 Aug. 39/1 This should scupper the laser idea, and yet, with no other explanations on offer, it's the only show in town.

SHOW someone a clean pair of heels retreat speedily; run away. *informal*

SHOW someone the door dismiss or eject someone from a place.
> **1991** M. CURTIN *Plastic Tomato Cutter* (1996) xv. 119 Mr Yendall, would you credit I had applicants who scorned the wages? I showed them the door.

SHOW one's hand (or cards) disclose one's plans. ● With reference to players revealing their cards in a card game.

SHOW a leg get out of bed; get up. *Brit., informal, dated* ●Used in imperative as a wake-up call, believed to be naval in origin.

SHOW of hands the raising of hands among a group of people to indicate a vote for or against something, with numbers typically being estimated rather than counted.

SHOW one's teeth reveal one's strength; be aggressive. *Brit.*

SHOW (noun) ▶ *see* **all over the SHOP**.

SHOW (verb) ▶ *see* **SHOW one's hand**; ▶ *see* **show one's COLOURS**; ▶ *see* **show one's FACE**; ▶ *see* **show the FLAG**.

a thing of SHREDS and patches something made up of scraps, patched together. *literary* ●After Shakespeare (*Hamlet* III. iv. 102): 'A king of shreds and patches'; parodied by W. S. Gilbert in *The Mikado* i. as 'A thing of shreds and patches'.

be (*or* get) lost in the SHUFFLE be overlooked or missed in a confused or crowded situation. *N. Amer., informal*

SHUFFLE the cards change policy etc.

SHUFFLE ▶ *see* **shuffle off this mortal COIL**.

be (*or* get) SHUT of be (*or* get) rid of. *informal*

SHUT up shop **1** cease trading, either temporarily or permanently. **2** *informal* stop some activity.

SHUT ▶ *see* **close the DOOR on**; ▶ *see* **close one's EYES to**; ▶ *see* **close one's MIND to**; ▶ *see* **shut the STABLE door after the horse has bolted**.

put up the SHUTTERS (of a business) cease trading either for the day or permanently.

have a SHY at try to hit something, especially with a ball or stone.

SICK and tired annoyed about or bored with something and unwilling to put up with it any longer. *informal*

(as) SICK as a dog extremely ill. *informal*

(as) SICK as a parrot extremely disappointed. *jocular* ●An L20 British catch-phrase, often associated with disappointed footballers.

> **1998** *New Scientist* 5 Sept. 54/1 Many of my MP colleagues are as sick as the proverbial parrot that Lord Sainsbury has been appointed to succeed John Battle as Britain's science minister.

the SICK man of — a country that is politically or economically unsound, especially in comparison with its neighbours in the region specified.
●Following a comment by Tsar Nicholas I of Russia about the moribund state of the Turkish empire, *sick man* was frequently applied in L19 to the Sultan of Turkey, later extended to Turkey and to other countries.

SICK to death very annoyed by something and unwilling to put up with it any longer. *informal*

SICK to (*or* N. Amer. at) one's stomach **1** nauseous. **2** disgusted.

worried SICK so anxious as to make oneself ill. ● Often used for emphasis.

let the SIDE down fail to meet the expectations of one's colleagues or friends, especially by mismanaging something or otherwise causing them embarrassment. *Brit.*

on the — SIDE rather —. ● Used with an adjective to indicate that the quality specified is manifested as a tendency rather than absolutely, e.g. *on the slow side*.

on the SIDE **1** in addition to one's regular job or as a subsidiary source of income. **2** secretly, especially with regard to a sexual relationship in addition to one's legal or regular partner. **3** *N. Amer.* served separately from the main dish.

SIDE ▶ *see* **the other side of the COIN**.

on (*or* from) the SIDELINES in (*or* from) a position where one is observing a situation but is unable or unwilling to be directly involved in it. ● A sporting metaphor: the sidelines mark the long edges of a playing area, behind which spectators, coaches, and other non-players must remain.

SIDEWAYS ▶ *see* **KNOCK someone sideways**.

out of SIGHT, out of mind one soon forgets people or things that are no longer visible or present. *proverbial* ● A saying that has been around in various forms since M13, but in this form since at least M16.

a SIGHT for sore eyes a person or thing that one is extremely pleased or relieved to see. *informal*

a SIGHT more — (*or* **a sight — than** *or* **a sight too —**) someone or something has a great deal or too much of a particular specified quality. *informal* ● Used for emphasis, e.g. *a sight too clever.*

SIGHT ▶ *see* **HEAVE in sight**.

in (*or* within) one's SIGHTS within one's expectations; close to achieving. ● With allusion to having one's target visible through the sights of one's gun; cf. next two entries.

raise (*or* lower) one's SIGHTS become more (*or* less) ambitious; increase (*or* lower) one's expectations.

set one's SIGHTS on have as an ambition; hope strongly to achieve or reach.
| **1996** *Home* Oct. 501 Within ten minutes I had made an offer … But another couple has also set their sights on the cottage, so sealed bids were submitted.

SIGN of the times something typical of the nature or quality of a particular period. ● In Matthew 16:3 'the signs of the times' (Tyndale's translation of 1525 and AV) are equated with weather indicators. The singular *sign of the times* is the usual modern form, and the emphasis is somewhat different.

SIGN on the dotted line agree formally. ● The space on a document for a signature is often indicated by a line of small dots or dashes.
| **1921** P. G. WODEHOUSE *Indiscretions of Archie* xvi. 184 I spoke to him as one old friend to another … and he sang a few bars from 'Rigoletto', and signed on the dotted line.

SIGNED, sealed, and delivered (or signed and sealed) formally and officially agreed and in effect. ● With allusion to the processing of official documents: the parties put their signatures to them, seal them with their official seals, and finally have them proclaimed or delivered.

SILENCE is golden it's often wise to say nothing. *proverbial* ● The fuller form of the saying is *speech is silver, but silence is golden*; Carlyle, in introducing it into English, alludes to what he calls 'the Swiss Inscription ... : *Sprechen ist silbern, Schweigen ist golden'* (in *Fraser's Magazine*, 1834).

the SILENT majority the majority of people, regarded as holding moderate opinions but rarely expressing them. ● Originally associated especially with US President Richard Nixon who claimed in his 1968 presidential election campaign to speak for this segment of society.

| **1998** *Spectator* 25 Apr. 55/2 Independent-thinking columnists claimed a silent majority loathed Di mania and maybe they were right.

SILENT ▶ *see* **silent as the GRAVE**.

make a SILK purse out of a sow's ear turn something inferior into something of top quality. ● Always in negative contexts. The observation that *one can't make a silk purse out of a sow's ear* has been proverbial since L16 but the saying is older (E16) with *a goat's fleece* in place of *a sow's ear*.

— oneself SILLY be unable to act rationally because of doing something to excess, e.g. *drink oneself silly*.

the SILLY season the months of August and September regarded as the time when newspapers often publish trivia because of a lack of important news. *chiefly Brit.* ● The concept and phrase date back to M19; in high summer Victorian London was deserted by the wealthy and important during the period in which Parliament and the law courts were in recess. Cf. *Saturday Review* (13 July 1861): 'the Silly Season of 1861 setting in a month or two before its time'.

be born with a SILVER spoon in one's mouth be born into a wealthy family of high social standing. ● E19.

on a SILVER platter (or salver) without having been asked or sought for, without requiring any effort or return from the recipient, in ready-to-use form. ● From a butler or waiter presenting something on a silver tray.

a SILVER lining a positive or more hopeful aspect to a bad situation, even though this may not be immediately apparent. ● Alluding to the proverb *every cloud has a silver lining*. Milton used the phrase *silver lining* in *Comus* (1634) I. 93, but the figurative use is apparently M19.

the SILVER screen the cinema industry; cinema films collectively. ● In the early days of cinematography, a projection screen was covered with metallic paint to give a highly reflective, silver-coloured surface.

have a SILVER tongue be eloquent or persuasive.

the real SIMON Pure the real or genuine person or thing. ● After a character in S. Centlivre's *A Bold Stroke for a Wife* (1717), who is impersonated by another character during part of the play.

(as) — as SIN having a particular undesirable quality to a high degree. *informal*
| 1991 R. R. MCCAMMON *Boy's Life* I. i. 13 Everybody knew Saxon's Lake was as deep as sin.

like SIN vehemently or forcefully. *informal*

SING a different tune (*or* song) change one's opinion about or attitude towards someone or something.

SING from the same hymn (*or* song) sheet (*or* book) present a united front in public by not disagreeing with one another. *Brit., informal*
| 1998 *Spectator* 9 May 10/1 Had he been working for a centrist minister, he would have been singing from a very different songbook.

SING ▶ *see* **sing for one's SUPPER**.

SINGE one's wings suffer harm especially in a risky attempt.

all-SINGING, all-dancing having a large number and variety of impressive features. *Brit., informal* ● Cf. ▶ **BELLS and whistles**.

SINK or swim fail or succeed entirely by one's own efforts.

SINK ▶ *see* **everything but the KITCHEN sink**.

a (*or* that) SINKING feeling an unpleasant feeling caused by the realization that something unpleasant or undesirable has happened or is about to happen. ● Cf. ▶ **one's heart sinks into one's BOOTS**.

for one's SINS as a penance. *chiefly Brit.* ● Used humorously to suggest that a task or duty is so onerous or unpleasant that it must be a punishment.

SIREN song (*or* call) the appeal of something that is also considered harmful or dangerous. ● In classical mythology, the Sirens were sea nymphs who lured sailors to their doom by the beauty of their song; cf. Homer *Odyssey* xii.

SIT at someone's feet be someone's pupil or follower.

SIT loosely on not be very binding.

SIT on one's hands take no action.
| 1998 *Times* 22 July 39/1 The England selectors, historically, find reasons to sit on their hands.

SIT (heavy) on the stomach (of food) take a long time to be digested.

SIT on someone's tail drive extremely close behind another vehicle, typically while waiting for a chance to overtake.

SIT tight **1** remain firmly in one's place. **2** refrain from taking action or changing one's mind. *informal*
| 1 1984 S. TERKEL *Good War* (1985) IV. i. 415 Our colonel told everyone to sit tight, don't leave the camp.

SIT up (and take notice) suddenly start paying attention or have one's interest aroused. *informal*

SIT ▶ *see* **sit on the FENCE**.

hit (*or* knock) someone for SIX affect someone very severely; overwhelm someone. *Brit., informal* ● *Six* is elliptical for *six runs*. With allusion to a forceful hit in cricket which propels the ball clear over the boundary of the ground for a score of six runs.

SIX feet under dead and buried. *informal* ●With reference to the traditional depth of a grave.

(it's) SIX of one and half a dozen of the other (there is) no real difference between the alternatives.

at SIXES and sevens in a state of total confusion or disarray. ●Originating in gamblers' jargon, the phrase may be an alteration or corruption of Old French *cinque* and *sice*, these two being the highest numbers on the dice. From the idea of hazarding all one's goods on the two highest numbers came the idea of carelessness and neglect of one's possessions and hence the modern usage.

| **1998** *Oldie* Aug. 18/1 But if you arrive in the afternoon we may be a bit at sixes and sevens as we're doing a wedding reception.

on a SIXPENCE (of a stop or turn) within a small area or short distance. *Brit., informal* ●The old sixpenny coin was one of the smallest in circulation prior to decimalization in Britain; ●Cf. ▶ **on a DIME** sense **1**.

the SIXTY-FOUR thousand dollar question the crucial issue, a difficult question, a dilemma. ●From the top prize (originally $64) in a US radio quiz show (M20).

that's about the SIZE of it said to confirm a person's assessment of a situation, especially of one regarded as bad. ●*informal*

get one's SKATES on make haste; hurry up. *Brit., informal*

SKATING ▶ *see* **on thin ICE**.

a SKELETON in the cupboard (or US in the closet) a discreditable or embarrassing fact that one wishes to keep secret. ●Brought into literary use by Thackeray in 1845 ('there is a skeleton in every house'), but certainly current at an earlier date.

SKELETON ▶ *see* **a ghost at the FEAST**.

hit the SKIDS begin a rapid decline or deterioration. *informal* ●The origin of *skid* is uncertain, but it may be connected with the Old Norse word from which English *ski* is derived. It is used here and in the next two entries in the sense of a plank or roller on which a heavy object may be placed in order to move it easily (E18). These figurative uses are E20 US in origin.

on the SKIDS (of a person or their career) in a bad state; failing. *informal* ●Cf. preceding entry.

| **1989** T. BERGER *Changing Past* ii. 101 Jackie arrived at middle age with a career on the skids.

put the SKIDS under hasten the decline or failure of. *informal* ●Cf. preceding entries.

to the SKIES very highly; enthusiastically. ●Usually in *praise someone to the skies*.

be SKIN and bone be very thin. ●Cf. ▶ **a BAG of bones**.

by the SKIN of one's teeth by a very narrow margin; only just.

get under someone's SKIN **1** annoy or irritate someone intensely. **2** fill someone's mind in a compelling and continual way. **3** reach or display a deep understanding of someone. *informal*

> **3 1998** *Times* 17 July 22/3 A student of the Method school, he has to get under the skin of the character he portrays.

give someone (some) SKIN shake or slap hands together as a gesture of friendship or solidarity. *US, black slang*

have a thick (*or* thin) SKIN be insensitive (*or* over-sensitive) to criticism or insults. ●Hence the adjectives *thick-skinned* and *thin-skinned*.

it's no SKIN off my nose (*or* US **off my back *or* US, *slang* **off my ass)** it's a matter of indifference to me; I am unaffected by something. *informal*

there's more than one way to SKIN a cat there's more than one way of achieving one's aim. ●There several traditional proverbs along these lines: e.g. *there are more ways of killing a cat than choking it with cream*.

under the SKIN in reality, as opposed to superficial appearances.

SKIRT ▶ *see* **a BIT of fluff**.

out of one's SKULL **1** out of one's mind; crazy. **2** very drunk. *informal*

the SKY is the limit there is practically no limit.

> **1991** *Nation* 14 Oct. 444/2 Now … he proudly proclaims that today in Russia the sky is the limit to what a person can earn.

SKY ▶ *see* **out of a clear BLUE sky**.

cut someone some SLACK allow someone some leeway; make allowances for someone's behaviour. *N. Amer., informal*

> **1998** *Times* 19 Aug. 26/4 Most, though, are willing to cut Spielberg some slack for the sake of cinematic interpretation.

take (*or* pick) up the SLACK use up a surplus or improve the use of resources to avoid an undesirable lull in business. ●Also literally, 'pull on the loose end or part of a rope in order to make it taut'.

a SLAP in the face (*or* eye) an unexpected rejection or affront.

> **1996** *Independent* 18 Jan. 10/1 The move was seen as another slap in the face for the monarchy in Australia.

SLAP someone on the back congratulate someone heartily. ●Hence *a slap on the back* and *back-slapping*.

SLAP on the wrist a mild reprimand or punishment.

> **1997** *New Scientist* 20–27 Dec. 3/2 Last week, in a Washington district court, [a judge] ordered software giant Microsoft to stop forcing PC-makers to install both Windows 95 and its Web browser, Internet Explorer. So far, though, it is just a slap on the wrist.

on the (*or* one's) SLATE to be paid for later; on credit. *Brit.* ●With allusion to the tablet of slate formerly used as a writing surface in shops and bars on which a record would be kept of what a customer owed.

SLATE ▶ *see* **WIPE the slate clean**.

take (or use) a SLEDGEHAMMER to crack a nut use disproportionately forceful means to achieve a simple objective. ●A *sledge* or *sledgehammer* is a large heavy hammer wielded by blacksmiths. *Sledgehammer* has been used figuratively in the context of heavy-handed or brutal criticism since L18.

| **1998** *New Scientist* 14 Mar. 33/2 Fighting tooth decay by annihilating mostly harmless bacteria in your mouth is like taking a sledgehammer to crack a nut.

one could do something in one's SLEEP one regards something as so easy that it will require no effort or conscious thought to accomplish. *informal*

SLEEP like a log (or top) sleep very soundly.

the SLEEP of the just a deep, untroubled sleep. ●From the idea that only those with clear consciences can expect untroubled repose.

SLEEP with one eye open sleep very lightly so as to be aware of what is happening around one.

SLEEP ▶ *see* **sleep EASY**; ▶ *see* **sleep ROUGH**.

let SLEEPING dogs lie avoid interfering in a situation that is currently causing no problems, but may well do so as a consequence of such interference. ●Cf. the E14 French advice *n'esveillez pas lou chien qui dort* (do not wake the sleeping dog). Chaucer has 'It is nought good a slepyng hound to wake' (*Troilus and Criseyde* iii. 764), but the present form of the proverb seems to be traceable to Scott in 1824 (*Redgauntlet* I. xi).

up one's SLEEVE (of a strategy, idea, or resource) kept secret and in reserve for use when needed. ●Cf. ▶ **have an ACE up one's sleeve**.

SLEEVE ▶ *see* **have an ACE up one's sleeve**; ▶ *see* **have a CARD up one's sleeve**; ▶ *see* **LAUGH up one's sleeve**; ▶ *see* **wear one's HEART on one's sleeve**.

SLEEVES ▶ *see* **ROLL up one's sleeves**.

take for a SLEIGH-RIDE mislead. ●A *sleigh-ride* here is an implausible or false story, a hoax. M20 US slang. A *sleigh-ride* can also mean 'a drug-induced high', so *take a sleigh-ride* (E20 US slang) means 'take drugs, especially cocaine'.

SLEIGHT of hand the display of skilful, especially deceptive, dexterity or cunning. ●Originally (M15 onwards) with reference to a conjuring trick.

a SLICE of the cake a share of the benefits or profits. *informal*

| **1991** R. REINER *Chief Constables* III. ix. 215 Perhaps it's because they're such good spenders that our slice of the cake is sufficient for all we want.

SLICE ▶ *see* **a PIECE of the action**.

let something SLIDE negligently allow something to deteriorate.

put someone's (or have one's) ass in a SLING land someone (or be) in trouble. *N. Amer.*, *informal*

SLING beer work as a bartender. *N. Amer.*, *informal*

SLING hash (or plates) serve food in a cafe or diner. *N. Amer.*, *informal*

SLING ▶ *see* **sling one's HOOK**.

SLINGS and arrows adverse factors or circumstances. ●With reference to Shakespeare's *Hamlet* III. i. 58 'the slings and arrows of outrageous fortune'.

give someone the SLIP evade or escape from someone. *informal*

let something SLIP **1** reveal something inadvertently in the course of a conversation. **2** fail to take advantage of an opportunity.

let something SLIP through one's fingers (*or* **grasp**) **1** lose hold or possession of something. **2** miss the opportunity of gaining something.

> **2 1925** W. S. MAUGHAM *Of Human Bondage* xlvii. 236 He was mad to have let such an adventure slip through his fingers.

SLIP of the pen (*or* **the tongue**) a minor mistake in writing (*or* speech). ●The equivalent Latin phrases, *lapsus calami* and *lapsus linguae*, are also sometimes used in formal English.

SLIP on a banana skin make a silly and embarrassing mistake.

a SLIP of a — a young, small, and slim person. ●In this sense since L16, *slip* is now rare outside this expression, which itself is M17. Cf. the horticultural sense of *slip* as a cutting taken for grafting or planting.

> **1980** P. LARKIN *Letter* 15 Mar. After all you are a very young 51! Hardly 51 at all! A slip of a thing!

there's many a SLIP ('twixt cup and lip) many things can go wrong between the start of something and its completion; nothing is certain until it has happened. *proverbial* ●Cf. Latin *saepe audivi inter os atque offam multa intervenire posse* 'I have often heard that many things can come between the mouth and the morsel'. (Aulus Gellius *Noctes Atticae* XIII. xviii. 1). The form with 'many a slip' is referred to as 'an old proverb' in 1783.

SLIP ▶ *see* **slip through the NET**.

SLIPPERY slope an idea or course of action which will lead inevitably to something unacceptable, wrong, or disastrous.

> **1998** *Spectator* 15 Aug. 12/2 Those of us who feared that devolution would not assuage nationalist sentiment but turn out to be the slippery slope to separatism have a good chance of being proved right.

SLOW but (*or* **and**) **sure** not quick but achieving the required result eventually. *proverbial* ●The saying *slow and steady wins the race*, possibly quoting from R. Lloyd *Poems* (1762), has given rise to *slow and steady* as a common variant of this expression. Both variants also exist as adverbial phrases: *slowly but surely* and *slowly but steadily*.

a SMACK in the face (*or* **eye**) a strong rebuff. *informal* ●Cf. ▶ **a SLAP in the face**.

have a SMACK at make an attempt at or attack on. *informal*

the SMALL hours the early hours of the morning immediately after midnight. ●An informal variant is *the wee small hours*.

SMALL is beautiful the belief that something small-scale is better than a large-scale equivalent. ● The title of a book by E. F. Schumacher (1973). Best known through its adoption as a slogan by environmentalists, it is now also used in other contexts.

SMALL potatoes insignificant; unimportant. ● Originally M19 US, especially in *small potatoes and few in the hill.*

look SMART be quick. *chiefly Brit.*

SMELL blood discern weakness or vulnerability in an opponent.

live (*or* survive) on the SMELL of an oil rag live in conditions of extreme want. *orig. Austral.*

SMELL of the lamp show signs of laborious study and effort. ● *Lamp* here is an oil-lamp for use while working at night. Used especially of uninspired works of literature.

SMELL a rat begin to suspect trickery or deception. *informal* ● Current in this figurative sense since M16.

SMELL the roses enjoy or appreciate what is often ignored. *N. Amer., informal*

come up (*or* out) SMELLING of roses (*or* violets) make a lucky escape from a difficult situation with one's reputation intact. *informal* ● Explained by a slang elaboration, which is also sometimes used: *fall in the shit and come up smelling of roses.*

come up SMILING recover from adversity and cheerfully face the future. ● *informal*

> **1989** *Woman's Realm* 11 Apr. 23/1 But despite her ordeal courageous Kelly has come up smiling and is now looking forward to a bright future.

go up in SMOKE (of a plan) come to nothing. *informal* ● From the literal sense of 'be destroyed by fire'.

no SMOKE without fire (*or* where there's smoke there's fire) there's always some reason for a rumour. *proverbial* ● In this form in English since L16, but much earlier in French (L13).

> **1998** *Times* 11 Mar. 15/4 This is not saying that there is no smoke without fire—which sentiment underlines why bogus claims can do so much irrevocable damage—but that this is always, necessarily, going to be an incendiary issue.

SMOKE and mirrors the obscuring or embellishing of the truth of a situation with misleading or irrelevant information. *chiefly N. Amer.*

> **1998** *Times* 13 Apr. 45/2 Accordingly, past stimulus packages have all been done with smoke and mirrors.

SMOKE like a chimney smoke tobacco incessantly.

watch someone's SMOKE observe another person's activity. ● The fanciful implication is that the activity will be so fast and furious that it will cause smoke, which will be the only thing visible. E20 US slang.

> **1947** P. G. WODEHOUSE *Full Moon* ii. 27 Look at Henry the Eighth ... And Solomon. Once they started marrying, there was no holding them—you just sat back and watched their smoke.

a SMOKING gun (*or* pistol) a piece of incontrovertible evidence. ● Drawing on the assumption, a staple of detective fiction, that the person found with a recently fired gun must be the guilty party. The currency of the phrase in L20 is particularly associated with the Watergate scandal in the early 1970s involving US President Richard Nixon. When one of the Watergate tapes revealed Nixon's wish to limit the FBI's role in the investigation, Barber B. Conable famously commented: 'I guess we have found the smoking pistol, haven't we?'

> **1998** *New Scientist* 11 July 38/1 This genetic smoking gun is evidence of a migration out of Asia that is hard to refute.

in SMOOTH water in quiet and serene circumstance, especially after difficulties.

SMOOTH ▶ *see* **smooth someone's RUFFLED feathers**.

a SNAKE in the grass a secret enemy, a lurking peril. ●After Virgil *Eclogues* iii. 93 (*latet anguis in herba* there is a snake hidden in the grass). Since L17 this expression has entirely superseded the earlier idiom *a pad in the straw* (M16–M17). (A toad or *pad* was formerly considered to be a venomous creature.)

in a SNAP in a moment; almost immediately. *chiefly N. Amer., informal*

SNAP ▶ *see* **snap one's FINGERS at**; ▶ *see* **bite someone's HEAD off**.

make it SNAPPY be quick about it.

> **1994** D. HAMILL *Drinking Life* I. ii. 9 Into bed! he said. Make it snappy! I retreated into the darkness of the second floor from the kitchen.

not to be SNEEZED at not to be rejected without careful consideration; worth having or taking into account. *informal*

cock a SNOOK openly show contempt or a lack of respect for someone or something. *chiefly Brit., informal* ●Literally, the gesture of placing one's hand so that the thumb touches one's nose and the fingers are spread out, in order to express contempt. Recorded from L18, this expression is of obscure origin— as is the gesture itself, which occurs under a variety of names and in many countries, the earliest definite mention of it being by Rabelais (1532). Suggestions as to the origin of the gesture include a mimicry of the erect comb of a fighting cock or the making of a grotesque nose in reference to the long-nosed effigies that are part of folk tradition in many cultures.

SNOW ▶ *see* **PURE as the driven snow**.

SNOWBALL ▶ *see* **not a hope in HELL**.

up to SNUFF **1** up to the required standard. **2** in good health. *informal*

SNUG as a bug (in a rug) extremely comfortable. *humorous*

no SOAP no chance of something happening or occurring. *N. Amer., informal* ●The origin of this expression, used to refuse a request, may be in the M19 US slang use of *soap* to mean 'money'.

> **1929** E. WILSON *I Thought of Daisy* iii. 153 If he tries to cut in on you, don't letum—I'll just tellum, no soap.

(as) SOBER as a judge completely sober.

knock (or blow) someone's SOCKS off amaze or impress someone. *informal* ● Also *knock the socks off someone* is to surpass or beat them.

| **1991** B. ANDERSON *Girls High* (1992) iii. 21 Years ago she saw a Hockney ... the few lines which sketched the owlish face knocked her socks off.

— one's SOCKS off do something with great energy or enthusiasm. *informal*

pull one's SOCKS up make an effort to improve one's work, performance, or behaviour. *informal* ● Recorded in L19, but apparently still a novelty in 1906, when it was glossed in the *Daily Mail* as 'Never mind' or 'Pull yourself together'.

put a SOCK in it stop talking. *Brit., informal* ● E20, usually in imperative.

SOCK it to someone attack someone vigorously or make a forceful impression on them in some other way. *informal*

from SODA to hock from beginning to end. ● In the game of faro, *soda* is the exposed top card at the beginning of a deal, *hock* the last card remaining in the box after all the others have been dealt.

have a SOFT spot for be fond of or affectionate towards.

SOFT ▶ *see* a soft **TOUCH**.

come (or play) the old SOLDIER use one's greater age or experience of life to deceive someone or to shirk a duty. *informal* ● In US nautical slang an (*old*) *soldier* was a worthless seaman. With *come* often followed by preposition *over*.

and then SOME and plenty more than that. *mainly US, informal*

| **1998** *New Scientist* 25 Apr. 34/2 But by simply sitting still and digesting, a chick could double this rate and then some.

thirty-SOMETHING (or forty-something, etc.) an unspecified age between thirty and forty (forty and fifty, etc.). *informal* ● The construction '—something' has long (since at least M18) been used in other contexts, such as times or names, in which *something* is a substitute for a detail that is immaterial or not remembered, e.g. 'the five something train' (Baden Powell *Matabele Campaign*, 1896). In L20 *thirty-something* etc. is particularly used to designate a person as a member of a social age-set, assumed to have characteristic interests, aspirations, etc.

SON of a gun a jocular or affectionate way of addressing or referring to someone. *informal* ● With reference to the guns carried aboard ships: the epithet is said to have been applied originally to babies born at sea to women allowed to accompany their husbands.

for a SONG very cheaply. *informal* ● Old ballads were sold cheaply at fairs. *Song* was used by Shakespeare in *All's Well* to mean 'an item of trifling value' and this idiom (or *for an old song*) was current by M17.

| **1985** N. HERMAN *My Kleinian Home* 78 The place was going for a song, since anyone in his right mind would have steered well clear of it.

on SONG performing well; in good form. *Brit., informal* ● Used especially in sports journalism. Its apparent earliest appearance (1967) was as *on full song*, used in the context of a car engine.

| **1996** *Times* [The horse] is in pretty good shape. I rode him out at Haydock and he felt on song.

SONG and dance **1** a fuss or commotion. **2** *N. Amer.* an long explanation that is pointless or deliberately evasive. *informal*

a SOP to Cerberus something offered in propitiation. ●In Greek mythology, Cerberus was the three-headed watchdog which guarded the entrance of Hades. Virgil (*Aeneid*) describes how the Sibyl guiding Aeneas to the underworld threw a drugged cake to Cerberus, thus enabling the hero to pass the monster in safety.

SORCERER's apprentice a person who having instigated a process is unable to control it. ●Translating French *l'apprenti sorcier*, a symphonic poem (1897) by Paul Dukas after *der Zauberlehrling*, a ballad (1797) by Goethe.

stand (*or* stick) out like a SORE thumb be very obviously different from the surrounding people or things.

more in SORROW than in anger with regret or sadness rather than with anger. ●With allusion to Shakespeare's *Hamlet* I. ii, describing the countenance of the ghost of Hamlet's father.

SORT ▶ *see* **separate the MEN from the boys**.

out of SORTS **1** slightly unwell. **2** in low spirits; irritable.

it takes all SORTS people vary greatly in character, tastes, and abilities. *proverbial* ●Often used as a comment on what the speaker feels to be unconventional behaviour. The more complete form of the expression is *it takes all sorts to make a world*.

> **1975** J. I. M. STEWART *Young Pattullo* iii. 'My father's a banker during the week and a country gent at week-ends. Takes all sorts, you know.' 'Takes all sorts?' 'To make a world.'

a lost SOUL **1** a soul that is damned. **2** *chiefly humorous* a person who seems unable to cope with everyday life.

work the SOUL case out of put under severe stress or work very hard.

SOUL ▶ *see* **BARE one's soul**; ▶ *see* **the LIFE and soul of the party**; ▶ *see* **SELL one's soul**.

from SOUP to nuts from beginning to end; completely. *N. Amer., informal* ●From the menu of a formal meal with soup as the first course and nuts and other sweetmeats as the last.

in the SOUP in trouble. *informal* ●Originally L19 US slang.

SOUR grapes an attitude in which someone disparages or affects to despise something because they cannot have it themselves.   ●With allusion to Aesop's fable *The Fox and the Grapes*, in which the fox, unable to reach the grapes, disparages them as being sour. Used of a situation when someone sneers at something which they have recently coveted.

> **1998** *New Scientist* 5 Sept. 54/1 At 66, I can be acquitted of any sour grapes, but I feel sorry for younger MPs … [who] have all been passed over.

down SOUTH to or in the south of a country. *informal* ● Cf. ▶ **up NORTH**.

> **1995** B. BRYSON *Notes from Small Island* (1996) xxvii. 330 'Ah, you're the chap from down south,' he said, remembering, which threw me a little. It isn't often you hear Yorkshire referred to as down south.

have the right SOW by the ear have the correct understanding of a situation. ● Proverbial since M16; also formerly *have the wrong sow by the ear*.

SOW the seed (*or* seeds) of do something which will eventually bring about (a particular result).

SOW ▶ *see* **make a SILK purse out of a sow's ear**.

watch this SPACE used to indicate that further developments are expected and more information will be given later. *informal* ● *Space* is an area of a newspaper available for a specific purpose, especially for advertising. E20.

> **1979** J. RATHBONE *Euro-Killers* iv. 44 Where is he? Watch this space for exciting revelations in the next few days.

call a SPADE a spade speak plainly or bluntly, without avoiding unpleasant or embarrassing issues. ● The ultimate source of this is Plutarch's *Apophthegmata*, where the Greek word for 'basin' is used. Erasmus in translating this into Latin either deliberately or through a misunderstanding used *ligo* 'a mattock'. Udall translated this Erasmus text into English (1542) using 'spade', and it was in this form that the saying became current in English. A colloquial variation on this, used for humorous emphasis, is *call a spade a (bloody) shovel* (E20).

> **1998** *Spectator* 30 May 54/2 [A] man whom I might not agree with where politics are concerned, but one who calls a spade a spade.

in SPADES to a very high degree; as much as or more than could be desired. *informal* ● Originally US. Spades is the highest-ranking suit in the card game bridge.

> **1997** *Times* 28 Nov. 39 (heading) Tears in spades for the queen of hearts.

old SPANISH customs (*or* practices) long-standing though unauthorized or irregular work practices. ● Current in printing circles since at least M20; often used jocularly of practices in the formerly notoriously inefficient British newspaper printing houses in Fleet Street, London.

> **1998** *Spectator* 11 July 22/3 [Outsourcing] can do much for flexibility and more for costs and it is a proven cure for quaint old Spanish customs.

a SPANNER (*or* mainly N. Amer. monkey wrench) in the works an event, person, or thing that prevents the smooth or successful implementation of a plan; a drawback or impediment. ● A *monkey wrench* (M19) is a spanner or wrench with adjustable jaws. *Throwing a monkey wrench in(to) the works* (E20) is thus a metaphor for wrecking plans or activities. The variant with *spanner* is slightly later (M20). Edward Abbey in his anti-technology novel *The Monkey Wrench Gang* (1974) applied the metaphor to systematic industrial sabotage, and *monkey-wrenching* is now a colloquial term for such activity.

> **1997** *Spectator* 8 Nov. 34/3 Pretty well all the newspapers ... are now adversarial in tone, conceiving their basic purpose as throwing spanners in the works almost as a matter of principle.

go SPARE **1** become extremely angry or distraught. *Brit., informal* **2** be unwanted or not needed and therefore available for use.

| **1 1991** R. DOYLE *Van* (1992) 145 Remind me to replace this one … Veronica'll go spare if she goes to get it on Sunday and it's not there.

(and) to SPARE in addition to what is needed; left over.

SPARE ▶ *see* **spare someone's BLUSHES**; ▶ *see* **spare the ROD and spoil the child**.

SPARKS fly a discussion becomes heated or lively.

strike SPARKS off each other (or one another) (of two or more people) creatively inspire each other while working on something.

SPEAK for oneself give one's own opinions.   ●The exclamation *speak for yourself!* indicates to someone that what they have said may apply to themselves but does not apply to others and is resented by them.

SPEAK in tongues speak in an unknown language during religious worship.   ● Speaking in (or with) tongues, the phenomenon known more formally as *glossolalia*, was a practice recorded of the apostles in the Bible (e.g. Acts 10:46, 19:6) and is still a component of charismatic Christian worship.

SPEAK one's mind express one's feelings or opinions frankly.

| **1982** M. Z. BRADLEY *Mists of Avalon* IV. i. 655 Someday she would be too weary or too unguarded to care, and she would speak her mind to the priest.

SPEAK volumes **1** (of a gesture, circumstance, or object) be very expressive (of); convey a great deal (about). **2** be good evidence (for).

| **1 1998** *New Scientist* It was a minor scandal … , but it spoke volumes about the world's shifting relationship with its favourite illicit drug.

SPEAK ▶ *see* **speak of the DEVIL**.

one SPEAKS as one finds one's opinion of someone or something can or should only be based on personal experience. *proverbial* ●Mainly used in situations in which someone's (usually bad) reputation is belied by one's personal experience of that person.

it SPEAKS well for something places someone or something in a favourable light.

on SPEC in the hope of success but without any specific plan or instructions; on the off chance. *informal* ●The colloquial abbreviation of *speculation* to *spec* was originally US, but it has been current in English since E19, and the phrase *on spec* itself is M19.

SPECTRE ▶ *see* **a ghost at the FEAST**.

up to SPEED **1** operating at full speed. **2** (of a person or company) performing at an anticipated rate or level. *informal* **3** (of a person) fully informed or up to date. *informal*

| **2 1998** *Times Magazine* 15 Aug. 55/1 Penati advises on menus and drops in occasionally to check that everything is up to speed. **3 1998** *New Scientist* 28 Mar. 18/2 It's well known to anyone who is up to speed with e-mail.

under someone's SPELL so devoted to someone that they seem to have magic power over one.

SPEND ▶ *see* **spend a PENNY**.

SPIKE someone's guns take steps to thwart someone's intended course of action. *mainly Brit.* ●First recorded in English in L17, the expression then refers literally to the practice of hammering a metal spike into the touch-hole of a captured enemy cannon to render it unusable.

SPILL the beans reveal secret information, especially unintentionally or indiscreetly. *informal* ●Originally E20 US slang.

SPILL one's guts reveal information to someone in a copious and uninhibited way. ●*informal*

SPIN ▶ *see* **spin one's WHEELS**; ▶ *see* **spin a YARN**.

enter into the SPIRIT of join wholeheartedly in (an event). ●Used especially of a celebratory and festive mood.

the SPIRIT is willing (but the flesh is weak) someone has good intentions (but yields to temptation and fails to live up to them). ●Quoting the words of Jesus to his disciples in the Garden of Gethsemane when he found them asleep after he had told them to stay awake (Matthew 26:41).

the SPIRIT moves someone someone feels inclined to do something. ●A phrase originally in Quaker use, with reference to the inspiration of the Holy Spirit.

be the SPIT (or the dead spit) of look exactly like. *informal* ●Cf. the colloquial expression *spitting image*.

SPIT blood (or nails or *Austral.* **chips)** feel or express vehement anger.

SPIT (out) the dummy behave in a bad-tempered or petulant way. *Austral., informal* ●With allusion to the action of a spoilt baby or toddler in spitting out its dummy.

SPIT in the eye (or face) of show contempt or scorn for.

SPIT and polish extreme neatness or smartness. ●From the cleaning and polishing duties of a serviceman.

SPIT and sawdust (of a bar or other place) old-fashioned, run-down, or dirty. *Brit., informal* ●Until M20 the general saloon of a public house would often have sawdust sprinkled on the floor, onto which the clientele would spit. Often as modifier: *spit-and-sawdust*.

SPITTING in (or into) the wind a futile or pointless activity.

make a SPLASH attract a great deal of attention.

> **1996** A. GHOSH *Calcutta Chromosome* (1997) ix. 55 This was just about the time that new sciences like bacteriology and parasitology were beginning to make a splash in Europe.

SPLIT one's sides (N. Amer. *also* **split a gut)** be convulsed with laughter. *informal* ●The expression *to split with laughter* dates from L17. *Side-splitting* (adj.) and *side-splitter* ('a very funny joke or story') are both M19.

SPLIT the ticket (*or* one's vote) vote for candidates of more than one party. *US*

SPLIT the vote (of a candidate or minority party) attract votes from another candidate or party with the result that both are defeated by a third. *Brit.*

SPLIT ▶ *see* split **HAIRS**.

be SPOILT for choice have so many attractive possibilities to choose from that it is difficult to make a selection. *Brit.*

SPOIL ▶ *see* spare the **ROD** and spoil the child; ▶ *see* too many **COOKS** spoil the broth.

put a SPOKE in someone's wheel prevent someone from carrying out a plan. *Brit.* ●It is not clear why a *spoke*, a normal component of many wheels, should have such a deleterious effect, and it has been suggested that *spoke* here is a mistranslation of Dutch *spaak* meaning 'bar' or 'stave', which occurs in the identical Dutch idiom. The idiom and various allusive phrases with *spoke* and *wheel* have been current since E17, although there is a L16 usage with *spoke* and *cog*.

SPONGE ▶ *see* **THROW** in the sponge.

make a SPOON or spoil a horn make a determined effort to achieve something, whatever the cost. *orig. Scottish* ●With reference to the practice of making spoons out of the horns of cattle or sheep.

win the wooden SPOON be the least successful contestant; win the booby prize. ●Originally a wooden spoon presented to the candidate coming last in the Cambridge University mathematical tripos (examination).

SPOON ▶ *see* **GREASY** spoon.

the SPORT of kings horse racing.

a SPORTING chance some possibility of success.

hit the SPOT be exactly what is required. *informal*

put someone on the SPOT force someone into a situation in which they must make a difficult decision or answer a difficult question. *informal*

SPOT ▶ *see* a **BLIND** spot.

SPOTS ▶ *see* **KNOCK** spots off.

up the SPOUT **1** no longer working or likely to be useful or successful. **2** not accurate; wrong. **3** (of a woman) pregnant. *Brit., informal*

a SPRAT to catch a mackerel a small expenditure made, or a small risk taken, in the hope of a large or significant gain. *Brit.* ●A *sprat* is a small marine fish, a *mackerel* rather larger. Current since M19; also with *whale* instead of *mackerel*.

SPREAD oneself too thin be involved in so many different activities or projects that one's time and energy are not used to good effect.

SPREAD ▶ *see* spread like **WILDFIRE**; ▶ *see* spread one's **WINGS**.

SPRING a leak develop a leak. ● Originally a phrase in nautical use, referring to timbers springing out of position.

on the SPUR of the moment on a momentary impulse; without pre-meditation.

> **1988** R. HALL *Kisses of Enemy* (1990) IV. lxxx. 461 Now that was a witticism, an inspiration on the spur of the moment.

SPURS ▶ *see* **WIN one's spurs**.

get SQUARE with pay or compound with (a creditor).

have SQUARE eyes habitually watch television to excess.

on the SQUARE **1** honest(ly), fair(ly). **2** having membership of the Free-masons. ● Sense 1, used especially in the context of gaming, has been current from L17; sense 2 is recorded from L19.

> **1 1997** *Spectator* 29 Nov 14/2 [H]is joke has taken on a whole new meaning. As they say over here [in the US], he may have been kidding on the square.

SQUARE the circle do what is impossible. ● In the literal sense, 'construct a square equal in area to a given circle'; since this problem is incapable of a purely geometrical solution, the phrase has become generally used in the context of attempting the impossible.

SQUARE (noun) ▶ *see* **BACK to square one**.

SQUARE (verb) ▶ *see* **settle ACCOUNTS with**.

put the SQUEEZE on someone coerce or pressurize someone. *informal*

> **1993** J. GREEN *Sex since Sixties* 164 One day two characters walked into my studio and tried to put the squeeze on me for protection money.

SQUEEZE ▶ *see* **squeeze someone until the PIPS squeak**.

SQUIB ▶ *see* **a DAMP squib**.

a STAB in the back a treacherous act or statement; a betrayal. ● *Stab someone in the back* is also used figuratively.

STAB ▶ *see* **a shot in the DARK**.

shut (*or* lock) the STABLE door after the horse has bolted take preventive measures too late. *proverbial* ● A saying known in Middle English and current until L19 with the conclusion ... *after the steed is stolen*.

the odds (*or* cards) are (*or* deck is) STACKED against one circum-stances are such that someone is unlikely to succeed.

hold the STAGE dominate a scene of action or forum of debate.

STAIR-RODS ▶ *see* **RAIN cats and dogs**.

go to the STAKE for do anything to defend a specified belief, opinion, or person. ● With reference to the Roman Catholic Church's former practice of burning heretics at the stake if they refused to recant their opinions.

pull up STAKES (of a person) move or go to live elsewhere. *N. Amer.* ● *Stakes* refers to the pegs or posts securing a tent or put up as a palisade around a temporary settlement.

| **1817** J. K. PAULDING *Letter from South* I. 83 When they have exhausted one hunting-ground, [the Indians] pull up stakes, and incontinently march off to another.

STAKE a claim declare one's right to something. ● With allusion to the practice of putting stakes around the perimeter of a piece of land to which one is laying claim. The expression *stake (out) a claim* was originally US, dating from the Californian gold rush of 1849 when the prospectors registered their claims to individual plots of land in this way.

set out one's STALL make one's position on an issue very clear. *Brit.*

STAND on one's own (two) feet be or become self-reliant or independent.

STAND up and be counted state publicly one's support for someone or something.

STAND ▶ *see* **stand someone in good STEAD**; ▶ *see* **stand out a MILE**; ▶ *see* **stand out like a SORE thumb**; ▶ *see* **stand PAT**.

leave someone/thing STANDING (of a person or thing) be much better or faster than someone or something else.

STANDS ▶ *see* **it stands to REASON**.

someone's STAR is rising someone is becoming ever more successful or popular.

reach for the STARS have high or ambitious aims.

see STARS see flashes of light, especially as a result of being hit on the head.

have STARS in one's eyes be idealistically hopeful or enthusiastic, especially about one's future in entertainment or sport.

take the STARCH out of someone shake someone's confidence, especially by humiliating them. *US* ● Cf. ▶ **knock the STUFFING out of someone**.

be STARING someone in the face (of a fact or object) be right in front of someone; close enough to be very obvious to someone.

be STARING something in the face (of a person) be on the verge of defeat, death, or ruin.

START ▶ *see* **start a HARE**.

under STARTER's orders waiting to start. *informal* ● Used literally of horses, runners, or other competitors ready to start a race on receiving the signal from the starter. Sometimes with preposition *for* and the name of the destination.

STATE of the art the most recent stage in the development of a product, incorporating the newest ideas and the most up-to-date features. ● Often as modifier *state-of-the-art*.

STATE of grace a condition of being free from sin. ● Originally and especially a Christian concept. Cf. ▶ **fall from GRACE**.

STATE of play **1** the score at a particular time in a cricket or football match. **2** the current situation in an ongoing process, especially one involving opposing or competing parties. *Brit.*

STAY the course (*or* distance) **1** hold out to the end of a race or contest. **2** pursue a difficult task or activity to the end.

a STAY of execution a delay in carrying out a court order. ●M18.
| *figurative*

STAY put (of a person or object) remain somewhere without moving or being moved.
| **1994** *Sunday Times: Style & Travel* VIII. 49/4 Despite firm intentions to explore, campers tend to stay put, especially if there are lots of activities and a good pool.

STAY ▶ *see* **stay one's HAND**; ▶ *see* **hang LOOSE**.

stand someone in good STEAD (of something learned or acquired) be advantageous or useful to someone over time or in the future.

STEADY as she goes keep on with the same careful progress. *informal*
●In nautical parlance *steady* is the instruction to the helmsman to keep the ship on the same course.
| **1998** *Bookseller* 3 Apr. 12/1 [H]is boss set him one task: 'steady as she goes, but more so'.

go STEADY have a regular romantic or sexual relationship with a particular person. *orig. US, informal*
| **1905** E. WHARTON *House of Mirth* II. xiii. 493 I thought we were to be married: he'd gone steady with me six months and given me his mother's wedding ring.

STEAL someone blind rob or cheat someone in a comprehensive or merciless way. *informal*

STEAL someone's clothes appropriate someone's ideas or policies. *Brit., informal*

STEAL a march on gain an advantage over someone, typically by acting before they do.

STEAL the show attract the most attention and praise.

STEAL someone's thunder win praise for oneself by pre-empting someone else's attempt to impress. ●The critic and playwright John Dennis (1657–1734) invented a new method of simulating the sound of thunder in the theatre, which he employed in his unsuccessful play *Appius and Virginia*. Shortly after his play had finished its brief run, Dennis attended a performance of *Macbeth* in which the improved thunder effect was used, and he is reported to have exclaimed in a fury: 'Damn them! They will not let my play run, but they steal my thunder.'

get up (*or* pick up) STEAM **1** generate enough pressure to drive a steam engine. **2** (of a project, plan, or process in its early stages) gradually gain more impetus and driving force.

have STEAM coming out of one's ears be extremely angry or irritated. *informal*

let (or blow) off STEAM get rid of pent-up energy or emotion. *informal* ● With allusion to the release of excess steam from a steam engine through a valve.

run out of (or lose) STEAM lose impetus or enthusiasm. *informal*

> **1992** J. TORRINGTON *Swing Hammer Swing!* v. 39 Eventually I ran out of steam and came to a halt.

under one's own STEAM without assistance from others. ● Used especially in the context of travelling somewhere.

STEER ▶ *see* **steer a MIDDLE course**.

from STEM to stern from the front to the back, especially of a ship.

mind (or watch) one's STEP be careful.

STEP on it (or *orig. US* **on the gas) 1** make a motor vehicle go faster by pressing down on the accelerator pedal with one's foot. **2** hurry up. *informal*

STEP out of line behave inappropriately or disobediently.

STEP ▶ *see* **step into the BREACH**; ▶ *see* **TREAD on someone's toes**.

be made of STERNER stuff (of a person) have a stronger character and be more able to overcome problems than others.   ● From Shakespeare's *Julius Caesar* (ii. 93), with reference to ambition.

> **1998** *Spectator* 29 Aug. 7/1 Unlike the Americans, who are inclined to pull all their personnel out of a country at the first hint of trouble, the British foreign service is made of sterner stuff.

STEW in one's own juice suffer the unpleasant consequences of one's own actions or temperament without the consoling intervention of others. *informal*

a STICK to beat someone/thing (with) a fact or argument used to hold over someone or something as a threat or an advantage.

STICK at nothing allow nothing to deter one from achieving one's aim, even if it means acting wrongly or dishonestly.

STICK it to someone treat someone harshly or severely. *chiefly US, informal*

STICK one (or it) on someone hit someone. *informal*

STICK one's neck out risk incurring criticism, anger, or danger by acting or speaking boldly. *informal* ● In 1926 the University of Virginia magazine described this expression as 'Absolutely original slang at the University of Virginia'.

> **1969** B. HEAD *When Rain Clouds Gather* (1989) iv. 60 Things are so bad that if anyone sticks his neck out for a refugee, he's not likely to get promoted for five years.

STICK to one's ribs (of food) be very filling.

STICK to someone's fingers (of money) be embezzled by a person. *informal* ● Also, referring to a dishonest person: *have sticky fingers*.

STICK it on 1 make high charges. **2** tell an exaggerated story. ● *informal*

STICK one's chin out show firmness or fortitude.

STICK ▶ *see* **stick one's BIB in**; ▶ *see* **stick in one's THROAT**; ▶ *see* **stick in one's CRAW**; ▶ *see* **stick in one's GIZZARD**; ▶ *see* **stick one's OAR in**; ▶ *see* **stand out a MILE**; ▶ *see* **stand out like a SORE thumb**; ▶ *see* **stick to one's GUNS**.

in the STICKS in a remote rural area. *informal* ●Originally E20 US.

up STICKS go to live elsewhere. *Brit., informal* ●Cf. ▶ **pull up STAKES**.

STICKY ▶ *see* **a sticky WICKET**.

a STIFF upper lip a quality of uncomplaining stoicism. ●A characteristic particularly associated with the British, although the phrase is apparently M19 N. Amer. in origin (it is used for example in Harriet Beecher Stowe's *Uncle Tom's Cabin* (1852)).

| **1998** *Spectator* 7 Feb. 12/2 The Princess, … as her final gift to the British people, had unstarched their stiff upper lips.

STILL small voice the voice of one's conscience. ●With allusion to the voice of God as described in 1 Kings 19:12.

STILL waters run deep a quiet or placid manner may conceal a passionate nature. *proverbial* ●A commonplace in English since the Middle Ages. Cf. Latin *Adjicit deinde, quod apud Bactrianos vulgo usurpantur: … altissima quaeque flumina minimo sono labi* he then added what is commonly said among the Bactrians … that the deepest rivers glide with least sound (Quintus Curtius *De Rebus Gestis Alexandri Magni* VII. iv. 13).

STING in the tail an unpleasant or problematic end to something.

| **1992** R. WRIGHT *Stolen Continents* (1993) v. 132 At last Hendrick came to the sting in the tail of his speech.

like STINK extremely hard or intensely. *informal*

STIR one's stumps (of a person) begin to move or act. *Brit., informal, dated* ●*Stump* is used jocularly for 'leg'. The collocation of *stir* and *stumps* dates from M16.

STIR ▶ *see* **LIFT a finger**.

in STITCHES laughing uncontrollably. *informal* ●*Stitch*, in the sense of 'a sudden localized jabbing pain' such as might be caused by a needle, is recorded from Old English. It is now generally used of a muscle spasm in the side caused especially by exertion. Shakespeare seems to have been the first to note *stitches* brought on by laughter; in *Twelfth Night* (1601) Maria invites her fellow conspirators to observe the love-lorn Malvolio with the words: 'If you … will laugh yourselves into stitches, follow me.'

| **1981** D. M. THOMAS *White Hotel* IV. i. 139 She had them in stitches with her absurd—but true—anecdotes.

a STITCH in time if you sort out a problem immediately, it may save a lot of extra work later. *proverbial* ●With allusion to the old (M18) couplet *a stitch in time saves nine*. *Nine* here has no particular significance as a number but is used for assonance.

put (*or* take) STOCK in believe or have faith in. ● Often with negative.

> *1870 MARK TWAIN in *Galaxy* Oct. 575/1 The 'chance' theory ... is ... calculated to inflict ... pecuniary loss upon any community that takes stock in it.

take STOCK review or make an assessment of a particular situation, typically as a prelude to making a decision. ● Literally, 'make an inventory of the merchandise in a shop'.

on the STOCKS in construction or preparation. ● Used literally since E15 in shipbuilding: the *stocks* were the wooden frame or scaffolding used to support a ship while it was being built.

an army marches on its STOMACH soldiers or workers can only fight or function effectively if they have been well fed. ● The saying has been attributed to both Frederick the Great and Napoleon I, more particularly the latter in that it paraphrases a long passage in E. A. de Las Cases' *Mémorial de Ste-Hélène* (1823).

on a full (*or* an empty) STOMACH having (*or* without having) eaten beforehand.

a strong STOMACH an ability to see or do unpleasant things without feeling sick or squeamish.

pick up STOMPIES break into a conversation of which one has heard only the end. *S. Afr.* ● A *stompie* is Afrikaans for a cigarette butt.

be carved (*or* set *or* written) in (*or* on) (tablets of) STONE be fixed and unchangeable. ● The allusion is to the biblical Ten Commandments, written on tablets of stone by God and handed down to Moses on Mount Sinai (Genesis 31:18). Mainly used to emphasize that particular rules or ways of doing things are absolutely inflexible.

cast (*or* throw) the first STONE be the first to accuse or criticize. ● With reference to the incident in the New Testament when a group of men preparing to stone to death an adulterous woman were addressed by Jesus with the words, 'He that is without sin among you, let him first cast a stone at her' (John 8:7). Also more generally, *cast a stone* or *throw stones*. Cf. the proverb *those who live in glass houses shouldn't throw stones*.

leave no STONE unturned try every possible course of action in order to achieve something.

a STONE's throw a short distance.

> 1989 J. TROLLOPE *Village Affairs* viii. 111 Can't tell you the difference it will make, having you a stone's throw away.

STONE ▶ *see* **have kissed the BLARNEY stone**; ▶ *see* **mark with a WHITE stone**.

fall on STONY ground (of words or a suggestion) be ignored or badly received. ● With allusion to the biblical parable of the sower (Mark 4:3–20, esp. verse 5).

fall between two STOOLS fail to be or to take one of two satisfactory alternatives. *Brit.* ● With allusion to the proverb *between two stools one falls to the ground*. The proverb was known to Gower (*Confessio Amantis*, (c.1390): 'Thou

farst as he betwen tuo stoles That wolde sitte and goth to grounde'. (iv. 626))
and also existed in medieval Latin and in E16 German.

pull out all the STOPS make a very great effort; go to elaborate lengths. ●With
allusion to the stops of an organ. An E20 colloquialism, but earlier in figurative use by Matthew Arnold who refers in the Preface to *Essays in Criticism*
(1865) to making himself unpopular by trying 'to pull out a few more stops
in that ... somewhat narrow-toned organ, the modern Englishman'.

STOP at nothing recognize no obstacles or reasons for not doing something;
be utterly ruthless or determined.

> **1991** *Time* 11 Feb. 36/1 Seen simplistically and from afar, Saddam Hussein comes across as
> ... the villain who will stop at nothing.

STOP one's ears **1** put one's fingers in one's ears to avoid hearing. **2** refuse
to listen. ●Cf. Psalm 58:4 'the deaf adder that stoppeth her ear'.

STOP a gap serve to meet a temporary need. ●Also *stopgap* noun and adjective.

STOP someone's mouth induce a person by bribery or other means to keep
silent about something.

STOP the show (of a performer) provoke prolonged applause or laughter,
causing an interruption.

put a (*or* the) STOPPER on cause something to end or become quiet.

set (*or* lay *or* put) STORE by (*or* on) consider (something) to be of importance
or value, especially to a specified degree.

go down a STORM be enthusiastically received by an audience.

the lull (*or* calm) before the STORM a period of unusual tranquillity or
stability that seems likely to presage difficult times.

a STORM in a teacup (*or* N. Amer. a tempest in a teapot) great anger or
excitement about a trivial matter.

> **1998** *Times* 3 July 31/1 A storm in a teacup? Who cares about a bunch of seeds?

take something by STORM have great and rapid success in a particular place
or with a particular group of people. ●From literally capturing a military
objective by a sudden and violent attack.

> **1998** *Times* 3 July 31/6 Round-up Ready soya has taken America by storm.

— up a STORM do something with great enthusiasm and energy. *chiefly N. Amer.*

end of STORY (that's) the end of the matter. *informal* ●Used to emphasize that
there is nothing more to add on the subject just mentioned.

> **1998** *Times* 20 May 48/5 Parents are role models. Footballers are picked for teams because
> they are good at football. End of story.

it's (*or* that's) the STORY of one's life something disagreeable or disappointing keeps on happening. *informal* ●Used to complain that a particular
misfortune recurs in one's experience.

to cut (*or* N. Amer. make) a long STORY short to make a rapid conclusion
to an account of events.

a **STOUT heart** courage or determination. *literary* ● Cf. also the E18 Scottish proverb *put a stout heart to a stey brae* (i.e. steep hillside).

slave over a hot STOVE work very hard preparing a meal. *informal* ● Often used humorously.

keep a STRAIGHT face not show any facial expression, even though one is amused.

the STRAIGHT and narrow morally correct behaviour. ● Used elliptically for *the straight and narrow path* or *way*. A misunderstanding of Matthew 7:14 'strait is the gate, and narrow is the way, which leadeth unto life'.

a **STRAIGHT fight** a contest between just two opponents, especially in an election. *Brit.*

STRAIGHT from the shoulder   **1** (of a blow) well delivered.   **2** (of a verbal attack) frank or direct.

STRAIGHT off (*or* out) without hesitation, deliberation, etc. *informal*

STRAIGHT up truthfully, honestly. *chiefly N. Amer., informal*
> **1994** I. WELSH 'Shooter' in *Acid House* 2 Naw, this is legit. Straight up, I smiled. My bullshit was authentic enough to give Gary confidence.

STRAIGHT ▶ *see* **a straight ARROW**; ▶ *see* **straight as a DIE**.

STRAIN at a gnat make a difficulty about accepting something trivial. *literary* ● With allusion to Matthew 23:24 'Ye blind guides, which strain at a gnat, and swallow a camel'. Even if the second half of the biblical quotation is not made explicit, the contexts in which *strain at a gnat* is used generally imply that the person concerned has already *swallowed a camel*.

STRAIN at the leash be eager to begin or do something. ● With allusion to a dog pulling on its lead in its eagerness to get free to run or hunt something. Often with present participle: *straining at the leash*.

STRAIN ▶ *see* **strain every NERVE**.

draw the short STRAW be the unluckiest of a group of people, especially in being chosen to perform an unpleasant task. ● With allusion to a method of drawing lots that involves holding several straws of varying lengths with one end concealed in the hand and inviting other members of the group to take one each.

the last (*or* **final**) **STRAW** a slight addition to a difficulty or annoyance that ultimately makes it unbearable.   ● With allusion to the proverb *the last straw breaks the* (*laden*) *camel's back*. The modern version of the proverb is traceable to Dickens in *Dombey and Son* (1848), but the idea antedates this; for example, an M17 version refers to *the last feather breaking a horse's back*.

a **STRAW in the wind** a slight but significant hint of future developments. ● From the action of throwing a straw up into the air to test which way the wind is blowing. 'Straws served to show which way the wind blows' was described by William Cobbett in *Porcupine's Works* (1799) as 'an old hackneyed proverb'.

clutch (or grasp or catch) at STRAWS (or a straw) do, say, or believe anything, however unlikely or inadequate, which seems to offer hope in a desperate situation. ● Originally with reference to the proverb *a drowning man will clutch at a straw*, recorded in various forms since M16.

STRAWS in one's hair a state of insanity. ● Formerly a supposed characteristic of a deranged person as straw was put on the floor of a madhouse.

like a STREAK (of lightning) very fast. *informal*

against (or with) the STREAM against (or with) the prevailing view or tendency.

on STREAM in or into operation or existence; available. ● Cf. ▶ **on TAP**.

not in the same STREET far inferior in terms of ability. *Brit., informal*

STREETS ahead greatly superior. *Brit., informal*
> **1991** A. CAMPBELL *Sidewinder* vii. 94 He has his shortcomings, sure, but he's streets ahead of Dr Nada.

up (or right up) one's STREET (or N. Amer. alley) well suited to one's tastes, interests, or abilities. *informal*

go from STRENGTH to strength develop or progress with increasing success. ● Perhaps originally with allusion to Psalm 84:7.

a tower (or pillar) of STRENGTH a person who can be relied upon to be a source of strong support and comfort. ● Perhaps originally alluding to the Book of Common Prayer 'O Lord ... be unto them a tower of strength'.

STRENGTHEN someone's hand (or hands) enable or encourage a person to act more vigorously or effectively.

at full STRETCH **1** with a part of one's body fully extended. **2** using the maximum amount of one's resources or energy.

at a STRETCH **1** in one continuous period. **2** with much effort or difficulty.

by no (or not by any) STRETCH of the imagination (something is) definitely not the case. ● Used for emphasis.

STRETCH one's legs go for a short walk, typically after sitting in one place for some time.

STRETCH a point allow or do something not usually acceptable, typically as a result of particular circumstances.

STRETCH ▶ *see* **stretch one's WINGS**.

STRICKEN in years (of a person) old and feeble. ● Used in several passages of the Bible (e.g. Joshua 13:1). Used euphemistically and now somewhat dated.

take something in one's STRIDE deal with something difficult or unpleasant in a calm and competent way. ● Also literally, 'clear (an obstacle) without changing one's gait to jump'.

STRIKE it rich find a source of abundance or success. *informal*

STRIKE lucky (or strike it lucky) have a lucky success. *Brit.*

STRIKE oil attain prosperity or success.

> **1994** *Nature* 24 Nov. 315/2 S. P. Goldman ... seems to have struck oil in the search for better ways of computing electronic states.

STRIKE while the iron is hot act promptly at a good opportunity. ●With reference to the process of working iron at a blacksmith's forge: the metal can only be hammered into shape while it is hot.

STRIKE ▶ *see* **strike at the ROOT of**.

STRIKING ▶ *see* **within striking DISTANCE**.

have a second STRING to one's bow have an alternative resource that one can make use of if the first one fails. *Brit.* ●A metaphor from shooting with a bow and arrow, most commonly in this form with *second string*, but also in other related expressions, e.g., *have several strings to one's bow*. Hence *a second string* (M17) is a person or thing regarded as a second choice.

how long is a piece of STRING? something by its nature cannot be measured or quantified. *informal* ●Used a rejoinder to indicate that it is unreasonable for someone to expect the speaker to be more precise about something.

on a STRING under one's control or influence. ●The idea is of a puppeteer controlling a puppet through its strings.

no STRINGS attached no special conditions or restrictions apply to an offer or opportunity. *informal*

STRINGS ▶ *see* **PULL strings**; ▶ *see* **PULL the strings**.

not (or never) do a STROKE (of work) do no work at all. ●Often shortened to *not do a stroke*, with *of work* understood.

put someone off their STROKE disconcert someone so that they do not work or perform as well as they might; break the pattern or rhythm of someone's work.

STROKE of genius an outstandingly brilliant and original idea.

STROKE of luck (or good luck) a fortunate occurrence that could not have been predicted or expected.

STROKE someone (or someone's hair) the wrong way irritate a person.

different STROKES for different folks different things please or are effective with different people. *chiefly US*, *informal* ●Used as a slogan in the early 1970s in a Texan drug abuse project.

come it STRONG indulge in exaggeration. *Brit.*, *informal*

come on STRONG **1** behave aggressively or assertively. **2** make great efforts or advances. *informal*

going STRONG continuing to be healthy, vigorous, or successful. *informal*

STRONG on **1** good at; expert in. **2** possessing large quantities of; rich in.

STRONG meat ideas or language likely to be found unacceptably forceful or extreme. *Brit.*

STRUT one's stuff display one's ability; dance or behave in a lively, expressive way. *informal* ● Originally E20 US slang, now used more widely.

| **1998** *Country Life* 4 June 85/1 London is a place to hide in, to get lost in; New York is a stage on which to strut your stuff.

in a brown STUDY in a reverie; absorbed in one's thoughts. ● The earliest sense of *brown* in English is simply 'dark' (cf. ▶ **BROWN as a berry**), hence 'dusky' or 'gloomy'.

| *1532 Dice-play* 6 Lack of company will soon lead a man into a brown study.

STUFF ▶ *see* **a BIT of stuff**.

knock (or take) the STUFFING out of someone severely impair someone's confidence or strength. *informal* ● Cf. ▶ **take the STARCH out of someone**.

beyond the black STUMP beyond the limits of settled, and therefore civilized, life. *Austral.* ● From the use of a fire-blackened stump as a marker when giving directions to travellers.

on the STUMP going about the country making political speeches or canvassing. *orig. US* ● In rural America in L18 the *stump* of a felled tree was used as an impromptu platform for an orator. In Britain the expression tends to be mildly derogatory, but this is not necessarily the case in the US.

up a STUMP in a situation too difficult for one to manage. *US*

SUCK someone dry exhaust someone's physical, material, or emotional resources.

SUCK it and see the only way to know if something will work or be suitable is to try it. *Brit., informal*

(all) of a SUDDEN quickly and unexpectedly; suddenly. ● *Sudden* as a noun is now found only in this phrase, but was formerly (M16–E18) used in the sense of 'unexpected danger, emergency'. The variant form of the phrase *on a sudden* is now archaic.

SUFFER fools gladly be patient or tolerant towards people one regards as unwise or unintelligent. ● With allusion to 2 Corinthians 11:19. Usually with negative.

SUGAR ▶ *see* **sugar the PILL**.

SUIT the action to the word carry out one's stated intentions at once. ● With allusion to Hamlet's instructions to the actors in Shakespeare's *Hamlet* III. ii: 'suit the action to the word, the word to the action'.

SUIT someone down to the ground be extremely convenient or appropriate for a particular person. *Brit.*

SUIT ▶ *see* **FOLLOW suit**.

SUITS ▶ *see* **MEN in suits**.

SUMMER ▶ *see* **INDIAN summer**.

the SUN is over the yard-arm it is the time of day when it is permissible to drink alcohol. *slang* ● Alluded to by Kipling (L19) as a British naval expression.

| **1992** A. LAMBERT *Rather English Marriage* (1993) iii. 50 'Have a snifter? Sun's over the yard-arm, as they say in the senior service.'

under the SUN on earth; in existence. ● From Ecclesiastes 1:3, 9, and *passim*. Used for emphasis.

someone's SUN is set the time of someone's prosperity is over.

SUN ▶ *see* **CATCH the sun**; ▶ *see* **make HAY while the sun shines**.

SUNNY SIDE up (of an egg) fried on one side only. *N. Amer.*

SUNSET ▶ *see* **RIDE off into the sunset**.

SUP ▶ *see* **sup with the DEVIL**.

sing for one's SUPPER do a service in order to earn a benefit or favour. ● After the nursery rhyme *Little Tommy Tucker*.

(as) SURE as eggs is eggs (*also* **sure as fate)** without any doubt; absolutely certain. ● In L17 in the form *as sure as eggs be eggs*. The non-standard form of the verb is found in Thomas Hughes's *Tom Brown's Schooldays* (1857).

SURE thing **1** a certainty. **2** *informal* certainly; of course. ● In sense 2 used in North America as an exclamation to indicate agreement or acquiescence.

SURF the net explore the resources of the international computer network by browsing at will through the available sources for information or entertainment. ● *Surf* here is from *channel-surfing*, the practice of switching between channels on a television set to discover things of interest.

SURVIVAL of the fittest the continued existence of organisms which are best adapted to their environment, with the extinction of others, as a concept in the Darwinian theory of evolution. ● The phrase was coined by the English philosopher and sociologist Herbert Spencer (1820–1903) in *Principles of Biology* (1865). Besides its formal scientific use, the phrase is often used loosely and jocularly in contexts relating to physical fitness (or lack of it).

on SUSS on suspicion of having committed a crime. ● *Suss* (earlier (M20) and more correctly spelt *sus*) is the abbreviation of *suspicion*. In Britain until 1981 there was a law (nicknamed the *sus law*), effective since the Vagrancy Act of 1824, that allowed the police to arrest a person on suspicion that they were likely to commit a crime.

one SWALLOW doesn't make a summer a single instance or indicator of something is not necessarily significant. ● Cf. Latin *una hirundo non facit ver* one swallow does not make spring (Erasmus *Adages* I. vii), translating the Greek of Aristotle (*Nicomachean Ethics* I. 7. 16). Proverbial in English since M16. Used mainly to caution that a single auspicious event doesn't mean that what follows will also be good (but cf. quot.).

| **1998** *Spectator* 14 Mar. 16/3 One swallow doesn't make a summer, ... nor one instance of police dereliction of duty, incompetence, laziness and stupidity a complete breakdown in law and order.

cut a SWATHE through pass through something causing great damage, destruction, or change. ● A *swath(e)* was the area cut by a sweep of a mower's scythe, hence the width of a strip of grass or corn thus cut.

SWEAR blind (*or* N. Amer. **swear up and down)** affirm something in an emphatic manner. *Brit.*, *informal*

SWEAR like a trooper swear a great deal. ● A *trooper* was originally (M17) a private soldier in a cavalry unit. Troopers were proverbial for coarse behaviour and bad language at least as early as M18 (a version of this simile was used by Richardson in *Pamela*, 1739–40). Cf. ▶ **LIE like a trooper**.

by the SWEAT of one's brow by one's own hard work, typically manual labour. ● Cf. God's sentence on Adam after the Fall, condemning him to toil for his food: 'In the sweat of thy face shalt thou eat bread' (Genesis 3:19).

don't SWEAT it don't worry. ● *US*

no SWEAT without any difficulty or problem. *informal* ● Often as an exclamation of confidence or reassurance.

SWEAT blood 1 make an extraordinarily strenuous effort to do something. **2** be extremely anxious. ● *informal*

SWEAT bullets be extremely anxious or nervous. *N. Amer.*, *informal*

SWEAT it out 1 endure an unpleasant experience, typically one involving extreme physical exertion in great heat. **2** wait in a state of extreme anxiety for something to happen or be resolved. *informal*

SWEAT the small stuff worry about trival things. *US*

SWEAT ▶ *see* **sweat one's GUTS out**.

SWEEP the board win all the money in a gambling game; win all possible prizes etc.

SWEEP (noun) ▶ *see* **make a CLEAN sweep**.

SWEEP (verb) ▶ *see* **sweep something under the CARPET**.

keep someone SWEET keep somone well disposed towards oneself, especially by favours or bribery. *informal*

she's SWEET all's well. *Austral.*, *informal*
| **1964** K. TENNANT *Summer's Tales* 67 'Everything O.K.?' 'Yep,' said the scrawny man beneath us. 'She's sweet.'

SWEET Fanny Adams absolutely nothing at all. *informal* ● Fanny Adams was the youthful victim in a famous murder case in 1867; her body was cut up by the murderer, which gave rise to the naval slang use of her name to refer to tinned meat, esp. mutton. *Sweet Fanny Adams* is often abbreviated in speech to *sweet FA*, which is vulgarly understood to be a euphemism for *sweet fuck all*.

the SWEET spot A particularly fortunate or beneficial circumstance or factor. ● Alluding to the point on the tennis racket believed by players to deliver the maximum power to the ball when it is hit off that point. In 1997 a physicist in Australia claimed to have disproved its existence.
| **1997** *Times* 5 Sept. 27 Enjoy the 'sweet spot' now, but don't expect a boom.

SWEETEN ▶ *see* **sugar the PILL**.

SWEETNESS and light **1** social or political harmony. **2** reasonable and peaceable behaviour. ●A phrase used by Swift in *The Battle of the Books* (1704) and taken up by Matthew Arnold: 'The pursuit of perfection, then, is the pursuit of sweetness and light' (*Culture and Anarchy*, 1869).

in the SWIM involved in or aware of current affairs or events. ●This metaphorical use of *swim* dates from M19.

SWIM ▶ *see* **go with the TIDE**.

get (back) into the SWING of things get used to (*or* return to) being easy and relaxed about an activity or routine one is engaged in. *informal*

in full SWING (of an activity) proceeding vigorously. ●*Swing* occurs in various colloquial expressions indicating brisk or lively activity (cf. ▶ **get into the SWING**, ▶ **go with a SWING**). *Full swing* was in use earlier (M19) as an adverbial phrase meaning 'at full speed'.

go with a SWING (of a party or other event) be lively and enjoyable. *informal*

SWING the lead malinger; shirk one's duty. *Brit., informal* ●*Lead* here is probably a sounding-lead suspended on a line to test the depth of water, with the notion of influencing the result shown. An E20 armed forces expression, it is one of a number of idioms depending on the idea of the inertness of lead; cf. ▶ **get the LEAD out**. Hence also the nouns *lead-swinging* and *lead-swinger*.

SWINGS and roundabouts a situation affording no eventual gain or loss, whatever action is taken. *Brit.* ●From the proverbial saying *you lose on the swings what you gain on the roundabouts*.

> **1983** P. LIVELY *Perfect Happiness* (1985) xi. 137 I have always reckoned on a fair share of that—swings and roundabouts, rough with smooth.

have a SWOLLEN head be conceited. ●Also in this metaphorical use *swelled head* (L19–E20).

SWOOP ▶ *see* **at one FELL swoop**.

SWORD of Damocles an imminent danger. ●When the courtier Damocles called Dionysius I, tyrant of Syracuse (405–367 BC), the happiest of men, Dionysius gave the flatterer a graphic demonstration of the fragility of a ruler's happiness: he invited Damocles to a banquet in the middle of which he looked up to see a naked sword suspended over his head by a single hair.

he who lives by the SWORD dies by the sword those who commit violent acts must expect to suffer violence themselves. *proverbial* ●Originally with allusion to the incident in the Garden of Gethsemane, when Jesus rebuked the disciple who cut off the ear of one of those who had come to arrest him: 'all they that take the sword shall perish with the sword' (Matthew 26:52). In contemporary versions *sword* is sometimes replaced by *gun*, *bomb*, etc.

put to the SWORD kill, especially in war.

SWORD ▶ *see* **a DOUBLE-EDGED sword**.

beat (*or* turn) SWORDS into ploughshares devote resources to peaceful rather than aggressive or warlike ends. ● With allusion to the biblical image of God's peaceful rule: 'they shall beat their swords into plowshares, and their spears into pruninghooks' (Isaiah 2:4).

SWORDS ▶ *see* **CROSS swords**.

SYDNEY or the bush all or nothing. *Austral.*

in words of one SYLLABLE using very simple language; expressed plainly. ● Often in the context of stressing a message that is unwelcome to the hearer.

in (*or* out of) SYNC working well (*or* badly) together; in (*or* out of) agreement. ● *Sync* is the abbreviation of *synchronization*. An E20 US abbreviation used in various technical contexts and now in more general use. Also spelt *synch* and *sink*.

get something out of one's SYSTEM get rid of a preoccupation or anxiety. *informal*

| **1988** E. SEGAL *Doctors* xxiv. 382 First she let her get the crying out of her system.

all SYSTEMS go everything functioning properly, so ready to proceed. ● Originally M20 US, used especially of the systems on a spacecraft.

T

to a T exactly; to perfection. *informal* ● Also in the form *to a tee*. The origin of this idiom (first recorded from L17) is disputed, and attempts to link *T* with either a golfer's tee or a builder's T-square are unconvincing. The underlying idea may be that of completing the letter T by putting in the cross-stroke, but the earlier (E17) expression *to a tittle*, now rarely heard, was identical in meaning, and it is possible that *T* may be an abbreviation of *tittle*.

| **1898** C. G. ROBERTSON *Voces Academicae* 29 SECOND SLEEK YOUNG CURATE I came here— FIRST SLEEK YOUNG CURATE To see the dear old Warden. My case to a T.

pick up the TAB pay for something. *chiefly N. Amer., informal* ● Used literally in the sense of picking up a bill or account that has been presented to one, as after a restaurant meal, with the intention of paying it, but also used figuratively of taking financial responsibility for something.

lay something on the TABLE **1** make something known so that it can be freely and sensibly discussed. **2** *chiefly US* postpone something indefinitely. ●If something is *on the table* it is offered for discussion. Cf. ▶ **on the TAPIS**.

under the TABLE drunk to the point of unconsciousness. *informal* ●Also ▶ **DRINK someone under the table**.

| **1921* W. S. MAUGHAM *Trembling of Leaf* 28 Walker had always been a heavy drinker, he was proud of his capacity to see men half his age under the table.

turn the TABLES reverse one's position relative to someone else, especially by turning a position of disadvantage into one of advantage. ● Until M18 *tables* was the usual name for the boardgame backgammon. Early instances of the use of this phrase (M17) make it clear that it comes from the turning of the board so that a player has to play what had hitherto been their opponent's position. With preposition *on*.

keep TABS (*or* a tab) on monitor the activities or development of; keep under observation. *informal* ●A figurative use of *tab* in the sense of 'account' (cf. the US sense 'bill' in ▶ **pick up the TAB**). Originally a L19 US colloquialism.

| **1978** M. PUZO *Fools Die* ii. 18Jordan knew that Merlyn the Kid kept tabs on everything he did.

a piece of old TACKIE an easy task. *S. Afr., informal* ●*Tackies* are plimsolls. Alternative spellings are *takkie*, *tack(e)y*, *teckie*, and *tekkie*; the last two reflect an Afrikaans or strong South African English accent, and the *-ie* endings suggest that the word is considered to be Afrikaans. However, its origins are uncertain, though there may be a connection with the English adjective *tacky*, meaning 'slightly sticky', perhaps referring to the effect on the plimsolls' rubber soles of extreme heat.

| **1979** *Cape Times* 18 Dec. 2 Getting the news of the Zimbabwe Rhodesian ceasefire to the ... guerilas might well make Paul Revere's famous midnight ride look like a piece of old tackie.

tread TACKIE drive; accelerate. *S. Afr.* ● See preceding entry.

> **1989** *Daily Dispatch* 13 May 8 By the time they finally trod tackie on the road out, a full week had gone by.

TACKS ▶ *see* **come down to BRASS tacks**.

TAG, rag, and bobtail the rabble. ● A *bobtail* (E17) is a horse or dog with a docked tail. *Tag* and *rag* express the same idea of 'tatters'. Thus literally the phrase means 'people in ragged clothes and their curs'. It has occurred since M17 in various forms; also *rag, tag, and bobtail*, *tagrag and bobtail*.

chase one's (own) TAIL keep on doing something futile. *informal* ● Like a puppy or kitten going round in circles in a futile effort to catch its own tail.

the TAIL wags the dog the less important or subsidiary factor or thing dominates a situation; the usual roles are reversed. ● Generally as noun phrase (see quot.).

> **1997** *Spectator* 29 Nov. 63/1 What is wrong is the almost total lack of artistic leadership, the administrative tail wagging the dog.

with one's TAIL between one's legs in a state of dejection or humiliation. *informal* ● With reference to the action of a frightened, hurt, or unhappy dog.

with one's TAIL up in a confident or cheerful mood. *informal* ● With reference to the attitude of a happy or excited dog.

TAIL ▶ *see* **a PIECE of ass**.

on the TAKE taking bribes. *slang*

> **1990** M. TORGOV *St. Farb's Day* ii. 168 I seen plenty of cops drive Mercedes. The ones that're on the take.

TAKE apart **1** beat or defeat conclusively. **2** criticize severely. *informal* ● These two M20 figurative senses are hyperbolical extensions of the literal sense of 'dismantle'.

TAKE (it) as read accept (something) without reading or discussing. *Brit.* ● Used in connection with the minutes of a meeting if a subsequent meeting does not consider it worth reading them out in the full.

TAKE the biscuit (*or* bun *or* cake) be the most remarkable. *informal* ● *Biscuit*, *bun*, and *cake* here are all metaphorical for 'the prize'. The *cake* (M19 US *cakes*, now obsolete) version is earlier than the one with *biscuit* (E20); *take the bun* is L19 US. (*Biscuit* in North American usage (since E19) can be taken to mean a 'small round cake', so the two are more closely synonymous in US English than they are in British.) All these phrases tend to be used in contexts indicating surprise or irritation.

> **1925** P. G. WODEHOUSE *Letter* 30 Mar. (1990) i. 38 Of all the poisonous, foul, ghastly places, Cannes takes the biscuit with absurd ease.

TAKE it or leave it an expression of indifference or impatience about another's decision after making an offer. ● Especially in imperative.

TAKE ▶ *see* **take it into one's HEAD**; ; ▶ *see* **take it on the CHIN**; ▶ *see* **take something LYING down**; ▶ *see* **take someone's name in VAIN**; ▶ *see* **take no PRISONERS**; ▶ *see* **take someone's POINT**; ▶ *see* **take STOCK**; ▶ *see*

take someone to the CLEANERS; ▶ *see* **take to HEART**; ▶ *see* **take to one's HEELS**; ▶ *see* **take someone to TASK**; ▶ *see* **throw down the GAUNTLET**.

have what it TAKES have the necessary qualities etc. for success. *informal*

for the TAKING (of a person or thing) ready or available for someone to take advantage of.

> **1994** J. HAMILTON *Map of World* x. 154 I try to imagine the land for the taking, and what it must have meant to have space for as far as the eye can see.

herein (or therein) lies a TALE there is a story connected with this.

> **1998** *Spectator* 25 Apr. 55/1 Now it has decided to fight back and clear its name. And herein lies a tale, however ludicrous.

an old wives' TALE an ancient but untrue story; superstitious non-sense. ●Reflecting the idea, current especially since the Reformation in England, that old women relating the stories and beliefs of their childhoods are the major force maintaining the currency of ancient superstitions.

TALK the hind leg off a donkey talk incessantly. *Brit.*, *informal* ●In 1808 *talking a horse's hind leg off* was described as an 'old vulgar hyperbole' (*Cobbett's Weekly Political Register* XIII. ii. 47), but the version with *donkey* was current by M19. In 1879 Trollope mentioned *talk the hind-legs off a dog* as an Australian variant (*John Caldigate* III. ix. 122).

> **1970** N. BAWDEN *Birds on Trees* (1991) viii. 139 Talk, talk—talk the hind leg off a donkey, that one.

TALK through one's hat (or the back of one's neck or *Brit.* **arse** or **backside** or *US* **ass etc.)** talk foolishly, wildly, or ignorantly. *informal*

TALK ▶ *see* **CHALK and talk**; ▶ *see* **talk a BLUE streak**; ▶ *see* **talk DIRTY**; ▶ *see* **talk nineteen to the DOZEN**; ▶ *see* **speak of the DEVIL**; ▶ *see* **talk SHOP**; ▶ *see* **talk TURKEY**.

a TALL order something difficult to accomplish. ●*Tall* in the sense of 'big' was originally US slang; the phrase is recorded from L19.

> **1998** *Times* 24 Aug. 41/7 But the UK economy had to slow down somewhat, and gliding it down to exactly the right spot was a tall order.

a TALL poppy a privileged or distinguished person. ●Originally in allusion to the legend of the Roman tyrant Tarquin striking the heads off poppies to demonstrate how to treat the eminent men of a conquered city.

> **1998** *Times* 5 Mar. 23/5 Why do we in Britain so resent the prescience of the 'tall poppy' and delight in cutting everyone down to size?

in TANDEM **1** one behind another. **2** alongside each other; together. ●The Latin word *tandem* means 'at length', used punningly here to describe a way of hitching two horses to a carriage one behind the other or the carriage drawn by horses harnessed thus. Sense 1 preserves the original L18 meaning, but since M20 the phrase has been commonly used imprecisely in sense 2 'functioning as a team'. *Tandem* is used as an adjective in sense 1 in *tandem bicycle* to describe a bicycle with seats one behind the other.

a TANGLED web a complex, difficult, and confusing situation or thing. ●With reference to Walter Scott's *Marmion* (1808): 'O what a tangled web we weave, When first we practise to deceive!' (vi. 17).

it takes two to TANGO both parties involved in a situation or argument are equally responsible for it. *informal* ●*Takes Two to Tango* was the title of a song by Hoffman and Manning (1952); the expression has since achieved proverbial status.

> **1996** *Washington Post* (*Washington Business*) 12 Feb. 19 It takes two to tango in this refresh business. Both your computer's video card and your monitor must be capable of a given rate to achieve it.

on TAP 1 freely available whenever needed. *informal* **2** on schedule to happen or occur. *N. Amer., informal* ●Used literally of water as being supplied ready to be poured from a tap.

have (*or* get) someone (*or* something) TAPED understand a person or thing fully. *Brit., informal* ●Early instances of the use of the phrase (E20) do not make clear its development: the sense could have come either from the action of measuring someone with a measuring tape (thus 'sizing them up') or from the sense of tying someone or something up with tape (and thus getting them under control).

> **1919** 'War Slang' in *Athenæum* 18 July 632/2'I got you taped,' an N.C.O. may say to a man, meaning 'I know what you are up to.'

on the TAPIS (of a subject) under consideration or discussion. ●A partial translation (L17) of the French phrase *sur le tapis*, literally 'on the carpet (i.e. tablecloth)'. Cf. ▶ **on the CARPET** and ▶ **on the TABLE**.

TAR and feather smear with tar and then cover with feathers as a punishment. ●The punishment was prescribed in an ordinance (1189) of Richard I for naval personnel guilty of theft, and seems to have been intermittently imposed upon other wrongdoers in Britain. The actual phrase, however, is particularly associated from M18 onwards with mob punishments of unpopular or criminal characters in the US.

> **1981** A. PRICE *Soldier no More* 161 The Russians ... wouldn't have cared less if we'd tarred and feathered Nasser and run him out of Suez on a rail.

TARRED with the same brush having or considered to have the same faults. ●Scott (*Rob Roy*, 1818) has *tarred with the same stick* and Cobbett (*Rural Rides*, 1823) has the version with *brush*.

TARTAR ▶ *see* **CATCH a Tartar**.

a bad (*or* bitter *or* nasty) TASTE in the (*or* someone's) mouth a strong feeling of distress or disgust following an experience. *informal*

TASTE (noun) ▶ *see* **a dose of one's own MEDICINE**.

TASTE (verb) ▶ *see* **taste BLOOD**.

not for all the TEA in China not at any price; certainly not! *informal* ●Identified by Partridge (1937) as an Australian colloquialism dating from the 1890s. Used to emphasize that there is nothing at all that could induce one to do something.

TEA and sympathy hospitality and consolation offered to a distressed person.

a whole TEAM and the dog under the wagon a person of superior ability; an outstandingly gifted or able person. *US*

TEAR one's hair out show extreme desperation. *informal*
> **1991** J. CHURCHILL *Farewell to Yarns* ix. 66 Someplace people were having nervous break-downs and tearing their hair out in a desperate effort to please Phyllis.

TEAR someone off a strip (*or* tear a strip off someone) rebuke someone angrily. *informal* ● Originally M20 RAF slang.

without TEARS (of a subject) presented so as to be learnt or achieved easily.

TEARS ▶ *see* **shed CROCODILE tears**.

TEETH ▶ *see* **ARMED to the teeth**; ▶ *see* **CAST something in someone's teeth**; ▶ *see* **rare as HEN's teeth**; ▶ *see* **sow DRAGON's teeth**.

bush TELEGRAPH a rapid informal spreading of information or rumour; the network through which this takes place. ● Originally (L19) referring to the network of informers who kept bushrangers informed about the movements of the police in the Australian bush or outback. Cf. ▶ **hear on the GRAPEVINE**.

TELL tales (out of school) make known or gossip about another person's secrets, wrongdoings, or faults. ● As telling tales to school authorities is a heinous offence in the eyes of schoolchildren, this expression is often used in the context of declining to supply information or gossip: *that would be telling tales out of school*. Often followed by preposition *on*.
> **1990** M. STALEY in A. Parfrey *Apocalypse Culture* (rev. edn) 175 Crowley … seems to some extent to have encouraged people to tell tales on each other.

TELL someone where to get off (*or* where they get off) angrily rebuke someone. *informal*

TELL someone where to put (*or* what to do with) something angrily or emphatically reject something. *informal*

TELL ▶ *see* **see something a MILE off**; ▶ *see* **tell that to the MARINES**.

that would be TELLING that would be divulging secret or confidential information. *informal* ● Used often humorously to convey that one is not prepared to betray a secret.

there's no TELLING it's impossible to know what has happened or will happen.

TEMPEST ▶ *see* **a STORM in a teacup**.

TEMPT fate (*or* providence) act rashly. *informal*

count (up to) TEN pause for long enough to enumerate the numbers one to ten in order to prevent oneself from speaking or acting impetuously.

TEN out of ten complete success has been achieved. ● Literally, ten marks out of ten, a perfect mark. Used to congratulate someone or indicate that they have done something well.

TEN ▶ *see* **be ten a PENNY**.

on TENTERHOOKS in a state of suspense or agitation because of not knowing what will happen. ● A *tenter* was a frame on which cloth was stretched after fulling, and *tenterhooks* were the hooks or bent nails set in the tenter to hold the cloth in position. The metaphorical use of the phrase for a state of mind dates from M18.

on TERMS **1** in a state of friendship or equality. **2** (in sport) level in score or on points.

TERMS ▶ *see* **in no UNCERTAIN terms**.

go (*or* come) with the TERRITORY be a unavoidable result of a particular situation. ● *Territory* here is probably in its E20 US sense of 'the area in which a sales representative or distributor has the right to operate'.

TEST the water judge people's feelings or opinions before taking further action.

TEST ▶ *see* **the ACID test**.

TETHER ▶ *see* **at the END of one's tether**.

THANK one's lucky stars feel grateful for one's good fortune. ● The *stars* here are regarded as influencing someone's fortunes and character.
> **1998** *Times* 11 Aug. 40/6 All Alec Stewart can do is thank his lucky stars that his main strike bowler is fit again.

no THANKS to not because of; despite.
> **1993** C. MACDOUGALL *Lights Below* 11 'How's your mother?' 'Our mother's fine. No thanks to you. She was worried sick.'

THANKS for the buggy-ride an expression of thanks for help given. *chiefly N. Amer.* ● A *buggy* is a light horse-drawn vehicle.

and all THAT (*or* and that) and that sort of thing; and so on. *informal* ● Often used flippantly or dismissively, as in the title of the classic comic history by Sellar and Yeatman: *1066 and All That* (1930).

been THERE, done that used to express past experience of or familiarity with something. *informal* ● Often now used as a flippant expression of boredom or world-weariness; a L20 elaboration is a parody of the blasé tourist's attitude to experience: *been there, done that, got the T-shirt*.
> **1997** *Neon* Sept. 77/2 [Taking acid] was a bad experiment … But I've had enough of that now. Been there, done that, got the T-shirt.

be THERE for someone be available to provide support or comfort for someone, especially at a time of adversity.
> **1998** *Spectator* 25 Apr. 16/2 Elegant, determined and intelligent, she was the perfect tycoon's wife: always there for her husband and ready to defend him.

have been THERE (*or* here) before know all about a situation from experience. *informal*

a bit THICK more than one can tolerate; unfair or unreasonable. *Brit., Austral., & NZ, informal*
> **1991** A. CAMPBELL *Sidewinder* i. 3 'Tia is a healthy girl can have lots of babies, but can you give her babies? No.' … I thought this was a bit thick.

give someone (*or* get) a THICK ear punish someone (*or* be punished) with a blow, especially on the ear. *Brit., informal*

in (*or* into) the THICK of something in (*or* into) the busiest or most crowded part of something; deeply involved in something.

THICK and fast rapidly and in great numbers.

(as) THICK as thieves (of two or more people) very close or friendly; sharing secrets. *informal*

(as) THICK as two (short) planks (*or* a brick *or* N. Amer. a plank) very stupid. *informal* ● There is a play on *thick* in its basic sense 'of relatively great depth from side to side' and its colloquial sense of 'stupid' (L16).

through THICK and thin under all circumstances, no matter how difficult.

THICK ▶ *see* **have a thick SKIN**; ▶ *see* **as THICK as two planks**; ▶ *see* **thick on the GROUND**.

have a THIN time have a wretched or uncomfortable time. *Brit., informal*

into (*or* out of) THIN air into (*or* out of) a state of being invisible or non-existent.

THIN on top balding. ● Used euphemistically.

THIN ▶ *see* **on thin ICE**; ▶ *see* **the thin end of the WEDGE**; ▶ *see* **thick on the GROUND**; ▶ *see* **have a thick SKIN**.

do the — THING engage in the particular form of behaviour typically associated with someone or something. *chiefly N. Amer., informal*

have a THING about be obsessed or prejudiced about. *informal*

make a THING of **1** regard as essential. **2** cause a fuss about. *informal*

teach (*or* tell) someone a THING or two impart experience. *informal*
| **1998** *Spectator* 13 June 34/2 A docker of the 1950s, ... a sailor of any previous age could tell you a thing or two about job insecurity.

THING ▶ *see* **a thing of SHREDS and patches**.

be all THINGS to all men (*or* people) **1** please everyone, typically by regularly altering one's behaviour or opinions in order to conform to those of others. **2** be able to be interpreted or used differently by different people to their own satisfaction. ● Originally probably in allusion to 1 Corinthians 9:22, 'I am made all things to all men'.

THINGS that go bump in the night supernatural beings; ghosts. *informal* ● From *The Cornish or West Country Litany*: 'From ghoulies and ghosties and long-leggety beasties And things that go bump in the night, Good Lord deliver us!' A humorous way of referring to nocturnal disturbances of all sorts.

THINGS ▶ *see* **other things being EQUAL**.

give someone furiously to THINK give a person cause to think hard. ● Literal translation of French *donner furieusement à penser*.

have (got) another THINK coming be about to be forced to reconsider. *informal* ● Used to express the speaker's disagreement with or unwillingness to do something suggested by someone else.

THINK twice consider a course of action carefully before embarking on it.

THINK ▶ *see* **think NOTHING of it**; ▶ *see* **think on one's FEET**; ▶ *see* **think the WORLD of**.

put on one's THINKING cap meditate on a problem. *informal*

THIRD time lucky (or US third time is the charm) after twice failing to accomplish something, the third attempt may be successful. ● *Third time lucky* has been proverbial since M19; this is one of several optimistic expressions about third attempts to do something; cf. *third time pays for all*.

THOMAS ▶ *see* **a DOUBTING Thomas**.

a THORN in someone's side (or flesh) a source of continual annoyance or trouble. ● *A thorn in the side* is after Numbers 33:55, while *a thorn in the flesh* quotes 2 Corinthians 12:7.

THORN ▶ *see* **no ROSE without a thorn**.

on THORNS continuously uneasy, especially in fear of being detected.

a second THOUGHT a moment's further consideration; any worry or concern. ● Usually with negative: 'not give something a second thought'. Also *have second thoughts about*.

hang by a THREAD be in a highly precarious state.

lose the (or one's THREAD) be unable to follow what someone is saying or remember what one is going to say next.

THREE musketeers three close associates, three inseparable friends. ● Translation of French *Les Trois Mousquetaires*, the title of a novel (1844) by Alexandre Dumas père.

THREESCORE and ten the age of seventy. ● With reference to the biblical span of a person's life: see Psalm 90:10.

THRILLS and spills the excitement of dangerous sports or entertainments, especially as experienced by spectators.

be at each other's THROATS (of people or organizations) quarrel or fight persistently.

> **1990** R. MALAN *My Traitor's Heart* (1991) 300 'It's not only difficult for people outside to understand why blacks are at each others' throats,' he says. 'It's difficult for ourselves.'

cut one's own THROAT bring about one's own downfall by one's actions.

force (or ram or shove) something down someone's THROAT force ideas or material on a person's attention by repeatedly putting them forward.

stick in one's THROAT (or gullet) be difficult or impossible to accept; be a source of continuing annoyance. ● The literal sense refers to something lodged in one's throat which one can neither swallow nor spit out. Also ▶ **stick in one's CRAW** and ▶ **stick in one's GIZZARD**.

THROW dust in someone's eyes mislead a person by misrepresentation or distraction.

THROW one's hand in give up; withdraw from a contest. ●In card games, especially poker, to *throw one's hand in* is to abandon one's chances.

THROW in the towel (or sponge) abandon a struggle; admit defeat. ●Boxers or their seconds literally throw the towel or sponge used to wipe a contestant's face into the middle of the ring to signal defeat.

THROW stones cast aspersions. ●Cf. the proverbial saying *those who live in glass houses should not throw stones*, a variant of which is recorded in G. Herbert's *Outlandish Proverbs* (1640). See also ▶ **cast the first STONE**.

THROW one's weight about (*or* around) act in a domineering or over-assertive manner. *informal*

THROW one's weight behind use one's influence to help support. *informal*

THROW ▶ *see* **throw the BABY out with the bathwater**; ▶ *see* **pour COLD water on**; ▶ *see* **throw down the GAUNTLET**; ▶ *see* **throw good MONEY after bad**; ▶ *see* **throw in one's LOT with**; ▶ *see* **throw someone to the DOGS**; ▶ *see* **throw someone to the WOLVES**.

THUMB one's nose at show disdain or contempt for. *informal* ●Cf. ▶ **cock a SNOOK**.

under someone's THUMB completely under someone's influence or control.

THUMBS up (or down) an indication of satisfaction or approval (*or* of rejection or failure). *informal* ●With reference to the signal of approval or disapproval, used by spectators at a Roman amphitheatre; the sense has been reversed, as the Romans used 'thumbs down' to signify that a beaten gladiator had performed well and should be spared, and 'thumbs up' to call for his death.

THUMBS ▶ *see* **be all FINGERS and thumbs**; ▶ *see* **TWIDDLE one's thumbs**.

THUNDER ▶ *see* **STEAL someone's thunder**.

what makes someone TICK what motivates someone. *informal*

on TICK on credit. *informal* ●*Tick* is an abbreviation of *ticket*, a memorandum of money or goods received on credit.

TICK (noun) ▶ *see* **TIGHT as a tick**.

punch one's TICKET deliberately undertake particular assignments that are likely to lead to promotion at work. *US, informal*

work one's TICKET contrive to obtain one's discharge from prison or the army.

write one's (own) TICKET dictate one's own terms. *chiefly N. Amer., informal*

TICKET ▶ *see* **SPLIT the ticket**.

be TICKETS be the end. *S. Afr., informal*

have TICKETS on oneself be excessively vain or proud of oneself. *Austral., informal*

on a TICKEY in a very small area. *S. Afr.* ●In the period before South African coinage was decimalized, a *tickey* was a very small silver coin worth three pennies.

be TICKLED pink (*or* to death) be extremely amused or pleased. *informal*

> **1992** G. VANDERHAEGHE *Things as they Are* 189 She made a big show of not being taken in by him, but I could see that [she] was tickled pink by his attentions.

go (*or* swim) with (*or* against) the TIDE act in accordance with (*or* against) the prevailing opinion or tendency.

TIE one on get drunk. *chiefly N. Amer., informal*

the old school TIE the attitudes of group loyalty and traditionalism associated with the wearing of such a tie. *Brit.* ●From the necktie with a distinctive pattern worn by former members of a particular (usually public) school.

TIE ▶ *see* **bind someone HAND and foot**; ▶ *see* **tie the KNOT**; ▶ *see* **tie oneself in KNOTS**.

TIED ▶ *see* **FIT to be tied**; ▶ *see* **have one's HANDS tied**.

have a TIGER by the tail have embarked on a course of action which proves unexpectedly difficult but which cannot easily or safely be abandoned. ●L20; an alternative way of referring to the same predicament is *ride a tiger* (E20), with allusion to the Chinese saying *he who rides a tiger cannot dismount* (in a collection of Chinese proverbs in English, 1875); a similar difficulty confronts those who ▶ **have a WOLF by the ears**.

a TIGER in one's tank energy, spirit, animation. ●From a 1960s Esso petrol advertising slogan, 'Put a tiger in your tank.'

(as) TIGHT as a tick extremely drunk. ●The simile *as full as a tick* occurs in a L17 proverb collection, referring to the way in which the blood-sucking insects swell as they gorge themselves. In the modern variant there is a play on *tight* as an informal synonym (M19) for 'drunk' and as 'stretched taut' like a blood-gorged tick.

run a TIGHT ship be very strict in managing an organization or operation.

a TIGHT corner (*or* spot *or* place) a difficult situation.

> **1994** *Interzone* July 28/3 The temptation to also invent some kind of magical McGuffin to get his hero out of a tight corner is something he works hard to avoid.

TIGHTEN ▶ *see* **tighten one's BELT**; ▶ *see* **tighten the SCREW**.

on the TILES away from home having a wild or enjoyable time and not returning until late in the evening or early in the morning. *chiefly Brit., informal* ●With allusion to the nocturnal activities of cats. Current since L19.

have (*or* with) one's fingers (*or* hand) in the TILL stealing from one's employer. ●Cf. ▶ **with one's hand in the COOKIE jar**.

(at) full TILT with maximum energy or force; at top speed.

> **1912** E. WHARTON *Letter* 29 June [J]ust after we left Modena a crazy coachman drove full tilt out of a side road.

TILT at windmills attack imaginary enemies or evils. ●With allusion to the activities of the hero of Cervantes' mock-chivalric novel *Don Quixote*, who attacked windmills under the delusion that they were giants.

know the TIME of day be well informed.

(only) TIME will tell the truth or correctness of something will only be established at some time in the future.

pass the TIME of day exchange a greeting or casual remarks.

TIME and tide wait for no man if you don't make use of a favourable opportunity, you may never get the same chance again. *proverbial* ●In Middle English *time and tide* was an alliterative reduplication, as *tide* simply meant 'time, occasion'; however, from the sixteenth century it has often been understood to mean 'the tide of the sea'.

from TIME immemorial (or N. Amer. **time out of mind)** from so long ago that people have no knowledge or memory of it. ●Legally in Britain, the time up to the beginning of the reign of Richard I in 1189.

TIME is money time is a valuable resource. *proverbial* ●Used to urge that things are done as expeditiously as possible. The present form of the expression seems to originate with Benjamin Franklin in 1748, but the sentiment goes back to ancient Greece.

TIME was there was a time. ●Often followed by *when* (see quot.).
> **1998** *Times* 25 May 46/1 Time was when venture capital was shunned by self-respecting, ambitious corporate financiers … .No longer.

TIME ▶ *see* **in the NICK of time**; ▶ *see* **take time by the FORELOCK**; ▶ *see* **TIME immemorial**.

have a TIN ear **1** be tone-deaf. **2** be insensitive to a particular person or thing.

TIN ▶ *see* **put the LID on**; ▶ *see* **little tin GOD**.

not give (or care) **a TINKER's curse (or** cuss *or* damn**)** not care at all. *informal* With reference to tinkers' supposed habit of casual bad language. ●Earliest as *tinker's damn* (in Thoreau's *Journal* 1839). Since L19 also often shortened to *not give a tinker's*.
> **1984** P. O'BRIEN *Far Side of World* v. 179 When I was a squeaker nobody gave a tinker's curse whether my daily workings were right or wrong.

be on the TIP of one's tongue **1** be almost but not quite able to bring a particular word or name to mind. **2** be about to utter a comment or question but then think better of it.

TIP one's hand (or mitt**)** reveal one's intentions inadvertently. US, *informal* ●E20 US slang. The opposite of ▶ **keep one's CARDS close to one's chest**.
> **1966** M. WOODHOUSE *Tree Frog* xviii. 133 We couldn't very well oppose it without tipping our hand.

TIP one's hat (*or* cap) raise or touch one's hat or cap as a way of greeting or acknowledging someone.

TIP (*or* turn) the scales (*or* balance) (of a circumstance or event) be the deciding factor; make the critical difference.

TIP someone off give someone information about something, typically in a discreet or confidential way. *informal* ●L19 US slang, used especially in the context of criminal activity. The phrase has given rise to the noun *tip-off* for information supplied in this way.

TIP someone the wink give someone private information; secretly warn someone of something. *Brit., informal*

TIP ▶ *see* **the tip of an ICEBERG**.

TIRED and emotional drunk. ●A humorous euphemism, from its use in newspapers in contexts where the word *drunk* would lay the publication open to a libel charge; it was popularized (M20) by the British satirical magazine *Private Eye*.

TIT for tat a situation in which an injury or insult is given in return or retaliation. ● Also as modifier: *tit-for-tat* (see quot.).
| **1998** *Spectator* 21 Mar. 26/1 [A] series of tit-for-tat woman-stealing episodes—Greek Io stolen by Phoenicians, Phoenician Europa stolen by Greeks, ...

be TOAST be or be likely to become finished, defunct, or dead. *chiefly N. Amer., informal*
| **1998** *Times* 17 Mar. 32/8 A new star has entered the financial firmament. Look to your laurels, George Soros, Warren Buffett, you're toast.

have someone on TOAST be in a position to deal with someone as one wishes. *Brit., informal* ● With allusion to having an item of food served up to one on a slice of toast.
| R. KIPLING *'Stellenbosch'* The General 'ad the country cleared—almost; The General ''ad no reason to expect', And the Boers 'ad us bloomin' well on toast!

on one's TOD on one's own; alone. *Brit., informal* ● Rhyming slang: *on one's own | Tod Sloan* (1874–1933), the name of a US jockey.

a TOE in the door a (first) chance of ultimately achieving what one wants; a position from which further progress is possible. *informal* ● Literally, placing one's foot on a threshold in such a way as to prevent a door being closed in one's face.

TOE the line accept the authority, principles or policies of a particular group, especially under pressure. ● Literally of competitors in a race, line up at the start with toes on the starting line. Also *toe the mark* and, less commonly, *toe the trig* (all E19). (*Trig* in the sense of 'a line cut or marked on the ground' is now confined to dialect; it was used particularly of a mark on a playing field from behind which a ball etc. was to be thrown or of the starting line in a race.)
| **1998** *Times* 31 Mar. 18/5 An insider suggests ... that the said minister is ... on the skids. The minister smarts, and toes the line.

make someone's TOES curl bring about an extreme reaction in someone, either of pleasure or of disgust. *informal*
| **1984** P. PRUDHOMME *Louisiana Kitchen* iii. 111 This is so good it'll make your toes curl!

on one's TOES ready for any eventuality. ● Also *keep someone on their toes* 'keep someone on the alert'. Cf. ▶ **catch someone FLAT-FOOTED**.
| **1921 J. DOS PASSOS *Three Soldiers* II. i. 56 If he just watched out and kept on his toes, he'd be sure to get it.

turn up one's TOES die. *informal* ● An M19 expression, of which a more elaborate version was *turn one's toes up to the daisies*.

TOES ▶ *see* **DIG in one's heels**.

not be able to do something for TOFFEE be totally incompetent at doing something. *Brit., informal*
| **1914 *Illustrated London News* 12 Sept. 380/1 Their opponents cannot 'shoot for nuts' (or 'for toffee', as one Tommy more expressly put it).

by the same TOKEN in the same way; for the same reason.
| **1975** F. EXLEY *Pages from Cold Island* (1988) ix. 154 The student could ask anything he chose, and by the same token Wilson could if he elected choose not to answer.

as if there was (or as though there were) no TOMORROW with no regard for the future consequences. ● Used in various phrasings since M19.
| **1980** *Guardian Weekly* 3 Feb. 1/3 Oil supplies that Americans at home continue to consume as though there were no tomorrow.

TOMORROW is another day the future will bring fresh opportunities. ● Known since E16 in the form *tomorrow is a new day*, which is now (since E20) apparently superseded by the version with 'another'. Used especially after a bad experience to express one's belief that the future will be better.

TOM, Dick, and Harry undifferentiated ordinary people. ● Earliest in an M18 song as typical names: 'Farewell, Tom, Dick, and Harry. Farewell, Moll, Nell, and Sue.' It is generally used in mildly derogatory contexts (*every Tom, Dick, and Harry*) to suggest a large number of ordinary people.

TOM Tiddler's ground a place where money or profit is readily made. ● With allusion to a children's game in which one player tries to catch the others who run onto his or her ground calling out, 'We're on Tom Tiddler's ground, picking up gold and silver.'

TON ▶ *see* **come down like a ton of BRICKS**.

(with) TONGUE in cheek without really meaning what one is saying or writing; with sly irony. ● Putting one's tongue in one's cheek is a gesture of contempt or sly humour; cf. Smollett in *Roderick Random* (1748) liv: 'I signified my contempt of him by thrusting my tongue in my cheek.'

someone's TONGUE is hanging out someone is very eager for a drink or something else. ● Alluding to the lolling tongue of a dog panting for water.

TONGUE ▶ *see* **with FORKED tongue**; ▶ *see* **have a SILVER tongue**.

the gift of TONGUES the power of speaking in unknown languages, regarded as one of the gifts of the Holy Spirit. ●One of the manifestations by the disciples of Jesus that they were filled with the Holy Spirit after Pentecost (Acts 2:1–4); cf. ▶ **SPEAK in tongues**.

fight TOOTH and nail fight very fiercely. ●That is, even to the extent of using one's teeth and fingernails as weapons.

at the TOP of the tree in the highest rank of a profession etc.

on TOP of the world exuberant. *informal*

over the TOP to excess, beyond reasonable limits; outrageous. ●Theatrical in origin; hyphenated when attributive. The specialist military sense, dating from the 1914–18 war, of going over the parapet of a trench to attack the enemy is now historical.

TOP and tail **1** remove the top and bottom of (a fruit or vegetable) while preparing it as food. **2** wash the face and bottom of (a baby or small child). *Brit.*

TOP (noun) ▶ *see* **off the top of one's HEAD**.

TOP (verb) ▶ *see* **top the BILL**.

carry a TORCH for feel (esp. unrequited) love for. ●The idea of *the torch of love* was a commonplace: e.g., in the Epilogue to Sheridan's *Rivals* (1775).
| *1927 Vanity Fair* (N.Y.) Nov. 132/3 When a fellow 'carries the torch' it doesn't imply that he is 'lit up' or drunk, but girl-less.

hand on (*or* pass) the TORCH pass on a tradition, especially one of learning or enlightenment. ●With allusion to the passing of a torch between runners in a relay, as happened in ancient Greece and as happens with the Olympic torch for the modern Olympic games. Cf. Latin *vitai lampada tradunt* 'they hand over the torch of life', Lucretius' metaphor for the transmission of life through the generations (*De Rerum Natura* ii. 78).
| **1887** *Quarterly Review* Oct. 276 [Italy's] work has been done among the nations, and in their turn France, England and Germany hand on the torch.

put to the TORCH (*or* put a torch to) destroy by burning.

give (*or* care) a TOSS care at all. *Brit.*, *informal* ●Usually with negative. A similar US expression, now dated, is *not give a whoop*.
| **1998** *Country Life* 25 June 98/3 I have swum in the Dart only a few yards from a mink, and the mink has not given a toss.

TOSS one's cookies vomit. *N. Amer.*, *informal*

lose one's TOUCH not show one's customary skill.
| **1991** *Times: Review Supplement* 33/2 The guv'nor is a former pork butcher who has clearly not lost his touch.

TOUCH bottom **1** reach the bottom of water with one's feet. **2** be at the lowest or worst point. **3** *Brit.* be in possession of the full facts.

a soft (*or* easy) TOUCH someone who is easily manipulated; a person or task easily handled. *slang* ●A *touch* was M19 criminal slang for the act of getting money from a person, either by pickpocketing or by persuasion. *Touch* was later extended to refer also to the person thus targeted, and a *soft touch* (M20) was specifically a person from whom money could easily be obtained, though it is now used in other contexts, such as sport (see quot.).

| **1998** *Times* 23 Mar. 37/1 Henman can be something of a soft touch. For every leading player who touts his potential, two from the basement would relish his name in the draw.

a TOUCH of the sun a slight attack of sunstroke.

TOUCH (noun) ▶ *see* **the MIDAS touch**.

TOUCH (verb) ▶ *see* **touch BASE**; ▶ *see* **touch WOOD**; ▶ *see* **would not touch someone/thing with a BARGEPOLE**.

TOUCHPAPER ▶ *see* **LIGHT a fuse**.

(as) TOUGH as old boots very sturdy or resilient. ●With reference to the strength and resistance of leather; *as tough as leather* was current earlier (M19) than the *old boots* version (L19), which has generally superseded it.

| **1967** *Listener* 7 Dec. 765/1 This is no sweet old dolly … She is tough as old boots, working for a living.

TOUGH it out endure a period of difficult conditions. *informal* ●Mainly US.

| *1852 Knickerbocker* XXXIX. 26 You don't need no medicine; you'll tough it out, I dare say.

TOWEL ▶ *see* **THROW in the towel**.

TOWER ▶ *see* **tower of STRENGTH**.

go to TOWN do something thoroughly or extravagantly, with a great deal of energy and enthusiasm. *informal*

| **1996** D. BRIMSON & E. BRIMSON *Everywhere We Go* xiv. 196 When there is a major incident, the press still go to town and we are bombarded with graphic images of bloody faces.

on the TOWN enjoying the entertainments, especially the nightlife, of a city or town. *informal*

TOWN and gown non-members and members of a university in a particular place. ●*Gown* with reference to the academic dress of university members. The distinction was made in these terms in E19 Oxford and Cambridge, but arose much earlier through the traditional hostility between the native inhabitants of the two cities and the incoming students. For instance, in Oxford the St Scholastica's Day riot in 1354 was a town vs gown affair.

TOWN ▶ *see* **PAINT the town red**.

kick over the TRACES become insubordinate or reckless. ●With reference to an ill-disciplined horse or other draught animal that kicks out over the harness straps (*traces*) that attach it to the vehicle that it is pulling, thus becoming uncontrollable.

make TRACKS (for) leave (for a place). *informal*

| **1984** D. BRIN *Practice Effect* IX. vii. 210 We have another big climb ahead of us and another pass to get through. Let's make tracks.

the wrong side of the TRACKS a poor or less prestigious part of town.

informal ● Originally US, the expression was explained in 1929 with reference to a town divided by a railroad track: 'There is the right side and the wrong side. Translated into terms of modern American idealism, this means, the rich side and the side that hopes to be rich.'

| **1977** *Listener* 13 Oct. 478/2 Eva Duarte Peron ... came from the wrong side of the tracks.

TRACK ▶ *see* **JUMP the track**; ▶ *see* **off the BEATEN track**.

TRACKS ▶ *see* **COVER one's tracks**.

as much as the TRAFFIC will bear as much as the trade or market will tolerate; as much as is economically viable.

TRAGEDY of the commons the inevitable damage done to a limited resource when too many people try to avail themselves of it. ● Arising from the ancient English custom by which villagers were allowed to graze their animals on common land; the thoughtless or greedy put too many animals on the commons, impoverishing the land, and thus the whole community.

| **1998** *New Scientist* 21 Feb. 40/1 All Web users are modern players in an old social dilemma known as the tragedy of the commons. By blindly acting in their own interests they are spoiling a valuable common resource.

TRAIL (or drag) one's coat deliberately provoke a quarrel or fight. ● Trailing one's coat (or coat-tails) is likely to result in someone's stepping on it, either intentionally or unintentionally, thus enabling one to pick a fight. This behaviour was traditionally associated with Irishmen at Donnybrook Fair: cf. C. M. Yonge (*Womankind*, 1877): 'Party spirit is equally ready to give offence and to watch for it. It will trail its coat like the Irishman in the fair' (xxv. 216).

| **1980** J. DITTON *Copley's Hunch* I. ii. 35 I was trailing my coat ... Trying to get the Luftwaffe to come up and fight.

TRAIL ▶ *see* **BLAZE a trail**.

over the TRANSOM offered or sent without prior agreement; unsolicited. *US, informal* ● A *transom* is a cross-beam, especially in a boat or dividing a window.

| **1976** P. ANTHONY *But What of Earth* (1989) 8 Editors claim to be deluged with appallingly bad material 'over the transom' from unagented writers.

TREAD (or step) on someone's toes offend someone, especially by encroaching on their privileges.

TREAD water fail to advance or make progress. ● Literally, 'maintain an upright position in the water by moving the feet with a walking movement and the hands with a downward circular motion'.

TREAD ▶ *see* **tread the BOARDS**; ▶ *see* **walk on AIR**.

— a TREAT someone or something does something specified very well or satisfactorily. *Brit., informal*

out of one's TREE completely stupid; mad. *chiefly N. Amer., informal*

up a TREE in a difficult situation without escape; cornered. *chiefly US, informal*

TREES ▶ *see* **GROW on trees**.

TRIAL and error the process of experimenting with various methods of doing something until one finds the most successful.

in a TRICE in a moment; very quickly. ● *Trice* comes from the ME verb *trice* (*tryce*, *trise*), cognate with words in various Germanic languages meaning 'hoist'. *Trice* as a noun meaning a 'single pull or attempt' is now obsolete in this sense, and the word occurs only in this phrase. The earliest form of this phrase (M15), now obsolete, was *at a trice*; *with a trice* (also obsolete) and *in a trice* are recorded from E16.

do the TRICK achieve the required result. *informal*
> **1990** N. HILL *Death Grows on You* (1992) viii. 101 I figured a box of candy would do the trick, would bring some colour back.

a TRICK worth two of that a much better plan or expedient. *informal* ● From Shakespeare 1 *Henry IV* II. i. 41.

every TRICK in the book every available method of achieving what one wants. *informal*

the oldest TRICK in the book a ruse so hackneyed that it should no longer deceive anyone.

turn a TRICK (of a prostitute) have a session with a client. *informal*

TRICK ▶ *see* **not MISS a trick**.

TRICKS of the trade special ingenious techniques used in a profession or craft, especially those that are little known by outsiders.

up to one's (old) TRICKS misbehaving in a characteristic way. *informal*

TRICKS ▶ *see* **a BAG of tricks**; ▶ *see* **a BOX of tricks**.

TRIED and true proved effective or reliable by experience.
> **1967** *Listener* 6 Apr. 474/3 Miss Aukin had the good sense to use the tried and true concealment gambit by which eventually two young officers, bent on cuckolding a greengrocer, were compelled to hide in the same grandfather clock.

in TRIM slim and healthy. ● *Trim* originally had various technical nautical senses, relating to the sails or balance of a ship (latterly to the balance of an aircraft), hence the general sense of *good order*. Cf. next entry.

TRIM one's sails make changes to suit one's new circumstances.

TRIP the light fantastic dance. *humorous, dated* ● Cf. the invitation to dance in Milton's 'L'Allegro' (1645): 'Come, and trip it as ye go On the light fantastic toe.'

(as) right as a TRIVET perfectly all right; in good health. *Brit., informal* ● In reference to a trivet's always standing firm and steady upon its three legs.

like a TROJAN in a brave, stalwart, and honorable manner. ● The inhabitants of the ancient city of Troy were proverbially brave and trustworthy.
> **1974** W. FOLEY *Child in the Forest Trilogy* (1992) 161 She put me to clean out all the fowls' cotes, and I worked at it like a Trojan.

a TROJAN horse 1 a person or device deliberately set to bring about an enemy's downfall or to undermine from within. **2** in computing, a program that breaches the security of a computer system, especially by ostensibly functioning as part of a legitimate program, in order to erase, corrupt, or remove data. ●The original Trojan horse (described in Virgil's *Aeneid* ii) was a huge hollow wooden statue of a horse in which the Greek soldiers are said to have concealed themselves to enter Troy by subterfuge.

off one's TROLLEY crazy. *informal* ●The *trolley* in this case is the pulley running on an overhead track that transmits power from the track to a vehicle; the idea is similar to that in ▶ **go off the RAILS**. L19 slang.

| **1983** N. R. NASH *Young and Fair* II. ii. 66 If you suspect Patty, you're off your trolley.

TROOPER ▶ *see* **LIE like a trooper**; ▶ *see* **SWEAR like a trooper**.

on the TROT **1** in succession. **2** continually busy. *informal*, *Brit.*

TROTH ▶ *see* **PLIGHT one's troth**.

meet TROUBLE halfway distress oneself unnecessarily about what may happen.

wear the TROUSERS be the dominant partner in a marriage or the dominant person in a household. *informal* ●Used particularly of a woman who is the dominant partner.

TROUSERS ▶ *see* **catch someone with their PANTS down**.

old TROUT an old woman, especially an unattractive or bad-tempered one. *informal*, *derogatory* ●Possibly developed from *trot* (ME *trat(te)*), a disparaging term of uncertain origin for an old woman; *trout* was also applied to a person in the obsolete phrase *trusty trout* (M–L17), meaning a 'confidential friend'. *Old trout* is L19, apparently coming into use around the time *old trot* was passing into obsolence.

| **1972** V. CANNING *Rainbird Pattern* iii. 50 She wasn't such a bad old trout. For all her money and position, life hadn't been all good to her.

TROWEL ▶ *see* **LAY something on thick**.

have (or want) no TRUCK with **1** avoid dealings or being associated with. **2** be unsympathetic or opposed to. ●The earliest sense of *truck* was 'trading by exchange of commodities' (from French *troquer* to barter), from which developed the sense of 'communication' or 'dealings'.

out of TRUE (or the true) not in the correct or exact shape.

| **1984** J. GASH *Gondola Scam* (1985) xii. 96 They all look scarily out of true, and I do mean a terrible angle. Pisa's got one sloper.

TRUE as Bob (or God) absolutely true. *S. Afr.*, *informal*

blow one's own TRUMPET talk openly and boastfully about one's achievements. ●Cf. ▶ **blow one's own HORN**.

| **1998** *Spectator* 11 Apr. 30/1 I only mention this to blow my own trumpet … it was a source of great pride to be reinstated at the specific behest of Britain's most celebrated black radical journalist.

come (or turn) up TRUMPS **1** (of a person or situation) have a better

performance or outcome than expected.   **2** (of a person) be especially generous or helpful. *chiefly Brit., informal* ● *Trumps* are playing-cards of whatever
suit has been designated as ranking above the other suits.

the TRUTH, the whole truth, and nothing but the truth the full and
unvarnished truth. ● The words form part of a statement sworn by witnesses
in court. Used informally to emphasize the absolute veracity of a statement.

TRUTH ▶ *see* **ECONOMICAL with the truth**; ▶ *see* **GOSPEL truth**; ▶ *see*
NAKED truth.

TRY a fall with contend with.

TRY (something) for size try out or test for suitability.

TRY one's hand see how skilful one is, especially at the first attempt. ● Usually
with preposition *at*.

TRY ▶ *see* **try CONCLUSIONS with**.

go down the TUBE (or tubes) be completely lost or wasted; fail utterly.
informal ● M20 US slang. Cf. ▶ **down the DRAIN**.

TUG of love a dispute over the custody of a child. *Brit., informal* ● The phrase,
formed on the pattern of *tug of war*, is particularly associated with L20 newspaper reports of divorced or separated parents fighting over rights of access
to their children, but it originated much earlier in the title of a comedy by I.
Zangwill (1907).

there's many a good TUNE played on an old fiddle someone's abilities
do not depend on their age. *proverbial*

> **1997** *Times* 25 Oct. 16 [O]ld Star remained as cool and collected as if he had been training for
> this day for months. Which only goes to show that there is many a good tune played on an old
> fiddle.

to the TUNE of amounting to or involving the considerable sum of. *informal*

TUNE ▶ *see* **CALL the shots**; ▶ *see* **CHANGE one's tune**.

TUNED in aware of or able to understand something. *informal*

> **1966** L. DAVIDSON *Long Way to Shiloh* (1968) V. iv. 79 I couldn't see much of her face … .
> What I could see looked merely tuned-in, which bothered me all the more.

TUNNEL ▶ *see* **LIGHT at the end of the tunnel**.

talk TURKEY talk frankly and straightforwardly; get down to business. *N. Amer.,*
informal

TURKEY ▶ *see* **go COLD turkey**.

like TURKEYS voting for Christmas totally unlikely as being hopelessly
self-defeating. *informal*

Buggins's TURN appointment in rotation rather than by merit. ● *Buggins* here
is a 'typical' surname used generically.

one good TURN deserves another if someone does you a favour, you should
take the chance to repay it. ● Cf. E14 French *lune bonté requiert lautre*; the
proverb has been known in English since E15.

to a TURN (especially cooked) to exactly the right degree etc.

| 1931 *Good Housekeeping* Dec. 28/1 The meal began with a magnificent bass, broiled to a turn over heart-wood coals.

TURN the corner pass the critical point in an illness, difficulty, etc. ●The use of this expression to mean 'start recovering from an illness' dates from M19, though the literal sense was current much earlier.

TURN ▶ *see* **turn one's BACK on**; ▶ *see* **turn CAT in pan**; ▶ *see* **turn a DEAF ear**; ▶ *see* **not turn a HAIR**; ▶ *see* **turn one's HAND to**; ▶ *see* **turn someone's HEAD**; ▶ *see* **earn an HONEST penny**; ▶ *see* **turn in one's GRAVE**; ▶ *see* **turn on one's HEEL**; ▶ *see* **turn the other CHEEK**; ▶ *see* **turn over a new LEAF**; ▶ *see* **turn the SCALES**; ▶ *see* **tip the SCALES at**; ▶ *see* **turn the TABLES**; ▶ *see* **turn to ASHES**; ▶ *see* **turn a TRICK**; ▶ *see* **turn TURTLE**; ▶ *see* **turn up one's NOSE**.

a TURN-UP for the book a completely unexpected (especially welcome) result or happening. ●*Turn-up* is the turning up of a particular card or die in a game; the *book* here is a book of bets.

turn TURTLE turn upside down. ●From turtle-hunters' flipping over turtles onto their backs to render them helpless. Used figuratively from E19 for turning upside down something of similar shape to a turtle, such as a boat or a hammock. The E19 version *turn the turtle* is now obsolete.

| 1990 s. KING *Stand* (rev. edn) II. xiv. 496 His tractor turned turtle on him and killed him.

never the TWAIN shall meet two people or things are too different to exist alongside or understand each other. ●From Kipling's 'Ballad of East and West' (1892): 'Oh, East is East and West is West, and never the twain shall meet.'

TWELVE good men and true a jury. *dated* ●A jury in a court of law was traditionally composed of twelve men. Political correctness may be combining with the fact of the presence of women on juries to push this phrase towards obsolescence; cf. *Spectator* 21 Mar. 1998: 'He added that if I did not apologise, "I would be regretfully prepared to have the evidence weighed by 12 good people".'

TWICE ▶ *see* **THINK twice**.

TWIDDLE one's thumbs be bored or idle because one has nothing to do. ●The action of rotating one's thumbs round each other with the fingers linked together is traditionally symptomatic of boredom.

in a TWINKLING (*or* the twinkling of an eye) in an instant; very quickly. ●*Twinkling* is the time taken by a wink or blink of the eye. Used since ME in this figurative sense; cf. also 1 Corinthians 15:52.

TWIST someone's arm persuade someone to do something that they are or are thought to be reluctant to do. *informal*

TWIST in the wind be left in a state of suspense or uncertainty.

TWIST (noun) ▶ *see* **round the BEND**.

TWIST (verb) ▶ *see* **twist someone round one's little FINGER**.

put TWO and two together draw an obvious conclusion from what is known or evident.   ●An extension of this is *put two and two together and make five*, meaning 'draw a plausible but incorrect conclusion from what is known or evident'.

that makes TWO of us one is in the same position or holds the same opinion as the other person. ●Used in spoken English to identify oneself with the position or views of the previous speaker.

TWO can play at that game one person's bad behaviour can be emulated to that person's disadvantage.

TWO heads are better than one it's helpful to have the advice or opinion of a second person. *proverbial*   ●In this form since M16. A similar saying is *four eyes see more than two*.

> **1994** J. KELMAN *How Late It Was, How Late* 354 Cause it's hard to do it yerself Keith, two heads are better than one.

TWO ▶ *see* **a bite at the CHERRY**; ▶ *see* **two a PENNY**; ▶ *see* **for two PINS**; ▶ *see* **in two SHAKES**; ▶ *see* **it takes two to TANGO**.

TWO-EDGED ▶ *see* **a DOUBLE-EDGED sword**.

add (or put in) one's TWOPENN'ORTH contribute one's opinion. *informal*   ●As much as is worth or costs two pence, i.e. a paltry or insignificant amount.

TWO-WAY street a situation or relationship between two people or groups in which action is required from both parties; something that works both ways.

U

an **UGLY duckling** a young person who shows no promise at all of the beauty and success that will eventually come with maturity. ● In allusion to a tale by Hans Andersen of a cygnet in a brood of ducks.

UNACCEPTABLE ▶ *see* **the acceptable FACE of**.

in no **UNCERTAIN terms** clearly and forcefully.

> **1991** K. GIBBONS *Cure for Dreams* iii. 23 My mother got the doctor back out to our house and told him in no uncertain terms to do what he was paid to do.

cry (*or* **say** *or* **yell**) **UNCLE** surrender or admit defeat. *N. Amer., informal*

> **1989** G. VANDERHAEGHE *Homesick* X. 141 Beat him six ways to Sunday and he still would never cry uncle or allow that there was an outside chance of his ever being wrong.

UNCLE Tom Cobley (*or* **Cobleigh**) **and all** a whole lot of people. *Brit., informal* ● *Uncle Tom Cobley* is the last of a long list of men in the English song 'Widdicombe Fair' (*c*.1800). Used jocularly to indicate an assorted crowd of people.

the **UNCO guid** those who are strictly religious and moralistic. *Scot., chiefly derogatory* ● *Unco* is a Scottish and northern dialect shortening of *uncouth*, used here as an adverb in the sense of 'unusually' or 'extremely'; *guid* is the Scottish form of *good*. The phrase originally alluded to Robert Burns's *Address to the Unco Guid, or the Rigidly Righteous* (1787), and generally carries an implicit charge of hypocrisy.

UNDER age not yet adult according to the law. ● Cf. ▶ **come of AGE**.

the **UNIVERSITY of life** the experience of life regarded as a means of instruction. ● Cf. ▶ **the school of hard KNOCKS**.

the late **UNPLEASANTNESS** the war that took place recently. ● Originally used of the American Civil War (1861–5).

get UNTRACKED get into one's stride or find one's winning form, especially in sporting contexts. *US*

the (great) **UNWASHED** members of the working class as viewed by those in higher social strata; the multitude. *dated, derogatory* ● A M19 expression, now only used facetiously.

> **1997** *Spectator* 29 Nov. 10/2 Early piers tried to be rather socially exclusive, but the need to maintain revenue soon opened the gates to the great unwashed.

be all UP with be disastrous or hopeless for (a person). *informal* ● Used with *it* as subject: *it's all up with —*.

on the UP and up 1 steadily improving. 2 *chiefly N. Amer.* honest(ly); on the level. *informal*

something is UP something unusual or undesirable is afoot or happening. *informal*

> **1994** M. WILLIAMSON *Illuminata* I. i. 5 It feels as though something is up, as though something significant and big is about to happen.

UP against it facing some serious but unspecified difficulty. *informal*

UP and about (*or* doing) having risen from bed; active.

UP and running taking place; active.

> **1998** *New Scientist* 22 Aug. 47/1 The arms race may be up and running again.

UP for it ready to take part in a particular activity. *informal*

> **1998** *Times* 15 Sept. 18/3 Women … say poor stupid guy, the girl was clearly up for it.

UP hill and down dale up and down hills, or confronting many obstacles, on an arduous journey or in the fulfilment of an arduous task.

be UP on be informed about (a matter or subject). ● Cf. the originally US slang expression *bone up on*, meaning 'study hard to make oneself thoroughly acquainted with something'.

UP ▶ *see* **up the ANTE**; ▶ *see* **up in ARMS**; ▶ *see* **up the SPOUT**; ▶ *see* **up STICKS**; ▶ *see* **up to the MARK**; ▶ *see* **up to SNUFF**; ▶ *see* **up to one's TRICKS**.

on the UPGRADE improving; progressing.

have (*or* gain) the UPPER hand have (*or* gain) advantage or control over someone or something.

the UPPER crust the aristocracy and upper classes. *informal* ● In A. E. Baker's *Glossary of Northamptonshire Words and Phrases* (1854) the nickname for 'any female who assumes unauthorised superiority' is 'Mrs Upper Crust', but it was also current in US colloquial speech in M19. The French word *gratin* has a similar pair of literal and metaphorical senses, being literally 'a crust of crumbs and cheese on top of a cooked dish' and metaphorically 'the highest class of society'.

on one's UPPERS extremely short of money. *informal* ● With reference to worn-out shoes as an indicator of someone's poverty: the *upper* is the part of a shoe above the sole, which is all that is left after the sole has been worn away.

UPSET ▶ *see* **upset the APPLE CART**.

be quick (*or* slow) on the UPTAKE be quick or slow to understand something. *informal*

UPWARDLY ▶ *see* **downwardly MOBILE**.

V

take someone's name in VAIN use someone's name in a way that shows a lack of respect. ●Cf. the third of the Ten Commandments: 'Thou shalt not take the name of the Lord thy God in vain' (Exodus 20: 7).

VALE of tears the world regarded as a scene of trouble or sorrow. *literary* ●This phrase M16; earlier as *vale of trouble*, *vale of weeping*, or *vale of misery* (cf. Psalm 84:6 in the Book of Common Prayer version). *Vale of tears* appears in the poetry of Cowper and Shelley.

> **1997** *Shetland Times* 21 Nov. 4/2 Then by God's grace we'll meet again, Beyond this vale of tears.

the VALE of years the declining years of a person's life; old age. ●Often as *decline(d) into the vale of years*, quoting Shakespeare *Othello* III. iii. 269–70.

VANISHING ▶ *see* **do a DISAPPEARING act**.

VARIETY is the spice of life new and exciting experiences make life more interesting. ●In this form originally with reference to Cowper's *Task* (1785): 'Variety's the very spice of life, That gives it all its flavour' (ii. 606).

beyond the VEIL in a mysterious or hidden place or state, especially the unknown state of existence after death. ●Various passages in the Bible mention the veil that concealed the innermost sanctuary in the Temple in Jerusalem, later taken as referring to the mysterious division between the next world and this.

draw a VEIL over avoid discussing or calling attention to (something), especially because it is embarrassing or unpleasant.

take the VEIL become a nun.

with a VENGEANCE in a higher degree than was expected or desired; in the fullest sense.

VENT one's spleen scold or ill-treat without cause. ●Followed by preposition *on* or *upon*.

VEST ▶ *see* **keep one's CARDS close to one's chest**.

VICTORY ▶ *see* **PYRRHIC victory**.

take a dim (*or* poor) VIEW of regard with disfavour or pessimism.

> **1996** C. J. STONE *Fierce Dancing* iv. 62 He says that ... the Home Office ... take a dim view of lifers talking to the press.

a Potemkin VILLAGE a sham or unreal thing. ●Count Potemkin (1739–91), favourite of Empress Catherine II of Russia, reputedly ordered a number of sham villages to be built for the empress's tour of the Crimea in 1787.

the VILLAIN of the piece the main culprit. ●With reference to the character in a play or novel important to the plot because of his or her evil motives or actions.

a VIPER in one's bosom someone who injures or betrays a benefactor. ●From the idea that a kind-hearted person warming a snake in their bosom is likely to be bitten. The idea is found in Latin (*in sinu viperam habere*) and the expression appears in various forms in English from L16.

make a VIRGINIA fence walk crookedly because drunk. *US* ●A *Virginia fence* is a rail fence made in a zigzag.

make a VIRTUE (out) of necessity derive some credit or benefit from an unwelcome obligation. ●A concept found in Latin in the writings of St Jerome (died 420): *facis de necessitate virtutem* you make a virtue of necessity (*In Libros Rufini* iii. 2). It passed into Old French (*faire de nécessité vertu*) and was apparently first used in English *c.*1374 by Chaucer (*Troilus and Criseyde* iv. 1586).

> **1997** *Spectator* 15 Nov. 60 How important it is for humanity always to make a virtue out of necessity.

VISITING fireman a visitor to an organization given especially cordial treatment on account of his or her importance. *US*

VOICE ▶ *see* **STILL small voice**; ▶ *see* **a voice in the WILDERNESS**.

VOTE with one's feet indicate an opinion by being present or absent or by some other course of action.

> **1991** J. HALSTEAD in Hampson & Maule *After Cold War* 145 Once the Berlin Wall had been breached ... the East Germans voted with their feet in an irresistible move toward freedom.

VOTE ▶ *see* **SPLIT the vote**.

W

WAG(s) ▶ *see* **the TAIL wags the dog**.

on the WAGON teetotal. *informal* ●Originally E20 US slang in the form *on the water wagon*; this is now less usual than the shorter form.

| **1989** M. NORMAN *These Good Men* iv. 111 I'll just have a club soda with a twist of lime … . I'm on the wagon.

WAGON ▶ *see* **FIX someone's wagon**; ▶ *see* **HITCH one's wagon to a star**; ▶ *see* **a whole TEAM and the dog under the wagon**.

WAKE up and smell the coffee become aware of the realities of a situation, however unpleasant. *chiefly N. Amer., informal* ●Usually in imperative.

be a WAKE-UP be fully alert or aware. *Austral. & NZ, informal* ●Also *be awake up*.

WALK all over **1** defeat easily. **2** take advantage of. *informal*

WALK the chalk have one's sobriety tested. ●A traditional method of testing whether someone is sober is making them walk along a chalked line.

WALK someone off his (*or* her) feet (*or* legs) exhaust a person with walking.

WALK of life the position within society that a person holds or the part of society to which they belong as a result of their job or social status.

WALK on eggs (*or* eggshells) be extremely cautious about one's words or actions.

WALK one's talk suit one's actions to one's words. *chiefly N. Amer.* ●Also as *walk the walk*.

WALK Spanish made to walk under compulsion. *informal* ●With reference to walking on tiptoe like a Spanish dancer (because one's collar and trousers are being held in order to propel one in a particular direction). M19 US slang.

WALK tall feel justifiable pride. *informal*

WALK ▶ *see* **RUN before one can walk**; ▶ *see* **tread the BOARDS**; ▶ *see* **waltz MATILDA**; ▶ *see* **walk on AIR**; ▶ *see* **walk the PLANK**.

go WALKABOUT wander around from place to place in a protracted or leisurely way. *orig. Austral.* ●A pidgin English expression used literally of the practice of Australian Aboriginals who go off into the bush away from white society in order to re-establish contact with spiritual sources.

go WALKIES go missing, especially as a result of theft. ●*Walkies* is a childish or jocular form of *walk*, used mainly in the context of taking a dog for a walk.

a WALKING — someone who notably embodies the characteristics of an inanimate object, especially a book. *informal* ●For example, someone described as *a walking encyclopaedia* has an impressive knowledge of facts.

drive someone up the WALL make someone very irritated or angry. *informal*

go to the WALL **1** (of a business) fail; go out of business. **2** support someone or something, no matter what the cost to oneself is. *informal*

off the WALL **1** eccentric or unconventional. **2** (of a person) crazy or angry. **3** (of an accusation) without basis or foundation. *N. Amer. informal* ●Often attributive: *off-the-wall*.

up against the WALL in an inextricable situation, in great trouble or difficulty. ●With allusion to the situation of someone facing execution by a firing squad.

WALL-to-wall **1** (of a carpet or other floor covering) fitted to cover an entire floor. **2** *informal* of great extent or number; allowing no unfilled space or interval.

> **2 1982** S. PARETSKY *Indemnity Only* vi. 74 Why would he agree to see me? He'd never heard of me, he has wall-to-wall appointments.

WALL ▶ *see* **between you and me and the BEDPOST**.

WALLS have ears used to warn someone to be careful what they say as people may be eavesdropping. *proverbial* ●Used in this form since L16. The older saying *fields have eyes, and woods have ears* (E13) is now less common.

on the WALLABY (*or* wallaby track) (of a person) unemployed and having no fixed address. *Austral., informal*

WALTZ ▶ *see* **waltz MATILDA**.

a WAR of nerves a struggle in which opponents try to wear each other down by psychological means.

a WAR of words a prolonged period during which two people or groups engage in a strong dispute about a certain issue.

a (*or* the) WAR to end all wars a war intended to make subsequent wars impossible, in particular the First World War.

keep something WARM for someone hold or occupy a place or post until another person is ready to do so.

make it (*or* things) WARM for someone cause trouble or make things unpleasant for someone.

(as) WARM as toast pleasantly warm. ●Also *toasty warm* (mainly US).

> **1991** W. P. KINSELLA *Box Socials* iv. 81 Scrunched down, warm as toast, between the cookstove and the woodbox, I couldn't see that getting something for nothing could be all that bad.

WARM ▶ *see* **warm the COCKLES of someone's heart**.

WARN someone off notify someone to keep at a distance. ●Specifically in horse racing, the British Jockey Club prior to 1969 had a rule empowering it to *warn someone off the course*, that is prohibit someone who had broken Jockey

Club regulations from riding or running horses at meetings under the club's jurisdiction.

on the WARPATH in a state of anger about something; expressing antipathy or hostility towards a decision or action. ● Formerly used literally of American Indians when heading towards a battle with an enemy.

have been in the WARS have been hurt or injured. *informal*

WARTS and all including or with no attempt to conceal features or qualities that are not appealing or attractive. *informal* ● Said to originate from a remark made by Oliver Cromwell to the portraitist Peter Lely: 'Remark all these roughnesses, pimples, warts, and everything as you see me' (quoted in Horace Walpole *Anecdotes of Painting in England* III (1763). Generally used postpositively (see quot.), but also as a prepositive modifier, e.g. in *a warts-and-all portrait*.

| 1998 *Times* 20 Feb. 40/2 We painted Fayed, warts and all; Fleet Street denounces us for not painting just the warts.

come out in the WASH be clarified, or (of contingent difficulties) be resolved, in the course of events. *informal* ● E20, but L19 in the form *come out in the washing*.

| 1993 *Canadian Living* May 69/4 We could all benefit from borrowing her philosophy: be cheerful and worry sparingly. In the end, it will all come out in the wash.

WASH one's hands of renounce responsibility for. ● Originally with reference to the biblical description of Pontius Pilate's symbolic action of washing his hands before the crowd to declare himself innocent of the blood of Jesus (Matthew 27:24).

won't WASH will not be believed or accepted. *informal* ● Used especially of an argument, proposal, plan, etc.; often with preposition *with*.

| 1998 *New Scientist* 19 Sept. 3/3 In the end, however, this argument won't wash.

WASH ▶ *see* **wash one's dirty LINEN in public**.

WASTE of space someone who is perceived as useless or incompetent. *informal*

WASTE not, want not if you use a commodity or resource carefully and without extravagance you will never be in need. *proverbial* ● *Want* can be understood as either 'lack' or 'desire' according to context. Apparently already standard in this form in 1800 when quoted by Maria Edgeworth as a slogan put up over a kitchen chimney piece.

WATCH one's (*or* someone's) back protect oneself (*or* someone else) against danger from an unexpected quarter.

WATCH the time ensure that one is aware of the time, typically in order to avoid being late.

WATCH ▶ *see* **watch the PENNIES**; ▶ *see* **watch someone's SMOKE**; ▶ *see* **watch this SPACE**; ▶ *see* **mind one's STEP**.

the WATCHES of the night night-time, especially viewed as a time when one cannot sleep. *literary* ● A *watch* was originally each of the three or four periods of time into which the night was divided by the Jews and Romans, during which a watch or guard was kept.

like WATER in great quantities.

> **1991** M. TULLY *No Full Stops in India* (1992) x. 321 Digvijay's supporters allege that George spent money like water to bribe the local leaders.

of the first WATER extreme or unsurpassed of their kind. ●The sense of *water* as 'the brilliance and transparency of a jewel' is found in other European languages (Ger. *wasser*, French *eau*), and may derive from Arabic. *Of the first water* used of a diamond or pearl denotes one that possesses these qualities to the highest degree, but in transferred use it often refers to someone or something perceived as extremely undesirable, e.g. *a bore of the first water*.

WATER under the bridge (*or* N. Amer. **over the dam**) events or situations in the past that are consequently no longer to be regarded as important or worth discussing. ●The related expression using this metaphor (*there's been*) *a lot of water under the bridge since* — is used to indicate that a lot of time has passed and a great many events have occurred since a particular event.

WATER ▶ *see* **like water off a DUCK's back**; ▶ *see* **on the WAGON**.

meet one's WATERLOO experience a final and decisive defeat. ●With reference to the battle of Waterloo (1815), which marked the final defeat of Napoleon.

WATERS ▶ *see* **cast one's BREAD upon the waters**.

make WAVES **1** create a significant impression. **2** *informal* cause trouble.

> **1 1997** *Spectator* 1 Nov. 25 Perhaps unsurprisingly, it is the old pros disguised as new boys and girls who are making the biggest waves.

WAX (noun) ▶ *see* **be PUTTY in someone's hands**.

WAX (verb) ▶ *see* **wax LYRICAL about**.

WAX and wane undergo alternate increases and decreases. ●Used especially of the apparent size of the moon as observed through the course of a month.

go out of one's WAY make a special effort; act gratuitously or without compulsion. ●Often followed by *to* and infinitive.

on the WAY out **1** going down in status, estimation, or favour; going out of fashion. **2** dying. *informal*

put someone in the WAY of give a person the opportunity of.

the WAY of the world the customary manner of proceeding, behaving, etc.

WAY to go used to express pleasure, approval, or excitement. *N. Amer., informal*

> **1990** R. OLIVER *Making Champions* ii. 187 You had Bechard shakin'. He wasn't gonna mess with you. Way to go! Play mad, hoo boy!

WAYS and means methods of achieving something. ●In the British parliamentary system this phrase is used specifically of the various methods of raising government revenue.

WAYS ▶ *see* **have it BOTH ways**.

fall by the WAYSIDE **1** fail to persist in an endeavour or undertaking. **2** be left without attention or help. ●In sense 1 with allusion to the biblical parable of the sower (Mark 4:3-20, esp. verse 4).

the WEAK link the point at which a system, sequence, or organization is most vulnerable; the least dependable element or member. ● Cf. the saying *a chain is only as strong as its weakest link*.

WEAK ▶ *see* **weak at the KNEES**.

WEAR (or **wear one's years) well** remain young-looking.

WEAR ▶ *see* **wear one's HEART on one's sleeve**; ▶ *see* **wear the TROUSERS**.

fine (or **lovely) WEATHER for ducks** wet, rainy weather. *humorous*

keep a WEATHER eye on observe very carefully, especially for changes or developments. ●Also *keep a weather eye open*.

make good (or **bad) WEATHER of it** (of a ship) behave well (or badly) in a storm.

make heavy WEATHER (or **work) of** have unnecessary difficulty in dealing with (a task or problem). *informal* ●*Heavy weather* has the specific nautical meaning of violent wind accompanied by heavy rain or rough sea.

under the WEATHER **1** slightly unwell. **2** in low spirits. *informal*

get WEAVING set briskly to work; begin action. *Brit., informal*

> 1992 G. M. FRASER *Quartered Safe Out Here* 199 'Come on, come on, come on! ... Let's get weaving!'.

the thin end of the WEDGE an action or procedure of little importance in itself, but likely to lead to more serious developments. *informal*

WEIGH ▶ *see* **weigh in the BALANCE**.

a WEIGHT off one's mind an anxiety has been relieved. ●Used to indicate that one is now reassured after having been very anxious.

worth one's (or **its) WEIGHT in gold** exceedingly useful or helpful.

WEIGHT ▶ *see* **THROW one's weight about**.

and WELCOME as far as one is concerned someone is welcome to (do) something. ●Used, often dismissively, at the end of a statement to indicate that the speaker is happy for the person addressed or talked about to have or do something.

outstay one's WELCOME stay as a visitor longer than one is wanted.

WELCOME ▶ *see* **join the CLUB**.

make the WELKIN ring make a very loud sound. ●*Welkin* (OE *weolcen*) is a poetic term for 'the vault of the sky', now obsolete apart from literary contexts and this expression.

give it some WELLY exert more effort or strength. *slang* ●*Welly* or *wellie*, the

informal abbreviation of *Wellington boot*, has developed (L20) the slang sense
of 'kick' or 'force'.

the great WEN London. *literary* ● From William Cobbett *Rural Rides* (5 Jan. 1822)
'But what is to be the fate of the great wen of all'.

go WEST be killed or lost; meet with disaster. *Brit., informal* ● With reference to
the sun's setting in the west.

all WET completely wrong. *N. Amer.*

WET the baby's head celebrate a baby's birth with a drink, usually an alcoholic
one. *Brit., informal*

WET behind the ears lacking experience; immature. *informal* ● Like a baby or
young animal still damp after being born.

a WET blanket someone who has a depressing or discouraging effect on others.
● With allusion to a dampened blanket used to smother a fire.
| **1991** M. CURTIN *Plastic Tomato Cutter* (1996) xx. 164 When in the company of those of us
who do succumb to the occasional dram Father Willie was never a wet blanket.

WET one's whistle have a drink. *informal*

out of WHACK out of order; not working. *chiefly N. Amer. & Austral.*
| **1998** *Bookseller* 28 Aug. 21/3 [T]here's been a fair amount of jeering … at the *Sunday Times*
for getting its figures so comprehensively out of whack, by a factor of about 100 if memory
serves.

top (or full or the full) WHACK the maximum price or rate.
| **1998** *Country Life* 26 Mar. 63/2 [At a new restaurant] one must expect to pay top whack.

a WHALE of a — an exceedingly good or fine example of the thing specified.
informal

WHAM-BAM-thankyou-ma'am sexual activity conducted roughly and
quickly, without tenderness. ● M–L20 US.

and/or WHAT have you and/or anything else similar. *informal*

and WHAT not and other similar things. *informal*
| **1992** N. BHATTACHARYA *Hem & Football* ix. 111 Has anyone ever seen such a selfish
daughter? Gorging herself on eggs, milk and what not while others in the house don't even get
two square meals?

WHAT with because of. ● Introducing a list of several relevant factors.

WHAT ▶ *see* **KNOW what's what**.

separate (or sort) the WHEAT from the chaff distinguish valuable people
or things from worthless ones. ● The metaphorical contrast of *wheat* and *chaff*
appears in several biblical passages (e.g., Matthew 3:17 '[Christ] will gather
the wheat into his garner; but the chaff he will burn with fire unquenchable').

silly as a WHEEL very silly. *Austral.*
| **1985** J. CLANCHY *Lie of Land* 112 Father Tierney was mad. Cracked as an egg, some boys
said, silly as a wheel.

WHEEL and deal engage in commercial or political scheming. ●*Wheel* here has the sense of 'control events', as in *a big wheel* meaning an important person who makes things happen. Often as noun phrase: *wheeling and dealing*.

the WHEEL of Fortune the wheel which the personification of Fortune was fabled to turn as a symbol of random luck or change.

WHEEL ▶ *see* **a BIG cheese**; ▶ *see* **a FLY on the wheel**; ▶ *see* **REINVENT the wheel**.

spin one's WHEELS waste one's time or efforts. *N. Amer., informal*

WHEELS within wheels complications and secret or indirect influences affecting a situation. ●With reference to the cogs of intricate machinery.

WHEELS ▶ *see* **GREASE the wheels**.

WHET (some)one's (*or* the) appetite make someone want more.

WHIP ▶ *see* **a fair CRACK of the whip**.

WHIPS of large quantities of. *Austral. & NZ*

give it a WHIRL give it a try. *informal* ●Originally a US colloquialism (L19); cf. ▶ **give it a BURL**.
| 1979 s. WILSON *Greenish Man* 11 You've nothing to lose. Give it a whirl, try it for a month.

reap the WHIRLWIND suffer serious consequences as a result of one's actions. ●With allusion to the proverb *they that sow the wind shall reap the whirlwind*, based on Hosea 8:7.
| 1998 *Spectator* 15 Aug. 12/1 A [political] party that thought all it had to do to keep Scotland happy was deliver devolution is instead reaping the whirlwind it sowed in the Eighties.

within a WHISKER of extremely close or near to doing, achieving, or suffering something. *informal*

have (*or* have grown) WHISKERS (especially of a story) be very old. *informal*

blow the WHISTLE on expose (someone's) illegal or secret actions to public scrutiny or investigation with the intention of having them stopped. *informal* ●An idiom from football, in which the referee blows a whistle when the rules of the game are infringed. The idiom has given rise to *whistle-blower* (a person who exposes such actions) and *whistle-blowing*.

(as) clean as a WHISTLE 1 extremely clean or clear. 2 *informal* free of incriminating evidence.

WHISTLE something down the wind let something go; abandon something. ●With reference to the falconer's action in letting a trained hawk loose by casting it off with the wind.

WHISTLE in the dark pretend to be confident or unafraid. ●Often *whistling in the dark* (M20).
| 1996 B. CONNOLLY *Rotten Heart of Europe* (ed. 2) viii. 189 Swedish authorities had, whistling in the dark, spoke of ERM 'association'—but nothing had come of it.

WHISTLE in the wind try unsuccessfully to influence something that cannot be changed.

WHISTLE ▶ *see* **WET one's whistle**.

mark with a WHITE stone regard as specially fortunate or happy. ●With allusion to the ancient practice of using a white stone as a memorial of a happy event; cf. Latin *albo lapillo notare diem* 'to mark the day with a white stone' (Pliny *Natural History* VII. xl. 41).

show the WHITE feather appear cowardly. *Brit., dated* ●A white feather in a game-bird's tail was considered to be a mark of bad breeding.

a WHITE elephant something useless or a nuisance to its possessor. ●The rare albino elephant was much prized in former times by the kings of Siam. As it was the object of special veneration, its upkeep was very costly, so it was likely to ruin any courtier to whom the king gave it as a gift.

a WHITE knight a company that makes a welcome bid for a company facing an unwelcome takeover bid. ●The metaphor is of the traditional chivalric figure who rides to the rescue of someone in danger; also ▶ **a KNIGHT in shining armour**.

WHITE ▶ *see* **big white CHIEF**; ▶ *see* **BLEED someone dry**; ▶ *see* **the white man's BURDEN**; ▶ *see* **white man's GRAVE**.

a WHITED sepulchre a hypocrite; someone who is ostensibly virtuous or agreeable but inwardly corrupt. *literary* ●After Matthew 23:27 'Woe unto you ... for ye are like unto whited sepulchres, which indeed appear beautiful outward, but are within full of dead men's bones, and of all uncleanness.'

WHITER than white 1 extremely white. 2 morally beyond reproach. ●In modern use after its popularization as a slogan advertising Persil soap powder.

WHO ▶ *see* **who GOES there?**

out of (the) WHOLE cloth wholly fabricated; totally false. *N. Amer., informal*

the WHOLE nine yards everything possible or available. *N. Amer., informal*

WHOLE ▶ *see* **go the whole HOG**; ▶ *see* **a whole new BALLGAME**.

WHOOP it up 1 enjoy oneself or celebrate in a noisy way, usually in a group. 2 *US* create or show excitement or enthusiasm. *informal*

WHOOP ▶ *see* **give a TOSS**.

make WHOOPEE 1 celebrate wildly. 2 make love.

the WHYS and wherefores reasons; details.

> **1991** *Gramophone* Jan. 1350/2 At this time I was desperate to know all the whys and wherefores of a really advanced technique.

dip one's WICK (of a man) have sexual intercourse. *vulgar slang*

get on someone's WICK annoy someone. *Brit., informal*

no peace (*or* rest) for the WICKED someone's heavy workload or lack of tranquillity is punishment for a sinful life. *humorous* ●With allusion to Isaiah 48:22 'There is no peace, saith the Lord, unto the wicked.' Used especially in spoken English as an expression of humorous resignation on the part of the speaker or of ironic comment on another's activities.

a sticky WICKET a tricky or awkward situation. *informal* ●Used literally in cricket of a pitch that has been drying out after rain and is therefore difficult to bat on.

WIDE ▶ *see* **give a wide BERTH to**; ▶ *see* **off the MARK**.

a WIDOW's cruse a seemingly meagre resource which is in fact not readily exhausted. *literary* ●In allusion to the biblical story of the container of oil that was miraculously replenished in a prolonged period of drought (1 Kings 17).

a WIDOW's mite a person's modest contribution to a cause or charity, representing the most the giver can afford. ●From the biblical story of the poor widow who donated two mites (coins of low value), representing her entire fund of money, to the treasury of the Temple in Jerusalem (Mark 12:41–4).

WIG ▶ *see* **FLIP one's lid**.

get a WIGGLE on get moving; hurry. *informal* ●Often imperative.

WIGS on the green a violent or unpleasant altercation; ructions. *orig. Anglo-Irish* ●From the idea of wigs falling off or being pulled off during a brawl.

WILD and woolly uncouth in appearance or behaviour. ●Originally applied to the American West; cf. 1891 title *Tales of the 'Wild & Woolly West'*. The adjective *woolly* probably refers to sheepskin clothing, worn with the wool still attached to it, seen as characteristic garb of the pioneers and cowboys who opened up the western US.

WILD ▶ *see* **sow one's wild OATS**.

a voice in the WILDERNESS an unheeded advocate of reform. ●In the Bible, the person who announced the coming of the Messiah (Isaiah 40:3), identified with John the Baptist (Matthew 3:3).

spread like WILDFIRE spread with great speed.

a WILD-GOOSE chase a foolish, fruitless, or hopeless quest, a pursuit of something unattainable. ●Earliest (L16) as the term, now obsolete, for a kind of equestrian sport in which the second or any succeeding horse had to follow accurately the course of the leader, like a flight of wild geese; later, an erratic course taken by one person (*or* thing) and followed (*or* that may be followed) by another.

1998 *Spectator* 5 Sept. 32/3 The 'struggle to align the clock and the heavens', then, is ultimately the story of mortal vanity, or at least a wild-goose chase.

where there's a WILL there's a way determination will overcome any obstacle. *proverbial* ●This form of the saying was quoted by Hazlitt in 1822, but George Herbert recorded a variant as one of his *Outlandish Proverbs* in 1640: *To him that will, wais are not wanting.*

WILL o' the wisp an elusive or deceptive person, idea, or goal. ●Literally, a phosphorescent light seen hovering or floating over marshy ground, perhaps due to the combustion of methane.

with the best WILL in the world however good one's intentions. ●Used to imply that success in a particular undertaking, although desired, is unlikely.

with a WILL energetically and resolutely.

> **1984** B. MACLAVERTY *Cal* 68 Dunlop told Cal to muck out the byre and because it was something he could do he went at it with a will.

wear the green WILLOW grieve for the loss of a loved one; suffer unrequited love. *literary* ● A willow branch or leaves were a symbol of grief or unlucky love; cf. the Willow Song in Shakespeare's *Othello*.

WIN (*or* earn) one's spurs gain one's first distinction or honours. *informal* ● In the Middle Ages gilt spurs were the distinguishing mark of a knight, and to *win one's spurs* was to gain a knighthood by an act of valour.

you can't WIN them all (*or* win some, lose some) no one can be successful on every occasion. *informal* ● Said to console someone for a failure or as an expression of resignation at one's own lack of success.

WIN ▶ *see* **win by a NECK**; ▶ *see* **carry the DAY**; ▶ *see* **win the wooden SPOON**.

between WIND and water at a vulnerable point. ● A nautical metaphor referring to that part of a ship's side near the waterline that is sometimes above the water and sometimes submerged; damage to the ship at this level is particularly dangerous. The phrase is first recorded in its literal sense at the time of the Spanish Armada (1588): 'One of the shot was betweene the winde and the water, whereof they thought she would haue sonke.' It was applied metaphorically to people from M17.

> **1967** M. GILBERT *Dust and Heat* iii. 239 Mallinson *must* have guessed what was coming. Nevertheless, it hit him between wind and water.

get WIND of begin to suspect that (something) is happening; hear a rumour of. *informal*

gone with the WIND gone completely; disappeared without trace. ● From Ernest Dowson's poem 'Cynara' (1896): 'I have forgot much, Cynara, gone with the wind'; also the title of Margaret Mitchell's novel (1936) on the American Civil War.

it's an ill WIND few things are so bad that no one profits from them. *proverbial* ● A nautical saying; in full, *it's an ill wind that blows nobody any good or that profits nobody.* Current since M16, the saying is used especially as a comment on someone's good fortune when it has been occasioned by someone else's misfortune.

put (*or* have) the WIND up alarm or frighten (*or* be alarmed or frightened). *Brit., informal*

> *1918 W. OWEN *Letter* 11 Oct. Shells so close that they thoroughly put the wind up a Life Guardsman in the trench with me.

sail close to (*or* near) the WIND verge on indecency, dishonesty, or disaster. *informal* ● A nautical expression, meaning 'sail as nearly against the wind as is consistent with using its force'. In its figurative euphemistic sense since M19.

> *1865 H. KINGSLEY *Hillyars and Burtons* iv. A certain kind of young English gentleman, who has sailed too close to the wind at home, and who comes to the colony to be whitewashed.

take the WIND out of someone's sails frustrate a person by unexpectedly ith the consequence that when a wolf did actually appear no one came to help him.

e (or hold) a WOLF by the ears be in a precarious position. ● The saying became current in English in M16, but the comic playwright Terence (195–159 BC) alluded to its Latin equivalent (*lupum auribus tenere*) as an old saying in his (*Phormio* (III. ii. 21). Cf. ▶ **have a TIGER by the tail**.

1631 F. QUARLES *Samson* xi. 63 I have a Wolfe by th'eares; I dare be bold, Neither with safety, to let goe, nor hold: What shall I doe?

p the WOLF from the door have enough money to avert hunger or starvation. ● Used hyperbolically in this sense since M16, but the image of the wolf as the embodiment of devouring and destructive forces is much earlier and has biblical warrant (e.g. Matthew 10:16).

OLF in sheep's clothing a person or thing that appears friendly or harmless but is really hostile and dangerous. ● With allusion to Jesus' admonition: 'Beware of false prophets, which come to you in sheep's clothing, but inwardly they are ravening wolves' (Matthew 7:15).

w someone to the WOLVES sacrifice a friend or ally to their enemies in order to avert danger or difficulties from oneself or a group of people. *informal* ● Probably in allusion to tales of packs of wolves pursuing travellers in horse-drawn sleighs, when one person would be pushed off the sleigh to allow it to go faster, thus enabling the others to make their escape.

1958 *Listener* 6 Nov. 743/2 This able and agreeable doctor was thrown to the wolves by a Prime Minister who had good reason to know that his own position was desperate.

MAN ▶ *see* **a man of LETTERS**; ▶ *see* **a man of the WORLD**.

ne days' WONDER a person who or thing which is briefly famous. ● The period during which a novelty is proverbially said to attract attention.

k (or do) WONDERS have a very beneficial effect (on someone or something).

1995 K. ISHIGURO *Unconsoled* v. 57 On the contrary, Father's worked wonders, made enormous strides!

see the WOOD (or N. Amer. the forest) for the trees fail to grasp the main issue because of over-attention to details. ● Current since M16. The North American version makes clear the sense in which *wood* is to be taken in this saying.

of the WOOD (or woods) out of danger or difficulty. ● Cf. the proverbial warning against *hallooing before you are out of the wood* (L18).

h (or US knock on) WOOD touch something wooden with the hand to avert ill luck. *chiefly Brit.* ● Often as an exclamation accompanying the action.

DEN ▶ *see* **accept a wooden NICKEL**; ▶ *see* **a wooden NUTMEG**; ▶ *see* **in the wooden SPOON**.

thing nasty in the WOODSHED a shocking or distasteful thing kept cret. *Brit., informal* ● A catch-phrase taken from Stella Gibbons's comic assic *Cold Comfort Farm* (1932); the shock of seeing *something nasty in the*

anticipating an action or remark. ● With allusion to the position of the wind in relation to a sailing vessel, used figuratively since E19.

1977 E. FIGES *Nelly's Version* (1988) I. i. 14 She could so easily have taken the wind out of my sails and put me in my place for good.

to the WIND(s) (or the four winds) **1** in all directions. **2** so as to be abandoned or neglected. ● The *four winds* are the north, south, east, and west winds.

WIND (noun) ▶ *see* **RAISE the wind**.

WIND (verb) ▶ *see* **twist someone round one's little FINGER**.

fling (or throw) one's cap over the WINDMILL(s) act recklessly or unconventionally. *dated* ● Translating French *jeter son bonnet par-dessus les moulins*.

1933 J. GALSWORTHY *One More River* xxxii. 305 I suggest that both of you felt it would be mad to fling your caps over the windmill like that?

WINDMILLS ▶ *see* **TILT at windmills**.

out (of) the WINDOW completely lost or abandoned. *informal* ● Used to emphasize how totally and irrevocably something, such as a plan or a way of acting or thinking, has disappeared.

1998 *Economist* 14 Mar. 35/2 In the ensuing struggle between the two groups [of councillors], the public interest goes out of the window.

WINDOW of opportunity a favourable opportunity for doing something that must be seized if it is not to be missed.

WINDOW of vulnerability an opportunity to attack something that is at risk. ● Especially associated with a cold-war claim that America's land-based missiles were easy targets for a Soviet first strike.

WINDS ▶ *see* **to the WIND**.

to WINDWARD of in an advantageous position in relation to. *dated* ● A sailing metaphor. Used literally in nautical contexts, and in this figurative sense from L18.

new WINE in old bottles something new or innovatory added to an existing or established system or organization. ● With allusion to the proverb *you can't put new wine into old bottles*, itself a reference to Matthew 9:17 'Neither do men put new wine into old bottles: else the bottles break, and the wine runneth out, and the bottles perish.'

WINE and dine (of people) have a meal with wine. ● Also used transitively, meaning to entertain someone to a meal with wine.

WINE, women, and song the hedonistic life of drinking, sexual pleasure, and carefree entertainment proverbially required by men.

on a WING and a prayer relying on hope; with only a slight chance of success. ● With reference to a song (1943) by H. Adamson about an aircraft making an emergency landing, 'Comin' in on a Wing and a Prayer'.

under one's WING in or into one's protective care so as to help face new experiences or challenges.

> **1991** M. MANTLE *My Favorite Summer: 1956* ii. 23 He kind of took me under his wing and showed me the ropes in my first year.

WINGED words highly significant or apposite words. *literary* ●The image, taken from Homer's *Iliad* (*passim*), is of the words travelling as directly as arrows to their mark.

in the WINGS ready to do something or to be used at the appropriate time. ●A theatrical metaphor: *wings* here are the areas screened from public view where actors wait for their cue to come on stage.

spread (or stretch or try) one's WINGS extend one's activities and interests or start new ones.

in the WINK of an eye (or in a wink) very quickly.

not sleep (or get) a WINK (or not get a wink of sleep) not sleep at all.

as easy as WINKING very easy or easily. *informal*

WINKS ▶ *see* **FORTY winks**.

WIPE someone's eye get the better of a person. ●*Brit., informal, dated*

WIPE the floor with inflict a humiliating defeat on. *informal*

WIPE the slate clean forgive or forget past faults or offences; make a fresh start. ●Shopkeepers and pub landlords used formerly to keep a record of what was owing to them by writing on a tablet of slate; hence a *clean slate* was one on which no debts were recorded.

down (or up) to the WIRE (of a situation) not decided or resolved until the very last moment. *orig. US, informal* ●The *wire* here is the finishing line on a racetrack.

under the WIRE at the last possible opportunity, just before a time limit. *N. Amer., informal*

WIRES ▶ *see* **get one's wires CROSSED**.

in someone's WISDOM ill-advisedly. ●Used ironically to suggest that an action is not well judged.

be WISE after the event understand and assess an event or situation only after its implications have become obvious. ●The French chronicler Philippe de Commynes used the phrase *saiges après le coup* in his *Mémoires* (*c.*1490), remarking of it *comme l'on dit des Bretons* (as the Bretons say). Although there are other allusions to *wise after the event* in the intervening period, the actual saying *it is easy to be wise after the event* is not recorded in English before E20.

be none (or not any) the WISER know no more than before.

put someone WISE give someone important information. *informal* ●Often with preposition *to*.

> **1950** G. GREENE *Third Man* ii. 21 He was a year older and knew the ropes. He put me wise to a lot of things.

a WISE man of Gotham a fool. *dated* ●*Gotham* was a vil[lage?] the folly of its inhabitants. Any link with Gotham in N[ew York?] uncertain. In E19 US *Gotham* became a nickname for New [York.]

the WISH is father to the thought we believe a thing b[ecause we wish it] true. ●With allusion to Shakespeare 2 *Henry IV* IV. v. 93 ('Th[y wish was] Harry, to that thought'), although observations on such [are] much older, occurring for example in the writings of Juliu[s Caesar (*De Bello*] *Gallico* iii. 18) and Demosthenes (*Olynthiaca* iii. 19).

> **1980** A. T. ELLIS *Birds of Air* 40 Somewhere in that area of the human mi[nd where the wish is] father to the thought activity was taking place. Hunter, Barbara decide[d ...] invitation in order to be with her.

if WISHES were horses (beggars would ride) if you coul[d obtain your] aims simply by wishing for them, life would be very easy. *p[roverb]* ●[First] recorded (E17) as a Scottish proverb. The first clause is now o[ften used expan-] sively on its own.

be at one's WITS' end be overwhelmed with difficulties and [not know] what to do next.

be frightened (or scared) out of one's WITS be extremely fr[ightened.]

gather (or collect) one's WITS bring oneself back to a state of [composure.]

> **1984** G. MCCAUGHREAN *Canterbury Tales* (1988) 46 Poor old man, he was to[o ... to] speak. And before he could collect his wits, he was sitting at table ... with his l[ord on one side] and his daughter on the other.

have (or keep) one's WITS about one be constantly alert and [ready.]

live by one's WITS earn money by clever and sometimes dish[onest means,] having no regular occupation.

pit one's WITS against compete with (someone or something).

> **1996** E. LOVELACE *Salt* xi. 201 Michael ... would be the one to make mone[y ... some] greater cause or adversary to pit his wits and slickness and spite against.

the WITCHING hour midnight. ●Cf. Shakespeare *Hamlet* III. ii. 4[06 'Tis now the] very witching time of night, When churchyards yawn and he[ll itself breathes] out contagion to this world.' Hamlet is referring to the ancien[t super-]stition that witches and other powers of darkness are active a[t night.]

WITHDRAWAL symptoms a feeling of being depressed b[y the absence of] something one has previously enjoyed. *informal* ●Used ori[ginally and] literally of the unpleasant physiological reactions that acco[mpany the process] of ceasing to use an addictive drug.

WITHER on the vine perish from neglect or inaction. ●W[ith allusion to an] abortive crop on a grapevine, probably referring to variou[s biblical passages] in which a withered vine is a metaphor for physical or [spiritual impover-]ishment.

cry WOLF call for help when it is not needed; raise a [false alarm. ●With] reference to the cautionary tale of a shepherd boy who c[ried wolf with false] alarms with cries of 'Wolf!', until people no longer too[k him seriously.]

woodshed was used by Aunt Ada Doom as her pretext for her emotional blackmail of her family.

take someone to the WOODSHED reprove or punish someone, especially discreetly. *US, informal* ● Now old-fashioned, this expression alluded to the practice of taking a naughty child to the woodshed for a beating out of sight of others.

vanish into (or come or crawl out of) the WOODWORK disappear into (or energe from) obscurity. *informal* ● Used of something unwelcome, with the implication that the persons or things concerned are like cockroaches or other unpleasant fauna that live in crevices of skirting-boards, cupboards, etc.

all WOOL and a yard wide of excellent quality, thoroughly sound. ● Literally, with reference to top-quality cloth.

| **1974** 'A. GILBERT' *Nice Little Killing* iii. 40 No one will ever catch her … with an alibi all wool and a yard wide.

pull the WOOL over someone's eyes deceive someone, especially by telling untruths. ● Originally an M19 US colloquialism.

| **1997** *Spectator* 8 Nov. 34/2 On no occasion do I remember Ridsdale trying to pull the wool over my eyes but rather trying always to remove the wool that journalists … pull over their own eyes.

have a WORD in someone's ear speak to someone privately and discreetly, usually to give them a warning. *informal*

| ***1599** W. SHAKESPEARE *Much Ado* IV. ii. 27Come you hither, sirrah; a word in your ear, sir.

a man (or woman) of his (or her) WORD a person who keeps the promises that they make.

take someone at their WORD interpret a person's words literally or exactly, especially by believing them or doing as they suggest.

take someone's WORD (for it) believe what someone says or writes without checking for oneself.

the WORD on the street a rumour or piece of information currently being circulated.

| **1992** V. HEADLEY *Yardie* (1993) 167 The word on the street was that Roy was hooked and had smoked a fair amount of the crack himself.

someone's WORD is their bond someone keeps their promises. ● Especially in the somewhat dated saying *An Englishman's word is his bond*.

someone's WORD is law someone must be obeyed without question.

(by) WORD of mouth (by) the use of speech rather than writing. ● Often as modifier (*word-of-mouth*) of a personal spoken recommendation.

| **1987** B. DUFFY *World as I Found It* (1990) 5 His ideas were repeated by word of mouth or passed around as transcripts of the shorthand notes that his students doggedly took down during his lectures.

a WORD to the wise a hint or brief explanation given when that is all that is required. ●Cf. the equivalent Latin phrase *verbum sapienti sat est*, the humorous abbreviation of which, *verb. sap.* (E19), is used in similar contexts.

> **1983** P. LIVELY *Perfect Happiness* (1985) iv. 40 A word to the wise. If you don't know the place I'm told the thing to do is steer clear of the guided tours.

not the WORD for it not an adequate or appropriate description. ●Often following a word that has been ironically quoted back at a previous speaker.

eat one's WORDS retract what one has said, especially under compulsion.

a man (*or* woman) of few WORDS a taciturn person.

too — for WORDS extremely —. *informal*

WORDS ▶ see **EAT one's words**; ▶ see **in words of one SYLLABLE**; ▶ see **put words into someone's MOUTH**; ▶ see **WINGED words**.

have one's WORK cut out be faced with a hard task.

WORK one's ass (*or* butt) off work extremely hard. *N. Amer.*, *vulgar slang*

WORK to rule (especially as a form of industrial action) follow official working regulations exactly in order to reduce output and efficiency. *chiefly Brit.* ●Also as noun.

WORK ▶ see **work one's fingers to the BONE**; ▶ see **work like a BEAVER**; ▶ see **work one's TICKET**.

a bad WORKMAN blames his tools someone who has done something badly will seek to lay the blame on the equipment rather than admit to a lack of skill. *proverbial* ●Cf. L13 French: *mauveés ovriers ne trovera ja bon hostill* bad workmen will never find a good tool. In English, variants of this French saying predominated, until M19; the current version, with *blame*, is modern.

give someone the WORKS **1** *informal* give or tell a person everything. **2** *informal* treat a person harshly. **3** *slang* kill a person.

in the WORKS being planned, worked on, or produced. *chiefly N. Amer.*

carry the WORLD before one have rapid and complete success.

come up in the WORLD rise in status, especially by becoming richer.

go down in the WORLD drop in status, especially by becoming poorer.

look for all the WORLD like look precisely like.

> **1993** *New Scientist* 26 June 17/1 Fossil imprints that look for all the world like motorcycle tracks have been explained.

a man (*or* woman) of the WORLD a person who is experienced and practical in human affairs.

out of this WORLD extremely enjoyable or impressive. *informal*

think the WORLD of have a very high regard for.

(all) the WORLD and his wife everyone; a large number of people. *Brit.* ●Cf. Swift: 'Pray, Madam, who were the Company? ... Why, there was all the world, and his wife' (*Polite Conversation*, 1738). As used in M18, the phrase applied particularly to people who had pretensions to fashion or high society, but it is now also used more generally for a large crowd.

the WORLD, the flesh, and the devil all forms of temptation to sin.

a (*or* the) WORLD of a very great deal of.

WORLD ▶ *see* **set the world ALIGHT**; ▶ *see* **not be LONG for this world**; ▶ *see* **the world is one's OYSTER**.

the best of both (*or* all possible) WORLDS the benefits of widely differing situations, enjoyed at the same time. ●The variant *all possible worlds* alludes to the catchphrase of the eternally optimistic philosopher Dr Pangloss in Voltaire's *Candide* (1759): *Dans ce meilleur des mondes possibles ... tout est au mieux*, usually quoted in English as 'Everything is for the best in the best of all possible worlds.'

(even) a WORM will turn even a meek person will resist or retaliate if harassed too much. *proverbial* ●Recorded from M16. Often used allusively, as in *the worm turns*.

a WORM's-eye view the view looking up at something from ground level. ●Formed (E20) after the pattern of ▶ **BIRD's-eye view**, it is very generally used of the viewpoint of a humble or insignificant person witnessing important events or persons.

food for WORMS a dead person.

WORMWOOD and gall a source of bitter mortification and grief. *literary* ●*Gall* is bile, the secretion of the liver; *wormwood* is an aromatic plant with a bitter taste. They occur together in the Bible as a metaphor for vexation and affliction (Lamentations 3:19).

none the WORSE for **1** not adversely affected by. **2** not to be considered inferior on account of.

> **1 1991** A. CAMPBELL *Sidewinder* i. 14 Two days have passed, and I am up and about, feeling none the worse for my attack of sunstroke.

so much the WORSE for — that's —'s problem. ●Used when the speaker considers that an unfortunate event or situation is the fault of the person specified, about whom the speaker feels little concern.

the WORSE for wear **1** damaged by use or weather over time; battered and shabby. **2** rather unwell. ●A euphemistic development of sense 2 is 'drunk'.

do one's WORST do as much damage as one can. ●Often used to express defiance in the face of threats: *do your worst!*

get (*or* have) the WORST of it be in the least advantageous or successful position; suffer the most.

if the WORST comes to the worst if the most serious or difficult circumstances arise.

WORST ▶ *see* **be one's own worst ENEMY**.

for all someone is WORTH **1** as energetically or enthusiastically as someone can. **2** so as to obtain everything one can from someone. *informal*

WORTH ▶ *see* **not worth a plugged NICKEL**; ▶ *see* **worth one's SALT**; ▶ *see* **worth one's WEIGHT in gold**.

WRAP (it) up be quiet. *Brit.*, *informal* ● Usually in imperative.

WRAP ▶ *see* **twist someone round one's little FINGER**.

keep (something) under WRAPS conceal; be secretive about. *informal*
| **1998** *New Scientist* 22 Aug. 13/3 The key to the fuel is a catalyst that the Navy is keeping under wraps.

WRING one's hands show great distress. ● From the action of clasping and twisting one's hands together as a gesture of anguish and frustration.

WRING someone's withers stir the emotions or conscience. ● After Shakespeare: 'let the galled jade wince, our withers are unwrung' (Hamlet's comment on guilty conscience in the play scene at *Hamlet* III. ii). The *withers* are the bony ridge between the shoulders of a horse which is liable to be chafed by an ill-fitting saddle.

put someone through the WRINGER (or the mangle) subject someone to a very stressful experience, especially a severe interrogation. *informal* ● The version with *wringer* appeared as US slang in M20, but is now widely used.
| **1984** L. ERDICH *Love Medicine* (1989) iv. 72 I saw that he had gone through the wringer. He was red-eyed, gaunt, and he was drunk.

WRINKLES ▶ *see* **IRON out the wrinkles**.

one's WRIT runs one has authority. ● Usually in clauses with a specification of where the legal authority mentioned is valid or acknowledged.

WRIT large in magnified or emphasized form. ● The literal sense of *written in large characters* has long been disused. As the past participle of *write*, *writ* is now generally superseded by *written* except in this phrase, in analogous phrases such as *writ small*, or as a deliberate archaism.

nothing to WRITE home about of little interest or value. *informal*
| **1970** N. BAWDEN *Birds on Trees* (1991) viii. 131 I daresay what I did was nothing to write home about, but it put food in her belly and shoes on her feet!

WRITE ▶ *see* **write one's TICKET**.

the WRITING (or N. Amer. handwriting) is on the wall there are clear signs that something unpleasant or unwelcome is going to happen. ● Ultimately from the biblical episode of Belshazzar's feast, at which a disembodied hand appeared and wrote a message on the wall foretelling the fall of the Babylonian kingdom to the Medes and Persians (Daniel 5:5, 25–8).
| **1998** *Spectator* [W]e ought to have spotted the writing on the wall when the dear old Ministry of Works became 'English Heritage', packaging the past as a set of limited-edition, special-offer collectables.

get in WRONG with (or on the wrong side of) someone incur the dislike or disapproval of someone. *informal*

get someone WRONG misunderstand a person, especially by falsely imputing malice.

get (hold of) the WRONG end of the stick misunderstand someone or something completely.

go down the WRONG way (of food) enter the windpipe instead of the gullet.

WRONG ▶ *see* **born on the wrong side of the BLANKET**; ▶ *see* **get out of BED on the wrong side**; ▶ *see* **in the wrong BOX**; ▶ *see* **the wrong side of the TRACKS**.

Y

by the YARD in large numbers or quantities.

> **1977** W. FOLEY *No Pipe Dreams for Father* in *Forest Trilogy* (1992) 236 Granny mixed her puddings in her huge bread-crock, then stuffed them by the yard down the stockings.

spin a YARN tell a story, especially a long and complicated one. ● With reference to a *yarn* in rope-making, one of the long fibres of which a rope is made. The expression is nautical in origin and current in this figurative sense since E19.

YEA and nay shilly-shally.

YEAR ▶ *see* **the year DOT**.

put YEARS on (*or* take years off) someone make someone feel or look older (*or* younger).

YEARS ▶ *see* **for DONKEY's years**; ▶ *see* **the VALE of years**.

YES and no partly and partly not. ● Used to express qualified assent to an idea or proposal.

YESTERDAY's man a man, especially a politician, whose career is finished or past its peak.

YESTERDAY's news a person or thing that is no longer of interest.

YONDER ▶ *see* **the wide BLUE yonder**.

YOU and yours you together with your family and close friends.

> **1937** *American Home* Apr. 113/1 (*advertisement*) So it's natural … to take good care of the home that gives you and yours this steadfast protection.

the YOUNG idea the child's mind. *dated* ● From James Thomson *Seasons* 'Spring' 1152.

Z

catch some (*or* a few) Zs get some sleep. *chiefly N. Amer., informal* ●Z (US pronunciation *zi:*) represents the sound of snoring.

> **1989** G. KEILLOR *Yon* in *We Are Still Married* (1990) 328 The subway was peaceful so early ... I even squeezed in some Zs myself.